The Virgin
Alternative
Guide to
British
Universities

The Virgin Alternative Guide to British Universities

First published in Great Britain in 1997
by Virgin Books
an imprint of
Virgin Publishing Ltd
332 Ladbroke Grove
London W10 5AH

A catalogue record for this title is
available from the British Library.

ISBN 0 7535 0110 4

Typeset by Roger Kohn Designs

Printed and bound by Mackays
of Chatham plc

W

Y

INTRODUCTION

THE VIRGIN ALTERNATIVE GUIDE *is a response to the huge changes going on in Higher Education and the challenge these changes represent to* **YOU** *making what so many insist is 'the most important decision you will ever make in your life.' Whether that is true or another symptom of the high pressure marketing by some universities is debatable.*

What is true is that the recent increase in the number of colleges and universities offering degree courses, the influence of top employers on what and how you will learn, the sophisticated marketing techniques being employed by some universities to ensure as large a share of the H.E. funding cake as they can get, and the increasingly outmoded advice of parents who argue for prestige over expediency, all combine to justify an **ALTERNATIVE** *approach which hands the choice back to you.*

We began our research with the official Uni-admin prospectuses, the students' own alternative prospectuses and the world wide web pages (http://www.ja.net/janet-sites/sites.html). Then we went to visit sixth-form careers officers (who have off-the-record gut feelings often more valuable than much of the Uni-hyped gloss) and consulted independent employer researchers who have another view again. Next we went to the government agencies. We sifted through all the assessments of courses undertaken by HEFCE (for England and Northern Ireland), SHEFC (for Scotland) and HEFCW (for Welsh universities), and analysed the Research Assessment carried out by the Joint Funding Council in 1996, which shows where Unis have strength in depth. Finally we went to HESA, the government statistics agency, which has (besides much else) unique material on where students from particular universities end up in the job market.

To restore a sense of balance, we then sent out letters to attract student moles. Our contacts came via school careers officers lively enough to keep tabs on where their students went, via Uni media editors, Student Unions, Media/ Journalism departments, and a network of friends of friends of friends. We wanted information and, in many cases, we managed to seduce our informers with offers too good to refuse to provide full-length records of their experiences. We visited some Unis (not enough) and sat in bars until copy deadline fears drove us - just the two of us - back to our computers. We learned a lot, not least how to get what we (and you) want to know with a good deal less fuss next time.

THE VIRGIN ALTERNATIVE GUIDE *seeks to give sixth-formers and mature students bases on which to make the BIG decision. We are not convinced that the variation of 10p or even 25p in the price of a pint lies at the real root of that choice.*

There are important general differentiations - Oxbridge, London Unis, Specialist Unis, Campus Unis, Civic Unis, Technological Unis, converted Polys or skills-obsessed new Unis. Whether a Uni is based in clubland or has a well-organised ents programme of its own is important. Whether it is full of chemical engineers or 'highly motivated' city types (or both or neither or whatever) is of interest. Whether it is a basically formal scene or a tight - some might say friendly, some claustrophobic - environment, like far-flung St Andrews, is also worth knowing.

No earth-shattering judgements are made as to which universities are overall best because it takes all sorts... But we do print what people we talked to feel - for example, Nottingham comes in for a bashing for its stuck-up attitudes but appeals to a great number of students. We leave you to make up your mind, for there is, indeed, something out there for everyone. You can spend three years campaigning about rents in Aber, hang out in laid-back Lampeter equally unaware that there's a world outside, get high in the bar (of all places) at SOAS, live it up in Manchester, Leeds, Newcastle or Birmingham, or move from public school to Durham and barely notice the change.

What we believe people want from us, is:

❶ A SENSE OF THE ATMOSPHERE AND SOCIAL SCENE
❷ A FEEL OF WHAT A UNI SPECIALISES IN OR IS GOOD AT TEACHING
❸ AN IDEA OF HOW SUCCESSFULLY (and to what end) A UNI PREPARES ITS STUDENTS FOR THE FUTURE

'Alternative' once spelled Revolution. Today's undergraduate students are part of a revolution of a different sort. Employers are increasingly in charge, and universities are becoming sophisticated in their marketing techniques. Who, a few years ago, would have credited a university advertising itself on TV? Remember, as you sift through the gloss, that Higher Education is fast becoming a business like any other, and that you are cast in the role of consumer. Your choice will ultimately determine where the revolution leads - not the employers, not the marketing men.

We hope this book will help to make the choice your own.

THE MODULAR SYSTEM, CATS AND PTS

Increasingly students are aware of what a modular system is, and the Credit Accumulation and Transfer System (CATS) which goes along with it. A module is a unit of study. You can set up a programme of them for either a single honours, joint honours or combined honours degree. What each module consists of will be limited by timetables, but the idea is that they allow inter-departmental mixes (science with arts, arts with social studies, humanities with maths or computer sciences, etc).

Adding a language or computer science to business, for example, may widen your choice of jobs. At the same time, mixing modules for ultimate flexibility can make it very confusing for employers to know what you have studied in depth. Beware those Unis who go on about flexibility. Freedom is great, but freedom per se is an empty concept. The question you should ask is, freedom to do what? The best Unis demonstrate their educational flair in their modular programmes as well as their commitment to getting you a job at the end of the degree. They marry one subject to another so that your interest and understanding of your main subject is actively enhanced. They allow you to look at it from another point of view. We realise today, for example, that scientific research often fails to take into account moral issues. At root level the modular system offers you an opportunity to look at science from a humanities point of view, at arts from a scientific point of view, and so on. It is a great principle, but not all universities have cottoned on to this fundamental principle of the modular system. Choice for choice's sake is pointless. What the choice implies is what is at issue. Judge universities on that basis and you will become actively involved in the evolutionary process of Higher Education.

The idea of CATS is that each module is accorded a number of points; if you pass the module you get the points, and you build up your programme of modules so that you make the requisite number of points for a degree (360). With the CATS system you don't necessarily have to do your course at one 3 or 4-year period, you could always come back to it later - the points you have achieved for the early modules remain in the bank, as it were.

PTS stands for 'personal transferable skills'. It is the opposite of 'ivory tower'. These are skills of communication, marketing yourself, presentation, etc. The concept is all the rage, particularly among the newer universities and those university sector colleges who want to become universities. Some universities try to tack them on to your course; others offer special dedicated courses running in parallel. That PTS has come to the fore is a sign of the degree to which employment is now reckoned to be the result of the equation of Higher Education. In many cases you might do better to join the Drama Soc. of your university, or work out your PTS in your social life. We believe that PTS are important for getting a job. We also believe that in terms of PTS, Higher Education can never substitute for the experience of working, and that jobs in the vacs, job placements, etc, are more important for PTS than going to university will ever be. Don't get hung up on PTS. It is a buzz phrase that very often demonstrates a lack in another department. Colleges can become good at PTS quicker than they can develop educational flair. Too many are looking for a fast route to success. There are rich spoils in Higher Education these days.

FACTS ABOUT FACTS

Courses listed with 'A' level grades or 'A' level points ***(A Grade = 10pts, B = 8, C = 6, D = 4, E = 2)*** *in* ***The Academic Profile*** *indicate the academic character of the university and 'A' level requirement.*

They should be compared with the government ***(HEFCE/SHEFC/HEFCW)*** *assessments below them. Be aware, however, that only government-funded institutions are subject to assessment (Buckingham, for example, escapes it) and that we have only included those courses which have achieved distinction.*

The government assessments are derived from an analysis ('informed by statistical indicators') of each institution's self-assessment and from visits by teams of assessors. The following are the assessment parameters:

❶ CURRICULUM DESIGN, CONTENT AND ORGANISATION
❷ TEACHING, LEARNING AND ASSESSMENT
❸ STUDENT PROGRESSION AND ACHIEVEMENT
❹ STUDENT SUPPORT AND GUIDANCE
❺ LEARNING RESOURCES
❻ QUALITY ASSURANCE AND ENHANCEMENT

Part way through their programme of assessment (which continues today), ***HEFCE*** *(for England and Northern Ireland) changed their marking system. They began with three grades: Excellent, Satisfactory, Unsatisfactory. Recently they have accorded points (maximum 4) to each of the six assessment parameters* *listed above (top marks 24 points). We have included courses rated Excellent and 18 or over.* ***SHEFCE*** *(Scotland) marked their assessments Excellent, Highly Satisfactory, Satisfactory, Unsatisfactory. We have included courses rated Excellent or Highly Satisfactory.* ***HEFCW*** *(Welsh) assessments were marked Excellent, Satisfactory, Unsatisfactory, and we have included those rated Excellent.*

The Joint Funding Council's Research Assessment for 1996, which gives an idea of a university's strength in depth, rated subjects on an ascending points system of quality: ***1, 2, 3a, 3b, 4, 5 and 5*****. We have included those courses given* ***5*** *or* ***5*****. 5 indicates 'International Excellence in some sub-areas [for example 'high energy physics in a Physics submission or the disparate research interests of an individual'], National Excellence in virtually all others'; 5* indicates 'International Excellence in a majority of sub-areas and attainable levels of national excellence in all others'.*

The PIP Employers' Survey for 1996, extracted under each Uni's ***Employment Profile****, is published annually and is wholly independent.*

Unlike the MPW table, PIP is strictly subject related. PIP sends to Graduate Recruitment Officers of some 400 leading companies and seeks to find which universities are most popular providers across 10 subject areas: Engineering & Technology, Construction & Civil Engineering, Languages, Law, Electrical Engineering, Science, Computing, Business, Accountancy, Finance & Banking, and Social Science/Economics.

PIP stands for Performance Indicator Project and is the brainchild of Dr Cliff Pettifor, who can supply copies of the full survey for a fee at Harlaxton College, Grantham, Lincs, NG32 1AG (Tel: 014765 64541; Fax: 70730).

The report reflects the opinions of a substantial section of major recruiters of graduates, but it is important to be aware that subject areas are limited. Also, as Dr Pettifor is at pains to point out, some subjects receive more feedback than others. Beware drawing too many conclusions from low level positions in Languages, Law and Electrical Engineering because they reflect the views of far fewer correspondents than, say, Engineering & Technology.

Dr Pettifor allowed us to quote the top three positions for any one institution, but we have tended to quote fewer or avoid quoting at all when response levels become less dependable (i.e. form a less profitable means for extrapolation).

What the inclusion of this PIP league table does for us, within the caveats mentioned above, is to give a national perspective to the HESA-derived ***Principal Job Market Destinations*** *material. When, for example, Computing is listed 5th most popular recruitment subject at a particular university and the same Uni appears nationally in the PIP survey at 12th position, you can bet that Computing is very strong and, indeed, that any subjects above Computing in the HESA-derived table, which are not covered in the limited course structure of the PIP survey, are pretty safe bets recruitment-wise.*

HESA *(the Higher Education Statistics Agency), provided us with a specially tailored draw-down of their research into first destinations of 1995 graduates, which are the latest figures available. Figures of undergraduate employment by university provided us with the basis of a top-down listing of the areas of employment into which students fell (or were pushed).*

HESA's research is unique. It is framed in what is called the Standard Industrial Classification of Economic Activities and we pulled out Agriculture; Manufacturing (with a special note about Pharmaceuticals and Electrical & Electronic); Construction (the Building Industry); the Wholesale and

Retail trade; Hotels and Restaurants; Financial Activities, with a special intake of figures on Accounting and Business - we call it Commerce; Public Admin, which includes central, regional, local government, and, when specifically mentioned, Law (though many lawyers don't go straight into employment); Health; Computer-related activities; Engineering activities such as Eng. Design, Geodetic Surveying, etc; Industrial Design; Architecture; Advertising; Market Research; Veterinary; Arts/Media (which includes Performance and Creative Arts, such as Design, TV/Radio, Journalism, Publishing, Printing); and finally Sports-related activities.

The destinations listed for each Uni are the principal destinations and not all categories of employment entered into by graduates. Don't fall into the trap of thinking that employment strengths always indicate course strengths, for an engineering graduate is as likely to end up in Manufacturing as in any of the Engineering categories, and a businessman can go most anywhere. The Job Market Destinations give what they promise: destinations. We list them top-down in order of strength and highlight where a university has a strong or good record as a provider in a particular category of employment.

John O'Leary broke the news of the ***MPW*** *National League Table in* The Times *on August 20th 1996. The research was conducted at the behest of Joe Ruston, the recently retired Chairman of the leading independent group of sixth-form colleges, Mander Portman Woodward. In the words of Mr Ruston, the MPW colleges 'specialise in helping students to win places on the most popular courses (e.g. Medicine) and at the most prestigious universities.' (If you are a prospective medical undergraduate get hold of a copy of his book,* Getting Into Medical School, *Trotman & Co. Tel: 0181 332 2132; Fax: 948 9267. It's the most incisive guide about how to choose a Medical School and how to prepare yourself for acceptance.)*

The MPW survey showed that the UK's leading industrial and commercial employers concentrate on a select group of premier universities for their graduate intake, which makes the MPW philosophy a sensible one and a big problem for some new universities. However, at 15th place, Glasgow Caledonian has clearly found a way to beat the problem. See, too, our assessments of universities like Sheffield Hallam, University of the West of England, Oxford Brookes and De Montfort for business. They may not have made the Top 20 in the MPW listing but they are offering the kind of vocational courses which will soon have them there.

Again, sponsorship is an increasing force. Unis in an area of big industry score well on recruitment because local industry is being pulled in to course planning and you will be learning what they, the companies, can use. You may not think that's the kind of dedicated teaching line you want to follow at university, and I wouldn't argue with it, but if employment in industry is an important aim, you may think you should play the game.

Apropos the new universities, when we spoke to students going for jobs in local media (radio in particular) we also discovered that a vocational course at a new university, plus hands-on experience at a Uni radio station, will stand you in better stead than a high-flying non-media course at a pukka university. Budding journalists rarely get the chance these days to train on a local paper (most of which are cut to the bone staff-wise), so if that's what you're about, look for those unis which are strong providers in this area and forget whatever pangs of shame mummy and daddy may feel when they are asked where you ended up.

Alternatively, why not consider a

vocational course like journalism after you have attained a degree in Psychology, or whatever, elsewhere? Cardiff Uni offers a very good course for this.

The hoary old chestnut roasting in the brazier of academia is about mind-train versus skills, and the advent of the old polys on to the scene has lifted the temperature ten-fold. But if you play your cards right they are not necessarily mutually exclusive.

This being a guide for students by students, we thought we'd leave you with a final word about strategy (and the ultimate inevitability of failure of even the best-laid plans) from Ben Jones and Chris Wilding at ***Warwick University****, who show that the game doesn't end with the UCAS form:*

STUFF THAT GOES ON

At the start of term you will be stranded in an island of grey, concrete, sixties architecture, a veritable continent-load of drinking establishments and a group of peculiar individuals that you don't know from Adam. ***BEWARE!***

These are the crewmates with whom you will sink or float. Over the next few months you will eat, sleep, drink, shag, bathe, read poetry, fight, bond, snog, argue, play indoor cricket, launder and socialise with these people. ***BEWARE!***

Your first night will consist of going to the SU bar with the people from your corridor. There will be a Chemistry student from Cheshire, called Anna; two clubbers from Birmingham (Kate and Mel), who will spend the whole night dancing and sleep with the rugby team by nine o'clock; the future hall Romeo from Leeds (Graham), who will wear a black shirt open to the navel; a nice girl/boy called Sue/Ben; and a Computer Science student from Woking called Bill. ***BEWARE!***

You will fancy the pants off Sue/Ben, who breaks your heart by getting off with Graham, who turns out to be bisexual. Anna will drink half a snakebite and black before falling off a table and collapsing paralytically in a corner. This will leave you with Bill, who will follow you like a lost sheep. You will end up being his only friend. You will live with him next year. When you marry, he will come on honeymoon with you. ***BEWARE!***

Your first day of lectures will see you talking to as many people as possible. You will write down everything the lecturer says and will leave feeling like a proper academic and everything. Then it will be time to join some societies. ***BEWARE!***

You will join the Socialist Worker's Student Society and be confronted every Saturday morning by a dirty, faintly must-smelling militant with bad breath and German army boots trying to get you to go on marches with him in Krakow. ***BEWARE!***

That afternoon you will buy a house plant from The Market Place. You will return to find three girls dying their hair purple and a large barbarous character from Exeter will have taken up residency in your room. He will be a friend of a finalist on the next floor and will compensate you by offering a supply of cannabis resin. This attractive arrangement will fall through when he gives you an Oxo cube covered in Patchouli Oil. ***BEWARE!***

Fresher's Ball will dominate the next night's proceedings. You will watch Right Said Fred, Carl Cox, Menswear, D-Ream and Mike Flower's Pops. You won't remember anything, but will wake up next morning with Graham from Leeds and spend the next week in solitary confinement. ***BEWARE!***

The next three years will be the best days of your life times ten. But don't rush. You have three years to do it all. You could have four babies in that time. You get less for GBH!

THE TEAM

We would like to thank everyone unreservedly for helping out, both those who submitted to an interview - students, school careers department teachers, employers, researchers - and those who actually wrote copy. To those who supplied copy, which we couldn't include, either because we chose someone else's, or because it didn't meet the brief, our thanks and commiserations. To all those Open University students who shared their innermost thoughts - nearly 100 - what can I say? I'd consider a book of them if I thought they'd get past the censor. Special thanks to Dee Dudgeon for her dogged research and to Sophie Vokes-Dudgeon for her tough interviewing, copy writing and editing.

STUDENT CONTRIBUTORS

★ Aberdeen University - *Kevin Walsh and Allan Tanner*
★ Askham Bryan College - *Ruth E.C.Furness and Peter Franks*
★ Birmingham University - *Ruth Hay*
★ Birmingham College of Food, Tourism and Creative Studies - *Patricia Magee*
★ Bradford University - *Andi Callan*
★ Bristol University - *Tony Dunkels*
★ Brunel University - *Kay Collins*
★ Cambridge University - *Liz Wade*
★ Cardiff Institute - *Jon Ruch*
★ Chester, University College - *Alastair Coles*
★ De Montfort University - *Amanda Dodson and David Naylor*
★ Durham University - *Sophie Vokes-Dudgeon*
★ East Anglia Universtiy - *Daniel Trelfer*
★ Edge Hill, University College - *Peter Cooper*
★ Edinburgh University - *Holly Crane*
★ Exeter University - *Jo Moorhouse*
★ European Business School - *York Zucchi*
★ Goldsmiths College - *Steven Paul Davies*
★ Hull University - *Adam Ford*
★ Imperial College - *Sarah Playforth*
★ Kent Institute - *Liz Wallace*
★ King Alfred's College - *Stephanie Kirk*
★ Lampeter University - *Sarah Vanstone (interviewed by Sophie Vokes-Dudgeon)*
★ Leeds Metropolitan University - *Rebecca O'Neil*
★ Leeds College of Music - *Sue-Lee Freeman*
★ Liverpool John Moores University - *Nicholas Wallis*
★ London Guildhall University - *Stuart Harkness*
★ Loughborough College - *Ayshea Corrigan*
★ Luton University - *Scott Williams*
★ Manchester University - *Nicola Chapman*
★ Manchester Metropolitan University - *Anna Sargent*
★ Middlesex University - *Helen Gibbons*
★ Newcastle-upon-Tyne University - *Miles Starforth*
★ Nottingham University - *Joanna Witt*
★ Northumbria University - *Susannah Bell*
★ Open University - *Dee McArthur*
★ Oxford University - *Fern Miller*
★ Oxford Brookes University - *Ed Balleny*
★ Roehampton Institute - *Gina Wright*
★ Royal Free School of Medicine - *James Varley*
★ Salford University - *S.M. Ashton*
★ University College Scarborough - *Ian Montgomery*
★ School of Oriental and African Studies - *Peter Beveridge and Catherine Wynne.*
★ School of Slavonic and East

European Studies - *Gideon Dewhirst*
★ Scottish Agricultural Studies - *Doug Page*
★ Sheffield University - *Emily McGarr*
★ Sheffield Hallam University - *Ian Montgomery*
★ South Bank University - *Richard Neville*
★ Southampton University - *Tristan Negus*
★ Stirling University - *Suzanne Bush*
★ Thames Valley University - *Ian Draysey*
★ Trinity College Carmarthen - *Robin Zulkiffly Rowlands*
★ Warwick University - *Ben Jones and Chris Wilding, Emma Burhouse*
★ West of England University - *Richard Silver*
★ Westminster University - *Calvin Holbrook*
★ Wye College - *Chloe Shears*
★ York University - *Kevin Murphy*

ABERDEEN UNIVERSITY

University of Aberdeen
Regent Walk
Aberdeen AB24 3FX

TEL 01224 272090
FAX 01224 272576

University of Aberdeen
Student Representative Council
50/52 College Bounds
Aberdeen AB2 3DS

TEL 01224 272965
FAX 01224 272977

UNIVERSITY OF ABERDEEN

Founded	**1495**
Situation/style	**City sites**
UNDERGRADUATE PROFILE	
Application acceptance rate	**14%**
Medical AAR	**11%**
Population	**7,900**
Mature student population	**25%**
Overseas student population	**10%**
Male/female ratio	**50:50**
1st year institut. accommodation	**100%**
Approximate cost	**£45-£65 pw**
ACADEMIC PROFILE	
A-level requirements:	**High**

Medicine ABB:
★ Science 'A's required **Chemistry + 2 of Biol., Maths, Physics**
★ Non-Science 'A's acceptable **Possibly**
★ Retakes considered **No**
★ Clinical contact **Phase II/2nd year**

Student/staff ratio	**11:1**
1st class degree pass rate	**7%**
SHEFC assessments (18 subjects assessed/approved):	
1994 **Civil Eng.**	Highly satis.
1995 **Economics, Geography**	Excellent
Chemistry, Geology, Maths, Statistics, Mechanical & Manufacturing Eng.	Highly satis.
1996 **Sociology**	Excellent
Theology, Finance & Accounting, History of Art, Law, Philosophy, Politics	Highly satis.
Joint Funding Council's research assessment 1996 (31 subjects assessed):	
Law	Grade 5*
EMPLOYMENT PROFILE	
Employability in Industry:	
MPW national league table (1996)	**31st**

Principal job market destinations:
Health, Commerce, Retail/Wholesale, Education, Public Admin/Law, Hotel/Restaurant, Manufacturing, Agriculture (strong), **Arts/Media, Property Development** (strong)

PIP 1996 employers' survey:	
Top 3 subjects/national ranking	
Law	10th=
Languages	12th=
Accountancy/Finance & Banking	22nd=
Approximate % unemployed	**5%**

VAG VIEW

Aberdeen is Britain's North Sea Oil capital, a busy city with a great deal of money flowing through it. The university was founded in 1495 and is the oldest university institution outside Oxbridge. Other than that and the fact that it has a very good medical school - Aberdeen was the first Chair of Medicine in the English-speaking world - we have precious little to add to our correspondents' excellent analysis.

GETTING THERE

★ By road: approach from the South on the A92, thence on to the ring road where you'll pick up signs. From the North, approach on the A96 or the A92 and follow signs to Old Aberdeen.
★ Aberdeen itself is a compact city with a good bus service and there is no need for a car.
★ By air: Aberdeen International Airport links with Heathrow, Gatwick, Stansted and Luton - just over one hour's flight time. Manchester, Newcastle, Belfast, Birmingham, Bristol and Norwich, and European destinations include Amsterdam,

Copenhagen and Stavanger.
★ Taxis from the airport cost about £8.
★ By rail: links via Edinburgh and Newcastle find their way in just under 7 hours to London King's Cross. The line from Edinburgh to Aberdeen can be very slow.

VIEW FROM THE GROUND
by Kevin Walsh and Allan Tanner

Aberdeen is situated 140 miles north of Edinburgh on the north-east coast and is currently the most northerly seat of Further Education in the UK. Because of this it is easy to feel far removed from where it's at in the rest of the country. A cosmopolitan mix of students, however, couples with the influx of people who work in the oil industry to ensure that the city and particularly the area surrounding the university gives the impression of being some sort of displaced cultural outpost, Doric nutcases notwithstanding. (Note - Doric is the term used to describe the local dialect).

The university recently celebrated its Quincentenary (with something of a whimper, it might be said) and the grand age of the establishment is not lost on even the greenest Fresher. A mere glance at the sheer gothicness of Marischal College is enough to suggest creaky old professors and academic intensity.

There are two campuses: the Medical School at Foresterhill beside the Aberdeen Royal Infirmary, and the main campus at King's College in the heart of Old Aberdeen where all the real action takes place. Painful as it is for a cynic's calloused heart to express, King's campus is truly stunning when it's not actually raining. When the weather takes a turn for the worse, however, the north of Scotland is a bleak and unforgiving climate, so perhaps those longjohns aren't such a bad idea.

STUDENTS
Aberdeen has a truly diverse student population. Your correspondents have so far encountered visitors from not only every European territory (with the exception of Russia for some reason) but also from even more exotic climes. The university is a keen participant in the ERASMUS exchange scheme and consequently there is ample opportunity for Aberdeen students to take time off to study abroad - an increasingly popular option. That said, around half the students hail from Scotland, from Lerwick to Stranraer. It's a bit of a haven for Edinburgh public school sorts and they comprise a small but highly visible group of Yas. The general consensus appears to be, however, that if you ignore them then they'll get bored and head off to the Bobbin (see below).

ACCOMMODATION
Students from outwith the city are guaranteed a place in halls of residence in their first year, should they wish to take it. Opinion varies as to the quality of university-owned accommodation in Aberdeen, but the private sector remains a popular and economically viable alternative. Hillhead Halls comprises around 3,000 students, spread through a mixture of catered and self-catering halls and flats, making it the largest student accommodation site in Europe. We challenge you to walk through every corridor without hearing Pearl Jam/a philosophy debate or an amorous encounter... As for the other halls, Crombie Johnston is visited with the same unfortunate plague of Yas, as mentioned above, and Dunbar has a reputation for eerie cosiness, the reasons for which are unfathomable. As in halls of residence all over the country, the atmosphere generated enables those less gregarious individuals to socialise easily, even if it is just to tell someone to turn their music down. In order to cope with the sudden increase in the intake of undergraduates, several new blocks have been built in the last five years. These large and expensive sites have proved popular despite being beset initially by problems and criticism from many students, and have provided much needed extra accommodation.

WHAT GOES ON
For its size (population around 220,000) Aberdeen has a disproportionate amount of pubs and clubs, and over the course of a degree, students tend to find their own

particular haunts, generally around the east end of Union Street in the city centre. Each band of students will have a number of regular hostelries with which they tend to stick for the duration of their university sojourn. The King Street Mill, however, universally known as the Bobbin, is the place where not only do those pesky Yas show off their Burberry tops and Barbarians jumpers, but where practically every section of the student body comes to hang out of an evening. Because of its ubiquitousness in Aberdonian student life, the crown in this, the most profitable Alloa pub in Britain, changes bewilderingly from night to night. This is by virtue of it being the closest pub to campus, apart from the notoriously minuscule St Machar Bar which is popular with teaching staff and stovies eaters.

Over the past few years, city centre pubs and clubs, and even some of the shops, have centred their attention on the student pound. This has seen a decrease in people frequenting the Student Union, despite its recent refurbishment, the cheap drink and the odd band or comedy night. As with most other cities, there has been a recent explosion in nightclubs in particular. New clubs such as The Works, however, have found difficulties in attracting large numbers of students, most of whom stick to tried and tested boogie zones. These include the sado-masochistic deathtraps such as Zuu and Smart Alex, as well as the more self-consciously trendy Pelican Club. The gaudier Ministry of Sin and the ever-popular Mudd Club account for the remainder of student clubbers, with an honorary mention perhaps for Oh Henry's, where the motto 'cheap and cheesy' becomes something of a doctrine.

You may have noticed that intoxication plays a large part in student social life. This is due, in part, to the large amount of free time available and also perhaps to the dearth of alternative activities in the city, not to mention the atrocious form of the once-great Aberdeen FC. Basically, it's the same old small-town story, despite the size of the city: Drink Beer, Take Drugs, Worship Satan. Out of town there are various interesting diversions, such as quad-biking, and both the Grampian Hills and Cairngorm Mountains are nearby, but, the chances of the average fey indie-boy student dying to claim another Munro are about as likely as a rise in the student grant. Bear in mind that Aberdeen is reckoned to be one of the most expensive cities outside London, so hedonism is an even more expensive pastime here than in most places.

Perhaps because the city is close to the coast and also only 40 miles away from south-central Peterhead, where more substances pass unnoticed than in Bogota, there is a laid back atmosphere around campus, as well as a plethora of torn folders in every student holdall.

Slightly more wholesome pursuits can be found in the form of any one of the many clubs and societies affiliated to the university. Popular ones are the Cinema Club, the Celtic Society and the Wine Club. There is everything from the Metabisulphate Club (home brewing) to Witchcraft and Battle Re-enactment. There's also the usual round of musical and theatrical societies, who perform regularly within the city. The university newspaper, Gaudie, recently celebrated its sixtieth birthday, and is always popular with the university's more coldly ambitious denizens. More recently established is the university's own radio station, Slick FM, which is currently struggling with teething troubles but has committed itself to rapid improvement in its next temporary licence.

Politically Aberdeen is a conservative city, but, divisions between the major parties not being what they once were, the Labour students are perhaps the most numerous at this moment in time. The Scottish National Party are obviously also well supported, and both groups are highly visible. At the moment the Students' Representative Council is firmly dominated by Labour activists, although students seem to have little trouble with the fact that posts on the SRC have become somewhat politicised.

This brings us on to perhaps the most striking aspect of Aberdeen students. Apathy (red letters dripping blood optional) permeates the student body to an alarming extent, as evinced by increasingly lower turnouts for the myriad of elections that the University bureaucracy necessitates. Nobody is quite sure why Aberdeen students don't seem to care who represents them, but we might suggest that the fact that the representation does not always seem to produce tangible results is a factor in this unfortunate trend.

SPORT

The University Athletics Association plays a large part in the lives of many Aberdeen students, and whilst there is no one one area in which the university excels, the clubs are well organised and coordinated. This means that trips and excursions to all parts of the UK and beyond are frequent, and a price which is not prohibitive. Butchart Recreational Centre, situated just on the edge of campus, offers cheap tuition in a wide range of disciplines as well as the usual round of aerobics, circuits and fitness classes.

ACADEMIA

Academically, the University is distinguished in various areas, perhaps most famously, Law, while close ties with the oil industry ensure prominence for Engineering and Geology. Most popular, however, are probably English and principally Psychology, which attracts a first year intake of around 600. All disciplines are linked by the Common Assessment Scale, a marking scheme which the University introduced to provide a consistency of grades between all degree courses. Whether all tutors and markers are playing with the same dimensions of goalposts is quite another matter, but it does provide a way for the student to gauge his/her own strengths and weaknesses in a particular subject.

THE FUTURE

The appointment of a new Principal who has pledged to raise Aberdeen's profile as much as possible in the term of his office, ideally to a level of parity at least with Edinburgh and Glasgow, if not Oxbridge, is a welcome development in such an environment. Generally the Aberdeen student of the present day floats through four years of university life, with the only imprint of the University's identity being delineated by the absence of any distinguishing features. This is more a symptom of the current mentality rather than the reality. There is an upside to this in that, unlike the stuffed-shirt traditionalism of Oxbridge, the opportunities are carved out by the student himself or herself, rather than being laid out on a plate by the establishment itself. And as we're all Thatcher's children now, isn't that the way things are meant to be?

UNIVERSITY OF ABERTAY DUNDEE

University of Abertay Dundee
40 Bell Street
Dundee DD1 1HG

TEL 01382 308080
FAX 01382 308877

University of Abertay Dundee
Students Association
158 Marketgait
Dundee DD1 1HG

TEL 01382 227477
FAX 01382 206569

UNIVERSITY OF ABERTAY	
Founded	**1888**
Situation/style	**City sites**
UNDERGRADUATE PROFILE	
Application acceptance rate	**22.5%**
Population	**3,300**
Mature student population	**28%**
Overseas student population	**10%**
Male/female ratio	**47:53**
1st year institut. accommodation	**100%**
Approximate rent	**£40 pw**
ACADEMIC PROFILE	
A-level requirements:	**Low**
Law CD, **Mech. Eng.** CD-D, **Chemistry** CC-DD	
Student/staff ratio	**18:1**
1st class degree pass rate	**3%**
SHEFC assessments (8 subjects assessed/approved):	
1995 **Chemistry, Maths, Statistics, Mechanical and Manufacturing Eng.**	Highly satis
Joint Funding Council's research assessment 1996 (12 subjects assessed):	
Grade 5/5*	None
EMPLOYMENT PROFILE	
Principal job market destinations:	
Health, Retail/Wholesale, Manufacturing, Commerce	
Approximate % unemployed	**10%**

VAG VIEW

Dundee is Scotland's fourth largest city. It is also quite a centre for learning. Allegedly 10% of the city's population are studying at one of its two universities or other colleges. Abertay Dundee was made a university three years ago and comes out of the Dundee Institute of Technology, which explains why a number of its students are local to the university. One result of this is that Abertay is much more savvy about the city than Dundee University. It also makes for a fairly integrated city/campus ethos, and is the source of its academic emphasis on 'skills development, work experience and the preparation for the world of work'. Links with local high-tech industries are good. Academic entry requirements are fairly low. Once there you'll find yourself submitting to a 'flexible course structure', in effect an inter-disciplinary modular approach combining languages with science, engineering, management, etc. Thick and thin sandwich courses bring the university and commerce industry together; thin courses normally involve students in two 6-month periods of professional training, the thick courses a full year. Subject areas include Business (with a European edge), Physical and Biological Sciences, (Ecology, Environment, as well as Chemistry, Biology, etc), Engineering, Social Studies (Economics, Psychology, Law).

There's a nice, fresh feel about Abertay. It is very much a 'new' university in terms of its concentration on work skills, etc, and being small there's a good community spirit. Sound, if not brilliant, performance in the academic assessments.

SITUATION

Abertay Dundee is located in the centre of the city with all its buildings within a quarter of a mile of each other. The city, on the north bank of the Firth of Tay, places the Uni further north even than St. Andrew's but not as far gone as Aberdeen, Robert Gordon, or Northern College (see entries). It is surrounded by some stunning countryside, mountains, glens - it's a walker's/ mountaineer's paradise. Golfers will be in their element too, as will skiers. It is the city closest to the majority of Scotland's ski slopes.

GETTING THERE

★ By road: From the South, A85 off Junction 10 of the M90, or over the Tay Bridge via the A91 and A914. From the North, the A9 and then the A85, or the A929 down from Forfar.
★ By rail: The journey from London takes just under six hours and you'll need to change at Edinburgh for Dundee.
★ There is a city airport.

ACCOMMODATION

The university offers all first years accommodation either in converted houses or purpose-built halls of residence. The houses comprise self-catering flats, where students have their own study bedroom and share a communal living/kitchen area. The halls are fully catered.

UNION AND ENTS

The Students' Association has recently been refurbished, and if you manage to make it up the many flights of stairs in Marketgait House you'll find a large licensed bar and disco, an all-day food service, fully equipped fitness centre, snooker, pool and table tennis rooms, and a recently added arcade - games machines, pinball tables, etc. Among ents on offer are the usual hypnotists and quiz nights, theme nights (blind date, fancy-dress parties etc), live bands, discos. They even served up strippers to the last Fresher intake - male and female, of course, to keep things well balanced.

Dundee's pubs are the city's live band focus - they've produced groups such as Deacon Blue and the Associates. In the summer there's the Dundee Jazz and Blues Festival. Dundee University, Abertay's much younger neighbours, recently engaged in an in-depth research project into the pubs in the area - see Dundee entry - though quite honestly, if you come here your average Abertay student knows the place better and you won't want for what goes on. There's also The Rep theatre in Tay Street (former members include Glenda Jackson, Hannah Gordon, Nicol Williamson), and The Whitehall for pro touring companies and amateur productions. It is also home to the Scottish Ballet Company, Scottish Opera and the Royal Scottish National Orchestra, which plays autumn and winter, and a proms season in early summer. The Steps Film Theatre balances the Odeon Multiplex with alternative and foreign films. Recommended student clubs in Dundee include Mardi Gras, De-Stihls and Fat Sams.

SPORT

Abertay have been champions at Ju-jitsu (kick boxing) and have won national and international competitions in Rugby Union and Rugby League, without any sporting facilities other than the fitness centre. Students use local amenities and there are plenty of those - 5 sports or leisure centres for swimming, indoor games - they recently added a basketball team to the University League - weights, saunas, spa pools, etc. Pitches are readily available for football, rugby, hockey and cricket and there are two golf complexes at Caird Park Stadium (championship-class greens include St. Andrew's and Carnoustie). In winter it's off to the ski runs at Glenshee, and the nearby hills of Angus at any time for walking.

ABERYSTWYTH UNIVERSITY

The University of Wales
Old College
King Street
Aberystwyth
Ceredigion SY23 2AX

TEL 01970 622021
FAX 01970 627410

University of Wales
Guild of Students
Penglais
Aberystwyth
Ceredigion SY23 3DX

TEL 01970 624242
FAX 01970 625028

UNIVERSITY OF WALES, ABERYSTWYTH

Founded	**1872**
Situation/style	**Campus**
UNDERGRADUATE PROFILE	
Application acceptance rate	**15%**
Population	**4,900**
Mature student population	**18%**
Overseas student population	**11%**
Male/female ratio	**50:50**
1st year institut. accommodation	**100%**
Approximate cost	**£30-£60 pw**
ACADEMIC PROFILE	
A-level requirements:	**High-medium**

Law BBB, **Geography & Combinations** 20-22/CCD, **English** BBB, **Politics** BCC, **Accountancy/Finance** 10, **French** 20

Student/staff ratio	**12:1**
1st class degree pass rate	**4.5%**

HEFCW assessments (15 subjects assessed/approved):

1994/5 **English, Info/Library Studies, Welsh, Earth Studies**	Excellent
1995/6 **Politics**	Excellent

Joint Funding Council's research assessment 1996 (22 subjects assessed):

Applied Maths, Politics, Celtic	Grade 5

EMPLOYMENT PROFILE

Principal job market destinations:
Retail/Wholesale, Commerce, Public Admin./Law, Manufacturing, Education, Arts/Media, Hotel/Restaurant, Agriculture

PIP 1996 employers' survey:
Top subject/national ranking

Accountancy/Finance & Banking	22nd=
Approximate % unemployed	**10%**

VAG VIEW

Aberystwyth is a long way away from anywhere and the Uni academics get on with what they are good at almost, but not quite, oblivious to its 'revolting' students. Perhaps the students are part of their research, for Politics is one of this uni's great strengths.

There has been a strong Welsh Nationalist element in Aberystwyth for ages; strong as in voluble, but very much in a minority. Students coming to Aber from outside sense this undertow but few take much more than a curious interest in it, and certainly don't vote for the party in any numbers.

Naturally the student media fan these flickers of curiosity in the hope that they will take light, but they rarely do, and when they don't - as in the last Union elections - the Uni rag, The Courier, put their failure down to their inability to push candidates rather than party politics. This may well have been true - personality politics is not really the Welsh Nationalists' thing.

Nevertheless there is at Aber a certain activist gumption which is to be applauded in these days of self-seeking Union politics (the SRC/Union political platform is seen elsewhere increasingly as a springboard to a real-life political career within the Establishment).

In June of last year the Queen was forced to cancel an engagement at the university amidst chaotic scenes of demonstration and strife. She was there to open a new building when some 200 demonstrators ambushed her car. It was the first time in QEII's reign that she had to cancel such an engagement. A month earlier the Union had passed a motion demanding an apology from the Queen for the past treatment of the Welsh language.

As in all the Welsh universities Aber is heavily into promoting its own national/cultural identity. If occasionally this spills over into activism we should not be surprised. Arrogance is a principal characteristic of British Establishment politics, so it is only to be expected that the underdogs will occasionally bite back. There is at least vigour at the core at Aber, and even if most students do adhere to the more usual apathy, it all keeps The Courier *alive with letters decrying it.*

When, not so long ago, a departing editor of The Courier *was asked what he would miss about the place, he revealed the almost innocent, heart-warming emotional sensitivity out of which this recipe of apathy and aggression is concocted:'To paraphrase Dr. Johnson, a man who is tired of Aberystwyth is tired of skiving. I would just like to say that I can't think of anywhere else I'd rather have constructively dossed for five years and although I'll miss the sea, the scenery, the town, the bars and the general air of squalor, the best thing about Aber is the people and anyone who argues otherwise is a bottom-feeding primaeval life form.'*

Only 10% of students speak Welsh as a first language, but the Aber Guild of Students' policy is that 'all its written administration and written dealings with students and all other bodies' be couched in both Welsh and English, 'with Welsh given obvious priority'. Fortunately there is a Guild translator at hand to implement this piece of positive discrimination.

According to The Courier, most of the protesting students who saw off the Queen were more concerned about budget cuts than they were about the Welsh language. Six months earlier 100 people turned up for a march against university rent increases, getting themselves on television for their efforts, though the rent strike which followed was eventually aborted. Since 1990, the University has invested more than £20 million in new residential accommodation, and it fell to this lot to help pay for it. Perhaps they sensed that universally this drive to improve accommodation in our universities is not only for students' benefit - the great Conference market in the vacs is the real money spinner and motivator. But if this is seen as exploitation, the universities know that they will always win, because undergraduates live in a very short timescale and the authorities are dealing with the university's future which does not include them.

The most pressing political issue these days is the threat of the Government's withdrawal of funding for students' course fees. This got Aber into a particular tangle with the NUS National Executive. Aber's Guild President rather unwisely took it upon himself to vote against Aber policy at an NUS Wales conference and, as a result, was banned from attending future conferences, leaving Aber powerless in the national political context and forcing the university to look, as it were, into a mirror, at its increasing isolation.

It did not go down well.

SITUATION

Aber's isolation begins with its position half way down the West Wales coastline. Most of the university, including the main Union building, is contained within the Penglais Campus, set on a hill above the beautiful Cardigan Bay. But there is another campus for approximately 150 students at Llanbadarn, less than a mile away. The Llanbadarn Campus is home to the Department of Information and Library Studies, the Institute of Rural Studies and the College of Further Education. It has its own

Union shop and bar, and its own entertainment facilities, discos and pool room.

The University's main sites are linked by a common telephone system, and there's a good bus service, though they are within walking distance.

GETTING THERE

★ By road: Approach via the A484 from North or South, or along the A44 from the East.

★ By rail: Approx. time from London Euston (5 hours). Chart your route carefully or you will end up on a local line which takes ages through the mid-Wales countryside.

ACCOMMODATION

Llanbadarn has five Halls of Residence, but the majority of student accommodation is at Penglais. All first years are guaranteed campus accommodation. There are also seafront residences, terraced houses painted in colourful pastel shades, near the original university buildings, which offer a welcome opportunity for some to delineate their own space and breathe in the fresh, unadulterated air from the sea.

ARTS AND ENTS

The Arts Centre Complex is the largest in Mid and West Wales. There are three art galleries, an on-campus cinema, a theatre, numerous choirs and orchestras, and key local events include the International Film Festival and Aber Jazz Festival.

On a more frenzied level the on-campus Joint provides the usual music nights, comedy acts and other events. The town has a large range of pubs, clubs and eating places, but naturally the campus provides the cheapest bars. The Joint Cafe Bar and the Take-Away/Eat-In Munchies in the main Union bar is open in the evening.

The Guild boasts a fine range of entertainment but students complain of the dearth of recognised live acts. The problem seems to be its isolation and lack of a large enough venue to make top events pay. It's no better in the town: 'Apart from Andy's, the new music supply in Aber is pretty abysmal'. There have been moves to sort this out - suggestions that students from relatively nearby Lampeter be bussed in to listen to bands which, otherwise, can't justify a trip to the University. In recent years top theatre companies and comedians like Lenny Henry, Jo Brand, Jeremy Hardy and Sean Hughes have played the town Arts Centre and there is a feeling that the Union hasn't done enough in pulling big acts in. Perhaps it's a question of priorities.

At Llanbadarn I note a rather different response. Their ents team list 26 separate events in the month of March, and the bar is about to make a profit for the first time ever.

There are around 50 clubs and societies from War Gaming and Role Playing to Vegan and Vegetarian, and of course plenty of politics - the Anti-Racism/Anti-Federalist League, the Anti-Nazi League, Aberystwyth Hunt Sabateurs, International Politics Society, Student Tories, the Student Labour Club and Plaid Cymru. The Student Community Action Group is, in comparison, a fairly new innovation. Dim Probe began as late as January 1984, but it now has over 200 registered volunteers working in the local community with people disadvantaged either economically, socially or physically. On the charity front Aber has Europe's largest fundraising Uni event in its Rag. It raises, on average, more than £200,000 a year. A well attended Debating Society offers a nice mix of beer debates: from *This House believes that Red Dwarf is better than Star Trek* to *This House would cancel Third World Debt.*

SPORT

Cardigan Bay and Snowdonia offer windsurfing and skiing opportunities respectively, and there is orienteering. mountain biking, rambling, sub-aqua and hang gliding too. Sport is a big thing at Aber, there are 50 acres of pitches and specialist facilities for water sports, including a boat house, an indoor swimming pool, 2 sports halls, a new all-weather floodlit sports pitch, squash courts and indoor facilities for football, badminton, basketball, hockey and tennis.

ACADEMIA

Besides Politics, Aber scored 5 with Applied Maths and with Celtic Studies in the recent research facility assessment, and both History and Computing Science scored an impressive 4. As an undergraduate at Aber you have free access to the National Library of Wales, which is one of the five great libraries in the country with over six million books, maps and prints available. The University's own library is also good with over 700,000 volumes and 4,000 current periodicals in stock, as well as CD ROMS, Network data bases and other electronic sources.

The academic year is divided into two semesters, which run from September to February and February to June with breaks at Christmas and Easter. They are into the modular system. On the undergraduate teaching assessment front 33% of subjects assessed achieved an 'Excellent' rating, which places it fourth after Bangor, Swansea and Cardiff in Wales.

Anglia Polytechnic University

Anglia Polytechnic University
Brentwood Campus
Sawyers Hall Lane
Brentwood
Essex CM15 9BT

TEL 01277 264504
FAX 01277 211363

Anglia Polytechnic University
Cambridge Campus
East Road
Cambridge CB1 1PT

TEL 01223 363271
FAX 01223 352973

Anglia Polytechnic University
Chelmsford (Central) Campus
Victoria Road South
Chelmsford
Essex CM1 1LL

TEL 01245 493131
FAX 01245 490835

Anglia Polytechnic University
Chelmsford (Rivermead) Campus
Bishops Hall Lane
Rivermead
Chelmsford
Essex CM1 1SQ

TEL 01245 493131
FAX 01245 495419

Anglia Polytechnic University
Danbury Park Conference Centre
Danbury
Chelmsford
Essex CM3 4AT

TEL 01245 222141
FAX 01245 224331

Anglia Polytechnic University
Student Union
East Road
Cambridge CB1 1PT

TEL 01223 460008/460009
FAX 01223 356558

Anglia Polytechnic University
Student Union
Victoria Road South
Chelmsford
Essex CM1 1LL

TEL 01245 258178
FAX 01245 490835

Anglia Polytechnic University
Student Union
Sawyers Hall Lane
Brentwood
Essex CM15 9BT

TEL 01277 217421
FAX 01277 211363

ANGLIA POLYTECHNIC UNIVERSITY

Founded	**1989**
Situation/style	**Campus**
UNDERGRADUATE PROFILE	
Application acceptance rate	**14%**
Population	**6,700**
Mature student population	**37%**
Overseas student population	**6%**
Male/female ratio	**43:57**
1st year institut. accommodation	**30%**
Approximate cost:	
Cambridge (Uni)	**£45-£55 pw**
(City)	**£50+ pw**
Chelmsford (Uni)	**£40-£50 pw**
(Town)	**£40+ pw**
ACADEMIC PROFILE	
A-level requirements:	**Low**

Law, Sociology, French, Music, Psychology etc. combos 12-16,

Student/staff ratio	**20:1**
1st class degree pass rate	**5%**

HEFCE assessments (14 subjects assessed/approved):

1994 **Social Work, Music**	Excellent
1995 **English**	Excellent
1996 **Sociology** 20, **Modern Languages** 21	

Joint Funding Council's research assessment 1996 (17 subjects assessed):

Grade 5/5*	None

EMPLOYMENT PROFILE

Principal job market destinations:

Education, Health, Retail/Wholesale, Manufacturing, Commerce, Health, Public Admin./Law, Computer, Arts/Media, Personnel, Hotel/Restaurant

Approximate % unemployed **11%**

VAG VIEW

Anglia became a university five years ago. It has four sites, in Brentwood, Cambridge and Chelmsford (2), as well as the Danbury Park Conference Centre.

The university also partners a wider group of 16 colleges, which goes by the name of The Anglia Regional University - the Colchester Institute (see separate entry), Norfolk School of Art and Design (Norwich and Great Yarmouth), City College (Norwich) and Writtle College (also a separate entry).

The unifying factor of this diverse conglomeration is its provision of 'vocationally relevant education'. Anglia is the only university among the Polys recently awarded university status to have retained 'Polytechnic' in its title - 'We respect the values that the polytechnics stood for.' Lecturers have professional experience and close links with local industry; student employment is the aim.

Roots are in the past - earlier incarnations reach back into the 19th century - but they're moving forward fast. The final approval for the college to call itself a polytechnic only came through in May 1991. When it happened Anglia geared itself up for a major building programme which included a new hall of residence on the Cambridge site (Swinhoe House). Following its recognition as a Uni in June 1992 it brought in staff from schools of nursing to form part of the faculty of Health, Nursing and Social Work. That month also saw the first steps in the development of the Brentwood site.

In 1990 and 1991 they introduced a modular course structure and the Credit Accumulation Transfer (CATS) assessment scheme, seeing the advantage of the scheme in terms of the richer perspectives it gives a Single Honours student on his chosen subject, and in terms of career opportunity. Each undergraduate, with the help of a field adviser, works up a programme of module subjects designed not just to complement the main study area but to encourage an appreciation of it from different points of view, and, in the case of language and technology modules, for example, simultaneously to increase the student's employability. Anglia's association with its many affiliated colleges allows students to draw on wider educational resources than Anglia could provide on its own and at the same time enables students from the other colleges to study for undergraduate and postgraduate courses, validated by Anglia, which they would not otherwise have been able to do. Anglia likes to think of itself as 'a people's university', and it is from that ideal that its whole strategy flows.

CAMBRIDGE CAMPUS

★ By road (from London): M25 (J27), M11 (J11), A10. From West or East, A45. From North-West, A604. Stansted Airport, M11.
★ By train: London's Liverpool Street - under the hour; Nottingham - 2:30; Sheffield, Birmingham New Street - 3:00.

On campus are the Mungford Theatre and Student Union HQ - bar, cafe and recreational facilities. Magazine, Apex, links all sites and provides information on ents, which are typical: live bands, comedy, discos, etc.

Accommodation for students is Anglia's main problem at the moment. Swinhoe Hall can take only 117 students; Bridget's and Nightingale Halls can accommodate 39 and 69 students respectively; a further 620 beds are available in houses leased or owned by Anglia.

There is a multigym, and tennis courts, on campus, and 100 metres away lies the Kelsey Kerridge Sports Centre with a large gym and nearby swimming pool. Half a mile north of the campus there are 3 football pitches, a rugby pitch and a cricket square. Rowing crews rack their eights at Emmanuel College Boat House.

Included among the Cambridge courses are Art History, Environmental Biology, Ecology and Conservation, Biological

Sciences and Animal Behavior, Biomedical Sciences, Business and Economics (including a good course on European Business), Chemistry and Medicinal Chemistry, Communication Studies, Computer Science, Electronics and Instrumentation, English, Geography, Geology, Earth Sciences, Graphic Art and Illustration, History, etc.

CHELMSFORD CAMPUSES

★ By road: A12, A130 or A414.
★ By rail: 35 mins away from London Liverpool St.
★ Being only 10 miles from the M25 there is ready access to Stansted Airport and Heathrow.

Sports building, SU bar, language centre, computer lab. Central campus for Business, Computing, Law, Technology, Environment, Housing and Planning, Health. Rivermead Campus for the Learning Resource Centre (library etc) and student village. Opened in 1995, it accommodates 500+ students in single study bedrooms with en suite bathrooms. There's also Mildmay Hall, which accommodates 100 students, 5 minutes away from Central, plus Uni-owned houses.

Besides the sports building on campus there are two leisure centres in the town and a number of sports pitches, indoor and outdoor swimming pool, plus competition-size ice rink.

BRENTWOOD CAMPUS

★ By road: M25, A12, A127.
★ By rail: fast rail links with London, Stansted, City and Southend airports, 30-40 minutes.
★ Heathrow and Gatwick via M25.

Campus dedicated to Teacher Training, Primary and BEd. On-site Student Union, common room, bar, plus gym, refectory, library, etc. Accommodation very limited - 14 study bedrooms in adjacent houses.

ASKHAM BRYAN COLLEGE

Askham Bryan College
Askham Bryan
York YO2 3PR

TEL 01904 772277
FAX 01904 772288

Askham Bryan College
Student Union
Askham Bryan
York YO2 3PR

TEL 01904 707398

ASKHAM BRYAN COLLEGE	
Founded	**1948**
Situation/style	**Campus/farm**
UNDERGRADUATE PROFILE	
Application acceptance rate	**10%**
Population	**55**
Mature student population	**97%**
Overseas student population	**9%**
Male/female ratio	**56:44**
1st year institut. accommodation	**60%**
Approximate cost (College)	**£36-£64 pw**
(City)	**£35-£40 pw**
ACADEMIC PROFILE	
Land Management and Technology (BSc)	
Requirement:	**HND** in Agriculture, Horticulture, professional experience
Business Management (BA)	
Requirement:	**HND,** professional experience

VAG VIEW

An Agricultural college just outside York, offering degrees in Business Management, and Land Management and Technology, but building a teaching expertise in other areas through its HND and DipHE courses. The college has 244 single study bedrooms with shared bathrooms, showers and kitchens, and 24 self-catering units. The bar is open in the evenings and is a regular venue for discos and live bands. There are sporting activities including soccer, rugby, hockey, tennis, cricket, volleyball, badminton, squash, and that's about it unless you count a four-hole pitch and putt.

GETTING THERE

★ By road: Make for the A1237 ring road (part of which is the A64) from any of a dozen routes which lead to the city. Heslington is on the south-east side and the university is well signposted.
★ By train: York is on the main East Coast line, the fastest in Britain. Leeds, 30 mins; Sheffield, 1:15; Manchester 1:30; London Kings Cross, 2:00; Birmingham New Street, 3:00.
★ Buses from the station are Nos. 4 and 5; a taxi will take about 15 minutes.
★ By air: Nearest airport is Leeds.

VIEW FROM THE GROUND

by Ruth E.C. Furness and Peter Franks

Askham Bryan College is situated 4 miles from the historic City of York. Located close to the motorway network, it provides easy access to the outstanding scenery of the North Yorkshire Moors, Yorkshire Dales and the coastal towns of Whitby and Scarborough.

Since its establishment in 1948 the college has expanded rapidly. It has lost its image as an agricultural and horticultural college and now focuses on all land-based industries, including leisure, tourism and business.

Many students like the college because it is small and friendly. Everybody knows everybody else. You don't feel lonely here because all the students have common interests. You'll find the lecturers are accessible, friendly and willing to help with anything. Living on campus is great because everything you need is just a few hundred yards away and of course you are in close contact with students and lecturers.

One of the college's greatest assets has to be the grounds. They are beautiful and there are plenty of places you can escape to if you want time to yourself. If you're into exploring then there are some lovely walks you can do around the local villages and countryside.

The main weakness of the College is the lack of variety of activity. Unless you're into rugby, football, hockey, badminton and squash then there's very little else to do. Sport plays a key role at the college, and is dominated by the rugby players.

The college canteen operates a Girovend system. A card is loaded with money you can spend when and how you want. The food is generally of good quality and there is catering for different tastes and nutritional needs. Light snacks are on offer all day so you can grab yourself a bite to eat during your coffee break. Alternatively, if you fancy something different then there are all sorts of take-aways nearby.

SOCIAL SCENE

The college bar is open six days a week from eight until eleven (half past ten on Sundays) and is a great student attraction. Students are able to take part in pub games such as pool and darts whilst in the bar. All of the social events that are organised by the Students Union take place in the college bar and it is an excellent location for social events such as quizzes, discos and hypnotists. There is a brand new SU building being planned for next year that will upgrade the facilities. There will be a new gym and snooker hall amongst other things.

ACADEMIC FACILITIES

There's a Resource Centre where books, videos, periodicals and computers are available for student use, and the college is linked to the Internet. Students can contact people or companies all over the world by using the E-mail facility. All students have their own password and E-mail number.

Students can also use York City and University libraries which are only a bus ride away and the British Library [an outpost of London's Bloomsbury/Kings Cross Mecca] is only twenty minutes away by car. Here you will definitely be able to find what you want.

ASTON UNIVERSITY

Aston University
Aston Triangle
Birmingham B4 7ET

TEL 0121 359 3611

Aston University
Students Guild
Aston Triangle
Birmingham B4 7ET

TEL 0121 359 3611
FAX 0121 333 4218

UNIVERSITY OF ASTON	
Founded	**1966**
Situation/style	**Campus**
UNDERGRADUATE PROFILE	
Application acceptance rate	**12%**
Population	**4,000**
Mature student population	**9%**
Overseas student population	**2%**
Male/female ratio	**54:46**
1st year institut. accommodation	**100%**
Approximate cost	**£25-£45 pw**
ACADEMIC PROFILE	
A-level requirements:	**Medium**
Law/Legal Practice Management BBB-BBC, **German** BCC, **Chem., E & E Eng., Computing Sci.** 20, **Accounting for Management, Marketing, Int. Business/ French/German, Psychology & Management** BBB-BBC	
Student/staff ratio	**17:1**
1st class degree pass rate	**6.8%**
HEFCE assessments (14 subjects assessed/approved): 1995/6 **German** 22, **Chemical Eng.** 19, **French** 22	
Joint Funding Council's research assessment 1996 (8 subjects assessed):	
Grade 5/5*	None
EMPLOYMENT PROFILE	
Employability in Industry:	
MPW national league table (1996)	**15th**
Principal job market destinations: **Manufacturing, Retail/ Wholesale, Commerce, Computer, Health, Education, Public Admin./Law, Market Research/Advertising**	
PIP 1996 employers' survey: Top 3 subjects/national ranking	
Business	5th=
Engineering & Technology	14th
Electrical Engineering	17th=
Approximate % unemployed	**5%**

VAG VIEW

Aston is slap bang in the middle of the city and proud of it, more or less. Just as Birmingham University is keen to point out in its seduction address to students that it is not actually in Birmingham, but in the leafy suburb of Edgbaston, so Aston is understandably wary of emphasising that the teaching area is right on that inner city motorway system, a hot, dusty, noisy place in summer, or that its high rise buildings do little to charm the eye. But its spirit remains proudly technological, civic, engineeringified, and it has no qualms about pushing that at you. Indeed why should it? Its history is all Technology.

Aston began life as a Technical School and by the time it switched to being a University in 1966, it was a College of Advanced Technology. Today there is more to Aston than science, engineering and technology, but it is no less urban in outlook.

Basically Aston consists of three faculties: ***Life & Health Sciences*** *(Pharmaceutical & Biological Sciences, Vision Sciences);* ***Engineering and Applied Science*** *(Civil Engineering, Chemical Eng. and Applied Chemistry, Mechanical & Electrical Eng., Electronic and Applied Physics, Computer Science and Applied Maths); and* ***Management Languages & European Studies.***

You can choose to study for a Single Honours degree, Joint, or Combined, the difference between Joint and Combined being that in Joint Honours the combination subjects are taught as an integrated whole - you explore how one impinges on the other, whereas in Combined they're treated as quite distinct.

The interesting thing about Aston is this third faculty - Management Languages and European Studies, which includes the Aston Business School and the School of Languages and European Studies. The Business School is one of the largest in Europe, with 80 teaching and research staff, and 2,500 undergraduate, postgrad. and management development students. From the start the School has been managed in partnership with industry, commerce and the public sector, here and abroad, particularly in Europe. It is, in fact, a wholly integrated part of Birmingham city's drive to be the business focal point of Europe. Aston has not just traded on that, it is an integral part of it.

High on Erasmus study-abroad programmes, sandwich courses and language combinations, everything is aimed at employment here and in the New Europe. If you think this is just Uni hype, look at its employment record so far - 15th on the MPW National league table, 5th in business on the PIP survey, 5% unemployed etc. Aston is the model on which all those new Unis/ex-Polys are building their own business schools.

And it is developing further. This emphasis on languages will soon take it into a new School of Humanities, and you can bet that it won't be offering the same combinations as Oxbridge.

GETTING THERE

★ By road: M1, M5, M6 and M40 all give ready access to the city, but the easiest route to the Uni is via the M6 (J6), A38M. Ignoring the signs to Aston, leave the A38M at the 3rd exit and take the first exit at Lancaster Circus roundabout.

★ By rail: Intercity to Birmingham New Street - Bristol Parkway or Sheffield, 1:30; London Euston, 1:40; Liverpool or Manchester, 2:00; Leeds, 3:00.

★ By air: Regular internal and international flights to Birmingham International Airport, 15 mins journey time by train to New Street (12 mins walk from campus).

ACCOMMODATION

Guaranteed to all first years if they get their accommodation form in by 1st September. Three high rise and four low rise halls on campus - the triangle, as they call it, because it is one. All self-catering. Four miles away from campus is more accomm. in The Village, set in 18 acres of parkland (so don't worry when you hear it's called Handsworth Wood). There's parking space here, a pub (The Village Inn), all the usual facilities and a good bus service to and fro. First years tend to go into Handsworth Hall or Oak and Ash houses, which offer single study bedrooms with breakfast and evening meals on weekdays and brunch on Saturdays. There are also self-catering flats.

SOCIAL SCENE

See Birmingham Uni and Birmingham College of Food for a fuller treatment of the city, but this is a place with too much for everyone - music, theatre, cinema, creative arts of all kinds, clubs, pubs and ethnic eateries. Birmingham is one of the liveliest places outside London and possibly easier to find your way about in once you're inured to living on a Scalextric track.

The Guild offers 3 bars and all the usual facilities. The rag is *The Birmingham Sun*. Ents include the usual range of discos, pub quizzes, cabaret, comedy and live bands - Credit to the Nation, Pato Banton, Utah Saints, Blur, Bootleg Beatles, etc have graced Aston in recent years; plus acoustic nights - a novel non-technological idea, student and local bands. Annual May Ball and various other key-event Balls-ups.

SPORT

Two sports centres on campus - indoor football, hockey, cricket, volleyball, Basketball etc; also squash courts, multigyms, climbing walls etc; swimming pool; 3/4 size floodlit synthetic soccer, hockey, tennis pitch. Green pitches 8 miles away - a 90-acre rec. centre, cricket, rugby, plus 4 squash courts, large pavilion with bars, dining room etc.

BANGOR UNIVERSITY

University of Wales
Bangor
Gwynedd LL57 2DG

TEL 01248 351151
FAX 01248 370451

University of Wales
Student Union
Deiniol Road
Bangor
Gwynedd LL57 2TH

TEL 01248 353709
FAX 01248 361418

UNIVERSITY OF WALES, BANGOR

Founded	**1884**
Situation/style	**City sites**
UNDERGRADUATE PROFILE	
Application acceptance rate	**13%**
Population	**4,500**
Mature student population	**32%**
Overseas student population	**8%**
Male/female ratio	**46:54**
1st year institut. accommodation	**100%**
Approximate cost	**£60 pw**
ACADEMIC PROFILE	
A-level requirements:	**Low-medium**
Law CCC, **Chemistry** 14, **Ocean Studies** CCC, **Teacher Training** 8-12	
Student/staff ratio	**13:1**
1st class degree pass rate	**6%**

HEFCW assessments (14 subjects assessed/approved):	
1993/4 **Chemistry**	Excellent
1994/5 **Welsh, Music, Ocean Studies**	Excellent
1995/6 **Religious Studies, Psychology, Russian**	Excellent
Joint Funding Council's research assessment 1996 (21 subjects assessed):	
Psychology	Grade 5
EMPLOYMENT PROFILE	
Principal job market destinations:	
Education, Retail/Wholesale, Commerce, Public Admin./Law, Manufacturing, Health, Agriculture	
PIP 1996 employers' survey:	
Top subject/national ranking	
Finance, Banking & Accountancy	28th=
Approximate % unemployed	**10%**

VAG VIEW

Bangor is in North Wales just across the Menai Strait from the Isle of Anglesey. North Wales is different from the rest of Wales; they're the real Welsh up here. Try struggling with the natives over a road map up through Gwynedd or better still, the Lleyn Peninsula, and you'll see what I mean. But I am assured they are a friendly bunch in Bangor, an idyllic spot which masquerades as a cathedral city heaving with history, but is really no more than a town-size place heaving with history. It's a small community which manages not to protest at the regular incursion of a student population which now totals, in all, some 7,000 under- and post-grads and swells the status quo by around 50% at the start of each term. In fact city-Uni relations couldn't be better. Perhaps it has something to do with living between inspirational Snowdonia and the sea.

The university started life on 18th October 1884 in an old coaching inn, a promising beginning, particularly as half the student intake was women (which was swimming against the tide in 1884). Today, possibly surprisingly to some, Bangor takes its place as an academic high achiever - 43% of subjects assessed attained an 'Excellent' rating - in a range of subjects which seems to strike almost the perfect balance: Finance and Accounting/Theology, Chemistry/Ecology, Engineering/Ocean Studies,

Welsh/English, and so on. There is also a healthy emphasis on, well, health - from Nursing & Midwifery to Sport and PE Sciences - and on the Earth Mother Sciences too. For besides the ocean, which is on their doorstep, they have all kinds of Environmental courses and Agricultural courses, and so good are they at the Arts (Music rates 'Excellent') and languages (Russian also made top marks), you begin to wonder what their secret might be. Then you look at Bangor's performance in the Joint Council's Research assessment, notice that they rated a 5 in Psychology - that's international notoriety - and you are forced to the conclusion that someone here knows how to make people tick. In percentage terms, Bangor leads the academic ratings among Welsh universities.

SITUATION

While not exactly a campus university, all the various university buildings, with the exception of the school of Ocean Sciences which is a few miles from the 'city' at the Menai Bridge, are within easy walking distance of one another.

GETTING THERE

For such an out of the way place, Bangor is actually very accessible, provided you don't enjoy yourself ambling through Gwynedd from the South.

★ By road: 90 minutes from the M56, which links with the M6.

★ By rail: There is a fast train service to Bangor from London Euston (4:00), Birmingham New Street (3:00), Manchester Oxford Road (2:30), Liverpool Lime Street (2:15).

ACCOMMODATION

Nice, confident touch in offering summer vacation bed and breakfast accommodation to prospective undergraduates - with or without their parents - to get a taste of the place. One hall exclusively for Welsh speakers (or those in the process of becoming Welsh speakers); one exclusively for women. Large number of en-suite rooms.

ACADEMIA

There are all the usual Erasmus projects, and their Multi-Media Language Centre is a pioneer of digital language laboratory technology in Britain. Yet still Bangor remains a university true to its cultural roots in a place where Welsh remains the mother tongue - they offer Single Honours degree courses in a number of subjects through the medium of Welsh, as well as informal tuition in Welsh in various subjects.

SOCIAL SCENE

Finally, after sustained protest from a large section of the population, there is an indie night in the Guild Refectory. If that isn't to your taste then it's off to the Barrells in the High Street, where entry is free. Near the Pier in Garth, at the Tap and Spiel, is 'the best pint in Bangor'. It may even sometimes be preferable to the Union bar which is generally bursting at the seams. Wednesday is now student night at The Octagon in town with a student/local mix, cheap beer and loud music - student discount with Union card. Fridays is Jukebox night at the Union main bar - '60s, '70s, '80s; Dance in the refec. is the alternative. The bar also has pool tables and arcade machines. Jazz Sundays. If you're a hard working lad or lass, and these students obviously are some of the time, what more could you want in the midst of some of the most beautiful scenery in Wales? The union runs a bussing service after. It's free, or 10p a mile for towns far away.

SPORT

Great emphasis on sport. Sports Sciences degree ensures top facilities for all major games. Outward bound activities, mountaineering, etc. popular, as well as rowing, sailing and canoeing.

Barnsley College

Barnsley College
Old Mill Lane Site
Church Street
Barnsley
S. Yorks S70 2AX

TEL 01226 216216
FAX 01226 216166

Barnsley College Students' Association
Old Mill Lane Site
Church Street
Barnsley
S. Yorks S70 2AX

TEL 01226 731 546

BARNSLEY COLLEGE	
Founded	**1990**
Situation/style	**Town site**
UNDERGRADUATE PROFILE	
Application acceptance rate	**46%**
Population	**800**
Mature student population	**58%**
Overseas student population	**1%**
Male/female ratio	**47:53**
1st year institut. accommodation	**15%**
Approximate cost(College)	**£35-£40 pw**
(Town)	**£35 pw**
ACADEMIC PROFILE	
A-level requirements:	**Low**

Combined Studies (Design/Social Science), Business & Mgt., Humanities, Pop Music, Music Technology, Engineering EE, **Combined Studies: Journalism, Media** CC, **Combined Studies: Performing Arts, Sport** DD

VAG VIEW

Barnsley is a town in South Yorkshire just north of Sheffield. It has a theatre, an Odeon cinema, two night clubs, one of which is called Club Hedonism, a collection of pubs, a Leisure Centre, and Barnsley FC. Allegedly it came 127th out of 127 in a recent poll about the best place to live.

One piece of good news for Barnsleyites, and for you if you'd like to avail yourself of it, is that the college is offering a passport out of the place to California. This has nothing to do with Club Hedonism, as far I am aware, though you may think it rather suspicious that it - Barnsley that is - also offers a degree course in Pop Music.

Barnsley is not the only college to offer such a course, and a recent article in The Independent *put the idea in a correct light by pointing out that if you accept degree courses in culture and society, how can you possibly leave out Pop Music, which has had such a seminal influence over the past 40 years? As for the trip to California, it has been on offer for the past three years, and is an exchange study scheme which can last anything up to twelve weeks.*

GETTING THERE

★ By road: M1 (J37).
★ By rail: London Kings Cross (via Leeds), just under 4 hours; Newcastle (via Leeds), 3:00; Birmingham New Street (via Sheffield), 2:00.

ACCOMMODATION

One hall of residence, Leecrest, situated out of town on a dual carriageway on the Doncaster Road, Ardsley, near the Barnsley crematorium. Preference is given to first years and 'students with acute medical conditions'. You may prefer to join the majority of students in shared housing nearer the centre of town.

SOCIAL SCENE/SPORT

Barnsley students are catered for generously by Club Hedonism, which offers them 'a pint for a pound and a shot for a pound'. They also have their own Student Union, which provides the largest venue for live bands in the town. The Union bar has video games, pool, Sky TV, pinball, and judging by a well produced concertina-style alternative prospectus, Barnsley students make for themselves a fair old time. Wednesday afternoons is given over to sport. The Metrodome Sports Centre offers students club membership for a pound.

ACADEMIA

Combined BA Hons degrees, all validated by the University of Leeds (15 miles to the north) include Design, Fine Art, Journalism, Media, Performing Arts, Social Science, Sport, Recreation and Tourism. Single Hons include Business, Band Studies (brass bands are big in this area), the aforesaid Pop Music (2 E Grades required), Technology, Engineering, etc.

BATH UNIVERSITY

University of Bath
Claverton Down
Bath BA2 7AY

TEL 01225 826826
FAX 01225 826366

Bath University Student Union
Claverton Down
Bath
BA2 7AY

TEL 01225 826612
FAX 01225 444061

UNIVERSITY OF BATH

Founded	**1966**
Situation/style	**Campus**
UNDERGRADUATE PROFILE	
Application acceptance rate	**9%**
Population	**4,800**
Mature student population	**16%**
Overseas student population	**6%**
Male/female ratio	**55:45**
1st year institut. accommodation	**100%**
Approximate rent	**£40 pw**
ACADEMIC PROFILE	
A-level requirements:	**High**

Architectural Studies 24, **Int. Business & Modern Languages** BBB, **Mech. Engineering** ABB, **Sociology** 22, **Computer Software Technology** 22

Student/staff ratio	**9:1**
1st class degree pass rate	**2%**
HEFCE assessments (10 subjects assessed/approved):	
1993 **Mechanical Eng.**	Excellent
1994 **Architecture, Business & Management Studies, Social Policy & Administration**	Excellent
1995/6 **Modern Languages** 19, **Sociology** 19, **Chemical Engineering** 20	

Joint Funding Council's research assessment 1996 (21 subjects assessed):	
Mechanical/Aeronautical/ Manufacturing Engineering	Grade 5*
Pharmacology, Biological Sciences, Pure Maths, Applied Maths, Statistics, Computer Science, Chemical Engineering, Social Policy & Admin, Business &Management, European Studies, Education	Grade 5
EMPLOYMENT PROFILE	
Employability in Industry:	
MPW national league table (1996)	**19th=**
Principal job market destinations:	

Manufacturing (strong on **Pharmaceutical, Electronic & Electrical**), **Commerce, Retail/ Wholesale, Health, Public Admin., Education, Computer, Architecture, Engineering Design**

PIP 1996 employers' survey: Top 3 subjects/national ranking	
Engineering & Technology	5th
Electrical Engineering	5th=
Business	14th=
Approximate % unemployed	**5%**

VAG VIEW

'Bath is one of the newer universities which has made it. One of our very best mathematicians bound for Cambridge has just come back from a visit to Bath and liked it very much. Of the newer Universities, I'd say it was number one.'

'I wouldn't call it a new university any more, it is very good, always has been very good for combined courses. It was quite radical in its thinking about modern languages and engineering or accountancy; it really was very forward thinking when it started all that.'

These views from schools advisers confirm that Bath has arrived. The Uni doesn't cover the full range of subjects, but what it does cover it succeeds at in a thoroughly professional and pleasant manner. Student life here is inspiring, fulfilling and clean.

SITUATION

Bath stone/concrete campus (60s design not to everyone's taste), set on a hill outside the city.

As long ago as the Iron Age, Bath, with its natural hot springs, was a place of pagan spiritual significance. Geoffrey of Monmouth (12th century) gives the founding of the city to Bladud, 'a most ingenious man who encouraged necromancy throughout the kingdom of Britain.' The Romans' Aquae Sulis took up where Bladud left off, but long before Jane Austen's *Northanger Abbey* (1818) the baths had lost their original 'gateway to the Underworld/fount of inspiration' associations and become a health spa meeting place for the society set. In 1687 Celia Fiennes described the King's Bath, 'which ye Company drinks of', as tasting like 'the water that boyles Eggs.'

Today tourists are the problem. They no longer sup the waters, but still flock to the baths and other city sites from all over the world. The cost for students living or playing in this beautiful and historic city is high prices and crowd/traffic congestion. Campus is a mile out, centred around The Parade, an area which includes the 24-hour library, Students Union and admin offices. The Uni is in a constant state of evolution, and it is impossible to be certain what you will find when you get there.

Note that parking is limited on campus and first years are not permitted to bring cars. There's a Uni bus service for town and a tradition of hitching from the bottom of the hill up to campus, so well established that students form a queue.

GETTING THERE

★ By road: M4 (J18), A46; at A4 turn right to Bath; after 3/4 mile turn right at traffic lights (signposted City Centre A36). After 700 yards turn left at r/about to Warminster, then right into North Road (signposted Claverton Down).

★ By rail: Bath Spa station - London Paddington or Southampton (1:30); Birmingham (2:15); Cardiff (1:50). Paddington - Bristol line. From Midlands, North and South West travel to Bristol and thence to Bath (15 minutes journey).

★ Frequent bus service (No. 418) from outside Berni Royal Hotel opposite station to university. The campus is only a mile or so from the city, but it is an uphill walk.

WHAT GOES ON

Although a relatively small university, if you add in the students at Bath College and Bristol Uni, you will appreciate why this area is student- as well as tourist-orientated, and being small and just that mile or so out, there's a friendly, close-knit community feel on campus. (See also rivalry with Bristol Uni, Bristol entry.)

The centre for arts is The Arts Barn - drama, dance, music, studio workshop space for visual arts and crafts. At the time of writing they had applied for a National Lottery grant to extend their arts facilities. Plenty of activity in music and drama, and opportunities to become involved in the Bath Fringe and Edinburgh festivals. Various art galleries in the city, 3 cinemas plus arthouse productions at the Little Theatre cinema. Dance and pre-run West End plays at Theatre Royal plus experimental theatre as part of Fringe Fest.

Student *Spike* mag. runner-up in 1995 NUS/Guardian Media Awards. Student-run 12-hour-a-day CTV (Campus TV), which has won awards, was launched in 1989. Called 'a dazzling piece of hypermedia' by Net Magazine. URB 963 is student radio station with 3 studios, 2 for broadcasting, 1 for production - extensive record library and roadshow.

Union ents - dance, indie, chart and busy Friday Freak Out (70s/80s) plus regular high profile live bands and imported club scenes-Ministry of Sound, Cream etc.

SPORT

Current projects include a £6 million range of astro pitches, athletics track (8-lane and floodlit, just completed), indoor tennis courts, 50m swimming pool, etc. Sport is very strong at Bath and given a high priority by University and union. There are over 50 sporting clubs and every opportunity to play any sport you fancy, from sub aqua to air ballooning to women's rugby.

ACCOMMODATION

First-year accommodation exclusively on campus, most others live out. All first-year accommodation is self-catering, either high rise blocks or low rise terraces, 8 to 13 study bedrooms centred on communal kitchen. Two of the accommodation blocks, Norwood and Wessex House, are adjacent to The Parade.

ACADEMIA

Bath concentrates on three areas - Sciences, Social Sciences and Technology. Very high percentage of 'Excellent' or high scoring ratings in HEFCE course assessments, backed by good performance in depth in terms of research. Go there for anything technical or computer-based, or for modern languages and business. The student computer facility is excellent - 254 in the library alone; the majority of student PCs are connected to Uni mainframe computers and a campus-wide network.

Strong on sandwich courses and very involved with industry. Job prospects very high.

Bath knows what it is good at and makes sure it is better than more or less anyone else at it: 'We have had experience in the last few years of girls who have been Cambridge entrants, but who have been interviewed earlier by Bath and given a two E offer to encourage them to go there,' recalls one sixth-form adviser. 'In one case a girl didn't want to go to Cambridge afterwards because the whole process, including the interview, was so welcoming.'

BATH COLLEGE OF HIGHER EDUCATION

Bath College of Higher Education
Newton Park Campus
Newton Park
Bath BA2 9BN

TEL 01225 875875
FAX 01225 875444

Bath College of Higher Education
Sion Hill Campus
Sion Hill Place
Lansdown
Bath BA1 5SF

TEL 01225 425264
FAX 01225 445228

Bath College of Higher Education Student Union
Newton Park
Newton St Loe
Bath
Somerset BA2 9BN

TEL 01225 872603
FAX 01225 874765

BATH COLLEGE OF HIGHER EDUCATION

Founded	**1983**
Situation/style	**Campus**
UNDERGRADUATE PROFILE	
Application acceptance rate	**10%**
Population	**2,100**
Mature student population	**38%**
Overseas student population	**8%**
Male/female ratio	**28:72**
1st year institut. accommodation	**100%**
Approximate rent	**£35-£40 pw**
ACADEMIC PROFILE	
A-level requirements:	**Medium**
Teacher Training CCC-CD	
Student/staff ratio	**17:1**
1st class degree pass rate	**6%**
HEFCE assessments (6 subjects assessed/approved):	
1994 **English, Environmental Studies**	Excellent
1995/6 **Sociology** 22	
Joint Funding Council's research assessment 1996 (12 subjects assessed):	
Grade 5/5*	None
EMPLOYMENT PROFILE	
Principal job market destinations: **Education, Retail/Wholesale, Manufacturing, Arts/Media**	
Approximate % unemployed	**10%**

VAG VIEW

Bath College may have less pretensions to greatness than Bath University (see entry), but it is really a quite different operation, appealing largely to women and mature students, and with a great deal going for it in both academic and social terms.

SITUATION

Two campuses. Newton Park is situated approximately 4 miles west of the centre of the city in a landscaped saucer of beautiful Duchy of Cornwall countryside, with a Georgian manor house as its administrative hub. Sion Hill is within walking distance of the city on its north side - this is reserved for Art and Design.

GETTING THERE

★ By road **Newton Park:** From London and East - by road: M4 (J18), A46, A4 through Bath towards Bristol. A39 to Wells, turn left after 200 yards into Newton Park estate. From South - A39 from Wells, after Corston Village turn right into Newton Park Estate. From South Wales and North - M4 (J19), M32, A4 through Bath, then as From London directions.

Sion Hill: From North, East and West - M4 (J18), A46, A420 (Bristol), first left to Hamswell, at second give-way take a right and 2nd right into Landsdown Crescent, over crossroads, first right to Sion Hill on your right. From South - A39, A4, left turn into

Marlborough Lane, at second crossroads, left then right: entrance to Sion Hill on your right.
★ By rail: Bath Spa station - London Paddington or Southampton (1:30); Birmingham (2:15); Cardiff (1:50). Paddington - Bristol line. From Midlands, North and South West travel to Bristol and thence to Bath (15 minutes journey).
★ Frequent bus service (No. 418) from outside Berni Royal Hotel opposite station to university. The campus is only a mile or so from the city, but it is an uphill walk.

ACADEMIA

Three of the six subjects assessed by HEFCE - English, Environmental Studies, Sociology - received the highest rating. Degree courses include Fine Art, Creative Arts, Graphic Design, Ceramics. Single Honours in Music, Ecology, Food Management, Environmental Science. There is a 17-subject modular programme (BSc/BA) available in Joint or Major/Minor combinations - including Business, Maths, History, English (plus Creative Writing), Environmental Biology, Health, Psychology, Sociology, Geography, Food, Music, etc.

ACCOMMODATION

Campus accommodation, available to all first years, ranges from rooms in a Georgian Crescent in Bath to purpose-built residences in Royal Newton Park. All with adequate self-catering facilities.

SOCIAL SCENE

Union ents include the usual comedians - recently Alan Parker Urban Warrior - hypnotists, discos, theme nights, and all-night parties. There are at least two events each week at the Union and regular live bands - Julian Cope, Urban Species, Hot Chocolate, Transglobal Underground are big names of recent years, though local fare is more likely. Eagle-eyed socialites will have noted the preponderance of females (F/M 72/28), but also the mature population, 38%. An emphasis on music on the academic side is reflected in the Michael Tippett Centre - an auditorium seating up to 200, and a venue for choirs, orchestras, etc.

SPORT

Not quite the pulling power among students as at the university, but there's a sports hall, tennis courts, gym, etc.

BIRKBECK COLLEGE

Birkbeck College
University of London
Malet Street
London WC1E 7HX

TEL 0171 631 6000
FAX 0171 631 6270

Birkbeck College, London
Student Union
Malet Street
London WC1E 7HX

TEL 0171 631 6000
FAX 0171 631 6349

BIRKBECK COLLEGE	
Founded	**1823**
Situation/style	**City site**
UNDERGRADUATE PROFILE	
Population/Full time	**150**
Part time	**3,300**
Mature student population	**95%**
Male/female ratio	**50:50**
1st year institut. accommodation	**N/A**
ACADEMIC PROFILE	
A-level requirements:	
No formal requirements for Mature Students; under 21:	**2 'A's + test**
Student/staff ratio	**17:1**
1st class degree pass rate	**13%**

HEFCE assessments (12 subjects assessed/approved):	
1995 **English**	Excellent
1995 **Linguistics** 19	
1995/6 **German** 20, **Iberian** 19, **French** 19	
Joint Funding Council's research assessment 1996 (20 subjects assessed):	
Psychology, Crystallography, Law, Economics, French, History, Philosophy	Grade 5
EMPLOYMENT PROFILE	
Principal job market destinations: **Manufacturing, Arts/Media, Commerce, Public Admin., Personnel**	
Approximate % unemployed	**15%**

VAG VIEW

A postgrad/research set-up which offers part-timers who missed out on Higher Education first time round an opportunity to make up for lost time in the evenings. Course/assessments are good, lecturers well qualified, and it works, too, because anyone who enrols is going to be highly motivated. Have you ever tried to hold down a job and get a degree in the evening?

LOCATION

Wedged behind the British Museum between Euston Road and Montague Place. Same building as University of London Union (ULU).

GETTING THERE

★ Circle/Metropolitan - Euston Square; Victoria - Warren Street; Northern - Goodge Street; Piccadilly - Russell Square.

ACADEMIA

First Degree courses offered only to part-time students, most over 21. Formal teaching after work hours, leaving the day for the serious stuff - postgrad teaching and research. Evening nursery facilities available.

Fees - Self-financing students get a concessionary rate, anything from £600 to £1,200 p.a.; LEA sponsored students, it's a couple of hundred more.

Subject areas: Biology, Physical Sciences, Computer Sci., Social Studies (Geog., Psychol., Law, Politics), Business Mgt, Economics, Languages (incl. Eng.), Humanities, Linguistics etc. Fair performance in assessment, good teaching and strong in-depth research scene.

ENTS

Tie-up with ULU means all the usual benefits - sports, leisure facilities, clubs and socs., discounted shops and services plus live bands, Indie Night, Gorgeous Night, etc.

Birkbeck not known for the best Ents in town, but things have improved over the past few years - better acts, more balls. Friday night main event - disco, jazz night, comedy, occasional live bands, plus promise of quiz nights Thursdays, pool tournaments, spoken word evenings, regular JCR events with late extensions on Fridays. Not exactly overawing but they're getting there.

BCLSU

Special office of the Union - MSU - looks after the 'complex problems faced by mature students', fitting round pegs into square holes for virtually everyone.

Recently ran a 'green practices' year - the Year of the Cycle: new cycle racks and a new recycling programme for paper to cans.

BCLSU pages on the web are among the best and getting better all the time. No surprise for a college which has run its own Virtual University courses on the Internet for the past few years. Try

http://www.bbk.ac.uk/Departments/bcsu

SPORTS, CLUBS, SOCIETIES

Recently appointed new BCLSU sports officer, but not because demand is high, just that the admin for the other clubs and socs are too demanding. Dwindling sports interest not helped by college withdrawing sports ground funds. Never mind, there's always ULU - int-length pool, health spa, fitness centre, plus everything from Shiatsu massage to chiropody. Though watch out, incredibly ULU recently tried to ban Birkbeck from using them until a new financial package was negotiated. Perhaps the college is worried about arterial trauma amongst all those wrinklies.

Other clubs mainly academically orientated, but plenty of discussions and lectures and - you'll be ready for it - the odd blow-out.

ACCOMMODATION

Full-time students only can take up college accommodation, so that means all undergrads are on their own...

BIRMINGHAM UNIVERSITY

University of Birmingham
Edgbaston
Birmingham B15 2TT

TEL 0121 414 3374
FAX 0121 414 3850

Birmingham University
Guild of Students
Edgbaston Park Road
Birmingham B15 2TU

TEL 0121 472 1841
FAX 0121 471 2099

UNIVERSITY OF BIRMINGHAM

Founded	**1900**
Situation/style	**Campus**
UNDERGRADUATE PROFILE	
Application acceptance rate	**8%**
Medical AAR	**10%**
Population	**12,500**
Mature student population	**11%**
Overseas student population	**7%**
Male/female ratio	**52:48**
1st year institut. accommodation	**100%**
Approximate cost	**£37-£76 pw**
ACADEMIC PROFILE	
A-level requirements:	**High**
Medicine (under review) ABB**:**	
★ Science 'A's required **Chemistry + 1Sci. + 1 other**	
★ Addit. Non-Science 'A's acceptable **Yes**	
★ Retakes considered **Rarely**	
★ Clinical contact **1st year**	
Student/staff ratio	**11:1**
1st class degree pass rate	**9.7%**
HEFCE assessments (20 subjects assessed/approved):	
1993 **History**	Excellent
1994 **Music, Geography**	Excellent
1995 **English, Geology**	Excellent
Italian 22, **German** 19, **Russian** 23	
1995/6: **Sociology** 24, **Chemical Engineering** 21	
1996: **French** 18, **Iberian** 22	

Joint Funding Council's research assessment 1996 (50 subjects assessed):	
Anatomy, Metallurgy & Materials, Middle East & African Studies, European Studies	Grade 5*
Clinical Lab. Sciences, Bio-chemistry, Chemistry, Physics, Chemical Eng., English, German/Dutch/ Scandinavian, Iberian/ Latin American, Byzantine/ Ottoman/Mod. Greek, History, Theology, Music, Education, Sport	Grade 5
EMPLOYMENT PROFILE	
Employability in Industry:	
MPW national league table (1996)	**6th=**
Principal job market destinations: **Health** (incl. **Dentistry**), **Manufacturing** (strong on **Pharmaceutical**), **Commerce, Retail/Wholesale, Public Admin/Law, Education, Personnel, Arts/Media, Computer, Construction, Sport**	
PIP 1996 employers' survey:	
Top 3 subjects/national ranking	
Electrical Engineering	7th
Science	9th=
Computing	9th
Approximate % unemployed	**5%**

VAG VIEW

Birmingham is the original Redbrick University with all that entails beyond its masonry - none of the snobbery attached to Oxbridge and a refreshingly laid-back approach to life, light years away from Durham and not as self-conscious as Manchester. If you don't enjoy a 3-year spell here, it won't be Birmingham's fault.

Birmingham itself offers the sort of night-time rapture and daylight utility you'd expect from England's second city. It's accessible, desirable and relatively trouble free.

Unlike Aston, which is in the eye of the whirling urban vortex, the self-contained campus is a couple of miles south of the city 'in leafy Edgbaston', a phrase which you'll hear from school careers staff and the Uni prospectus until you're sick of it. But what it gives is a wonderfully objective appreciation of the goodies on offer in the city. You can use it, abuse it and retreat to semi-rural bliss to get the brain cells back in some sort of working order for the occasional sortie into academia, a well-organised world in which good results are the norm.

GETTING THERE

★ Brum is at the confluence of the M40, M42, M5, M6, M69, M1, M45, well served by rail (London Euston, 1:40; Bristol Parkway or Sheffield, 1:30; Liverpool Lime Street or Manchester Piccadilly,1:40; Leeds, 2.15), coach and air. The campus is 2.5 miles from the city centre on the A38. Avoid entry through suburbia from the M40; instead join M42 and connect with A38 at J1.
★ Taxi to Uni from airport 30 mins, from city centre 10 mins.
★ Frequent trains from New Street to University Station.

WHAT GOES ON

'Birmingham isn't just about getting rat-arsed and going for a closing time curry, but more students do that than spend their time in an art gallery,' is one student analysis, but in truth there is more to life here than it suggests, for Birmingham is big enough to absorb, supply and satisfy a multiplicity of tastes among the straights and misfits, artistes and piss artistes, boffins and gifted layabouts, who end up here.

Sure, omnipresent Balti restaurants mop up the small change - a fiver will put the food question out of the way - and there is no shortage of choice among ethnic eateries (Chinese, Italian, Kebab Greek, Thai, Mexican, Japanese or fish 'n' chips).

True, there are pubs galore - the Hibernian in the Stirchley student area is one of the best places in Brum for live music, and real ale tapsters roll out their own lethal brews at the Flapper & Firkin, shaping the experience with a rich variety of gigs.

True, too, you can club out in Brum every night without deja vu (even without change of venue), and the NEC, Aston Villa Leisure Centre, Wolverhampton Civic Hall and NIA play host to a rich miscellany of live bands.

But theatre and classical music thrives as well. The Hippodrome, the Rep and the Old Rep boast West End tours and supply top-flight native productions and plenty of fringe. The Symphony Hall at ICC is home to Sir Simon Rattle's Birmingham Symphony Orchestra, and the Hippodrome to the Birmingham Royal Ballet. And art galleries do pull - the Barber Institute, Gas Hall and City among them.

Likewise, on campus, artistic input is high. There's a Chamber orchestra and choir, an orchestra of 100, a choir of 220, and a Guild musical theatre group, which milk the astonishing musical talent that abounds among students here. Again, if you're into drama this is one of THE places to be. There's a Guild group and a Drama dept group in the Uni's Studio Theatre; students perform all over the city and there's a student humour night at the Glee Club (Brum's stand-up comedy scene). Then, for Shakespeare freaks, Stratford is but 20 miles down the road.

For a full run-down on Birmingham night and day, see Patricia Magee's piece - *What Goes On* - under Birmingham College of Food immediately after this entry. Here's a taster: 'The list of clubs goes on forever but to name a few - The Steering Wheel (home to Slag and Fun), Bonds (home to Miss Moneypenny's), Bakers (home to Renaissance), The Que Club (often housing Liverpool's Cream), the new Sanctuary, Wobble & Crunch, Snobs, System, Liberty's, Subway, The Dome II, Pulse, Exile, XL's, The Nightingale (Gay), The Church, Ronnie Scotts (Jazz), Bobby Browns, The Surfer's Paradise (Australian), Gary Owen (Irish), Claridges (Soul), etc., etc., etc. And, of course, there's always the underground all-night venues.

'However, this does create severe problems. Why do I feel my head has exploded? Where the hell do we go? When am I ever going to study? When exactly *was* that appointment with my bank manager?'

Fact is that weight of student numbers - more than 18,000 here, a figure which approaches 40,000 with the other Unis and colleges - helps tailor the city to student tastes. And because Brum is so cosmopolitan it can take them in its stride with no more aggro than you might expect in any city.

Back on campus the University Guild converts, of an evening, to a passable potted version of the city scene, presumably for those hard-grinders who have lost the use of their legs. The Guild was the first Student Union, which they say with touching pride and baffling logic is why it is called a Guild.

BUGS for short, it sounds like a training ground for CIA agents, and there's clearly a feeling from our correspondent, Ruth Hay, that the appelation may not be entirely inappropriate. However, here entertainment *is* cheaper than in the city, the main caveat being that, for live bands it's too small for the biggies and too big for the smaller ones. It's Fingal's for a quiet drink, Old Joe's and Berlin's for events licensed to 2 am or longer. A recent menu included: Monday bar quiz, Tuesday Planet of Sound indie night, Wednesday sports night (drink and debauchery in all its livid forms), Thursday Club Tropicana 70s/80s disco, Friday Lush & Frenzy. All this peppered with Society nights like Roscoe or Spanish Society's Latin American or the upfront girations of the Kinky Sex Soc.

ACCOMMODATION

Officially all 1st years are guaranteed a place in hall or in a self-catering flat, 'subject to certain conditions'. So, if Birmingham wasn't your first choice and you are late returning your form, you may have to mark time in the city until a hall place falls free, which can take anything from a few days to a term.

In hall there are singles and shared, some singles with en-suite. There's a space on the form for 'interests', but don't be duped into thinking you're about to form a meaningful relationship with the admin. department. Given half a chance they'll match you up with some weirdo, so if you want a single, say you're a tooth-grinder.

Four halls are mixed: Chamberlain, Manor, Mason, University. Lake is trumpeted as men only, Wyddrington women only, but they're linked by communal eating/bar/ games rooms, and if there's a fire alarm, it's odds on more men will come out of the women's wing.

University is near BUGS, has the smallest intake, is difficult to get a place in, but has good sized rooms, bar, 2 TV rooms, good food, an active JCR and disabled access.

Manor is two miles from campus, an old characterful building, and has some decent sized rooms and en-suites, waiter-served dinner, loads of formal meals, balls, a garden party, a bar, and is good for sport.

The rest are in the Vale, 20 mins from campus centre. Mason has 3 TV rooms, games room, 2 launderettes, fitness room, sunbed, music practice rooms, shop, photocopiers, bar. Chamberlain has an en-suite wing with Sky TV points, fitness room, sunbed, baby grand, launderette and the most unsociable bar in the Vale. Lake/Wyddrington has the best bar in the Vale, games room, shop, CD library, multigym, 2 TV rooms, 1 with Sky, photocopiers, darkroom, launderette, and high reputation theatre company - Madsoc.

Fees include 'breakfast and dinner Monday to Friday, and breakfast and lunch on Sunday'. In fact you get fed twice on Saturday too, but as anywhere it's a poor investment if you don't rise before 9 for breakfast or eat out a lot in the evening. The single-sex self-catering flats in mixed blocks (there are 6, Griffin Close, Tennis Courts, Beeches, Hunter Court, Queen's Hospital Close, Maple Bank) are a better bet; a half-way house to living out.

Lower band fees don't include gas or electricity; you get en-suite facilities, 'background heating' and hot water for the higher prices. The real bonus is that you can use your flat during the Christmas and Easter vacs for no extra.

Selly Oak, Stirchley, Balsall Heath and Harborne are the 4 city student ghettoes for living out. Selly, the closest, has the largest student population in turn-of-the-century slums, good corner-shop shopping, a curry-house haven, a park and 3 OK pubs (but avoid the OVT if you're allergic to Chemical Engineers).

Stirchley is close too, about half a mile

away. It has the Hibernian, OK shopping and plenty of fast-food outlets.

Balsall Heath, 2-3 miles from campus, the redlight area, is cheap and a Mecca for curry houses.

Harborne is posher, with proper High Street shopping, loads of pubs, quite close to campus, but closer to Medical School.

To find out what's available go to Uni housing services where landlords advertise, or get in touch with BUGS, who specialise in filling vacant rooms in student houses. Sign nothing until you have full psycho-profile on prospective flatmates.

ACADEMIA

Subject areas with the largest full-time undergraduate take-ups are Engineering & Technology (1,847), Languages (1,350), and Medicine & Dentistry (1,178). The courses favoured most by employers are Electrical Engineering, Science and Computing. Chemical Engineering is also a strength.

A full-time post-graduate population of 3,201, second only to Oxford and Cambridge, is a good indicator of academic depth of field. Medicine, Biological & Physical Sciences, Engineering & Technology, Business & Administrative Studies and Education are especially strong.

Medicine/Dentistry is the 4th largest faculty in the country and there are a number of bonus points worth mentioning about it. For example, when it comes to offers, preference is given to applicants with no alternative offer from elsewhere. Mature applications are welcomed and there is no special entrance requirement.

Although, as elsewhere, the A-Level requirement is high, particular attention is placed on what applicants have done extra-curricular to show commitment and motivation to the care of others. And this emphasis on practical clinical experience is immediately a feature of study in Year 1. Attachment to a family in need of medical counsel is one aspect of this, and 1st years are also affiliated to local general practices.

This practical emphasis and involvement with the real world beyond campus is an impressive aspect of a number of courses at Birmingham. And the proximity of important industries and businesses, as well as artistic nucleae, is key. In practical terms the Arts faculty has woken up to the fact that non-vocational courses can prepare students for employment provided attention is given not just to what they study but how they study. Organisation, analysis, presentation, communication and problem-solving are all skills to the fore whether it is Business Studies, Music or Languages. Both Music and Drama are particular strengths, and performance is a significant aspect of both.

SPORT

The large Munrow Sports Centre on campus offers facilities and classes in every conceivable sport and exercise with a 25m pool, 2 gyms, climbing wall and all kinds of courts. Next to it is one of only two full-size running tracks in the country (the other is at Loughborough).

170 miles away, by Lake Coniston in Cumbria, is a Centre for Outdoor Pursuits (watersports, mountaineering, mountain biking etc). Nearer home are 2 floodlit synthetic pitches and tennis courts, and 5 miles away (served by coaches and mini-buses) 70 acres of rugby and soccer pitches. It's all here to national squad/professional level (sports scholarships are offered), and in the unique Active Lifestyles Programme every opportunity for amateurs simply to enjoy.

VIEW FROM THE GROUND

by Ruth Hay

This is one big university, with approximately 18,000 students - and quite a high intake of foreign and mature students.

The campus is lovely with plenty of greenery and some great red-brick architecture. The library is very big and very useful, although the books are not always what I would call up to date.

The university accommodation varies greatly, with University House - right next to campus - having the appearance and atmosphere of an upper-middle-class boarding school. Tennis Courts, just up the road, are self-catering flats, simple but homely. Nelson Hall is probably the liveliest, and Hunter Court - a fairly new complex - is good but expensive and approximately 25 minutes from campus.

Recently there has been increasing action among the students - involving demonstrations and occupations - in a battle to stand up against accommodation rent-rises.

These activities have led to widespread disillusion in the Guild - being the oldest Student Union building in the country it is buried in antiquity, apparently unwilling to change its name and acknowledge its role.

The Guild is supposedly student-run by representatives we vote in, but it seems more and more that they are merely the Vice-Chancellor's henchmen. They may provide good, if naff, nights of beer and 70s disco, but they are not willing to support students where more profound issues are at stake.

But enough of politics! The Guild usually has a good atmosphere, catering for the drunken debauchery of Sports Night, to the acid jazz groovings of Martha's Yard. The main bar, Old Joe's, is usually open and usually full.

There are only a few good pubs in Selly Oak - the main student area around campus - and these are generally heaving, but fortunately, being in the city, anything from all-night techno to traditional Irish bars are easily accessed.

Birmingham University is a great place to study. You'll meet a wide range of people and all tastes, races, colours and creeds are fairly well catered for. However, unless the University authorities and the Guild start listening to students (and that means YOU) these varieties may begin to disappear as university becomes once more only for the rich and elite.

BIRMINGHAM COLLEGE OF FOOD, TOURISM & CREATIVE STUDIES

Birmingham College of Food,
Tourism & Creative Studies
Summer Row
Birmingham B3 1JB

TEL 0121 693 5959
0121 604 1000
FAX 0121 608 7100

Birmingham College of Food,
Tourism and Creative Studies
Student Union
Summer Row
Birmingham B3 1JB

TEL 0121 236 6104

BIRMINGHAM COLLEGE OF FOOD, TOURISM & CREATIVE STUDIES

Founded	**1961**
Situation/style	**City sites**
UNDERGRADUATE PROFILE	
Application acceptance rate	**18%**
Population	**2,000**
Mature student population	**20%**
Overseas student population	**20%**
Male/female ratio	**36:64**
1st year institut. accommodation	**50%**
Approximate cost (College)	**£35-£52 pw**
(City)	**£35 pw**
ACADEMIC PROFILE	
A-level requirements:	**Low**
Food & Consumer Management 8, **Food & Retail Management, Tourism, Business Management** 12	
EMPLOYMENT PROFILE	
Principal job market destinations:	
Hotel/Restaurant, Leisure, Tourism & Business	

VAG VIEW

Can't think there's much to add to Patricia Magee's piece except that this foodies' paradise began life in 1961 as the Birmingham College of Domestic Arts, and if you're going to Aston, Birmingham Uni or Central England, get yourself along there to one of their halls parties and find a pie for the proverbial finger - if nothing else, you can bet they can cook. So, for prospective undergrads of BCFT and evil strategists from other Brum haunts, here's how to get first to the city and then to the bar...

GETTING THERE

★ Brum is at the confluence of the M40, M42, M5, M6, M69, M1, M45, well served by rail (London Euston, 1:40; Bristol Parkway or Sheffield, 1:30; Liverpool Lime Street or Manchester Piccadilly,1:40; Leeds, 2.15), coach and air. The campus is 2.5 miles from the City Centre on the A38. Avoid entry through suburbia from the M40, instead join M42 and connect with A38 at J1.

★ Taxi to Uni from airport 30 mins, from city centre 10 mins.

★ Frequent trains from New Street to University Station.

The bar: No parking on campus, but plenty of car parks and on-street parking close by. Ref: Birmingham A to Z Street Atlas, page 73, Ref 3G - find your way to Paradise Circus - just go on round until you find a way into Great Charles Street following signs to The North M6, and you'll whiz past the college on your left. That's as it should be. Take first left at lights into Newhall Street, then left again at next lights into Lionel Street and suddenly you'll see the college again on your left. Park. Cover up that wasted lean 'n' hungry look and make your way to the bar in the college basement. A whole new lifestyle lies in wait.

VIEW FROM THE GROUND
by Patricia Magee

Talk about a mish-mash...Birmingham itself is home to an extensive range of ethnic groups.

The college is no exception. It has students from everywhere in the UK; from every background, race and creed. There is quite a large number of Irish students in the college too.

There's students from Europe and even further afield, such as South Africa, America, Hong Kong, Indonesia and Malaysia. This is mostly due to the college's great reputation in the Hospitality arena. There are always students on exchange programmes, like the ERASMUS project, with large groups coming from France, Spain, Scandinavia and the Netherlands.

English students also get the chance to study abroad. There are a number of clubs and societies at the college where these groups get to know each other.

There's a mix of ages attending the college too. Not only do they run Higher Education courses but there are also programmes for Further Education.

Age ranges from 16 upwards, but for those of you trying to get away from this kind of thing, there's no need to worry...everything is based on separate floors, so you don't have to mix unless you want to.

Everyone usually fits in. Whether you're rich or skint, lazy or a swot, stuck-up or down-to-earth, male or female, gay or straight, black or white, young or old, if you're also open minded then you will. And, if you're looking for a city life to match your independence, then Brum's a great place to do it.

WHAT GOES ON

There's plenty of the opposite sex to keep everyone amused! With courses like hair & beauty, caring and nursery nursing, tourism and leisure, it's clear to see what a mix there is. Each course has males and females but there's a definite difference in some areas.

The BCFTCS Student Guild has a bar in the basement of the college. This is open as a common room and smoking area during the working day. At 5 o'clock it becomes a hive of activity usually packed with the regular, on the way to the detox clinic crowd. There are events organised regularly and if it's just a normal night the variety of DJs will keep you occupied.

There's usually someone playing pool or everyone's screaming at the sports channels.

Boxing and football nights are very well attended, but not generally well behaved. If this isn't for you there are two prominent bars about 30 seconds away. Why not follow the pattern and do all three!

The city is overwhelmed with bars, restaurants and clubs to suit every taste, and there are still new ones opening. The list of clubs goes on forever but to name a few: The Steering Wheel (home to Slag and Fun), Bonds (home to Miss Moneypenny's), Bakers (home to Renaissance), The Que Club (often housing Liverpool's Cream), the new Sanctuary, Wobble & Crunch, Snobs, System, Liberty's, Subway, The Dome II, Pulse, Exile, XL's, The Nightingale (Gay), The Church, Ronnie Scotts (Jazz), Bobby Browns, The Surfer's Paradise (Australian), Gary Owen (Irish), Claridges (Soul), etc., etc., etc. And, of course, there's always the underground all-night venues.

However, this does create severe problems. Why do I feel my head has exploded? Where the hell do we go? When am I ever going to study? When exactly was that appointment with my bank manager?

Birmingham Uni, Aston Uni and the University of Central England also share this modern city which leads to a big student presence and sometimes very long queues at popular nights. It's always worth the wait though, because there's just so many rugby teams to work through!! If you don't find the man or woman of your dreams in one club there's always the next one to try. Most clubs cater for a range of tastes most nights of the week so there is always somewhere to go...coursework permitting of course. Prices aren't bad and more venues are offering student rates at weekends.

Birmingham is definitely a city of entertainment as well as a centre for education. If you decide to dry out for a week you could always go to the cinema (Virgin or Odeon!), or one of the many museums on offer.

The national centres usually have concerts or performances on every night and Birmingham is the home of the National Ballet, Welsh National Opera and the Birmingham Symphonic Orchestra. The city also has loads of theatres showing a range of West End shows such as *Grease,* etc.

Birmingham is the birth place of the Balti.

These are cheap, tasty and you usually get one at any time of the night. It's a favourite with students as a three-course jobby is so cheap. There's loads more diners, restaurants and fast food places. You can basically get everything, even Mongolian foods.

The tourist guides available give addresses, typical menus and listings of nearly all restaurants, cheap and expensive. Sandwiches are easy to find because recently there's loads of new snack places opening. It's not just the city centre that's packed with food shops; nearly every area has a couple on the main streets and there are McDonald's everywhere. The college also organises its own functions, as it is one of the best catering colleges in the country.

The Student Guild organises nights out regularly and often gets together with the other Unis to organise mega events such as the recent club-crawl, where any student card would get you into any participating club in the city for £1. The Guild is also responsible for parties or get-togethers in the halls of residence, the most memorable this year being the 'getting to know you' marquee party on the halls' green. Everyone brought their own drink as well as the Guild supplying about 100 bottles of wine (more like vinegar) and DJs and party games to get everyone in the mood. The lecturers at college are quite good for helping to organise nights out. A pub crawl was organised at the beginning of the year with three coaches of third years eagerly taking part. Some of the lecturers actually came along. They're not all the serious type. Other trips such as 'end of course weekends' to Butlins or Belgium, are also happening this year thanks to some Year Managers.

ACCOMMODATION

The accommodation for the college has all changed recently. New halls of residence have been built on the same campus as the University of Birmingham within a 5 minute walk of the city centre, the college and the main entertainment centre, Broad Street. The accommodation is mixed sex, en-suite and all amenities are on site. The students there this year have been very pleased. The security of the campus is pretty tight but once you're there you will get to know the security staff; they're a pretty good bunch really. Not only does the college have students on this site it also has a number of rooms in other campuses. The standard is generally very satisfactory and, after all, life on campus is what the students make it! There has been rumour of more new accommodation on the new site soon.

There are loads of other residential areas with a high population of students due to the city having three large universities and many higher education colleges. Selly Oak is one having a high student density. As with all big cities there are areas that are not as desirable as others. There are no real danger spots but you have to keep your wits about you in some suburbs. Handsworth was one once, because of rioting in the 80s. This is not really the case anymore, and many students enjoy living there. Some areas are more culturally mixed than others and if you're small-minded you'll notice this before you sign any rent contracts.

ACADEMIA

The Birmingham College of Food, Tourism and Creative Studies, as the name suggests, is a specialist provider of courses for Hospitality and related service industries. It offers vocational programmes which have achieved national and international recognition. There are strong links with industry, both in the UK and overseas. Most students come to the college because of this reputation and take pride in being associated with it.

The college is well equipped and has a brilliant Resource Centre with more than 300 computers that can be used on a drop-in basis. Currently there are computers. The library, recently refurbished, is a specialist national centre for hotel and catering, tourism and leisure courses. There is good access to CD ROMs and the Internet and the staff are helpful.

There is also a centre for student study support. The staff are exceptional there and there's no stigma attached to using it. Again, every student is encouraged to attend the Modern Languages Department and the college offers workshops in addition to lectures.

Most courses arrange work placements, mostly in Hotel and Catering. Others have yearly overseas visits as far afield as Goa, the Gambia, Tunisia, Israel, Spain, the Canaries, Poland, the Czech Republic etc., as well as in the UK or Ireland.

Career prospects are good owing to the college's reputation and links with industry, a relationship which spills over into award ceremonies sponsored and attended by big organisations such as the English Tourist Board. The college is also one of those invited to exhibit at trade fairs and big exhibitions like Hospitality Week at the NEC. Contacts can be really productive.

All Higher Education courses are semesterised and subjects modularised. This, I find, makes it easier to focus.

SPORT

All the sports clubs and societies are run by the Student Guild. The teams - football, rugby, volleyball, hockey, netball, etc - are all in the BUSA League but were out of the championships this year. There is also Gaelic football, and at the Fitness Centre classes are organised in self-defence and aerobics.

When, alas, it's all over, the Guild always organises a big bash for Graduation Ball - loads of fancy clothes, beer and snogging!!! But you've got three years to get through first. Good luck!

BISHOP GROSSETESTE COLLEGE

Bishop Grosseteste College
Newport
Lincoln LN1 3DY

TEL 01522 527347
FAX 01522 530243

Bishop Grosseteste College
Student Union
Newport
Lincoln LN1 3DY

TEL 01522 544378

BISHOP GROSSETESTE COLLEGE	
Founded	**1862**
Situation/style	**Campus**
UNDERGRADUATE PROFILE	
Application acceptance rate	**11%**
Population	**850**
Mature student population	**15%**
Male/female ratio	**13:87**
1st year institut. accommodation	**100%**
Approximate cost	**£55-£60 pw**
ACADEMIC PROFILE	
A-level requirements:	**Low**
Teacher Training CD-DD, **Arts in the Community** CD, **Heritage Studies** 8	
Student/staff ratio	**19:1**
1st class degree pass rate	**0.65%**
EMPLOYMENT PROFILE	
Principal job market destinations:	
Education, Personnel, Holy Orders	

VAG VIEW

Fairly low profile, mainly teacher training establishment with strong Anglican Christian roots. There's a good practical emphasis on the TT courses (working with children, schooling in motivation, self-esteem, etc) and whatever you're up to you'll find a quietly experienced, rather efficient little set-up that will almost certainly find you a job at the end (strong links with particular schools and placements abroad). They may not be into any hype, but they know what they are about and are good at it. No swingers need apply.

SITUATION

★ Up Riseholme Road (10 mins walk) from Lincoln Castle and Cathedral. Approachable from out of town from the North (Hull) along the A15 which becomes Riseholme; from Sheffield way (NW) via the A57 on to A46 Lincoln by-pass (left at r/about when you hit it and then right at next r/about on to Riseholme). In fact wherever you're coming from, get on to that A46 by-pass, nose round to the north of the city to the intersection with the A15, then drop down Riseholme and you'll see the college on your left.

ACADEMIA

Founded in 1862 to 'train young women of the Anglican religion to be teachers'. Still a preponderance of young women, but it is up to more than teacher training now - three new 3-year BA courses in Heritage Studies, Arts in the Community and Christian Studies.

Its name was bestowed on it in 1962 as part of the centenary celebrations - Robert Grosseteste was Bishop of Lincoln in the 13th century and the first Chancellor of Oxford Uni. There's an international focus these days, but no figures available on numbers of students from overseas.

Since 1987 it's been a school of Hull University, where the main subject in the 4-year teacher training BA/BSc (Hons) course is studied in the 2nd year. The main TT subjects offered include History, Geography, Religious Studies, Drama, Music, Maths/Technol., Science, English, Art. There's also a new 3-year BA in primary education and a part-time BPhil course in primary education.

ACCOMMODATION

On-campus single study bedrooms for first year, then it's probably Hull and off to a bijou apartment perhaps in Lincoln.

ENTS ETC

College bar opens lunchtimes and evenings. Rest of the day it's a coffee area. There's a TV lounge, reading room and laundry... get the picture? There's not much to say about ents in Lincoln either, but it's a historic (pre-Roman even) and beautiful city with state of the art cobbled streets, decent pubs and restaurants, the odd club (very odd).

SPORT

On-campus gym, playing fields, tennis courts, and 'a working relationship with Yarborough Sports Centre'.

BLACKBURN COLLEGE

Blackburn College
Feilden Street
Blackburn
Lancs BB2 1LH

TEL 01254 55144
FAX 01254 682700

Blackburn College
Student Union
Feilden Street
Blackburn
Lancs BB2 1LH

TEL 01254 57211

BLACKBURN COLLEGE	
Founded	**1888**
Situation/style	**Town sites**
UNDERGRADUATE PROFILE	
Population	**700**
Mature student population	**30%**
Male/female ratio	**40:60**
1st year institut. accommodation	**30%**
Approximate cost (College)	**£40 pw**
(Town)	**£30-£35 pw**
ACADEMIC PROFILE	
A-level requirements:	**Low**

Law/Legal Studies 18/12, **Business & Management** EE, **Fine Art** 2-4

HEFCE assessments

(1 subject, **Computing/Business & Management Studies**, assessed/approved 1994*)*

EMPLOYMENT PROFILE

Principal job market destinations:

Education, Industry, Commerce

VAG VIEW

This is a town campus (with a tiny accommodation facility nearby) in the NE Lancashire town south of the Forest of Bowland. In 1995 it became an associate college of Lancaster Uni, three junctions up the M6 motorway. There are also tie-ups with Huddersfield Uni, Glamorgan, Central Lancs, Salford and St Martin's to produce its degree course curriculum, which includes Business, Accounting, Law, Leisure Mgt, Media, Fine Arts, Electronics, and Plant Engineering. There's also a good foundation degree course in Science and Humanities for students with no A-levels - this in cahoots with Lancaster.

What's impressive is the line it has into Europe. Language courses are available with most subjects, there's a state-of-the-art Sony language laboratory, there are partnerships with colleges and agencies in Belgium, Denmark, Spain, Greece, Poland and the Netherlands, and projects and exchanges are undertaken, which bear fruit in academic and career contexts. For a college this size the computer facility is also impressive - more than 1,000 stations, 700 on the college network.

Excellent results, particularly in the non-HE sector (incl 85% passes at A-level – this out of more than 800 pupils), suggest that the newish HE adjunct will be handled with some style. Every HE student is assigned a personal tutor, the purpose being to develop communication (career) skills on a one-to-one basis.

What's more, the college was overall winner in the Association of Hairdressers Championships. Conclusion: A college to watch.

GETTING THERE

★ By road: From North, South and West, M6 (J31), A677; From East, M65.
★ By rail: Manchester Piccadilly, 1:00 (change Salford Crescent); London Euston, 3:30 (change Preston).

BLACKPOOL & THE FYLDE COLLEGE

Blackpool & The Fylde College
Ashfield Road
Bispham
Blackpool
FY2 OHB

TEL 01253 352352
FAX 01253 356127

BLACKPOOL AND THE FYLDE COLLEGE	
Founded	**1937**
Situation/style	**Town sites**
UNDERGRADUATE PROFILE	
Application acceptance rate	**15%**
Population	**500**
Mature student population	**40%**
Male/female ratio	**60:40**
1st year institut. accommodation	**None**
Approximate rent	**£35-£40 pw**
ACADEMIC PROFILE	
A-level requirements:	**Low**
Design, Hotel Management & Tourism 10	
EMPLOYMENT PROFILE	
Hotel/Restaurant, Public Admin.	

VAG VIEW

This is another associate college of Lancaster Uni (see Blackburn) and is nearer to it by one junction on the M6. Blackpool, an essential part (if not the flagship) of the once proud great British holiday-by-the-sea culture, may not be the first place you'd think of when consigning your future to an establishment of Higher Education, but more than 20,000 students are there to prove you wrong, so we're told. There are four campuses - Palatine Road in the centre and Bispham to the north of the town, with its three piers, 'Pleasure Beach', famous tower and Wintergarden Complex; another in Lytham St Anne's (about seven miles to the south along the coast); and the fourth, Fleetwood, about seven miles from Blackburn in the other direction, to the north of the Fylde, which is the name given to the chin of land jutting out over the Ribble Estuary.

The main thrust of full-time courses is Business & Finance and Leisure & Tourism, both features arising out of the culture of the area. The degree courses however, are confined to Design, Hotel & Catering, Hospitality Management and Food Manufacturing, and with that in mind it is perhaps not so bad a place to be. There is a new multimedia building for a BA Foundation Course in Art & Design, and there are placement links for Design students in Europe.

GETTING THERE

★ By road: M6 ((J32), M65.

★ By train: Manchester Piccadilly, 1:15; London Euston, 2:25.

BOLTON INSTITUTE OF HIGHER EDUCATION

Bolton Institute of
Higher Education
Deane Road
Bolton BL3 5AB

TEL 01204 528851
01204 900600
FAX 01204 399074

Bolton Institute of
Higher Education
Student Union
Deane Road
Bolton BL3 5AB

TEL 01204 389024
FAX 01204 371493

BOLTON INSTITUTE OF HIGHER HIGHER EDUCATION

Founded	**1982**
Situation/style	**Campus**
UNDERGRADUATE PROFILE	
Application acceptance rate	**15%**
Population	**3,100**
Mature student population	**69%**
Overseas student population	**12%**
Male/female ratio	**58:42**
1st year institut. accommodation	**100%**
Approximate cost	**£40 pw**
ACADEMIC PROFILE	
A-level requirements:	**Low**

Civil Engineering 12, **Electronic, Mech. Eng.** E/EE, **Combined courses** featuring **Computing, Environmental Studies, Creative Writing, History, Law, Psychology, Maths, Biology, Business, Management, Marketing, Textiles, Tourism,** etc CD-E

Student/staff ratio	**21:1**
1st class degree pass rate	**4.7%**
HEFCE assessments (6 subjects assessed/approved):	
Mechanical Engineering on 2nd visit, 1995	
Joint Funding Council's research assessment 1996 (10 subjects assessed):	
Grade 5/5*	None
EMPLOYMENT PROFILE	
Principal job market destinations:	

Retail/Wholesale, Manufacturing, Public Admin/Law, Commerce, Construction, Health

Approximate % unemployed	**17%**

VAG VIEW

Politically correct prospectus hype vies against what is nevertheless an up and coming institution going for Uni status.

SITUATION

Bolton is an old Lancashire industrial town a few miles north-west of Manchester, though the institute's prospectus describes it as 'a modern, lively market town, famous for its hospitality.' The truth falls somewhere in amongst the two.

Its proximity to Manchester and to the Pennine Moors makes for a nice balance. A couple of nights of Mancunian debauchery followed by a soul-searching chill-out on the wilderness Tufton Moor might be just the thing if you ever manage to tear yourself away from 'the award winning shopping centre' and 'excellent leisure facilities' which apparently make Bolton such a joy to live in.

It's a three-site campus, with on-street, Victorian redbrick Great Moor Street, home of the Art & Design 'Division', looking rather less campusy than others.

ADDRESSES

(Tel/Fax same for all, see above):

Deane Campus, Deane Road, Bolton BJ3 5AB, is for Business, Engineering, Textile Studies, Psychology, Biology, Maths.

Chadwick Campus, Chadwick Street, Bolton BL2 1JW, is for Humanities, Education, Health.

Great Moor Street Campus, Great Moor Street, Bolton BL1 1NS.

GETTING THERE

★ M62 and M61 provide contact with the outer world. M61 (J3) then A666 for Chadwick, or M66 (J2) then A58 from Bury to the East. M61 (J5) then A58 (from West) for Deane. You could use either route in for Moor Street, and there are many other routes in. Bolton is a sort of traffic island in the midst of the most complex pattern of motorways in Britain.

★ Rail connections with Manchester frequent. Bolton station is close to Moor Street and midway (a short distance) between the other two campuses. No problems by rail, whereas by road you may discover things about your navigator you'd rather not. Good map in official prospectus.

★ Manchester airport 30 mins from Bolton.

★ Coach station close to Deane.

ACCOMMODATION

Halls of residence for first years - Hollins on Chadwick campus, Orlando on a roundabout south of Moor Street campus and equidistant between the other two. Both within walking distance. No self-catering.

ACADEMIA

Institute on verge of being awarded university status as I write. They offer a wide range of degree courses and most are part of the modular framework/Credit Accumulation and Transfer Scheme. 'Flexible' approach to entry qualifications. 'It is what you are capable of doing, rather than what you have already done, which interests us.' Accepts BTEC National Certificates and Diplomas, Irish and Scottish Leaving Certificates, International Baccalaureat, City & Guilds Certificates and GNVQs, as well as A-levels. 'Applications encouraged from members of groups traditionally under-represented in higher education.' That means mature, overseas, underprivileged presumably. Most students are from the north-west.

Sound career base through close contact with industry and commerce.

STUDENTS UNION

Bistros, restaurants and snack bars at both Deane and Chadwick campuses. Major new development underway to provide bar, ents venue, 'and a cafe for those students who do not wish to associate with alcohol' - pity the poor student with a hangover. Bolton itself offers a handful of clubs and the odd student night, a Cannon cinema complex, live music venues. Octagon Theatre and Albert Hall, which includes comedy, jazz, classical music, and I hear tell of a north-west Beer Fest. But basically it's Manchester for your ents.

SPORT

Large multi-court sports hall, fitness centre, specialist coaches, access to playing fields, all-weather pitches, swimming pool. Relative proximity to Lake District encourages interest in orienteering, rock climbing, etc.

BOURNEMOUTH UNIVERSITY

Bournemouth University
Talbot Campus
Fern Barrow
Poole
Dorset
BH12 5BB

TEL 01202 524111
FAX 01202 513293

Bournemouth University
Student Union
Talbot Campus
Fern Barrow
Poole
Dorset BH12 5BB

TEL 01202 523755
FAX 01202 535990

BOURNEMOUTH UNIVERSITY

Founded	**1976**
Situation/style	**Campus**
UNDERGRADUATE PROFILE	
Application acceptance rate	**11%**
Population	**6,500**
Mature student population	**27%**
Overseas student population	**5%**
Male/female ratio	**53:47**
1st year institut. accommodation	**100%**
Approximate cost	**£40-£55 pw**

ACADEMIC PROFILE
A-level requirements:
Law 18, **Business Studies** 14-16, **Multimedia Journalism** BBC, **Public Relations** 18-20, **Advertising Mgt, Communication** BB-BBC, **Media Production** 18-22, **Retail Management**, **Leisure Marketing** 14-22, **Computer Sci. & Engineering** 10-12, **Clinical Nursing/Midwifery** 12-14, **Land-based Enterprise (Agric.)** 12-14

Student/staff ratio	**17:1**
1st class degree pass rate	**2.5%**
HEFCE assessments (6 subjects assessed all approved)	
Joint Funding Council's research assessment 1996 (14 subjects assessed):	
Grade 5/5*	None
EMPLOYMENT PROFILE	
Employability in Industry:	
MPW national league table (1996)	**44th=**

Principal job market destinations:
Manufacturing (strong on **Electronic**), **Commerce** (strong on **Finance & Business Management**), **Arts/Media** (strong on **Publishing & Radio/TV**), **Retail/Wholesale, Hotel/Restaurant, Computer, Public Admin/Law, Education, Advertising**

PIP 1996 employers' survey:	
Top subject/national ranking	
Business	21st=
Approximate % unemployed	**10%**

VAG VIEW

Bournemouth is something of a niche university which happens to be set in one of the more congenial parts of the south (given that you will probably not be around when the tourist season is in full flow). Serious work/career orientated students are appreciated here, and the area caters for a range of less bizarre obsessions.

SETTING

Premier seaside resort, miles of golden sand and clean bathing, between Poole to the west and Christchurch to the east. Two campuses, Talbot (2 miles from Bournemouth town centre) is the main one. Bournemouth campus is more of a collection of town sites, a relatively recent acquisition with teaching facilities for Business, Health, Design, Engineering, Computing, Conservation. No parking rule within a mile of town campus. Students discouraged to bring cars. Even visitors to Talbot need a parking permit. Free bus service between campuses.

GETTING THERE

★ By road from East or North M3/M27/A31/A338, which turns into The Wessex Way. Leave it at 2nd r/about and follow Uni signs to Talbot campus. From West A35 then A3049 (Wallisdown Road). For Bournemouth campus, leave A338 at St Paul's r/about (Travel Interchange junction) on to St Paul's road and find a car park.

★ By rail, it's 96 minutes from London Waterloo, Bristol under 3 hours, Birmingham or Cardiff less than 4, Manchester about 5.

★ Take a taxi from station to Talbot (7 mins) or Bus No. 69. Bournemouth campus 5 mins walk away.

ACADEMIA

Bournemouth out on its own with courses such as Public Relations, Advertising, Communications, and emphasis on Business, Journalism, etc. Course on Taxation & Revenue Law first of its kind in UK. Strong emphasis on future careers. Communication skills, enterprise, problem-solving strategies couple with close ties with industry. Lecturers drawn from the world of work and a strong diet of sandwich courses (50%) characterise this establishment as the modern answer to more traditional forms of HE. Took 2nd place in one (1995) employment survey of graduate employment after six months. But not a great performer in HEFCE assessments yet.

ACCOMMODATION

Guaranteed accommodation arrangements for 1st years but places in Student Village on Talbot and Hurn House at town campus are limited (to 250 and 155 respectively). New student housing development on its way. Like most seaside places town accommodation is plentiful and good.

ENTS

Get hold of *The Punter - Student Guide,* Southampton Edition. Not only is it useful about what's on in Bournemouth, but it's tip top on more personal advice: On sleeping with your flatmate: 'Like milk, sex on your doorstep seems like a good idea, but you've got to pay for it sooner or later.' On sex with your letcherer - 'If your lecturer offers to help you pass your oral, don't go to their room wide-eyed or mouth - get them into a compromising position and introduce them to Mr Polaroid. Now that's what we call a graduation ceremony.'

Bournemouth is bursting with gays, population apparently triples in size to 15,000 in the summer. Start at The Triangle Club. Look further with a copy of The Pink Gay Map. Everybody will find low prices at The Old Fire Station - disco, live music, Indie nights, etc, etc. This is the main social focus for students. Known as TOFS, it's just round the corner from the town campus and includes nightclub, bar, bistro and allegedly the longest fireman's pole in Britain. Also explore Madisons, Gardening Club (see London University, a sibling of the Covent Garden enterprise), Hot n' Horny at The Academy, Boscombe (between Bournemouth and Christchurch), The Zoo & Cage, and many more.

Students Union attracts wide range of live bands (Lush, Menswear, Dubstar, Sunscream and Ocean Colour Scene), DJ club nights, comedy nights, and the ubiquitous hypnotists.

Live bands/top acts at Bournemouth Int. Centre (Oasis, Pulp, Bjork and The Cranberries), and Pool Arts Centre. Locals at Mr Smith's Piano Bar, Gander on the Green.

NUS discounts at Pool Arts Centre (theatre and arthouse cinema) and at Regent Centre, Christchurch (arts, theatre, cinema) plus commercial cinema (ABC, Odeon etc). Some restaurants also offer student discounts. See also Southampton.

SPORT

Proximity to sea encourages windsurfing, sailing, paragliding, jet ski, etc. Uni provides full-time instructors and facilities for wide range of sports. Sports hall includes squash courts and multi-gym. Cricketers use the county standard Dean Park ground.

BRADFORD UNIVERSITY

University of Bradford
Richmond Road
Bradford BD7 1DP

TEL 01274 733466
FAX 01274 305340

Bradford University Union
Richmond Road
Bradford BD7 1DP

TEL 01274 383300
FAX 01274 385530

UNIVERSITY OF BRADFORD

Founded	**1966**
Situation/style	**Campus**
UNDERGRADUATE PROFILE	
Application acceptance rate	**13%**
Population	**6,000**
Mature student population	**22%**
Overseas student population	**11%**
Male/female ratio	**56:44**
1st year institut. accommodation	**100%**
Approximate cost	**£35-£60 pw**

ACADEMIC PROFILE

A-level requirements: **High-medium**
Cellular Pathology, Nutrition, Biomedical Sciences BB-CCD, **Physiotherapy** BCC, **Chemistry with Pharmaceutical and Forensic Science** BCC, **Modern Languages** BCC, **International Management** BBC, **Chem., Civil/Environmental Eng.** CCC, **Civil/Structural Eng.** BB-CCD, **E & E** 12-ABB, **Mech, Manufac. Eng.** 14-18, **Computer Sciences & Eng.** 18-22, **Sociology** BB-CCC, **Media Technology & Production** BCC

Student/staff ratio **16:1**

1st class degree pass rate **7.4%**

HEFCE assessments (10 subjects assessed/approved):
1995/6: **Chemical Engineering** 20, **Modern Languages** 18, **Sociology** 17

Joint Funding Council's research assessment 1996 (18 subjects assessed):
Civil Engineering, European Studies, Archaeology Grade 5

EMPLOYMENT PROFILE

Employability in Industry:
MPW national league table (1996) **41st**

Principal job market destinations:
Manufacturing (strong on **Electronic & Electrical**), **Retail/Wholesale, Commerce, Health, Education, Public Admin., Arts/Media, Construction, Hotel/Restaurant, Computer**

PIP 1996 employers' survey:
Top 3 subjects/national ranking

Business	17th=
Engineering & Technology	19th=
Accountancy/Finance & Banking	22nd=

Approximate % unemployed **7%**

VAG VIEW

Bradford Uni is rooted in the Industrial Revolution which made this city. A Uni since 1966, it emerged out of the Bradford Technical College, which itself grew out of the textile industry in the 1860s. Today the connection between Higher Education and the workplace remains key. Bradford is one of the leading sandwich course specialists, and it offers a heavily career-orientated curriculum with a science/technology bias, welcoming GNVQ and BTEC students.

First degree subject areas include Engineering, Science, Health, Mgt and Languages, Social Sciences, and it has been a pioneer in such courses as European Studies, Environmental Studies, Technol. & Mgt, Peace Studies, Electronic Imaging and Media Communications.

The campus is part of the city geographically, culturally and in every way and all the accommodation is either on it or nearby. It is a relatively small Uni with a close-knit student community, which in 1996 comprised 26% from Yorkshire, 20% Midlands/E. Anglia, 18% north-west, 13% London/South-East, 11% overseas, 12% the rest, and it is committed to widening its cultural base still further.

There's crime in the city, but there's a safety bus at night to truck you anywhere from campus within a 7-mile radius. Groups of more than two males may be refused admittance, however, 'as they may constitute a problem for the female driver...' (An insight perhaps into your average Bradford student.) Unfortunately, with crime comes a light-fingered police presence, but again the Union provides a safety net - a 7-point plan for if you're arrested or stopped on the street.

GETTING THERE

★ M62 and M606 connect you to the national motorway network, but from the North take the A629/A650 via Skipton and Keighley. From the North-East, the A1 or A19, then the A59 and A658 south of Harrogate.
★ Finding your way to the campus is mindblowing; either get a street map or have the Uni send you one.
★ By train it's 3 hours from London Kings Cross, 4 hours from Edinburgh, 3 hours from Birmingham, 1 hour from Manchester.
★ Leeds/Bradford Airport is 7 miles from the campus.

VIEW FROM THE GROUND
by Andi Callan

Although only a small university, Bradford has much to offer both the gregarious and the introverted scholar alike.

The main campus is compact, bounded by roads on all four sides, with many halls of residence on site.

Four other halls are situated less than half a mile away, near to those of the local Health College, which has recently been integrated into the University. All teaching within the University is carried out on the main campus, except for Business Studies, whose students have a short bus ride to the highly rated Management Centre at Emm Lane.

A 10 minute downhill stroll into town takes in such glorious landmarks as the beautifully restored Alhambra Theatre, the imposing Town Hall and the National Museum of Photography, Film and Television, not forgetting the crustie who's always pan handling by the Greek restaurant. One of the first things you'll notice about this West Yorkshire mill town is that it seems to be in a perpetual state of redevelopment, which has been the case since the 196s.

The ugly legacy of this decade can be seen in the shape of both the offices of the Yorkshire Building Society, which dominate the cold night skies habitually experienced here, and the main university building, the Richmond. This is a fifteen storey monument to crap concrete construction so popular at the time, with a strangely shaped foyer, allegedly representing a frog - don't ask me why!

It was supposedly meant as a temporary structure, but it is still here, and rumour has it that it advances down the hill at a rate of several millimetres per annum.

The Richmond is well known to both students and cab drivers alike, and houses a Nat West cash point and the only Union bar to be awarded a CAMRA "Pub Of The Year" plaque. It is also from this landmark that several of the local clubs run a free bus service, even though some of them are little more than half a mile into town.

WHAT GOES ON - THE CITY

The two biggest club nights are Monday and Wednesday. Monday's big night out is 'Belief' at Maestros, the biggest club in the country, with goldfish ponds in the toilets. Ideal for those nights when all you've got left in your wardrobe is a thigh high mini and a pair of strappy sandals, it appears to have a sexist policy of only letting girls dance on top of the speakers, but I put that down to good taste.

Maestros is a definite 'dress up to get down' venue, not recommended other nights of the week due to its student unfriendly pricing policy, and the desire of some locals to give you a hard time. Two less salubrious, but still eminently enjoyable venues also open on Mondays, and operate almost on campus.

Tumblers is tucked away behind the Richmond, whilst Club Rio is practically next door to the Longside halls of residence. They offer a different ambience to that provided by Maestros. People here think you've made an effort if you iron your shirt. They both play the formulaic 'Student/Indie' dance tunes, so musically there is little to choose between the two, except for Rio's superior sound system and spacious dance floor. The entry charge at Tumblers is £2.50 (expensive for Bradford!), but its main attraction is that pints and spirits are only 60p all night. Many a Tuesday morning lecture absence bears living testimony to this! Wednesday is the student night out, especially for all those involved in the numerous and varied sporting activities on offer at the university, no doubt refuelling after a hard afternoon's exertion. Traditionally the place to go to, if society jumpers and drill tops are your idea of club wear, is Pickwicks on Morely Street, which is open all week, but Wednesday is the night it's best known for. Little more than a converted house, run by one of the most miserable doormen I've ever met, this is the place where all the jock and jockesses hang out. It operates a fairly relaxed music policy with only Tuesday being a dedicated 'Indie/Brit Pop' student night. However, these days it's Lingards, which seems to hold the mantle of 'best Wednesday night out'. This is yet another club that runs a free bus to and from the Richmond, and with dancing on two of its three floors and bars on each, it is different things to different people. It can get a little claustrophobic due to its 'free entry with a flyer' policy, and that fact that pints are 80p, but at prices like these who cares about a little pushing and shoving? There are also some big weekend dance nights held at the Windsor Baths, notably 'SMILE'. Just look out for the flyposters which litter the roads around campus.

Live music venues in town include St George's Hall, which has attracted top names like Suede, Ocean Colour Scene and Terrorvision, and the north's premier rock club, Rios, which seems to be the final resting place of spandex trousers! It has also put on some superb British and American metal and hardcore bands, with Fear Factory, The Misfits, Cradle Of Filth and Downset performing here recently. Of course there is always the short train journey to Leeds (£1.05 return with a rail card), where you'll find many major bands stopping off on tour.

There are many student pubs close to campus, one of the most popular being the Westleigh, where you might find Terrorvision supping the odd ale, between touring and recording.

Other highly recommended watering holes include, The Peel Hotel, The Willowfield, MacCrorys, Delius Lived Next Door and The Queens Hall. There are several new pubs in town; O'Neills and the new Firkin are the pick, although the Vaults is good, but pricey.

The single most redeeming feature about 'Bratford' (learn to pronounce the 't') is how far your money goes, a very important factor in these days of reduced grants. But be warned, after the pubs and clubs kick out, there is mortal danger waiting for you on every street corner. Something your parents will probably warn you against, something so addictive that after your first fix you'll find yourself hopelessly hooked for life. Others will always try and offer you harder, stronger stuff, like...vindaloo...because as you may know Bradford is curry central and people are always amazed by the cost, quality and number of eateries. You'll never visit them all, but they are a joy, especially when you find one still open at 4am as the munchies take hold. Prices range from £2.50 to £3.50 for a basic chicken dish with chapatis. Treat curry with respect and don't dive head first into vindaloo territory; build up slowly. The best of the student curry houses are the Shabina, Shimla, Shezan, Eastern Tandoori and Mr Pappadoms! Avoid the cunningly named International and the Evershine, often referred to as the Evershite, or you'll find out why it's so called!

WHAT GOES ON - THE UNI

The entertainments entry in the University prospectus reads like a Reading Festival line up, with Nirvana, Terrorvision, Therapy, Echobelly and Ice Cube all having played here in the past. Well that was a while ago, but 1996 saw gigs from Space, Stereolab, The Cardigans, Dreadzone, Silver Sun, Mansun, The Longpigs, Collapsed Lung and Heavy Stereo, to name but a few. Comedy also features regularly, and all the Union events are held in the Communal Building, a 1200 capacity venue.

Of course, your evenings don't have to be spent in search of shameless hedonism. For instance, the excellent Theatre In The Mill, based on campus, stages a number of professional dance and theatre productions each year, as well as several by our own students. It not only offers workshops in design, writing and directing, but also lets people experience other aspects of the dramatic arts, such as advertising and publicity.

With no formal music courses undertaken at the University, it is left to the students and staff, with the aid of the Fellow in Music, to cater for the creative needs of musicians around campus. There are five music societies which you can get involved in, the Chamber Choir, the Choral Society, the Jazz Ensemble and both Wind and Full Orchestras.

Of course, if you enjoy being entertained rather than entertaining, then these groups give performances every term. If that's all a little too high brow for you, you could always try the Bradford Student Cinema. Three times a week they show some of the latest blockbuster and art movies, many only a few months after general release, and all for a couple of quid. Showings are held in the Great Hall, and on Sundays there is a double bill for an extra pound.

If money is short and that essay hand-in date is getting ever closer, you can always have a quiet drink in either of the two campus bars and slip off home to listen to 'the UK's leading Student Radio Station', RAMAIR. The presenters are never further than a phone call away, and will play requests and dedications, often less than 20 minutes after you've rung up. The station was established sixteen years ago, the first of its kind in the UK, and is a fun thing to get involved with, being run by students for students. Twice a year, for a month, the good ship RAMAIR slips its moorings and becomes a 'real' radio station, broadcasting 24 hours a day in stereo FM, with adverts, jingles and campus news, to the whole of Bradford and not just the student population. Sixteen of these special licences have now been completed, more than by any other UK student radio station.

THE UNION

There are many clubs and societies you can join, anything from Karate to Ultimate Frisbee. The more unusual clubs seen here in recent years include, The Vampire Society, The Geoff Thomas Appreciation Society and a strange group of people extolling the virtues of SPAM - I kid you not. All you need are 20 members and you could set up your own 'Richard Branson Society', with funding from the Student Union, although probably not enough to earn you any air miles! Many courses have their own societies, including Chemistry, Applied Social Studies, Modern Languages and the intriguingly named BUMS, which I'm reliably informed is short for Bradford University Maths Society. And whatever religious denomination you are you'll surely find it here, with the Catholic, Anglican, Methodist, Jewish, Islamic, Baptist, Lutheran, Quaker, Sikh, Hindu and Greek Orthodox faiths all represented.

The Student Union is quite active in both local and national issues, and often organises cheap coach trips to major demonstrations. There are lots of projects which tie in with the local community, but to try and list them all would probably result in me missing a very worthy cause, so I won't try. There are plenty of opportunities to have your voice heard in the Union, either by standing for one of the sabbatical or non-sabbatical positions, or coming along and getting involved in one of the campaign groups.

ACCOMMODATION

Accommodation in Bradford is probably cheaper than anywhere else in the country. For first years, there is a choice of halls, the most expensive being Trinity, as it offers en-suite facilities and is much more modern than the rest.

Trinity is at the Laisteridge Lane site, opposite The Westleigh, and is overshadowed by the two tower blocks, Revis and Dennis. These two halls are catered and will set you back around £60 a week. The halls on the main campus are cheaper and uncatered, and there is little to choose between Shearbridge Green, Longside and Kirkstone. However, Bradford and University Halls are terrible, and I've yet to meet one person with anything good to say about them. If you're a mature or post graduate student, there is much to be saved and gained by living off campus in private housing. Do not be panicked into looking for a house at the beginning of the summer term; there are literally hundreds of landlords who make a very nice living out of people paying large retainers for houses over the summer. It is very easy to find a good, cheap house at the end of August, often one that's just been redecorated or refurbished.

Rents range from £20 to £35 a week, depending where you are situated. The closer to the university, the higher the premium, and a ten minute walk could well save you £10 a week, so it's worth considering. The biggest, most sought after student area is to the east of the university, from Great Horton Road to Little Horton Lane. Here you will find many take-away food places and corner shops, opening late. However it is one of the most frequently burgled areas. One place which seems popular with students, but can be quite dangerous to live, is south west of the university, along Woodhead Road. Attacks on students have often been reported here in recent years and it does not make for a restful place to live. I think it's far better to live somewhere a bit further out and less studenty, where you aren't so obvious.

ACADEMIA

Finally, I suppose I have to mention the real reason you want to come to Bradford – *study*. The University of Bradford has an excellent reputation in the fields of Management, Civil Engineering, Pharmaceutical Chemistry and Modern Languages. It also offers the Peace Studies course, the only one of its kind in the UK (although King's College runs one called War Studies). I myself studied Environmental Science, which means about 18 hours a week of lectures and workshops. Some courses, such as Social Science and Peace Studies, have less than 10 hours, whilst some Computing and Pharmacy courses have over 20. Of course, you are supposed to do more reading if you have less lectures, or so I'm told. The University operates in two semesters, but has three terms, which is slightly confusing. The latest rule to hit Bradford students is zero marking for late submissions, even by 5 minutes! In the past it was always a 25% penalty, but now it seems they want us to do some work! Many courses have second and third year options to work in industry or to travel and study or work abroad, especially Business Management, Chemical Engineering, European Studies and Environmental Science. This provides a good opportunity for further life experience, to pay off some debt or to save some extra money for your final year, and of course is great CV material.

Bradford can be a fun place to live and study and there's always something to do, even if it means visiting the beautiful surrounding countryside, of which there is plenty. Yorkshire folk have got it right when they call it God's own country. Come to Bradford, and tell them Andi sent you.

BRADFORD & ILKLEY COMMUNITY COLLEGE

Bradford & Ilkley
Community College
McMillan Building
Trinity Road
Bradford
West Yorkshire BD5 0JD

TEL 01274 753203
FAX 01274 307828

Bradford & Ilkley
Community College
Bradford Campus Student Union
The Sound Gallery
Great Horton Road
Bradford
West Yorkshire BD7 1AY

TEL 01274 753007
FAX 01274 414316

BRADFORD & ILKLEY COMMUNITY COLLEGE	
Founded	1982
Situation/style	2 urban sites
UNDERGRADUATE PROFILE	
Application acceptance rate	19%
Population	2,300
Mature student population	95%
Overseas student population	10%
Male/female ratio	35:65
1st year institut. accommodation	65%
Approximate cost (College)	£30-£45 pw
(City/town)	£30-£40 pw
ACADEMIC PROFILE	
A-level requirements:	Low
Teacher Training 8, **Law & European Business** 6, **Community Studies** 8	
HEFCE assessments (2 subjects assessed/approved):	
1994 **Applied Social Work**	Excellent
EMPLOYMENT PROFILE	
Principal job market destinations:	
Education, Health, Business	

VAG VIEW

The name of this community college reminds idle readers of this guide, moving spellbound from one entry to the next, that Bradford City is on the edge of some beautiful countryside. The Ilkley site, where the health and community aspect of the curriculum is run, pulls us 15 miles NNW of the city into some sublime granite-black West Riding countryside. Ilkley Moor is but one of its delights. Going south over Rombalds Moor and thence over Keighley and Haworth Moors you come to the heart of Brönte country, where Emily set Wuthering Heights, choosing the adjective wisely as 'descriptive of the atmospheric tumult to which its station is exposed in stormy weather' - six layers of clothing in winter is not inadvisable.

The college offers degree courses in cahoots with Bradford Uni in Art & Design, European Textile Design, Business Admin., Law & European Studies, Organization Studies (a kind of preparation for Mgt.), Social Work, Health & Community Studies, etc., and a Combined Hons. course which brings the modular structure of all its courses to its zenith with more than 300 modules offered within the Credit Accumulation and Transfer Scheme. Entry requirements may be low but so far their course assessments are admirable.

Both sites offer limited accommodation, all self-catering. Non-Uni accommodation is plentiful and cheap in Bradford, but if you're not one of the 190 live-in students at Ilkley, you'll almost certainly need a car. The Bradford sites are scattered around the Bradford Uni area. Ilkley is on the A65 between Skipton and Otley. Both campuses have their own Student Unions.

BRETTON HALL

University College
Bretton Hall
West Bretton
Wakefield
West Yorks WF4 4 LG

TEL 01924 830261
FAX 01924 830521

Bretton Hall Students Union
West Bretton
Wakefield
West Yorks WF4 4LG

TEL 01924 832012
FAX 01924 832014

BRETTON HALL	
Founded	**1949**
Situation/style	**Campus**
UNDERGRADUATE PROFILE	
Application acceptance rate	**11%**
Population	**1,900**
Mature student population	**32%**
Overseas student population	**1%**
Male/female ratio	**30:70**
1st year institut. accommodation	**100%**
Approximate cost	**£65 pw**
ACADEMIC PROFILE	
A-level requirements:	**Medium Low**
Performance Management BB, **Performing Arts** CC, **Social Studies** CD-CC	
Student/staff ratio	**23:1**
1st class degree pass rate	**7.4%**
HEFCE assessments (3 subjects assessed):	
Music, English, Applied Social Work, approved satis. 1994/5	
Joint Funding Council's research assessment 1996 (5 subjects assessed):	
Grade 5/5*	None
EMPLOYMENT PROFILE	
Principal job market destinations:	
Education, Arts/Media, Retail/Wholesale	
Approximate % unemployed	**9%**

VAG VIEW

Sixteen miles from Leeds, 18 miles from Sheffield, 5 miles from Wakefield - Bretton Hall is a real find. Five hundred acres of landscaped parkland, rooted in the 13th century, now supports an 18th century Palladian Mansion, lakes, woods, a nature reserve with many species of animal and wild fowl, and gardens replete with astonishing statuary. It has to be the most beautiful campus in the country, and is just about the only place that made me want my time again.

As a college of Leeds University, Bretton Hall offers 'a dynamic learning experience' in Performing Arts *(including Dance, Theatre, and yes, as Barnsley College, Pop Music),* Design, Ceramics, Performance Mgt *(there has to be a place for you on that),* Social Studies, Arts & Education, Cultural Studies... *It's a kind of Dartington Hall of the north. And those sculptures in the park are a permanent feature, for Bretton Hall is also the home of the acclaimed Yorkshire Sculpture Park.*

Needless to say, with all this creative inspiration on tap, student organised social life is imaginative. Accommodation is on campus or in college-managed buildings in towns and villages around, or in Manygates, a Victorian estate, 10 minutes from Wakefield town centre, with 360 study bedrooms, en-suite of course. College performance facilities sited in Wakefield include a 136-seater theatre and dance studio used as a city showcase for student work. Get there - at all costs - from Junction 38 of the M1, the A637 to West Bretton, and a left turn by the War Memorial.

BRIGHTON UNIVERSITY

University of Brighton
Mithras House
Lewes Road
Brighton BN2 4AT

TEL 01273 600900
FAX 01273 642825

University of Brighton
Student Union
Cockcroft Building
Lewes Road
Brighton
East Sussex BN2 4GJ

TEL 01273 642870
FAX 01273 600694

UNIVERSITY OF BRIGHTON

Founded	**1970**
Situation/style	**4 town sites**
UNDERGRADUATE PROFILE	
Application acceptance rate	**9%**
Population	**7,500**
Mature student population	**35%**
Overseas student population	**12%**
Male/female ratio	**45:55**
1st year institut. accommodation	**55%**
Approximate cost (Uni)	**£42-£63pw**
(Town)	**£40pw**
ACADEMIC PROFILE	
A-level requirements:	**Medium-low**

Generally 'a flexible admissions policy'
Teacher Training 8, **Law, Accountancy/Finance, Business Studies** 18, **European Nursing Studies** 16, **Pharmacy** 20, **Computer Science, Software Eng.** DDD, **Maths & Statistics** DD, **Environmental Sciences** CCC, **Geography** DDD, **Electronic Eng.** CC, **Mech., Civil Eng.** 10-16,18, **Media** 18, **Art & Design** Unspecified

Student/staff ratio	**16:1**
1st class degree pass rate	**6.4%**

HEFCE assessments
(7 subjects assessed/approved):
1995/6 **Modern Languages** 20
Joint Funding Council's research assessment 1996
(19 subjects assessed):
Grade 5/5* None

EMPLOYMENT PROFILE
Principal job market destinations:
Education, Retail/Wholesale, Health, Manufacturing (strong on **Electronic**), **Commerce, Arts/Media** (strong on **Creative Arts**), **Public Admin./Law, Hotel/Restaurant, Computer, Personnel, Sport**
PIP 1996 employers' survey:
Top subject/national ranking
Social Science/Economics 36th=
Approximate % unemployed **10%**

VAG VIEW

Brighton, though once labelled London-by-the-sea, is still a fairly well-kept secret and there can be few better ways to spend three years as an undergraduate than in attempting to discover it.

It is an energetic, laid-back, imaginative, vibrant, artistic, commercial, alternative coastal culture, but still known by many, who merely visit it, as just another seaside resort. There are many different sides to Brighton, from the recently renovated seafront, to the North Laine area (the hub), to that self-contained little bit of it, Kemptown, redolent of the spirit of Graham Greene's Brighton Rock *perhaps, the village within the town, where real Brighton (shorn of students and tourists) still lies closest to the surface.*

As for the University, some of its parts - Fashion, Business - already have the recognition they deserve, but we think overall it's unfairly dismissed as Sussex Uni's poor neighbour.

SITUATION

Brighton University is a split site. Art and Design has a town location opposite the Royal Pavilion, near the Museum and Art Gallery and within 200 yards of the sea. The main site is on the northern edge of Brighton in Moulsecoomb, a stop on the rail line from Brighton to Falmer, where Sussex University is to be found and where Brighton Uni has its third campus (Teacher Education). There is a fourth site in Eastbourne, 20 miles east along the coast (Sport & Leisure). There's a shuttle bus between campuses.

ADDRESSES

(all telephone numbers the same, see above):
Grand Parade Campus, Grand Parade, Brighton BN2 2JY.
Moulsecoomb Campus, Lewes Road, Brighton BN2 4GJ.
Falmer Campus, Falmer, Brighton BN1 9PH.
Eastbourne Campus, Gaudick Road, Eastbourne BN20 7SP.

GETTING THERE

★ The University is within easy reach of London, and Gatwick and Heathrow Airports.
★ By road: M23 (past Gatwick), A23 to Brighton, on to A27 eastbound for Falmer, taking right turn (south on B2123) for Moulsecoomb. Dreadful roads in summer. Drivers from the east or west enter via A27, etc. For Eastbourne, stay on A27 and follow signs south on to A22.
★ Frequent trains from London Victoria (1:10). Change at Brighton for Moulsecoomb and Falmer. Frequent local trains - the journey to Falmer takes about eight minutes. Taxis available at Brighton Station. It is about 4 miles from the centre of Brighton to Falmer.
★ Coaches to Brighton leave from London Victoria Coach Station and arrive at Brighton Pool Valley Coach Station. Services depart every hour during the day (1:45).

ACADEMIA

Six faculties: Art, Design & Humanities; Business; Education, Sport & Leisure; Engineering & Environmental; Health; Information Technology.

Strong tradition of vocational - work-orientated - degree courses. Large number of sandwich courses - work placements. High proportion of mature students (35%), for whom work experience is a contributory factor to acceptance at Brighton. Part-time courses also on the increase.

Brighton and Sussex Unis have a close working relationship and aim to complement each other in the courses they provide. Collaboration also takes place in research and services for industry (see Sussex for this) as well as in student social and support services.

The Art & Design faculty is one of the best in the country. It includes Fine Art Painting/Printmaking/Sculpture, Dance, Music, Theatre, Graphic Design, Illustration, and a particularly good course in Fashion Design with Business Studies. Link-ups all over the world with this faculty, exposure on TV, close links with the artistic community in Brighton (a thriving scene) all combine to generate an enormous amount of imaginative energy. Other aspects of faculty are in sympathy, with courses in Cultural and Historical Studies, History of Design, Visual Culture, Humanities (analytical approach to social, political change/historical, ethical evaluation).

The Business School is high on links with Europe - languages are an increasingly important element, their BSc European Business with Technology breaking further ground with two European Unis (in France and Italy) and demanding fluency in two languages. Sponsorship by Coopers Lybrand Deloitte and Unilever, and the Rover Group, typifies two-way interest between Brighton and Industry & Commerce. Good also on Leisure & Tourism; links again with Brighton's commercial base.

Education, Sport & Leisure is a faculty collaboration between the Falmer and Eastbourne sites, which makes use of Eastbourne gym, swimming pool, labs and dance studios.

The Engineering & Environmental faculty offers a mix of traditional and modular structured courses in areas concerning natural and built environments - distinctive characteristic is their design orientation.

Health faculty is in cahoots with five local hospitals and embraces courses ranging from biology to occupational therapy and nursing.

The Faculty of Information Technology thrives on innovative post-grad research, and also has key links with Europe (BSc Informatique a collaboration with Paris). Close contacts again with industry, commerce, professions for research, work placement and consultancy purposes.

ENTS

The Student Union runs Brighton's longest established night club, the Basement (with a soft spot for Indie) and bars at Falmer and Eastbourne. The Basement is closed for developments as I write, but it will, I'm sure, only be better for it.

For the nightlife in Brighton, get hold of a copy of *Punter Student Guide, Brighton/Sussex edition.* It's worth its weight in whatever you value. The club scene is among the best in the country, although most close at 2. Sample The Jazz Place, Enigma, The Concorde, The Zap, The Escape, The Richmond, The Beachcomber etc. *Punter* gives you all the low-down on these and many more.

There are a dozen or more gay bars in town and Sussex Students Union has a particularly lusty line in gay, lesbian and bisexual groups (see Sussex). Clubs WonderBar, Simone on Top, Skirt and Just Sisters made for women. 'Outside of maybe Manchester and London, it really is one of the best places to be if you are gay,' Ella Jackson (WonderBar). If you're still not satisfied stick around for summer time – Brighton Gay and Lesbian Pride.

Cinemas: ABC, Odeon, Virgin, arthouse/alternative Duke of York's, Cinematique. Also cheap viewing at Gardner Arts Centre, Sussex Uni Campus (Falmer).

Comedy at Crocodile Club and Gardner Arts, latter also for theatre. Seek out Komedia too, and mainstream at Theatre Royal.

The pubs in Brighton offer everything from student discounts to alternative cabaret and theatre. They are at root what the whole place is about.

Bristol University

University of Bristol
Senate House
Tyndall Avenue
Bristol BS8 1TH

TEL 0117 928 9000
FAX 0117 925 1424

Bristol University Union
Student Union
Queens Road
Clifton
Bristol BS8 1LN

TEL 0117 973 5035
FAX 0117 946 6952

UNIVERSITY OF BRISTOL

Founded	**1876**
Situation/style	**City sites**
UNDERGRADUATE PROFILE	
Application acceptance rate	**7%**
Medical AAR	**6%**
Population	**8,000**
Mature student population	**13%**
Overseas student population	**9%**
Male/female ratio	**50:50**
1st year institut. accommodation	**100%**
Approximate cost	**£45-£68 pw**
ACADEMIC PROFILE	
A-level requirements:	**High**

Medicine ABB:
★ Science 'A's required **Chemistry + 1other Sci.**
★ Additional Science 'A's preferred **Biology**
★ Addit. Non-Science 'A's acceptable **1 only**
★ Retakes considered **Ext. circs.**
★ Clinical contact **1st year**

Student/staff ratio	**7:1**
1st class degree pass rate	**12.4%**
HEFCE assessments (15 subjects assessed/approved):	
1993/4 **Law, Mechanical Engineering, Chemistry**	Excellent
1994 **Geography, Applied Social Work**	Excellent
1995 **English**	Excellent
1995 **Sociology** 21	
1995/6: **Russian** 20, **Iberian Studies** 22	
1996: **French** 20, **Italian** 21	
Joint Funding Council's research assessment 1996 (43 subjects assessed):	
Geography	Grade 5*
Physiology, Pharmacology, Biochemistry, Chemistry, Physics, Earth Sciences, Applied Maths, Statistics, Computer, Civil Eng., Electrical & Electronic Eng., Economics, Social Policy & Admin., French, Italian, Classics, History, Education	Grade 5
EMPLOYMENT PROFILE	
Employability in Industry:	
MPW national league table (1996)	**9th=**

Principal job market destinations:
Commerce (strong), **Health** (incl. **Dentistry**), **Manufacturing, Personnel, Retail/Wholesale, Arts/Media** (strong), **Education, Computer, Veterinary, Dentistry**

PIP 1996 employers' survey: Top 3 subjects/national ranking	
Science	4th
Law	4th=
Accountancy/Finance & Banking	6th
Approximate % unemployed	**3.6%**

GETTING THERE

★ By train to Bristol Temple Meads from most anywhere other than Wales (which is Bristol Parkway). London Paddington or Birmingham New Street (1:30); Nottingham (3:00).
★ Get a cab from the station; the one-way system can be a nightmare.
★ By road: Bristol is at the intersection of the M4 and M5. The M32 runs off into the city from Junction 19 of the M4, but Clifton is also readily accessible from Junction 17 of the M5 through Westbury on Trym - just follow the signs to the zoo (an elephant).
★ Coach services from everywhere you'd expect - 2:30 hours from London.
★ Then there's the airport for European and inland destinations.

VAG VIEW

The first point about Bristol is that it is a great city. Perhaps its special spirit has something to do with being a gateway both to the sleepy West Country and the anxiety-ridden M4 corridor. Bristolians do seem to have got city-living about right.

The University and the city are all one. There is no real campus, it is all jumbled up together, which means that you won't find yourself dumped in an insular, campus-studenty environment like an extension of school.

Academically it offers courses which its league table equivalent in the north, Durham, does not - Medicine, Dentistry and Veterinary Science for a start, and its Economics courses explore a range of interesting combinations, two 4-year courses with a particularly intriguing European connection. Equally, Durham has its own strengths, which Bristol lacks, such as its Arabic, Chinese, Japanese connections.

Bristol has a reputation for being a place for Oxbridge rejects or for people not quite what Oxbridge want. Some would say that the latter is to recommend it. In fact the two experiences are so different that you would be wise to make plain to yourself what it is that you are after. Its sporting excellence, though it receives unconventional treatment by our mole, is, like everything else here, of the highest quality (its Boat Club, which trains on the Avon, together with its Sailing Club, is enjoying particular success right now). Academically, Bristol's HEFCE assessments (see box) confirm its place at the top of the tree. Perhaps the real difference is that Oxbridge belongs to academics, Bristol to undergraduates. The undergraduate teaching may even be better here. Oxbridge has overall a better reputation in terms of research, but it may well be that the lecturers and professors at Bristol see undergraduates as less of a necessary evil than do their Oxbridge counterparts.

Leaving aside the question of prestige - which for historical reasons Oxbridge answers with greater credibility - many will tell you that Bristol is a far better place to be between the ages of 18 and 21 than either Oxford or Cambridge. Certainly our correspondent discovered avenues of exploration and discovery which could, arguably, last a lifetime.

A few years back, so we heard from various schools careers teachers, Bristol was a bit like Nottingham is today - 'There was a time,' said one, 'when Bristol was a little bit arrogant. But they've actually learned a lesson, they are levelling out.' He was talking about the university authorities - schools liaisons' take-it-or-leave-it attitude,– not the students, although they suffer their own particular brand of stereotyping...

VIEW FROM THE GROUND
by Tony Dunkels

Bristol University has the reputation, especially among some of its more northerly competitors, as being a bit of a 'shandy drinkin', southern poof's university', comprising mostly ex-Oxbridge wannabes and the like. However, I shall now try to convince you that the only part of this summing up that is correct is the University's location. Bristol city is located fairly centrally in the south, being equidistant from London in the east (for a bit of high class, high cost action), and Devon and Cornwall down in the south-west (erm... for a quiet weekend with the missus maybe?!!). One of the principle advantages about its location is its proximity to other popular universities such as Bath or Exeter (both only about half-an-hour away). This means there is a lot of mixing that goes on as friends go to visit friends from old schools and so on.

Bristol's central location also has the

advantage of ensuring that most students don't have that far to travel to get to home base in times of clean clothes shortage, or when a decent Sunday lunch beckons. However, conveniently, it's usually far enough from home not to warrant unwanted parental visits that all students know so well and hate (unless cash donations are involved).

Many of the University's clubs and societies gain an advantage over many other universities via Bristol's location. Clubs such as the Hiking Club are forever taking groups of intrepid explorers up into Wales and even further afield. Among others, the Windsurfing Club often brave the cold of the Exmouth coast in Devon to test their skills. But everyone knows why it's best to be one of the most southerly universities. Very simply, because we're furthest away from where Oasis were created!! Pheww!

STUDENT PROFILE

As with all universities, Bristol is what you choose to make it. There is something and someone here for absolutely everyone if they are prepared to go and look. If a student isn't enjoying the university life then chances are that it's no fault of the university, more likely a fault of the student.

The best time to meet like-minded students is in the first week at the Freshers' Fair, when most of the looking is done for you. If you want to try every lager under the sun then there will be people embarking on the same mission (joining the bottled beer society would be a good place to start!). If you would rather be a bit of a recluse then fellow recluses will be banging on your door faster than you can shout 'Piss off!'

It is true, however, that there are a lot of 'Hooray Henrys' at Bristol...but probably not in greater numbers than at most other universities. It doesn't take long for all new students to settle into their own group of friends, and fortunately most groups seem to mix pretty freely. It really makes no difference as to whether a student is state or independently educated, foreign or native, and so on.

In conclusion, the best way to survive at Bristol is to be outgoing and open-minded; find who and what interests you, but certainly don't let that restrict your social circle. Remember that your Uni mates are going to be the ones that you are most likely to keep for life...SO DON'T HOLD BACK!!

SOCIAL LIFE

Unfortunately, the Students Union isn't the centre point for social activity that it might be. This could have something to do with the fact that there is no form of nightclub whatsoever in the building. NUS presidents, past and present, have campaigned to get this changed, but are fighting against the local residents who are concerned about noise levels - drunken students leaving in the early hours of the morning. (It was probably a little silly of them to get a house next to a student union!)

The Epi bar is the closest you'll get to socialising in the Union and is a popular starting point for nights on the town. This is probably for convenience sake more than anything else, as drink prices are easily challenged by some of the local bars, and the decor leaves a lot to be desired, showing possible signs of underfunding. There are, however, pool tables, a big-screen TV and a small arcade to keep you amused. If you're a keen sportsman (especially a rugby player) then Wednesday night is the one for you. The bar is transformed into a rowdy display of testosterone, team ties, drinking games, sweat and vomit.

There is another smaller, quieter bar in the Union called the Mandela Bar. This is a lot smarter than the Epi (not having to put up with such a regular trashing) and has more of a wine bar decor. As for the Union food, Cafe Zuba, situated next to the Epi, serves up a basic range of meals and snacks through the afternoon and into the evening. The food is cheap and student friendly, being high in taste and even higher in cholesterol; useful if the need arises.

The Anson rooms at the top of the building provide the ideal venue for balls and large gigs. The biggest event of the year is the Freshers' Ball at the beginning of the autumn term. This is the opportunity for all Freshers to mix and snog. But make sure you get your ticket early, preferably before the beginning of term, as they do sell out very quickly.

There is always a programme of entertainment going on; last year there was the Jool's Holland Band, a cinema, bungie running and much more. A large range of international bands gig there. Over recent years The Wildhearts, The Cardigans, Dodgy, Ocean Colour Scene and more have used the Anson rooms as their venue.

Once they've drunk their fill at the Epi most students then move out to the various pubs, bars and clubs in the town. A lot of these move in and out of fashion faster than boy-bands, but there are a few long-timers that I will try to list.

Most of the pubs and bars are found on Whiteladies Road and Park Street. Quite an absurd amount actually (and conveniently), so many in fact that the locals are complaining that the route is turning into a continuous pub crawl every evening. Recently, numerous super-pubs have opened on Whiteladies. These spectacular alcohol heavens are every student's dream; taps as far as the eye can see, walls of bottled lager, comfy sofas, big-screen TVs, AND the gents' toilet is always clean which is extremely rare these days! These super-pubs include The Rat and Parrot, The Fraternity House and the most recent, and spectacular, addition, The Bohemia, which apparently took £3 million to convert from the previous pub.

There are, of course, some more standard pubs along this stretch of road. The most popular of these include The Steam Tavern, well known for the fact that everything in this pub is upside down, from the labels on the beer taps to the 'Please wash your hands' sign in the toilet. This bewilders first-timers, but is actually because the owners are Australian. Hmmm, how imaginative. It's a very pleasant place to drink all the same.

For a slightly rowdier atmosphere, the Irish pub, Finnegan's Wake, on Cotham Hill, is the place to go. Lively Irish folk bands regularly turn the place into a stomping frenzy. Don't go there in your best strides as you're likely to get them covered in beer. Other popular pubs along Whiteladies Road and Park Street include The Jersey Lilly, The Bristol Blue, The Dog and Duck and The Berkeley. Of course, there are other popular pubs in other areas. The most notorious pub in Bristol, The Coronation Tap, is situated out in Clifton Village, and is definitely worth a visit. However, don't expect to go anywhere afterwards, as the lethal and infamous Exhibition Cider pretty much takes care of the rest of the evening.

The nearby Footbridge and Firkin is also a popular pub, probably because of its giant game of Jenga. Indeed a Jenga brick is an impressive trophy after a night out and nearly rates as highly as a bar stool as far as acknowledgement from fellow drinkers is concerned. Two other popular Clifton pubs, especially on Saturday nights, are The Channings Hotel, which has a bizarre selection of 20 flavours of vodka, and the much more traditional Albion. A pub more popular at lunch time, because of its cheap bar snacks, is The White Bear on St. Michael's Hill, and The White Hart and The Berkeley are two other popular lunchtime venues.

For a more up-market, costly drink, there are numerous bars in an area which might take your fancy. The most popular of these is Henry J. Beans, right at the top of Whiteladies. This nationally successful bar serves up a wide range of brightly coloured cocktails and is reasonably full most nights. Another good choice is the Square Bar just off the triangle. This was made famous among students for its jugs of Jellybean, which for a relatively low price gets you absolutely hammered. Other bars include Boom, The Tequila Worm and numerous others.

After the pubs and bars have been depleted of alcohol it's off to the clubs. There is pretty much something going on every night at the clubs. To name a few: Lakota is said to be the best club in the south-west, and for students its Shaft night on Tuesdays does go off a treat, playing mostly funky mixes. It's also one of the only clubs to have a weekend 6am licence. IQ and Odyssey are Bristol's answer to cheesy clubs; lots of pop, lots of snogging; great stuff!! Wedgies and Kickers aren't nearly as impressive as the aforementioned, but don't be too hasty to judge, especially if you're hideously drunk, play rugby, and it's Wednesday night.

The Steam Rock down near the waterfront also offers a great student night on Mondays, but be prepared to queue, because no matter how early you get there you can guarantee that 200 people will have beaten you to it. If you've got a mobile phone and are from one of the stylish areas of London then Poo-Naa-Naa or The Blue Mountain are the places for you. You'll get lots of kisses on the cheek in there if nothing else.

As for those who like to eat out every now and again there are restaurants to suit every taste in Bristol, especially on and around the Whiteladies Road area. To name the most popular: Bella Pasta provides a very tasty Italian, but Pizza Express makes pizza for the gods! The Balti House do the best curries in town, and never complain when their restaurant is repeatedly trashed! For oriental, The Orchid, although expensive, shows that what you pay for is what you get. Chiquito's offers a blinding South American. But most importantly I hastily press on to kebabs, the essential ingredient to any good night out (that is, if you failed to pull)! The crown has to be shared on this one between The Triangle Sandwich Bar and Flippers.

This is, of course, only a mere handful of the restaurants around Whiteladies alone. There are probably enough cheap eateries in the student areas of Bristol to feed all the starving nations of the world.

Bristol also has a generous lashing of cinemas covering all the student areas. These all show the latest releases at a decent price, and most offer a student discount. However, if it's more culture that you're after, there are also numerous theatres around the city centre and the campus. The biggest, The Hippodrome, shows everything from West End shows to touring acts such as Bottom. Numerous other theatres, most notably the Glynn-Wickam Studio, also stage student productions which are usually of a very high standard.

SPORT

One very excellent aspect of student life in Bristol is the harmless competition between the Bristol students and the University of the West of England students. This competition ranges from the sportsfield to the nightclubs but is nearly always friendly. Students from both universities mix freely, and most Bristol students have good friends at UWE and vice versa.

DRUGS

Like all universities, drugs, soft and hard, are frowned upon greatly. However, the biggest punishment is probably the social one, with users becoming an extremely insular crowd that is hard to escape from.

ACCOMMODATION

At Bristol it's definitely better to go into one of the halls of residence for your first year as this is where most friendships are forged. There are basically two groups of halls. The first are the Clifton halls, more popular with second and third years. These halls have the advantage of being closer to the university, but the disadvantage of being further away from the majority of first year students, which if you are a first year is a bit of a bummer. These halls comprise Clifton Hill House, Manor Hall and the recently converted Goldney Hall.

The second group are the Stoke Bishop halls, about 40 minutes' walk from the university. These halls are generally more popular with first year students. They consist of Baydock and Churchill halls (the party halls), Hiatt Baker (nick-named rather appropriately, shite-bunker), Wills Hall (the mobile phone hall) and Durdham Hall, and finally the quiet hall, University Hall. All the halls are very unassuming and most students will make friends and have fun wherever they go. There is a lot of friendly rivalry, especially sportswise, between Wills and Churchill hall. However, Baydock has the greatest sporting reputation, especially for rugby (which is probably why it's such a nut house!).

Whether you should choose self-catering or catering depends on how much confidence you have in your own cooking abilities; but try not to have too much faith in the expertise of the University's cooking, as the food on the whole is absolutely appalling!

When it comes to getting your own house in the second year you have to be shrewd and fast. It's a dog eat dog world in the field of rented accommodation. There are numerous ways to get houses,– through the University's own accommodation bureau, through friends who are moving out, through letting agencies or even by buying accommodation on the market. Try to get it sorted out in the spring term so that you don't have to worry about it during exams in the summer. The most popular student areas to live in are down Whiteladies Road, in Redland and Clifton, as these are all nice areas and close to the university.

POLITICS

The spring term, in some ways, can be the most irritating time of the year, as it's election time. You can't walk across campus without being badgered by various candidates. Yet the best line I've ever heard is still only, 'Oh, go on, please vote for me'. Not particularly persuasive! There are several positions to be voted for, including Union President and Vice-President, General Secretary, blah, blah, BORING! Luckily some more inventive candidates, such as Darth Vader, also join in and hold speeches on ridding the Earth of the Force once and for all!! YEAH, up with the darkside!

British Institute in Paris

British Institute in Paris
Departement d'etudes
Francaises
Institut Britannique de Paris
9-11 Rue de Constantine 75340
Paris 07
France

TEL 00 331 45 55 71 99
FAX 00 331 45 50 31 55

BRITISH INSTITUTE IN PARIS	
Founded	**1894**
Situation/style	**City site**
UNDERGRADUATE PROFILE	
Application acceptance rate	**8%**
Population 3rd-yr UK U/Gs	**125**
BA (Hons) U/Gs	**15**
Mature student population	**20%**
ACADEMIC PROFILE	
A-level requirements:	**High**
French Studies ABB,	
HEFCE assessments (1 subject assessed/approved):	
1996 **French** 18	
Joint Funding Council's research assessment 1996 (1 subject assessed):	
Grade 5/5*	None

VAG VIEW

This is part of The University of London, originally set up to teach French to English students and vice versa. One hundred plus British students spend their year abroad here; then there is a handful of students following a full-time BA degree. It is also a centre for research into language translation and the two cultures. It publishes an academic journal called Franco-British Studies.

Paris is a great city in which to be an impoverished student or to be rich and successful; less good if you're in between. The really extraordinary thing is that the institute only scored 18 on the HEFCE French assessment and came close to bottom in the 1996 research assessment with a 3b rating. No LEA grants. Full fees - over £2,000 payable.

BRUNEL UNIVERSITY

Brunel University
Uxbridge
Middlesex UB8 3PH
TEL 01895 274000
FAX 01895 232806

Brunel University
Union of Brunel Students
(Uxbridge and
Runnymede Area)
Cleveland Road
Uxbridge
Middlesex UB8 3PH

TEL 01895 462200
FAX 01895 810477

Union of Brunel Students
Twickenham Campus
300 St Margaret's Road
Twickenham
Middlesex TW1 1PT

TEL 0181 892 6085

Union of Brunel Students
Osterley Campus
Borough Road
Isleworth
Middlesex TW7 5DN

TEL 0181 560 2984
FAX 0181 568 3741

BRUNEL UNIVERSITY

Founded	**1966**
Situation/style	**4-site campus**
UNDERGRADUATE PROFILE	
Application acceptance rate	**10%**
Population	**7,725**
Mature student population	**45%**
Overseas student population	**3%**
Male/female ratio	**75:25**
1st year institut. accommodation	**100%**
Approximate cost	**£35-£50 pw**
ACADEMIC PROFILE	
A-level requirements:	**High-medium**

Law BBC-BBB, **Computer Science** BBC-BCC, **Mech. Eng with Aeronautics** BCC, **E & E Eng.** BBC, **Thick/thin SW General Eng. courses** BBB-CCC, **Mech./Manufac. Eng** BCC/CCC, **Politics & Social Policy** BCC, **Sociology & Communication** BCC, **Film & TV Studies** 22

Student/staff ratio	**16:1**
1st class degree pass rate	**8.3%**

HEFCE assessments (11 subjects assessed/approved):

1995 **Anthropology, Social Policy & Admin.**	Excellent
1996 **Sociology** 22	

Joint Funding Council's research assessment 1996 (21 subjects assessed):

Art & Design	Grade 5*
Anthropology	Grade 5

EMPLOYMENT PROFILE

Employability in Industry:

MPW national league table (1996)	**26th**

Principal job market destinations:

Manufacturing (strong on **Electronic & Electrical,** good **Pharmaceutical**), **Commerce, Education, Computer**

PIP 1996 employers' survey:

Top 3 subjects/national ranking

Engineering & Technology	18th
Electrical Engineering	23rd=
Computing	28th
Approximate % unemployed	**6.5%**

VAG VIEW

Out of a technical background, its roots in the 19th century, Brunel established itself as a science/technology/engineering Uni in the late 60s, as a pioneer of the thin sandwich course, but recently it has spread its wings, quadrupled in size and taken on a broader academic brief - Social Work, Sociology, Politics, Law, Psychology, Health and Arts (from English to Film/TV Studies, from American Studies to Drama), and Sports Studies/Sciences, where it has scored very big owing to its merging with Brunel University College - or Borough Road, as it is affectionately known by its students, a college with an exceptional record in sport, as our correspondent will tell us.

BUC accounts for Brunel's Twickenham and Osterley campuses.

And the expansion doesn't stop there. Buckinghamshire College of Higher Education is now affiliated to Brunel University. It offers degrees in Building (Design & Processes), Business, Engineering, Engineering Design, Business Information Technology, Criminology/ Criminal Justice, Film/Media/Culture, Literature/Art History/Culture, Design, Health, Leisure. It is situated at Newland Park, near Chalfont St Giles, and at two sites in High Wycombe. Phone 10494 5221141 (Fax: 01494 871954) for prospectus and information.

Brunel's assessments are extremely impressive in some of the new subject areas it has taken on, but it remains true to the career-orientated principles (and technology assisted learning processes) on which it built its earlier success, demonstrated in the employment league tables. Rightly it trumpeted its presence at the top of The Financial Times *League Table six times in the last decade.*

At its Twickenham and Osterley campuses Brunel makes its mark as one of the leading Unis for Sports Studies and sporting performance. The Rugby Union Club were British University Champions in 1995. In 1993/4 Brunel won the overall Small University Championships against teams such as Durham and Swansea, and the year earlier it took the honours for the women's Championship. In the same years they won at men's volleyball, were finalists in netball, runners-up in athletics, and so it goes on. This, as our correspondent says, is one of the places for sport, and they have the requisite facilities and staff (among them ex-Olympic and World Championship contenders).

SITUATION

Since 1995 Brunel has been sited at four campuses - Uxbridge (main site), Runnymede, Twickenham and Osterley. They like the idea of themselves as perched on the edge of London, not suffocating in the Metropolis but near enough to take advantage of it - 'The hustle and bustle of city life is not for everyone.' Students agree.

ADDRESSES

Uxbridge Campus (as above);
Twickenham Campus, 300 St Margaret's Road, Twickenham, Middx, TW1 1PT (Tel: 0181 891 0121. Fax: 0181 891 8270);
Osterley Campus, Borough Road, Isleworth, Middx, TW7 5DU (Tel: 0181 891 0121. Fax: 0181 891 8211);
Runnymede Campus, Englefield Green, Egham, Surrey TW20 OJZ (Tel: 01785 431341. Fax: 01784 472879).

ACCOMMODATION

Uxbridge: Five halls with single study bedrooms (635 with en-suite), self-catering. Runnymede: Ten self-catering halls, some shared rooms. Osterley and Twickenham: 340 places in hall with small kitchenettes, but rents include five main meals a week. All four campuses have refectories.

GETTING THERE

★ Uxbridge by road: Leave M4 at Junction 4 and follow signs to Uxbridge (A408). Cross two roundabouts then turn right, A408. Continue across one set of traffic lights and almost immediately take right filter at traffic lights into Station Road. After 300 metres turn left into Cleveland Road and then right into University.
★ A40/M40: At M40/A40 interchange (Swakeleys Roundabout) take B483 exit to Uxbridge. Follow signs across two mini-roundabouts. At major road bear left on to A4020 (Brunel sign), then at first traffic lights turn right into The Greenway. At first crossroad, turn left into Cleveland Road, and, after 150 metres, into the University.
★ By Underground: Metropolitan Line from Baker Street (and Piccadilly Line during peak hours). Then bus, U3 or U5. By Rail: Trains to West Drayton. U3 to campus or U5 to Cowley Road.
★ Runnymede by road: M1/M25 (Junction 13) A30 then A308 and A328, signed Air

Force Memorial.
★ M4/M25/A30 or A4/A30 west towards Staines, then A308 etc as above.
★ A4 or M4 (Junction 6) then A332 and A308 as above.
★ A30 or M3 (Junction 3) to Bagshot then A30 to Englefield Green traffic lights, and left signed Air Force Memorial. Ignore Runnymede sign on A30 to Egham.
★ By rail: To Egham, changing at Staines or Ascot if necessary. Walk from Egham Station can take 30 minutes.
★ Twickenham by road: Chertsey Road (A316) to St. Margaret's Road (A3004) north. The college is 300 yards on right.
★ By Underground: Richmond (District Line) then H37 bus; or Hounslow East (Piccadilly Line) then H37 bus.
★ By rail: St. Margaret's Station then H37 bus or 15 minutes walk; or Richmond Station (North London Link Line) then H37 bus.
★ Osterley by road: Great West Road (A4) to Wood Lane (traffic lights). The college is 500 yards west of A310 junction at Gillette Corner.
★ By Underground: Osterley (Piccadilly Line) then left out of station, 15 minutes walk on south side of Great West Road.
★ By rail: Isleworth Station and five minutes walk.

VIEW FROM THE GROUND AT BUC

by Kay Collins

Brunel University College, or BUC for short, has undergone many name changes since its foundation years and years ago, but one thing that has not changed is its close-knit student community. BUC, or 'Borough Road' - BUC's traditional name (which comes from its location on Borough Road!) - is part of Brunel University. But students are determined that certain traditions remain, namely that of its sporting excellence which means for students: It's not the winning that counts (as we nearly always do) but the style in which the winning is achieved.

BUC boasts the B.U.S.A. (British Universities Sports Association) champions in hockey and netball last season (3 times in a row), as well as rugby in the previous season; not surprising with the 1sts, 2nds, and 3rds all reaching the finals (as well as countless other individual elite athletes, some of whom were followed closely in the 'Olympics' this year by the rest of us aspiring-to-be-elite sports players).

If sport is your domain BUC is definitely the place to be. Wednesday nights are legendary with *all* clubs celebrating victories together. *No* rivalry between clubs exists here; everyone meets up after respective games and celebrates, singing traditional Borough songs.

But BUC is not just about sports orientated students, it also boasts some history... Borough Road is one of the oldest educational establishments in the country and still turns out dedicated, fun-loving teachers, as well as being the home of the Rambert School of Ballet.

The facilities at BUC are what you would expect of a small university - quite limited, but bars are what you make them and the atmosphere in the Student Union bars can be electrifying. BUC is also under a period of expansion at present with a new nightclub just having been installed - entertainments are looking promising and many more developments are in the pipeline. The SU shop is well equipped for those chocolate moments in between lectures and if you find yourself short of stationery, food, or a T-shirt, you can also buy them in there relatively cheaply.

BUC is served by many student-type eateries, many of which have to be visited after a Wednesday night out. Michelle offers a running commentary on the local talent (male and female) - but if you can endure this the Chinese is second-to-none. Mr. Wurabo offers an eat-as-much-as-you-can! for £5, which is excellent value. Pizza Hut buffet is also a favourite - eat as much as you can for £4.99 - as is the £2.50 option of the Ice-Cream Factory. The Shack is also a Borough tradition where many a student can be found eating an English breakfast before a game on Wednesday.

I guarantee you will enjoy yourself here. And if you leave without knowing the words to our song - Borough Blazer - something's got to be wrong!!!

BUCKINGHAM UNIVERSITY

The University of Buckingham
Buckingham
MK18 1EG

TEL 01280 814080
FAX 01280 822245

University of Buckingham
Student Union
Buckingham MK18 1EG

TEL 01280 822522

UNIVERSITY OF BUCKINGHAM	
Founded	**1966**
Situation/style	**Campus**
UNDERGRADUATE PROFILE	
Application acceptance rate	**8%**
Population	**880**
Mature student population	**51%**
Overseas student population	**65%**
Male/female ratio	**55:45**
1st year institut. accommodation	**100%**
Approximate cost	**£60 pw**
ACADEMIC PROFILE	
A-level requirements:	**Low**
Law 12-18, **Psychology** 14, **Accounting & Financial Management** 16, **Business Studies** 14	
Student/staff ratio	**10:1**
FEES	
Approx. annual fees	**£9,750**
EMPLOYMENT PROFILE	
PIP 1996 employers' survey:	
Top subject/national ranking	
Law	36th=

VAG VIEW

This is Britain's only independent university. All students are charged the cost of their studies. Grants available from LEA (in 1996, £2,176 per student from UK and EU) make barely a dent in the tuition/residency costs. Clearly it is not a university for the impoverished.

Degree courses are completed in two years rather than three - 'to gain the same degree as elsewhere, yet to graduate a year earlier than your contemporaries.' There I was thinking the 2-year degree made it better value for money - going on for £20,000 for a degree rather than some £30,000.

But could it be the way of things to come for all Unis? If it is possible to work a degree in two years, why isn't everyone doing it? The questions are endless, and it is too simplistic to say that this is a Uni for rich also-rans because Buckingham is gaining quite a reputation in some areas - 'It is a very intensive experience,' said one independent school careers master. 'In Biological Sciences and some other research areas it's got a very good reputation.' Okay, I hear you say, but most people that study as undergraduates here are into Business and Social Studies.

The Uni itself doesn't submit to the government's academic assessments for the simple reason that they are carried out by the funding body (HEFCE) which doesn't fund Buckingham. The government might consider the downside of spending masses of money tooling up funding bodies for academic assessment when/if they are about to consign them to the dust heap. Perhaps academic assessment should be carried out by a wholly independent body.

Buckingham has this way of getting us looking into the future. It has its own independent Advisory Committee and since it must realise that its future depends on its results, you can bet that this body is independent and earns its fees. We're not into a Holborn College experience here. Sir Richard Luce, the Vice Chancellor of Buckingham, may well go down in history as the man who led the way. (He is being succeeded by Professor Bob Taylor (ex-SOAS) by the time we publish. Perhaps Prof Taylor's Oriental and African contacts will be just the thing to boost intake.)

Meanwhile, the present is with us and Buckingham is out on its own, a fact which had one sixth-form careers adviser give other than a financial or academic reason for her pupils rejecting it as an option - 'It's a two-year course, January to January. With traditional exams in June it puts them out of kilter with their friends.' What this means to Buckingham is that their short-term market is outside the UK and outside the mainstream tradition HE student market. So it is that 65% + of their students come from overseas and more than half their intake are wrinklies, which in turn influences the kind of life you can expect to find there, which may be good or bad, depending on where you are coming from. Undergraduates will have to contend with a quiet rural setting, a high pressure, concentrated academic scene. There will not be much time for the three-year exploration of the bottomless pit of your needs and desires, which, let's face it, most undergraduates are looking for. I mean, what do you think's going down between Oxford and Milton Keynes?

SITUATION

Oxford (23 miles), London (58 miles), Cambridge (63 miles), Milton Keynes (14 miles). You need a car (and you probably have three).

Two sites, Hunter Street (south-west of town centre, caught rather attractively in a loop of the Ouse) and 8-acre Verney Park (smack on The London Road). They're within walking distance of one another. A third development down the road from the Hunter Street precinct is under construction on Chandos Road.

Business and Humanities are at Hunter Street. Law, computer rooms, library teaching rooms are found at Verney Park and 'recreational activities in the cellars of the Franciscan Building' (sounds more promising).

Chandos Road will give them a new library by a Language Centre and more lecture rooms.

GETTING THERE

★ By road: Make for Buckingham by-pass. M40 (J9) from South, then A41, A421 or the scenic route M25 (J20), A41, A413 which will carry you straight to Verney Park (on your right) after crossing the by-pass. Town also fed by A422, A421, as well as A413 from North.

★ By rail: Frequent services to Milton Keynes and Bletchley from London, Euston (1:00), Birmingham New Street, 1:20).

★ Bus service to Buckingham from both destinations. Taxis also available.

★ By air: Heathrow or Gatwick to London (train, underground, taxi as appropriate) then by rail.

ACCOMMODATION:

Guaranteed first-year accommodation (*shared* bathroom/showers, would you believe?) at around £60 a week.

SPORT

Four all-weather tennis courts, one all-weather 5-a-side pitch. Fields for rugby, football, cricket, hockey. Stowe Estates and Sports Club for swimming, tennis, badminton, squash.

ACTION

The Union organises regular social functions such as the Graduation Ball and the August Rag Week. Then there's those cellars in the Franciscan Building, and 'the multi-national student community has led to the formation of a large number of overseas clubs which promote cultural events.' Ah, now we have it - these include the Arab Society, the African Students' Association, the Caribbean Society, the Greek Society, the Indian Society, the Islamic Society...

Cambridge University

Cambridge Intercollegiate
Applications
Kellet Lodge
Tennis Court Road
Cambridge CB2 1QJ

TEL 01223 333308
FAX 01223 366383

Cambridge University (CUSU)
Student Union
11/12 Trumpington Street
Cambridge CB2 1QA

TEL 01223 356454/333313
FAX 01223 323244

UNIVERSITY OF CAMBRIDGE

Founded	**13th century**
Situation/style	**City collegiate**

UNDERGRADUATE PROFILE

Application acceptance rate	**29%**
Medical AAR	**25%**
Population	**10,800**
Mature student population	**6%**
Overseas student population	**9%**
Male/female ratio	**57:43**
1st year institut. accommodation	**95%**
Approximate cost (College)	**£70 pw**
(City)	**£50+pw**

ACADEMIC PROFILE

A-level requirements: **Very high**

Medicine AAA**:**

★ Science 'A's required **Chemistry**

★ Additional Science 'A's preferred **Physics, Biol., Maths** or at GCSE

★ Addit. Non-Science 'A's acceptable **Yes**

★ Retakes considered **No**

★ Clinical contact **4th year**

Student/staff ratio	**5:1**
1st class degree pass rate	**27%**
3rd class rate	**0.97%**

HEFCE assessments
(12 subjects assessed/approved):

1993: **Chemistry, History, Law**	Excellent
1994: **Computer Science, Architecture, Music**	Excellent
1995: **English, Geography, Geology, Anthropology**	Excellent
1996: **Modern Languages** 22	

Joint Funding Council's research assessment 1996
(46 subjects assessed):

Clinical Lab. Sciences, Hospital/Clinical, Physiology, Pharmacology, Biotechnology, Pure Maths, Applied Maths, Chem. Engineering, Built Environment, Economics, Middle Eastern/African, Asian, Russian, Linguistics, Philosophy, Theology, Music	Grade 5
Community/Clinical, Anatomy, Biochemistry, Psychology, Chemistry, Physics, Earth Sciences, Genetics, Statistics, Computer, Engineering, Metallurgy, Geography, Law, Anthropology, English, French, German/Dutch/ Scandinavian, Italian, Iberian, Classics, Archaeology, History, Hist. of Art/Architecture/Design, Philosophy (Hist. & Phil. of Science), Zoology	Grade 5*

EMPLOYMENT PROFILE

Employability in Industry:

MPW national league table (1996) **2nd**

Principal job market destinations:

Commerce (very strong)**, Manufacture, Health, Education, Arts/Media** (strong)**, Public Admin/Law, Computer, Veterinary, Retail/Wholesale, Market Research/ Advertising**

PIP 1996 employers' survey:

Top 3 subjects/national ranking

Science	1st
Computing	1st
Law	2nd
Approximate % unemployed	**4.6%**

VAG VIEW - THE OXBRIDGE EXPERIENCE

Everything that is happening in Higher Education seems to be happening outside Oxbridge. Today Thatcher's children have a clear choice, which no longer turns simply on their ability to make the Oxbridge grade. 'We have very bright students who don't want the traditional Oxford and Cambridge experience,' said one school careers adviser. 'They would prefer something more progressive in the sense of preparing you for the world. People are looking more widely now; they realise that Oxbridge isn't the key to quality.'

The much publicised Target School Scheme for a bigger dose of State School sixthformers in the Oxbridge intake recipe seems quaintly out-of-date as a solution to their increasing isolation from what is at root a re-definition of the entire higher education programme, and has little to do with privilege or class.

Certainly there is also a drive among new and not so new (see York) universities to widen their intake, by means of the GNVQ route and so on, but the reasoning behind it has to do with the course and assessment structure of GNVQs being more suited to the new modular scheme, which is meeting the needs of employers nationally and internationally.

Again, people look at the employer tables and marvel at the success rating of places such as UMIST and Bath. But the real choice today is not between vocationally and non-vocationally led universities, but between universities which see the academic virtues of inter-disciplinary course schemes, and those which remain blind to it.

The modular approach isn't just a question of broadening higher education for those who can't take the depth, nor is it about shovelling in a spadeful of languages or computing to prepare graduates for a career or give them an opportunity to work in Europe.

What is being schemed by those who are using the new system adventurously and in an inter-disciplinary way is a resolution of the traditional opposition between two ways of looking at the world and its problems - the scientific way and the artistic way, a resolution which the traditional, specialist approach disallows. Even medical schools and university departments are now allowing an Arts element in their A-level requirements. Perhaps soon they will actively encourage one.

Another debate is aired in the current Cambridge University Student Handbook, *about the fact that female undergraduates are far less likely to be awarded a First Class degree than male undergraduates. The question is raised as to how a First Class degree can reflect true excellence if it discriminates by gender. Does the statistic suggest that, to be fair, no exam paper should carry the name or gender of the examinee? Or does it suggest that there is a gender difference in the way students tackle a subject and that the Cambridge system favours a male approach? Or does it suggest that men, at this level, are brighter than women?*

It is, as with the debate about specialisation, tempting to argue that what this fact suggests is that we have reached a crucial stage in the evolution of Higher Education. Newnham College, an all-female college, was founded in 1871, but it was not until 1948 that they were awarded Cambridge degrees. It will be fascinating to see where Oxbridge will take us in the next fifty years. What is certain is that they will fiercely protect their position, whatever it is, and that there will continue to be reason to opt for the Cambridge experience, not limited, I hope, to what a student of St. John's admitted in the Cambridge Alternative Prospectus, *namely that there is 'a kick knowing that you live in a place other people visit on holiday!'*

GETTING THERE

★ By road (from London): M25 (J27), M11 (J11), A10. From West or East, A45.
From North-West, A604.
★ Stansted Airport, M11.
★ By train: London's Liverpool Street - under the hour; Nottingham - 2:30; Sheffield, Birmingham New Street - 3:00.

CAMBRIDGE COLLEGES

CHRIST'S
Cambridge CB2 3BU
TEL 01223 334953
Founded 1448. Local situation. Beautiful grounds, gardens, courts, fifteenth Century chapel and Master's Lodge. Good mix of students. Good on sport, music and drama. Football, rugby, hockey and rowing are particular strengths, twice termly bops, biannual May Ball. Law Library and theatre. Accommodation offered throughout. All non-overseas applicants invited for interview.

CHURCHILL
Cambridge CB3 0DS
TEL 01223 336202
Founded 1960. Spacious grounds with playing fields on site. Situated away from the centre, though only about a five minute bike ride. Modern buildings mean modern facilities and the accommodation is very good indeed. College founded for anoraks, and scientists and engineers still abound. First college to admit women (1972). Fifty per cent intake from comprehensive schools. Film society and boat club are key. Huge bar where Thursday night is disco night plus other engineering delights such as Blind Date night and karaoke sessions.

CLARE
Cambridge CB2 1TL
TEL 01223 333246
Founded 1326. Located in the centre of Cambridge straddling the River Cam. Life centres on seventeenth century Old Court. Accommodation across the river (Memorial, Ashley, Thirkill Courts) is modern. Further accommodation ten minutes away. Friendly, tight-knit community. Very strong on music, choir in particular, allegedly the best live ents nights in town. Clare cellars home to jazz, blues, rock events and Indie nights. Good facilities for photography, drama (Clare Actors' Society), pottery, sport (including Clare Rats - mountaineering, trekking etc). Recent sport successes include women's rugby. Strong academic competition in Arts area, they encourage applicants to take a gap year.

CORPUS CHRISTI
Cambridge CB2 1RH
TEL 01223 338056
Founded 1352. Strong in History, English and Law. The majority of intake are immediate entrants (no gap year). Enthusiastic music contingent. Organ and choral scholarships. College located in centre of city, friendly, a-political, cosy (some might say claustrophobic). Accommodation throughout in fourteenth century Old Court; New Court (1830s); Beldam Court (1996) includes en-suite facilities. No great space for ents but recently bands have been allowed into the bar and karaoke nights are the thing. Good reputation for food but high Fixed Kitchen Charge.

DOWNING
Cambridge CB2 1DQ
TEL 01223 334826
Founded 1800. Neo-Classical architecture in the centre of town away from the Backs (back of colleges stretch of river). Spacious accommodation, some en-suite. New Library 1993, law collection a fine one. Academically strong in Law, Medicine and Engineering. Scholarships for Creative Writing, awards for distinction in Law or Medicine, Choral and Instrumental awards annually. High involvement in University activities (sport, journalism, drama). Claims best boat club and strong women's rugby team. College multi-gym. Regular bops and films. Candlelit Formal Hall three times a week.

EMMANUEL
Cambridge CB2 3AP
TEL 01223 334290.
Founded 1584. Friendly, unpretentious, the College (known as Emma) actively recruits from the whole spectrum of schools. Accommodation self-catering facilities poor,

but it's the only college with a weekly laundry service. Well equipped computer room. Active drama society (REDS) went to Edinburgh recently. Music strong. Sport - successful in ladies' rowing and women's football (Pink Panthers). Two squash courts and open air swimming pool on site. Rich college with hardship fund, scholarships, prizes. Almost everyone is interviewed.

FITZWILLIAM
Cambridge CB3 0DG
TEL 01223 332030
Founded 1869. Some might say it's a bit like a multi-storey car park; present buildings date from 1963. But, despite lack of funds, gardens tended with t.l.c. Set apart from the centre of town, Fitzwilliam has less of a traditional/ self-conscious feel about it than most colleges. Stands about midway in the academic table and students have a reputation for being relaxed and sociable. The bar is the fulcrum of social activities. Though ents appear only twice a term, toga parties have caused a stir. Cinema, dark room. They do well in football (men and women). College library good and separate law library. Most candidates interviewed and they seem to be trying to recruit more mature students. Higher than average intake from state sector. Accommodation limited, many live out after first year.

GIRTON
Cambridge CB3 0JG
TEL 01223 338972
Founded 1869. Set in 50 acres of beautiful grounds two miles out of the city of Cambridge, well away from the crowds of tourists. Originally a women only college, it first admitted men in 1979. Men now slightly dominate women, in numbers only. Egalitarian approach to student recruitment in line with otherwise unpressured, friendly atmosphere. Accommodation initially in College then in Wolfson Court, near University Library, or in college houses nearby. Cellar bar is the focus for socialising and ents nights. Sports facilities include large indoor heated swimming pool in the college grounds. Rowing popular. Not the most academic of colleges.

GONVILLE & CAIUS
Cambridge CB2 1TA
TEL 01223 332447
Founded first as Gonville Hall in 1348 then, in 1558, re-filed as G & C by John Caius, Royal Physician. Two sites: King's Court by the Market Place in the centre, Harvey Court (number 62) across the river, a few minutes walk away (with faith). Accommodation not Gonville & Caius's strong point. The library, however, is undergoing a big re-development and computer facilities are to be installed. Re-development on the social side of things will bring a new bar, much needed apparently as the Buttery, which closes at 10pm, lacks vigour, although bops are popular. Sport strong - a licensed sports pavilion helps. Music and Drama also strong (22 choral awards available). More than half the intake is science orientated.

HOMERTON
Hills Road
Cambridge CB2 2PH
TEL 01223 411141
Founded in 1695, a college wholly devoted to education. Wide spread of student intake; State school predominates; mature population relatively high. Strong on men's rugby and women's rowing. Grounds in the process of being sold off but sporting facilities remain with gym, squash court and a sports field.

JESUS
Cambridge CV5 8BL
TEL 01223 357626
Founded in 1496. Spacious grounds five minutes from city centre. Accommodation in college or houses across the road. Music and drama strong; organ scholarships and choral exhibitions available. Bar open until 11.30 pm, but poor ents due to lack of room. Strong on sport - soccer, rugby, cricket, hockey pitches on site, also squash and tennis courts. Boat house a short walk away.

KING'S
Cambridge CB2 1ST
TEL 01223 331417
Founded in 1441. Alleged contradiction (due to its famous chapel and choir) between

public perception as prestigious/traditional and down-to-earth actuality. King's claims 75% intake from state schools, has no formal arrangements for meals (no connection divined in this, but College is reported to be obsessed with political correctness). Claims to operate one of the best ents scenes in the university from its Cellar. Arts Centre and computer room. Active drama as well as music. Sport not strong.

LUCY CAVENDISH
Cambridge CB3 0BU
TEL 01223 332190
Founded 1965. This is a college for mature female students. English, Law and Veterinary Science traditionally strong. College situated minutes from city centre but tucked away in a cul-de-sac. Recent accommodation block has en-suite bedrooms. Sport weak. Recently started its first rowing crew and opened a gym, but predominantly academically orientated.

MAGDALENE
Cambridge CB3 0AG
TEL 01223 332135
Founded in 1542. Quiet, riverside site north of city centre. Magdalene stereotype is public school - traditional candlelit Formal Dinner every evening in Hall - but students claim no overpoweringly arrogant ethos. Strong involvement in wider Uni activities - sport, drama, journalism. Playing fields shared with St. John's.

NEW HALL
Huntingdon Road
Cambridge CB3 0DF
TEL 01223 351721
Founded in 1954. All women college. Not academically high flying but strong in Medicine and Economics. Situated at least ten minutes walk from the centre of town. Newest accommodation facilities offer 112 en-suite bedrooms. Formal Hall nights. Garden Party a key event. Enthusiastic involvement within drama (Madhouse), music, and sport - currently four eights on the river and a football club in the First Division. Has tennis, squash, netball courts.

NEWNHAM
Cambridge CB3 1DF
TEL 01223 335783
Founded 1871. All women college, conveniently sited near Uni's Arts Faculties and not far from the river. Academically competitive. Well-balanced intake with 10% from overseas and fair mix of state and independent. Anything but insular, students very much involved in Uni life outside. College gardens lead to playing fields, tennis courts, croquet lawn, pitches for cricket, hockey, lacrosse, football and occasionally rugby. Newnham boat club is the oldest women's boat club in England. Boat house shared with Jesus, squash courts with Selwyn.

PEMBROKE
Cambridge CB2 1RF
TEL 01223 338154
Founded in 1347. City centre location but off the tourist track. High academic standards and sporting enthusiasm - rowing, rugby, football, netball, hockey and women's football well represented. Good bar, regular ents, closing time late. Accommodation either in college, in houses a short way away or near the sports ground/Grantchester Meadows; new building due to be finished this year. Well supplied with computers - student network. Music strong, as is journalism and theatre (Pembroke Players). Almost all candidates interviewed.

PETERHOUSE
Cambridge CB2 1RD
TEL 01223 338223
Founded 1284. Oldest and smallest undergrad. college. Choosier than most, yet diverse student body and no Peterhouse stereotype, so be very good at what you're good at. Majors in History, Natural Sciences, Engineering, English, Law, Medicine, Classics, Maths. Fairly but not too central a location. High involvement in wider Uni activities. Thriving boat club, rugby, football teams. Despite publicity to the contrary students claim this is not a wholly right-wing place.

QUEEN'S
Cambridge CB3 9ET
TEL 01223 335540
Founded in 1448. Compact site over the Cam. In-college accommodation. Well above average facilities. Well-balanced intake. High involvement in Uni and college activities. Strong sport, drama, music; academically competitive too. Good bar (pool table, arcade bandit, etc.). Capacious Fitzpatrick Hall good for theatre, bops, films. High standard ents. Currently strong in rowing, basketball and football.

ROBINSON
Cambridge CB3 9AN
TEL 01223 339143
The newest of Cambridge's colleges (brick), founded 1979, situated behind the University Library near Arts Faculties, Music School and Uni rugby ground. Shares sports ground with Queen's, boat house with Downing. Ents include karaoke, quiz nights, music 'from pop to jazz'. Low on tradition, high on deriding Cambridge stereotypes. Accent on personal freedoms. Students Association meetings open to all.

ST. CATHARINE'S
Cambridge CB2 1RL
TEL 01223 338319
Founded 1473. Small, friendly college with good social mix though much fewer women than men. High academic achievers, recently second in exam league tables. Formal dinners legendary, three times a week. Centrally sited next to King's. Good sporting tradition, particularly rugby, hockey and athletics. Astro-turf pitch; squash, badminton courts, cricket, tennis and football all catered for. Recent improvements include new library, JCR and bar, but ents programmes relatively poor. Notable theatrical/musical productions at the Octagon Theatre (capacity 150).

ST. JOHN'S
Cambridge CB2 1TP
TEL 01223 338685
Founded in 1511. The founder, Lady Margaret Beaufort, King Henry VII's mother, is remembered in the name of the drama society - The Lady Margaret Players - and in that of the boat club (LMBC). Situated by the river, within walking distance of anywhere. Academically strong and strong too on sport (pitches adjacent to college) and music. Thriving Christian Union. All male college choir world class. Also run an orchestra, a second choir, a jazz band and other groups. Regular ents events, Clubclass and Funkdafied. May Ball is key. In 1994 they opened a new multi-million pound library with state-of-the-art computer facilities. Fisher Building has auditorium, games rooms, music rooms, arts studio and an architectural/engineering drawing office. All this within the precincts of the Bridge of Sighs.

SELWYN
Cambridge CB3 9DQ
TEL 01223 335896
Founded 1882. Centrally located. Broad based intake. Not known for its academic prowess but strengths include Engineering, History, Natural Science - even balance between Arts and Science undergraduates. Freshers accommodated in the '60s' Cripps Court, otherwise accommodation in Old Court and College-owned houses in or near the grounds. Some rooms in Cripps have a living area as well as a bedroom. College rooms gradually being computer networked. The Mitre Players (drama) do their thing in The Diamond in Cripps Court; music, film societies also active. Not known for sport, but boat club recently awash with fresh talent. Bar good, several bops each term, May Ball a bi-annual event.

SYDNEY SUSSEX
Cambridge CB2 3HU
TEL 01223 338872
Founded in 1596. The College seeks a good balance of male/female, Arts/Sciences. City centre site, buildings range from sixteenth Century to 1983. First year accommodation within College. Student-run bar, well equipped sound system, pool table, quiz machine, table football. Frequent bops. Food voted second worst in 1993. Not pro-sporty but strong enthusiasms. Shares its sports ground with Christ's. Academically good.

TRINITY
Cambridge CB2 1TQ
TEL 01223 338422
Founded 1546 by Henry VIII. Beautiful situation/architecture - Wren Library magnificent, overlooking the Backs. Largest Cambridge college, claims diverse undergraduate profile: overseas contingent relatively high (10%+); but women appear under-represented (around 35%). Academic record sound, bias towards Science (especially Mathematicians and Natural Scientists), but large enough to cater for all sorts. Well supplied with computer technology in College and University Library. Book grants for all students, library very well stocked. Room rents among the lowest in the University. Renowned mixed-voice choir (broadcasts, recordings, etc.) Proud sports tradition, but rugby currently on the wane - nevertheless superb facilities. Small, pleasant college bar but hopeless for large scale events. Plans in motion for new JCR ents complex.

TRINITY HALL
Cambridge CB2 1TJ
TEL 01223 332535
Founded 1350, traditionally famous for Law. Prides itself in having all the best facilities of the other colleges while maintaining a unique sense of 'community', encouraged by the cultural focus of the college - the bar, the JCR, the library - being also architecturally at the centre of things. It is indeed a close, friendly community and not at all insular. Heavily involved in wider Uni activities. Enlightened intake policy. Good ents - Varsity described them in 1995 as 'the busiest and best in Cambridge'.

WOLFSON College,
Cambridge
CB3 9BB
TEL 01223 335900
and
HUGH'S HALL,
Cambridge CB1 2EW
TEL 01223 334893
Both principally graduate colleges.

VIEW FROM THE GROUND
by Liz Wade

Cambridge. Choir boys singing out from King's College chapel as young intellectuals in tweed go cycling by in soft-focus. Glasses clinking as lazy students punt down the Cam with their Pimms and lemonade... This is the point at which I'm supposed to turn round and tell you that it's not really like that. Well, actually it pretty much is. Something like half of everyone here has been to public school, and while some of them are relatively normal, others continue to eschew the real world and spend their time forming organisations dedicated to kicking all women out of the university, for instance. Mind you, you could argue that's hardly surprising when it's only been five or so years since Magdalene, the last remaining all male college, went mixed in the first place. I thought Cambridge would be on the cutting edge; in fact, it is probably the least innovative or progressive university in the country (apart from Oxford, of course). The problem is that although there is now little difference in entrance requirements between Cambridge and other top universities like London, even very intelligent people think they won't get into Cambridge because they're not Stephen Fry, so they don't apply. As a result, things don't change, or they change infuriatingly slowly, and the problem continues. In the last couple of years, the university has finally recognised that taking only 45% of its undergraduates from state schools when 60% of UK students who get three As or higher come from them is a bit obscene, and the Target Schools campaign has been set up to try to encourage more State School students to apply. I am writing this piece largely with the same end in mind. You might think Cambridge doesn't need you but it does.

Before I start, I should tell you, in traditional Cambridge essay fashion, what I can't do. I can't tell you which college to apply to, you'll have to work that out for yourself, although you might find it useful to consult CUSU's *Alternative Prospectus* (send a £4 cheque to Cambridge University Student Union, 11-12 Trumpington Street, Cambridge,

CB2 1QA) as well as the official one when weighing it all up. I know everyone says this, but it really is important to come here and look, either on an Open Day or independently. Some of those beautiful old colleges just may not appeal in the flesh, as it were, and that ugly one might bowl you over. I can't tell you what subject to do either, although for most people the choice is pretty easy as they're only good enough at one thing. Cambridge subjects are famously straight - none of your fancy Media Studies or your Psychology with French here. In fact, this doesn't much matter as there are a million and two media societies to join, and excellent facilities for learning or improving your language skills; it's just that you do it in your spare time, off your own initiative, which is a bit of a bummer if you're the kind of person who needs a good kick to get things done, but certainly character-building. Finally I should remind you that, of course, I can only write from my own experience, and the reality might not quite match if you're going to be a scientist, say. If your supervisions aren't quite how I've described them, please don't beat me up. Okay.

COLLEGES

At Cambridge, you generally live in your college. This is probably the most important difference between here and anywhere else. Colleges are mini-communities, and they really are quite mini - most take about a hundred undergraduates each year and many not even that. Colleges are like halls of residence, but ones in which you work, eat, sleep, socialise, everything. The lack of a central student union building (we're currently trying to procure one, but I wouldn't hold your breath) places even more emphasis on college as the basis of Cambridge life. It can be wonderful. Never before have you had so many people around you all the time to sit up all night, talk philosophy and eat toast with. Never before have you had such opportunity for bumping into that one you fancy every day and every night. On the other hand, never before have you been so surrounded by busybodies watching your door to see what time in the morning that one you fancy leaves, and when the romance is over it can be a bit of a pain to carry on bumping into them every day for three years. If the college you're considering can only provide accommodation for two years, don't let that put you off, because living out in the second year can be (was for me, at least) a liberating experience. There's something reassuringly normal about slobbing around in your house, doing a bit of work and watching a bit of telly, without being surrounded by the ancient stones and spires that testify to your utter insignificance.

Life in college can get introspective, even oppressive at times; it's frightening how a few hundred square yards (or miles, if you're at Trinity) can become a vacuum, outside of which nothing exists. It's not unusual for Cambridge students to remain totally unaware of major news stories for days, as they move from college library to college canteen to college bar and back again without newspapers, televisions, or contact with the outside world. This goes some way to explaining why we are quite an apathetic lot on the whole, just about bothering to vote, and mostly voting Labour, but not getting terribly wound up about politics. Having said that, the surprisingly large turnout at the recent protest against education cuts may indicate a change is on the way. The response may also have something to do with the fact that there are fewer and fewer of those traditional Cambridge rich kids coming here every year, and just like students at any other university, we have to worry about money. There's a myth that you need to be rich to come here. Although house rents can be higher than in a big city, it's not true; in fact, Cambridge has more money to give you in hardship funds than most places, and if you go for a rich college like Trinity or St John's, you can look forward to three years of big, cheap rooms, travel grants, and large financial rewards for good results.

Of course, rich, old colleges have their drawbacks too. They tend, for instance, apart from the famously subversive King's, to be more traditional, although they really are trying to move into at least the nineteenth century. Many people would rather be at a poorer but more 'normal' modern college like Robinson or Fitzwilliam, and if you're thinking 'but that's not really Cambridge', then bear in mind that the supervision system means you will still get plenty of chances to amble arrogantly over the Bridge of Sighs.

Supervisions are the root of Cambridge education; they usually take place in the college of whoever is supervising you, and you have different supervisions with different teachers for each of your papers. Supervisions are the weekly sessions in which you (and often one other person) have to spend an hour defending your work to the man (or woman, but usually man) who, often as not, wrote the books you've been reading all week. It's daunting at first, but you shouldn't let it worry you; they're not as bad as films make out. I don't know anyone who's ever had to read an essay out on the spot, and most of the dons I've had dealings with have been well-organised, professional teachers rather than dotty old academics. Their eccentricities tend to extend no further than occasionally making you cakes to eat whilst you mull over Milton or macro economics.

ACADEMIA

As you would expect, work is pretty intense here, but it's really up to you how much you do; you'll probably get a 2:1 anyway. Depending on your subject you are expected to put in anything up to 12 hours a day, although there may well be a considerable contrast between your supervisor's and your own opinion of what is enough. The Cambridge system of testing three years' learning with a series of three hour exams (with a couple of coursework papers if you're lucky), makes for frightening finals, but does allow for a certain amount of dossing throughout your degree, and the good thing about Cambridge is the number of things you can do with the time you make for yourself.

SOCIETIES

There are societies of all shapes and sizes here as you will quickly discover. If you make it out of the packed Freshers' Fair alive then you're doing well. If you've managed to hold on to some of the rain forest of flyers you were given by those weird people who wanted you to be in the Hang-gliding Soc or join that club where people sit around with teddy bears and cocoa reading bedtime stories to each other, then you're doing even better. The next stage is to sift through them all, chuck the guff in the bin (except the Green Soc flyer which you guiltily put in your recycling box) and decide which ones are actually worth joining.

One of my favourites is the Chocolate Society, the gateway to chocolate buffets, chocolate formal halls and trips to Cadbury's world, but there really are loads, and many of them have encouragingly famous alumni. Footlights was the first port of call for many of the alternative comedians we know and love. Cambridge University Radio has spawned Radio One DJs. And there's hardly a cabinet minister who wasn't in the Union Society, although that in my opinion is only one of several reasons for not joining it.

CITY LIFE

What of Cambridge as a place? Well, the city of Cambridge is the university - there is really little life outside of it. Of course, I say that from the limited perspective of an undergraduate, but in a place where the reason for building the railway station a mile out of the centre was to stop degenerate young students disappearing off to London all the time, it's pretty obvious that gown has always come before town. The drawback of this situation, apart from the fact that the townies hate you (be careful which pubs you wear that college scarf into), is that Cambridge is hardly the most buzzing of places, as a few minutes of watching Anglia News will confirm. Their most exciting story last year was about some people who had written a song about a local roundabout. This has its up side: it's a peaceful place where you don't have to live in fear of being beaten up or having your stuff nicked.

Unfortunately, all peacefulness is shattered as soon as the tourists come out of hibernation each year, and although your insurance might be cheap, the tiny town is so short of accommodation that, if you live out, your rent will more than make up for it. Less the city that never sleeps than the one which never quite wakes up, there is only one (incredibly tacky) nightclub that most of us never make it to. Should you choose to frequent this cattle market, then on leaving at 1 am you will notice that pretty much all of East Anglia is safely tucked up in bed; the only thing you can get is a chip butty from Gardenia's on the way home (go easy on the mayonnaise; it can make you quite sick). If at this point you find yourself wishing you were in Manchester or somewhere with a bit more life, do remember that in its moments of tranquil beauty, little Cambridge is rather lovely. True, this might be poor consolation for a dedicated clubber, but there are places to go if you're prepared to explore. The mile trek to the station is less of an impediment for this generation of degenerates, and from there London is only an hour away. Alternatively, you could keep cycling right past the station and you will, eventually, reach The Junction which hosts some good medium-sized bands, as well as respected club nights.

COLLEGE LIFE

There are loads of social activities going on within the university itself which will probably provide quite enough diversion for the average student. Most colleges hold 'ents' twice a term or more, which means there are several to choose from every week. They vary immensely from college to college, from the small, hip and sweaty club atmosphere of Trinity Hall's Ascension to the relaxed ambience of jazz night in Clare Cellars; from the three-hall dance/indie/ chill-out extravaganza of Fitz End to the sleazy pulling-ground that is Caius's Orgasm, complete with red, amber and green sticker system to indicate each punter's availability. On top of this there are numerous other things, of various degrees of intellectual stimulation, going on all the time: plays, comedy shows, music recitals, cheap film screenings, and debates. If those fail to satisfy there are lots of very nice (but expensive) pubs, and your good old college bar (generally less nice, but unfortunately not much less expensive), where, let's be honest, you will spend a fair proportion of your evenings sitting and chatting with your mates. If you think the work/socialising ratio sounds a bit less appealing than at other higher educational institutions, then do bear in mind the unbelievable carnival of carnage that is May Week, that wonderful week (actually in June) after your exams are over. Kicking off with Suicide Sunday, on which it is obligatory to drink yourself 'to death', you get to spend seven wonderful days playing up the Cambridge thing for all it's worth, punting drunkenly and lolling around in the sunshine. For this one week, students everywhere will flock to the Mill, and the pub of the same name will take more money than the rest of the year put together. May Week, if nothing else, is truly a cross-college phenomenon. At the end of it all there's an Event waiting for you (a massive, marqueed club night), or if you can afford it, and suspend your social conscience for a few hours, a Cambridge May Ball, which, honestly, has to be experienced to be believed.

A seven hundred year history can be a pain at times, and sometimes you feel like you don't have the right to be treading the same paths as Wordsworth, Darwin and Norman Lamont, but in its sublime moments, it can give you a wonderful sense of past achievements and present possibilities. Cambridge is the best university in the world, it gives you the best education in the world, and when you leave you will have the best opportunities in the world - don't you want a bit of that?

CANTERBURY CHRIST CHURCH COLLEGE OF HIGHER EDUCATION

Canterbury Christ Church
College of Higher Education
Canterbury
Kent
CT1 1QU

TEL 01227 767700
FAX 01227 470442

Canterbury Christ Church
College of Higher Education
Student Union
North Holmes Road
Canterbury
Kent CT1 1QU

TEL 01227 782416
FAX 01227 458787

CANTERBURY CHRIST CHURCH COLLEGE OF HIGHER EDUCATION

Founded	**1962**
Situation/style	**Campus**
UNDERGRADUATE PROFILE	
Application acceptance rate	**11%**
Population	**4,000**
Mature student population	**30%**
Overseas student population	**10%**
Male/female ratio	**25:75**
1st year institut. accommodation	**100%**
Approximate cost	**£45-£65 pw**
ACADEMIC PROFILE	
A-level requirements:	**Low**
Teacher Training, Media Studies, Music, Geography, History, Business, Applied Social Sciences, etc CC	
Student/staff ratio	**26:1**
1st class degree pass rate	**4.5%**
HEFCE assessments (8 subjects assessed/approved):	
1995 **Geography, History**	Excellent
Joint Funding Council's research assessment 1996 (8 subjects assessed):	
Grade 5/5*	None
EMPLOYMENT PROFILE	
Principal job market destinations: **Education, Health, Public Admin., Arts/Media, Commerce, Retail/Wholesale**	
Approximate % unemployed	**11%**

VAG VIEW

Not to be confused with Uni Kent at Canterbury, or indeed with the College of Further Education, the College of Art, the School of Architecture (all of which, just to confuse you, are part of the Kent Institute of Art & Design, see entry), CCCC is a college in the university sector, i.e. it offers degree courses but is not strictly yet a university.

There's a BA/BSc Hons scheme with Science (incl. Sport), Media (Radio, Film & TV), Business, Art & Design, Languages (incl. here American Studies), Health, Social Studies (Geog., Psychol.), Tourism, Music, etc. Plus BA in Primary School Teaching, BScs in Midwifery, Nursing, Radiography, Occup. Therapy. It's really quite a good package.

It's a music loving city and the college music - particularly the 30-strong Chamber Orchestra (C4CO as it's called) - carries through the culture of the place well. It has a well-equipped Language Centre, a 160,000-book library, computer facilities (incl. open access to the Internet), and the technical equipment and facilities for the media course are good. They have their own radio station, C4, which broadcasts about 40 hours of music, news, features, drama, etc every week. There is also continuous information about what is happening in college and in Canterbury in the station's 'What's On' bulletins.

Canterbury, one of our oldest and most historic cities, is dominated by the cathedral and more or less surrounded by mediaeval walls. It's a good place to be if not exactly jumping with action. There are theatres, cinemas, museums, libraries, art galleries and bookshops, and a venue for leading orchestral and choral groups (see Uni Kent at Canterbury). For students there's also the Union - discos seem to be the main thing. There are the usual bars and other games/leisure rooms, and, thanks to the Sports Science course, there's action to be had on their 16 acres of playing fields. Various sports societies add badminton, netball, karate, riding and sailing to the cricket, rugby and soccer sports agenda.

It offers accommodation to all first years either on campus or in a hall of residence (largely self-catered) nearby.

GETTING THERE

★ By road: M2 and A2 connect Canterbury to London and beyond.
★ By coach: There are fast coaches between Canterbury and London Victoria both ways, every hour for most of the day. Journey time, 1 hour 45 minutes.
★ By rail: Trains leave for Canterbury East or West two or three times an hour from Victoria, Charing Cross and Waterloo East stations. The fast service takes 1 hour 20 minutes.
★ Once in Canterbury the college is 10 - 15 mins walk from the coach and rail stations. Main entrance to college in North Holmes Road.

Cardiff University

University of Wales, Cardiff
PO Box 494
Cardiff CF1 3YL

TEL 01222 874404
FAX 01222 874130

University of Wales,
Cardiff Student Union
Park Place
Cardiff CF1 3QN

TEL 01222 396421
FAX 01222 344140

UNIVERSITY OF WALES, CARDIFF

Founded	**1883**
Situation/style	**City site**
UNDERGRADUATE PROFILE	
Application acceptance rate	**14%**
Population	**11,000**
Mature student population	**19%**
Overseas student population	**13%**
Male/female ratio	**52:48**
1st year institut. accommodation	**100%**
Approximate cost	**£36-£56 pw**
ACADEMIC PROFILE	
A-level requirements:	**High**

English, Language & Communication ABC, **Law** AA-BBB, **Accounting, Business Admin.** BBB-BBC, **E & E Engineering** BBB, **Pharmacy** BBC, **Archaeology** BCC, **Journalism, Communication, Social Policy, Sociology** BBC, **Marine Geography** BCC-CCC, **Architecture** 22, **Chemistry** 16-18

Student/staff ratio	**12:1**
1st class degree pass rate	**7.6%**
HEFCW assessments (31 subjects assessed/approved):	
1993/4: **Mechanical Eng., Chemistry**	Excellent
1994/5: **Architecture, Environmental Engineering, Maritime Studies, English Language**	Excellent
1995/6 **Opthalmics, Philosophy, Psychology, Town & Country Planning, Pharmacy, Electrical & Electronic Engineering, Archaeology & Ancient History**	Excellent
Joint Funding Council's research assessment 1996 (29 subjects assessed):	
English	Grade 5*
Pharmacy, Subjects allied to **Medicine, Psychology, Pure Maths, Civil Engineering, Mechanical/Aeronautical/ Manufacturing Eng., Town & Country Planning, Law, Business/Management, Celtic, Theology**	Grade 5
EMPLOYMENT PROFILE	
Employability in Industry:	
MPW national league table (1996)	**22nd**

Principal job market destinations:
Retail/Wholesale, Manufacturing (strong on **Pharmaceutical, Electronic & Electrical**), **Commerce, Health, Public Admin./ Law, Education, Hotel/Restaurant, Arts/Media** (strong on **Publishing**), **Architecture, Computing, Market Research/Advertising**

PIP 1996 employers' survey:	
Top 3 subjects/national ranking	
Law	22nd=
Business	24th=
Electrical Engineering	27th=
Approximate % unemployed	**6%**

VAG VIEW

One of the best deals going. Tip-top Uni academically, not the hardest to get into, fantastic ents scene.

SETTING

Cardiff, population 300,000, is a modern capital city with masses to offer by way of artistic and hedonistic experience. It's a compact city and prices are not outrageous. The Uni lies just a few minutes walk away.

Countryside around encourages all kinds of outdoor pursuits (hiking, rambling, rock climbing). The Gower Peninsula to the west is one of the loveliest sea-coast stretches in the entire country, immortalised by Dylan Thomas in his 'Who Do You Think Was With Us?'; The Brecon Beacons are due north up the A470, with their sublime neighbours, The Black Mountains; seaside resorts, Penarth and Barry Island are nearby, and of course Cardiff dockland once gave teeth to the Bristol Channel, on whose shores the city is set. Carleon, five junctions up the M4, gives the area its (Arthurian) mythic status, and Uni Arthurian Society - Llys y Brenin Arthur yng Ngaerdydd is your entry to the Underworld.

GETTING THERE

★ By car: Travelling eastbound on M4, take Junction J32, A470 signposted Cardiff into the Cathays area of the city. Travelling westbound leave at Junction 29, follow the A48(M)/A48, signposted Cardiff East and South, to the A470 signposted City Centre, into the Cathays area of the city.
★ By rail: London Paddington, 2:30.
★ Airport for USA and inland. City centre coach station. Good local bus services to campus.

ACCOMMODATION

All first years guaranteed a place in university-owned accommodation. Most of the accommodation is on campus, otherwise situated close to it. 64% of the individual study bedrooms have their own en suite shower and toilet. Most are self-catering flats; catered accommodation is also available - University and Aberdare Halls. Aberdare is a no-smoking, women-only hall on campus. There's even a Woy Jenkins Hall which has flats with dining rooms (would you believe?) and, no doubt, claret decanters. Free mini bus service between Union and halls; service is women-only after 11pm.

ACADEMIA

Nigh a million books and journals in the Uni Library and fully computerised reservation and ordering system, the network also allows access to a wide range of CD Roms. This is but one aspect of its excellent computing facilities - the Uni is one of only twelve regional centres for Super Janet, the educational and research network. If you haven't already locked into at school, do yourself a favour and do it now.

Many degrees include a sandwich option, and Cardiff has strong links with local commerce and industry. It's a career organised curriculum but with the kind of academic depth which you'd expect from a 1st division Uni (see Academic Profile, especially the research results - they came 16th overall). Yet it's not *that* demanding of entry requirements among Unis within the High Band.

Courses are modular, and they operate a points scheme compatible with CATS, all based on an annual 2-semester timetable.

One area in which Cardiff has a particularly good reputation is Journalism, but don't confuse the BA in Journalism, Film and Broadcasting with the postgraduate Diploma in Journalism Studies, which is so popular. Both courses are good, and the BA is a fine preparation for the postgrad. course, but it is not a vocational course (more social role, history, etc, though there is some teaching of writing skills in Part II). Incidentally, the Union launched X-Press Radio in 1996.

ENTS

Pubs, wine bars, lounge bars, nightclubs enough to suit every deviant taste. Live venues include The National Stadium, International Arena and University Union (a major venue on the national tour circuit). St. David's Hall and The University Concert Hall are the classical music venues - regular recitals and concerts. The Welsh National Opera has its home in Cardiff, and there are two theatres - alternative theatre and student drama at the Sherman Theatre - and an arts centre, various multi-screen cinemas, museums and art galleries.

Terminal 396, with state of the art sound and lights systems, is the students' very own nightclub, with a varied menu of live bands and club-discos. Dance, chart, indie, party music, occasional 70p a pint nights, Gaggin' for it comedy every other week, 'Paaar-taay 60s, 70s, 80s nights, Cloud 9 injections of cheese - 'Only at C9 can you hear Take That mix into The Prodigy, and Nirvana alongside

Abba,' they tell us. Also at T396 Club EZ on Sunday afternoons, a hangover hair of the dog experience. Tafarn, quaint Tudor style pub with extensive Real Ale selection at 15% lower cost than outside, hosts Disco Inferno and regular Tafarn Quiz. The Finistere is a French-style bistro with disco dance floor (capacity 300+). The Junction (railway theme) has two bars. The Great Hall is the 1,500-capacity venue for mainstream live acts (25-odd big name concerts a year; recently Paul Oakenfold, and Kula Shaker). Newly refurbished Starlight Club at The Great Hall (recently cultural icon DJ Carl Cox did his stuff under starlit canopy with mammoth inflatables) - 'Definitely one of Cardiff's top venues,' according to leading monthly magazine Buzz. Union ents activities climax occasionally in 'Spectaculars' - 3,000 can attend these wild, all-night orgies of entertainment.

Buzz is the mag to get as soon as you land in Cardiff. It has all the city listings, major Uni events (and Swansea and Newport too) and much more - sound informative/evaluative youth culture journalism. In the city, the club scene is terrific - student nights at The Astoria, The Emporium, Zeus; NUS concessions at Club Metropolitan, Sam's Bar; then there's Newport nearby (The Cotton Club, TJ's) or if you really haven't had enough you could lock into the scene up the road apiece at Glamorgan Uni or stagger over the Severn Bridge to Bristol, Bath...

SPORT

Cardiff Arms Park is of course the sporting and spiritual home to Welsh Rugby. There's league soccer at Ninian Park and first class cricket at Sophia Gardens. The Welsh Institute of Sport, the National Athletics Stadium and the Olympic-standard Empire offer exceptional facilities. Cardiff is one of the few places that offers baseball (The Cobras) and ice hockey. Within the Uni all traditional sports are catered for, and the Uni's Talybont Sports Centre has a £2 million multi-purpose sports hall and 33 acres of pitches. Sports bursaries are available.

Cardiff Institute

University of Wales Institute
Western Avenue
Cardiff CF5 2SG

TEL 01222 506070
FAX 01222 506911

University of Wales Institute
Cardiff Student Union
Central Student Union Offices
Cyncoed Campus
Cyncoed Road
Cardiff CF2 6XD

TEL 01222 506190
FAX 01222 506199

UNIVERSITY OF WALES INSTITUTE, CARDIFF

Founded	**1976**
Situation/style	**City site**
UNDERGRADUATE PROFILE	
Application acceptance rate	**9%**
Population	**4,000**
Mature student population	**30%**
Overseas student population	**3%**
Male/female ratio	**40:60**
1st year institut. accommodation	**90%**
Approximate cost (Uni)	**£35-£65 pw**
(City)	**£35-£40 pw**

ACADEMIC PROFILE

A-level requirements: **Low**

Teacher Training 12, **Business Studies, European Admin** 10, **Biomedical Sciences, Dental Technology, Podiatry** EE, **Psychology & Communication** 16-18, **Art & Design** EE, **Sports Sciences** 14-20

Student/staff ratio	**25:1**
1st class degree pass rate	**5.4%**
HEFCW assessments (9 subjects assessed/approved): 1995/6: **Psychology, Art & Design (Ceramics/Fine Art/ Internal Architecture)**	Excellent
Joint Funding Council's research assessment 1996 (8 subjects assessed): **Grade 5/5***	None

EMPLOYMENT PROFILE

Principal job market destinations: **Education, Health, Manufacturing, Retail/Wholesale, Hotel/Restaurant, Sport** (strong)

Approximate % unemployed **10%**

VAG VIEW

Obviously draws more locally than Cardiff Uni and appeals to more mature students, but there's a kind of academic symbiosis between the two institutions, and some would prefer the smaller, very friendly environment of UWIC. Also the sports courses and special facilities look very good indeed. VAG found contact with UWIC open, natural and very friendly. Sounds a good place to be especially if you prefer to look out from a peaceful safe haven at the more riotous Uni life, dipping into it when and where you want. There's good interaction between the two places, in particular their Unions.

SETTING

There are four teaching campuses at UWIC, all city based.

ADDRESSES

(Telephone number as above):
Colchester Avenue Campus, Colchester Avenue, Cardiff CF3 7XR;
Cyncoed Campus, Cyncoed Road, Cardiff CF2 6XD;
Howard Gardens Campus, Howard Gardens, Cardiff CF2 1SP;
Llandaff Campus, Western Avenue, Cardiff CF5 2YB.

GETTING THERE

See also Cardiff Uni. UWIC's buildings are all within a short distance of the centre.
★ From the A48(M) Eastern Avenue turn

into Newport Road (A4161) heading from the city centre. The turning for **Colchester Avenue** is on the right.
★ **Cyncoed Campus**: From the A48(M) Eastern Avenue, travel via Llanedeyrn Road to Cyncoed Road.
★ **Howard Gardens Campus**: From the A48 Eastern Avenue, follow signs for Newport Road (A4161) and the city centre. Nearing the city centre follow the direction for the Howard Gardens Gallery; the turning is on the left.
★ **Llandaff Campus** is located on Western Avenue (A48).
★ **Fairwater Campus** (accommodation only): Travel along the A48 Eastern/Western Avenue dual carriageway, turn right into St. Fagans Road, then into Plasmawr Road - the Hall of Residence is on the right hand side, opposite a health centre.
★ By rail: Major destination; 2+ hrs London Paddington.
★ Airport for USA and inland.
★ City centre coach station. Good local bus services.

ACCOMMODATION

No guarantee that all first year students will have a place in hall. Mainly catered accommodation at The Cyncoed Centre - single-study bedrooms in purpose-built units, but some newly built self-catered flats. Also small number of self-cater houses, flats and bedsits. A limited number of self-catered units are also available at Llandaff, and plans are afoot for 275 more by October 1997. A fifth - mainly accommodation - campus is **Fairwater** (also used for conferences and seminars); it is located in its own attractive grounds, has a lounge and gym, and is close to the artificial ski slope - smart single study bedrooms, but mainly reserved for mature or postgrad students.

ACADEMIA

Colchester Avenue Campus for Business, Leisure and Food; **Cyncoed Campus** for Education and Sport, part of Art; Design and Engineering is at **Howard Gardens**; **Llandaff Campus** is Art, Design, Engineering, Community Health Sciences.

Some but not all courses are modular based. They run access programmes for mature students returning to education. Big emphasis on employer links, sandwich courses, European dimension etc. Sound external assessments, and a relaxed, friendly and useful place to study.

SPORT

Cycnoed again the centre for this - floodlit astroturf, athletics track, rugby/football/cricket pitches, indoor/outdoor tennis courts, gym, indoor cricket nets, swimming pool, volleyball, netball, basketball, badminton, squash courts, dance studio. And as The Wales Sports Centre for the Disabled is also here, they've got some of the best resistance training equipment available anywhere. UWIC offer degrees in Sport and Exercise Sciences, Sport and Human Movement Studies, so the whole thing is well-organised and top class. Sports scholarships available.

ENTS

Jon Ruch, VP Students Union tells all:

VIEW FROM THE GROUND
by Jon Ruch

Social life at UWIC combined with Cardiff city life make an amazing combination, that can cater for your every need, guaranteed to turn your 3 years studying into an experience that you will never forget!

Social events at UWIC are run by the Students Union based at the Cyncoed Campus. At Cyncoed, Taffys Bar is well renowned by students for its easy going atmosphere - a great place to unwind after a hard day of lectures. Friday night discos are not to be missed amongst band nights, karaoke nights, and promotion nights. Drink prices are kept as low as possible, so without putting a dent in your wallet, you are in for a great night! If it's your birthday watch out - custom and tradition ensures that the Yard of Ale must be attempted!! At the start of the academic year Taffys hosts a great freshers line up - hypnotists, bands, and games nights ensure that you quickly meet new friends, and guaranteed tonsil hockey is a favourite for most!

For the Art students based at the Howard

Gardens campus - Tommys Bar offers the alternative scene - dark and dingy, out of the smoky atmosphere weird bands and dance nights emerge. Friday nights is where you see it happening - black clothes, black make-up, extreme hair colours, extreme students having an extreme night!

If these don't interest you look no further than Cardiff itself with its huge spectrum of pubs, clubs, restaurants and theatres. St. Mary's Street is not so much a street but a haven of drinking outlets that span the entire length of the street on both sides; it provides the focal point of the annual student union fancy dress five legged pub crawl during freshers! In addition the pubs surround the Arms Park so on International weekends the pubs are packed and the atmosphere electric with Welsh voices in drunken song heard from outside every pub! There is a huge range of clubs in Cardiff, and for your average student night the favourites include; Zeus, Astoria, Escape and Winstons, who compete heavily for the student market - hence crazy prices on beer and entrance fees ensuring that you get a great night at a great price.

If you are looking for a more active life then the Student Union runs a large number of clubs and societies, ranging from rock climbing to canoeing. The Athletic Union runs a large number of sports clubs at a very successful level, with squash, rugby, football and ladies hockey all reaching semi finals and squash becoming BUSA champions. The sports facilities offered by the University are first class (indoor tennis, floodlit astro hockey and football pitches, floodlit rugby stadium, in addition to a fitness suite and swimming pool).

For students seeking a little more culture Cardiff has plenty of reasonably priced restaurants offering great food. The three main theatres offer student tickets for plays, comedy, musicals and opera at amazing value, whilst the nearby museums offer good value for interesting art and history.

Cardiff has something about it which cannot be described; its atmosphere reaches out to everyone offering warmth and friendliness, so if you are looking for fun, beer, and great mates to accompany your studies, then UWIC is for you and awaits your arrival!

CENTRAL ENGLAND UNIVERSITY IN BIRMINGHAM

University of Central England
in Birmingham
Perry Barr
Birmingham B42 2SU

TEL 0121 331 5000
FAX 0121 331 6358

University of Central England
in Birmingham
Students Union
Franchise Street
Perry Barr
Birmingham B42 2SU

TEL 0121 356 8164
FAX 0121 344 3670

UNIVERSITY OF CENTRAL ENGLAND IN BIRMINGHAM

Founded	**1971**
Situation/style	**City sites**
UNDERGRADUATE PROFILE	
Application acceptance rate	**9%**
Population	**9,000**
Mature student population	**4%**
Overseas student population	**9%**
Male/female ratio	**50:50**
1st year institut. accommodation	**75-80%**
Approximate cost (Uni)	**£40-£45 pw**
(City)	**£35 pw**
ACADEMIC PROFILE	
A-level requirements:	**Low-medium**

Law 14-18, **Computer Sci. and Engineering, General, Mech., Manuf. and E & E Engineering combinations** (incl. **Visual Communication** - 18) 2-12, **Architecture, Housing, Planning** 12-18, **Accountancy, Finance, Business & Management, Marketing,** etc 12-16, **Combined Health Studies** 8-12, **Sociology** CC

Student/staff ratio	**25:1**
1st class degree pass rate	**4%**
HEFCE assessments (8 subjects assessed/approved):	
1995 **Music**	Excellent
Sociology 18	
Joint Funding Council's research assessment 1996 (12 subjects assessed):	
Grade 5/5*	None
EMPLOYMENT PROFILE	
Principal job market destinations:	

Manufacturing, Education, Health, Retail/Wholesale, Commerce, Arts/ Media, Computer, Hotel/Restaurant, Public Admin/Law, Architecture, Property Development

PIP 1996 employers' survey:	
Top subject/national ranking	
Business	39th=
Approximate % unemployed	**8%**

VAG VIEW

Ex-Birmingham Poly, multi-faceted, thoroughly professional, proud to maintain its links with its poly past in terms of the lively, academic/vocational nature of its courses, work placement ideology, strong links (especially through research programmes) with industry, enlightened entry requirements (GNVQ and access courses), part-timer education, etc.

It may be difficult to get a handle on UCE overall because of its diverse setting across so many sites, but conversely its integrity lies in its diverseness. It is in touch with this great city through its disparate city sites, through its intake policy which draws 25,000 students through its doors, many of the city, and through its 'contact' academic policy, and it has a healthy respect for students' views. Since 1989 it has been random sampling student views and incorporating analysis of them into Uni strategy. That seems a fair basis for recommendation.

In any case, UCE got Nigel Mansell into the fast track, so why not you?

SITUATION

Seven teaching sites, all but Edgbaston (see also Birmingham Uni) and the main UCE campus site (Perry Barr) are in the city centre. There are recreational facilities and Union bases at both Perry Barr (northern city suburb) and Edgbaston (southern city suburb). The local bus service is excellent and gets you to the central sites in 15 minutes or so. You'll need a Student Travelcard.

GETTING THERE

★ Perry Barr by road: Junction 7 M6, then A34. See Birmingham Uni for other info. and routes to Edgbaston.

ACADEMIA, TEACHING SITES AND CAMPUSES

Art & design, Built Environment, Business, Law and Social Sciences, Computing and Information Studies, Education, Engineering & Computer Technology, Health & Social Sciences, Music at the Birmingham Conservatoire.

The 'contact' principle on which all courses are designed is that they should 'relate theoretical study to real life situations so that they combine an academic with a vocational approach.'

The Birmingham Conservatoire was formerly the Birmingham School of Music. Note (fact box) they have an Excellent rating for this and it's one of the jewels in the crown of UCE. Strong links with Birmingham Symphony Orchestra, and they have two performance venues (Adrian Boult Hall seats 530), 4 organs, sound recording studio, etc. Rich and varied performance opportunities and touring possibilities.

The Conservatoire, located in Paradise Place, is in the middle of town, but not alone - Fine Arts at the Margaret Street site, the real jewel - The Jewellery School (founded 1890) - in the Birmingham Jewellery Quarter (Vittoria Street), and Design (Fashion, Textiles, Visual) at Gosta Green on the edge of the city centre (Aston), are none of them far away.

Perry Barr is the main campus, however, and is located in leafy suburbia to the north of the city. It houses Built Environment (Architecture, Building/Surveying, Estate Mgt., Planning, Landscape, etc - a very comprehensive range), Computing (this extends interestingly into the fields of linguistics and the media), Engineering/ Computer Technology (high on modules, sandwich courses, etc), Health (one of the largest non-Medicine HE health faculties, it also operates on the Edgbaston campus and at Good Hope Hospital in Sutton Coldfield, offering anything from Sociology to Radiography, Nursing to Speech and Language Pathology), Business (Accountancy, Economics, Finance, Int. Bus. & Language, Marketing, Mgt., as well as Bus. Studies), Law and Social Sciences. Edgbaston, a suburb to the south (see Birmingham University), also has Education.

Each faculty has computing resources. Most courses have a computing element. Several data networks available. The Uni Library is one area where the annual sampling of student views (see *VAG View* above) has born visible fruit - following the 1993 survey, the Uni invested a million quid on books for the library.

See also Birmingham College of Food, Tourism & Creative Studies, an associate college of UCE.

ACCOMMODATION

There are three self-catering halls of residence, one on the Edgbaston Campus, one in the city centre and one adjacent to Perry Barr. In addition there are Uni-managed houses and flats, most within easy reach of your particular base.

ENTS

With almost 25,000 students all told, UCE makes a great contribution to student life in this city, which, as you'll see from the Birmingham entry, is a big focus.

The UCE Union has two bars - one at Perry Barr, one at Edgbaston. Wide range of live bands, cabaret, quizzes, club nights on offer, and it is Union policy to ensure that all groups, however, much in the minority, get their own bash. There's a definite policy against discrimination of any kind at UCE - what they call their 'Safe Place' policy.

CENTRAL LANCASHIRE UNIVERSITY

University of Central
Lancashire
Preston PR1 2HE

TEL 01772 201201
FAX 01772 892935

University of Central
Lancashire Student Union
Fylde Road
Preston PR1 2TQ

TEL 01772 258382
FAX 01772 882689

UNIVERSITY OF CENTRAL LANCASHIRE

Founded	**1828**
Situation/style	**Campus**
UNDERGRADUATE PROFILE	
Application acceptance rate	**18%**
Population	**8,000**
Mature student population	**45%**
Overseas student population	**2%**
Male/female ratio	**50:50**
1st year institut. accommodation	**90%**
Approximate cost (Uni)	**£57-£67 pw**
(Town)	**£35-£50 pw**
ACADEMIC PROFILE	
A-level requirements:	**Low-medium**

Law BCC-CCC, **Psychology** 18, **Business Studies** BC-CCD, **Accounting/Finance** 14, **Computing Sci. & Eng.** 10-14, **Electronic Eng.** DD, **Design & Manufac. Eng.** CCC-DD, **Italian** (Combined Honours prog.) 8, **Sociology** (Combined Honours prog.) 18, **Linguistics** (Combined Honours prog.) 16, **Film & Media, Media Tech., Journalism, PR** 16-24

Student/staff ratio	**24:1**
1st class degree pass rate	**4.5%**

HEFCE assessments (13 subjects assessed/approved):
1996: **Linguistics** 22, **Sociology** 18, **Modern Languages** 21

Joint Funding Council's research assessment 1996 (22 subjects assessed):
Grade 5/5* None

EMPLOYMENT PROFILE

Principal job market destinations:
Manufacturing, Retail/Wholesale, Public Admin./Law, Commerce, Hotel/Restaurant, Arts/Media (strong on **Publishing**), **Education, Personnel, Health**

Approximate % unemployed **11%**

VAG VIEW

It has to be mentioned - UCL has the 'best student dance club in the UK', 'one of the top 30 clubs in the country.' No-one writes anything about UCL these days without including one or both of these quotes, the first from The Observer, *the second from* DJ Magazine. *It is a mark of their excellent PR - well, they run among the best BA Public Relations and BA Journalism courses in the country, didn't you know? - that a. they got these quotes, and b. everyone who knows anything about the place, knows this too.*

They probably also know that the VC is a soccer nut - some might say that if you're a long-term fan of Preston North End it has to be an obsession. But here is a powerful man. He's got UCL into a joint project with the Football Museum, situated in the new Tom Finney Stand at Preston North End's Deepdale Stadium. Called The Institute of Football Studies, its purpose is to 'further the academic study of football at local, regional and national levels.' Nice work if you can get it, I'd say. But UCL is on a bit of a roll at the moment sportswise. It just received £8 million from the Lottery and is developing an 'Outdoor Multisport Complex'. They'll show you an artist's impression of it, brilliantly designed to maximise space and to include rugby pitches, cricket pitches, athletics track, football pitches (natch), tennis courts, cricket nets and much, much more, including a 'closed circuit' cycle track (well, you know what they mean).

So this is what goes on in Higher Education in the forgotten northern reaches of Lancs, I hear you mutter. Well, it is, but it's only the cream on the cake. The real key to the success of UCL since it became a university is its academic approach. Strong vocational bias of course - ex-Lancashire Poly, ex-Preston Poly - but they underwrite their career-orientated academic policy with an assumption that the job market is not just Preston, or Lancashire, or even the UK or the EC. They have undergrad. exchange arrangements with America and Europe, and co-ordinate their partnership policy as far afield as Romania and Russia. 'On virtually all our programmes of study you will have the opportunity to take up a European or USA exchange,' UCL announce. And this cuts two ways. Being an exchange, the campus is a thoroughly cosmopolitan place.

SETTING

UCL is situated in the centre of Preston, the commercial, administrative and cultural capital of Lancashire. The town lies in a valley at the head of the Ribble Estuary, which flows past Lytham St Anne's into the sea. It is north-west of Manchester, west of Bradford and Leeds, and south of Kendall (gateway to the Lake District).

In the 12th century, Henry II gave it the right to have a Guild Merchant, and since 1500 they've been holding Guild Celebrations every 20 years. The last spectacular was in 1992, the very year in which UCL was awarded university status. But there's no need to defer entry until 2012, for this historic market town (which is remembered by most only on account of its pre-eminence in the dark Satanic days of the Industrial Revolution) can't resist celebrating on a much more regular basis. The Heineken Music Festival, the Annual Egg Rolling event, music events in Avenham Park, circuses, fun runs on Moor Park, the Pot Fair, Town Criers Competition and Historical Fayre in The Flag Market - the impression one is left with is of a market town. It's open market is just as historic - permanently possessed of mediaeval madness.

GETTING THERE

★ By road: Travelling South, M6 (J32/M55). Exit 1 (A6) to Preston/Garstang. Six traffic lights on, following signs for Liverpool turn right into Moor Lane. Pick up Uni signs and find UCL at r/about at end of Moor Lane. Travelling North, M6 (J31), A59 towards Preston. Bear left at first r/about, still following signs for Preston and you'll pick up Uni signs. Turn right at T-junction (traffic lights) and proceed past first traffic lights at the ring road on to dual carriageway. Turn right at next set of lights and immediately left into Walker Street. Find UCL at end of Walker Street over r/about.

★ By rail: mainline station half a mile from campus. Less than 3 hours from London.

★ By coach around 5 hours.

ACADEMIA

Business (including International Tourism as well as the usual stuff, also Journalism and PR comes under this); Cultural, Legal & Social Studies (which heads off with your passport to the USA, American Studies - go for it, it's only 3 Cs, and also includes Film & Media Studies, and some good language-related courses), Design & Technology; Health; Science; Combined Hons (60+ subjects). Emphasis on international job market, exchanges and work placements abroad (see VAG view above) brings languages to the fore throughout and at all levels. Note very good score, 21/24 Modern Languages in government assessments.

ACCOMMODATION

Self-catering halls of residence and university-controlled flats and houses. Most recent halls en-suite.

ENTS

No shortage of pubs or bars, some live music. Clubs offer dance, indie, period rock/pop, no dress restrictions. Guild Hall for orchestral and rock, televised sport (snooker, bowls). Regular Student Union Ents include Free 2 Dance, intended as something to drop in on - late bar with DJs - but has become a focus in its own right and is now 9pm to 2am Tuesdays. Wednesday is Prize Bingo, believe it or not, in the Polygon bar - the rules (and £50 prizes) bring them in: a stamp for every drink you buy; more drinks, more stamps, more winning. You can't fault it. Thursday drinks promo night. in all three bars from 9pm to 2am. Friday is Timetrip - DJs go retro, and in The Polygon it's gaming at Double Six Club. Sunday is film night in The Venue. Otherwise special events, such as Billy Bragg or the Super Furry Animals.

SPORT

Badminton, basketball, volleyball, rugby, hockey, netball, fencing, martial arts. Until the Outdoor Multisport Complex opens, outdoor facilities are off campus - soccer, hockey, tennis, netball and cricket, rugby league. Lancashire is the home of rugby league (Wigan, St. Helens), but also rugby union at Preston Grasshoppers (remember Wade Dooley?). Also Classic Golf at Royal Lytham St. Anne's. Preston's Guild Hall for World Championship Snooker.

★ *Note: UCL Preston operates a No Smoking policy throughout the university*

CENTRAL SCHOOL OF SPEECH & DRAMA

Central School of Speech
& Drama
Embassy Theatre
64 Eaton Avenue
London NW3 3HY

TEL 0171 722 8183
FAX 0171 722 4132

Central School of Speech
& Drama
Student Union
Embassy Theatre
64 Eton Avenue
London NW3 3HY

TEL 0171 483 0144

CENTRAL SCHOOL OF SPEECH & DRAMA	
Founded	**1906**
Situation/style	**City sites**
UNDERGRADUATE PROFILE	
Application acceptance rate	**7%**
Population	**470**
Mature student population	**45%**
Overseas student population	**8%**
Male/female ratio	**30:70**
1st year institut. accommodation	**None**
Approximate rent	**£55-£70 pw**
ACADEMIC PROFILE	
A-level requirements: performance related + **Clinical Communications Sciences** CCC, **Drama & Education** BCC	
Student/staff ratio	**11:1**
1st class degree pass rate	**1%**
Joint Funding Council's research assessment 1996 (3 subjects assessed):	
Grade 5/5*	None
EMPLOYMENT PROFILE	
Principal job market destinations: **Arts/Media, Health, Education**	
Approximate % unemployed	**7.5%**

VAG VIEW

Two sites - the main site at Swiss Cottage (Finchley Road), the second at 1-5 St Pancras Way, Camden, London NW1 OPB. Both are within easy reach of Central London.

This is a drama school with a long and fine reputation, which in 1992 came under the auspices of the Higher Education Funding Council of England (HEFCE), which funds all but one of the universities in this country.

Central offers first degrees in Acting (BA), Theatre Studies (Design) (BA Hons), Drama & Education (BA Hons), Clinical Communication Sciences (BSc Hons). The BSc Clinical Communication Sciences course is accredited by The Royal College of Speech and Language Therapists. The BA in Acting and the Stage Management courses are accredited by the National Council for Drama Training. The development out of drama into education and speech & language therapy is a natural progression, the BSc course involves work in hospitals, schools, health centres and Central's own on-site clinic, opened in 1995.

No residential accommodation, but assistance to students in finding a place to lay their heads. The union provides a range of sporting activities (including netball, squash, yoga, basketball), but sport is probably not high on the list of priorities for prospective students.

★ *The school operates a No Smoking policy.*

GETTING THERE

★ Jubilee line (Underground) to Swiss Cottage (or Metropolitan line to nearby Finchley Road station). Northern line to Camden Town.
★ No car parking at the school.

Charing Cross & Westminster Medical School

Charing Cross & Westminster
Medical School
The Reynolds Building
St Dunstan's Road
London W6 8RP

TEL 0181 846 1234
FAX 0181 846 7222

CHARING CROSS & WESTMINSTER MEDICAL SCHOOL

Founded	**1918/1834**
Situation/style	**City sites**
UNDERGRADUATE PROFILE	
Application acceptance rate	**6%**
Population	**900**
Mature student population	**10%**
Overseas student population	**7%**
Male/female ratio	**50:50**
1st year institut. accommodation	**100%**
Approximate cost	**£46-£55 pw**
ACADEMIC PROFILE	
A-level requirements: **AAB**	

★ Science 'A's required **Chemistry**
★ Additional Science 'A's preferred **Biology**
★ Addit. Non-Science 'A's acceptable **1 only**
★ Retakes considered **Yes**
★ Retake offer **AAB**
★ Clinical contact **1st term**

Student/staff ratio	**3:1**
1st class degree pass rate	**4.8%**
Joint Funding Council's research assessment 1996 (3 subjects assessed):	
Grade 5/5*	None
EMPLOYMENT PROFILE	
Approximate % unemployed	**0%**

VAG VIEW

The merger of Charing Cross and Westminster Medical Schools in 1984 is to be followed, this year, by the further merger with Imperial College School of Medicine. However, the first joint undergraduate intake will not occur until October 1998. The new school will also incorporate The Royal Postgraduate Medical School, based at Hammersmith Hospital and The National Heart and Lung Institute, based at The Royal Brompton Hospital.

Following a paper by the GMC - Tomorrow's Doctors, *it was agreed that all medical schools would work towards a revision in the curriculum. The move looked at the time as if it would favour a greater emphasis on clinical training and problem-solving skills. At time of writing it isn't possible to say what the outcome will be. Certainly Charing Cross is working towards the new curriculum, like all the rest, and in their case jointly with Imperial. 'As the joint curriculum is developed,' they say, 'so new course material and new concepts in teaching, and learning will be introduced into our current undergraduate teaching.'*

Charing Cross is in fact on the Fulham Palace Road, a great area of London in which to be, round the corner from some of the best pubs and restaurants in Fulham and near to Hammersmith and exits west out of London. The hospital has a club with squash and badminton courts and a 25m metre indoor pool on site. The Union and recreation areas (including a gym and a bar) are in The Reynolds Building, also on site. Playing fields, however, are in Cobham, Surrey, which on busy days can be more than the 30 minutes away they tell you in the prospectus. This part of London and out Surrey way can be very road-busy. Hockey, rugby, soccer, cricket, tennis, croquet are all catered for and there's a club house and bar. Most of the Union societies are sports orientated, but there is music too, and at least four dramatic productions a year. There are regular bops in The Reynolds Building and winter and summer balls.

'If you go to a university to study medicine you have some chance to mix with students from other disciplines, at least for the first year or two,' said one sixth-form careers mistress, 'but if you go to a hospital-based school you'll be in only with medics right from the start.' It is probably true, but there are many other points to consider wherever you apply to study medicine, which are probably as important. Not being institution specific, they are beyond the brief of this book. We recommend you to read: The UCAS Students' Guide to Entry To Medicine *and Joe Ruston's* Getting Into Medical School *(Trotman: 0181 332 2132).*

GETTING THERE

★ Nearest Underground station, Hammersmith (Metropolitan, Piccadilly and District Lines).

Cheltenham & Gloucester College of Higher Education

Cheltenham and Gloucester College of Higher Education
PO Box 220
The Park
Cheltenham
Gloucestershire GL50 2QF

TEL 01242 532825
FAX 01242 256759

Cheltenham & Gloucester College of Higher Education Student Union
PO Box 220
The Park (Elwes Building)
Cheltenham
Gloucestershire GL50 2QF

TEL 01242 532848
FAX 01242 261381

CHELTENHAM & GLOUCESTER COLLEGE OF HIGHER EDUCATION

Founded	**1990**
Situation/style	**3 campuses**
UNDERGRADUATE PROFILE	
Application acceptance rate	**9%**
Population	**4,600**
Mature student population	**40%**
Overseas student population	**1%**
Male/female ratio	**40:60**
1st year institut. accommodation	**60%**
Approximate cost (College)	**£53-£67 pw**
(Town)	**£40-£45 pw**
ACADEMIC PROFILE	
A-level requirements:	**Low**

Teacher Training 12, **Business & Finance** 6, **Hotel & Marketing Management** 12, 200+ combinations **Computer Sci & Eng.** 8-18, **Sport Sciences with Finan. Mgt.** 12-16, **Geography with Social Studies** 12, **Media Communications** and **Art & Design** combinations 8-16

Student/staff ratio	**26:1**
1st class degree pass rate	**4.7%**
HEFCE assessments (10 subjects assessed/approved):	
1995 **Geography**	Excellent
1996 **Sociology**	20
Joint Funding Council's research assessment 1996 (11 subjects assessed):	
Grade 5/5*	None
EMPLOYMENT PROFILE	

Principal job market destinations:
Education, Retail/Wholesale, Commerce, Sport (strong), **Manufacturing, Hotel/Restaurant, Arts/Media, Health**

Approximate % unemployed	**8%**

VAG VIEW

I can imagine some parents coming to the module scheme, in which this Uni claims to be an acknowledged specialist, and reaching for the gin bottle. The idea of a modular education is to give students more flexibility, so they can broaden their education by choosing their own programme of study from a number of possible subjects. Cheltenham & Gloucester gives you something like 1,000 modules from which to select a programme to study, which puts them in the Oxford Brookes league. Even De Montfort offers a mere 650. C&G's 1,000 are pushed at us as a bonus, but while this strategy broadens your choice in theory, there is little to convince that there is the necessary flair to make the choice worthwhile.

In the Big Official UCAS Guide, C&G takes up pages of space, offering literally hundreds of possible combinations with this and that; it is mindblowingly complex, and you search for a rationale behind it all.

The questions are: Do students want such a choice? and Do students need *such a choice? It's got to the point now where employers can't tell what a student has taken his or her degree in, or what their specialism is. But there's more to it than that. Given the shift towards vocational training in the Higher Education sector, shouldn't they be looking at what the New World employers want - suggesting combinations that will be of use to their students (like Essex University does, for example)? Pushing a rationale as to why such and such a combination will give you a deeper understanding of your main-interest subject(s)? Oxford Brookes does this with its Languages for Business combinations, where the whole culture of a country is explored, the foreign university is actively involved and the student can end up with a thorough cultural/linguistic/ social knowledge of the field in which he intends to do his business. The first thing you look at it when judging a university is its courses - What are they aiming at? What is the thought that has gone into this or that particular course combination to enliven and enhance the main subject? What is their strategy and where will it lead?*

SETTING

The academic choice isn't the only confusing aspect of the C&G prospectus. We read that it is a split campus college and when we are told all about Gloucester being able to trace its history back to the 1st century we expect to hear that some parts of it are *in* Gloucester. Only gradually does it become apparent that Gloucester has nothing whatsoever to do with this Uni. The sites are all in Cheltenham. It is most confusing.

There is also much talk about how near everywhere else is to where they are, which rather seems to imply that you're going to feel a bit isolated, even perhaps out of place as a student in Cotswoldian green wellie land. They could be right.

What seems to be the case is that there are three sites. The main one is called Park Campus, near the A46, leading south west out of the town. Then there is Francis Close Hall, which is shown on a map at the end of the prospectus to be in the vicinity of the road leading north-west out of the town to Junction 10 of the M5 - the A4109. In fact that road is really the A4019. Finally, appropriately enough, there is Pittville, which is off to the north-east.

GETTING THERE

★ By road: From the West, North or South, Junction 11, M5. From the East M40/A40 or Junction 15, M4 and A419.
★ National Express and local bus/coach services to Cheltenham town centre.
★ By rail: Cheltenham Spa is well served. Station about a mile from Park Campus. Bristol Parkway, 45 mins; Birmingham, 1.00; London Paddington, 2:30.

ACADEMIA

You may think we have covered this, but for the record, Cheltenham and Gloucester operate three faculties - Arts & Education (split between Park and Pittville), Business & Social Studies (Park), Environment & Leisure (Francis Close).

ACCOMMODATION

Can't guarantee first years a place in Uni accommodation, but those who do get into a hall will find them on four sites around town. There is also self-catering en-suite accommodation at Hardwick, and at Pittville, which also does some half-board accommodation.

SPORT

Hardwick campus for sports hall, swimming pool, and a sports science laboratory (they offer a degree base in sport and exercise sciences).

ENTS

The Elwes Building on Park Campus (opened in 1994) is where the Union does its stuff. 'If you are looking for somewhere to eat, drink and be merry...the SU will provide.' There are weekly SU discos, the most popular band on the SU jukebox in 1995 was Oasis, the best club in Cheltenham is Enigma (Wednesday night, student night), and the best place to eat is Balti Walla.

C&G tell us that there are *better quality clothing shops* in Cheltenham than anywhere in Britain. Their student population clearly wants to know this. Suddenly the whole thing falls into place.

CHESTER UNIVERSITY COLLEGE

University College Chester
Cheyney Road
Chester CH1 4BJ

TEL 01244 375444
FAX 01244 373379

University College, Chester
Student Union
The De Bunsen Centre
Cheyney Road
Chester CH1 4BJ

TEL 01244 390093/382212
FAX 01244 382212

UNIVERSITY COLLEGE CHESTER

Founded **1839**

Situation/style **Campus**

UNDERGRADUATE PROFILE
Application acceptance rate **7%**
Population **2,900**
Mature student population **30%**
Overseas student population **1%**
Male/female ratio **28:72**
1st year institut. accommodation **70%**
Approximate cost (Uni) **£40-£60 pw**
(City) **£35 pw**

ACADEMIC PROFILE
A-level requirements: **Low**
Teacher Training 12, **Health & Community Studies** 6, **Social Sciences combinations**10, **Sports Science** 10-12, **Modern Language combinations** 12/CC, **Environmental Science (plant/animal Biol.)** 10
Student/staff ratio **19:1**
1st class degree pass rate **33%**
HEFCE assessments
(5 subjects assessed/approved):
1995 **English** Excellent
1996 **Modern Languages** 19
Joint Funding Council's research assessment 1996
(12 subjects assessed):
Grade 5/5* None

EMPLOYMENT PROFILE
Principal job market destinations:
Education, Retail/Wholesale, Health, Public Admin., Manufacturing
Approximate % unemployed **7%**

VAG VIEW

Founded in 1839 as Chester College, the institution adopted the title of University College, Chester in 1996. It is a University Sector College on a 30-acre campus, half a mile from the City Walls.

The curriculum majors on Education, but the college is active in many other areas. UCC has forged a partnership with 400+ employers and involved them in the design and assessment of its modular courses. This facilitates work placements which is one ingredient in the career-based learning recipe which characterises the BA/BSc degree programme.

Sport is especially strong and there are constantly evolving facilities to support it - for example a newly refurbished all weather soccer pitch, a 25m pool, a new fitness suite and aerobics arena. 'Many of our students excel at sport after they have arrived here. Others, like Alwyn Cosgrove (British Taekwondo Champion) and Jon Sleightholme (England Rugby Union player) improve their training programmes to enable them to progress to even higher standards.'

The college was founded by the Church of England and it maintains contact with its roots. Every morning there is a short informal service.

Finally, if you want a First, come here (see fact box).

GETTING THERE

★ By road: The city is fed by the A540 (North-west), M53 (it ends on the North-east outskirts), A51 (from East), and A483 (from South). The college is situated at the junction of the A540 and Cheyney Road.
★ By rail: Chester is also well fed by trains

and coaches from all major cities: London Euston, 2:45; Sheffield, 2:25; Birmingham New Street, 1:45; Liverpool Lime Street, 0:40; Manchester Oxford Road, 1:00. The railway station is 20 minutes walk from the campus.
★ A taxi costs around £3.00.

VIEW FROM THE GROUND
by Alastair Coles

The introduction in the official prospectus proudly states that 'University College Chester is one of the leading colleges in the country'... More than one Freshers' edition of the college student newspaper has said that 'you will develop a sense of pride and loyalty for this flower-diseased, old farty, titchy-tiny, pompously pooey, but truly excellent establishment.' Both of the above may well be true, but if you can make sense of what the latter wonderfully descriptive image really means, you're probably already half way to getting a degree at Chester - if not, prepare to be enlightened.

If you come to UCC, the first thing that will strike you is its size. The college is a tight, compact unit, with only a small number of other sites and associated institutions away from the main campus. This, however, is one of the main contributing factors to the overwhelming friendly and relaxed atmosphere. There are just over 5,000 students at Chester, of which only around half study full time. So, unlike the relative anonymity you might suffer at a larger establishment, you'll find it very hard not to see a plethora of people you know walking around campus and even the city centre. The obvious downer to this 'family' environment is that everyone will know what you did last night by the following morning...at the latest.

The other thing that becomes immediately obvious is that the campus always looks 'nice'. It is rumoured that the many welcome security cameras are primarily there to make sure you don't pick, trample on, or generally desecrate the award-winning flower arrangements.

When it comes to the buildings, there is a mixture of both old and modern styles, all of which appear quite homely - we can match the widespread 'concrete jungles' of Higher Education only with a rather meagre 'concrete tree' in the form of a towering teaching block at the centre of our campus.

OUR KIND OF STUDENT

If you are considering coming to Chester, you are most likely to be white, northern, female, not the sort of person who got two As and a B at 'A' level, and probably sporty. This may perhaps seem a sweeping generalisation, but a whacking 72% of full-time students are female, and almost a quarter come from Cheshire, never mind the rest of Northern England. There are staff and students representing over thirty-two different countries, but these are in a definite minority, while almost three-quarters of full-time students are under 21; however, with most part-timers being older and a high proportion of postgraduates to undergraduates, you will find not a small amount of mature students walking around.

CHESTER AND ITS MINOR PLEASURES

Moving away from the campus into Chester itself, you'll find one of the most picturesque city centres in the country. It has shopping opportunities second only to London, and if you have the frequent urge to rush out and see something of extreme historical importance during a break from lectures, you won't be let down by the architectural minefield dating back to Roman times. You can get to almost anywhere within about twenty minutes, leaving the (nevertheless cheap) public transport to those with extreme couch-potato-like tendencies.

For those interested in the arts, the Gateway Theatre is just one of a multitude of theatres and cinemas - with the famous medieval 'Mystery Plays', produced every five years, proving a major attraction. Another bonus is that there are always plenty of part-time jobs available for the financially burdened student, as well as a fair amount of student discounts to be found in the city centre shops, pubs and restaurants. However, all these positive points lead, almost inevitably, to a negative one... there are tourists and shoppers everywhere - especially on a Saturday, when you will need either the patience of a two-toed sloth or a particularly evil body odour to make your way through the crowds.

COMMUNICATION

When you come to UCC, you will be bombarded with abbreviations and strange words that are otherwise meaningless to the casual onlooker. Having updated your 'P3' you might very well go to the 'DB' or 'SU' to check you 'piggies' to see if you have anything from 'SGSS', or the 'SAC', or maybe even your 'PAT'! Confusing as it may all seem, you'll get used to it, and you'll get a lot of advice. This is worth mentioning - the majority of staff, from porters to lecturers, from gardeners to the administration, are all very friendly and helpful. While many students at university complain of 'feeling lost' and 'people not really caring about what the students think or do', the atmosphere at Chester is pleasantly different, and as far as keeping the students 'informed' is concerned, the Union produces a weekly newsletter. The ridiculously good Collegian newspaper is released monthly, and there are year and module representatives, house managers, a students handbook, an alternative prospectus, a sports handbook and finally the piggies, the internal pigeon-holes, in which you'll find all your library fines, fan-mail, etc.

WORK, REST & PLAY: The UCC Degree

Despite the above sub-heading, there really is no such thing as a University College Chester degree. Putting the new improved title aside, Chester is still an accredited college of the University of Liverpool, and as such, degrees are awarded by the University and not the college itself. With the college having been 'semesterised' and 'modularised' many find it easier to monitor their progress, but really it depends on your preferred method of study and assessment... the modular system certainly puts more emphasis on 'on-going assessment' (coursework); so if you live in fear of long 'do or die' exams, there's less to worry about. There are two semesters per year, and you are required to take four modules per semester. When choosing your course, especially those with combined subjects, be wary: even if you only want to do two subjects, you may have to follow three for the first year....and make sure you find out the 'weighting' of the course in the later years (i.e. will you be able to take subjects at a major, equal or minor level?)

Be aware that college policy, departmental ideals and tutors' discretion will, invariably, clash. However, where administration is lacking in some areas, in others it is very good; the majority of departments provide handbooks for each separate module taught, which give you every conceivable piece of information you might want to know. Again, tutors are always willing to give one-to-one advice if needed. Perhaps the most prominent of all of the departments is Physical Education/Sports Science - it is very popular, with a large intake every year, made obvious by the overwhelming amount of lary green, white and black college sportswear to be seen around campus!

PLACES TO LIVE

There is a wide range of accommodation on campus and around Chester. The big plus is that in comparison to the rest of the country, Chester is relatively cheap and definitely a cheerful place in which to live. Even if you don't get a college-owned room/house in your first year (not everyone does), you'll be given a lot of help by the accommodation office.

Astbury & Fisher: the two largest halls (around 60 people in each). Both mixed, they have three floors of smallish single rooms, with shared bathroom facilities. Be prepared for a lot of friends and a lot of noise.

Margaret, Alexandra & Catherine: three small halls. Margaret and Alexandra are female-only. Again on three floors, with single rooms. Quieter, and a little more refined than the above - but not much!

Old college: old! Adjoins administration and teaching block. Female-only. Single and shared rooms. Lots (and lots) of stairs to climb. Beware of the pigeons!

John Douglas Court: female-only. Nice and modern. Slightly isolated from the centre of campus.

Parkgate Road: self-catering houses. Some nice, some pretty depressing! Single and shared rooms. Cheaper. Consider learning to cook before taking the college meal-scheme option - it's cheaper and often more convenient.

Finally, if you are in halls, you will have the enviable pleasure of being able to sample all of the wonderful delicacies provided by the college dining hall/cafateria - which is modern, comfortable and relatively inexpensive. There is a wide selection of food from 'proper' nutritional meals to salads, burgers, chips and beans, with ample vegetarian alternatives and by the end of the year, you may well have worked out one or two of the many ingredients which comprise 'Red Dragon Pie'... or not, as the case may be.

CLUBS & SOCIETIES

Sport, sport and more sport! If you're a sports fanatic, it's all here for you - squash courts, fitness suite, astroturf pitch etc, etc... both the college and Chester itself are home to literally hundreds of sports clubs and centres. The UCC clubs are relatively cheap to join, very successful in both regional and national competitions (especially considering the size of the college), and have a good 'team spirit' with lots of club socials. However, sport as a casual/recreational activity is not actually that well catered for, with facilities almost always fully booked for squad training or matches.

Away from sport, UCC is lacking a little on the clubs and societies front. You won't find any political groups, because the Chester Student Union is apolitical and on occasions nationally outspoken.

Having been founded by the Church of England, the college's links with the church still prevail, with a large Christian community on campus and a well attended Christian Union. Even in this domain, the dominance of sport in the college is underlined with a 'Christians in Sport' group.

The arts are well provided for, with both the drama department and club putting on frequent productions.

SOCIAL SCENE: On-Campus

To be fair, the entertainment facilities at UCC could be better....a lot better! The main venue on-campus (in fact the only venue except for the bar!) is 'Small Hall' - and that's essentially all it is; the hall is home to a small makeshift, bar, a stage, a couple of lovely flashing and coloured lights and massive queues which invariably leave you freezing by the time you get in. There is, however, one positive point...the hall's size can sometimes lend itself to an excellent atmosphere, especially with a live band. Events are usually laid on once a week, on a Friday, in the form of a 'bop' (which usually entails a DJ, a theme, and a cheap entry fee), and live bands appear fairly infrequently (about once a month). The bands that do appear, though, are very well received, with attractions over the past year encompassing Irish, soul, funk and indie music. A Beatles cover band, 'Beatlemania', is a definite UCC favourite, with at least two appearances a year, and a highlight of 1996 was the Dharmas, fresh from the Phoenix Festival.

The Student Union bar, having been recently refurbished, is popular, very modern, and has all the usual facilities; cheap drink, pool tables, arcade machines, jukebox, table football, etc. However, as the college rapidly expands, the bar is becoming far too small to cater for the crowds of students that pile in every night.

Entertainment at UCC is at its best during Freshers' Week and RAG Week. Freshers' Week (which sees just as many second, third and fourth years as Freshers!) provides seven nights of events in a row, which have, in the past, included bands, comedians, hypnotists, and theme nights. RAG Week at UCC is big, raising just as much, if not more, money for charity than many of the big universities (usually over £17,000!).

OFF-CAMPUS

Pubs - Once you get bored of squeezing your way through the throngs of over-enthusiastic karaoke-goers in the Student Union bar, with over sixty pubs in Chester, you can't really go wrong. Most of them are within easy walking distance - The Bouverie Arms (or the Bouv) - *the* student pub, lively, generally crowded and full of sports clubs; The George & Dragon - more refined, but if you like your real ales, this is definitely the place to go; Telford's

Warehouse - overlooking the canal, an excellent venue for live bands and good music; Scruffy Murphy's - an Irish bar with a wonderful atmosphere, often with live Irish music and excellent Guinness.

Clubs - Chester is a bit weak on the ground in this department. However, while you might have to travel to Liverpool or Manchester for a serious night on the dancefloor, there are some clubs well worth trying out. By far the most popular with UCC students are Blimpers and Rosies, both of which provide student nights with cheap entry and cheap drinks. Rosies liaises with the college to provide a 'Feel It' night, once a month - three floors (one disco, one dance, one indie) of fun and frolics with advance tickets.

CHICHESTER INSTITUTE OF HIGHER EDUCATION

Chichester Institute of
Higher Education
Bishop Otter Campus
College Lane
Chichester
West Sussex
PO19 4PE

TEL 01243 816000
FAX 01243 828351

Chichester Institute of
Higher Education
Bognor Regis Campus
Upper Bognor Road
Bognor Regis
West Sussex
PO21 1HR

TEL 01243 865581

Chichester Institute of Higher
Education Student Union
Bishop Otter Campus
College Lane
Chichester
West Sussex PQ19 4PE

TEL 01243 787137
FAX 01243 532658

CHICHESTER INSTITUTE OF HIGHER EDUCATION

Founded	**1839**
Situation/style	**2-site campus**
UNDERGRADUATE PROFILE	
Application acceptance rate	**11%**
Population	**2,400**
Mature student population	**64%**
Overseas student population	**5%**
Male/female ratio	**30:70**
1st year institut. accommodation	**50%**
Approximate cost (Institute)	**£60 pw**
(Town)	**£35 pw**
ACADEMIC PROFILE	
A-level requirements:	**Low-medium**

Teacher Training & Education Studies combinations CCC-DE, **Language Studies** EE, **Social Studies** 6, **Sports Studies** 14, **Media Studies** 8-12, **Related Arts (Art, Dance, Music with Humanities/Arts/ Geography** combs., or as majors) 6-8

Student/staff ratio	**21:1**
1st class degree pass rate	**5.6%**
HEFCE assessments (4 subjects assessed/approved):	
English on 2nd visit, 1996	
Joint Funding Council's research assessment 1996 (8 subjects assessed):	
Grade 5/5*	None
EMPLOYMENT PROFILE	

Principal job market destinations:
Education, Retail/Wholesale, good record **Sport**

Approximate % unemployed	**13%**

VAG VIEW

A well-worked modular course structure with an interesting bias towards physical and spiritual health. Nice situation. Not a place for the riotous or wicked.

SETTING

The institute is situated between the South Downs and the sea in Chichester (The Bishop Otter Campus) and Bognor Regis (the less imaginatively named Bognor Regis Campus). The walled, cathedral city of Chichester is the county town of West Sussex and is widely known for its annual Festival of Music and Arts. Bognor Regis lies 5 miles south-east of Chichester and is a seaside resort.

GETTING THERE

★ By road: The easiest route to Bishop Otter Campus is along the A286 from the North, which brings you in to Chichester on Lavant Road, parallel to College Lane. From East and West the city's main feed road is the A27. The road between Chichester and Bognor is the A259.
★ By rail: To Chichester, London Victoria: 0:45; Birmingham: 4:00.
★ Frequent trains to both sites from Gatwick Airport.

ACCOMMODATION

Catered accommodation available in halls of residence on each college site.

ENTS

Besides The Chichester Festival Theatre, which opened in 1962, there's the Minerva Studio Theatre with more alternative theatrical fare and films. There is also The New Park Film Centre. The Union, which operates a bar on each campus, also organises regular discos, bands and balls. Sculptures by Henry Moore, Geoffrey Clarke, Willi Soukup and others are a feature of the Mitre Gallery at Bishop Otter, which also supports regular exhibitions by artists connected with the institute. Bognor, being a resort, has a few night clubs and a 2-screen cinema. Besides the pubs, that's about it.

Portsmouth is some 15 miles away; Southampton 25, where a brighter nightlife may be had.

ACADEMIA

The institute is a college of Southampton Uni. Single Honours first degrees are offered in Health Studies and Sports Studies (BSc) and Geography, History, Religious Studies , and a Social Sciences degree awaits validation (BA). Well worked out Major/Minor combinations are offered with Art, Dance, English (Creative Writing is a particular strength), Geography, History, Mathematics, Music, and Religious Studies (some with optional QTS for primary teaching). The same are available in Joint Honours courses, as are English, Environmental Science, Media Studies, Women's Studies, and there's a BSc Joint combination of Health and Psychology.

You may have noticed the ubiquitous Religious Studies. The institute traces its history back to 1839 when Bishop Otter College was founded by the Church of England as a teacher training establishment; there is a striking, modern chapel in the grounds of the Chichester campus.

Current developments include a learning resources centre, which will house the library and a media and computer centre.

SPORT

A sporting tradition is strong - boxing, football (women's and men's), volleyball, cricket, rugby (their sevens' team went farther than any other Uni or college side in the 9915 Middlesex Sevens and were knocked out by the pro winners, Leicester). Windsurfing and sailing are also popular. The BSc Single Hons in Sports Studies sustains a Centre for Sports Science, where champion boxer Richard Woodhall is on the receiving end of a specialist regime. Lynda Moore, a mature student on the BSc course, found fame on TV's Gladiators after her training programme was devised here. A new sports hall is in the planning stage.

CITY UNIVERSITY

City University
Northampton Square
London EC1V OHB

TEL 0171 477 8000
FAX 0171 477 8559

City University Student Union
Northampton Square
London EC1V 0HB

TEL 0171 505 5600
FAX 0171 505 5601

CITY UNIVERSITY

Founded	**1894**
Situation/style	**City sites**
UNDERGRADUATE PROFILE	
Application acceptance rate	**8%**
Population	**3,500**
Mature student population	**35%**
Overseas student population	**15%**
Male/female ratio	**53:47**
1st year institut. accommodation	**65%**
Approximate cost (Uni)	**£67-£74 pw**
(City)	**£55-£70 pw**
ACADEMIC PROFILE	
A-level requirements:	**Medium high**

Law BBB, **Banking & Int. Finance, Bus. Studies** BBB, **Business Computing Systems** BBC-BCC, **Nursing** 16-24, **Psychology & Health** BCC, **Speech/Language Therapy** 22, **Sociology** BCC, **Civil Engineering** CCC, **Music** BBC-BCC

Student/staff ratio	**18:1**
1st class degree pass rate	**8.9%**
HEFCE assessments (6 subjects assessed/approved):	
1994 **Business & Management, Music**	Excellent
1996 **Sociology** 19	
Joint Funding Council's research assessment 1996 (19 subjects assessed):	
Library & Info. Management	Grade 5*
Music, Civil Engineering	Grade 5
EMPLOYMENT PROFILE	
Employability in Industry:	
MPW national league table (1996)	**31st=**
Principal job market destinations:	

Commerce, Health, Retail/Wholesale, Manufacturing, Arts/Media, Education, Property Development, Public Admin./Law

PIP 1996 employers' survey:	
Top 3 subjects/national ranking	
Accountancy/Finance & Banking	8th=
Construction & Civil Eng.	23rd=
Business	24th=
Approximate % unemployed	**6%**

VAG VIEW

The University, formerly the Northampton Institute, places great emphasis on links with the city, industry and the professions. There is a truly cosmopolitan atmosphere here and its professional and unpretentious approach, along with its position in one of London's choice areas for having a good time, makes it a very attractive proposition.

SETTING

The main University buildings form part of a square (Northampton Square) in the North London Borough of Islington. Main library, lecture theatres and StudentUnion are here. The Business School and Department of Arts Policy and Management are nearby in The Barbican Centre. The Dept of Radiography and halls of residence are also within walking distance. The St. Bartholomew School of Nursing (part of Bart's Hospital but also part of City), is situated in Whitechapel.

ADDRESSES:

City University (above);
City University **Business School**, Frobisher Crescent, Barbican Centre, London EC2Y 8HB; Tel: 0171 477 8000.
St Bartholomew **School of Nursing and Midwifery**, City University, 20 Bartholomew Close, London EC1A 7QN; Tel: 0171 505 5721.

Department of Radiography, City University, Rutland Place, Charterhouse Square, London EC1M 6PA; Tel: 0171 410 0105.

GETTING THERE

★ All sites are well served by buses.
★ Parking difficult and expensive.
★ Nearest underground stations to main sites are Angel (Northern line), Farringdon and Barbican (Metropolitan and Circle). Moorgate (Metropolitan, Circle & Northern) is also close to the Business School.
★ For the School of Nursing, it's either Whitechapel (District & Metropolitan), Aldgate (Metropolitan), Aldgate East (Metropolitan & District), or Tower Hill (District).
★ All the University buildings are 5-10 minutes walk from the nearest underground station.
★ Coaches, trains, airports link with Underground and bus networks.

ACADEMIA

Full-time courses are offered in Business and Management; Computing; Engineering; Health Sciences; Law; Maths, Actuarial and Statistical Sciences; Music; Social Sciences and Media Studies. Note assessment strengths in fact box above.

The Business School has a high profile, attracts top class visiting lecturers, often prominent in the media, and there is a strong European orientation and emphasis on work placement. In Computing, excellent facilities combine with City's internationally recognised research in this area (see fact box) and a one to one tutor system to produce an impressive course. In Engineering, strong links with industry and professional institutions foster a career-orientated approach (strong Maths capability required). In Health Sciences a wide range of specialisms are taught and City has useful links with the major London teaching hospitals. City Law graduates are guaranteed a place at The College of Law to complete Legal Practice training, and 'performance' skills are encouraged (e.g. debating). Almost half the staff in the Actuarial Science & Statistics Department are Fellows of The Institute of Actuaries and there are strong professional and international links. Performance tuition in Music (see assessment fact box) is by the excellent Guildhall School of Music & Drama nearby. Social Sciences & Media Studies is a large faculty: Social Sciences include Economics, Philosophy, Psychology, Sociology; Media courses include the broad-based BA course in Journalism which has a particularly fine reputation.

ACCOMMODATION

All first years from outside Greater London are accommodated.

ADDRESSES

Halls of residence:
Finsbury and Heyworth Halls (catered), 15 Bastwick Street, London EC1V 3PE.
Peartree Court, Finsbury Residences (self-catering), 15 Bastwick Street, London EC1V 3PE.
Walter Sickert Hall (self-catering), 29 Graham Street, London N1 8LA.
Francis Rowley Court (self-catering), 16 Briset Street, London EC1M 5RN.

ENTS

See London.

City's immediate neighbourhood is Islington. Galleries, cinemas, theatres and the Barbican Arts Centre are within walking distance. Islington is one of the best 'village' places to live in London, accessible and replete with great pubs, live music venues and clubs. City SU organises ents in its new £1.5 million Union building in Northampton Square.

SPORT

Wednesday afternoons are free for sport. Sub-aqua, canoeing and swimming in the Uni's 33m pool, rowing on the Thames, sailboarding and sailing at the Queen Mary Sailing Club. Shared sports fields (in South London unfortunately), with facilities for rugby, hockey, football, tennis and cricket. Uni's own Sports Centre for squash, badminton, football, netball, tennis, aerobics and yoga.

COLCHESTER INSTITUTE

Colchester Institute
Sheepen Road
Colchester
Essex CO3 3LL

TEL 01206 718000
FAX 01206 763041

Colchester Institute
Student Union
Sheepen Road
Colchester
Essex CO3 3LL

TEL 01206 572462/718705
FAX 01206 573838

COLCHESTER INSTITUTE	
Founded	**1886**
Situation/style	**Campus/ town site**
UNDERGRADUATE PROFILE	
Application acceptance rate	**26%**
Population	**600**
Mature student population	**35%**
Overseas student population	**2%**
Male/female ratio	**50:50**
1st year institut. accommodation	**30%**
Approximate cost (Institute)	**£28-£38 pw**
(Town)	**£35pw**
ACADEMIC PROFILE	
A-level requirements:	**Low**

Design, Freshwater & Marine Biology, Environmental Biology DE-EE, **Humanities combs** (incl **Media, English, History, Sociology**), **Leisure Studies** 12+, **Music, Occupational Therapy** EE

HEFCE assessments
(3 subjects assessed/approved):

English	after 2nd visit, 1996
Music	Excellent

VAG VIEW

The institute offers a few degree courses in interestingly diverse areas - Design, Health, Environment, Business.

SETTING

The institute operates from campuses at Colchester in Essex and, 12 miles to the south-east, at Clacton-on-Sea. In addition the institute has amalgamated with The Essex School of Occupational Therapy, based at Witham, 10 miles south-west of Colchester along the A12. A total no-smoking policy is under consideration.

ADDRESSES

Colchester Campus (as above).
Clacton Campus, Colchester Institute, Marine Parade East, Clacton-on-Sea, Essex CO15 6JQ; Tel: 01206 718000.
Colchester Institute, **Essex School of Occupational Therapy**, Collingwood Road, Witham, Essex; Tel: 01376 532540.

GETTING THERE

Essex is commuter distance from London.
★ Trains are regular and the A12 feeds Colchester from south-west and north-east.
★ The road from Colchester to Clacton is the A133, and a free bus service runs twice a day between the two campuses.
★ There is free student car parking on the Colchester campus, but none at Clacton.

ACADEMIA

The institute offers degree courses in the following subjects: Design (BA Hons) - a Graphics, Fashion and Industrial Design course with a study abroad semester in the 2nd year; Environmental Monitoring & Protection (BSc Hons), validated by Anglia Polytechnic Uni and incorporating 2 summer work placements; Fresh Water and Marine Biology (BSc Hons) for mature students – a practical path to careers in the water industry or environmental mgt.; Business Studies (BA Hons), a 4-year sandwich course; Humanities (BA Joint Hons), 2 out of English, History, Communications & Media, Sociology; Leisure Studies (BA Hons); Music (BA/BA Hons), a first degree in a subject at which The Institute excels (see assessment) and for which they also offer an MA and MPhil/PhD postgraduate degree; Occupational Therapy (BSc Hons) at the Witham School.

ACCOMMODATION

Clacton Halls of Residence for 200+; Colchester for 12, self-catering.

ENTS

Colchester has a few clubs, and restaurants, pubs, and cinemas - see Essex University, Union and Ents. Clacton plays host each year to a Real Ale and Jazz Festival, an Air Show and a Classic Vehicle Show. There are theatres, a cinema and nature reserves. Social events at the Union include comedy nights, live bands, discos, barbeques and arranged outings.

SPORT

Sport is big in Colchester itself. There is a multi-million pound sports and leisure complex. Clacton has opportunities for windsurfing, sailing etc.

Courtauld Institute of Art

Courtauld Institute of Art
Somerset House
The Strand
London WC2R ORN

TEL 0171 873 2645
FAX 0171 873 2781

Courtauld Institute of Art
Student Union
Somerset House
The Strand
London WC2R 0RN

TEL 0171 873 2717

COURTAULD INSTITUTE OF ART	
Founded	**1932**
Situation/style	**City site**
UNDERGRADUATE PROFILE	
Application acceptance rate	**10%**
Population	**115**
Mature student population	**20%**
Overseas student population	**19%**
Male/female ratio	**26:74**
1st year institut. accommodation	**35%**
Approximate cost (ULU)	**£70-£80 pw**
(City)	**£55-£70 pw**
ACADEMIC PROFILE	
A-level requirements:	
History of Art BBC, (Relevant 'A's **History, History of Art, English, Euro Langs; Art** excluded when in addition to **History of Art**)	
Student/staff ratio	**5:1**
Joint Funding Council's research assessment 1996 (1 subject assessed):	
History of Art	5*

VAG VIEW

The institute is the international centre for the study of Art History; its library, together with the institute galleries and the quality of its own scholarship, makes it a magnet for scholars from all over the world. The institute was founded on a magnificent collection of French Impressionist and Post-Impressionist paintings donated in 1932 by Samuel Courtauld.

In this book it is something of an island in a sea of change. Appropriately, its situation in Somerset House describes an island too, surrounded by busy, if elegant, streets - The Strand, Victoria Embankment, and Lancaster Place.

Part of the federal University of London, students may avail themselves of its Student Union and other facilities, such as the Intercollegiate Halls of Residence (see London).

Undergraduates are taught in small groups of around eight and there is a one-to-one relationship between each student and his or her personal tutor. Besides the scholarship of the institute itself, students enjoy ready access to other centres of artistic interest nearby, such as The National Gallery, The National Portrait Gallery, The Royal Academy and The Hayward Gallery, to name but a few.

European art and the culture of which it is an integral part is the focus of degrees and naturally includes European languages. Students go on to teach or work in museums, galleries, auction houses and publishing, as well as in other areas. There is a modular structure to the first degree in The History of Art (BA), but the course remains clearly focused on the subject in hand.

GETTING THERE

★ Underground stations nearby include Aldwych (Piccadilly), Temple (Circle, District), Holborn (Central, Piccadilly), Covent Garden (Piccadilly).

COVENTRY UNIVERSITY

Coventry University
Priory Street
Coventry CV1 5FB

TEL 01203 631313
FAX 01203 838793

Coventry University
Student Union
Priory Street
Coventry CV1 5FJ

TEL 01203 221167
FAX 01203 559146

COVENTRY UNIVERSITY

Founded	**1970**
Situation/style	**Campus**
UNDERGRADUATE PROFILE	
Application acceptance rate	**12%**
Population	**12,150**
Mature student population	**44%**
Overseas student population	**15%**
Male/female ratio	**57:43**
1st year institut. accommodation	**100%**
Approximate cost (Uni)	**£45-£63 pw**
(City)	**£35 pw**

ACADEMIC PROFILE

A-level requirements: **Medium**

Law CCC, **Mech., E & E Engineering** 8-18, **Building Surveying** 14, **Manufacture/ Business Studies** 8-18, **Maths** 16-24, **Computer Sci. & Eng.** 12-16, **Sociology** 12, **Geography** 12-14, **Communication Studies** 16-22

Student/staff ratio	**20:1**
1st class degree pass rate	**4.6%**
HEFCE assessments (10 subjects assessed/approved):	
1993 **Mechanical Engineering**	Excellent
1995 **Geography**	Excellent
1995 **Sociology** 21, **Modern Languages** 21	
Joint Funding Council's research assessment 1996 (22 subjects assessed):	
Grade 5/5*	None

EMPLOYMENT PROFILE

Principal job market destinations:

Manufacturing (strong on **Electrical & Electronic**), **Retail/Wholesale, Health, Commerce, Public Admin./Law, Computer, Construction,** good record **Industrial Design**

PIP 1996 employers' survey:

Top subject/national ranking	
Electrical Engineering	39th=
Approximate % unemployed	**6.5%**

VAG VIEW

In 1970 the Coventry College of Art merged with Lanchester College of Technology and Rugby College of Engineering Technology to form Lanchester Polytechnic, named after Dr Frederick Lanchester, a leading industrialist. In 1987 its name was changed to Coventry Polytechnic. Then, in 1992, the poly became Coventry University. Its continuing connection with industry helps mould its course character, and keeps its employment record good and inward investment healthy.

Dr Michael Goldstein, Vice Chancellor, reaffirms Coventry's continuing aim to satisfy both the 'educational and vocational needs of students'. It is a curriculum shaped to that end; subjects and course structures are designed to educate and to prepare students for the world of work. One schools careers master said, 'They have deliberately gone for the vocational - that was their background. We have students for whom Coventry is exactly right.' It is an impressive set-up, and offers much, much more than the old poly, both from the academic and social point of view.

But all you shrinking violets be aware; you are entering the real environment of Coventry City. VAG correspondents at Warwick Uni (also in Coventry) tell us that the city has 'the highest inner-city violent crime rate per head of population in Europe'. On the Internet, Coventry SU describe their Union as 'your safe environment in a dynamic but very real city.' Elephant & Castle, *the student newspaper, describe the opening of Planet - the Uni's new live band venue - as an 'attempt to break the barrier between locals and students'.*

SETTING

The purpose-built, 25-acre Uni site is well placed near the modern cathedral in the central area of this moderate-sized city (population around 300,000), rebuilt after its almost total destruction during the Second World War. Mediaeval ruins of the old city remain a constant reminder of its past glory, however, and no-one is allowed to forget the legend of Lady Godiva who rode naked through the streets in protest at the high taxes imposed by her husband, Leofric. 'Naked she rides still, in statue form, between two of Coventry's shopping centres.' Nevertheless, today Coventry is above all else a city of modern engineering, known for its car industry - Rolls-Royce, Jaguar, Rover and Peugeot Talbot all have bases here.

GETTING THERE

★ By rail: Trains from London Euston (80 mins) leave every 30 mins.; Manchester Piccadilly, 2:30; Nottingham, 1:45; Bristol: 2:30. Also good services from most other places.
★ Taxi to Uni, approx. £2.00.
★ By air: Birmingham Airport - internal UK flights and flights to Europe - is just 15 minutes away by road or rail.
★ By road: From London M1 (J17), M45, A45, signs for City Centre. From the South, M40 (J15), A46, signs for City Centre. From the Southwest, M5, M42 (J6), A45. From South Wales, M4, M5, then as above. From Northwest, M6 (J2), City Centre signs. From the North, M1 (J21), end of M69, signs to City Centre.
★ Car parking spaces at Uni limited; public car parks close at hand.

ACCOMMODATION

Uni accommodates all first years in Uni-owned or managed houses, or Halls of Residence. **Caradoc Hall**: 1 or 2-bedroomed flats in city tower block. **Priory Hall**: On-campus single bedrooms, traditional catered hall. **Singer Hall**: On-campus, self-catered, single bedrooms.

UNION AND ENTS

The Students Union offers a busy entertainments calendar. Newly opened Planet is the focal point, a 4-storey entertainment venue, a colossal creation, a club for both students and locals (takes 2,000), designed - despite its purple colour theme - to put Coventry back on the map by attracting really big name bands. Also used for comedy nights, dance nights, etc. It's the biggest development in 20 years of Union history. Then there are the bars - annual consumption estimated at over one million pints, the snackbars and restaurants, where more than 75,000 meals are served annually.

Right now Coventry Union is the most active it has ever been. There's to be a Student Development and Activity Centre, which will include computer facilities for preparing promotion material for student activities, training rooms and all kinds of back-up facilities for non-academic activities, a new office for the Union newspaper, music practise rooms, etc, etc.

In the city cinemas, restaurants, bars, nightclubs abound. See also Warwick entry for much more.

ARTS

Shakespeare's Stratford-upon-Avon is 20-odd miles down the road. Coventry's Belgrade Theatre for more eclectic fare - popular/pioneering dramas. Music is the Uni's boast. David Poulter, Organist and Director of Music at Coventry Cathedral, is in charge: chamber orchestra, string orchestra, concert Band (wind, brass), choir.

SPORT

Former international athlete David Moorcroft is now Uni sports consultant. The thirty-seven acres of Uni playing fields four miles from the city centre - rugby, soccer, hockey, netball, tennis, cricket, and a 9-hole golf course. New Uni sports complex with facilities for 5-a-side football, martial arts, table-tennis and weightlifting. Touring opportunities in the hockey, rugby and football clubs. Next door to campus is the city sports complex, squash courts, international pool, etc.

ACADEMIA

In subject terms the emphasis is on Engineering and Technology, Social Sciences, Health Sciences (very popular), but a wide range of other subjects are also offered, from Communication Studies to Art & Design. Entry requirements remain realistic, as the fact box shows. Courses are modular; contact with the real world is key. 'Coventry University is not cocooned in a world of its own, ignoring outside influences, but knows how to take advantage of the expertise on its doorstep. We play a leading role in industrial liaison and are proud of our working partnerships with employers, both large and small, local, national and international. We help companies with research, development and training; in turn, they offer work placements to students, and provide up-to-the-minute expertise to ensure our courses meet the needs of today.'

CRANFIELD UNIVERSITY

RMCS Shrivenham
Cranfield University
Shrivenham
Swindon
Wiltshire SN6 8LA

TEL 01793 785400
FAX 01793 783966

Silsoe College
Cranfield University
Silsoe
Bedfordshire MK45 4DT

TEL 01525 863318
FAX 01525 863316

Cranfield University
Association of Students
RMCS Shrivenham
Cranfield University
Shrivenham
Swindon
Wiltshire SN6 8LA

TEL 01793 785704
FAX 01793 785702

Cranfield University
Union Society
Silsoe
Bedford MK45 4DT

TEL 01525 863075

CRANFIELD UNIVERSITY	
Founded	**1953**
Situation/style	**Campus**
UNDERGRADUATE PROFILE	
Application acceptance rate	**13%**
Population	**638**
Mature student population	**36%**
Overseas student population	**11%**
Male/female ratio	**74:26**
1st year institut. accommodation	**100%**
Approximate cost	**£40-£75 pw**
ACADEMIC PROFILE	
A-level requirements:	**Medium**
Command & Control, Communications & Info. Systems CCC-CC, **Aeromechanical Systems Eng.** BCC-BC, **Mech. Eng.** BCC, **Management & Logistics** CCC-CC,	
Student/staff ratio	**9:1**
1st class degree pass rate	**8.8%**
HEFCE assessments (3 subjects assessed/approved):	
1993 **Mechanical Engineering**	Excellent
1994 **Business & Management**	Excellent
EMPLOYMENT PROFILE	
Principal job market destinations: **Public Admin./Defence, Health, Manufacturing**	
Approximate % unemployed	**2%**

VAG VIEW

Military and students mix in a bizarre and potentially explosive situation.

SITUATION

RMCS Shrivenham: RMCS stands for Royal Military College of Science; Shrivenham is a spot in the Vale of the White Horse, Oxfordshire, a few miles north-east of Swindon, where the college is set in more than 650 acres. Sounds beautiful, doesn't it? And it is, except for the high security fence which surrounds it.

Silsoe College is set many miles away to the east, about 7 miles south of Bedford, just off the A6.

GETTING THERE

★ You are best to get to either of these places by road, and if possible to keep a car with you at all times. The A420 passes Shrivenham North and South, and basically if you can find your way to Swindon, you will have no difficulty finding your way on this road to the village of Shrivenham, which is about 5 miles out. The nearest motorway is the M4, exit at Junction 15 on to the A419, thence the A420. Drive through the village and the college is on the right past the Golf Club. Silsoe is on the A6,

almost exactly mid-way between Bedford and Luton.
★ By rail: Swindon station is nearest to Shrivenham, with good connections to London Paddington, Bristol, Reading. Flitwick is the nearest to Silsoe, but Luton is the best line: London Kings Cross Thameslink: 0:40; Nottingham, 1:45; Birmingham New Street, 2:30.

RMCS SHRIVENHAM

This is *not* only for the military, although the army and the RAF make up roughly half the student contingent. One girl is quoted as saying that as a new student at Shrivenham you may feel the military presence a bit 'intimidating' at first, but it doesn't last. She said this before the college was rocked back on its heels when three officer cadets were charged with raping a woman here, something more than a blip on the propaganda screen. Normally everyone 'mixes in', half the student population dressing up in uniform occasionally and entertaining themselves in the Officers' Mess, to which ordinary students might be invited, and then again, apparently, might not. The academic curriculum revolves around The College of Aeronautics, The Institute of BioScience and Technology, The School of Mechanical Engineering, The School of Industrial and Manufacturing Science, The School of Defence Management and The School of Engineering and Applied Science.

I looked these up on my friend's powerful computer and it was noticeable that we couldn't access certain subject areas. Like the Ballistics Group, for example, or The Department of Defence Management & Policy Studies, or The Cranfield Security Studies Institute.

The real secret of Cranfield's effectiveness is (as you might have guessed) not its civvy street undergraduate population, but its serious minded post-grad researchers, who, they will tell you, attend 'Europe's largest centre for applied research'. The specialist end, you see, is Defence under the auspices of the MoD, but they also broaden their brief with a bit of engineering, radiography, etc on the side. It is a marvellous principle - the best way to keep something out of the public eye is to put it out in the open under camouflage; it's a time-worn military tactic.

You may feel you need to spend a little time the other side of the fence - even 650 acres can seem small when you know it's secure. If so, you'll find Swindon isn't a bad place for clubs and pubs, and The Link Centre offers an ice rink and swimming pool and all sorts of sports. The Oasis Leisure Centre is more of an entertainment sports complex. And The Milton Road Baths and Health Hydro might be just the thing, with its Turkish baths, solarium and jacuzzi, to release those repressed tensions.

There are of course sporting facilities inside too - a golf course, swimming pool, even a beagle pack and riding stables. Then there's a regular party on Wednesdays and 3 balls a year (students and staff attend). You have to admit it would make for a different experience, this Shrivenham.

SILSOE COLLEGE

Silsoe is punted as the soft alternative to Shrivenham. It's not an RMCS for a start. What goes on here is said to be essentially different. There's The School of Agriculture, Food and Environment and The Cranfield School of Management. But watch out for the Trans-Campus Initiatives, and if you try, as I did, to access the Centre for Developing Personal Effectiveness, I'm afraid you'll find no joy at all.

On the outside, however, this is, as they will tell you, the place to 'develop a career in agriculture, food, business, environmental management or agricultural environmental engineering.' Sounds harmless enough. Why not give it a try?

Well, one reason might be the Students Association - or CSA, as they like to call it (their proof reading is impeccable). In an extraordinary message to Freshers, the CSA advises that lecturers should be treated with 'respect', otherwise it will be reflected in your grades! I couldn't believe it, but it was there, on my friend's computer. 'Yes, yes, I know that's called bias,' was the Union exec's rationale, 'but it's also called Human Nature.' At Silsoe, perhaps.

Further on, in a piece entitled 'The CSA -

Who we are, what we do and what we offer' - this same fella suggests to his wide-eyed Fresher audience that 'If you want to look hip, come and hang around with us'. The less than tempting invitation was issued from Building 114 (that's the seductive name of the safe haven the Union occupies). Then, in another message, this Union gaffer starts oiling it with the post-grads. *We* both know that undergrad Union reps only come on 'radical and hip' to further 'their fledgling political careers... we won't be wasting your (and our) time and energy campaigning for or against things which don't affect you as Cranfield postgrads - even if the rest of student-kind is doing so'.

It's an interesting interpretation of Union representation; revolutionary even. I sort of hoped it might be a joke, but there was more to come. Perhaps the problem is like at Shrivenham - all this pent-up aggression. It's understandable; they've only recently been allowed a bar of their own. It's downstairs in Building 114, in amongst the Union Shop, the Common Room, the Function Room. They call it The Cuckoo's Nest... 'for reasons which will become apparent to you after being here for a little while.'

There is one outlet for student views, a magazine, but I couldn't help feeling there was a bit of deliberate irony in its name. They call it *Carte Blanche*!

At the end of this fella's piece came a personal *crie de coeur* from an ordinary member of the rank and file (I hestitate to call him a student), who clearly wasn't enamoured of the scene at Silsoe, though our man in the CSA didn't realise or couldn't have cared a damn, for he dedicated it to all those 'unfortunate human beings' who had come to the conclusion that signing up for Cranfield was signing up for 'a life of untold misery and depression'. Extraordinary insight.

The student began, 'Never one to criticise this glittering example of a cutting-edge, frontier breaking, money spinning research institution, I nevertheless felt that it was my duty as a fellow student...to tell of a not-too-distant land flowing with milk and honey...' He went on to describe what this might be – Bedford. **Bedford!**

DARTINGTON COLLEGE OF ARTS

Dartington College of Arts
Dartington
Totnes
Devon TQ9 6EJ

TEL 01803 862224
FAX 01803 863569

Dartington College of Arts
Student Union
Higher Close
Totnes
Devon TQ9 6EJ

TEL 01803 865008

DARTINGTON COLLEGE OF ARTS	
Founded	**1961**
Situation/style	**Campus**
UNDERGRADUATE PROFILE	
Application acceptance rate	**12%**
Population	**450**
Mature student population	**39%**
Overseas student population	**2%**
Male/female ratio	**43:57**
1st year institut. accommodation	**95%**
Approximate cost (College)	**£37-£40 pw**
(Town)	**£35-£45 pw**
ACADEMIC PROFILE	
A-level requirements:	**Medium**
Theatre BC, **Music with Performance Writing** CD, **Visual Performance** BE	
Student/staff ratio	**17:1**
1st class degree pass rate	**4.5%**
EMPLOYMENT PROFILE	
Principal job market destinations:	**Arts/Media**
Approximate % unemployed	**12%**

VAG VIEW

Dartington in south Devon is a lovely part of the country, and friendly too. The saying round here is that you can tell the difference between people from north and south Devon by looking at their cows. In the north they are angular, lean and temperamental, influenced perhaps by the more sublime spirit of the place, the iron north coast with its crashing Atlantic swell, the stark lonely spaces of Exmoor and Dartmoor. While in the south the herds are fat and contented, producers of the famously thick Devonshire cream.

Dartington, just south-east of Buckfast Abbey and a couple of miles north-west of a town called Totnes, is an ideal setting, a village in the shadow of Dartmoor but nestling in the valley of the River Dart. There's nothing fat and contented about the gaffers at the college, however, who offer a close-knit, intense, artistic experience, not at all your average higher education. It had an exciting reputation in the existential and permissive 60s, which they are never allowed to forget, thanks to people like me.

All that has changed unfortunately. Now, the college not only awards university degrees in Performance Arts, but is committed to a programme geared to working (Heaven forbid). Link-ups with professional companies and projects with clients, both local and European, are part of the experience.

GETTING THERE

★ By road: A38 from Exeter (20+ miles away to the north-east), left along the A384 two miles after Ashburton or, if coming from Plymouth (20+ miles away to the south-west), take a right two miles after the (A385) turn-off to Totnes.

★ By rail: Trains to Exeter are very good. From London, Paddington is the departure point: 2:30 (Exeter); from Birmingham, 3:00. Sometimes trains go through to Totnes, sometimes you'll need to change and take a local train.

ACCOMMODATION

First years given priority for hall residence, but not guaranteed on-site accommodation. Some halls are ten to fifteen minutes walk away, through the Dartington Hall Estate.

ENTS

Just about the only institution not to mention bops, which is quite a relief. There is, however, no shortage of entertainment, much made by the students or the nearby Dartington Arts, who put on all kinds of concerts, exhibitions, films and theatre. There's also a 5-week Arts Fest. at Dartington College in the summer. Pubs in the area are very good, though you're not into student concessions round here. Totnes is within walking distance, while Torbay, Exeter and Plymouth are nearest for the club scene, etc. See Exeter University, Plymouth University.

ACADEMIA

Not hung up on academic qualifications for entry. They'll want to meet you and see what you've got to offer personally and artistically. Modular course structure. Single Honours (BA) offered in Music, Performance Writing, Theatre, Visual Performance. Combined Honours (BA) in Music (Major) with Theatre (Minor), or any of all subjects taught with Arts Management.

SPORT

Not seen by the college as part of its brief.

De Montfort University

De Montfort University, Leicester
The Gateway
Leicester LE1 9BH

TEL 0116 255 1551
FAX 0116 255 0307

De Montfort University, Milton Keynes
Hammerwood Gate
Kents Hill
Milton Keynes MK7 6HP

TEL 01908 695511
FAX 01908 695581

De Montfort University, Bedford
Lansdowne Road
Bedford MK40 2BZ

TEL 01234 351966
FAX 01234 350833

De Montfort University, Lincoln School of Applied Arts and Design
Lindum Road
Lincoln LN2 1NP

TEL 01522 512912
FAX 01522 542167

School of Agriculture and Horticulture
Caythorpe Court
Caythorpe
Grantham
Lincs NG32 3EP

TEL 01400 272521
FAX 01400 272722

DE MONTFORT UNIVERSITY

Founded	**1969**
Situation/style	**Campus**
UNDERGRADUATE PROFILE	
Application acceptance rate	**12%**
Population	**14,365**
Mature student population	**25%**
Overseas student population	**6%**
Male/female ratio	**50:50**
1st year institut. accommodation	**63%**
Approximate cost (Uni)	**£35-£50 pw**
(City/town)	**£30-£40 pw**
ACADEMIC PROFILE	
A-level requirements:	**Medium**

Law BBC, **Pharmacy** 18-22, **Biomedical Sciences** 12-14, **Accounting & Finance** 14, **Business Studies** 22, **Computer Science & Engineering** 8-18, **Electrical Engineering, Electronics, Industrial Design** 18, **Combined/Joint Humanities** BCD-CCD, **Sports Engineering** 16, **Sociology** 12, **Arts Mgt.** BCD-CCD, **Media & Pop Culture** 12, **Performing Arts (Dance)** BBC-EE

Student/staff ratio	**10:1**	
1st class degree pass rate	**5.7%**	
HEFCE assessments (11 subjects assessed/approved):		
1994 **Business & Management**	Excellent	
Joint Funding Council's research assessment 1996 (34 subjects assessed):		
Grade 5/5*	None	
EMPLOYMENT PROFILE		
Employability in Industry:		
MPW national league table (1996)	**49th=**	

Principal job market destinations:
Education, Manufacturing (strong on **Pharmaceutical**), **Retail/Wholesale, Commerce, Arts/Media** (strong on **Publishing & Creative Arts**), **Public Admin/Law, Health, Computer, Architecture, Market Research/Advertising, Sport** (strong)

PIP 1996 employers' survey: Top 3 subjects/national ranking	
Business	20th
Languages	29th=
Computing	35th=
Approximate % unemployed	**10%**

VAG VIEW

De Montfort is in the vanguard of universities which have defined Higher Education as a business with students its market. Their TV advertisement was a first and it worked. One careers master told me that interest and intake increased dramatically when the ads were running, but fell away shortly afterwards. That could be sour grapes. For, as I discovered, not quite everyone is convinced that the slogan lives up to the reality. You may remember the ad. It made use of Attenborough film footage which showed a whale coming up on a beach and attacking a seal. Dramatic stuff. The message was that De Montfort prepares you for the Trials of Life.

We had a number of pieces from

Leicester campus students, but none from any other. The message about the Uni's academic approach was that the teaching is good, but as in any other Uni, success is down to self-motivation in the end. Students study eight modules a year. Some claimed that life was a doss; others that they wean you off the school ethos gently in the first year, giving you a light taste of what will be required later. None complained about high pressure. One school careers mistress said, 'I'd recommend it for someone who wanted to do something competitive like Pharmacy but didn't have the grades, say, for The School of Pharmacy in London.' Another at a smallish public school in the north was more positive: 'It's very, very popular, and we have a high regard for it for Business Studies. We are talking here about vocational training - they have sandwich courses and an impressive record on employment. They have links with industry and they have a named person who is responsible for these sandwich placements - it's not left to the students who haven't really got a clue.'

De Montfort has four centres of education on ten campuses, study links with 19 colleges, and franchise arrangements as far away as South Africa and Malaysia. In 1997 DMU celebrated its centenary, basing the date on its previous incarnation as Leicester Municipal Technical and Arts School. But their great expansion was seeded in more recent times.

The problem on which any fast expanding, acquisitional business must focus is raising standards (not only of facilities, but that too) in each new acquisition. Otherwise all the new business creates is more problems. There was a general feeling that De Montfort is only just managing to keep up with its extraordinary expansion rate. One student described your chances of finding decent accommodation in DMU's halls of residence as about the same 'as Linford Christie looking into his lunchbox and finding a bacon sarnie.' Still, business is De Montfort's thing, over-expansion does not seem to be a problem yet, and they are reported by The Independent *to be 'happily in the black'.*

Among DMU's recent improvements to the infrastructure is an electronic library facility which permits inter-campus communication and lends credence to their boast that however far apart their educational 'parts' may be, when you join one of them you can draw on the resources offered by the whole. It is a first principle which any orchestra conductor understands, and as it turns out the Vice Chancellor is a musician. Look too at the Employer League Tables, which are more relevant to De Montfort than to many another university - (student employment being an essential part of what drives De Montfort) - and you will see that the DMU recipe is working well.

SETTING

Leicester:

City Campus: City centre.

Scraptoft Campus: 6 miles from centre, edge of country, largely self-contained.

Charles Frears Campus: Out of town off the A6.

Bedford:

Lansdowne Campus: Quiet situation on north-west side of town.

Polhill Campus: North-east of town.

Lincoln:

Caythorpe Campus: Off the A17, south of Lincoln, near Caythorpe village. Includes 250 hectare arable teaching farm.

Riseholme Campus: Just north of Lincoln off the A46, old Bishop's Palace.

Holbeach Campus: Near Holbeach between the A16 and A17 at the heart of the Lincolnshire Fen.

City Campus: Close to Lincoln city centre.

Milton Keynes:

Kents Hill Campus, off the A421 south-east of Milton Keynes.

GETTING THERE

Leicester:

★ By road: M1 (J21) or M6 then M69.

★ By rail: from London St. Pancras 75 minutes.
★ By coach: readily accessible.
★ By Air: Birmingham International Airport, accessible via the M69/M6; East Midlands International Airport via M1 (J23a).

Bedford:
★ By road: 50 miles north of London on A6.
★ By rail: 50 minutes from London Kings Cross; good services elsewhere.
★ By coach: Direct from London, Luton and Heathrow airport.

Lincoln:
★ By road: A1M, A1.
★ By rail: On main East Coast line London Kings Cross and Edinburgh via Newark.
★ By air: Humberside Airport, 35 miles North, for regular internal and European city flights. East Midlands International Airport 45 miles to the West.

Milton Keynes:
★By road: M1 (J14), A509. A5 also runs through city.
★ By rail: Milton Keynes Station to London Euston 60 minutes; direct trains also to Birmingham, Glasgow and connections.
★ By coach: Good services from London but coaches stop M1 (J14); connecting shuttle.
★ By air: London Heathrow, Luton, Birmingham within one hour's drive. London's Gatwick via M25.

ACADEMIA

Fourteen schools. Subjects wide-ranging, from Law to Engineering, from Agriculture to the Arts. Modes of study include full time, sandwich and part time. Each department has its own computer network, and 24-hour computer accessibility at MK.

DEGREE FACULTY CAMPUS DISTRIBUTION

Leicester - Home of Applied Sciences, Arts and Multi-disciplinary Studies, Built Environment (see also Milton Keynes), Business (see also Milton Keynes), Computing Sciences (see also Milton Keynes), Design & Manufacture, Engineering and Manufacture (see also Milton Keynes), Health and Community Studies (Charles Frears Campus; see also Milton Keynes), Humanities, Law.
Bedford - Home of Humanities, and at the Polhill Campus, Sport and Education.
Lincoln - Applied Arts and Design (City Campus), Agriculture and Horticulture (including Agric. Engineering).
Milton Keynes - Built Environment (Architecture & Urban Studies, Land Mgt.), Business (Business Administration, Business Studies, and part-time degrees), Computing Sciences (Computer and Information Studies, Computing), Engineering and Manufacture (Information Systems with Mgt. or Electronic Library Services), Health and Community Studies (Applied Social and Community Studies), Social Sciences.

ACCOMMODATION

Leicester: 21 halls of residence, catered and self-catered.
Bedford: 3 halls of residence plus university-managed properties. All first year students guaranteed accommodation.
Lincoln: No DMU-owned residential accommodation at City Campus. School of Agriculture and Horticulture has halls of residence on its campuses.
Milton Keynes: One hall of residence close to Kents Hill Campus, plus a range of leased accommodation from Midsummer Housing. All self-catering.

ENTS

Leicester: See student piece - *View from the Ground* - below.
Bedford: Clubs include Winkles, indie night Thursday; Esquires, student haunt, live bands upstairs, dance floor down; The Plaza; Riviera Nights, open till 4; Chaplins, Karaoke night Wednesday. Recently built cinema complex, Aspects plus bowling alley, nightclub, bars, eateries. Union events include bands, hypnotists, comedians, quiz nights, theme discos. Wednesday discos at Polhill Campus, Friday night's Flipside, Christmas and summer balls.
Lincoln: Theatre Royal for pre-West End plays, etc. plus Ritz Cinema. The Lawn, the Castle and the Cathedral for concerts. Some nice pubs Union provides annual Halloween party and May Ball.
Milton Keynes: The Point, multi-screen cinema, restaurant, nightclub, bars.

Winter Gardens has nightclub, health

club, restaurant complex, wine bars and pubs. National Bowl for live music - REM, UB40, U2, also London Philharmonic. Union bar has local bands, cabaret acts, weekly disco. Couple of miles south-east lies Wavendon where Cleo Laine and Johnny Dankworth do their stuff at The Stables in the grounds of their home. The Stables also attracts top comedians, bands and offers concessionary rates for students.

SPORT

Leicester: Leicester City Football Club, Leicester Tigers RUFC, Leicestershire County Cricket Club. Saffron Lane Velodrome for championship cycling, athletics. Mallory Park and Donington Park circuits not too far for motor racing. Leisure centres for anything from roller skating to archery. Golf courses, and practice facilities at Humberstone Heights and Western Park - no membership required.

Leicester's Superbowl for Quasar, pool, ten-pin bowling. John Sandford Sports Centre on City Campus and at Scraptoft, a gym, fitness studio, solarium, weight training, and extensive playing fields.

Bedford: In-town Oasis Beach Pool for fun swims, Robinson Pool for serious. International standard Bedford Athletic Stadium. DMU's House of Sport for coaching by National Coaching Foundation sports developments officers. Plus DMU astroturf, football, rugby, cricket pitches.

Lincoln: City leisure centres for swimming, badminton, squash, tennis. Agri-campuses have football, rugby, hockey pitches, and tennis courts, floodlit all-weather playing surfaces and indoor sports halls. Horse riding is a popular pastime in the indoor and outdoor schools near Caythorpe Campus. Also facilities for sailing, canoeing and windsurfing not too far away.

VIEW FROM THE GROUND

by Amanda Dodson

'God, you must hate it there,' was what everyone used to exclaim in my first year of university, when I told them I came from London. I didn't at all - I thought Leicester was a good city for students but not somewhere that I would stay after my degree. I have since changed my mind about this last point, for Leicester has improved in the last year and a half and continues to do so, the most major development being a shopping complex in the centre, intended to make Leicester a rival to Birmingham and Nottingham. There was also little provision for those who liked bars as opposed to pubs - now we are spoiled for choice and the standard, diversity and appearance in both categories is much improved. However, if you still like a quiet pint in a dingy but cosy old man's pub, Leicester still has these in great supply. The fact that the city centre is not huge means that you can walk everywhere, or if you're lazy at least your cab fares will be kept to a minimum, which is crucial if you're on a budget (and you will be!).

One of the most fab things about Leicester is it's location right in the centre of the country, which means that nowhere seems that far away. No matter how much you want to get away from home initially, it is mentally and financially beneficial if home is not hundreds of miles away, especially in first year. From Leicester, Manchester, Sheffield and Liverpool are only about 2 hours away; so are London and Bristol. Nottingham, Birmingham, Loughborough and Derby can all be reached in under 3/4 hour. So if you want to visit a new friend or party in another city, it's easy.

If you're worried about the culture shock of university, Leicester is perfect again due to its location in the Midlands. Whether from the north or south, you will feel comfortable in Leicester, where there is an excellent mix of people from all over the country. Like anywhere you might experience some animosity, but what you never face is hostility for being from one side of the divide or the other.

ACCOMMODATION

The University is very close to the city centre and most buildings are located in one campus area. However there is Scraptoft campus about 7 miles away which has more disadvantages than advantages really. Many students live in Scraptoft Halls and have to travel in to city site to lectures, which in traffic takes about 3/4 hour. Public administration, dance and music courses primarily take place here. Buses servicing Scraptoft are quite regular but it can be an expensive business if you have to make the journey every day - it is a cost that other students don't have and the University unfortunately does not subsidise travel for Scraptoft people. A cab to or from Scrappie will cost you £5 minimum - work that out if you're going into town 4 nights a week, which you might have to do because there's not too much going on in Scraptoft Village. Neither is there a late University bus for Scraptoft people. If you want to save yourself the cab fare from the Union or town, there is a regular night bus which charges 50p to go anywhere, leaving from the Union, but the last one leaves at 1.40am, which means Scraptoft people always have to go home that little bit earlier.

Scraptoft is a beautiful green-field site with nice halls and it does have its own sports hall and Union which puts on good nights, but there is nothing much else up there, apart from a few country pubs, oh, and the stupendous summer ball! Having said all this, it is idyllic in summer and no one I've spoken to who was up there in their 1st year had a bad time.

De Montfort's other accommodation consists of a few poor-standard houses and Halls - accommodation is not it's strong point, unless you happen to be a foreign student, in which case you get gorgeous halls (but it WILL cost you). The halls are not pretty but most people just get on with it and being in Halls makes your first few months easier with regard to making friends.

SOCIAL SCENE

So to the most important matter of nitelife. Leicester definitely has everything but some things you might have to search for. The 2 biggest clubs are Krystals and the dreadfully named Le Palais de Dance. Both these have pretty big student nights, where the drink is cheap, there's loads of snogging and the music is fun. For the best laugh, go in a big group. Krystals has recently staked its claim as the better of the 2 with its Tuesday night Sugar Club, where the pints can sometimes be had for 50p. Its cheap to get in but there will be a top DJ playing (Jeremy Healy, Tony De Vit, Danny Rampling etc etc)!! You won't really want to go to these clubs unless it's a student night, so check the night.

Mosquito Coast on a Wednesday has been huge since I started. It suffers in trying to cater to too many tastes musically, but its pretty mad at times and you find yourself there having a good time despite any other intentions. With an NUS card you are automatically a member, which means its cheap to get in, if not free. MC also does an excellent Brit Pop/Indie/Alternative night on Mondays, and Fridays are fun too.

Streetlife is the place to be on a Friday - it is commonly said that you never have a bad night there. There is the large 'house' room where the atmosphere is sometimes great but most of the time absolutely amazing! They usually have well-known DJs, especially if Mixmag are throwing one of their famous all-nighters. Otherwise it's open until 3.30am. The large chill-out room plays jazzy stuff, 70s funk and disco and has a transvestite cabaret at midnight (self-conscious males beware as you may be hauled up on stage for a bit of audience participation!). Unfortunately it's quite expensive but well worth it, once every 2 or 3 weeks. For the rest of the week Streetlife is predominantly a Gay club.

The White Room has been criticised for the coldness of it's interior decor - white rooms - which can mean it lacks atmosphere but its gaining in popularity all the time despite this. Wednesday is Student night, playing House and Garage in one room, Soul, R&B, Hip Hop and Funk in the other. For the rest of the week it has Happy House through to Rave music, also getting in top DJ's.

Luxor is another club where you don't often have a bad night. Its Student Night died a sad death last year for no real reason, but it might be back, in which case it will be one of the best nights of the week - Luxor on a Tuesday was one of our reasons for living! It is also well worth a visit on Thursdays, when they do special party nights (see advertisements), which were never really busy but always brilliant. Fridays and Saturdays are also good if you like it quite glamorous and housey. Prices are pretty average and they always do a deal for students. The Starlight Club and the Underground Club (where nobody seems to go but it might be worth investigating) cater to harder tastes, the former putting on a hugely popular 'lose it' all-nighters once a month. There's also the Dielectric Club which is very hard and ravey.

If you like Soul, R&B, Jungle and Hip Hop, then Branigans is the best, if not the only, club. It's big, smartly decorated and averagely priced. Thursdays (student night) are soulful, sexy, casual and friendly. There's a mixed crowd and none of the 'attitude' which may (or may not) apply to other nights, but the rumours seems to put many off.

The Fan Club and Alcatraz cater to heavy metal, rock and indie tastes. These are the main clubs but there are a few others.

If you like jazz, several bars have live jazz nights, one of the most notable being the glamorous Cafe Bruxelles on Mondays. The Phoenix Theatre has Sunday afternoon jazz in its cafe, and the Uni now holds a good weekly jazz session, which is also a potential jam for musicians and singers.

If you like a bit of Irish, there are many Irish pubs in Leicester, the 2 central and most trendy being Molly O'Gradys and O'Neils. Both are big, with little 'snugs' here and there, serve delicious traditional Irish food, and have old pots and brooms and books everywhere. The former is the livelier with bands playing on certain nights and entertaining staff.

There are 4 or 5 Firkin pubs, which everyone knows about. Loads of wine bars; Vingt-Quatres, Weavers, and Fat Cats have a friendly, 20-30 somethings, trendy kind of crowd. The Bank and The 39 Steps are a bit noisier and less classy but are fun and play good music (the latter also serves good food); Morgans has a sports and young businessman crowd; Bossa has a gay and quite trendy crowd - shame it's so small. Le Bodega Espanola is no longer a well-kept late night secret - a small, very friendly, often completely barmy tapas bar complete with karaoke on request and perfect for small-ish meals/parties; The Rhythm Room is a very new, large restaurant-bar-club which is open till 2 am and gets you salsa-ing on the tables! You will undoubtedly spend time in Bar Gaudi which is open most nights until 2.0am and plays acid-jazz, funk, some Spanishy type tunes and mellow dance music. It's dingy and gothic and totally fab, if a bit expensive. Bar Europa also has to be visited for top cappuccinos and authentic Italian food. It's intimate and friendly, run by eccentric Italians, always smells of parmesan cheese (but not offensively so) and can often be relied on for a late night drink. There are of course other notable bars and pubs but I would be here for ever.

If you're into gigs you'll be pleased to know that Leicester has quite a large scene. You might even have heard of The Charlotte, which has seen many bands, such as Ocean Colour Scene go on to bigger things. Several of the pubs are gig venues, with bigger acts playing at The Venue (De Montfort Uni), Leicester Uni, or De Montfort Hall, which Oasis played about a year ago.

DMU has played host to loads of top acts - JTQ, The Lighthouse Family, The Prodigy, Dodgy, EBTG, Orbital, Pulp (to name but a few). Though the entertainments programme at De Montfort has come under a lot of criticism for not catering to enough needs, it's not bad. They do regularly have gigs and get in good DJs. There's something on every night of the week, even if it is just the football and a quiz in The Blues Bar, curiously named because they never play blues. The Uni is trying to attract thousands more students every year and is a bit behind in funding the Union to provide for them. If you're Gay, Asian or a rocker, you will find what you want in town but the Union will disappoint at this time - it caters to general tastes which is fine, but does not hold 'events' which satisfy these groups. Again this might change as ents caused uproar at the recent AGM with everyone clamouring for student representation on the ents team.

The 'big' nights at the moment are The Big Cheese (Sat) - snog-fest extraordinaire, party tunes, loadsa beer and cheer, karaoke downstairs and Hey Jude at the end of the night. You get sick of the Cheese but it's fab when you're not. Whatever (Fri) plays indie and alternative. It goes through phases of popularity but you usually have a good night because it's casual and friendly, even if you don't like the music. Karma Coma (Thur) can be mad or moderate, you can dance loads or just chat, and there's always a nice atmosphere. (Soul, funk, dance anthems, R&B, rap, trip hop, and acid jazz - FAB!) There's also a Madchester night every other Wednesday, which is Brit pop/indie sort of stuff. Friday afternoons in the bar can also be quite an event - nothing special, just pre-weekend drinking and excitement.

For non-drinking entertainment, Leicester has 2 great theatres, The Haymarket, which often previews big London shows, and The Phoenix, which has a packed weekly programme featuring contemporary dance, local film makers, writers' seminars, folk music, comedy, small operas, anything you want from traditional to alternative theatre. The YMCA gets forgotten behind these two but also has a diverse programme and is worth checking out, not least because De Montfort Student Theatre put their plays on there, and it has chilled out comedy and music nights.

There are 3 cinemas in Leicester central which have somewhat been usurped by the out-of-town Meridian leisure complex. It takes only 5-10 minutes and between £3.50-£4.50 in a cab. For that you get a glam cinema and Warner comfort and spaciousness. There are about 5 restaurants up there, a games arcade and a pub, so you can make quite a night of it. In terms of 'fun things to do' in town, there are 2 Quasar centres, 2 bowling alleys, an OK swimming pool and Gary Lineker's parents' market stall!! Leicester has a huge market selling fruit and veg, second hand clothes and all the usual market fare.

In general Leicester is a good place for students - it's culturally diverse and not expensively big, but certainly not small. Leicester Uni is close by if you need to use their library. The entertainments up there are open to De Montfort students.

De Montfort Uni is not the best university - it can be frustratingly disorganised and like a lot of Unis, often seems only concerned with attracting more students but not ploughing this money back into provision of books and aiding clubs and societies. A spanking new gym was added to the sports centre this year and more improvements are planned to start soon. A huge new library complex is currently under construction which will provide desperately needed computer and group-work facilities - it's long overdue. Maybe the motto is better late than never. Overall, I've enjoyed my course and am pleased with my choice of Uni and city.

DERBY UNIVERSITY

University of Derby
Kedleston Road
Derby DE22 1GB

TEL 01332 622222
FAX 01332 294861

University of Derby
Student Union
Main Site
Kedleston Road
Derby DE22 1GB

TEL 01332 622222 x1507
FAX 01322 348846

University of Derby
Student Union
Mickleover Site
Western Road
Mickleover
Derby DE3 5GX

TEL 01332 518150

DERBY UNIVERSITY

Founded **1851**

Situation/style **Campus**

UNDERGRADUATE PROFILE

Application acceptance rate **12%**
Population **7,160**
Mature student population **53%**
Overseas student population **3%**
Male/female ratio **42:58**
1st year institut. accommodation **90%**
Approximate cost (Uni) **£37-£54 pw**
(City) **£35 pw**

ACADEMIC PROFILE

A-level requirements: **Medium-Low**
Law 18-20, **Teacher Training** CC, **Chemistry** 10, **Occupational Therapy, Arts Therapy, Diagnostic/Therapeutic Radiography** 14, **Computer Sciences, Health Care Info. Management,** etc 8, **Business Studies** 14, **Applied Arts, Photography & Time-based Media Graphic Design** 18, **Sociology** CC, **Applied Community & Youth Studies** 8
Student/staff ratio **16:1**
1st class degree pass rate **4.3%**
HEFCE assessments (14 subjects assessed/approved):
Law and **Computing** on 2nd visit, 1994 and 1995 respectively, **Modern Languages** NYP,
1995 **Geology** Excellent
1995/6 Sociology 18
Joint Funding Council's research assessment 1996 (19 subjects assessed):
Grade 5/5* None

EMPLOYMENT PROFILE

Principal job market destinations:
Education, Retail/Wholesale, Health, Manufacturing, Hotel/ Restaurant, Arts/Media, Commerce
Approximate % unemployed **12%**

VAG VIEW

If the government should ever forget why they threw open Higher Education to the masses in 1992, they need look no further than Derby for a clear statement of the principles on which the decision was made.

SETTING

The University of Derby is situated at the southern edge of the Peak District, ten miles west of Nottingham. There are twelve sites scattered over the city, the Kedleston Road campus, one of the two furthest away from the city centre (but only 10 minutes walk), being the hub.

GETTING THERE

★ Kedleston Road campus is just off the A38 the main south-west/north-east thorough which goes south to Exeter and meets the M1 at Junction 28. M1 (J25) for access from the East, A6 from the south-east (Loughborough way).

★ Rail links with Derby easy. London is 2 hours away.

ACADEMIA

Since it became a university in 1992, Derby has expanded fast in this area. With three times as many students as it had then, a host of new departments have sprung up. There have been rocky moments - Law and Computing both required a second visit by the assessors in 1994 and 1995 respectively, but maybe that should be put down to growing pains - both had been introduced post-1992.

The Uni is committed to the ideal of Higher Education for all and keeps its entry requirements low to that end, proud that mature students now make up more than half their undergraduate population and that women now predominate in the gender ratio.

Societies dedicated to minority cultures in the university - their web page features a dazzling display by The Taiwan Society - reflect their drive to increase the overseas contingent too. For example, a 1-year Foundation course for international students at Buxton's High Peak College ensures a place in Derby's School of Engineering. There's also an awareness of the problems and advantages of the multi-racial society in which we live, new course strategies putting that awareness to work - the MA offered in Culture, Place and Identity by The School of European and International Studies comes to mind, as does the pastoral and mediation elements in some of their Social Science courses.

Meanwhile the bedrock - Engineering, the School of Environmental and Applied Sciences, Business, Art & Design, Education - remains firm alongside innovative courses such as Electronics with Music Technology, Biology with Visual Media.

A sixth-form college careers master we spoke to praised the modular structure because 'the modular system, with exams at the end of semesters rather than at the end of a course, now adopted by most universities, is the style of working in GNVQ,' but decried the posturing of 'places like Manchester, Birmingham, Leeds, Oxbridge, who say, "What's GNVQ?" - a gut feeling that GNVQs are rubbish and A-levels are OK. Now of course A-levels are becoming increasingly modular.' At Derby they are committed to GNVQ's, BTEC awards, NVQ units at level 3, and other equivalent qualifications ranging from the International Baccalaureate to a recognised Access course', because they are committed to the principle of Higher Education for all, presumably the reason why, in 1992, all those polys were given University status - Derby being the only HE college to make the grade. And they are underpinning the policy with investment in learning resources. This year a new Hi-Tech Learning Centre opens - 'from books (over 250,000 in stock) to periodicals (1,500 UK and overseas magazines subscribed to), from microfiches to CD-ROM, from audio-visual aids to the Internet, the new centre will support your learning in the fullest way.' There are plans, too, to install cable connections between halls of residence and the Learning Centre for out of hours access to information databases, and to install videos to record lectures, not so that students can stay longer in bed but to go back over stuff in their own time and make sense of notes taken in the heat of the moment.

If you're casting a wide net, it's as well to have the mechanisms in place to haul your catch up on to the boat.

ACCOMMODATION

Seven self-catering sites, not enough to guarantee first years accommodation.

STUDENT UNION

Active not only in Ents but, in line with the whole ethos at Derby, on the caring side too. They represent students not only in the sense that the Union bods are elected representatives of the student body. They will actually go in to bat for students on their behalf, whether it is a problem over housing, finance or an academic injustice (like an unfair put-down in exams). For every course offered, there is a student representative responsible for advising students on how to handle any problem that emerges. 'The Advice Centre [open daily from 9 to 5] is here to provide information and support on such matters.'

There is the usual complement of clubs - some 60 - ranging from The Chinese Society to The Hellenic Society, from Women's Groups to Drama. Among the strongest of the 30 sports clubs are Caving and

Mountaineering (in the nearby Peak District) and there are 'regular abseils from campus towers for charity'. In line with this interest - obsession? - they recently awarded a posthumous honorary degree to Derbyshire born Alison Hargreaves, the first woman to climb Everest solo, without oxygen.

ENTS

The Atrium at the Kedleston campus is the social focus, it takes up to 4,000 students for all-night extravaganzas, formal and informal, live bands and stage acts. There are, altogether, six bars in this Uni, one of which doubles as a 1,000-capacity venue for 'discos and bands - lately Lush, Chumbawamba'. There's a pub rock and indie scene in the city, but it's not Birmingham or Manchester or anything approaching them. Derby is relatively small, and there's none of the aggro you get in larger cities. Then there's the Metro Cinema with 250 different films each year from around 30 different countries - part of the Uni, housed in the School of Art and Design on Green Lane.

SPORT

Football, cricket, hockey, women's rugby, snowboarding, mountaineering, caving - the Peak District's the big attraction, the last wilderness left in Middle England and less than 20 miles to the north-west of the city. Gym facilitates badminton, volleyball, basketball courts and 5-a-side football, and includes a fitness room. Running track and 25m swimming pool.

DONCASTER COLLEGE

Doncaster College
Waterdale
Doncaster
DN1 3EX

TEL 01302 553755
FAX 01302 553704

DONCASTER COLLEGE	
Founded	**1915**
Situation/style	**Town site**
UNDERGRADUATE PROFILE	
Application acceptance rate	**11%**
Population	**530**
Mature student population	**85%**
Male/female ratio	**54:46**
1st year institut. accommodation	**90%**
Approximate cost (College)	**£32-£39 pw**
(Town)	**£30-£40 pw**

ACADEMIC PROFILE
A-level requirements: **Low**
Business Studies 12, **Computer Science** E, **Civil Eng., Environment & Resource Management** CC, **Mining & Elec./Mech. Engineering** CC, **Combined (Social/Literary) Studies** EE
HEFCE assessments
(3 subjects assessed):
Business & Management, Computer Science, English,
approved 1994/5

VAG VIEW

The college is based at four sites in and around this South Yorkshire town, which lies just north of the intersection between the M18 and the M1, about 15 miles north-east of Sheffield and 25 miles south-east of Leeds.

Degrees (BSc) are offered through The Faculty of Technology - Integrated Business Technology (it focuses on Information Systems and their applications) and Integrated Technology (entry requirements HND or BTEC), and BEng degrees in Mining & Electrical/Mechanical Engineering and Quarry & Road Surface Engineering. BA (Hons) degrees from The Faculty of Business include a Business Studies degree validated by Hull University, as well as courses in Business & Marketing, Admin., Social/Employment/Literary/Urban Studies. There is also a BEd (Hons) in Education, post 16.

College accommodation is provided on the High Melton site, 6 miles to the west of Doncaster. Doncaster provides a £22 million Dome leisure complex as the leisure focus in the town, which also boasts one of the largest open air markets in the country. There are clubs - Rocque, Karisma, Visage - a fair range of ethnic restaurants, a Warner multiplex cinema and of course the racecourse for which Doncaster is most widely known.

DUNDEE UNIVERSITY

The University of Dundee
Nethergate
Dundee
DD1 4HN

TEL 01382 223181
FAX 01382 201604

Dundee University
Students Association
Airlie Place
Dundee
DD1 4HP

TEL 01382 221841
FAX 01382 227124

UNIVERSITY OF DUNDEE

Founded	**1967**
Situation/style	**Campus**
UNDERGRADUATE PROFILE	
Application acceptance rate	**10%**
Medical AAR	**10%**
Population	**6,000**
Mature student population	**21%**
Overseas student population	**8%**
Male/female ratio	**49:51**
1st year institut. accommodation	**100%**
Approximate cost	**£35-£71 pw**
ACADEMIC PROFILE	
A-level requirements:	**High-Medium**

Law BBC, **Architecture** BCC, **Accountancy, Business Economics & Marketing** CCC, **Social Work** BCC, **Maths & Statistics** 14, **Civil Engineering** 12, **Tourism** 14, **Medicine** ABB**:**
★ Science 'A's required **Chemistry**
★ Additional Science 'A's preferred **Biology & Physics**
★ Addit. Non-Science 'A's acceptable **Yes**
★ Retakes considered **Ext. circs.**
★ Retake offer **AAB**
★ Clinical contact **2nd year**

Student/staff ratio	**7:1**
1st class degree pass rate	**9.3%**
SHEFC assessments (19 subjects assessed/approved):	
1994 **Civil Engineering, Physics**	Highly satis.
1995 **Environmental Science,**	Highly satis.
Hospitality Studies, Maths, Statistics	Highly satis.
Graphic & Textile Design	Excellent
1996 **History, Law, Politics, Social Work**	Highly satis.
Finance & Accounting	Excellent
Joint Funding Council's research assessment 1996 (27 subjects assessed):	
Biochemistry	Grade 5*
Computer, Civil Engineering, Art & Design	Grade 5
EMPLOYMENT PROFILE	
Principal job market destinations:	

Health (incl. **Dentistry**), **Commerce, Retail/Wholesale, Manufacturing** (strong on **Electronic & Electrical**), **Education, Public Admin./Law, Hotel/ Restaurant, Architecture**

PIP 1996 employers' survey: Top subject/national ranking	
Law	22nd
Approximate % unemployed	**10%**

VAG VIEW

'I suppose, if you are a Scot, Edinburgh would have to be high on the list, but people have had very good experiences of Dundee.' This was a sixth-form adviser talking about Medicine, but the same view might be held in other of its academic specialisms. This is a traditional premier-league University with a reputation in Medicine, Law, Finance/Accounting and Design (including Textiles). Where possibly it falls down in comparison with Edinburgh and Glasgow, at least as far as Sassenachs are concerned, is that it is far-flung and neither the city nor the artistic or social side seems to have quite the same bite.

SITUATION

Dundee is one of Scotland's four big cities, set amidst some impressive countryside. But the city hasn't exactly benefited from its inhabitants' strange obsession in times past and even today to destroy visible evidence of its history. However, the 'Jute, Jam and Journalism' survives, and connects it in the first place with its industrial fibre, which today translates into a partly American-inspired techno revolution, mostly confined to an industrial belt, where, among other things, it has been responsible for bringing us that cash-card 'hole in the wall'. The Jam recalls James Keillor's famous Dundee marmalade, and the Journalism of course that giant of the publishing industry, D C Thomson, who gave us naughty kids culture in the shape of the Beano and the Dandy.

The city is set in beautiful country, the Sidlaw Hills, the Braes of the Carse, the Carse of Gowrie, and the Firth of Tay. You can hear the music of the (inimitable) Dundee accent in the names of the places round here.

The Uni's landscaped campus, with buildings both new and old, is a 10 minute walk from the city centre.

GETTING THERE

★ By road: The M90 sprouts a shoot called the M85 before culminating in Perth, then it's the A85, A972.

★ By rail: On the East Coast line, Britain's fastest - Newcastle (3:00), London Euston (6:00). The station is a few minutes walk from Campus.

★ Coaches are no problem either.

★ By air: Dundee airport soon to connect with other internal city airports. Edinburgh International Airport is an hour away.

ACADEMIA

Traditional degree structure. Five faculties: Medicine & Dentistry, Science & Engineering, Law & Accountancy, Arts & Social Sciences, Art & Design.

Sound academic assessments (see fact box), good employment record.

Six computer work stations with more than 150 fully networked IBM PCs, which can be connected to the powerful SPAR centre 2000 UNIX multi-user computer. More computer wizardry at Medical School in Ninewells Hospital.

STUDENTS ASSOCIATION & ENTS

Annasach is the SA mag. for Union issues, *MacDougal* for a keener exploration into the culture of the place. Dundee was Chartist in the 19th century, but if you want to take up a cause today it's Scotland's freedom and future with the Student Nationalists Association - active campaigners for students rights and anything else you might want to get your teeth into.

Attempting to fill the cultural vacuum student-wise in the city, the Dundee SA supplies two disco venues, four bars, a fast food area and games room - NBA Jam, Quintoon, Mortal Combat II, Lethal Enforcers, Cup Final (ECT), plus 10 Pool Tables, pinball machines, etc. Also weekly film nights, quiz nights, bingo, comedy, cabaret nights, and something called All Building Events, which remains a bit of a mystery. To satisfy more sophisticated tastes, there are also coach trips to Glasgow and Edinburgh. (I bet they don't do a return trip here.)

A recent research project by the Association discovered a few haunts worth visiting in Dundee. They provide a list of pubs to pin on the back of your spanking new SA card, among them Wesport & Hawkhill, a studenty pub closest to the Union, The Globe for a friendly welcome and good beer, The Ascot for a great atmosphere at weekends, Lucifer's Mill for cheap cocktails, the Parliamentary Bar for quiet drinking during the week, The Phoenix for decent beer *and* food, Berts for breakfast, Laings for a sun tan in the beer garden, McGonagills (remember that Dundee poet, by name of William, the world's best worst poet?), where you'll mingle with artists just as suspect from the Art College across the road, The Tavern for serious drinking, and finally - though why it took them so long to find it I can't imagine - The Taybridge Bar which sells spirits in quarter gills.

Oh, and there's The Rep theatre in Tay Street (former members include Glenda Jackson, Hannah Gordon, Nicol Williamson), and The Whitehall for pro touring companies and amateur productions. The Royal Scottish National Orchestra plays autumn and winter, and a proms season early summer. Jazz, folk festivals too.

ACCOMMODATION

Catered and self-catered halls of residence and self-catered university houses. Most salubrious is the newly built Seabraes - 31 flats (seven in each) - en-suite shower and toilet, fully equipped kitchen/dining area. West Park self-catering hall also has en-suite, etc. For families (large mature population here) there are 24 two-bedroom flats and 6 one-bedroom flats within five minutes walk of the campus: large family common room for kids or playful adults.

SPORTS

Sports Union combines with PE Department to provide full programme of sports. Hillwalking, trekking, skiing country. Some of the best fishing anywhere on the Tay. Uni's outdoor facilities include a 33-acre sports ground, floodlit, artificial grass tennis courts, Water Activities Centre for sailing. Second sports hall and teaching area (Dept Physical Education) just completed, conditioning Room, 25-metre pool, etc. Golf Bursary Scheme part of a Uni partnership with the Royal and Ancient Golf Club of St. Andrews (10 miles away).

DURHAM UNIVERSITY

The University of Durham
Old Shire Hall
Old Elvet
Durham
DH1 3HP

TEL 0191 374 2000
FAX 0191 374 7250

Durham Student Union
Dunelm House
New Elvet
Durham City DH1 3AN

TEL 0191 374 3310
FAX 0191 374 3328

UNIVERSITY OF DURHAM

Founded	**1892**
Situation/style	**City collegiate**
UNDERGRADUATE PROFILE	
Application acceptance rate	**12%**
Population	**7,600**
Mature student population	**14%**
Overseas student population	**4%**
Male/female ratio	**49:51**
1st year institut. accommodation	**90%**
Approximate cost (Uni)	**£80 pw**
(City)	**£45 pw**
ACADEMIC PROFILE	
A-level requirements:	**High**

Law AAB, **Economics** (+ **Langs., Humanities, Social Sci.** combs: AAB-ABC) ABC, **Chinese/ Japanese Management Studies** BBC, **English Literature** ABC, **Psychology** BBB, **Latin** BCC, **Physics** 18-22, **Geography** BBC, **Geology** 6-20, **Anthropology & Archaeology** BBC, **Sociology** BCC, **Social Sciences combined** ABC, **Arts combined** (incl **Modern Langs.**) 24, **Manufac./E & E/Civil Engineering** 22

Student/staff ratio	**11:1**
1st class degree pass rate	**8.5%**
HEFCE assessments (17 subjects assessed/approved):	
1993 **Chemistry, History, Law**	Excellent
1994 **Anthropology, Applied Social Work, English**	Excellent
1995 **Geography, Geology**	Excellent
1995/6 **German** 22, **Italian** 20, **Linguistics** 22, **Russian** 20, **Sociology** 21	
Joint Funding Council's research assessment 1996 (31 subjects assessed):	
Geography	Grade 5*
Chemistry, Physics, Pure Maths, Applied Maths, Engineering, Asian Studies, Archaeology, History, Theology, Music	Grade 5
EMPLOYMENT PROFILE	
Employability in Industry:	
MPW national league table (1996)	**9th=**
Principal job market destinations:	

Commerce (very strong, especially **Accountancy**), **Education, Manufacturing** (strong on **Pharmaceutical**), **Retail/ Wholesale, Public Admin./Law, Arts/Media**

PIP 1996 employers' survey:	
Top 3 subjects/national ranking	
Law	3rd
Languages	4th
Social Science/Economics	5th
Approximate % unemployed	**5%**

VAG VIEW

Durham, like Bristol, has to suffer the jibe about mopping up the Oxbridge rejects, though 'suffer' may not be the right word. The University is very happy with its own selection procedure. It knows what kind of student it wants and if, in some cases, that means waiting until the Oxbridge results are in, so be it. It's a high-flying Uni academically, as if you didn't already know, and it's college structured, though not like Oxbridge - students are not college taught. There is a preponderance of Yahs, Rahs, or whatever you care to call them - in a sense it is like going from public school to public school with rather more freedom. But not all students are the same. What is the same is the place; it is small and rather insular, though there is nothing like being on an island of goodies, at least for a while. Certainly it is a very friendly place, and the system of non-academic tutors works well - 'it's a relaxed on-going relationship, useful for meeting people, and later for references,' said one student.

You know what you're getting at Durham - first class education and reputation, three cosy years, and a job in the city at the end. If the revolution ever comes, it won't start at Durham.

SETTING

Durham is a small, stunningly beautiful city, situated 258m north of London and 16m south of Newcastle. The nucleus of the medieval city, where five of the colleges and the Arts and Social Sciences departments are located, is formed by a sharp bend of the River Wear round a rocky peninsular, dominated by the 11th century cathedral and castle.

GETTING THERE

★ By road: Junction 6 of the A1 is minutes away. The city is well served by long-distance coaches and regional express services.
★ By rail: 3 hours from Kings Cross (London), 1 hour from Edinburgh. Direct services from Yorkshire, the Midlands, Manchester, Merseyside, and the North of Scotland. The railway station is 10 minutes walk from the centre and local bus and taxi services are good.
★ By air: International and domestic flights to Newcastle, Teesside (25m).
★ Once there, everything is within easy reach by foot or bicycle. There's no need for a car, though parking is ample.

ACADEMIA

Academically, it is up there with the best and A-level entry requirements are commensurately high. At interview they look for enthusiasm, motivation and work/practical experience. The University library is accessible via the University IT Network; personal computers are linked to Uni and national networks; and all students have their personal e-mail numbers.

Its assessment results are superb (see fact box). Most popular subject areas are Physical Sciences, Social Studies, Languages, Humanities, Maths Sciences, Biological Sciences. Interesting strengths include Chinese, Japanese, Arabic, and Latin combinations.

Durham has a fine reputation for getting students employed, and most of the students reveal their colours by falling for the lure of commerce (the city) and milkround industry, which laps them up. You get the feeling they would have come for them anyway, Durham selection procedure being the source of their reputation among prospective employers. University sponsorship and student recruitment figures indicate their approval of the ambitious, highly motivated student, which is the Durham ideal. 'Durham is a seriously city place,' one student said. Some feel they are on something of a conveyor belt. Future accountants, merchant bankers and management consultants sign here.

COLLEGES

There are 15 colleges, including the Graduate Society for post-grads, Ushaw Theological College and University College, Stockton, whose affiliation caused one or two turned-up noses when students were asked what they thought about Durham validating Stockton degrees. Only Stockton is both a residential and teaching college. The rest, unlike Oxbridge colleges, are all purely residential. Situated in an urban regeneration area, Stockton pioneers courses in regional development.

The crucial distinction between the mainstream undergraduate colleges is described in the rivalry between the so-called Bailey Colleges (John's, Chad's, Cuth's, University and Hatfield), situated in the Bailey area of the medieval city and the Hill Colleges (Trev's, VM, Mary's, Collingwood, Grey's and Aiden's), situated SW of the Bailey, on the other side of the river.

The Bailey colleges are older, more traditional, and generally more difficult to get into, especially for state school students. The Hill colleges are modern, have a higher State School intake, and are less the Durham stereotype. Hild Bede, second oldest and largest college, is situated on its own NE of the Bailey and offers a good balance.

Hatfield, Hild Bede and University

College (known as Castle) are best for sport. Hatfield and Castle are best academically. Best college bars are Collingwood, Hild Bede and Castle. Best food at Collingwood and Hatfield.

You can leave college choice to the University, but girls marking their application 'open' are consigned to Mary's (the only all-female establishment).

College accommodation is guaranteed only for Years 1 and 3.

ACTION

In the traditional Durham scene there is something of the dreamy spirit of Oxbridge, punting up the river and so on. And yet even at its best it isn't quite the same. There is a sense of privilege certainly - intake is weighted in favour of independent schools - and the formal social aspect is strong (don't underestimate the cost). Black tie formal dinners are held most weeks at the two most traditional colleges, Hatfield and Castle, and at Hild Bede three times a term. Hill college Collingwood fights back with bigger events known as 'mega formals'. Well-heeled, disenfranchised students (who live out permanently) operate a dinner party circuit. The biggest event in Durham's formal social calendar is the Castle summer ball (£70 a ticket).

Less formal are the discos and gigs at Dunelm House, the Student Union building, and at all the colleges. The Uni prospectus plugs Dunelm, which also offers cafes, bars, cabarets, office, launderette and travel services, a shop ('very competitive prices'), accommodation, legal, welfare support, etc. But some students would disagree - 'SU shop at Dunelm expensive', 'Long queues for travel shop,' etc - and in truth the colleges are the social hub.

'No atmosphere at Dunelm', 'Better bops at colleges, though some of those are pretty bad', 'Dunelm's Kingsgate bar's awful, you're quite sad if you go, but nice view in summer overlooking river' are some of the downside comments which suggest a 20-minute train ride to Newcastle for some real excitement.

But things may be changing. In '96 Dunelm was visited by Ease and the Ministry of Sound, and a group of students called Narcosis brought indie to Hill Bede. But honestly, if it's the club scene you're after, see Newcastle, Manchester or Birmingham. Don't get me wrong, there are plenty of students happy enough with life at Durham, but there are also those who travel the 15 minutes to Newcastle rather than suffer the sweatshop clubs of Durham - 'By the end of three years,' said one, 'most of your social life is in Newcastle; Newcastle becomes the focus.'

Student parties are few, except housewarmings at the start of the year. No raves, relatively few drugs; booze is the thing - so much so that someone has gone into print suggesting there's a real problem. Best publicised drink event (by ex-student Will Carling) is The Duncow challenge (10 pints in 2 hours) and the female equivalent, The Duncalf challenge (10 half-pints). There was a Uni motion to stop it recently.

Although ads focus principally on college/Uni discos, gigs etc, there are many plays, orchestral concerts etc in colleges or at the Uni Assembly Rooms. As with sport, college artistic activity encourages wider participation than at most Unis.

Whatever the shortcomings, there is a spirit about the place which many wouldn't trade - where else would students flock to Uni rugby matches and regattas in such numbers? - and a strong sense of belonging to this close community from the moment you arrive.

TOWN/GOWN

'Survivors of northern industrial wasteland meet yuppy interlopers after 10pm to contest socio-political differences. Taxi service benefits.' It's a tempting headline, and not too far from the truth.

There is a big town/gown problem, which regularly turns violent. One rugby player admitted unease at walking the city after 10. Everyone knows someone who's been attacked. Certain pubs are off-limits, everyone knows which. Female students confirm that you can't go to any pub at weekends. Student ghettoes are vulnerable to burglary, but so are some of the colleges, particularly St Hild & St Bede, situated near the notorious Sherburn Estate. A visiting mother told me about 'problems with knives, bricks through windows,' in the Gilesgate area (near the

Estate). 'I delivered my son to the door of his house there and asked his flatmate what the pile of glass was doing where we parked the car. He said that it was the windscreen of the last car that parked there.' Others see the problem in terms of the selection process preference for public school students and would-be yuppies. Certainly cultural differences between native and student are the main source of antagonism, made challenging by the sudden population swell - a third increase - in term-time. But it is a problem at many other Unis too.

The authorities are aware of it. They encourage students 'to develop good relations with their neighbours and other residents in the city'. As elsewhere volunteers of Student Community Action work with locals. Guidelines have been drawn up by staff and students to discourage harassment and are available from the Personnel Office.

SPORT

Durham is very sporty. Academic concessions for sporty types are apparent, though not admitted. High standards are encouraged by inter-college rivalry, especially Castle vrs Hatfield (rugby) and Castle vrs Hill Bede (rowing). College rowing crews are often better than other Uni crews. The river is a magnetic draw. There are fantastic opportunities for novice rowers. Such are the facilities at college level that it is perfectly feasible to be rowing for the University by your second year. Sixty acres of playing fields are maintained to first class standard. Durham CCC played here in '93. Newcastle United FC use the excellent Sports Centre for training.

VIEW FROM THE GROUND

by Sophie Vokes-Dudgeon

Lying on the banks of the River Wear after exams, sipping Pimms and watching the rowing boats (and lycra clad rowers) weaving their way through the arches. Wandering through the cobbled streets, wrapped up warm in hat and scarf, passing hundreds of familiar faces as the snow falls around you. Going round to tea with one of your course mates at their room in the Castle, overlooking the courtyard, with the cathedral in the background. Going out for a good old boogie in a small naff club, being certain of knowing about 70% of your fellow boppers, and certainly recognising the others. Dressing up in black tie gear for formal dinners and balls, in some of the most beautiful buildings in the country. And most of all, feeling all that hard work was worth while as you go about your daily life, in some of the most spectacular surroundings of any University city, in blissful ignorance of all the stresses and strains of big cities just a few minutes train journey away in Newcastle.

If this sounds like the ideal student life, then Durham's the place for you. But then there's the other side: Standing at the edge of Rixy's dance floor, being sandwiched against the walls literally dripping with sweat as half of the Uni rugby scrum bounce obliviously to 'Football's coming home...', waiting for some 'decent' music, but knowing it won't come. Dodging from lecture theatre to college with your head in your files, praying that that minger you snogged on Wednesday won't also be walking along Elvet too, but knowing they will. Going to the Freshers Fair hoping to join an active political group to actually make a difference, but suddenly becoming blatantly aware that apathy rules in Durham. When you don't even know what Daddy's paying for your education, why would you want to protest against increases? Or perhaps you have a particular aversion to baseball caps, red jeans and black puffa jackets topped off with a spiffing Rah accent, a couple of Golf GTIs and a mobile phone thrown in too. If this is your idea of hell, then whatever you do, don't put Durham on your UCAS form, even just to please Granny.

Of course, I don't mean to imply that if you're not a stinking Rah, that you shouldn't come here (although if you are, you'll certainly fit in). It's just that the abundance of public school luvvies could be stifling for someone who wants to live in the real world and experience all sides of life. If you're looking for the Manchester club scene, and hoping to fall into an 'alternative' way of life, you'll be hard pushed to find it. But there are plenty of normal people too, and the size of the University makes it certain you'll meet someone like you in a couple of days - you could meet *everyone* in a couple of weeks!

Freshers Week is an absolute breeze in Durham, or Freshers few days as it turns out, since Durham terms are only 9 weeks and they can't really spare you a whole ninth of the term to get drunk, go to Rixy's and pull - especially since you'll be doing that all term anyway! With the college system, Durham is one of the friendliest places to start life as a Fresher. All the second and third years come back early to 'help you settle in'. It's quite likely that in the couple of square miles that is Durham, you'll get lost on your way home, but fear not, many an offer to accompany you there will materialise as if by magic! Colleges aren't really like halls of residence, they're more like extended families. Within a couple of days you'll have learnt your college songs and rituals, and feel a strange affiliation with this quaint old set of buildings, which will manifest itself loudly on many a river bank or touch line throughout your life as a Durham student.

Pick your college carefully though. Some are small and cliquey; great if that's what you like, but too much for some people. The stereotypical image we have is of Rahs on the Bailey and Plebs on the Hill. And then there's Hild/Bede, the biggest college, a minute or two further out, perhaps with a more diverse mix than some of the others. Don't go entirely by the stereotypes though, and be sure to visit. I wouldn't suggest an open application either, as you're more than likely to end up in Mary's - the all girls college. Obviously that's more likely to happen if you're female, though rumour has it Hillary someone was designated there until Freshers Week when they realised she was a he!

Since practically all your socialising is done in college, the bar is a vital consideration. The Hill colleges are more like a campus, with Aidans, Mildert, Trevs, Collingwood, Grey and Marys all a drunken stagger from one another. Next to the science site, computers and library too, but what you gain in convenience you certainly lack in history and surroundings. not to mention their devastating distance from Rixy's and Klute! The Bailey colleges, Hatfield, Cuths, Johns, Chads and Castle, are also near enough for a bar crawl, and the cobbled streets and cathedral backdrop make it far more aesthetically pleasing. Chad's and John's bars are barely big enough to swing a cat, however, and you may be more likely to stumble upon Evensong than a pint of lager in St Johns. Hild Bede bar resembles an airport lounge, but the tow path leads to Klute and the beer's cheap so who complains?

Colleges also differ in facilities. Hild Bede has a brand new multi gym, an abundance of tennis courts, squash courts, gymnasiums, and beautiful if basic accommodation. Castle, on the other hand, offers third years the chance to live in a castle, while Collingwood gives you en-suite shower rooms and kettles. The choice is yours!

Another area where Durham excels is in sport. A recognised centre of excellence for cricket and up there with the best in Rowing, our women's eight has been asked to represent England at Henley. And then of course there's rugby. Will Carling - well, need we say more! If you play a sport, Durham will have a team, and a good one at that. What's more, the collegiate system allows all to participate. If you're not good enough for, or don't want to commit to, Uni level, join a college team, many of which play against other university sides, such is the standard. There's also plenty of opportunity to take up new sports: The Hatfield Cup is a very high profile Regatta at the end of the first term where novice rowers compete intercollegiately, taught from scratch by other students.

But no description of Durham would be complete without a mention of reputation. Fight as we may to get courses regarded as equal, and to raise the status of former Polys to universities to rid the system of bias, as yet, reputation sticks. Loathe as I am to put the idea of Accountancy and Management into your heads, a great number of Durham graduates fall into such, admittedly high salaried, questionably mundane employment. If this is your plan then a 'Durham' after your name will undoubtedly help. As many a friend has been informed in interview, 'We only look at Oxford,

Cambridge, Durham and Bristol'. Fair it may not be, but certainly worth considering.

To sum up, Durham has given me the most wonderful three years imaginable. It doesn't have the buzz and excitement of Birmingham, the alternative scene you could find in Manchester, or the work load of Oxford. What it does have is the ability to make you feel like you belong. Peaceful, but certainly not boring. If you've read this and not thought, 'What an absolute nightmare,' you'll love it. Most do.

Stop press: Rixy's has just been re-named Elysium

EAST ANGLIA UNIVERSITY

The University of East Anglia
University Plain
Norwich
NR4 7TJ

TEL 01603 456161
FAX 01603 458553

University of East Anglia
Student Union
Union House
Norwich
Norfolk NR4 7TJ

TEL 01603 503711
FAX 01603 250144

UNIVERSITY OF EAST ANGLIA

Founded	**1963**
Situation/style	**Campus**
UNDERGRADUATE PROFILE	
Application acceptance rate	**10%**
Population	**5,800**
Mature student population	**37%**
Overseas student population	**5%**
Male/female ratio	**51:49**
1st year institut. accommodation	**100%**
Approximate cost	**£40-£50 pw**
ACADEMIC PROFILE	
A-level requirements:	**High**

Law AAA, **English Literature** (also w. **Drama**) ABB-BBB, **Drama** BBB-BBC, **Sociology** BBC, **Applied Psychosocial Studies** BBC-BCC, **Environmental Chemistry** CCC, **Computing Science/Accountancy/Eng.** BBB-CCC, **Maths** BCC-BD, **French & German Lang. with Interp. & Translating** ABC

Student/staff ratio	**10:1**
1st class degree pass rate	**8.1%**
HEFCE assessments (10 subjects assessed/approved):	
1993 **Law**	Excellent
1994 **Applied Social Work, Environmental Studies, Developmental Studies**	Excellent
1995 **Sociology** 20	
1996 **Modern Languages & Linguistics** 19	
Joint Funding Council's research assessment 1996 (27 subjects assessed):	
Environmental Sciences, Scandinavian	Grade 5*
Biol. Sciences, Pure Maths, Social Work, History, Communication/Cultural/Media, Education	Grade 5
EMPLOYMENT PROFILE	

Principal job market destinations: **Commerce, Retail/Wholesale, Manufacturing** (strong **on Electronic & Electrical**), **Health, Education, Arts/Media** (strong), **Hotel/Restaurant, Public Admin./Law**

PIP 1996 employers' survey: Top subject/national ranking	
Science	32nd
Approximate % unemployed	**6.3%**

VAG VIEW

A university founded in the 1960s which has developed along its own paths. A lively atmosphere, set apart in rural Norfolk but reaching out to the world through innovation and flair.

SETTING

UEA campus is fifteen minutes by road from the centre of Norwich, a city less than 15 miles away from the Norfolk Broads, an area of outstanding beauty and tranquility. A bit like York, the city reads like a cultural palimpsest with its modern surface script looking for character in its secondhand stores, cobbled side streets, churches, the cathedral, and its lively street theatre which binds the whole together.

The nearby coastline boasts relics from the golden age of holiday-by-the-sea culture, such as Great Yarmouth to the east and Hunstanton to the north-west. But the whole area from the Wash to Great Yarmouth (including picturesque Cromer) is very worthwhile exploring. Hunstanton was the setting of *Go-Between* author L P Hartley's first novel, *The Shrimp and The Anemone*.

UEA campus has won a number of awards for its architecture, an intriguing foil to the natural beauty of this 320-acre sometime golf course. It revolves around the Square, a student rendezvous, transformed into an open-air disco at the end of the academic year.

GETTING THERE

★ By road: From London it's the A11(M), A47. From the North or the Midlands, A47 Kings Lynn or the new A14 as far as Newmarket and then the A11 to Norwich.
★ By rail: less than 2 hours from London (Liverpool Street); Intercity link via Peterborough with the Midlands (Birmingham New Street, 4:00), the North (Sheffield, 3:50) and Scotland.
★ By air: Norwich airport has regular flights inland and to 200 cities worldwide via Schipol Airport in Amsterdam.

ACADEMIA

UEA can call the tune in its Law department - it demands AAA at A Level - because of the department's American and European Law specialisms. The entry requirements are quite testing altogether, but the Uni has a policy to attract mature students, which it does very successfully, because it feels they enrich the culture of the place and much depends on what their interests are and what they have done. Our correspondent also noted, 'I like to think of UEA as being a fairly relaxed place that is not helplessly caught in the past like certain other establishments. It is not afraid to take a lead from America, and the use of semesters means that it is relatively easy to transfer to America to pick up credits, should your course allow that.'

There are twice yearly literary festivals; they have a professional writer in residence, and it is here that Malcolm Bradbury (author of the classic University novel, *The History Man*) set the literary firmament alight with his creative writing school. The late novelist Angela Carter was involved and Ian McEwan and Kazuo Ishiguro came out of here. Arthur Miller, Thomas Keneally, Fay Weldon, Paul Theroux and our Poet Laureate Ted Hughes have all visited.

Degree programmes are modular. 1,500+ computer workstations and many student bedrooms are connected to the campus network.

ACCOMMODATION

Norfolk, Suffolk and Waveney Terraces, Orwell Close and Wolfson Close provide self-catering accommodation in groups of up to 15 study-bedrooms, Nelson Court and Constable Terrace in slightly smaller groups with en-suite facilities. *The Independent* has described UEA as a 'model for university housing'. Since 1994 accommodation has also been offered in a university village; ten buildings with apartments for 6 to 8 students.

UNION AND ARTS

The Uni has been particularly active on the Internet, pulling together information from Unions throughout the country. The Union has a lively reputation for journalism - their TV station is Nexus TV, their radio station, Livewire. *Concrete* is the newspaper, *Bucket of Tongues*, the student magazine; both won the 1995 *Guardian*/NUS Media Award.

The Studio is the UEA theatre, used by students and outside companies. The city has the Theatre Royal (touring companies, RSC, National) and new repertory theatre, the Playhouse, also Sewell Barn and Maddermarket, smaller theatre companies. There are three cinemas, Cinema City for arthouse, and The Arts Centre for live music, from rock and jazz to chamber music.

SPORT

Good facilities. Eight-lane international athletics track, two floodlit artificial turf hockey pitches, indoor games sports hall, squash courts, tennis/netball courts, fitness centre, plus UEA sports park (40 acres). New indoor sports complex to include 25m swimming pool.

VIEW FROM THE GROUND
by Daniel Trelfer

The campus of UEA and the city of Norwich itself are strangely similar in that both are somewhere in the wilderness, miles away from anywhere. The fact that the nearest town is forty-five minutes away by train, and even then it's only Ipswich, gives you some idea how remote Norwich is. If you drive there you will see nothing but flat lands, tractors and trees for the last half an hour of your journey, a journey that might double in time if you get behind a hay cart, which is more than likely. The campus is three miles from the centre of Norwich, and was uninterestingly built on an old golf course. If you go to the top of the enormous library there, you can see where the bunkers would have been but obviously that is not a valid reason to choose UEA. Everything you need is on campus - there is a bar and another bar. On top of that I believe there are places to eat, a Post Office, a newsagent, some banks, a book shop, and a super market - well, they call it a supermarket, but that is a bit like calling a Mini Babybel a Dutch Edam. This self-containment is a good thing in a way, but while some people are happy to live for 12 weeks inside a square quarter mile, others go insane and have to run to town to feel free again. UEA is certainly the place to come and escape parents/annoying boyfriend or girlfriend/psycho siblings/smog, but be warned, once you come to Norwich you can never leave. That could be a myth, though I just don't know.

THINGS THAT GO ON - CAMPUS

Concert venues are about as common as people who aren't farmers in this part of the country, which actually turns out to be great news, because the LCR campus is the place where bands of reasonable fame will turn up. Face facts though, you won't ever see Noel and Liam there unless they claim they are bigger than Jesus and their whole career falters, but it was not so long ago that Pulp caused all skinny people to get really confident when the band invaded UEA, and The Stone Roses put in a highly-acclaimed appearance last year. Smaller bands such as Space or Fluffy in their fledgling status can be seen at the Union's venue in the city - The Waterfront. It is a smaller place, but bands tend to have a closer relationship with the crowd there as a result. For jazz and blues, the barely-surviving Norwich Arts Centre and Boswells are particularly good, if a little under represented by students. These places usually have older people in them, which can be a bit scary at first because some of them have beards.

The LCR does not only play host to gigs, though. Every Thursday the famous and cleverly titled disco - the 'LCR' (which for anyone faintly interested stands for 'Lower Common Room') staggers into action. It is too sweaty, it has a weird lagery smell to it, it is impossible (almost) to get a drink, and it ends too early (1.30am). Naturally, everybody attends. It is probably the top place to meet partners, and although you could do that at the launderette, it is generally thought odd if you make drunken passes at people, or 'accidentally' tip beer on someone's shoulder, or dance wildly to 'Saturday Night' while waiting for your washing to dry. Thursday nights at UEA are an institution: slagged off, yet appreciated by all. On Tuesday nights, the neighbouring bar, The Hive, presents 'Live in the Hive' which has different events each week, usually consisting of live bands, or weird items such as dodgy freak shows (one time they had a man whose entire act was based on farting), or that game where people put on big Sumo costumes and then fall over. This is not as big an event as the LCR which is just as well because the area is smaller.

CITY

Norwich city centre does offer a fair range of evening entertainment. The aforementioned Waterfront regularly has 80s nights, but then the LCR also has the famed 'Club Retro' (the same as the 'LCR' disco, but with older music). These nights are always popular because people get to wear their old fluorescent and luminous socks they used to wear when Madness were cool. Dance nights are regular, 'Milky Lunch' being the big club event at the Waterfront, and the LCR has presented club nights performed by both Miss Moneypennys and the Ministry of Sound. Apparently the lights are really good. The Waterfront sometimes comes across all generous and does all-nighters, which I'm told are quite good if your batteries are well charged. Of the four or five clubs that blot the city surface, Ritzy is the most popular, because you can get in for 50p on Mondays -

the student night. Ritzy and the couple that are very similar to it are the staple club you will find anywhere in the country - hotter than the inside of a recently roasted chicken, a floor that is worryingly sticky, and too much music by Whigfield. It is advisable to avoid this place at the weekend if you are in the habit of advertising yourself as a student, because the town's youth often become unreasonably riled. The area around Ritzy - eerily called Tombland - is probably the most dangerous in the city, but, again, most trouble will come from advertising your studentness by wearing clothes like Jarvis Cocker. The other dodgy area is near The Waterfront on King Street - it is the Red Light District of Norwich, so be prepared (I mean to be propositioned, not... anyway, it is not the best place to walk by yourself). Ironically, the worst place is 'The University Arms' near campus, where they throw pitch forks at you, should you breach their doorway. This report is unconfirmed because I've never had the guts to go in there and verify it, as it is on top of a hill, like Norman Bates's house was.

Apparently, Norwich has a pub for every day of the year. Unfortunately to describe all 365, although well within my capacity, would be over-long and over-dull. However, The Murderers is a popular venue for a pre-club beverage or two, and a good place to watch the football on Sky. Just outside the city The York Tavern comes highly recommended, but if you really are into town culture, Jampin' Jaks and Chicago Cafe are good options for loud music and no room to sit down. Failing that, the Union Bar has loud music, usually Oasis, but often taking a downward slide to Queen, or veering to The Stone Roses. There is a huge selection of drinks, but most people seem more than happy paying a measly £1 a pint for Heineken. They have two blue pool tables as well! And they're much better than the green type! If you simply can't be bothered to cook, The Diner serves up main meals of a reasonable standard, but the place does smell of primary school dinner halls (i.e. cabbage), while the controversial Piccolo's serves pizza and pasta, but is always ready with chips and beans if needs be. I say 'controversial' firstly because it makes me sound like Angus Deayton, and secondly because Piccolo's replaced the revered Breakers which sold junk food in large quantities, and some people became quite nostalgic and upset when it was binned. As a result there are rumours that a late night kebab place or a chippy might soon appear, but that's confidential information. The best place on campus is probably The Sainsbury Centre, which is really an arts centre, but has a cool cafe that not many people use. In town, students' favourites include Pedros, which serves Mexican food in quantities to satisfy Mr Creosote, the downside being you are forced to wear overlarge sombreros, the brim of which could blind someone should you choose to twist your head too quickly in the manner of The Exorcist Girl. Across the road from Ritzy is the ever-expanding restaurant. Originally called Pizza One, it has now settled on Pizza One, Pasta Too, and Pancakes Three. It is fairly priced, and often does special student offers. Apart from that it's the usual melting pot of fast-food and dodgy pub lunches you would find in any normal city, although there is a really expensive lobster place that no-one can afford to go to, so that was a bit irrelevant really.

ACCOMMODATION

Accommodation on campus has caused quite a rumpus recently because of rent increases, but it's still about a third cheaper than in London. There are different standards on campus. Waveney, Norfolk, and Suffolk Terraces are all very similar, although Waveney looks like prison, without bars on the windows, obviously. People in Waveney have a real community spirit because the space is small, and there are loads of people on each corridor. Nelson Court and Constable Terrace are the best places, but are subject to unreasonable rent increases, and prices are currently hovering at around the £50 a week mark, which is a little unbelievable when you realise that good houses in the city tend to average at about £36 a week. Having said this, the buildings are so white that they look like they have been cleaned in an oversized washing machine full of Daz Ultra, and you get your own en-suite bathroom so it feels like a hotel, a bit, anyway. The Village had a terrible start with damp problems, but now seems to have become quite civilised. Mary Chapman Court is actually in the city, which means you can be excluded from a lot of University activities such as drinking, but people who live there turn out to be much closer to each other than in any other accommodation; siege mentality, apparently. Incidentally, I should point out that there were bedbugs in some of the beds in Waveney Terrace this year, but, apparently, they only like human flesh, so...oh, no wait, that's bad. They'll be gone by the time you get there...

When you have to move off campus, it is advisable to aim for the legendary 'Golden Triangle' area where many students live. Unfortunately, no-one is sure where the boundaries lie.

ON THE WHOLE - SPORTS, MEDIA ETC.

There is an indoor sports centre on campus to complement the running track, two artificial pitches (well they're real, but the grass is, oh, you knew what I meant, sorry), and the large sports field area at the rear of the University. There is also a very deep lake on campus, but people tend to play weird dungeons and dragons games around it, or have barbecues, rather than go windsurfing or water ski-ing. However, whatever sports interest you have, UEA almost guarantees a society that deals with it. The media is quite strong, boasting a newspaper (Concrete), a television station (Nexus) and a radio station that broadcasts just to the campus (Livewire 945am). I have rarely found UEA lacking in any interests I have had in my time there (apart from the time I wanted a society that specialised in playing winter sports such as bobsleigh in the nude, and I couldn't find one nor generate any great interest in my idea), and although I admit to knowing little about religion and politics movements there, I am sure anyone can make the most out of what the various groups and parties have to offer. It does often seem to me, though, that there is a fair amount of apathy at UEA on the politics front, which may or may not reflect the youth of the whole nation. It appears that the only issues anyone becomes passionate about are rent increases, or, for example, earlier this year the Union voted to boycott 'Loaded' magazine, when most people, due to apathy, had no idea the motion was being put forward at the General Meeting. Of course, you are free to make your own judgements on UEA and Norwich, but remember, some excellent stars have emerged from this so-called sleepy area; famous TV fisherman, John Wilson, Delia Smith, and ...er....Alan Partridge. What better evidence of a fun, exciting and downright exhilarating place can you get than the stamp of approval from those three? The final message is clear, then: Come to UEA and mix with the STARS.

EAST LONDON UNIVERSITY

The University of East London
Romford Road
Stratford
London
E15 4LZ

TEL 0181 590 7000
FAX 0181 519 3740

University of East London
Student Union
(Barking Campus)
Union Building
Longbridge Road
Dagenham
Essex RM8 2AS

TEL 0181 590 6017
FAX 0181 597 6987

University of East London
Student Union
(Stratford Campus)
Maryland House
Manbey Park Road
Stratford
London E15 1EY

TEL 0181 555 8447/8
FAX 0181 221 1719

UNIVERSITY OF EAST LONDON

Founded	**1970**
Situation/style	**Campus, 2 sites**
UNDERGRADUATE PROFILE	
Application acceptance rate	**11%**
Population	**8,335**
Mature student population	**55%**
Overseas student population	**8%**
Male/female ratio	**50:50**
1st year institut. accommodation	**25%**
Approximate cost (Uni)	**£35-£55 pw**
(City)	**£45-£60 pw**
ACADEMIC PROFILE	
A-level requirements:	**Low**

Law, Architecture 6-20, **Psychology** 12-24, **Nursing** – no 'A's, but AGNVQ, **Physiology, Biological Sciences, Civil, E & E, Manufac. Eng, Computer-aided Eng. Design,** 100+ **Sociology/Anthropology combinations,** also **Social Policy, Business Studies combs., Modern Lang. combs., Media Studies combs.** 6-14

Student/staff ratio	**20:1**
1st class degree pass rate	**5.5%**
HEFCE assessments (11 subjects assessed/approved):	
1994 **Architecture, English**	Excellent
1996 **Sociology** 19, **Modern Languages** 18	
Joint Funding Council's research assessment 1996 (20 subjects assessed):	
Communication/Cultural/ Media	Grade 5
EMPLOYMENT PROFILE	
Principal job market destinations:	

Health, Retail/Wholesale, Manufacturing, Public Admin./Law, Arts/Media, Education, Personnel, Commerce

Approximate % unemployed	**12.5%**

VAG VIEW

In the University of East London we have a university truly of the people. Formerly East London Poly it operates, as its new name suggests, in the East End of London, traditionally one of the soul cultures of the Metropolis. Since the war the East End has enveloped into itself a diverse immigrant population. It is a lively, evolutionary culture and the Uni is an integral part of it, its stated mission 'to provide the highest possible quality of education in order to meet' - not the needs of the country or Europe or the world, but - 'the needs of individuals and of the communities and enterprises in our region.'

UEL draws a large proportion of its students from the area, and the needs it identifies are targeted specifically in a number of its courses. Of the twenty research subjects which it submitted for assessment last year to the Joint Funding Council, one only achieved a 5 rating. But it is wholly pertinent to UEL's ethos that the subject was Communication, Cultural & Media Studies.

One of our educational advisers said to us, 'Mistrust any course that has the word "studies" in it.' But at UEL things are a bit different. For their BA (Hons) Cultural Studies course, for example, they want students from diverse social, intellectual and cultural backgrounds and they find a number of them on their doorstep. 'The course,' said one graduate, who went on to edit Sky *magazine, 'gives fuel to things you're already thinking about and puts them in context.'*

SETTING

Its two sites are in Stratford, just off the Broadway at Romford Road and Water Lane, and in Barking, on Longbridge Road and Goodmayes Lane, to the north and south of which is green parkland. A third campus is under construction in London's Docklands and will open in 1999.

GETTING THERE

★ Stratford is on the Central Line, half an hour from Oxford Circus in the centre of the West End of London.
★ The closest overland rail station is Maryland (connect London Liverpool Street).
★ Barking Underground station (on the Metropolitan and District lines) is a bit of a hike away up Longbridge Road to the Barking Campus, and one station up the line (Upney) may even be a tad closer. Goodmayes overland station, five stops up from Maryland, is a short walk up Goodmayes Lane.

ACCOMMODATION

On-site student accommodation on the Barking Campus comprises groups of flats for 6 with shared kitchen/diner, shower, bathrooms and toilets. In Stratford it's either a university house or flat-share at one of two sites in the West Ham area nearby.

ACADEMIA

Four Schools - *Design, Engineering and the Built Environment*: Architecture, Art & Design, Fashion & Marketing, Civil, Manufacturing, Electrical & Electronic Eng., Surveying. *The Business School*. *Science and Health*: Environmental Sciences, Health and Life Sciences, Maths & Physical Sciences, Psychology. *Faculty of Social Sciences*: Cultural Studies, Economics, Education & Community Studies, Innovation Studies (range of undergraduate degrees in the study of the relationship between society and technical change), Languages & Linguistics, Sociology, Third World Studies, Women's Studies, Social Work, Politics, etc.

ENTS

There's not quite the same sense of separateness of student from town culture that you find in most Unis, so many of the students being of the area. There are good pubs and ethnic eateries, and clubs popular among students include the Island in Ilford, and Secrets and Ritzy in Romford. Just opening in Barking is Wild Styles. Some students take to the city centre and recommend SW1, the Satellite, the Gardening Club and Camden Palace. Coaches are sometimes arranged for mass student migration.

Bars at both campuses are transformed into clubs at night with bands, club nights - Indie, '80s, Jungle, Hip-hop, Ragga - comedy acts, talent contests, and special events - Spring Ball, Valentine's Bash, Diwali Rave, Hallowee'n Night/Rocky Horror Nite, Christmas Rave. Recent bands include Goats Don't Shave, Urban Species, General Levy.

On the representation front, the Students Union is active in sorting out students' hassles of any kind.

SPORT

Sport centres on the Barking campus - a swimming pool is used also for water polo, sub-aqua and canoeing; there are two gyms, facilities for aerobics, dance, badminton, table-tennis, karate, circuit training, volleyball, basketball, indoor football, a squash court, four tennis courts, a fitness centre. Playing fields are at Little Heath, 3 miles away. Badminton is available near the Stratford Campus and there are other recreational activities on offer - golf, sailing, windsurfing, skiing, sub-aqua, riding, and a variety of weekend and vacation courses are arranged.

EDGE HILL UNIVERSITY COLLEGE

Edge Hill University College
St Helens Road
Ormskirk
Lancashire
L39 4QP

TEL 01695 575171
FAX 01695 579997

Edge Hill University College
Student Union
St. Helens Road
Ormskirk
Lancs. L39 4QP

TEL 01695 575457/584255
FAX 01695 577904

EDGE HILL UNIVERSITY COLLEGE	
Founded	**1885**
Situation/style	**Campus**
UNDERGRADUATE PROFILE	
Application acceptance rate	**16%**
Population	**3,450**
Mature student population	**34%**
Overseas student population	**1%**
Male/female ratio	**32:68**
1st year institut. accommodation	**100%**
Approximate cost	**£31-£54 pw**
ACADEMIC PROFILE	
A-level requirements:	**Low**
Teacher Training CC-DD. Examples from BA/BSc Modular Scheme: **Afro Asian Studies** CD, **Applied Social Sciences** CC, **Drama** CC, **Geography** DD, **Sports Studies** CC	
Student/staff ratio	**20:1**
1st class degree pass rate	**1.4%**
HEFCE assessments (6 subjects assessed/approved):	
1995 **Social Policy & Administration**	Excellent
Joint Funding Council's research assessment 1996 (9 subjects assessed):	
Grade 5/5*	None
EMPLOYMENT PROFILE	
Principal job market destinations: **Education, Retail/Wholesale, Commerce, Public Admin, Health**	
Approximate % unemployed	**10%**

VAG VIEW

Situated fifteen minutes walk from Ormskirk in Lancashire - this is an area buzzing with action in Higher Education, Liverpool, Manchester, Preston, Blackburn, Blackpool, Lancaster are all centres nearby - Edge Hill is a university sector college, whose degrees are awarded by the University of Lancaster.

They offer degrees or diplomas in the Arts, Humanities, Management, Environmental and Social Sciences. Particularly interesting Single or Major Honours degree subjects are Applied Science for Environmental Mgt., Field Biology and Habitat Mgt., Gender & Development, and a range of Urban social studies which impinge on Race, Sport and Mgt. Edge Hill have already proved themselves in the Social Sciences area with an 'Excellent' in Social Policy & Admin two years ago. The preponderance of female students (see fact box) is down to the Health Faculty in Fazakerley, Liverpool, which offers diplomas in Nursing and Midwifery.

The BA/BSc degree scheme is strictly modular. Edge Hill is a slick set-up with its boss calling himself a Chief Executive and a team of marketing and communications executives backing him up.

Edge Hill has outstanding technological back-up, for example, the student:workstation ratio is apparently 7:1. With around a third of students being mature, and living locally, and with Ormskirk not being exactly a global centre of entertainment, prospective students shouldn't expect a wild time. The Rose Theatre on campus is used for student theatre and music events, and by visiting companies. Otherwise campus social life revolves around The Venue, which offers the usual fare, cheap beer, bar with ents such as discos and quiz nights. The campus social scene usually finishes at 11pm, but occasionally coach trips are laid on by the college to one of the big cities nearby - Preston, Manchester, Liverpool.

Accommodation is either mixed or single sex, some self-catering and some with breakfast and dinner included. Obvious advantages of living on the campus are proximity to lectures and libraries, and access to Uni amenities, including the 40 sporting and social groups on offer.

GETTING THERE

★ By road: M6 (J26), M58 (J3), A570 to Southport. The university is two miles along on the right.

★ By rail: Local Northern Line Merseyrail train connections to Ormskirk from Liverpool Central and Preston intercity stations. Alight at Ormskirk station, not Edge Hill.

VIEW FROM THE GROUND

by Peter Cooper

Edge Hill University is based in Ormskirk, a small town on the outskirts of Liverpool. It takes about thirty minutes by train into Liverpool city centre. The campus is about ten minutes walk from the centre of Ormskirk. Ormskirk has a thriving market on Fridays and Saturdays and is well served by supermarkets. It is a small friendly community that caters for the basics. Liverpool, Preston and even Manchester are easily accessible.

STUDENTS PROFILE AND SOCIAL SCENE

They basically fall into two categories, students who live on and off campus and enjoy the student social life, and mature students who live and commute locally to college. There are a large number of mature students at Edge Hill, and due to family commitments, the majority of them use the college only for its academic purposes. There is a common room where they can socialise during the day as well as all the catering amenities. In my experience the mature students who live locally with young families find the going tough. They have to be very determined and have supportive partners.

It is mainly younger students who enjoy the campus social life. The college bar is large and spacious with prices that are cheaper than most pubs. The Union has an elected Entertainments Officer who maps out the year's entertainment. The best nights are at the end of terms when everyone is in party mood. There are disco nights with local well-known DJs, party nights, quiz nights and unplugged nights where students can show off their musical talents. There are also occasionally live guest bands. Apart from these in-house entertainments, there are the cheap college nights out to a club in Southport, where the drinks are £1 all night, and various coach trips to Liverpool, Manchester and Leeds. The local pubs are varied but there are no night clubs in Ormskirk. There are several local takeaways, including one on campus, which are cheap. One of the local pubs does an excellent 3-course Sunday lunch for £4, and other bar meals for £1.99. Most pubs have cheap menus catering for students. The one complaint about the night life from the younger students, is the closing time of the college bar which is 11.00 pm, apart from the occasional extension.

It would be wrong to say that there is no tension between locals and students. But this is mainly on a Friday and Saturday night when people from the surrounding areas come in for a drink. There has been no major incident during the 12 months I've lived on campus. The only contentious issue is a local residency group who complain about the noise from the students when leaving the bar at closing time.

ACCOMMODATION

The halls of residence are situated on the campus. There is self-catering and packaged meals. The packaged meals are taken in the Terrace Cafe and consist of breakfast and evening meal. At weekends students get two meals. On Saturday they get a brunch and on Sundays they get an evening meal. The quality of the food is not considered to be very good by the majority of students. It is by far the most complained about facility.

What is the advantage of living on campus? The social life and access to University amenities. There are plenty of sporting and social groups that you can join. Fifty in total ranging from the Irish Society, Footlights (the amateur dramatic society), to football and badminton.

If you like a small community where you are likely to get to know everyone then this is a good campus. It is a relatively safe place and although it might not have all the facilities of a larger university it compensates with its friendly atmosphere.

EDINBURGH UNIVERSITY

The University of Edinburgh
Old College
South Bridge
Edinburgh
EH8 9YL

TEL 0131 650 1000
FAX 0131 650 2147

Edinburgh University Students Association
Student Centre House
5/2 Bristo Square
Edinburgh EH8 9AL

TEL 0131 650 2656
FAX 0131 668 4177

Edinburgh Uni. Students Ass.
King's Building House
King's Building
Mayfield Road
Edinburgh EH9 3JF

TEL 0131 650 5572
FAX 0131 650 6720

Edinburgh Uni. Students Ass.
PAMS House (Postgraduate and Mature Students)
22-24 Buccleuch Place
Edinburgh EH8 9LN

TEL 0131 650 4016

Edinburgh Uni. Students Ass.
Potterrow (Mandela Centre House)
Student Centre House
5/4 Bristo Square
Edinburgh EH8 9AL

TEL 0131 650 8091

Edinburgh Uni. Students Ass.
Teviot Row House
13 Bristo Square
Edinburgh EH8 9AJ

TEL 0131 650 4673
FAX 0131 650 6966

Edinburgh Uni. Students Ass.
Societies Centre
60 Pleasance
Edinburgh EH8 9TJ

TEL 0131 650 2349
FAX 0131 650 6383

UNIVERSITY OF EDINBURGH

Founded	**1583**
Situation/style	**City sites**
UNDERGRADUATE PROFILE	
Application acceptance rate	**10%**
Medical AAR	**10%**
Population	**12,800**
Mature student population	**12%**
Overseas student population	**7%**
Male/female ratio	**52:48**
1st year institut. accommodation	**100%**
Approximate cost	**£46-£72 pw**
ACADEMIC PROFILE	
A-level requirements:	**High**

Medicine AAB:
★ Science 'A's required **Chemistry + 2 of Biol., Maths, Physics @ 1 sitting**
★ Addit. Non-Science 'A's acceptable **Yes if academic**
★ Retakes considered **Ext. circs.**
★ Retake offer **AAA**
★ Clinical contact **3rd year**

Student/staff ratio	**7:1**
1st class degree pass rate	**8.6%**
SHEFC assessments (22 subjects assessed/approved):	
1994 **Civil Engineering, Music, Architecture**	Highly satis.
Computer Studies, Physics	Excellent
1995 **Business & Management, Geography**	Highly satis.
Chemistry, Electrical & Electronic Engineering, Geology, Maths & Statistics	Excellent
1996 **History of Art, Law, Philosophy, Politics, Theology**	Highly satis.
History, Finance & Accounting, Sociology, Social Work	Excellent
Joint Funding Council's research assessment 1996 (54 subjects assessed):	
Electrical & Electronic Eng., Geography	Grade 5*
Hospital/Clinical, Biol. Sciences, Agriculture, Chemistry, Physics, Earth Sciences, Pure Maths, Computer, Sociology, Accountancy, Economic & Social History	Grade 5
EMPLOYMENT PROFILE	
Employability in Industry:	
MPW national league table (1996)	**6th=**

Principal job market destinations:
Health, Commerce (strong), Manufacturing (strong on **Electronic & Electrical**), **Retail/Wholesale, Public Admin./Law, Education, Veterinary, Arts/Media** (strong), **Computer**

PIP 1996 employers' survey: Top 3 subjects/national ranking	
Accountancy/Finance & Banking	2nd
Languages	2nd=
Business	3rd
Approximate % unemployed	**7%**

VAG VIEW

'If you are looking at the employers' surveys or parents' perceptions, then it's Oxbridge then Durham and Bristol, and Edinburgh is the Scottish equivalent of these...Edinburgh, they know, is the place to be.' View from an English careers adviser.

The Students Association produces a Survival Guide to Edinburgh, the city, and student living, which runs to some 300 pages and answers just about every question a student, who knows little of Edinburgh, could possibly ask. Get hold of a copy from the Union. Four years seems barely sufficient to sample what is on offer - bars, cafes, bistros, restaurants, pubs, live music venues, clubs, theatre, commercial and art cinemas, galleries, sport facilities - all are described with great clarity and style, but with a kind of avuncular patronage which would remind me, if I were coming to Edinburgh from a different sort of home a long way away, that I was about to become but one insignificant particle in its long history. It is not patronising; on the contrary, there is a sense in which Edinburgh is more complex than even the authors have managed to suss. Indeed, any guidebook can only hope to scrape the surface of this intriguing city. A quest for its true spirit must be made in person.

On the surface Edinburgh is a clean, open, friendly city, redolent of its history. Our contributor, Holly Crane, the editor responsible for some of the best journalism that has come out of the University in recent times, makes the point that the city strikes a fair balance between big opportunities and friendliness. But the spirit of Edinburgh is a deep run thing, and its complexity has attracted the attention of writers for centuries. It is something of a split personality. Charting its dissipations have been Dunbar, Fergusson and their modern imitators; charting its guilty secrets under the heavy cloak of Calvinism have been writers such as Stevenson and McGaig. When you arrive you will be thrown into its dissipations in Freshers Week; a few of you may take the next four years to dig deeper for its real secrets.

Our image from afar - largely owed to the international impact of The Edinburgh Festival - is of an artistic city, and you will not be disappointed if that is what warms you to the idea of coming here. But art is often born out of the trauma of split, and rather appropriately we find evidence of the Jekyll and Hyde nature of the place in the Edinburgh University Theatre Company, which entertains its audience in what was once the site of Bristo Bedlam, where the 'mad, manic and mental' were locked away. Again, we find that none other than Robert Louis Stevenson, the author of 'Jekyll and Hyde', founded the student newspaper, Student, *in 1887. There is, as I say, much more to Edinburgh than meets the eye, though you can of course opt for the bops and let the challenge of its identity pass you by.*

SETTING

The Uni is set in the heart of this historic, capital city of Scotland, not all of it on a self-contained campus, though the focus is around George Square, where some of the buildings date from 1776.

GETTING THERE

★ By road: M90 from the north across the Forth Bridge or the M9 down from Stirling. The A1 up from Newcastle. The M8 from Glasgow.

★ By rail, part of the fast north-east line which leads eventually to London Kings Cross (4:30). Glasgow Central is 50 mins. away; Newcastle 1:30.

★ By air: Edinburgh Airport is a few miles to the West and offers inland and international flights.

ACCOMMODATION

Pollock Halls is the main residential complex, where most first years are accommodated. It is a group of rather ugly buildings but the ground of Holyrood Park rises up behind and makes something of a view, and you do get waited on hand and foot - cooking, cleaning, your bed linen is laundered, etc, and there are video nights and sport competitions, music rooms, squash courts, a computer room, and a bar of course. Now, too, they are providing single rooms with en-suite bathroom facilities.

Mylnes Court Halls are nearer the central Uni area, in the shadow of the Castle and within easy walking distance of Waverley Station, part of the Old Town, which is the most interesting area of the city. There is a lovely view over the New Town and the Forth. Alas, these halls, in one of the most sought after areas of the city, are reserved for postgraduate students. But maybe your day will come. You could, however, choose to live in a Uni-owned flat, which might be shared by as few as 3 or as many as 6, and in a few cases 12 students.

A compromise between halls and flats are Uni-owned student houses, which are part supervised (there's a warden, a cleaner and some senior residents), though they are very often positioned farther away from the main area than either of the other two types of accommodation.

UNION & ENTS

Everyone talks about The Edinburgh Festival, but the city also features the most popular student Hogmanay (New Year) celebrations anywhere in Britain - hundreds of thousands of students from all over the country congregate to express themselves (and a few other things besides).

Alongside the more administrative/student-political SRC (Students Representative Council) is Edinburgh's massively busy Student Association - it occupies no less than 8 buildings, and if you lock on to their web pages via JANET you will find a map which shows that they operate in more.

Teviot-Row House is the centre of many events. Sunday might see a drinks promotion in Teviot Sportsman's Bar, or a pool tournament, or Teviot Pursuit (a quiz). As the week gets going, there will be comedy, cabaret, leading to theme nights and club nights mid-week - 'Funk and hip-hop to alternative Indie: a musical pick 'n' mix.' Then perhaps it's off to the Pleasance Bar, the societies' centre of operations (there are over 130 clubs and societies), which, besides a bar, has a theatre and a function room used as a cabaret venue. Regular Friday nights at Teviot are disco or live bands, and Upstairs at PAMS - the postgrad and mature student Union - there'll probably be something to suit less frantic tastes. On Saturday it's off to the Potterrow, which has club nights, facilities for private parties, pool tables and games machines. Or maybe you'll brave the King's Buildings, set apart from the central university area. The King's Buildings are where the Science and Engineering students hang out. Unfortunately no-one could tell me what goes on there, because the media is of course run by Arts. You could say that this odd segregation is another example of the ever-present duality, characteristic of Edinburgh's spirit, a spirit which writers like Stevenson and Hogg (in his Private Memoirs and Confessions of a Justified Sinner) picked up on to such weird effect.

ACADEMIA

'An Edinburgh degree is a very good degree to have. They don't admit to offering a Scottish quota, but I think that it is still considered to be part of a Scottish person's birthright, if that is what they want. High qualifications are required by English students. But then you don't know what they actually take in Scottish Highers.'

Medicine, Veterinary Science, Health, Agriculture, Biological and Physical Sciences, Maths Sciences, Engineering, Social Studies (including Law, Politics), Languages, Humanities. There is little not represented, other than Mass Communications, Education.

They boast an incredible 2,275,000 volumes in the library, and excellent computer facilities and language laboratories. Yet there is a problem in getting to use some of these resources, so our contributor tells us.

SPORT

The University is pre-eminent in sport. Besides its 25-acres of playing fields and a residential centre on the shore of Loch Tay, there's a sports centre with conditioning gymnasia, a fitness and sports injury centre, and a wide range of team and individual activities. Sports bursaries are offered through the Physical Education Department.

VIEW FROM THE GROUND
by Holly Crane

There is a discernable buzz about Edinburgh University: a condensed feeling of potential, and energy. This is partly due to the city itself: there's just enough of the 'ivory tower' atmosphere to leave you inspired but not oppressed by your impending academia. But it's also to do with the type of people. With many doing four year (or longer) degrees, there is if not more time, then more reason, to get up off your arse and do something a bit different. There is a very active theatre society, radio station and newspaper, as well as over 160 other societies to choose from, before you even begin to go into the sports clubs. Every student at Edinburgh University seems to be involved in some activity or other, even if it's only because their flatmate drags them along to fundraising events from time to time.

It would be impossible for one Arts student to write anything too specific about the academic side of Edinburgh University that would be universally useful. The range of academic disciplines and methods is as wide as the range of opportunities coming to Edinburgh opens up to you.

There's a very real split in the campus between Science (Kings' Buildings) and the Arts (George Square). George Square is an easy walk from the centre of town, and surrounded by a vast choice of pubs, coffee houses and restaurants. The Scientists ('KB kids') get much the worse deal, as their campus, about one hour's walk from George Square, is out of the way. This means that the fairly reasonable catering and entertainment facilities provided for students and staff begin to pall after a while. Smaller faculties, such as Medicine and Law, are very active, and generate their own sense of community. With 17,000 students (and rising), however, you'd be hard pushed to find a sense of identity in the larger faculties.

That doesn't mean you're destined to get swallowed up by the anonymity of a big city, however. That's the beauty of Edinburgh: it gets the balance between big city opportunities and small town friendliness just right. Whatever it is you want to do, you're guaranteed to be able to find both it and a group of people who want to do it with you. Become a stand-up comic; go to the theatre; become a fine art, wine or food connoisseur; dig up roads for charity; discover your sexuality; start a band; debate international issues; explore religion, role-playing or politics; try them all. And, by the end of your three or four years, provided you make a tiny amount of effort, you'll have discovered a fair few things you didn't know you wanted to do, too. It's all out there, but you have to be prepared to look for it.

The same applies to socialising. The late licensing hours mean you can happily talk animatedly into the early hours over a bottle of wine or a string of pints. But this doesn't mean there isn't a clubbing culture - rather it gives you another option, or something to do beforehand, depending on which way you look at it. There are a lot of elegantly trendy clubs here, as well as your average cheesey sharking joint. And you have five separate Union buildings to choose from, just at *your* University. If you were rich enough, you could go out every night for a month and do something different (the average price of a pint is around £1.80 - £1.30 in the Unions - so start calculating). If you're not rich, there's plenty of cheaper ways to go about entertaining yourself, from walks and free entry galleries, to throwing yourself into a society and the social life that goes with that.

I know everyone is supposed to fall in love with their university city, but Edinburgh just makes it so easy. Like all universities these days, however, it is losing out because of government funding cuts. Not only are queues for the Crisis Loans lengthening, but study resources are being stretched to the limit, and lecture rooms seem to become more crowded even as you watch. The main library in George Square, in particular, is extremely understocked. If you want to study a course which relies heavily on books, you should be prepared either to buy your own, get up very early in the day, or become adept at hiding anything pertaining to your essays.

Rented accommodation is another hotly contested property up here, with £175 per month being fairly average rent. Although at some point during your laboured search for a home, you're likely to believe you'll end up on the streets, it never quite happens. Those who have the best deals rent-wise are those who can afford their own flats - or who've found a friend who can.

Despite the threatening shadows of decreasing funding and increasing prices, Edinburgh still manages to shine with that feeling of excitement and vitality peculiar to your university years. It's the ideal advert for Higher Education: a place where you learn not only facts and formulae from your academic studies, but also about what you can do, what you want to do - and what you don't want to do - with the rest of your life.

ESSEX UNIVERSITY

The University of Essex
Wivenhoe Park
Colchester
Essex
CO4 3SQ

TEL 01206 873333
FAX 01206 873598

University of Essex
Student Union
Wivenhoe Park
Colchester
Essex CO4 3SQ

TEL 01206 863211
FAX 01206 870915

UNIVERSITY OF ESSEX

Founded	**1964**
Situation/style	**Campus**
UNDERGRADUATE PROFILE	
Application acceptance rate	**17%**
Population	**4,100**
Mature student population	**33%**
Overseas student population	**28%**
Male/female ratio	**54:46**
1st year institut. accommodation	**100%**
Approximate cost	**£33-£52 pw**
ACADEMIC PROFILE	
A-level requirements:	**Medium-high**
Law BBB, **Accounting** 20, **Psychology** 22, **Sociology** 20, **English/French/German and Linguistics** 20, **Computer Science** 20	
Student/staff ratio	**8:1**
1st class degree pass rate	**8.1%**
HEFCE assessments (7 subjects assessed/approved):	
1993 **Law**	Excellent
1995/6 **Sociology** 22, **Linguistics** 21	
Joint Funding Council's research assessment 1996 (18 subjects assessed):	
Politics, Sociology	Grade 5*
Law, Economics, History of Art/Architecture/Design	Grade 5
EMPLOYMENT PROFILE	
Employability in Industry:	
MPW national league table (1996)	**49th=**
Principal job market destinations:	
Commerce, Retail/Wholesale, Public Admin./Law, Computer, Manufacturing, Education	
PIP 1996 employers' survey:	
Top subject/national ranking	
Social Science/Economics	18th=
Approximate % unemployed	**5%**

VAG VIEW

The move to a modular structure has brought a variety of responses from universities, some trying to tack it on to the traditional degree structure, some going mad with so many options that neither students nor their eventual employers know what their specialisms are. Essex proposes its own well thought out solution, which goes a long way to maintaining the advantages of both approaches.

Essex is also a great place to be if you're a student, and not only because you'll be so near London. The student scene here is great, an island haven in a sea of commuter anxieties.

SITUATION

Colchester, capital of Roman Britain, is today a regional centre of commerce, light industry and high technology (population 150,000). It is also a dormitory city for commuters to London, 55 minutes away by train. But more than this, nearby, to the east, there is a mass of delightful creeks, estuaries and villages and still plenty of gently rolling countryside all about.

The campus comprises 200 acres of landscaped parkland, two miles from the centre of Colchester. It is modern, not to everyone's taste perhaps, but it was conceived as a university town from the start and there's a good atmosphere as well as good facilities.

GETTING THERE

★ By road: Exit A12 for Colchester. Visitors car park Pay and Display.
★ Well served by coach services, either direct or via London.
★ By rail: Trains from London Liverpool Street (1:00) to Colchester North every half-hour - this is commuter territory. Connections to Norwich, Ipswich (0:25), Felixstowe, Harwich, Clacton/Walton.
★ Ten minute taxi run to Campus. Birmingham New Street (3:30); Sheffield (4:00).

ACCOMMODATION

Purpose-built accommodation, 70% of which is on campus. Off-campus accommodation is 10 to 30 minutes walk away, and well served by buses. There was a rumpus recently when an anonymous fax was sent to *Parklife*, the student newspaper alleging that university accommodation was being let off to the public sector when students were being refused it. But worry not, all first years are guaranteed a place.

ACADEMIA

Good undergrad. and research assessments. Note also large overseas student population. Traditionally strong links with Europe (ties with 50+ Euro Unis), and Socrates/Erasmus exchange schemes proliferate; also Tempus (East/West).

Modular course structure phased in from end-'95 (CATS system), but flexibility and choice bonus of modular structure has not been allowed to weaken the traditional coherence of degrees offered - you'll know what you'll come away with and employers will be in no doubt what you've been up to in the 3 or 4 years study. They do this by throwing open the first year to study of a grouping of four or five courses according to a strategy which will enable you to investigate your main subject from a variety of different but enlightening points of view. For example, in Social Sciences this may involve studying Sociology from an Economics point of view, History from a Psychology pov - wherever Social Science subjects intersect will be the focus. Then in the second year you can move forward to a specific degree (Single or Joint Honours) - Psychology, Economics, whatever you choose, with a far deeper understanding of it than if you had embarked on it straight away.

Five Schools of Study - Comparative Studies (Humanities, but with a cross cultural, internationalist approach), Social Sciences, Law, Maths & Computer Sciences, Science & Engineering.

Good central computing facilities, all connected to the Internet.

UNION AND ENTS

Societies: Music (Classical to Jungle), Religious (Chinese Christian to Gregorian), Political (Conservatives to Fifth Monarchists), Cultural (the widest selection: Afro Caribbean to Friends of Palestine), Campaigns (active: from Legalise Cannabis to International Women's, from Amnesty International to Shelter), Departmental, etc.

Parklife is the student newspaper, and Nicola Mends is the current editor, whose Student Handbook is about the clearest, well-paced, balanced, unpartisan one we've seen.

Excellent secondhand bookshop (student buy 'n' sell) operated by the Union. All-day opening student bar, refurbished and freshly equipped after a fire a year or so ago with more pool tables, better jukebox, etc. On the floor below is Level 2, an events venue come night club, with late bar extensions, comedy nights, society nights, local bands, discos, drink promotions, etc. Beware Wednesday evenings if you're allergic to rugger buggers - it's Sports Fed night. Otherwise it's the Dancehall for bigger bands and Hot 'n' Sticky Fridays.

The Union's programme of live bands is a deliberately broad-based mix - something for everyone out of club tours, discos, comedy, hypnotists, karaoke, theme nights. Summer Ball held in marquee on the sports fields after exams - an extravaganza of wild bands, casino, karaoke, fairground rides, etc.

High demand for Uni's superclub Rapture, capable of packing out Colchester's biggest club venue, The Hippodrome. City club venues include Valentinos for house, L'Aristo's near Campus, Kings in Copford, a few miles out of Colchester, Colchester Arts Centre for popular specialist club nights - indie night

Twisted Melon specially; also theatre and live bands here. Fine array of pubs, from real ale chains (Tap and Speil) to Irish pubs (Molly Malones) to club nights (The Castle Inn). Most are crowded out at weekends. *Parklife* gives up-to-date listings.

Besides Colchester Arts, for live venues there's The Oliver Twist, in Norwich (40+ miles away) the UEA Union (see East Anglia), and in Ipswich (15 miles) the Ipswich Regent.

Uni's Lakeside Theatre for popular Wednesday night touring company theatre slot. Also 15 student plays a year.

Wivenhoe, a 'quiet but trendy' fishing village/town a couple of miles to the south-east is also a popular quest. 'The Wivenhoe Run' is the traditional pub crawl, and has eateries too. Uni involved in town plan to convert a building next to the railway station into a theatre.

SPORTS

Forty+ Union sports clubs, from yoga to rugby, archery to gliding. Team sports - football, hockey, rugby, cricket - regionally and increasingly nationally competitive, but again emphasis on involvement by as much of the whole student body as possible. Recently extended sports hall with six badminton courts, fitness room, sauna, sun-bed, squash courts, table tennis, climbing wall. Then Sporturf pitch, floodlit tennis courts, 3 cricket pitches (one artificial wicket) plus nets, Squirrel Run circuit, 18-hole disc/frisbee-golf. Watersports centre.

City sports cubs offer sailing, windsurfing, canoeing. Uni swimming club uses pool at Colchester Leisure World. A new Masters degree in Sports Science (Fitness and Health) introduced autumn '95.

European Business School

The European Business School
Regent's College
Regent's Park
London
NW1 4NS

TEL 0171 487 7400
FAX 0171 487 7465

EUROPEAN BUSINESS SCHOOL	
Founded	**1981**
Situation/style	**Campus**
UNDERGRADUATE PROFILE	
Application acceptance rate	**8%**
Population	**600**
Mature student population	**15%**
Overseas student population	**80%**
Male/female ratio	**60:40**
1st year institut. accommodation	**35%**
Approximate cost (School)	**£135-£180 pw**
(City)	**£55-£70 pw**
ACADEMIC PROFILE	
A-level requirements:	**12**
FEES	
Approx. annual cost	**£7,500**
EMPLOYMENT PROFILE	
Principal job market destinations: **Finance & Banking, Manufacturing, Marketing, Consultancy, Retail, Property Management, Media/Leisure Industry**	
Approximate % unemployed	**0%**

VAG VIEW

This school is in London's Regent's Park'. It offers BA (Hons) degrees in the following subjects:

★ **European Business Administration**
(4 years; 48 weeks work experience)
★ **International Business Studies**
(4 years; 48 weeks work experience)
★ **Business Administration and Language Studies**
(4 years; 48 weeks work experience)
★ **International Business Administration**
(3 years; no work experience)

Two other courses were awaiting validation at time of writing:
★ **International Management and Business Studies**
(4 years; 48 weeks work experience)
★ **International Management Studies**
(3 years; 48 weeks work experience)

Strong links with the business world, both through those who teach and manage the school and through students, 75% of whose parents have businesses of their own, ensures a coherent and valuable pattern of student recruitment, course strategy and eventual employment.

Languages are a focus of academic life here, and the student body, which is thoroughly international, ensures plenty of practice.

Accommodation is available to some but not all undergraduates, either in the north wing of the main academic building or in an on-campus hall of residence with 12 double rooms. It doesn't come cheap, but this is an institution which confines itself to the job in hand - sport, for example, must be sought outside - and in any case it is probably rightly assumed that most students have the wherewithall to sort out their own lives.

AN INSIDER'S VIEW OF THE EUROPEAN BUSINESS SCHOOL

VIEW FROM THE GROUND
by York Zucchi

The school's buildings, set within the boundaries of majestic Regent's Park, are suitable for any reasonable academic performance. The lecture theatres (large Victorian rooms rather than classic amphitheatres, but well lit and ventilated) are fitted with all the expected lecturing facilities, and for the PC literate, there's a good intranet/internet set-up.

Architecture apart, let me begin with what EBS is not. For one thing it is not a research institution. Lecturers here lecture. They do not spend a great deal of time being theoretically original, they are more focused on making sure that the student has a practical understanding of the subject at hand. It is not the ideal base camp-site to go on to do a PhD, though some students merrily continue along the path to an MBA. Reputation-wise I'd say it's improving by the day. Our Dean's favourite statistic is that within six months all EBS grads are either in employment or in further education, though in terms of specialization it has quite a way to go before being on a par with the UK Ivy League (LSE, LBS, Cambridge)...

All right! Enough of the propaganda. Let's move on to the actual study material. Describing it in one word, I'd say 'encompassing' - the courses aim at developing the GM or CEO of tomorrow; at least that's what it says in the prospectus. They are certainly wide ranging and also specific - the beauty of the degree paths offered is that they are very flexible, offering the student wide choice in terms of modules. The work load is reasonable and I suppose a lazy student might get by with relatively little effort. If you only read the assigned material, without engaging in outside research, it is possible to walk away from Uni with a 'pass' class degree, though this kind of performance is far from encouraged, and is targeted by the academic troubleshooters (aka tutors). The comparatively small size of the school ensures a good student to tutor ratio.

The key characteristic is the incredible international atmosphere. For example, I came here after working as a banker for three years with a Swiss/German/Ital/South African/Cantonese educational/professional background. There are languages galore: many a student walks away with up to six and they don't let you loose with less than three. Another distinctive feature about the students is that many of them are closely related to present captains of industry - read: a fantastic networking foundation (just what the doctor-turned-broker ordered)...

Waiting list? Well, apart from the usual school qualifications, the filtering system relies principally on a £7,500/year invoice (regardless of origins - be they EC or not). You might argue that this is a trifle pricey but this is the 20th century, and flexibility, exclusivity (i.e. as many resources as possible dedicated to you alone) and individual attention do not come cheap, especially in London. You needn't have any fears about being ripped off; all the cash is poured back into the student's facilities... or so I am told.

Final verdict? If you'll allow me the metaphor, as a sailor riding the uncertain waters of business, I like it here. The ship's captains have plotted an interesting cruise and all evidence points to their intention to keep improving their ship's features. In fact, if current increase in passenger demand is anything to go by, there's every reason to expect that it won't be long before this ship's power turns from diesel to jet. Oh! by the way, should you ever hear rumours about an EBS student's party stamina - well, believe it.

EXETER UNIVERSITY

The University of Exeter
Northcote House
The Queen's Drive
Exeter
Devon
EX4 4QJ

TEL 01392 263263
FAX 01392 263108

Exeter Guild of Students
University of Exeter
Devonshire House
Stocker Road
Exeter
Devon EX4 4PZ

TEL 01392 263540
FAX 01392 263531

UNIVERSITY OF EXETER

Founded	**1955**
Situation/style	**Campus**
UNDERGRADUATE PROFILE	
Application acceptance rate	**8%**
Population	**6,500**
Mature student population	**12%**
Overseas student population	**6%**
Male/female ratio	**49:51**
1st year institut. accommodation	**100%**
Approximate cost	**£40-£85 pw**
ACADEMIC PROFILE	
A-level requirements:	**High**

Law AAB, **Psychology** AAB-BBB, **Accounting & Financial Studies** BBB, **Politics** BBB, **English Literature** BBB-BCC, **Drama** BBC, **Sociology** BBC-CCC, **Educational Studies** BCC-DD, **Modern Languages** 22-24, **Chemistry** CCC-CDD, **Civil, Electronic, Mech. Eng.** CCC

Student/staff ratio	**13:1**
1st class degree pass rate	**9.4%**
HEFCE assessments (16 subjects assessed/approved):	
Postgrad English on 2nd visit, 1995	
1995 **English, Geography**	Excellent
1995/6 **French** 22	
1996: **Russian** 20, **Sociology** 21, **German** 24, **Iberian** 20, **Italian** 22	
Joint Funding Council's research assessment 1996 (36 subjects assessed):	
Hospital/Clinical, Applied Maths, Economics, Accountancy, Classics/ Ancient History	Grade 5
EMPLOYMENT PROFILE	
Employability in Industry:	
MPW national league table (1996)	**19th=**

Principal job market destinations:
Commerce (very strong, especially **Accounting**), **Education** (strong), **Manufacturing, Retail/Wholesale, Arts/Media** (strong), **Public Admin./Law,** good record **Sport**

PIP 1996 employers' survey: Top 3 subjects/national ranking	
Accountancy/Finance & Banking	7th
Social Science/Economics	10th
Languages	11th
Approximate % unemployed	**7%**

VAG VIEW

The Streatham Campus is beautifully set on a hill, 15 minutes walk from the centre of this cathedral city, which itself lies close to the sea on one side and the wide open spaces of Dartmoor on the other. The School of Education is a mile away, but the Students Union operates a frequent minibus service between the two. There is also a base in West Cornwall - The Camborne School of Mines - well placed for the study of Environmental Science as well as Mining (Cornwall is famous for its tin and copper mining history since earliest times, and Imperial College London also owns a copper mine in the area).

Exeter became a university in 1955, but it came out of The University College of the South West, established in 1922, and before that The School of Art (est. 1855). In the 1970s, they took Exeter's St Luke's College of Education into the fold, a college notable in the 1950s for its excruciatingly cold (unheated) outdoor swimming pool, I am reliably informed. I see that the pool is now part of an indoor Fitness Education Centre.

Exeter has had a reputation as a haven

for the green welly brigade, Hoorays brought down from London by the Porscheful, future city slickers out for a last taste of freedom in the idyllic West Country before being tethered to their work stations earning millions of pounds. Certainly the Uni's performance in the Accountancy, Finance & Banking fields - it occupied 7th place in the PIP national survey - supports this. But such an attempt to pigeon-hole it denies Exeter its rightful place as one of our premier league establishments, in academic terms more or less across the board.

There is an interesting modern specialism, as one careers mistress told me: 'Exeter is very good on things Arabic. It has had a lot of inward investment from that direction. It is very good on Middle Eastern languages, there's a large teaching/library facility on that side. It is also very good on Law, and there's a very good theatre there.'

It has indeed. The Northcott Theatre is exceptionally well designed, very good acoustics and a high banked auditorium for maximum audience visibility. It must be one of the best campus theatres in the land and supports high quality outside productions as well as high quality student fare. Personal recollections include Diana Rigg's first (only?) appearance on stage in the buff, and a year when the National Finals of the NUS Drama Fest. were held there (they're now always in Scarborough, see Uni College Scarborough). I was unfortunate enough to be in a visiting finalist troupe actually booed off stage. But I don't hold it against the Uni, as I am sure you will tell.

GETTING THERE

★ By road: M5 (J30).
★ By rail: well served from all destinations - London Paddington, 2:30; Birmingham, 3:00; Plymouth, 1:15.
★ By air: Exeter airport offers flights inland, to Europe and on occasions across the Atlantic;
★ 15 minutes from campus by taxi.

ACCOMMODATION

Halls, all mixed. Older halls - Hope, Lopes, Kilmorie, Thomas - are converted large houses. Mardon Hall was purpose-built in the 1930s, Birks Halls and Duryard Halls in the 60s. Birks are 3 houses with shared bar, dining and common room. Duryard are 4 houses which have no bar. Hope, Kilmorie and Lopes (known as The Exeter Halls and a short way off campus to the east) have tennis courts, no bar. Mardon is most central and has tennis courts and bar. Thomas is in 14 acres of grounds beyond Duryard to the north of the campus and has tennis courts. Self-catered accommodation is also offered in Uni flats in various groves, courts and mewses. St Luke's Hall is in the St Luke's complex about half a mile from the city centre. The St Luke's brigade have a degree of autonomy, and en-suite rooms too.

ACADEMIA

Modular style credits system, but they don't let student choices dominate the timetable. A dedicated Modular Degree is also offered for students in their second year dissatisfied with the promise of their original degree selection. It is also seen as an opportunity to spice up a degree by adding, for example, Languages, Law or Computing. There's a strong emphasis on languages for all students and their Foreign Language Centre caters for an increasing number of students taking a European option in their degree programmes.

With an eye to the careers marketplace, departments 'are encouraged' to develop skills in problem-solving, communication, self-management etc.

Known as PTS - 'personal, transferable skills', a great piece of socio-psychological gobbledegook beloved of careers advisers (and another sign of the employment sector's power in Higher Education) - students are taught how to handle themselves in a work situation. The irony is that the newer universities, which tend to focus on vocational courses and PTS, are not the ones that appear in the employers' league tables. The wonder is that it can be done successfully here by academics on a departmental basis, rather than by specialist socio-psycho-mongers.

Fine library with over a million books and journals opened in 1983, plus specialist collections (Law, Education, Engineering, Mining, Maths, Music, Physics).

Choral and organ scholarships are available.

For information on Camborne School of Mines, contact Asst. Registrar, Camborne School of Mines, Pool, Redruth, Cornwall TR15 3SE. For information about St Luke's, which remains geographically distinct from the university, contact Exeter at the address above.

SPORT

Some 50 clubs, all major teams games well represented, also martial arts, watersports (rowing, canoeing, sailing - club keeps six Lark dinghies on the Exe Estuary) and even ultimate frisbee. On-campus facilities include sports hall (basketball, netball, volleyball, tennis, badminton, indoor cricket net), a climbing wall and traversing wall, rooms for fencing, martial arts, weights, etc. Pitches include 2 all-weather pitches, large grass pitch with nets area, and there are 60 off-campus acres of playing fields nearby.

VIEW FROM THE GROUND
by Jo Moorhouse

Exeter is very easy to fall in love with. This may sound like a subjective view, and of course it is, but as a besotted (and soon to be departing) third year I speak with knowledge. Exeter has one of the most beautiful campuses in the country, in one of the most beautiful counties in Britain. Added to which, revision for summer exams can either be done on Dartmoor or on the beach. How can you lose?

Of course, there is a downside: Exeter is small. Not tiny, but still a city with fewer inhabitants than some London boroughs. This does not seem to limit the number of pubs; there are hundreds, offering everything from a glass of Real Ale before a log fire, to dance and alternative nights, to dodging glasses thrown by enraged Marines (don't worry, you will be told how to avoid that last possibility). Unfortunately, though, those used to big cities may consider Exeter's clubs somewhat lacking in the 'sophisticated entertainment' department.

However, people willing to leave their preconceptions and snobbery at the door will find that 'small' and 'provincial' do not inevitably equal 'boring'. Virtually every kind of music is catered for at some point in the week, and cheap drinks and free admission are common. Added to this, the size of the city and the number of students out and about mean that it is almost impossible to go clubbing after two terms at Exeter and not meet someone you know.

The Guild (aka the Student Union) is responsible for the best-known and best-attended club in Exeter: the Lemon Grove, known to its friends as the Lemmy. It opens on Friday and Saturday nights, and is second in student hearts only to the Ram, the main campus bar. The Guild also oversees a thriving music scene (in the last eighteen months Tori Amos, the Stone Roses, Jamiroquai, Pulp, Dodgy, the Prodigy and Supergrass, to name but a few).

So what is the typical Exeter student like? Basically, just like anybody else. Most of our students come from the southern half of the country, but not all. We do have a sizeable share of the 'green welly' contingent, but they are firmly in the minority. Politically speaking, we are not at all militant; this may be because Exeter is consistently voted into the top five of 'quality of life' surveys.

Around one-third of Exeter students are involved in sport every Wednesday; thousands more give their free time to media, film, theatre, fund-raising or any one of the hundreds of societies. With over eight thousand students at the university, you are guaranteed to find like-minded people. And if you don't find the niche - create it! Some of Exeter's best-loved institutions were started by students, such as the legendary Cocktail Society (Coc-Soc).

After a term, you'll feel as if you belong, partly due to all the people before you who loved the place enough to put something back in. Our car stickers and sweat-shirts proclaim that Exeter is 'probably the best university in the world.' You'll end up agreeing.

FALMOUTH COLLEGE OF ARTS

Falmouth College of Arts
Woodlane
Falmouth
Cornwall
TR11 4RA

TEL 01326 211077
FAX 01326 211205

FALMOUTH COLLEGE OF ARTS	
Founded	**1938**
Situation/style	**Town site**
UNDERGRADUATE PROFILE	
Application acceptance rate	**10%**
Population	**680**
Mature student population	**38%**
Overseas student population	**2%**
Male/female ratio	**50:50**
1st year institut. accommodation	**None**
Approximate rent	**£35 pw**
ACADEMIC PROFILE	
A-level requirements:	**Low**
Graphics, Photography, Broadcasting, Journalism CC	
Student/staff ratio	**10:1**
1st class degree pass rate	**10%**
Joint Funding Council's research assessment 1996 (2 subjects assessed):	
Grade 5/5*	None
EMPLOYMENT PROFILE	
Employability in Industry:	
Arts/Media, Manufacturing	
Approximate % unemployed	**14%**

VAG VIEW

Falmouth is a fairly busy town below Wendron Moors in West Cornwall about 10 miles south of Truro. It looks out over a bay towards The Lizard peninsular and is a short way from the Helford Estuary where Daphne du Maurier set her stirring novel, Frenchman's Creek. *The college is, therefore, close to some of the most lovely countryside which this country has to offer, and it is itself set in 8 palm-tree spotted acres between the town, the harbour and the beach.*

BA (Hons) degrees are offered in Broadcasting Studies, English with Media Studies, Fine Art, Graphic Communication, Illustration, Journalism Studies, Photographic Communication, Studio Ceramics, and Visual Culture. Sports are organised by a Union representative and opportunities include football, rugby, cycling, horse riding, golf, tennis, sailing, hang gliding, surfing, rock climbing, canoeing and of course swimming.

Accommodation facilities will shortly be improved by the opening of new purpose-built halls of residence. But in any case it is not difficult to find accommodation in a part of the world which depends economically on tourism.

GETTING THERE

★ By road: A30 over Bodmin Moor, A3076 to Truro, A39 to Falmouth.
★ Trains run from all major cities to Truro (4 hours+ from London Paddington). Change there for Falmouth.
★ By air: Flights leave daily from Newquay on the north coast to Heathrow and take about an hour.

FARNBOROUGH COLLEGE OF TECHNOLOGY

Farnborough College of Technology
Boundary Road
Farnborough
Hampshire
GU14 6SB

TEL 01252 515511
FAX 01252 549682

Student Union
Farnborough College of Technology
Boundary Road
Farnborough
Hampshire
GU14 6SB

TEL 01252 517838
FAX 01252 517838

FARNBOROUGH COLLEGE OF TECHNOLOGY

Founded	**1957**
Situation/style	**Campus**
UNDERGRADUATE PROFILE	
Application acceptance rate	**15%**
Population	**440**
Mature student population	**45%**
Overseas student population	**3%**
Male/female ratio	**60:40**
1st year institut. accommodation	**70%**
Approximate cost (College)	**£25-£60 pw**
(Town)	**£40 pw**
ACADEMIC PROFILE	
A-level requirements:	**Low**

Media Technology 14, **Aerospace Engineering** 10, **Environmental Mgt. & Business** DE, **Computing** EE

HEFCE assessments (2 subjects assessed): **Computer Studies, Environmental Studies,** approved 1994

EMPLOYMENT PROFILE

Principal job market destinations: **Manufacture, Education**

VAG VIEW

Farnborough is situated just south of Junction 4 of the M3, about 35 miles from the centre of London, and is famous for its Air Show, so we shouldn't be surprised that a College which prides itself on its links with industry and business in the area offers a BEng (Hons) degree in Aerospace Engineering. The Engineering faculty is, however, but one arrow in Farnborough's quiver. Environmental Management is another. It offers two first degrees (BSc Hons), in Conservation Mgt. and Pollution Control. The School of Business, which claims to be the largest outside the University sector - its degrees are validated by Surrey University - offers BA (Hons) in Business Administration (with a special emphasis on personal skills development - communication, presentation, problem solving, etc), Accounting (a pathway to professional exams which can also be completed in the Business School), Marketing (earning major exemptions from the professional exams of the Chartered Institute of Marketing), Leisure Mgt (a degree awarded by Portsmouth Uni, and taught by lecturers with practical experience in the Leisure industry), and the Science & Mgt of Exercise and Health. They also offer BSc degrees in Computing and Media Technology.

The proximity of the college to London has obvious advantages and the Students Union has recently been enhanced by an investment of a million pounds and a full-time Ents officer put in place to develop a programme of events. Half board accommodation is offered in six halls of residence less than a mile from campus.

GETTING THERE

★ By road: M3 (J4).
★ By train: Fast trains from London Waterloo.

GLAMORGAN UNIVERSITY

University of Glamorgan
Pontypridd
Mid Glamorgan
CF37 1DL

TEL 01443 480480
FAX 01443 480558

University of Glamorgan
Student Union
Forest Grove
Treforest
Pontypridd CF37 1UF

TEL 01443 408227
FAX 01443 491589

UNIVERSITY OF GLAMORGAN

Founded	**1913**
Situation/style	**Campus**
UNDERGRADUATE PROFILE	
Application acceptance rate	**14%**
Population	**7,700**
Mature student population	**8%**
Overseas student population	**7%**
Male/female ratio	**40:60**
1st year institut. accommodation	**100%**
Approximate cost	**£35-£65 pw**
ACADEMIC PROFILE	
A-level requirements:	**Low**

Geological Sciences DD, **Pre-Clinical Sciences, Food Sci.** DD, **Chem., Mech., Manufac. Eng.** DD, **Law** 8-18, **Computer Studies and combinations, Electronics** 8-16, **Civil Eng.** 6-14, **E & E Eng.** CD, **Building Economics, Urban Studies** 8-16, **Sociology combinations** 12-16, **Business Studies, BS & Economics, Marketing, Management** 14-16, **English Studies/Theatre & Media Drama** 14, **Media Studies combinations** 12-14

Student/staff ratio	**31:1**
1st class degree pass rate	**3.9%**
HEFCW assessments (13 subjects assessed/approved):	
1993/4 **Business Studies**	Excellent
1994/5 **Mining Surveying, Creative Writing/Theatre, Media Drama**	Excellent
1995/6 **Electrical & Electronic Engineering**	Excellent
Joint Funding Council's research assessment 1996 (9 subjects assessed):	
Grade 5/5*	None

EMPLOYMENT PROFILE

Principal job market destinations:
Manufacturing (strong on **Electrical & Electronic**), **Retail/Wholesale, Public Admin./Law, Computer, Education, Commerce, Health, Arts/Media**

PIP 1996 employers' survey: Top subject/national ranking	
Social Science/Economics	36th
Approximate % unemployed	**10%**

VAG VIEW

Friendly atmosphere, pleasant setting and within 25 minutes of Cardiff's dens of iniquity by road; also easy access from station near campus. But the sport and ents at Glamorgan make it worthwhile sticking around.

SITUATION

On campus in Treforest in the Taff Valley, a couple of miles from the market town of Pontypridd. Treforest is an industrial estate - cum village, Cardiff is approximately 20-25 minutes by train from Treforest station, adjacent to Uni.

GETTING THERE

★ By road: M4 (J32), the University signposted from both directions on the A470. Take the exit marked Llantrisant, A473.
★ By train: London Paddington, 2:45; Birmingham, 2:15; York, 5.00.
★ Cardiff Airport for inland and international flights.

ACCOMMODATION

New (three years ago) en-suite residences, set in landscaped gardens overlooking the campus. Communal kitchen and dining area with fridge/freezers, microwave ovens, irons and kettles per six rooms. Other halls not en-suite but refurbished, up to date and cheaper.

THE UNION & ENTS

Night club, Shafts - indie nights alternate with best in alternative, Britpop and new music. Tuesdays Live - Collapsed Lung, Counterfeit Stones, Hom, Space, etc. Thursdays house, film shows, cabaret/comedy nights, The Regurgitator (self-explanatory; he vomits forth all over the Uni circuit), hypnotists etc. Two pubs, The George Knox, trad-style; Smiths, cafe bar. The club is great and a popular draw in the area, but Cardiff, 25 mins away, is a magnet: 'The Owain Glyndwr is a popular pub in the centre of Cardiff,' they'll tell you, 'and the Old Orleans is well known for its cheap cocktails, and the Astoria night club is famous for its late night dancing. However, as night clubs go in and out of fashion, you can't go wrong if you head down St Mary's Street and follow the crowd!' See also Cardiff University entry. The Bridge, the Forest, the Otley Arms, the Malsters are popular pubs with students in Pontypridd, where there's also a cinema in the Muni (Municipal Hall).

Drama and classical music (choir, orchestra) good in Uni. Sherman and New Theatre recommended for plays in Cardiff, St David's Hall for orchestras, jazz, rock bands, touring ballet, opera. Cardiff International Arena and National Stadium both major live band venues - e.g. Michael Jackson, U2, Bon Jovi, REM, Simple Minds.

SPORT

Top class facilities and coaching available. Sports Centre Main Hall has six badminton courts, climbing wall, all indoor sports. Smaller hall for keep fit, table tennis, martial arts, fencing. Four squash courts (1 glass-backed), two conditioning rooms, sauna/solarium suite. 30-acres floodlit pitches - football, rugby and hockey, plus trim trail, cricket pitch, archery. Sports Scholarship Scheme is available for students who are competing at national/international level. Also nearby swimming pools, golf courses, running tracks, and Brecon Beacons for horse riding, canoeing, mountaineering, hang gliding, walking. Also sailing, windsurfing.

ACADEMIA

200+ courses on offer, modular structure, emphasis on sandwich placement. Faculties include Arts, Humanities and Social Sciences; Business, Management and Law; Engineering and Technology; Languages; Mathematics, Computing and Information Systems; Nursing and Midwifery; Science. See fact box for strengths.

GLASGOW UNIVERSITY

The University of Glasgow
University Avenue
Glasgow
G12 8QQ
TEL 0141 339 8855

Glasgow University Union
32 University Avenue
Glasgow G12 8LX

TEL 0141 339 8697
FAX 0141 334 2216

Glasgow University
Queen Margaret Union
22 University Gardens
Glasgow G12 8QN

TEL 0141 339 9784
FAX 0141 357 3567

Glasgow University
Students' Representatives Council
John McIntyre Building
University Avenue
Glasgow G12 8QQ

TEL 0141 339 8541
FAX 0141 337 3557

UNIVERSITY OF GLASGOW

Founded	**1451**
Situation/style	**Campus**
UNDERGRADUATE PROFILE	
Application acceptance rate	**12%**
Medical AAR	**13%**
Population	**15,270**
Mature student population	**20%**
Overseas student population	**9%**
Male/female ratio	**48:52**
1st year institut. accommodation	**60%**
Approximate cost (Uni)	**£34-£59 pw**
(City)	**£35+ pw**
ACADEMIC PROFILE	
A-level requirements:	**High**

Medicine AAB:
★ Science 'A's required **Chemistry +1 of Maths, Physics or Biol.**
★ Addit. Non-Science 'A's acceptable **Yes**
★ Retakes considered **No**
★ Clinical contact **1st year**

Student/staff ratio	**8:1**
1st class degree pass rate	**11.2%**
SHEFC assessments (21 subjects assessed/approved):	
1994 **Civil Engineering, Music.**	Highly satis.
Computer Studies, Physics	Excellent
1995 **Maths & Statistics, Mechanical + Manufacturing Engineering**	Highly satis.
Chemistry, Geography, Geology	Excellent
1996: **History of Art, History, Finance & Accounting, Law, Politics, Social Work, Theology.**	Highly Satis.
Philosophy, Sociology	Excellent
Joint Funding Council's research assessment 1996 (51 subjects assessed):	
Computer Science.	Grade 5*
Biochemistry, Biol. Sciences, Electrical & Electronic Eng., Town & Country Planning, Politics, European Studies	Grade 5
EMPLOYMENT PROFILE	
Employability in Industry:	
MPW national league table (1996)	**19th**

Principal job market destinations:
Health (incl. **Dentistry**), **Commerce, Retail/Wholesale, Manufacturing** (strong on **Electronic & Electrical**), **Education, Public Admin./Law), Arts/ Media** (strong), **Veterinary, Engineering Design** (strong)

PIP 1996 employers' survey:	
Top 3 subjects/national ranking	
Computing	10th=
Languages	12th=
Social Science/Economics	13th=
Approximate % unemployed	**8%**

VAG VIEW

Glasgow is the total city, more like New York than London is today. In fact you might say that Glasgow is to Edinburgh what New York is to Paris. It is exciting, diverse, you can have a riotous time here certainly but there is also a creative precariousness, something of an edge to life, which sets it apart from Edinburgh and certainly from all those mindless middle England cities of bop. If you're up to it, Glasgow is more likely to bring the innovative artist out in you than most. And it is academically a very good Uni indeed. Sassenachs might be advised by one of the schools careers mistresses we interviewed: 'There is of course a high proportion of home-based students, so if you are going from England you should at least be aware of that, you'll want to befriend the Scots fairly quickly or set up your own more isolated social life - Glasgow rather more than Edinburgh in this...'

SETTING

'Very fine North part of the city. It's a very divided city. The Southern edge has really suffered from industrial recession (all the steel, the coal mining has gone, the shipbuilding also has declined a lot) and hasn't yet really been replaced with anything very much. It's a bit like Sheffield was, say 15 years ago. On the other hand it's really the commercial capital of Scotland, with all the big banks and money brokers, and there's a very fine city centre (and going northwards through the university) as a result.'

The campus, as you may have guessed from the foregoing - the lady, our guide, has a son-in-law teaching in the Chemistry department - is situated to the North of the city centre, about 3 miles away in fact.

GETTING THERE

★ By road: M8 (J19) if travelling East, J18 if travelling West. Other routes include the A82, the A814, the B808, Byres Road.
★ Car parking on campus difficult.
★ Good coach services nationally end up at Buchanan Street Bus station.
★ By rail: 50 minutes Edinburgh, 5 hours London. Two city stations, Queen Street and Central, served by Buchanan Street and St. Enoch underground stations respectively (main campus Underground station is Hillhead).
★ Bus routes 44 and 59 (orange Strathclyde buses) run through the main campus from the city centre.
★ By air: Major destination, airport bus service to city centre.
★ The taxi fare is around £15.

ACADEMIA

The Scottish way is a four-year first degree. Though A Level entrants can sometimes opt to go straight into the 2nd Year, life's so good up here it'd be a pity to miss a year, and you'll integrate better if you're in from the start.

The assessments speak for themselves, and, as our adviser assures us, you're not going to be taught by a lot of old codgers: 'Very good care for students. We've had people going there recently for Philosophy [note Excellent SHEFC rating], for Art History - it's good for the Artsy based degrees; outside London, Birmingham it's one of *the* places to go for anyone interested in Art, Art History. But it's good on the sciences too. Having experienced Cambridge, Montreal, Dublin and Glasgow, my son-in-law says that they are better focused on their students at Glasgow than at any of these. They are also making a deliberate effort to get more young staff in, because, like a lot of universities who took on a lot of lecturers in the '60s, they've stayed there and grown old together. There's going to be a phase, in a decade's time when a lot of people retire...but not at Glasgow. We had one student who went round York University with his mother and she recognised people who had taught her - an immediate put-off for the girl.'

Glasgow has a long record of involvement with the wider-than-campus community too. Recently launched campus-based SATRO (Science and Technology Regional Organisations) puts West Scotland on a national network map of organisations dedicated to enthusing young people about science, engineering and technology. The project involves the university, schools and industry to the clear additional advantage in the wider context of student recruitment and graduate employment.

STUDENT UNIONS & ENTS

There are four Union type bodies at Glasgow - the Students Representative Council (SRC), a kind of umbrella organisation or wise kindly parent for the two squabbling sibling organisations, Glasgow University Union (GUU) and Queen Margaret Union (QM). Then there is GUSA, founded in 1881 and the grandaddy of them all. GUSA administers the 45 sporting clubs - from Aikido to Curling, from the Boat Club to the Parachuting Club, from Cricket to Golf.

You can join GUSA and GUU or GUSA and QM, but you can't join both GUU and QM. Confused? Well don't be, because the rule only appertains to voting rights; every student is free to take advantage of the orgiastic opportunities which these two, mainly social beasts, will first present to you during Freshers' Week.

GUU's portfolio includes their own disco, The Hive, cheap nights from Thursday through Saturday, and live Basement Bar frolics on Wednesdays. They claim anything up to seven functional bars open for business on each night of the week, 10 full-size snooker tables, air hockey, games machines, annual games events and games of a competitive nature throughout the year. The Big Date is Daft Friday at the end of the first term - a wild extravaganza of discos, live acts, karaoke, ceilidhs (that's folk happenings to anyone from South of the border). But the really big GUU deal is their debating. It's serious stuff on a global scale. They've been World Champions on four occasions, and by all accounts, whether you are likely to participate or not, it's worth just going to watch..

For their part QM offers bars 11am till 11pm, three discos a week till 2 am, eateries, pool tables, slot machines and arcade games, a private (for hire) snooker room and, not to be outdone, Dafter Friday, again 8pm to 8am, bands, discos, comedy acts, etc, etc. Qudos is 'where most of the hedonism happens' - bar, cafe, stage, dance floor. A typical week's entertainment recently included Indie on Friday night; Handbag House on Saturday - 'Cute girly house with its hair in bunches and its hand down the front of your trousers'; Quiz night Sunday; Karaoke Monday; local bands in Jim's Bar Tuesday; Heckling Meeting (electioneering) Wednesday; pool competition, QM pub quiz, and Snap Crackle Pop (Cheese night) Thursday.

With all this activity on campus, it's a wonder anyone has time to sample the delights of Glasgow city, though this is another reason for recommending you get here as quick as you can. *The List* is what you'll need, Glasgow and Edinburgh's fortnightly events and listing magazine.

Cheap clubs include Hotshots, The Cathouse, The Arena, The Attic, The Garage, Sub Club, but there are many more and in fact the Uni's Hive and Qudos feature as heavily as anywhere in the listings.

There is probably nowhere better than Glasgow for pubs and the SRC see that you're equipped with a well worked out taster review listing at the start of Fresher's Week.

Above all, Glaswegians are performers, in case you hadn't noticed, and the theatre scene here is electric eclectic. No one big theatre but a host offering rep (cheapest: Gorbals-based Citizens'); coalface productions (cutting edge drama at Tramway); Opera, Ballet (at the Royal); nightclub turned theatre beneath Central Station: the Arches has its own company and touring productions; comedy and lightest entertainment at King's; pantos and hypnotists at Pavilion.

Among interesting cinemas, the Grosvenor near campus gives over to off-beat fare at weekends; the Glasgow Film Theatre for sheer variety - foreign to Hollywood gloss; plus the usual multi-screens.

Mention must be made too of the lively journalistic scene at Glasgow - SubCity Radio, only a year old, but already main focus of T in the Park, the big music fest.; *The Guardian*, finger on the student pulse fortnightly newspaper; *GUM*, the uni's older, 3 issues a year publication; *GUST*, which claims to be the largest student TV station in the UK; *Paper*

Cut, contributor magazine - poems, photographs, stories, etc. See what I mean about artistic?

ACCOMMODATION

Halls of Residence and Student Homes, catered and self-catered (all have kitchens), old and new. The SRC runs a mini-bus from campus to all halls.

Queen Margaret Hall: Large Hall, good social life. Fifteen minutes walk from Uni, on bus route to city centre, lively area. Breakfast, dinner weekdays; Continental breakfast, lunch, dinner weekends. Single rooms, Common room, library, TV, table tennis, snooker.

Wolfson Hall: Close to School of Veterinary Medicine and new Sports Centre, 3 miles from Uni, but regular buses. Breakfast, dinner weekdays; Continental breakfast, lunch, dinner weekends. Singles and twin rooms, common rooms, library, 2 TVs, games room. Good social life.

Horselethill House: Smallest Hall, well-integrated community, 5 minutes walk from Uni, on bus route to city, also close to Underground (Byres Road). Full breakfast, dinner weekdays; self-catering weekends.
Singles and twin rooms. Common room, TV.

Dalrymple Hall: Ten minutes walk from Uni, on bus route into city. Breakfast, dinner weekdays; Continental breakfast, lunch, dinner weekends. Singles and twin rooms. Common room, TV, games room.

Reith Hall: Fifteen minutes walk from Uni, on bus route into city. Breakfast, dinner weekdays; Continental breakfast, lunch, dinner weekends. Singles and twin rooms. Common room, 2 TVs.

Maclay Hall: Small and friendly, 10 minutes walk from Uni, on bus route into city. Self-catering. Singles and twin rooms. Common room.

Cairncross House: Newest, modern building, well equipped, less than a mile from Uni and on city bus route. Self-catering. Singles and twins. Common room.

Student Housing: Uni-owned/managed flats, some on campus, rest a short walk away. Self-catering. Unlikely for freshers.

Student Village: Fifteen minutes walk from Uni. Completed 1994. House units and flats. Sel-catered. Freshers mostly in flats (4 or 5 per flat). Also communal/Common room, TV, games room, snack bar, shop, etc. Good social scene.

SPORT

All the usual facilities for team sports, individual training, etc. including a 25m pool, steam room and sauna, two activity halls with sprung flooring, basketball, volleyball, 5-a-side soccer; a fitness and conditioning area, fully equipped. £1,500 p.a. bursaries offered in squash, athletics, rowing; £1,000 pa, golf: some 40 courses in the area.

GLASGOW CALEDONIAN UNIVERSITY

Glasgow Caledonian University
Cowcaddens Road
Glasgow
G4 0BA
TEL 0141 331 3000
FAX 0141 331 3005

Glasgow Caledonian University
Students' Association
City Campus
70 Cowcaddens Road
Glasgow G4 0BA

TEL 0141 332 0681
FAX 0141 353 0029

Glasgow Caledonian University
Students' Association
Park Campus
1 Park Drive
Glasgow G3 6LP

TEL 0141 339 9942
FAX 0141 337 2940

Glasgow Caledonian University
Students' Association
Southbrae Campus
Crawford Building
Southbrae Drive
Glasgow G13 3PP

TEL 0141 337 4703
FAX 0141 337 4600

GLASGOW CALEDONIAN UNIVERSITY

Founded	**1971**
Situation/style	**City sites**
UNDERGRADUATE PROFILE	
Application acceptance rate	**10%**
Population	**8,000**
Mature student population	**26%**
Overseas student population	**4%**
Male/female ratio	**44:56**
1st year institut. accommodation	**80%**
Approximate cost (Uni)	**£40-£55 pw**
(City)	**£35+ pw**
ACADEMIC PROFILE	
A-level requirements:	**Medium-low**

Accountancy, Finance BB,BC-CD, **Medical Physics Technology** BBC, **Nursing** CC, **Biomedical Sciences** DDD, **Nutrition** CC, **Physiotherapy, Radiography** CCC, **Law** BB-CC, **Social Sciences** CCD, **Computers Studies** CD-DDE, **Electronic, Civil Eng.** EEE,EE

Student/staff ratio	**19:1**
1st class degree pass rate	**4.8%**

SHEFC assessments (16 subjects assessed/approved):	
1994 **Physics**	Highly satis.
1995 **Consumer Studies, Maths & Statistics**	Highly satis.
Chemistry	Excellent
1996 **Finance & Accounting, Mass Communications, Sociology, Social Work**	Highly satis.
Joint Funding Council's research assessment 1996 (14 subjects assessed):	
Grade 5/5*	None
EMPLOYMENT PROFILE	
Employability in Industry:	
MPW national league table (1996)	**15th=**
Principal job market destinations:	

Health, Retail/Wholesale, Manufacturing (strong on **Electronic & Electrical**), **Commerce, Construction, Hotel/Restaurant, Public Admin./Law, Education**

PIP 1996 employers' survey:	
Top subject/national ranking	
Computing	35th=
Approximate % unemployed	**11%**

VAG VIEW

Glasgow Caledonian is in the growing pains stage of maturation. A careers teacher in a northern girls school described their school liaison department as 'completely out of touch, out of date', and the impression one gets is of a Uni still finding itself since being awarded university status in 1992. Or perhaps, of necessity, the Uni, in a state of enormous expansion, is simply having to make a few unpopular decisions about what is urgent and what is merely important, and the left hand isn't quite cognisant of what the right hand is doing.

The free student newspaper, UNI, was full of it at the end of last year, when cranes, workers, JCBs littered City campus and noise levels rose to such a degree that students and lecturers added their voices to it in protest.

It isn't only the library elongating itself Spiderman-like over what once was a car park to allow a third more students to use the facility, or the building of a much trumpeted (and delayed) new sports centre, or indeed any of the hush-hush building projects in planning stage that attest to the fact that Caledonian is on the move up, or at least out.

Students arrived back at the beginning of the year to find that they no longer belonged to a Uni with three sites, but to one with 5. The College of Nursing and Midwifery had been gobbled up by this insatiable monster.

The Scotsman newspaper reports that Caledonian is now the third largest university in Scotland behind Edinburgh and Glasgow, and its expansion has brought teething problems which present undergraduates with the undeniable, if unpalatable, truth that their 4-year stay is as nothing compared with the grand perspective of time (well into the next millennium), which preoccupies the University authorities.

Students may grouse that the influx of 1,000 extra nursing students coincides with a cut in the Student Association block grant (the already thinly spread welfare and hardship funds are particularly at issue), but the Uni is making a play for the future and what seems to some students today to be the conspiratorially 'low-key and hush-hush' way in which the Uni is going about change may soon be forgotten. In any case, as most everywhere these days - even at Aberystwyth - despite a voluble press, the student caucus takes whatever the authorities are prepared to dish out. Caledonian is not a markedly radical place, and there are already bonuses being dished out in one area that matters - Ents.

In 1996, for the first time, Ents Co-ordinator became a post distinct from Social Secretary at the Union. New sound systems were installed in Asylum, the main student venue at City. Shed Seven played the Freshers' Ball there. Upstairs a new nightclub opened, capable of transforming itself at will from games-room-cum-bar-cum-eaterie; and the then year-old Bedsit at Park Campus played host to Champagne Supernova.

These are landmark times for Caledonian, indeed perhaps for everyone. Twenty years ago there were only half a million students at university nationwide, whereas today there are 1.6 million - the reason, of course, why the JCBs are strutting their stuff at Caledonian, and acts, bigger than at any time in the last 30 years (when they had Hendrix, can you believe?), are playing at Asylum.

SITUATION

City Campus is on Cowcaddens Road, opposite Buchanan Bus Station. Cowcaddens and Buchanan Street Underground stations are nearby. This is the main university site, where the Student Association building is.

Park Campus is on Park Drive, where the West End starts and student life is most heavily concentrated. Nearest Underground is Kelvinbridge.

Southbrae Campus is on Southbrae Drive, some 5 miles from the city centre - take a train from Glasgow Central to Jordanhill Station. It is moving to City Campus in August 1998 when new buildings are complete.

The two College of Nursing and Midwifery sites are close to the Royal Infirmary and Stobhill Hospital, in St James's Road and Bolgrayhill Road. They are known as **St James'** and **Stobhill** campuses respectively, and they too will be moving to City Campus in August 1998.

GETTING THERE

★ Routes into Glasgow by road: M8 (J19) if travelling East, J18 if travelling West. Other routes include the A82, the A814, the B808, Byres Road.
★ Car parking on campus difficult.
★ Good coach services nationally end up at Buchanan Street Bus station.
★ By rail: 50 minutes Edinburgh, 5 hours London.
★ Two city stations, Queen Street and Central, served by Buchanan Street and St. Enoch underground stations respectively (main campus Underground station is Hillhead).
★ Bus routes 44 and 59 (orange Strathclyde buses) run through the main campus from the city centre.
★ By air: Major destination, airport bus service to city centre.
★ The taxi fare is around £15.

ACADEMIA

Caledonian offer courses from within three faculties - Business (some aspects at Park), Health (Southbrae, St James' and Stobhill), Science & Technology.

The academic year is structured out of two semesters, three modules per semester, and they encourage students not only to consider making a module mix from within a faculty but to cross faculty frontiers, for example BA/BSc combined. There are obvious advantages in this, Business combines well with Health if you have an eye to a management career in the Health area.

Entry-wise, as the academic side is so closely geared to employment, academic qualifications are not the only matter up for consideration. Caledonian offer vocational courses and they want students who are motivated with enthusiasm and drive, and in particular those who have made some effort to discover what their subject is about and what it will lead to - the successful student may, for example, have spoken with someone in the industry with which the course is directly connected.

For the same reason, entry requirements are relaxed for mature students who can show that they have knowledge, skills or experience in fields related to the course they want to study.

ACCOMMODATION

All within a 4-mile radius of the city. Caledonian Court consists of self-catering flats, 6 to 8 bedrooms. Gibson Hall is trad. catered hall of residence traditional residence. Gibson Hall is convenient for Park or Southbrae campuses. David Naismith Court and Red Road Court for self-catered accommodation north of City Campus. Shelley Court and Yorkhill Court, again self-catering - four rooms, kitchen and bathroom.

ENTS

Clubs, bars, eateries, discos, live acts, including comedy - recent rapturous reception for Alan Parker: Urban Warrior at Asylum's 'Haven' (City). The Bedsit at Park (see above). City clubs recommended by SA include Velvet Rooms, Garage, Art School, Reds (at top end of town); Tunnel, Archaos, Arches, Sub Club, Cathouse (at bottom end). Pubs are ubiquitous and splendidly specific reviews are given in a glossy hand-out to Freshers on arrival. See also Glasgow Uni entry.

Also worth noting, 2-year-old Untapped Theatre Club based at Park and offering students a chance to write as well as the rest of it. Also Debating Soc, only four years old, is mixing it with the big boys - Oxford, St Andrews, Birmingham, Southampton, etc in competition.

SPORTS

Sports hall on City Campus. Fitness Centre and gym at Park. 20+ sports clubs; rugby, soccer, hockey, athletics catered for. Uni pre-eminent in athletics. Bearsden dry ski slopes for GCU Club Ski and the real white stuff for weekends in Semester 2. Hillwalking and Mountaineering Club the largest, weekends away in Glen Coe.

GOLDSMITHS COLLEGE

Goldsmiths College
University of London
Lewisham Way
New Cross
London
SE14 6NW

TEL 0171 919 7171
FAX 0171 919 7113

Goldsmiths College
Student Union
Dixon Road
London SE14 6NW

TEL 0181 692 1406
FAX 0181 694 9789

GOLDSMITHS COLLEGE

Founded	**1891**
Situation/style	**Campus**
UNDERGRADUATE PROFILE	
Application acceptance rate	**10%**
Population	**3,400**
Mature student population	**40%**
Overseas student population	**15%**
Male/female ratio	**35:65**
1st year institut. accommodation	**100%**
Approximate cost	**£45-£60 pw**
ACADEMIC PROFILE	
A-level requirements:	**Medium**

Teacher Training CCC-DD, **Drama/English and Theatre Arts** BBC, **Art & Design** BBB-CC, **Psychology, Sociology** BBC, **Computing & Information Systems** CCC, **Modern Language Studies** CC

Student/staff ratio	**14:1**
1st class degree pass rate	**8%**
HEFCE assessments (7 subjects assessed/approved):	
1995 **Music**	Excellent
1995/6 **Sociology** 23	
Joint Funding Council's research assessment 1996 (22 subjects assessed):	
Art & Design	Grade 5*
Anthropology, Sociology, Music	Grade 5
EMPLOYMENT PROFILE	

Principal job market destinations:
Education, Retail/Wholesale, Arts/Media (strong), **Public Admin., Manufacturing**

PIP 1996 employers' survey: Top subject/national ranking	
Social Science/Economics	25th=
Approximate % unemployed	**10%**

VAG VIEW

Goldsmiths describes itself as a specialist university. But it is not so much specialist for the subjects it teaches as for the distinctive environment in which those subjects are taught. To understand what that environment is, you must first understand where Goldsmiths is coming from.

It was founded in 1891 by the Worshipful Company of Goldsmiths 'as the Company's Technical and Recreative Institute'. 'Technical' we can readily understand, but the word 'recreative' is chosen advisedly. What the Worshipful Company wanted, besides a continuing education for its local artisans, was not simply a wild recreational time, though no doubt they had that too, but a creatively invigorating time. The College's School of Art began life in the same decade. In the following decade its teacher education provision was added. In the 1930s the adult (evening) educational programme was instituted as part of the curriculum. In the 1960s (that great decade of innovation, artistic creativity, self-awareness and rejuvenation), the college's humanities, performing arts and social sciences programmes came to the fore. In 1988 it became a School of the University of London, and on the first day of 1990 Goldsmiths was granted its Royal Charter.

The key words in this truncated

history of Goldsmiths are 'local', 'continuing education', 'wild', 'creatively invigorating', 'adult', 'innovation', 'artistic' and 'self-awareness', for there is a continuity of purpose here which is traceable right back to its roots in the late 19th century.

Goldsmiths continues to draw students from the locality. It is involved in a process of continuing education of its students and its staff - 40% of its intake is 'mature' and there is a rolling Quality Assessment of its teaching through workshops and training programmes for staff, seminars and constant discussions about methods. In coursework their aim is to make you think about what, in reality, your subject entails, what the theory implies for society and for yourself. For example, Social Policy and Politics applies social and political theory to real issues of today; Psychology students are encouraged to consider the theory in terms of their own lives. But it isn't only these students who speak of their time at Goldsmiths as a period of discovery.

Their teaching methods are rigorously non-judgemental and while the college has adopted the same modular course-unit system as many other colleges, its subject combinations are very much its own, interdisciplinary, many encouraging innovative ideas - visual and performing arts exerting a liberating influence among mathematical or social scientists, for example.

It may sound a bit artsy fartsy but the proof that it works is in their assessment record, their employment statistics, and the high regard with which their graduates are held, particularly in the fields of Education and Arts/Media. Also, more to the immediate point, they have what has been described as the wildest student social scene in London.

VIEW FROM THE GROUND

by Steven Paul Davies

Situated in New Cross, south-east London, a semi-yuppified inner-city area, the campus comprises a huge modern library, halls of residence and the main Victorian college building. Greenwich and Lewisham are close by and trains from New Cross to Central London (twelve minutes to Charing Cross) run frequently. Great for those who love the freedom of city life.

Goldsmiths is predominantly an arts college, mostly attracting trendy laid-back arty types. The male/female ratio is 2:3 and there are many mature students and overseas students who help create a varied cultural mix. Previous Goldsmiths' 'stars' include Malcolm McLaren, Mary Quant, Damien Hirst, Lord Merlyn Rees.

Goldsmiths, SU organises a variety of guest speakers including recent attendances by Michael Winner, Michael Caine and numerous politicians. On the whole the college and student union are left wing although it is increasingly becoming a more social rather than political Union. The Union provides three bars, a student shop, clubs and societies (very popular Athletic Union, Drama Club and even a Crap Film Club - although don't imagine for a minute that joining the latter will enhance your credibility around the college), sports and entertainments. *Time Out* has called us 'the best student venue for bands in London'. Local pubs are friendly if you respect the locals. Of course, for the price of a train ticket (and an extended overdraft) scores of West End entertainments are on offer.

Accommodation is increasingly hard to find and many opt to squat. However, conditions have improved greatly and now all first years are guaranteed a hall place. Most halls have recently been renovated, are essentially quite attractive and are situated in nearby residential areas. The most popular hall is Raymont (en-suite rooms) with the average rent currently at £55 per week.

The Media & Communications course is extremely popular and has a good reputation within the media. If you'd rather watch telly than read a book, this course is for you! Many media students go on to work in public relations and the media. The Art course is also renowned for producing some of the most celebrated artists of the last ten years. Student art shows continue to thrill devotees of the avant-garde. In terms of work load, the Fine Arts course has the lowest - never arrange to meet Art students in the library...they'll never find it!

In short, Goldsmiths College, coupled with the experience of living in London, will offer you a variety of spices for you to mix into your life...and it's not a bad place to get a degree!

GREENWICH UNIVERSITY

The University of Greenwich
Bexley Road
Eltham
London
SE9 2PQ

TEL 0181 331 8000
FAX 0181 331 8855

University of Greenwich
Student Union
Bathway
Woolwich
London SE18 6QX

TEL 0181 331 8268
FAX 0181 331 8591

GREENWICH UNIVERSITY

Founded	**1970**
Situation/style	**City/urban sites**
UNDERGRADUATE PROFILE	
Application acceptance rate	**10%**
Population	**9,100**
Mature student population	**62%**
Overseas student population	**9%**
Male/female ratio	**52:48**
1st year institut. accommodation	**100%**
Approximate cost	**£45-£65 pw**
ACADEMIC PROFILE	
A-level requirements:	**Low**

Teacher Training 10-12, **Housing Studies, Architecture** 12,14, **Law** 20, **Environmental Sciences** 2-16, **Business Studies, Economics with Psychology** 16, **Computer Science combinations** 8-14, **Biological Sciences** 8-10, **Health with Sociology/Management** 12, **Sociology and combinations** 12-14

Student/staff ratio	**12:1**
1st class degree pass rate	**4.5%**
HEFCE assessments (13 subjects assessed/approved):	
1994 **Architecture, Environmental Studies**	Excellent
1996 **Sociology** 23	
Joint Funding Council's research assessment 1996 (31 subjects assessed):	
Grade 5/5*	None

EMPLOYMENT PROFILE

Principal job market destinations:
Education, Retail/Wholesale, Manufacturing, Public Admin/Law, Commerce, Health, Construction, Architecture, Hotel/Restaurant, Personnel, Market Research/ Advertising (strong), **Arts/Media**

Approximate % unemployed **12%**

VAG VIEW

Greenwich Uni is an umbrella organisation for teaching/ accommodation sites in various quite disparate parts of London and Kent. Maybe it hasn't quite recovered from its disparate rooting in Woolwich Poly, Avery Hill College of HE, Dartford College of Education and Garnett College. Certainly it is difficult to get a handle on the whole thing, and arguably most of its students have no need to - 63% of them are mature (there are good childcare arrangements incidentally, though stretched) and students probably go to a particular site for a particular reason - the site course or its geographical proximity. There are, however, attempts to bring a kind of coherence. The Student Union, for example. But even that focuses mainly on one of the sites.

Bearing the mature intake in mind, there is an academic emphasis on tailoring courses to individual requirements. 'Flexibility' and 'pathways' are the two buzz words, which don't take us a great deal further forward. Much more impressive is the Uni's HEFCE assessment record in Architecture, Environmental Studies and in Sociology. Two 'Excellent' ratings and a 23 out of 24 in Sociology suggest an academic strategy far above what one might expect from such a disparate grouping. Teaching excellence is the key to Greenwich, and there's something rather reassuring about that in terms of the government's desire to throw open Higher Education to mature students in a career context which can no longer reassure us with a job for life.

There is also an impressive emphasis on getting students jobs, which goes beyond the usual Erasmus, sandwich placements, or the PTS (the personal transferable skills that you hear about to the point of blurred vision from all non-traditional Unis). SCAMP is a scheme to develop skills required in the world of work, certainly - communication, mgt. skills, etc - but Greenwich is targeting students from ethnic minority groups and persuading managers in national companies to pair up with individuals to raise consciousness of what will be involved when they leave Greenwich.

You get the feeling that however disparate Greenwich may be geographically, there is someone behind it who has a clear and pragmatic strategy.

In addition to their own parts or colleges, Greenwich teams up with a range of associate colleges, 'who help to make the delivery of access, and the earlier years of Higher Education courses possible'. A lot of what they tell you about themselves is unfortunately framed in this kind of lingo. I take it to mean that they give non-degree establishments access to Greenwich's academic facilities and information, allow them to offer Greenwich awards and recruit 'foundation' students from them. If so, the liaison is another example of their enlightened espousal of the idea that in Higher Education today lies the hope not just of academic excellence for the few, but of the cultural, educational and economic regeneration of the country as a whole.

Seeming to confirm that the Uni is indeed operating at the sharp end is their involvement in the Greenwich millennium project. It organised a major architectural design competition for the Expo site and brought its environmental expertise to bear on the Millennium Fest. with the Millennium Tree Line project, which will see 2,000 trees planted, visible as a line from the air, in England, Europe and Africa. Questions as to why the Uni should even be called Greenwich (as no sites are there) would seem to be answered by its strategic position at some sort of ideological fulcrum of the Prime Meridian.

GREENWICH SITES

Accommodation, either in halls of residence or Uni-managed housing, is guaranteed to all first years.

Woolwich Site: Wellington Street, Woolwich, London SE18 6PF. This is the main site, which offers a wide range of courses and the delights of the Student Union, which is a converted Victorian swimming pool, hence The Deep End, a venue for discos, live bands, comedy, film nights, etc. There is also a sports hall, fitness room and 2 squash courts.

Avery Hill Sites: Bexley Road, Eltham, London SE9 2PQ, and Every Hill Road, Eltham, London SE9 2HB. Here you'll find Education (see also The Jewry Centre below), Law, Health, two gyms, soccer, rugby, lacrosse and hockey and cricket pitches, a running track and tennis courts.

Dartford Site: Oakfield Lane, Dartford, Kent DA1 2SZ. Schools of Architecture and Landscape, Land and Construction Mgt. There's a heated swimming pool here too, a sports hall, netball and tennis courts, soccer and cricket pitches.

Medway Site: Pembroke, Chatham Maritime, Kent ME4 4AW. Computing, a sports hall with badminton and basketball courts and a weights room.

Roehampton Site: Manresa House, Holybourne Avenue, London SW15 4JD. Business and Accounting, also football pitches, netball and tennis courts and a snooker room.

Kings Hill Site: 30 Churchill Square, Kings Hill, West Malling, Kent ME9 6DU. This is

where partnerships are developed with industry and commerce - education, training, consultancy, technology transfer and research (including research into 'the virtual classroom', allowing education students access to and communication within a classroom environment from a distance - sounds better than the real thing).
Jewry Street Centre: 31 Jewry Street, London EC3N 2EY. This is the School of Compulsory Education and Training.

GETTING THERE

★ By rail to main Woolwich site: Trains go from Charing Cross, Waterloo East and London Bridge (Dartford and Gillingham ultimate destinations). Make for Woolwich Arsenal station.

GYOSEI INTERNATIONAL COLLEGE

Gyosei International College
London Road
Reading
Berkshire
RG1 5AQ

TEL 0118 975 8281
FAX 0118 931 0137

GYOSEI INTERNATIONAL COLLEGE	
Founded	**1988**
Situation/style	**Campus**
UNDERGRADUATE PROFILE	
Population	**320**
Overseas student population	**80%**
Male/female ratio	**50:50**
1st year institut. accommodation	**100%**
Approximate cost	**£50-£85 pw**
ACADEMIC PROFILE	
A-level requirements:	**Medium**
Business Studies BCC	
FEES	
Contact Mr Reginald Hunt, Academic Registrar on 0118 975 8281 for 1998 fees.	
EMPLOYMENT PROFILE	
Principal job market destinations:	
Commerce, Industry	

VAG VIEW

The niche strategy, which millionaire businessman Jim Slater called the Zulu Principle, is the cornerstone of what Gyosei is offering. Edward de Bono, who coined the concept of lateral thinking, described it this way: 'Not many people know much about Zulus, Mr Slater would point out. But a lot of people make it their life's work to know all there is to know about, say, England or America. So it is very hard to make much impact as an expert about those countries. But if you were to find out only a fair amount about Zulus, you could probably become the world's top expert...In his case, the Zulus were obscure little companies that had been ignored by the stock market but had hidden potential.' (Tactics: The Art & Science of Success, *Collins 1985*).

The niche which Gyosei is offering first degree business students in England is delivered by what they call the 'bi-cultural education' at the college. Gyosei has a Japanese base. The courses offer something which probably no other business course in the UK does: 'firsthand knowledge and experience of Japanese business and culture...' As a non-Japanese student at Gyosei you will get 'invaluable links with Japan, with Japanese people, with Japanese companies, and with international companies that do business with Japan...', and, in particular with the Nozu Group of Japanese companies.
It's a pretty clear and impressive route to success. Three to four-year degree courses lead to BA degrees awarded by City University (see entry). Courses include Business Studies, Business with Cultural Studies, Business with Language Studies.

The college, which operates out of Reading University's original site on London Road, charges annual tuition fees of £9,145 (1996). A grant is available (around 10%), and there are international bursaries and scholarships.

GETTING THERE

★ By road: M4 (J11).
★ There is an express bus service to and from London, which stops outside the campus.
★ By rail: London Paddington, 30 mins; Bristol Parkway, 1:00; Birmingham New Street, 2:15; Sheffield, 3:45.
★ By air: Direct bus/train services from Heathrow and Gatwick.

HARPER ADAMS AGRICULTURAL COLLEGE

Harper Adams
Agricultural College
Edgmond
Newport
Shropshire
TF10 8NB

TEL 01952 820280
FAX 01952 814783

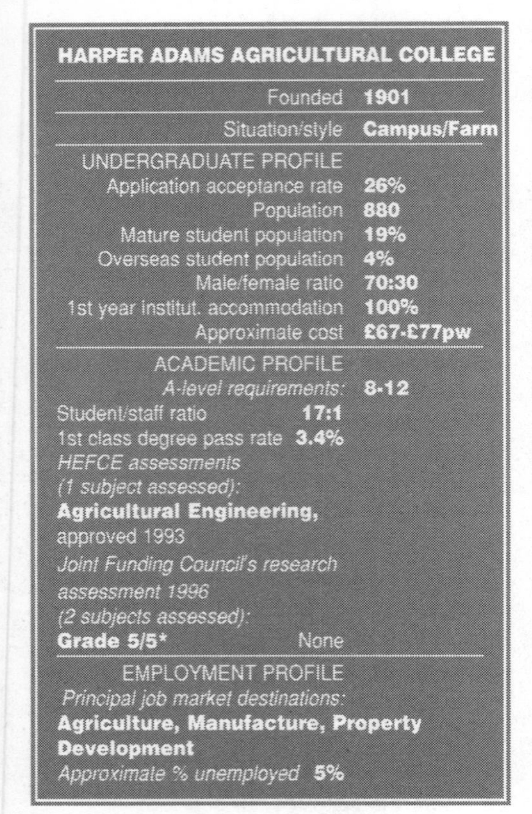

HARPER ADAMS AGRICULTURAL COLLEGE	
Founded	**1901**
Situation/style	**Campus/Farm**
UNDERGRADUATE PROFILE	
Application acceptance rate	**26%**
Population	**880**
Mature student population	**19%**
Overseas student population	**4%**
Male/female ratio	**70:30**
1st year institut. accommodation	**100%**
Approximate cost	**£67-£77pw**
ACADEMIC PROFILE	
A-level requirements:	**8-12**
Student/staff ratio	**17:1**
1st class degree pass rate	**3.4%**
HEFCE assessments (1 subject assessed):	
Agricultural Engineering, approved 1993	
Joint Funding Council's research assessment 1996 (2 subjects assessed):	
Grade 5/5*	None
EMPLOYMENT PROFILE	
Principal job market destinations: **Agriculture, Manufacture, Property Development**	
Approximate % unemployed	**5%**

VAG VIEW

Harper Adams is an agricultural college on the borders of Shropshire and Staffordshire, which also offers degrees in related fields. It's approach to agriculture is both academic and practical, full use being made of the college's 175-hectare farm.

Besides Agriculture, Animal Science, and Production, courses (all BSc, most involving work placement) are offered in Land and Crop Mgt., Marketing, and in International Agriculture, Agricultural Engineering & Engineering Mgt., Rural Enterprise, and Environmental Protection.

All first year students are accommodated and catered for in college.

There's a fully equipped sports hall with weights room, indoor swimming pool, snooker table, tennis and squash courts and students organise a range of otuward bound activities including mountaineering, orienteering and absailing.

GETTING THERE

★ By road: M6 (J 13 or J14), A518, A41, B5062.

★ By rail: To Shrewsbury from Birmingham New Street, 1:10; from London to Stafford, 1:40.

HERIOT-WATT UNIVERSITY

Heriot-Watt University
Riccarton
Edinburgh
EH14 4AS

TEL 0131 449 5153
FAX 0131 449 5111

Heriot-Watt University
Student Association
The Union
Riccarton
Edinburgh EH14 4AS

TEL 0131 451 5333
FAX 0131 451 5344

HERIOT-WATT UNIVERSITY

Founded	**1966**
Situation/style	**Campus**
UNDERGRADUATE PROFILE	
Application acceptance rate	**16%**
Population	**4,350**
Mature student population	**20%**
Overseas student population	**13%**
Male/female ratio	**58:42**
1st year institut. accommodation	**100%**
Approximate cost	**£28-£55 pw**
ACADEMIC PROFILE	
A-level requirements:	**Medium-High**

Int. Business & Finance BBC, **Architecture** BCC, **Town Planning** CDD, **Actuarial Maths & Statistics** BBC, **Computer Science & Engineering** CDD, **Chem., Civil, E & E, Mech. Eng.** CCD

Student/staff ratio	**12:1**
1st class degree pass rate	**9.8%**
SHEFC assessments (11 subjects assessed/approved):	
1994 **Civil Engineering, Computer Studies, Physics**	Highly Satis.
1995 **Chemistry, Maths & Statistics, Mechanical + Manufacturing Engineering.**	Highly Satis.
Electrical & Electronic Engineering.	Excellent
1996 **Finance & Accounting.**	Highly Satis.
Joint Funding Council's research assessment 1996 (15 subjects assessed):	
Mineral & Mining Engineering	Grade 5*
Applied Maths, Built Environment	Grade 5
EMPLOYMENT PROFILE	
Employability in Industry:	
MPW national league table (1996)	**22nd**
Principal job market destinations:	

Commerce, Manufacturing (strong on **Electronic & Electrical**), **Retail/Wholesale, Education, Computer, Construction**

PIP 1996 employers' survey:	
Top 3 subjects/national ranking	
Electrical Engineering	12th
Science	14th
Construction & Civil Engineering	15th=
Approximate % unemployed	**6%**

VAG VIEW

Heriot-Watt is on the up, both in this country and internationally, thanks in particular to its language courses. It has done what many other Unis are trying to do - it has captured the respect of the job market in the EC.

It also has an active and clear thinking Union, rather more prepossessing than Edinburgh in that this Uni is smaller, it is closer-knit, and it is easier to make your mark here. Nevertheless, the levels, for example of the journalism, are very good.

The Uni is also in Edinburgh. What else needs to be said?

SITUATION

Heriot-Watt Riccarton Campus, built around a loch, is on the west side of Edinburgh and has associations with three other academic institutions (see Academia below).

GETTING THERE

★ By road: Approach Heriot-Watt on the A71 or the A70, in which case turn off at Currie on to Riccarton Mains Road.
★ By rail: part of the fast north-east line, which leads eventually to London Kings Cross (4:30). Glasgow Central is 50 mins. away; Newcastle 1:30.
★ By air: Edinburgh Airport is nearby and offers inland and international flights.

ACCOMMODATION

Student village: three self-catering, en-suite halls of residence: Robert Bryson, Robin Smith and George Burnett Halls.

Leonard Horner Hall, elsewhere on campus, also self-catering, and there's a group of smaller halls fully catered, but some must share here.

University-owned furnished (4/5 person) flats on campus plus others around Edinburgh (mainly for 2nd+ years).

UNION & ENTS

Edinburgh Festival, Hogmanay (see Edinburgh Uni entry) plus everything that makes this the cultural capital of Scotland (Britain?). Heriot-Watt Students Association offers Liberty's cafe bar - lunch (home-bakes; no smoking), cocktail nights, live bands; Dr Connery's for club nights, especially Friday's Club FND (great lights system, top club venue plus drinks promotions); Jinglin' Geordies' bar with cast conditioned ales, fast food, T/time specials, The Big Breakfast - 11am to 12 weekends; Hustlers games arcade. Also usual quiz nights, comedy acts, etc.

Very sound welfare organisation and active campaigners - most recent success Anonymous Marking: the person marking the exam paper will not know who has written it (or at least the student's name won't appear) as from 1997 entry. Perhaps such an idea as this would cure Cambridge students' concern over female students being awarded fewer Firsts than male students. Also enlightened canvassing of students, in context of government cut-backs, for alternative ideas to funding education. Liveliness reflected in good *Watts On* student newspaper, particularly features and reviews; fair record for career prospects in journalism (e.g. *Scotsman*, *Guardian*, Channel 4).

SPORT

Student-run sports centre offers 30 clubs, squash, badminton, volleyball, basketball, climbing wall, indoor football, multi-gym, free weights and ergometer, sports doctor, physiotherapists, plus adjacent football pitches (6), rugby pitches (2), cricket square, all-weather tennis courts.

ACADEMIA

Degrees follow the usual credit-based modular system, but 'the University has safeguarded the quality and standing of specialist Honours degree courses by avoiding an unnecessary fragmentation of study.' Here is a Uni which can see the pitfalls of *ultimate* flexibility, which so many are promoting elsewhere. For those keen on a broad-based interdisciplinary course, the Faculty of Combined Studies (BA or BSc) caters for them.

'Modern languages are an outstanding strength,' confirmed one careers adviser. 'You can walk straight out of Heriot-Watt with a Modern Languages degree into European jobs in the EC. They have a translating/ interpreting element which is not quite unique but a great strength.'

Look also at the courses on offer in their Faculty of Environmental Mgt. and Technology, and the BSc programme in Actuarial Maths and Statistics.

Finally, the Uni has a close relationship with Silicon Glen and a good placement reputation in the high-tec/ computing/ electrical engineering field - see particularly their Computing Science and Electrical & Electronic Engineering programmes.

High A-level grades allow students to cut 4-year courses to three, but consider the social implications - you'll be a Fresher when your academic contemporaries are already well into the Edinburgh scene and friendships have been formed. In any case, aren't four years in Edinburgh, even on a grant, better than three?

Heriot-Watt also has The Edinburgh College of Art. Architecture has been offered here since its founding in 1907; there's also a BA course in Planning Studies, as well as Art & Design. Then there's Moray House (founded in 1835). Holyrood Campus is in the heart of the Old Town, Cramond Campus a bus ride away from the centre with playing fields on site. Accommodation provided. Moray House specialises in Education (including a good course in Physical Education) and Social Work. What's more it has an Outdoor Centre in Kingussie in the Scottish Highlands ostensibly for course work. Finally, H-W has The Scottish College of Textiles (founded 1883) 30+ miles to the South of Edinburgh in Galashiels. It constitutes H-W's Faculty of Textiles, offers its own accommodation, sporting facilities, wide-ranging ents programme, and has a good record of assessments in both Textile Design and its business side - Textiles with Marketing (BSc), Quality Mgt. (BSc).

Edinburgh College of Art
Lauriston Place
Edinburgh EH3 9DF
Tel: 0131 221 6000
Fax: 0131 221 6001

Moray House
Institute of Education
Holyrood Road
Edinburgh EH8 8AQ
Tel: 0131 556
Fax: 0131 557 3458

The Scottish College of Textiles
Netherdale
Galashiels
TD1 3HF
Tel: 01896 753351
Fax: 01896 758965

HERTFORDSHIRE UNIVERSITY

University of Hertfordshire
College Lane
Hatfield
Hertfordshire
AL10 9AB

TEL 01707 284000
FAX 01707 284115

University of Hertfordshire
Student Union
(Hatfield Campus)
PO Box 109
College Lane
Hatfield
Herts AL10 9AB

TEL 01707 285000
FAX 01707 251118

University of Hertfordsire
Student Union
(Balls Park Campus)
Hertford
Herts SG13 8QF

TEL 01707 285577

University of Hertfordsire
Student Union
(Wall Hall Campus)
Nr Aldenham
Watford
Herts WD2 8AT

TEL 01707 285780

UNIVERSITY OF HERTFORDSHIRE

Founded	**1952**
Situation/style	**City sites**
UNDERGRADUATE PROFILE	
Application acceptance rate	**14%**
Population	**10,250**
Mature student population	**40%**
Overseas student population	**12%**
Male/female ratio	**52:48**
1st year institut. accommodation	**100%**
Approximate cost	**£36-£46 pw**

ACADEMIC PROFILE

A-level requirements: **Low-Medium**

Pharmacology 12-14, **Nursing & Social Work** 14, **Applied Biology** 12-14, **Computer Science combinations** 12-20, **Maths & Statistics combinations** 12-20, **Aerospace, Civil Engineering** 18-22, **E & E Eng. combinations** 16-22, **Law** 16-22, **Politics, Social Policy, Sociology, Environmental Studies** 14, **Accounting, Financial Services** 18, **Business Studies and combinations** 12-20, **Linguistics and combinations** 14-16

Student/staff ratio	**17:1**
1st class degree pass rate	**5.5%**
HEFCE assessments (14 subjects assessed/approved):	
1995 **Environmental Studies**	Excellent
Linguistics 20	
Joint Funding Council's research assessment 1996 (17 subjects assessed):	
Grade 5/5*	None

EMPLOYMENT PROFILE

Principal job market destinations:

Manufacturing (strong on **Electrical/ Electronic, Pharmaceutical**), **Education, Retail/Wholesale, Commerce, Computer, Health, Public Admin./Law, Personnel, Arts/Media** (esp. **Publishing**), good record **Engineering Design**

PIP 1996 employers' survey: Top 2 subjects/national ranking	
Engineering & Technology	30th
Computing	33rd=
Approximate % unemployed	**6%**

VAG VIEW

Hertfordshire Uni, formerly Hatfield Poly, has various sites (see Addresses), all of them tracing an arc from Hertford through Hatfield through St Albans to Watford, some 7 miles north-west of Greater London.

The main site is known as the Hatfield Campus, but watch out!, so is another Uni site on the other side of Hatfield. It is, on the face of it, very confusing, particularly as 'Hertford' sounds a bit like 'Hatfield', there is more of the Uni of Hertfordshire in Hatfield than Hertford, and the St Albans campus is in Hatfield Road. But students capable of working out the intricacies of the modular system will no doubt cope.

Indeed they may not have to cope, as 'you will be based entirely on one campus.' But even that isn't quite true, because the Hatfield Campus (that is the main Hatfield Campus, not the other Hatfield Campus) is the one where most of the action is.

Hatfield itself is a dot on the map east of St Albans, two miles or so beyond the M25. People are presumably born there and some no doubt stay, but most are surely there for its convenient position vis a vis the metropolis, the A1M/M1 chimney to the north and the M25 ring around London.

The Hatfield Campus - the main one - couldn't be more convenient; it is slap bang on Junction 3 of the A1M.

ADDRESSES

Hatfield Campus: Most faculties, see address above.
Hatfield Campus, Manor Road, Hatfield, Herts AL10 9TL. Tel: 01707 285305.
Hertford Campus, Mangrove Road, Hertford, Herts SG13 8QF. Tel: 01707 285406.
St Albans Campus, 7 Hatfield Road, St Albans, Herts AL1 3RS. Tel: 01707 286210.
Watford Campus, Wall Hall Aldenham, Watford, Herts WD2 8AT. Tel: 01707 285606.

GETTING THERE

★ By road: The main **Hatfield** Campus - A1M (J3); the Art & Design Faculty - via Junctions 3 or 4 (it is midway between the two).
★ By rail: London (Moorgate, 40 mins), London (Kings Cross, 22 mins). The main campus is a few miles from the station, as is Art & Design, but in another direction. I would take a taxi.
Hertford is a town off to the West of the A10, about 6 miles north-east of Hatfield. They are joined by the A414. Mangrove Road, where the campus is set, runs off the A414 on the East side of the town.
★ By rail: There are 2 stations in Hertford (wouldn't you know?). Trains to Hertford North come out of London Kings Cross (25 mins) and London Moorgate (45 mins). Trains to Hertford East come out of London Liverpool Street (45 mins).
The **Watford** Campus is actually nearer Aldenham than Watford, so by road it's the M1 (J5).
★ By rail: It's either London Euston (20 mins) to Watford Junction or London Kings Cross Thameslink to Radlett (20 mins); the campus is about equidistant between the two.
The **St Albans** Campus is in the centre of St Albans, and the easiest route in from the South is probably the M25 (J22), A1081.
★ By rail: it's London (Thameslink) to St Albans City, journey time 25 mins.

ACADEMIA

Hatfield Campus: Faculties of Engineering, Health and Human Sciences, Information Sciences, Natural Sciences, Combined and Continuing Studies.
Watford Campus: Humanities and Education.
St Albans: Law.
Hertford Campus: Business.
Hatfield/Manor Road: Art and Design.
Part time and sandwich degree offered. Note assessment strengths in Environmental Studies and Linguistics.

ACCOMMODATION

All self-catering. All first years, who will live on or nearby the campus where they are taught, are guaranteed accommodation, most of which is purpose built.

SPORT

Hatfield Campus: tennis courts, playing fields, all weather, floodlit playing surface, sports hall, 2 squash courts, fitness centre, artificial hockey pitch, plus football, rugby and cricket pitches. The real prize is that the Hertfordshire Indoor Cricket School is situated in the centre of the campus and the Uni can use its top quality practice nets. *Hertford Campus*: indoor swimming pool, gym, soccer, tennis, netball, cricket facilities, fitness centre, trim trail, floodlit, all weather courts for tennis, netball, hockey, football. *Watford Campus*: rugby, football pitches, open air swimming pool, floodlit and other tennis, netball courts, gym, fitness centre, and the whole is situated on the edge of a golf course.

ENTS

Faced with the appalling job of bringing all this together the Union is doing an incredible job. Universe is their journalistic communication tool; Crush AM/FM plays reggae, classical, jazz, rap, indie, dance, bhangra, heavy metal and more besides - chat shows, comps., interviews, news, weather - it is a lively invigorating scene. Clubs and sports clubs abound (from Living Marxism to Tae Kwon Do, from Myth and Magic to American Football - the Hurricanes are their team). Ents include live bands (Counterfeit Stones, Fluke, Roy the Roach, etc), comedy (Jack Dee, Alan Parker etc), novelty theme nights, discos, cabarets (the ubiquitous Regurgitator, Stevie Starr) and balls.

Hatfield, which has the best technical facilities, hosts the main live music events and transport is laid on from the other sites. There are discos, quizzes, theme nights and the odd live band or comedy act at the Boathouse Bar on Hertford, and at Watford discos, themed party nights, bands and events such as Alternative Miss World. Balls at all except St Albans, with which the Union is just now getting to grips.

HOLBORN COLLEGE

Holborn College
200 Greyhound Road
London W14 9RY

TEL 0171 385 3377
FAX 0171 381 3377

HOLBORN COLLEGE	
Founded	1969
Situation/style	City sites
UNDERGRADUATE PROFILE	
Application acceptance rate	11%
Population	650
Mature student population	70%
Overseas student population	75%
Male/female ratio	55:45
ACADEMIC PROFILE	
A-level requirements:	Low
Law EE	
FEES	
From approx. **£400** to **£10,300** depending on course specification.	

VAG VIEW

A college exclusively for the study of Law. Degrees awarded by Wolverhampton University.

With basic entrance requirements of EE, and no LEA funding for the course, you would be forgiven for thinking this was a way to buy a Law degree if you've got the money and can't make the grades. This may be the case for some of the 650 students, but for others the flexibility and facility of this course makes it a practicable and welcome alternative to the traditional route. Everything you need is included in the price, from personal study timetable plans, to course route maps taking you step by step to your finals. There are summaries of casebooks, as well as revision books, mock exams and even ideal answers.

The main advantage of this college has to be the correspondence route. You can take up to seven years to complete your course, professional bodies complying, and if you fancy spending a year in college, and a few at home, you're more than welcome. Correspondence students attend a mid-sessional review course, and a final revision course, where lecturers go over all the material you were sent on tape. Throughout, correspondence students can use the Student Enquiry Service to contact their tutors if they encounter any problems.

For those choosing an in-house degree, accommodation is not offered but help is available to find it. You are entitled to a maintenance grant (usual conditions applying), and the LEA will give you a cost contribution towards the course of around £850, if you are eligible.

The degree is divided into three parts, each comprising four subjects. You can do two, three or four subjects a year. The first part gives you a Certificate of Higher Education, the second a Diploma of HE in Law, and the third the LLB Degree. Another valuable aspect of this college is its international relations. 75% of students are from overseas, and review and revision courses are held in Hong Kong, Kuala Lumpur and Johor Bahru. The King of Malaysia actually offers two Bar scholarships to promising Malaysian students to study at Holborn.

With international investment and all-inclusive fees, it seems more like a business venture than a university. However, they tell us it works - 'high pass rates and prize winning performances'.

GETTING THERE

★ Hammersmith Underground (Piccadilly, Metropolitan, District lines) or Barons Court (Piccadilly, District).

HUDDERSFIELD UNIVERSITY

The University of Huddersfield
Queensgate
Huddersfield
HD1 3DH

TEL 01484 422288
FAX 01484 516151

University of Huddersfield
Student Union
Milton Hall
Queensgate
Huddersfield HD1 3DH

TEL 01484 538156
FAX 01484 432333

UNIVERSITY OF HUDDERSFIELD

Founded	**1841**
Situation/style	**Campus**
UNDERGRADUATE PROFILE	
Application acceptance rate	**19%**
Population	**7,150**
Mature student population	**30%**
Overseas student population	**3%**
Male/female ratio	**52:48**
1st year institut. accommodation	**60%**
Approximate cost (Uni)	**£35-£57 pw**
(Town)	**£35 pw**
ACADEMIC PROFILE	
A-level requirements:	**Medium-Low**

Chem. Engineering 10, **E & E Engineering** 12, **Engineering Design, Mech. Eng.** CCC-EE, **Multimedia Tech., Music Tech.** 18, **Law** CCC, **Social Work** EE, **Health/Sports/ Community Studies combs.** 10-14, **Politics** 14, **Accountancy** 12-14, **Business Studies, Mgt., Marketing** 14-16, **Theatre Studies** BCC, **Music** (+ practical qualifications) CE

Student/staff ratio	**21:1**
1st class degree pass rate	**3.9%**
HEFCE assessments (13 subjects assessed/approved):	
1994 **Applied Social Work, Music**	Excellent
Joint Funding Council's research assessment 1996 (21 subjects assessed):	
Grade 5/5*	None
EMPLOYMENT PROFILE	
Employability in Industry:	
MPW national league table (1996)	**49th=**

Principal job market destinations:
Manufacturing, Retail/Wholesale, Commerce, Hotel/Restaurant, Education, Health, Public Admin/Law, Computer, Arts/Media, Architecture

PIP 1996 employers' survey:	
Top subject/national ranking	
Business	29th
Approximate % unemployed	**10%**

VAG VIEW

I get the feeling the University doesn't like its own students, but no doubt I've been listening to an unrepresentative few. There have certainly been rifts in the past and last year was no exception. There's a kind of leftover from the 60s feel about the place - poetry, drug busts et al - which is beguilingly quaint. But certain departments do seem to be making ground.

SITUATION

Huddersfield lies between Leeds to the north-east and Manchester to the south-west, about 15 and 25 miles respectively from these great centres of commerce and entertainment.

Two sites: Queensgate, the main campus, close to the centre of town (the focal point), and Holly Bank, two miles out and well set for an early escape to Manchester via Junction 24 of the M62.

GETTING THERE

★ By road: M62 (J24), M1 (Junctions 38-40).
★ Good coach facilities.
★ By train: Queensgate Campus is about 10

minutes walk from the station, which offers routes out in every direction (London via Wakefield, 3:30; Liverpool Lime Street, 1:45).
★ By air: Leeds-Bradford or Manchester airport.

ACCOMMODATION

Can't guarantee first years a place in hall - one catered, the rest not. Things will get better - they've bought a site to erect a student village south of the town.

UNION & ENTS

There have been strained relations between the university authorities and the Student Union of late, which came to a head over a drug bust in the SU nightclub, Eden, at the tail end of last year. The Union is of course anti-drugs, and the bust in itself was never an issue, rather the way the Uni authorities went about it without co-opting the support of the Union beforehand. *Udders*, the student rag, milked the situation for all it was worth, suggesting a Uni undercover operation as deft as that undertaken by the police, with the upshot that an executive member of the Union, who had allegedly been 'pressured', was reported afterwards to have been in some form of 'police protection'. My, my, and we thought the 60s were over.

In fact *Udders*, a new and sparkily conspiratorial student newspaper, makes Huddersfield seem quite an intriguing sort of place altogether. In the December 3 issue there was the drugs bust, the unveiling of a student stalker, the exposure of a student operation downloading pornography via the Uni's Internet, and a report that the university's resident Territorial Army was enhancing its security in preparation for 'a renewed bombing campaign by the IRA' at Christmas. That these were more than shadows was shown a few weeks later when the IRA campaign did happen.

Ents focus on Eden as nightclub - events include bar quizzes, discos, theme nights, bands, cabaret - and various haunts in town. The Albert pub is where all the interest in poetry emanates from - Huddersfield's annual poetry fest., in March, is a national institution. Then there are folk and jazz evenings (and recently gargantuan actor Brian Blessed did his one-man bearded mammoth show) at the Cellar Theatre, part of the Lawrence Batley Theatre - he of local Cash 'n' Carry fame. Fast-paced topical comedian Rich Hall played the cellar bar there not so long ago. Around the same time Red Dwarf Craig Charles played the Town Hall. The Arts Centre has gone, alas, pulled down last year to make way for a shopping precinct. The one cinema also closed, to be re-opened as a private business venture called The Tudor. Then there's a new pub right opposite the Uni which is just now managing to separate unwary students from their pitiful grant cheques, and old favourites, Yates's Wine Lodge and the Old Coach House among others. Award-winning club Beyond Beach Babylon tempts some away from the Eden in their own backyard, as occasionally do Ethos (purportedly for over-25s) and Visage (over 18s). Finally the football and rugby league stadium, the McAlpine, is the venue for music spectaculars - from classical concerts to top rock bands.

SPORT

Sports hall on campus plus a new fitness training centre and playing areas away from campus, which provide for football, rugby (league and union), hockey, cricket and tennis. There is also a new astroturf pitch and two new top quality soccer pitches. In addition, Huddersfield has a large student-discount sports centre with a swimming pool.

ACADEMIA

Music and Applied Social Work scored 'Excellent' in the HEFCE assessments, and you can't do better than that - these from among a range of subjects, all of them approved, the weakest being Modern Languages with a 15 out of 24. Since then Languages have become an integral part of the modular system which operates here, and no doubt that will have raised its profile accordingly.

The eight academic schools are: Applied Sciences (Transport and Logistics, Chemical and Biological Sciences, Geographical and Environmental Sciences), Computing and Mathematics, Design Technology (Textiles, Architecture), Education, Engineering,

Business, Human and Health Sciences, (Podiatry, Behavioural Science, Social Work, Health Studies, Careers Guidance), Music and Humanities.

'I went there,' said one sixth-form adviser, 'and spent a couple of days with the Department of Distribution.' *What?* 'The Department of Distribution - they've looked at the market very carefully and where there's a gap... in this case Transportation...they've gone hard for it.' He must have seen my eyes glaze over - 'I have to say, I have seen more enthusiasm among the staff at Huddersfield - both in this department and in Hotel and Catering - than at any other university in the land. I had thought, Oh, Huddersfield, can I really afford the time to go? And I was very surprised.'

I myself had encountered a similar example of inspired opportunism in connection with the Department of Politics. It was around the time of the Scott Report and I was being advised by one of this country's best informed sources on the Intelligence Services, a writer by the name of Stephen Dorril - no, not the MP, the author, rather, of *The Silent Conspiracy*, *Smear* and numerous other spycatcher tomes, the editor no less of *Lobster*, Britain's most authoritative journal on the security services at the forefront of exposing the MI5 plots against Harold Wilson. Stephen had been asked to lecture in the Politics Department and I thought, What an inspired move. A year or so afterwards, while enjoying the conspiratorial tone of *Udders*, I must say I wondered whether Stephen had taken the whole place over. It's a hand-in-glove fit.

Hull University

The University of Hull
Cottingham Road
Hull
HU6 7RX

TEL 01482 346311
FAX 01482 465936

Hull University Union
University House
Cottingham Road
Hull HU6 7RX

TEL 01482 445361
FAX 01482 466280

UNIVERSITY OF HULL

Founded	**1927**
Situation/style	**Campus**
UNDERGRADUATE PROFILE	
Application acceptance rate	**9%**
Population	**6,100**
Mature student population	**20%**
Overseas student population	**10%**
Male/female ratio	**50:50**
1st year institut. accommodation	**100%**
Approximate cost	**£40-£70 pw**
ACADEMIC PROFILE	
A-level requirements:	**Medium-High**

Aquatic, Environmental, Marine Biol. BCC-CCD, **Psychology and combinations** BBB-BCC, **Physical Science** CCC-CDD, **Math combs. and Statistics** BCC-BCD, **Computer Science & Eng.** BCC-CCC, **Electronic Eng., Robotics, Media Tech.** BCC-CCC, **History, Law** BCC-BBB, **Sociology, Anthropology, Social Policy** BBB-CCC, **Politics** BBC-BCC, **English, Modern Languages, & combs.** BBB-CCC

Student/staff ratio	**16:1**
1st class degree pass rate	**5.6%**
HEFCE assessments (16 subjects assessed/approved):	
(**Scandinavian Studies** NYP)	
1993 **Chemistry, History**	Excellent
1994 **Applied Social Work**	
Social Policy & Admin.	Excellent
1995/6 **French** 21, **German** 19	
1996 **Sociology** 20, **Italian** 22	
Joint Funding Council's research assessment 1996 (34 subjects assessed):	
History	Grade 5
EMPLOYMENT PROFILE	
Employability in Industry:	
MPW national league table (1996)	**26th=**
Principal job market destinations:	

Manufacturing (strong on **Electronic & Electrical**), **Retail/Wholesale, Commerce, Education, Public Admin./ Law, Arts/Media, Computer, Health**

PIP 1996 employers' survey:	
Top subject/national ranking	
Languages	20th=
Approximate % unemployed	**5%**

VAG VIEW

Hull's famous literary son, the late poet Philip Larkin, described the city as 'in the world, yet sufficiently on the edge of it to have a different resonance.' It is the sort of place once discovered that you are in danger of staying in for life. People talk about friendly places, but Hull really is one and the reason it is, is historical. For centuries it was cut off from the rest of the country, by the Humber to the south, the wide open agricultural Wolds to the north, and by a large expanse of nothing to the west. Then all the way from Liverpool on the opposite coast came the M62, which connects with the A1(M), north and south, and suddenly Hull became part of the rest of the world. But it didn't lose its community spirit. If you get lost in Hull, which is quite easy, you will immediately tune into this.

For many, however, Hull is still a bit off the map. Current student Adam Ford told me, 'You'd be surprised at the number of people in Liverpool who think that the M62 stops in Leeds. This is the essence of Hull - those who know it, love it; those

who don't, sneer at it as a fish 'n' peas Mecca.'

In Yorkshire there are even stranger reactions to Hull. 'Hull is separate culturally,' said a teacher at a sixth-form college just an hour away, who sends students to Newcastle, two hours further north; to York, an hour to the west; to Sunderland; to Teesside; but rarely, if ever, to Hull. Perhaps they never quite forgave Humberside for becoming part of the county. Another teacher, in the area of York, said rather grudgingly, 'Some of the management courses at Hull I am very impressed with.'

In fact Hull, as the fact box shows, has a high degree of teaching excellence in a number of subjects. It all seems very unfair, and there may even be an inferiority complex developing in people from Hull. A teacher at a girls' public school south of York said, 'We had a speaker in from Hull who has put my pupils off for life - he was selling Hull: if you haven't been to Hull you haven't lived. It is good that there are such critical consumers about.' Perhaps Hull would do better to sell itself outside Yorkshire. I can think of reasons why I'd buy it.

SITUATION

The campus is three miles to the north of Kingston-upon-Hull, more or less midway between the city and Beverley, a town/cathedral city, with its very small Minster. The city's name, perhaps a little confusing to people outside the area, means 'King's Town upon the River Hull', and the seal was set on it by Edward I in 1299. Generally, except in atlases and on formal occasions, the city is known just as Hull, and to be absolutely clear, the river on whose northern bank it is situated is the Humber. The River Hull flows down into the Humber to the east of the University.

GETTING THERE

★ By road: M62, A63, A1079, B1233.
★ By rail: Leeds, 1:00; Sheffield, 1:45; Manchester Piccadilly, 2:15; London Kings Cross, 4:30; Birmingham New Street, 3:00.
★ Fast connections to Cottingham; bus the 2 miles to Campus.
★ By air: Humberside airport; Leeds/Bradford airport.

ACCOMMODATION

Large, traditional (fully catered) halls and more beautifully set, part-catered halls in nearby Cottingham, self-catered student houses, on-campus flats and Uni-managed private properties.

UNION, ARTS & ENTS

Hull is a centre for the arts, particularly for music, poetry and theatre. The Hull Truck Company is one of this country's most highly renowned companies, a great seedbed of writing and acting talent, particularly drawn from the locality. They also stage one-night fringe and jazz productions and galvanise the city's annual festival. The Hull New Theatre looks after the more conventional drama and May St Theatre is the place for dance and mime. For films, the pioneering Take Two, with its classic cinema fare, and the arthouse/cult cinema, Hull Screen, balance the more commercial multiplex Odeon and UCI. All these offer student discounts.

Hull nightlife is so good that it was, a year or so ago, the subject of a TV documentary. All its clubs do at least one student night a week. LA's, Oasis and Eclipse satisfy chart/dance fans; Spiders for goths, crusties and indie kids; Welly for indie; the Room for ambient/techno fans; Silhouette for indie, 80s and gay nights. The Tower, with a wide menu of music, also does a gay night, but it is at other times student Hull's most popular hetero pulling shop and the place where all Freshers begin.

Because the Uni is so self-contained on its campus just north of the city, it is a humming hive of activity. There is a student radio station, URH, which serves the campus and most halls of residence and acts as a training ground for a radio club, heavily into deejaying and local hospital radio. There are openings for position heads in programme planning, engineering, marketing and managing, and among students who have served the station are some who have gone on to York's Viking FM, Hull's local station and the BBC. The Tech. Comm. is a parallel organisation heavily into sound and lighting systems and deejaying, which gets its performance kicks at the Friday Big Bang classic disco and live band, and the Saturday sell-out night Double Dipped disco, which caters for indie, dance, happy house and pop classics. There is also a magazine, HULLFiRE, produced by students from a busy DTP room, where you'll as likely find club secretaries using the equipment for posters, pamphlets and so on, for Hull is also something of a campaigning and fund-raising Union. Mainstream campaigns have included actions in support of Third World First, Animal Rights and Amnesty International, and there's a particularly active Women's Committee - 'not a gang of man-haters or bra-burners', so much as champions of women's welfare, health and safety, and really just having a good time.

There are 4 bars, two on the ground floor of the Union - Chico Mendes, used for local band nights, club and society parties, smaller discos and charity auctions, and the John McCarthy (he was a student here), used for Monday quiz nights, regular bar promotions, etc. A second floor has snooker and pool tables and games machines, and the fourth is to be found in the Sports and Fitness Centre. There is always something going down at each of these every night of the week.

SPORT

The sports centre has two large halls for indoor sports. There are 6 squash courts, a solarium, and a gym, and adjacent to the Centre are pitches for football, rugby, hockey, cricket, 9 tennis courts, and a floodlit all-weather surface. The Boat, Canoe and Sub-Aqua clubs have a boathouse on the Hull. Bursaries are available, some 20 a year, some for disabled athletes.

IMPERIAL COLLEGE LONDON

Imperial College of Science,
Technology & Medicine
Exhibition Road
South Kensington
London
SW7 2AZ

TEL 0171 589 5111
FAX 0171 584 7596

Imperial College Union
Beit Quad
Prince Consort Road
London SW7 2BB

TEL 0171 594 8060
FAX 0171 594 8065

IMPERIAL COLLEGE OF SCIENCE, TECHNOLOGY & MEDICINE

Founded	**1907**
Situation/style	**City site**
UNDERGRADUATE PROFILE	
Application acceptance rate	**12%**
Medical AAR	**5%**
Population	**5,200**
Mature student population	**15%**
Overseas student population	**30%**
Male/female ratio	**70:30**
1st year institut. accommodation	**100%**
Approximate cost	**£55-£75 pw**
ACADEMIC PROFILE	
A-level requirements:	**Very High**

Medicine ABB:
- ★ Science 'A's required **Chemistry**
- ★ Addit. Non-Science 'A's acceptable **Yes**
- ★ Retakes considered **Ext. circs.**
- ★ Retake offer **AAB**
- ★ Clinical contact **3rd year**

Student/staff ratio	**4:1**
1st class degree pass rate	**20%**
HEFCE assessments (6 subjects assessed/approved):	
1993 **Chemistry**	Excellent
1994 **Business & Management, Computing, Geology**	Excellent
1996 **Chemical Engineering** 22	
Joint Funding Council's research assessment 1996 (23 subjects assessed):	
Hospital/Clinical (National Heart & Lung Institute), **Pure Maths, Computer, Chemical Eng., Civil Eng., Mechanical/ Aeronautical/ Manufacturing Engineering.**	Grade 5*
Pre-Clinical, Biochemistry, Biol. Sciences, Chemistry, Physics, Applied Maths, Statistics, Engineering, Mineral/Mining Eng., History.	Grade 5
EMPLOYMENT PROFILE	
Employability in Industry:	
MPW national league table (1996)	**14th**

Principal job market destinations:
Health, Commerce (strong on **Accounting**), **Manufacturing** (strong on **Pharmaceutical**), **Engineering Design** (strong), **Computer**

PIP 1996 employers' survey: Top 3 subjects/national ranking	
Engineering & Technology	2nd
Science	2nd
Computing	2nd
Approximate % unemployed	**4%**

VAG VIEW

There's a welcome sense of continuity in the academic life of the college since its foundation in 1907, following the merger of the prestigious Royal College of Science, the Royal School of Mines and the City and Guilds College. Today these three constituents still identify three of the main areas of study in Imperial College: the RCS for pure science, the RSM for mining (and related fields such as geology) and the CGC for engineering.

A fourth constituent element in this impressive cocktail is Medicine. In 1988 St Mary's Hospital Medical School became part of Imperial and then in 1995 the National Heart and Lung Institute joined too. Together they formed the Imperial College of Medicine. Now, in 1997/8, Imperial College of Medicine is to merge with Charing Cross and Westminster Medical School to form the new Imperial College School of Medicine. As is the case with all medical schools and medical departments of universities, Imperial is in the throes of drawing up a new medical course to reflect the GMC's recommendations outlined in Tomorrow's Doctors *(1993).*

The subject assessments (see fact box) leave us in no doubt that Imperial's strength runs deep. Through its research departments it is operating at the very coal face of science, which is the reason why industry and government and the media call upon it and sustain it financially.

SITUATION

The Kensington site (on Queen's Gate, Prince Consort Road, Exhibition Road and Imperial College Road) of the 20 buildings which compose the college is no less impressive, including as it does in its vicinity the Natural History Museum, The Science Museum, The Victoria and Albert Museum, The Royal College of Music, the Royal College of Art, the Royal Geographical Society and the Royal Albert Hall. You might say that the scientific and artistic potential of this architectural conglomeration reduces (in comparison) the latent 'Magick' of Stonehenge to that of a pile of rubble.

GETTING THERE

★ South Kensington Underground station (Circle, District and Piccadilly lines).

SPORT

Imperial College is part of the federal University of London (see London). The Imperial College Sports Centre at Prince's Gardens (Exhibition Road) includes a 25m swimming pool, 4 squash courts, a gym, a 25m rifle range, a training studio, sauna, steam room and poolside spa bath. Nearby there are tennis and netball courts, and a weights room. At Harlington near Heathrow there's a 60-acre athletic ground, facilities for rugby, soccer (loaned to Chelsea FC for training), cricket and a floodlit multi-purpose surface often used for hockey. There are a further 15 acres at Teddington, a boathouse at Putney and a sailing club at Welsh Harp Reservoir in North West London.

VIEW FROM THE GROUND
by Sarah Playforth

I am a second year student studying biology at Imperial College, London. The college is located smack bang in the middle of London, in the attractive Kensington area. This is a far cry from the grubby, urban wasteland of *Eastenders*; you are far more likely to bump into Princess Di than Pauline Fowler with Kensington Palace and Harrods only a stone's throw away. At Imperial College you are surrounded by beautiful buildings, not least of these being the Royal Albert Hall and the Natural History Museum. But you don't need a love of architecture to appreciate this fantastic location. The shopping and night clubs of the West End are close at hand and the 'adult' delights of Soho are half an hour's walk away. This has got to be the best situated college in London, probably in England and perhaps even in the world. If you come from a small town like I do, you'll be blown away by it.

Now the negative point. If Daddy doesn't own half the oil fields in Texas you are likely to hit a major financial crisis if you eat out at anywhere other than McDonald's. Yes, central London is an extremely expensive place. By the time you graduate you will probably have acquired an overdraft equivalent to the annual budget of small a country. But what the hell! You'll have enjoyed yourself and the prestige of a degree from Imperial will get you a top job after which those student debts will vanish overnight.

STUDENT PROFILE

The bright lights of the big city are bound to attract the most beautiful, interesting, energetic people around, right? Wrong. Imperial College is the top engineering school in Europe and manly attracts one kind of person: boring computer spods who think it's okay to wear sandals with socks. Witness 1996's winning University Challenge team. The male:female ration is about 100:1 but, although that makes it very easy for most women to pull, what they pull is not guaranteed to be human. Blokes have practically no chance of getting a woman, ever, and consequently Imperial College is the sexual frustration capital of Britain.

The good thing about the student body is that the college's international reputation leads to a large cultural diversity and you can make friends from all over the world, so you can have a cheap holiday by going to visit them. To be fair, the people here aren't as bad as I've made out; I have managed to make a good many excellent friends here who I wouldn't trade for anyone.

THE UNION AND ENTS

Imperial College Union is probably not the best in the world. You can't buy books or stationery cheaper here than anywhere else and the range of entertainment isn't as varied as it could be - it's almost entirely devoted to dance and very little to guitar bands or other forms of music. If you want to see a band like Ash perform live, you have to go to the University of London Union at Russell Square.

Imperial College has three main bars. The Union bar tends to be too full of old people to promote a relaxed atmosphere. But, if you can stand the excitement, it is well worth a visit to see the largest collection of pewter tankards in Europe. Southside bar is also well worth a visit, because, although lacking in the pewter tankard department, it boasts the cutest selection of barmen (check) this side of the Watford gap. Southside also has a great atmosphere, especially if you live in the halls of residence above it because all your mates are down there. Beware the women's rugby team who inhabit Southside bar on Wednesday nights and whose raucous, sexist singing is enough to drown out Fulham brass band.

Da Vinci's is the third IC bar and is alright but lacks that good old pub atmosphere and you find yourself staring hypnotically at the giant MTV screen rather than talking to your friends. Da Vinci's does have a cocktail night on Thursday nights which is excellent, offering cheap, delicious cocktails. I heartily recommend 'Sex on a Beach'.

Another attraction of the Union is the cinema which has the advantage of being at least twice as cheap as the London cinemas. It shows films much later than elsewhere but only go if you think the film is worth getting an extremely sore bum for.

With the financial difficulties of eating out in Kensington, it is vital that you are briefed on the college's eating facilities. The JCR is yellow and horrid; Da Vinci's is cramped, clingy and smoky but does a nice selection of hot rolls. That just leaves Basics. I work there and endorse it because I want a pay rise. Look, you can't go wrong with pizza and baked potatoes, can you? And as long as you avoid the chilli con carne, you probably won't be hospitalised. Basics has a very limited sound system, the only CDs being 'Ultimate 80s' and 'Saturday Night Fever' but if you look closely behind the piles of washing-up you might see Kenny doing his John Travolta impression, the perfect accompaniment to any meal. The main social event at the Union is Friday night, when you can be deafened by loud bass and suffer attacks of claustrophobia whilst queueing for the bar. When you're a first year, it is a good place to go because it is cheap, nearby and full of other first years. It is especially good at the end of the year when you know most people there and you can get high on how popular you are. However, after the first year, it is generally considered quite sad to resort to the Union of a Friday (except for the end of term carnivals), and most tend to venture outwards to explore more fully what London has to offer.

THE CITY

London does indeed have a lot to offer, if you can afford it. There are pubs and clubs to cater for all tastes and sexual preferences. If you want to find the ideal night out to suit you, the best way is by word of mouth, as experimenting is expensive. A handy hint is to spend ten minutes a week wandering round Camden High Street where you will be forced to accept hundreds of flyers giving cheap entry to some of the best clubs around. Despite the large variety of pubs, it is not easy to find somewhere with a comfortable 'local' atmosphere and you just have to explore. We knew we'd found our local when we saw Adrian from Bread drinking there. I will make just one recommendation - Scruffy Murphy's on Fulham Road hosts traditional Irish storytelling evenings, which provide an alternative way to relax after a hectic weekend.

SHOPPING

The thing I most love about London is the shopping. When it comes to clothes and records you can find anything you want if you are prepared to hunt and, as far as I'm concerned, there is no end to the excitement of wandering around posh shops like Liberty's and Harrods. There are also markets galore. The atmosphere of Camden Market cannot be beaten, nowhere has a street-life like Camden Town and nowhere else will you see such a rich variety of body piercings. Although the more touristy markets like Camden have a reputation for being expensive, I find it unbeatable for suede, leather and tasteless Doc Martens. Greenwich is my favourite part of London, with its seaside atmosphere and quaint little craft markets. The problem is that it's difficult to get to and involves a train journey through the Isle of Dogs which is without doubt the most depressing place on earth; no wonder no-one lives there.

After a hard day's shopping, the best night out I can think of is to go to a gig by some pre-pubescent guitar band. This is a reasonably cheap way of enjoying yourself and, London being London, that band you really want to see is bound to be popping round your way.

JOBS

Another of London's strong points is the abundance of student jobs. You can slave away in a pizzeria like me or, with the right connections, you can land yourself something far more cushy. My friend earns herself £5.50 per hour for programming internet addresses in a building sandwiched between two male-model agencies. How lucky can you get?

ACCOMMODATION

Whichever university you settle upon, living in a hall of residence is going to be a laugh. Let's face it, anywhere with a hundred 19 year olds living under one roof is hardly going to be a den of abstinence. Imperial College residences have the bonus of being centrally located. I could see Harrods out of my bedroom window last year and it's pretty certain that no matter how hard I work for the rest of my life, I'll never afford to live in an exclusive area like that again. Facilities in halls are generally quite good, although they are nearly all self-catering and kitchens can be hectic, so label those saucepans if you don't want to lose them. My most missed 'facility' of halls is Sharon, the cleaning lady, who was almost a surrogate mother to me during my first year. I hope all future residents of Tizard Hall appreciate her as much as I did. Relations between students and locals are never harmonious but this is probably more true in posh areas such as this than anywhere else. There were repeated calls to the police during my stay.

LIVING OUT

Moving out of halls is expensive and finding the perfect student pad can take a lot of time which, due to the heavy workload at IC, is in short supply. You should always pick your flatmates carefully. Someone once said to me that it was the most stressful thing in the world telling your friends that you don't want to live with them but even so, you should *never* agree to let someone live with you just because you feel sorry for them. Down that road lie madness and murder.

Most Imperial students choose to live in Earl's Court or Fulham because, although it is a long walk to college, you can afford a house rather than a flat. Living in Earl's Court has allowed me to accumulate a large catalogue of local nutters; the man who sits on the pavement barking like a dog; the man who talks into his hat as if it was a mobile phone; and Mad Ken the puppeteer who has to be seen to be believed. Living out of college is a good option because it allows you to extend your social life beyond the Union.

ACADEMIA

Enrolling on a course at Imperial College is not a soft option. I am working a lot harder than my friends at other colleges, but this is to be expected, considering its excellent reputation. I am studying biology which makes me feel like an arts student among the engineering and computing students which abound here. Biology is a subject which will have something to interest everyone, particularly when it comes to evolution and natural history, which I am not ashamed to admit I find fascinating. The reputation of the department attracts many top-notch lecturers, but I sometimes feel that, as a student, I am getting in their way and they would much rather be in a darkened lab watching water fleas mating than teaching up the particulars of their subject. Thanks to the field-trips, biology is a particularly social department and we are able to form strong friendships. This is handy as our computing course got us so stressed we nearly killed each other.

CLUBS AND SOCIETIES

Like all universities, Imperial boasts a wide variety of clubs and societies. If you can afford it you can take part in many exciting outdoor activities such as diving or parachuting. If you prefer something more lively, the sports societies have excellent social lives with regular bar-nights where enough alcohol is consumed to make George Best look like a teetotaller. There is a huge number of international societies, the largest being the Chinese Society. Wherever you come from, you can find someone who talks your language.

Political societies are not a major feature and, unusually for a college, the most popular is the Conservative Society who get together occasionally for hideously expensive dinners and come back with Peter Liley's autograph. Despite the popularity of the right-wingers, the Imperial gaysoc, IQ (Imperial Queers), is quite well subscribed, although its name has caused at least one student to mistakenly believe he was joining Mensa! Members of IQ are undoubtedly the most fun people in college and provide the best shopping partners a girl could wish for.

The society I recommend most is the Pimlico Connection, which sends Imperial students out into local schools to provide tutoring. This doesn't have a great social life but it is fun, rewarding, challenging and looks great on your CV. Best of all, after a week of getting Ds in your coursework, the adoration of thirty 9-year-olds is the perfect confidence booster.

So, whatever you may think of Imperial College after reading this, remember Brian May from Queen came here so it must be alright.

KEELE UNIVERSITY

The University of Keele
Keele
Staffordshire
ST5 5BG

TEL 01782 621111
FAX 01782 613847

Keele University
Student Union
Keele
Staffs ST5 5BJ

TEL 01782 711411
FAX 01782 712671

KEELE UNIVERSITY

Founded	**1949**
Situation/style	**Campus**
UNDERGRADUATE PROFILE	
Application acceptance rate	**8%**
Population	**4,600**
Mature student population	**20%**
Overseas student population	**17%**
Male/female ratio	**40:60**
1st year institut. accommodation	**100%**
Approximate cost	**£27-£43 pw**
ACADEMIC PROFILE	
A-level requirements:	**High**

100+ **Politics combinations,** 100+ **Sociology or Anthropology combs.,** 50+ **Applied Social Studies combs.** BBB-BBC, 50+ **Psychology combs.,** mainly BBB, 100+ **Law combs.** ABB-BBB, 150+ **Business/Finance/Management combs.,** 50+ **French combinations,** 50+ **German combinations,** 50+ **Music combinations** BBC-BCC

Student/staff ratio	**14:1**
1st class degree pass rate	**6.6%**
HEFCE assessments (15 subjects assessed/approved):	
1994 **Applied Social Work, Music**	Excellent
1995 **German** 19	
1995/6 **French** 20, **Sociology** 22, **Russian** 20	
Joint Funding Council's research assessment 1996 (30 subjects assessed):	
Engineering	Grade 5*
American Studies	Grade 5
EMPLOYMENT PROFILE	
Principal job market destinations:	

Retail/Wholesale, Commerce, Education, Manufacturing, Health, Public Admin./Law, Personnel, Arts/Media

PIP 1996 employers' survey: Top subject/national ranking	
Social Science/Economics	34th
Approximate % unemployed	**7%**

VAG VIEW

Keele is in the area known as the Potteries, a b orough incorporated in 1907 to include Stoke-on-Trent, Hanley, Burslem, Tinstall, Longton, and Fenton. Its most famous literary son, Arnold Bennett (Clayhanger, Anne of the Five Towns - *he left Fenton out because he preferred the sound of 5 towns) couldn't get away fast enough, though to be fair he had been under pressure from his erstwhile potter and pawnshop-owning father to settle down as a solicitor, and the place did certainly inspire him as a writer.*

Key to this university is its academic strategy, considered in great depth, to plumb certain advantages of the modular system. You'll either like their ideas (see Academia) or you won't, but at least they make their strategy clear. Thousands do.

SITUATION

Rural campus by Keele village, near M6 and with easy bus access to Newcastle-Under-Lyme (2 miles), Stoke-on-Trent, Hanley (5 miles). M6 provides access to Manchester (40 miles).

GETTING THERE

★ By road: From the North M6 (J16), A500, A531, right onto A525, right through Keele village. From South, M6 (J15), A5182, left on

to A53, right at Whitmore following signs.
★ By rail: Good service more or less everywhere, London 1:30 to Stoke-on-Trent station, then taxi.
★ Stoke also the coach connection.

ACCOMMODATION

First years guaranteed accommodation in single study bedrooms.

Barnes Hall has flats as well, TV, bar, games room; Lindsay has en-suite (and Lindsay's Cafe Bar); Horwood has bar. Hawthorns is in Keele village.

ACADEMIA

Modular course structure, CATS points system, large number of combinations on offer, two semesters a year.

'At Keele we have always attached great importance to a broad education.' Four-year BA/BSc enables 'access to the full range of the undergraduate curriculum' in the first year (possibly as many as 12 modules). But you don't have to do this if you have a firm idea of where your degree is leading you career-wise. Dual Honours degrees (2 principal subjects, 4 modules in first year) are most popular, with possibility of crossing science with arts. But if you opt for this, you must also take at least 1 subsidiary course (2 modules), its purpose to add a skill (a language, say) that'll be useful in your career - they mean what they say about a broad education. You may take one principal course subject, but again it must be studied with 1 subsid. Emphasis on computer literacy throughout.

ENTS & UNION

Contrary perhaps to expectations, the area has quite a student focus, for, in addition to Keele, there's Staffs Uni, Stoke College, Newcastle-Under-Lyme College and Stafford College of Higher Education. A car would be useful, but student travel to Stoke, Newcastle, Hanley is made easy by a bus which actually goes through the campus.

The Firkin chain has quite a grip - Stoke, Newcastle, Hanley, Stafford, and pubs like The Terrace in Leek Road, Stoke, offer a week's worth of student nights round Freshers Week. There's The Market Tavern & Dew Drop (alternative and indie) at Hanley; the Locker Room, also in Hanley, has a student night Thursday, music till 2. There are student nights at club Zanzibar in Newcastle and various other clubs in Newcastle and Hanley.

Then there's Staffs Uni (Stoke) - Legends on its Beaconside site, pool competitions and bar promotions at its Sleepers Bar, a club venue and bar at Leek Road, and another, more alternative, venue and bar - Odyssey - in College Road (swing soul hip hop, alternative rock, metal, punk, indie).

There are theatres in both Newcastle and in Stoke. The King's Hall (Stoke) is a concert venue and there's the Trent Film Theatre, and at Festival Park there's a 10-screen cinema.

At Keele itself the Union does seem to be quite a dab hand at hauling in some good acts. They boast '7-day non-stop ents' throughout the academic year. There are 5 bars and two venues; at weekends they draw enough of a crowd to justify house in one venue, pop in the other. They can accommodate 2,500 on a night and do, which is probably the reason they can entice the likes of Human League, D:Ream, Jools Holland and U2. Regular club events include Under-Ground and Lurveshack - alternative and 70s/80s. Every second Thursday there's comedy. There's also a pub and restaurant in the village.

Students are very active in the journalistic field, they've had various magazines - *Grapevine* and now monthly *Concourse*, weekly newsheet *Junction 15* and radio station - KUBE. Also, the student music scene thrives with a sound (sorry) base in an academic department which is among the best in the land: folk, jazz, swing, classical (Keele Philharmonic, Concert Band, Bach Choir, etc).

SPORT

Sports facilities on campus include the gym, a newish sports hall (badminton, netball, basketball, judo and 5-a-side), and floodlit, synthetic sports pitch. Forty-six acres of grass pitches - athletics, lacrosse, soccer, rugby, 3 wickets, netball and tennis courts. A leisure centre includes a fitness centre, seven squash courts and a climbing wall. Newcastle has a 25m swimming pool.

KENT UNIVERSITY AT CANTERBURY

The University of Kent
at Canterbury
The Registry
Canterbury
CT2 7NZ

TEL 01227 764000
FAX 01227 452196

The University of Kent
at Canterbury
Student Union
Mandela Building
The University
Canterbury
Kent CT2 7NW

TEL 01227 765224
FAX 01227 464625

KENT UNIVERSITY AT CANTERBURY

Founded	**1965**
Situation/style	**Collegiate campus**
UNDERGRADUATE PROFILE	
Application acceptance rate	**12%**
Population	**5,700**
Mature student population	**21%**
Overseas student population	**14%**
Male/female ratio	**55:45**
1st year institut. accommodation	**100%**
Approximate cost	**£47-£64 pw**
ACADEMIC PROFILE	
A-level requirements:	**High**

Biological Sciences, Math Sciences, Computer Science BCC, **Electronic Engineering** BB-BCC, **Law** 22-26, **Psychology** BBC, **Sociology, Social Policy, Theology** 20, **Accountancy & Finance, Business combs.** 20, **Modern Languages combinations** BBB-BCC, **Drama combinations** 22-24

Student/staff ratio	**13:1**
1st class degree pass rate	**8.7%**

HEFCE assessments (13 subjects assessed/approved):

1994 **Computing**	Excellent
1995 **Anthropology, Social Policy & Administration**	Excellent
1995 **Sociology** 21	
1996 **Modern Languages** 19	

Joint Funding Council's research assessment 1996 (25 subjects assessed):

Social Policy & Admin	Grade 5

EMPLOYMENT PROFILE

Employability in Industry:

MPW national league table (1996)	**49th=**

Principal job market destinations:

Commerce, Retail/Wholesale, Manufacturing (strong on Electronic & Electrical), Health, Education, Arts/Media, Public Admin./Law, Computer

PIP 1996 employers' survey:

Top 2 subjects/national ranking

Accountancy, Finance & Banking	5th
Law	30th
Approximate % unemployed	**6%**

VAG VIEW

The students of Kent at Canterbury produce a very good alternative prospectus. It may not be the wackiest around, but for my purposes and, I suspect, for any Fresher, it is invaluable, and it's rather well written. For example, their guided tour of this great cathedral city begins - 'Canterbury is an old, proud and generally easy-going city, with a long tradition of murder, corruption and (of course) religion.'

These qualities, inseparable through history and finding ultimate expression in the murder of Archbishop Thomas Becket (1170) in the cathedral here, draw hundreds of thousands of tourists each year to gaze upon a stone which is supposed to bear the stain of Becket's blood. They come also because of the pilgrimage to Canterbury from Southwark described in Chaucer's Canterbury Tales *(1387), though again I'm sure what pulls them in is not so much a literary appreciation of Chaucer but a vague memory of some schoolday voyeuristic interest in the ribald fabliau told en route by the Miller and the Reeve.*

Everything in Canterbury is dedicated either to Becket or Chaucer, and there's no small irony in thousands making annual pilgrimages to the high seat of Anglicanism, inspired by such unholy thoughts. If Kent's eagle-eyed academics ever turned their attention to these tourists I feel sure that they would come up with a course in Leisure Studies which would turn what's available on its head. For Kent, whose principal preoccupation is society and culture, is, above all, innovatory.

The University is pre-eminent in the field of Social and Public Policy and Social Work, as both its teaching and research assessments (see fact box) show. Indeed, students at Kent and elsewhere are using books written by current Kent academics or those who went before.

Kent's degree in Urban Studies is another example of their research work which has led to a complete re-think about the processes underlying contemporary urban problems.

Kent has other more or less unique characteristics. It is one of the few universities to offer an American Studies programme which involves a year spent in the USA. They are also committed to encouraging the assimilation of European culture in almost any course they offer - by study in Europe, by taking on a European language, or by combining one of their innovative artistic or media packages with advanced work in a modern foreign language, as in their European Arts course.

It is also their policy to extend accessibility to Higher Education by offering foundation courses, for example in Biology, Chemistry, Physics, Computer Systems Engineering and Maths, which will lead to the commencement of a degree course in the second year. And there is a definite strategy to encourage mature students' re-education, or 'continuing education', by providing course programmes at times and in locations that are practicable, and by tailoring mature student entry requirements accordingly.

Another interesting thing about Kent's courses is that although they are, like many modern university courses, career orientated (work placements, etc), the teaching of PTS (the 'personal transferable skills', beloved of employers) is never seen as distinct from the principal course in hand. Inter-disciplinary course programming facilitates this strategy, their media arts and English courses informing social scientists on matters such as communication (their English course, for example, concentrates on creative writing, learning to analyse effectively and to construct coherent arguments). What we see at Kent is a university not just going with change, but making it happen.

SITUATION

Kent at Canterbury Campus is positioned a mile or so north-west of the city centre. It is a collegiate university, teaching and socialising being organised on a college basis - as at Oxbridge rather than as at Durham. There are four allusively named colleges: Darwin, Eliot, Keynes and Rutherford. Every student belongs to a college, whether or not they choose to live on campus.

GETTING THERE

★ By road: From the West, M2, A2. From the South, A28 or A2. From the East, A257. From the north-east, the A28. From the north-west, the A290.
★ By rail: London (Victoria) to Canterbury East (85 mins). London (Charing Cross or Waterloo East) to Canterbury West (90 mins).
★ By air: Heathrow, Underground to Victoria, overland train to Canterbury East.

Gatwick, express to Victoria, train to Canterbury East.
★ Parking permits required by students with cars, not granted if resident in a college room, Tyler Court or the houses adjacent to Eliot or Darwin Colleges.

ACADEMIA

Schools/Departments: Business, Maths & Statistics, American Studies (compulsory year in USA), Biosciences, Social and Public Policy and Social Work, Chemistry, Physics, Classics and Philosophy and Religious Studies, Arts and Image Studies, Computing, Electronic Engineering, Sociology and Social Anthropology, Economics, Law, English, European and Modern Languages, Geography, History, Politics and International Relations, Psychology, Sociology and Social Anthropology, Social and Public Policy and Social Work.

ACCOMMODATION

All first years live on campus, accommodation being mainly on a bed and breakfast basis, plus a 40% discount on the cost of other main meals.

ARTS AND ENTS

The Marlowe Theatre is the city tourist theatre, with acts like Eddie Izzard, Ben Elton and Jack Dee keeping the industry ticking over nicely after a drink at the Miller's Arms pub. The Gulbenkian Theatre on Kent's campus offers entertainment to a more discerning crew, with Cinema 3 - arthouse fare - being its filmic equivalent.

Popular city pubs among students are The Three Compasses, The Black Griffin, The Tap and Simple Simon's. On campus they have to hold their ents in college dining halls or JCRs because for 25 years they have been campaigning for a Student Union building better than the township hut they have at present - rather sweetly called The Mandela Building - and only recently have they had the go-ahead. Perhaps if the Uni had been doing research for industry rather than government they would have had it before. What's planned, and will likely be built by the time you get there, will include a nightclub with gallery area, a 'Mediterranean-style cafe-bar-bistro...overlooking the campus and the city.' Cost, £3.5m. I reckon the students deserve it, if only because recently they have shown an extraordinary facility for picking acts just before they break - acts like Kula Shaker before they made it. Well, they've had to, haven't they? In between the big discoveries have been smaller bands, discos, gameshows and collegiate balls. But any moment now, ents at Kent at Canterbury is going to be on the map. Let's hope The Regurgitator's not still doing his rounds.

Kent Union is also a campaigning body in more than entertainments. Their efforts have brought a minibus for night-time transportation of students to outlying areas, night security guards, spy-holes in doors, and on a nation scale they are particularly active in the campaign against government funding cut-backs.

SPORT

Multi-purpose halls for badminton (12 courts), basketball, volleyball, netball, 5-a-side football. Cricket nets and a climbing wall, squash courts, a weights room and outdoor tennis courts. Pitches include a floodlit all-weather pitch for hockey and soccer as well as grass for all team sports, including American football. £500 sports bursaries available.

KENT INSTITUTE OF ART & DESIGN

Kent Institute of Art & Design
Oakwood Park
Maidstone
Kent
ME16 8AG

TEL 01622 757286
FAX 01622 692003

Kent Institute of Art & Design
(Canterbury) Students Assoc.
New Dover Road
Canterbury
Kent CT1 3AN

TEL 01227 760463

Kent Institute of Art & Design
(Maidstone) Students Assoc
Oakwood Park
Oakwood Road
Maidstone
Kent ME16 8AG

TEL 01622 679685

Kent Institute of Art & Design
(Rochester) Students Assoc.
Fort Pitt
Rochester
Kent ME1 1DZ

TEL 01634 830022

KENT INSTITUTE OF ART & DESIGN	
Founded	**1987**
Situation/style	**City site**
UNDERGRADUATE PROFILE	
Application acceptance rate	**8%**
Population	**1,000**
Mature student population	**54%**
Overseas student population	**24%**
Male/female ratio	**55:45**
1st year institut. accommodation	**60%**
Approximate rent (Institute)	**£40-£45 pw**
(City)	**£45 pw**
ACADEMIC PROFILE	
A-level requirements:	**Low-Medium**
Architecture 16, **Art & design** 12	
Student/staff ratio	**16:1**
1st class degree pass rate	**6.3%**
HEFCE assessments (1 subject assessed/approved):	
1995 **Architecture**	
Joint Funding Council's research assessment 1996 (2 subjects assessed):	
Grade 5/5*	None
EMPLOYMENT PROFILE	
Principal job market destinations:	
Arts/Media, Architecture, Manufacturing	
Approximate % unemployed	**5%**

VAG VIEW

In 1987 three art colleges - Canterbury, Maidstone and Medway - merged to form the Kent Institute of Art & Design. They are based at Canterbury, Maidstone and Rochester. Its undergraduate degrees - Fine Art, Architecture, Communication Media, European Fashion, Fashion Design, Editorial & Advertising Photography, Three-Dimensional Design, Silversmithing, Goldsmithing and Jewellry Design - are validated by the University of Kent at Canterbury.

Communication Media concerns print, graphics, illustration, photography, film video and electronic media. Students may undertake specialist study or lock into a course which focuses on the shared concepts of these media.

SITUATION

Rochester Site:
Fort Pitt,
Rochester,
Kent ME1 1DZ.
Tel: 01634 830022. Fax: 01634 829461.
★ Fashion, Silversmithing etc, Three-Dimensional Design, Editorial & Advertising

Photography.

Canterbury Site:
New Dover Road,
Canterbury,
Kent CT1 3AN.
Tel: 01227 769371. Fax: 01227 451320.
★ Fine Art.

Maidstone Site:
Oakwood Park,
Maidstone,
Kent ME16 8AG.
Tel: 01622 757286. Fax: 01622 692003.
★ Communication Media.

GETTING THERE

★ Rochester: M20 (J4), A228. Maidstone: M20 (J6), A229. See also Kent University entry.

VIEW FROM THE GROUND
by Liz Wallace

Kent Institute of Art & Design, Maidstone. It is unlikely that anyone has ever applied to KIAD because the name sounded good. Institute! What's the first thing that springs to mind? Residence for the mentally ill? Exactly! Not an art college in the middle of a Kentish park. In fact the students at KIAD Maidstone would be better described as free thinking and creative, the mentality that gives the college its atmosphere and is its strongest feature.

The campus is not particularly old, bohemian or messy, as Maidstone runs photography, TBM, Graphic Design, Illustration and Foundation courses. So it's not all splattering paint. Students can cross the boundaries between these areas with ease and are encouraged to do so. This might not appeal to someone with more specialised ideas but most like the approach.

Working hard is important if you want to stay at KIAD. Just before assessments the pressure is strong and equipment is at a premium, as everyone tries to get work in on time. But this is also when the atmosphere at college is best (everyone is in for a start!).

It can be hard to get used to showing and sharing your work and it can become competitive. Nevertheless the students who come from many different backgrounds, cultures and countries, work together well.

However, if you are looking for the 'big city university-life', then don't expect to get it in a small town and college like Maidstone. You may not know everyone in college, but you will recognise most of them - and them you.

You don't have to be a party animal to fit in at KIAD, but it is possible to play hard here as well as to work hard. The town itself has plenty of pubs, some more frequented by students than others. (Incidentally, it isn't *the norm* for Maidstonians and students to socialise together.) 'Drakes' has a very long standing relationship with the college and has student nights, where the prices are more in keeping with our wallets, and students are welcome to DJ. There are four very 'handbag' clubs that don't attract many students, and a couple of other nightclub venues that have runs of good evenings, though they usually get closed down just as they get good. If you really want to club you have to go to London, and many do.

The good thing about the small size of the college and town is that the students are forced to provide their own entertainment. College parties are frequent, and licence extensions at the bar can be arranged. The bar itself is newly refurbished and looks really naff, but it's very functional and reasonably priced. At least once a term there are poetry and talent evenings there. It sounds a bit pretentious, but it is one of the best nights of the term, involving a lot of alcohol and watching your friends getting up on stage and either really impressing you, or making a total fool of themselves, which is even better.

The cinema in Maidstone is cheap, if you are a student, and runs pretty much in line with London showings. All the usual eating establishments exist, e.g. McDonald's, Pizza Hut etc. The museum and art gallery are best described as lame.

Other interests such as religion and sport are badly catered for in college, but KIAD has organised a deal with the large leisure/sports centre in Maidstone that lets students in free with an NUS card. This is a brilliant deal, as the facilities are excellent. Most students just use the gym and pool, but there are football and basketball teams that meet regularly from college. Basically there is plenty to do in Maidstone if you are prepared to find it. If you expect to have something laid on for you every night then don't come here. Maidstone town isn't most people's idea of a great place; it really is what you make it.

Accommodation varies, and we don't have the big university 'halls'. There are a couple of large houses, which hold between 10 and 16 students, but most live in student houses in two main areas of town. This type of accommodation can be organised through college or found independently. It is important to remember that no arrangement is permanent, and if you do find yourself living somewhere or with someone you can't stand then the college will help you do this. The advantage of using this college facility is that they, in effect, act as your landlord, and houses have to comply with many safety regulations before the college will represent them. Having an independent landlord is much more of a responsibility and isn't really advisable in your first year. If you did want to find yourself a house/flat, aim for the prison area! - near to the town centre, but a 40 minute walk to college. It is popular with students and reasonably priced. Or try and get somewhere near to college; the 'Upper Fant' area is a good enough description..

For those considering studying in Maidstone, the best and most useful advice I can think of is to come and find out for yourself.

KING ALFRED'S COLLEGE, WINCHESTER

King Alfred's College, Winchester
Winchester
Hants SO22 4NR

TEL 01962 841515
FAX 01962 842280

King Alfred's College Student Union
Sparkford Road
Winchester
Hants SO22 4NR

TEL 01962 827419/7
FAX 01962 827419

KING ALFRED'S COLLEGE OF HIGHER EDUCATION, WINCHESTER

Founded	**1840**
Situation/style	**Campus**
UNDERGRADUATE PROFILE	
Application acceptance rate	**16%**
Population	**3,250**
Mature student population	**37%**
Overseas student population	**3%**
Male/female ratio	**25:75**
1st year institut. accommodation	**100%**
Approximate cost	**£45-£70 pw**
ACADEMIC PROFILE	
A-level requirements:	**Low-Medium**
Teacher Training 10-12, **Archaeology, Psychology** 14, **Design & Technology** 14, **Drama, Theatre, TV** 20-24	
Student/staff ratio	**18:1**
1st class degree pass rate	**3%**
HEFCE assessments (5 subjects assessed/approved):	
Joint Funding Council's research assessment 1996 (10 subjects assessed):	
Grade 5/5*	None
EMPLOYMENT PROFILE	
Principal job market destinations:	
Education, Retail/Wholesale, Hotel/Restaurant, Commerce	
Approximate % unemployed	**9%**

VAG VIEW

King Alfred's was founded in 1840 as a Diocesan teacher training establishment (Church Elementary Schools). It has now become a University Sector College, which means that it is a sort of halfway house to becoming a University. It is working its way towards being a university. The fact that it and other non-universities can offer degree courses suggests that there is more to being a university than that.

In fact King Alfred's offers a whole host of degree courses, within the following schools: Education; Cultural Studies; Science; Technology and Design; Humanities and Social Sciences; Drama, Music and Sports Studies; Health and Community Studies. They are validated by Southampton University.

King Alfred's, which employs the modular/CATS system in its coursework and assessment, is making its own way in terms of its degree subjects - there is a good Drama, Theatre and Television Studies 'vocational' degree (and it has its own theatre on campus, as well as a dance studio for its Performing Arts course). There are interesting opportunities in its East Asian and Business Studies course, and in Honours combinations which include Japanese language. In 1994 the Basingstoke and Winchester School of Nursing and Midwifery became part of the college and they are developing multi-disciplinary courses in health care. They have also built an interesting course in Biopsychology on the back of research into the benefits of an interdisciplinary approach to that subject, and there is an Archaeology course which is being taught by people actively involved in archaeological research. Then there are the traditional subjects - History, Geography, American Studies, etc, which variously make use of this characteristic emphasis on an inter-disciplinary approach, or are simply a natural extension of King Alfred's vocational, teacher training past.

We may assume that only local students are interested in King Alfred's, but we would be wrong. Some students, like Stephanie Kirk (our correspondent), come to King Alfred's from a long way away for a specific course. Another student I know went there from London through Clearing after he missed Liverpool by a grade. He stayed only three days because it wasn't like a real university, it wasn't Liverpool, and it wasn't what he had in his mind a university should be. That is not to be critical of King Alfred's, which is pouring money into its student infrastructure, accommodation, sport, etc, and building up a students union on the caring principles which come naturally to a church foundation. It is just that King Alfred's is at a particular stage in its evolution and in its becoming a university.

SITUATION

King Alfred's is a campus university overlooking the historic cathedral city of Winchester in Hampshire, 15 miles north of Southampton.

GETTING THERE

★ By road: M3 (J10). From the North-west A272, B3041. From the South-west, A3090.
★ By rail: London (Waterloo) is an hour away, Bristol Parkway: 2:15; Birmingham New Street: 3:15; Southampton: 20 mins.
★ By air: Gatwick and Heathrow are just over an hour away. Southampton airport has inland flights and flights to Europe.

VIEW FROM THE GROUND

by Stephanie Kirk

Having just arrived home for Christmas, I realise exactly how much my life has changed in little more than a year. At the age of eighteen I left a small northern seaside town, where all the splendid hotels of the fifties are now lifeless, pillared rest homes for the elderly, and looked to Winchester, home of wine bars, cobwebbed inns and 'olde worlde' antique shops. Scarborough had been my home for all of my eighteen years, and the thought of leaving it behind set my pulse racing and my eyes twinkling. I had worked through my tedious A-levels, and now I was moving south to fortune and opportunity.

After completing four mindblowing terms at King Alfred's College in Winchester, Scarborough is actually a very nice place to come home to for the holidays. Winchester, however, has become like another home. Coming from a small town to a popular historical city has been much easier than I thought. Two years ago, the world seemed such a huge place. Now I travel nearly 700 miles in three days, just to go home for the weekend. My attitude to life has changed, as have my views on politics and the Arts. However, these are not things you can learn about in a book, and I have no handy hints on anything deep or meaningful; you'll have to learn through your own experiences. All I can do is offer practical advice; and I can tell you where to get the best kebab in Winchester!

WHERE IS IT AND WHAT IS IT LIKE?

If you have lived in a small town and feel threatened in a large city, Winchester may be the place for you. It is a city, not because of size, but because of its cathedral. It is quiet, picturesque and may prove to be a bit dull for some people, as it has only one nightclub. We had two last year, but, Murphy's Law, the good one closed. Do not despair, Winchester is very close to Basingstoke, Southampton and, of course, London. With a Young Person's Railcard a return trip to Southampton is currently £2.20. Trains normally run until quite early in the morning. Personally, since I got to college, I've gone off clubs anyway, the music not being to my taste, so I'm to be found most nights a week in one of Winchester's many pubs. In the north I pay around £1.60 for an average pint of lager. Watch out! Some places ask £2.10 a pint in Winchester. Some places do student discounts, and the cheapest, of course, is the Union bar - around £1.30 for a pint of weak beer in a plastic cup.

When I became seventeen, all I wanted was a car. Thank God my parents didn't succumb, as I would never use one here. Everything is close at hand and you won't find anywhere to park it anyway - special permits are needed everywhere.

Everyone seems friendly in Winchester, but watch out for 'Squaddies' from the nearby barracks. In general, they don't appreciate students, unless served on a plate with chips.

Winchester is steeped in history, not only due to King Alfred, but also to King Arthur. Allegedly, his famous round table is housed in the city's Great Hall. The cathedral, where our graduation ceremony takes place, is the main focal point of the city, along with Winchester boys' school, second only to Eton. Don't be too taken by the city's regal frontage; the cathedral makes a rather ornate backdrop to scenes of homelessness in Winchester. I have discovered that some of the nicest, most sincere people live on the streets, and they can invariably be found on Winchester High Street. I follow Drama, Theatre and Television Studies, and got to know this side of Winchester when we spent a term in community drama. A small group of us worked with a day centre. Most of the people who frequent it are homeless, or on a very low budget, some are ex-offenders, some drug addicts. None of them wanted anything to do with drama! It took us ten weeks to get a workshop up and running, but the course was so satisfying in the end.

WHERE DO WE KIP?

Most students I know don't really care where they live, as long as it's cheap and close to a bar, but your living arrangements can make or break your time at college.

At King Alfred's, we normally spend our first and last years in college halls. I refer to my first experience of halls as 'The Denstone Experience'.

Denstone Lodge was a building with thirteen rooms, two bathrooms, two kitchens, one shower, and twenty-six people! It was old, had peeling paint, and a fridge big enough for two yoghurts and a pint of milk. I shared a room with two other girls; fun for the first two weeks but I found myself needing privacy on occasions.

King Alfred's has two types of accommodation, catered halls and self-catering halls. The catered halls are in very basic condition, but it is a good idea to take one in your first year if only so as you won't worry about where your next meal is coming from.

Most of the college's self-catering accommodation is recently, or is still being, built. There is a large 'student village', containing over one hundred houses, each with seven rooms (mixed gender) and a large kitchen/dining room. About half the accommodation has en-suite facilities, and all the appliances in the kitchens and bathrooms are brand new - showers, fridges, freezers and microwaves. The only drawback is having to drag your laundry to the college washing machines, but it's not far.

Start looking early for accommodation when moving out of halls. Start looking straight after Christmas. You can find houses in Winchester town centre, just out of town, on the surrounding estates, or, out of Winchester, at Chalder's Ford and Southampton. Houses beyond the city tend to be bigger and detached; great for parties etc, but they can be expensive and you can feel cut off from everyone else. Many students live on the Stanmore estate. Houses here are cheaper, but two of my friends have had bad experiences - houses with no heating, or with paint peeling off the walls, and it takes around twenty to thirty minutes to walk to town or college from the estate.

Houses between town and college are quite rare, although I managed to find one last year. I share with four others, none of them on my course. The house is slightly higher than average in rent (£190 per month), but it is situated perfectly, with college five minutes in one direction and town five minutes in the other.

Beware very cheap prices, check gas certificates, insurance, heating and facilities like washing machines, showers and freezers. Ask to have any bills sent to you, not to the landlord, and it's a good idea to get in touch with the last people in the house and ask them how much their bills were. Look around as many places as you can and make sure you know exactly what you're paying for.

SOCIAL LIFE: Or where's the bar?

People (and students) in Winchester usually tend to go out on Wednesday and Friday nights. I prefer Saturdays, as Fridays are so busy in town that people crowd outside pubs to drink in the street.

As I mentioned, Winchester has one nightclub, so if clubbing's your thing, Southampton is a much safer bet. The pubs in Winchester, on the other hand, are excellent. For dance music and a really loud and bright atmosphere, the Guildhall is the trendy place to be, but what the city specialises in is old, comfortable inns, the oldest being the Wykeham Arms, near the boys' college, where you can sit at old candlelit school desks. A very popular student pub is the Mash Tun - for mad, but warm-hearted people! There are various pubs where you can get live music and theatrical entertainment, like the Railway Inn or the newly opened North Pole, which serves very good food, as does the Exchange - if you like kangaroo or crocodile burgers.

I have two local pubs, the Westgate, which has cheaper beer, fancy dress nights and karaoke, and the County Arms, which is opposite the main student accommodation and offers good food at budget-friendly prices. Other decent places to eat are Fatty Arbuckles, Muswells, Noahs or the bus station cafe, which offers cheap fry-ups.

We have a newly opened three-screen cinema in Winchester, and although they do get appearances from the stars (e.g. a talk from Terry Gilliam at the opening night of Twelve Monkeys), they have committed the worst sin of offering no student discounts. Basingstoke and Southampton to the rescue again.

For theatre we have the Tower Arts Centre and as the Theatre Royal won't re-open until 1998, King Alfred's College are taking on their productions in the John Stripe Theatre.

Winchester is generally a very safe and secure place to live. Some places are badly lit at night, so you have to work out your route before going out, or walk with a big group of people. The only thing to happen while I've been there is a few sightings of a flasher, who seems to have got bored and left now, or maybe it's too cold to show your bits in January.

In the Union bar there is different music most nights, karaoke, bar quizzes, college bands, and a disco in the exam hall every Friday night. The Christmas and Summer Balls take place in the Guildhall, a great venue, with a main hall and lots of smaller rooms with jazz, karaoke, live music, Tarot readings and a casino. The balls are certainly worth going to. Prices may seem expensive, but it's worth paying for the good night that you'll have.

CRAPS: Or, Clubs, Religion, Arts, Politics and Sport

When it comes to politics, students are normally seen as socialists - 'power to the people' etc. But at King Alfred's we have a mixture of views. Winchester is a wealthy, Liberal city. Some tutors may be perceived as 'right on Lefties', but no one imposes their views on others. In general students are not behind any political party; they want a new movement to vote for.

The college itself tends to have a very good reputation for theatre and film. We have our own dance studio and human movement centre. King Alfred's Performing Arts Company, (KAPAC), run by tutors, perform around three times a year. This includes an open air Shakespeare production, which happens normally once a year. The student led theatre company, KASPA (King Alfred's Society for the Performing Arts), which I am currently on the committee for, is putting on thirteen productions this year. We are backing directors from all years in all types of theatre. There is, too, an annual pantomime and a musical (this year it's "Jack the Ripper"), which are good to get started in. To be in productions you do have to audition, but you don't have to be brilliant, and getting involved in these is the best way to meet people from other courses and years.

Last year, KASPA entered a production of Terry Pratchett's 'Weird Sisters' into the Edinburgh Fringe Festival. It was highly successful, selling out for the whole week and was great fun to be a part of. It got a five star review in *The Scotsman* and a nomination for a Festival Fringe First Award. KASPA are looking forward to entering another production at this year's festival. Also, some students involved in KASPA are hoping to go to the National Student Drama Festival, held in Scarborough.

College sports cater for both genders in football, rugby, basketball and hockey. There is also a netball team. The college runs courses in aerobics etc, but Winchester's leisure centre is well equipped for a wider range of sports.

The college used to be a religious school for boys, so it still has some religious outlooks. There is a group of Christian Fellowship who are very active, and do try to impose their beliefs occasionally. When I started they came around to the halls with free chocolate drinks to entice people to join with them!

There are many different clubs at King Alfred's. The Lesbian, Gay and Bisexual Club run frequent trips to gay clubs in Southampton and London, and have meetings each week to freely express their sexuality. There is no violence towards gay people in the college; in fact, no noticeable distinction is made between gays and straights. The LGB notice board gets defaced occasionally, but only through ignorance and alcohol. There is a club to cater for mature students, who are many at King Alfred's. One of the best and probably most unusual clubs is the role-playing society. Nothing kinky, just good old Dungeons and Dragons etc. The film society run the latest films every Sunday in the theatre.

STUDENT PROFILE: Or what kind of weirdos are at this place?

Winchester is an affluent city, and there are more students from the area than from anywhere else in the country (there is talk of a Northerners Society!). The better off you are financially, the better you will survive in Winchester. The college welcomes foreign students, including Japanese as it runs a successful course in Japanese. Anyone who adores clubs will be disappointed with the city, because it is small, as is the college. However, any man will be quite happy here - the present ratio of women to men is twelve to one!

KING'S COLLEGE LONDON

King's College London
Strand
London
WC2R 2LS

TEL 0171 836 5454
FAX 0171 836 1799

King's College London
Student Union
Macadam Building
Surrey Street
London WC2R 2NS

TEL 0171 836 7132
FAX 0171 379 9833

King's College School of
Medicine and Dentistry
Student Union
Bessemer Road
London SE5 9JP

TEL 0171 737 4000 ext 4050

KING'S COLLEGE LONDON	
Founded	**1829**
Situation/style	**City sites**
UNDERGRADUATE PROFILE	
Application acceptance rate	**9%**
Medical AAR	**5%**
Population	**9,500**
Mature student population	**19%**
Overseas student population	**12%**
Male/female ratio	**45:55**
1st year institut. accommodation	**100%**
Approximate cost	**£44-£108 pw**
ACADEMIC PROFILE	
A-level requirements:	**High**
Medicine ABB**:**	
★ Science 'A's required **Chemistry**	
★ Addit. Non-Science 'A's acceptable **Yes**	
★ Retakes considered **Ext. circs.**	
★ Non-science 'A's acceptable **Possibly**	
★ Retakes considered **No**	
★ Clinical contact **1st year**	
Student/staff ratio	**8:1**
1st class degree pass rate	**10%**
HEFCE assessments (13 subjects assessed/approved):	
1993 **Law**	Excellent
1994 **Geography, History**	Excellent
1995 **Music**	Excellent
1995/6 **German** 20	
1996 **French** 21 **Portuguese** 23 **Spanish** 22	
Joint Funding Council's research assessment 1996 (30 subjects assessed):	
Community/Clinical (Institute of Psychiatry). **Mechanical/Aeronautical/ Manufacturing Engineering, Politics, Classics/Ancient History, History, Music, Education.**	Grade 5*
Nursing, Pure Maths, Applied Maths,Law, German/Dutch/ Scandinavian, Iberian, Philosophy, Theology.	Grade 5
EMPLOYMENT PROFILE	
Employability in Industry:	
MPW national league table (1996)	**36th=**
Principal job market destinations: **Health** (incl **Dentistry**), **Retail/ Wholesale, Commerce, Arts/Media** (strong), **Manufacturing, Public Admin./Law, Education, Computer**	
PIP 1996 employers' survey: Top 3 subjects/national ranking	
Law	10th=
Languages	3rd=
Social Science/Economics	13th=
Approximate % unemployed	**6%**

VAG VIEW

King's College London is one of London University's oldest and most prestigious institutions, and today their teaching and research record places them among the best in the country. Undergraduates feel part of this strong tradition, but the university is so scattered around that it is as unlikely that you will find a common denominator among KCS undergraduates as it is that you will find one among Londoners in general. And perhaps that is their characteristic feature, namely that they share in the special sort of existential anonymity which allows Londoners to be themselves and at the same time to be part of, and draw inspiration from, something that is bigger than the sum of its parts. In that sense, King's College might be said to be the truest London university of all.

There's an Alice in Wonderland feeling when you first walk through the narrow passage into the main Campus. At one moment you are part of the bustle of London's famous Strand, with its elegant buildings, its hotels, smart shops and theatres, and the next, as you emerge into the KCL Quadrangle, another world opens out before you. It seems, the first time, that you have uncovered a well-kept secret, particularly if you have walked past that entrance hundreds of times before and never noticed that this range of buildings is there. Those KCL students whose lives centre on this site no doubt soon become used to this. But, as at Oxford and Cambridge, so with the students at KCL, wherever they have studied within the precincts of the college, a feeling that they have this special entree does remain.

SETTING

Strand Campus (address above): Humanities, Law, pre-clinical medical and dental teaching.
Cornwall House, Waterloo Road, London SE1. Tel: 0171 836 5454; Fax: 0171 928 1395, just across the Thames by the Royal National Theatre. Houses Education and Nursing.
Kensington Campus, Camden Hill Road, London W8. Tel: 0171 836 5454; Fax: 0171 937 7783: Most Life Sciences.
Chelsea Campus, Manresa Road, London SW3. Tel: 0171 836 5454; and 552 Kings Road, London SW10. Tel: 0171351 3026; Fax: 0171 352 7376: Pharmacy and Pharmacology.
Denmark Hill Campus (as Medical Union address above): Medicine and Dentistry.

GETTING THERE

★ **Strand Campus**: Temple (District Line, Circle), Aldwych (Piccadilly), Holborn (Piccadilly, Central).
★ **Cornwall House**: Waterloo and Waterloo East overland, and Waterloo Underground (Bakerloo, Northern).
★ **Kensington Campus**: High Street Kensington (District, Circle), Notting Hill Gate (Central, District, Circle).
★ **Chelsea Campus**: Sloane Square (District, Circle).
★ **Denmark Hill Campus**: Denmark Hill overland.

ACCOMMODATION

All full time first years guaranteed accommodation in KCL or London Uni Intercollegiate residence (see London). KCL residences: Lightfoot Hall (Kings Road, Chelsea), breakfast weekdays. Malcolm Gavin Hall (Beechcroft Road, Tooting), breakfast weekdays. Queen Elizabeth Hall (Camden Hill Road, Kensington), self-catering. Hampstead Campus (Kidderpore Avenue, Hampstead), self-catering. King's College Hall (Champion Hill, Camberwell), breakfast and evening meals weekdays, all meals weekends. Wellington Hall (Vincent Square, Victoria), breakfast and evening meals weekdays. Stamford Street Apartments (Waterloo), en-suite, self-catering and newly equipped gym.

All residences mixed. New development to open September 1997.

UNION & ENTS

KCLSU is situated on the 3rd floor of The Macadam Building on the Strand Campus (far left - SE - as you walk in, on the far side of the main building). Every Friday Night is Shark! - the Waterfront is one of two bars. Every Saturday night Tutu's 'rocks to the sounds of the latest & greatest Britpop' - Tutu's is a cafe bar in the day, a club at night. Excellent draw on live acts, frequent balls. Regular Tuesday comedy quiz, Fridays - dance, Saturdays - indie; weekend bar closing time 1.30am. As part of London University, all students are entitled to use the ULU facilities, including ents. See London.

KCSMD is Student's Union of the Medical and Dental Students at the Denmark Hill Campus. Any member of KCL can participate. (The Guild can be found in The Penthouse top floor, old medical school.) The 'Penty' particular claim to fame is that it has the only 3rd-floor bar in London with a working fountain. Free house, Sky TV, The Blue Room ('sweetie', Pepsi and coffee machines, pool tables (20p a game) pinball and video games). Regular Friday and Wednesday late bar and disco, frequent dinners, balls, events - bands, comedy acts, etc.

SPORT

New Malden sports ground and KCSMD has Griffin sports ground in Dulwich Village. Hockey, Football, Rugby (KCL Rugby Club was one of the 12 founder members of the Rugby Union), Cricket and Netball, hard/grass tennis courts. KCSMD automatic members of Dulwich Hamlets Health Club. Two gyms on Chelsea Campus; squash courts, multi-gym at Kensington; rifle ranges at the Strand.

ACADEMIA

Traditional teaching methods, but modular course structures permit extensive interdisciplinary course programming; semester assessment system. Schools of Study: Education; Humanities (Greek, Classics, English Language Teaching, French, Geography, German, Language and Communication, Philosophy, Spanish, Theology, War Studies, Combined), Law, Life (Basic Medical and Health Sciences), Physical Sciences and Engineering (Chemistry, Computing, Engineering, Maths, Physics), Medicine and Dentistry.

Impressively efficient exploitation of research facilities: KCL Enterprises Limited, a wholly owned subsidiary of King's College London since 1993, established to market KCL's research in Europe, promote European collaboration, and monitor research opportunities and negotiate contracts for KCL academics.

KINGSTON UNIVERSITY

Kingston University
River House
53-57 High Street
Kingston-upon-Thames
Surrey
KT1 1LQ

TEL 0181 547 2000
FAX 0181 547 7093

Kingston University Guild of Students
Main Site
Penrhyn Road
Kingston-upon-Thames
Surrey KT1 2EE

TEL 0181 255 2222
FAX 0181 974 5336

Kingston University Guild of Students
Kingston Hill Centre
Kingston Hill
Kingston- upon- Thames
Surrey KT2 7LB

TEL 0181 541 0995

Kingston University Guild of Students
Knights Park Centre
Grange Road
Kingston-upon-Thames
Surrey KT1 2QJ

TEL 0181 547 2000

Kingston University Guild of Students
Roehampton Vale Centre
Friars Avenue
London SW15 3DW

TEL 0181 547 2000

KINGSTON UNIVERSITY

Founded	**1971**
Situation/style	**City sites**
UNDERGRADUATE PROFILE	
Application acceptance rate	**14%**
Population	**9,500**
Mature student population	**56%**
Overseas student population	**2%**
Male/female ratio	**55:45**
1st year institut. accommodation	**100%**
Approximate cost	**£47-£54pw**
ACADEMIC PROFILE	
A-level requirements:	**Medium-Low**

Business Studies CCC, **Accounting & Finance** CCD, **Architecture** 20, **Biomedical Science, Radiography** 12, **Pharmaceutical Science, Biochemistry** 8, **Applied Biology** 10, **Physical Sciences** 6-10, **Geology** 10-12, **Math Sciences, Computing** 10, **Aerospace Engineering** 10-12, **Electronic Eng., Mech. Eng.** 4-6, **Music & Technology** CD, **Law** CCC-BCC, **Sociology, Applied Social Science, Politics** 12-14, **Modern Languages combinations** 12-16, **Teacher Training** CD

Student/staff ratio	**20:1**
1st class degree pass rate	**6%**

HEFCE assessments (15 subjects assessed/approved):

1994 **Business & Management**	Excellent
1995 **English, Geology**	Excellent
1995/6 **Modern Languages** 21	
Sociology 21	
Joint Funding Council's research assessment 1996 (17 subjects assessed):	
Grade 5/5*	None

EMPLOYMENT PROFILE

Employability in Industry:	
MPW national league table (1996)	**49th**

Principal job market destinations:
Retail/Wholesale, Manufacturing (strong on **Electrical & Electronic**), **Education, Commerce, Computer** (strong), **Personnel, Arts/Media** (strong on **Creative Arts**), **Health,** good record **Construction, Architecture, Geodetic Surveying, Industrial & Engineering Design**

PIP 1996 employers' survey:	
Top 3 subjects/national ranking	
Construction & Civil Engineering	29th=
Languages	29th=
Accountancy/Finance & Banking	33rd=
Approximate % unemployed	**12%**

VAG VIEW

Whatever they tell you - and they will - about Kingston being the oldest Royal Borough, the place where Saxon kings were crowned (the Coronation stone lies in the Guildhall -King's Stone, geddit?), it is, in the cold light of reality, a monstrous suburban shopping centre, a housewife's paradise. Today, the Bentalls Centre rules. People come from miles, even - especially - from south-west London (Putney, Fulham, Barnes, Richmond, etc) to partake of the mall, the market and the endless chain-shops. For, whatever mass-market fashion shops they have in these places, in Kingston they have them in greater abundance and variety.

In fact Kingston has always had this role of supplier, as Charles I noted in 1628 when he gave it its Royal Charter. He described it as 'a very ancient and populous town...situated on the banks of the Thames, from which town by means of that river, different goods and merchandises, laden in wherries and boats, are daily transported..to our city of London and the adjacent parts.'

It is still as populous as ever and Old Father Thames still rolls majestically by, seeming to whisper something of Kingston's past. But instead of transporting their supplies by means of it, Kingstonians now play host to the crowds of shoppers, while its pubs and clubs, like Volts and Options, attract streams of youthful revellers, offering a sound return for the privilege of sharing reasonable portions of students' grant cheques.

Here, the sometime Kingston Poly explores a similar theme in the uptempo New World of Higher Education. On Kingston Hill the implications of supply and demand are studied in depth at its prestigious Business School, and at its Penrhyn Road site - the hub - a lively Students Guild is bent on turning student revelry into an art form.

SITUATION

Penrhyn Road: the centre of the Student Guild operation, Science and some Technology.
Kingston Hill: Business, Education, Music, Law, Social Work, and Healthcare Sciences.
Knights Park (near Penrhyn Road site): Art & Design, Architecture, Quantity Surveying, Estate Mgt.
Roehampton Vale: Mechanical, Aeronautical and Production Engineering.

GETTING THERE

★ There are fierce parking restrictions in Kingston; it is not a place to bring a car if you can avoid it. The university runs a free bus service between its sites.
★ Roehampton Vale site (Friars Lane) on the north-west side of Wimbledon Common and opposite Richmond Park, just off the A3, is a bit out on a limb, not served by trains. A car is really essential, though buses are good. The Vale (A3) leads into Kingston Hill (A308 - same road, different name), served by Surbiton Station (same line as Kingston).
★ By rail: Frequent trains from London Waterloo to Kingston. No Underground this far out, but it is well served by buses.
★ By road: M1 (J6a), M25 (J13), A30, signs to A308 (Kingston). From London: A3 to Robin Hood Roundabout, then A308.
★ By air: Heathrow is on the 111 or 285 bus route to Kingston.
★ Alternatively, Piccadilly line Underground to Earls Court, District Line to Wimbledon, overland to Kingston.
★ From Gatwick, overland train to Clapham Junction, change for Kingston.

ACCOMMODATION

Accommodation offered to all first years. Kingston Hill site has en-suite facilities. It is the only real campus - trees, hall of residence, tennis courts, etc.. Four other residential sites, including recently opened Middle Mill Hall, self-catering flats opposite Knights Park Campus.

ENTS

Penrhyn Road: Main KUGS (Guild) site. Bar offers sex (Sex on the Bar, a variant of the ubiquitous Sex on the Beach) plus other

dreamy cocktails.
Kingston Hill: Hannafords bar, good especially in the evening when ents programme is orchestrated by sound light system and heavy sound system.
Knights Park: Artistic bar and laid-back clientele, 'warm vibes'.
Roehampton Vale (engineers) seems to be a dry area, but there is another bar, at Tolworth Courts, the Uni's sports ground.

All the usual ents - anybody on the circuit including the Regurgitator, who must be permanently on the road, swallowing his goldfish and regurgitating them. Plus live bands, club nights 'almost every night of the week'. The full range, and that's before you sample the delights of Kingston and up-town London. If you're concerned that your grant won't stretch to it, the University has contacts with local employers, who will give you part-time work.

SPORT

Tolworth Court sports ground has tennis courts, soccer, rugby, hockey, cricket, netball pitches, and there's a fitness centre at Penrhyn Road. Also rowing on the Thames.

ACADEMIA

Faculty of Business (also includes Law, Education, Social Work).
Faculty of Design (also includes 3-D Design, Architecture, Fashion, Music).
Faculty of Human Sciences (includes Combined Studies, Economics, Eng. Lit. - with a sound novelist-taught creative writing course, Languages, Social Science).
Faculty of Science (includes Chemistry, Physics, Geography, Geology, Life Sciences, Maths).
Faculty of Technology (Engineering, Computer Science, Info Systems).
Faculty of Healthcare Sciences (Midwifery, Nursing, Radiography).
Faculty of Science offers extended degrees to allow for Foundation course. Sandwich courses available in Science and Science/Business subjects, also in Science/French programmes. Part time degrees popular.

LA SAINTE UNION

La Sainte Union College
The Avenue
Southampton
SO17 1BG

TEL 01703 216200
FAX 01703 230944

La Sainte Union College
Student Union
8 Archers Road
Southampton SO15 2LR

TEL 01703 904900
FAX 01703 904901

LA SAINTE UNION	
Founded	**1904**
Situation/style	**Campus**
UNDERGRADUATE PROFILE	
Application acceptance rate	**17%**
Population	**2,000**
Mature student population	**50%**
Male/female ratio	**32:68**
1st year institut. accommodation	**100%**
Approximate cost	**£57-£68 pw**
ACADEMIC PROFILE	
A-level requirements:	**Low**
Teacher Training CD-DE, **Modern Languages** DD-DE, **Sociology combs., Psychology combs., Humanities combs.** CD-DD	
Student/staff ratio	**23:1**
1st class degree pass rate	**3.5%**
HEFCE assessments (5 subjects assessed/4 approved): **Modern Languages** for reassessment in 1997; 1996 **Sociology** 18	
Joint Funding Council's research assessment 1996 (8 subjects assessed): **Grade 5/5***	None
EMPLOYMENT PROFILE	
Principal job market destinations: **Education, Health, Retail/Wholesale, Commerce, Hotel/Restaurant**	
Approximate % unemployed	**12%**

VAG VIEW

LSU is a Catholic Institution of 2,000 students, affiliated to the University of Southampton, which validates their degrees. Students from all religious backgrounds are welcome, but this does not mean that the college has moved away from its roots. The focus of an LSU education is not purely educational - they are on a mission - to teach you skills and get you to explore your beliefs, to realise your maximum potential, and to benefit society as a whole. The LSU Mission Statement encourages students to 'search for truth in a spirit of free enquiry... to learn the fundamental values of justice, integrity and respect for others and to search for a meaning by which to live.'

The offer is not a hollow one. Its programme has been recently developed to give students the chance to extend their personal horizons in five areas - Personal and Social Management, Beliefs and Values, Cultural and Recreational Activities, Careers Skills and Politics, Social and Community Awareness. You pursue the activities in term time and vacs, and decide on your own focus. With only 2,000 students, LSU is a friendly close-knit community, certainly not the 'impersonal, fragmented and competitive society' from which they aim to remove you.

Claustrophobia might become a bit of an issue, but students seem to focus on the opportunity to feel secure and gain self-confidence in a caring environment where close friendships are forged. With mature students making up a huge 50% of incomers each year, there is a range of age and experience.

SITUATION

Set on a 13-acre site, 5 minutes walk from the centre of Southampton, you have all the advantages of a major city on your doorstep and none of the cares.

GETTING THERE

★ By road: M3 (J14). National Express coaches to Southampton Coach Station.
★ By train: London Waterloo, 1:30; Bristol Parkway, 2:15; Birmingham New Street, 3:30. From railway station, take a right, then third left into Above Bar. At the crossroads, continue straight on to London Road. Second left into The Avenue. The main entrance is on your left.

ACCOMMODATION

Hall accommodation is provided for all first years, some in swish en-suite flats, others in hostel type study bedrooms.

ACADEMIA

As with most low entry requirement institutions, the emphasis is on breadth rather than depth: most of the degree subjects are Combined Honours courses, and the modular system allows a sampling of subjects prior to (optional) specialisation. Education is a major department with 58% of graduates going into teaching or lecturing. For mature students the general entrance requirement of two A-levels does not apply (relaxed entry requirements for part-timers too). The size of the college is an advantage for mature students apprehensive about their ability to get back into the swing of study, and with a full-time Pastoral Care Team of 10 tutors, any problems can be easily put right.

UNION & ENTS

Child care services are available both daily and in the evenings for parent students who want to make the most of the bar and events. Ents are in fact surprisingly evident despite the size of the college, with parties and discos held weekly and four balls a year. There are theme nights, firework parties and occasional bus trips to London clubs (or even Amsterdam or France). And with Southampton but a short walk from campus, you won't have any moans as far as nightlife is concerned. (See Southampton Uni entry.)

Environmental awareness and voluntary work in the local community are key. LSU Students Union is an 'environmentally friendly Union' in their purchasing, transport, energy saving policies and recycling. Saintly? LSU certainly lives up to its name!

LAMPETER UNIVERSITY

The University of Wales
Lampeter
Ceredigion
SA48 7ED

TEL 01570 422351
FAX 01570 423423

University of Wales, Lampeter
Student Union
Ty Ceredig
Lampeter
Ceredigion SA48 7ED

TEL 01570 422619
FAX 01570 422480

UNIVERSITY OF WALES, LAMPETER	
Founded	**1822**
Situation/style	**Campus**
UNDERGRADUATE PROFILE	
Application acceptance rate	**24%**
Population	**1,600**
Mature student population	**22%**
Overseas student population	**5%**
Male/female ratio	**49:51**
1st year institut. accommodation	**100%**
Approximate cost	**£50-£70 pw**
ACADEMIC PROFILE	
A-level requirements:	
Archaeology 16, **Humanities (History, Philosophy, Theology), Arts (English, Languages), Social Studies (Sociology, Anthropology, Women's Studies) combinations** 10-18	
Student/staff ratio	**16:1**
1st class degree pass rate	**3.8%**
HEFCW assessments (7 subjects assessed/approved):	
1995/6 **Archaeology**	Excellent
Joint Funding Council's research assessment 1996 (10 subjects assessed):	
Grade 5/5*	None
EMPLOYMENT PROFILE	
Principal job market destinations:	
Retail/Wholesale, Education, Public Admin., Manufacturing, Commerce	
Approximate % unemployed	**9%**

VAG VIEW

Lampeter has well-rooted traditions. It has been awarding degrees for longer than any other institution in England and Wales, other than Oxbridge. It is also a small university, and the other thing about Lampeter is that it is situated in a very beautiful and inspirational place, not far from the Preseli Mountains where the gigantic stones of the innermost sacred circle of pre-historic Stonehenge - once Britain's national necropolis - are supposed to have been cut.

This is mythic Wales, celebrated in the oldest story in the Mabinogion, *a magical collection of eleven stories sustained orally since earliest times and written down in the 14th century. The story which comes from this area (Pwyll, Lord of Dyved [Dyfed]) is probably the oldest of all, maybe as old as the second millennium BC.*

There is much in the University of Lampeter which reflects this historical backdrop. Its spiritual aspirations for a start. For years it was a Theological College, the gradual change into its present state as university first spurred in the 40s and 50s when Anglican Canon Henry Archdall was Principal and brought it into the 20th century. Today, courses still include Religion, but the traditional Theology and Divinity degree is regarded as a specialism. To the fore are courses in Ethics & Society, which is taught as often by lecturers in English, History and Philosophy as by lecturers in Theology, and there is even a course in Islamic Studies.

Also relevant is the emphasis on Ancient History and on Archaeology at Lampeter. The area is littered with burial mounds and cromlechs redolent of civilisations long past, and I imagine that its atmosphere must be conducive to such study, although today Lampeter is part of the modern world too. Classics & Classical Studies is a principal course in this faculty, but its prospectus description leads off with the sentence, 'Classics graduates get jobs.' This is indeed true, and a rather nice irony in the face of all this emphasis elsewhere on 'vocational training', which (again ironically) used to mean training for the priesthood rather than Business or Engineering.

Altogether at Lampeter there is a refreshing feel not of ivory tower academia but of a consistency of purpose and adapting to the needs of the modern world. Other courses include History, English, Informatics, and Management Techniques.

For teenage first degree students coming out of a rather different culture, a period of adapting to their new environment may be necessary, as Sarah Vanstone discovered:

VIEW FROM THE GROUND
by Sarah Vanstone

With only fifteen hundred or so students, Lampeter is not exactly a hive of activity, but once you're there, so long as you consider going to the pub and getting wasted a good time, there is plenty to be had. There aren't any clubs (though occasionally the Uni will lay on a bus to one), but on Wednesday and Friday there is a disco in the union until 1am. There are also bands in the Union on Tuesdays and a late bar until 1. Basically, everyone goes to the same place at the same time every week, which gives Lampeter a real family feel. The variety is not there, but you can guarantee that all your mates will be there and you're bound to have a good time.

There is a definite town/gown problem in town, so usually you stick to the student friendly pubs. The Quarry is the student pub in Lampeter. On Saturday, the landlord puts on a disco which is very popular. There is also a disco on Wed, Thurs and Fri, but these don't prove as popular as the Union ones. Wednesday though is Sports Night, and the allure of promotions on drinks, and the huge tradition of team socials means a Wednesday night out is often a mixture of the two venues, with, of course, a lot of ale being consumed by all. Sport is OK here. There's brilliant opportunities for everyone to have a go, and if you're half good at anything, chances are you'll get in a team. We compete in UAU matches, and cricket and football are particularly successful, especially considering the size of the Uni. We got to the quarter finals in the England UAU in cricket and have a first division football team. Most tastes are catered for too, and even if we don't do brilliantly, we have a real laugh, and are bloody good at celebrating or commiserating in style.

The setting of Lampeter is beautiful. Right in the middle of the Welsh Valleys, only 13 miles from the coast where there are some beautiful beaches. It's very rural, with millions of sheep. In fact, amidst the doctors and cinema numbers on the 'List of important phone numbers' each student is given, is 'Sheep Services'. Not sure exactly why we'd want to service a sheep, but that's something you wouldn't find on offer in England, isn't it!

Everything's on campus, never more than a five-minute walk away. This also adds to the friendliness of the Uni, everyone knowing everyone else. With the limited numbers of students, there's a lot of inter-year mixing which is nice too. Of course there is a drawback of being so intimate the whole time, and around week six or seven it can start to get a bit claustrophobic. You're more or less bound to see everyone you want to (and don't want to) at least twice a day, so by then you really need a break. But bear in mind, if things do get too much for you, our welfare services are really excellent!

Halls on campus differ in facilities and price. The newer halls are en-suite and more expensive (around £700 a term), whereas the self-catering ones can cost as little as £510. Usually first years go full board (only two halls are actually full board) and returning third and fourth years are more likely to self-cater. You live out in the second year and third year. You can get a nice place for around £40 a week, and you don't have to pay for the summer holidays. Again, the size of the town means you're never living too far away. Despite this though, quite a large number of students bring their cars with them, which also gives you the freedom to escape for a break. The bus service is seriously lacking too, so if you fancy a few trips to larger cities or into the country, a car is great.

The Uni library is OK, and whatever it lacks can be supplemented by inter-university loans, usually with Aberystwyth. Computing facilities are quite good, with two computer rooms and Internet access; it's always quite easy to get to a computer.

Academically, Lampeter is particularly strong in Philosophy and Theology, being purely a Theology college at one stage. Geography courses are good too, but Languages are pretty hopeless, reflected in the fact that the department is soon to close down.

There are quite a few international students here; perhaps surprisingly there are a lot of Greeks. Not quite so surprising is the large proportion of Welsh, probably around 40%, but there are plenty of English too.

Basically, Lampeter is a great place if you're not dead set on a bustling university with the opportunities of a big city and a club scene to rival Manchester. There's masses of boozing to be done, and loads of lectures to be missed due to stonking hangovers, just like everywhere else. Lampeter certainly isn't tame on that front. The drug scene is not extensive, sort of kept to those who want to and away from others. There's a wicked time to be had here though, and once you're here you settle in really quickly.

GETTING THERE

★ By road: From South M4, A483, A40, A482; From North, A485; From East, A40, A482.

★ By coach: the Traws Cambria service from Bangor via Aberystwyth to the North, and Cardiff, Swansea and Carmarthen to the South and East (Tel: 01970 617951).

★ By rail to Aberystwyth (25 miles), London Euston (5 hours); to Carmarthen, Cardiff Central, 1:30; Birmingham New Street, 4:10.

LANCASTER UNIVERSITY

The University of Lancaster
University House
Lancaster
LA1 4YW

TEL 01524 65201
FAX 01524 594294

Lancaster University
Student Union
Slaidburn House
Tower Avenue
Lancaster LA1 1YA

TEL 01524 593765

LANCASTER UNIVERSITY

Founded	**1964**
Situation/style	**City Collegiate**
UNDERGRADUATE PROFILE	
Application acceptance rate	**10%**
Population	**7,350**
Mature student population	**26%**
Overseas student population	**7%**
Male/female ratio	**50:50**
1st year institut. accommodation	**100%**
Approximate cost	**£36-£50 pw**
ACADEMIC PROFILE	
A-level requirements:	**High**

Advertising & Marketing ABB-BBB, **International Business** AAB, **Accounting and Finance** BBB, **English, History, Law** BBB, **Psychology** BBC, **Sociology** 20, **Social Work** BCC, **Environmental Sci., Biol. Sciences, Ecology** BBB, **Biochemistry, Computer Science** BCC **Physical Science** BCE-CCE, **French** BCC, **Electronic Engineering** 20

Student/staff ratio	**13:1**
1st class degree pass rate	**7%**
HEFCE assessments (17 subjects assessed/approved):	
1993 **History**	Excellent
1994 **Applied Social Work, Business & Management Studies.**	Excellent
1995 **English, Environmental Studies, Geography, Social Policy & Admin, Music**	Excellent
French 20 **Sociology** 21	
1995/6 **Italian with Iberian** 20	
Social Policy and Admin	Excellent
1996 **German** 19 **Linguistics** 23	
Joint Funding Council's research assessment 1996 (26 subjects assessed):	
Sociology, Business Management, Theology.	Grade 5*
Environmental Sciences, Computer, Engineering, Social Work, Education.	Grade 5
EMPLOYMENT PROFILE	
Employability in Industry:	
MPW national league table (1996)	**49th=**

Principal job market destinations:
Education, Manufacturing (strong on **Electronic**), **Commerce, Community Health, Retail/Wholesale, Public Admin./Law**

PIP 1996 employers' survey:	
Top 3 subjects/national ranking	
Social Science/Economics	13th=
Law	26th=
Languages	29th=
Approximate % unemployed	**7%**

VAG VIEW

There's a kind of experimental feel about Lancaster. It hasn't gone along the same lines as other universities established in the 1960s. The basic idea seems to have been to create a mini city in the countryside, which sounds like the old campus concept, but at Lancaster it goes further than that.

To begin with, take Lancaster's setting. The Uni is far away from the industrial Lancashire towns of popular imagination. It sits up to the north of the county, sandwiched between the Forest of Bowland, a huge open fell space giving life to myriad becks, and only five miles to the west from the sea. Lancaster itself, which is nearby, is a city, certainly, but it is small and has cobbled streets and its buildings are historic, well-maintained, indeed many are probably protected. Really the whole setting is almost too perfect, and it is at once clear that the street-wise club-loon who has pencilled in Manchester, Birmingham, London, Leeds would not be a happy bunny up here on the fells.

Within this setting they have created a city of their own on campus. There's a central square - Alexandra Square, a meeting place and market place, just like any other well-planned city has. There's even a parking problem. There are shops for all that you'll need, much at subsidised prices. Then there is the Spine. The Spine is a kind of 60s equivalent to the monastic cloisters you get in the older Oxbridge colleges. What it means in Lancaster is what it meant for the monks moving from vespers to their meagre repas - you don't have to scurry, you don't get wet when it rains, and outside and inside are, thereby, made one.

Nor is this feature the only thing they've borrowed from their more traditional forebears. Lancaster runs a collegiate system, like Oxford and Cambridge (and not like Durham), for here virtually everything is done with or for your college. Not only will you eat and sleep in college during your first year, but you will be entertained there and do much of your academic work there.

This an essential element in the Lancaster experience. You might think that college life among 500 or so (or less) student colleagues, while easing you in very successfully, could get a bit claustrophobic in time, but that is not the experience of students. The campus itself, being a relatively small, all-encompassing 'city' miles from anywhere, with no need to go off it for anything, might, without the loyalties and rivalries of the college system, preoccupy students with thoughts of wanting to get off it. As it is, any feelings of break-out are displaced by the two-tiered ecosystem. By your second year you will probably be ready to break out, but the urge is satisfied by leaving your college residence rather than the Uni as a whole. For in your second year accommodation in town is actively encouraged, while your continuing allegiance to your college is ensured by both sporting and course activities.

The result of this very successful organic experiment is that when you ask students what it's like at Lancaster Uni, the words that crop up time and again are, 'friendly', 'homely', 'relaxed', 'unintimidating'. The students here are healthy in body and mind and not at all the kind of things you'll find down in Huddersfield, and I can't imagine that the 'personal advisers' - a 1:5 staff to student ratio for welfare and educational advice - ever have much to do. It is just the sort of place parents would love to see their children go to.

There are, however, reasons for choosing Lancaster other than health and stability, which appertain to the extremely high teaching standards. It seems that the experiment works on the lecturers too, who are indeed part of the collegiate system.

The system is that your first year is a kind of taster year. They've woken up to the fact that a number of students study subjects at degree level that they haven't studied at school, and everyone must crack into three subjects at the start, with the option to change to anything they want within the timespan of a year - 'total freedom to adapt to your needs' is the slogan, and it appears to have put hundreds out of their misery. They also have secret weapons in their educational armoury like the Active Learning Unit, to which everyone is encouraged to submit. Special modules can be worked into your course-mix which will develop intellectual and personal skills beloved of employers. Again, there's a first-class placement system for a year abroad, and with specialisms in Chinese and Japanese we're not just talking about Erasmus or Socrates.

The proof that all this works is in the fact box above. Their teaching assessments are top of the range, their research facility a good deal better than solid, and their Employment Profile looks like that of an engineering college with local sponsors knocking at its door. Yet all this is done in the most beautiful surroundings away from such hassles, far away from gritty reality.

GETTING THERE

★ By road: M6 (J34), A683 from the north; M6 (J33), A6 from the south.
★ Good service National Express coaches.
★ By rail: London Euston, 3:30; Newcastle, 3:00; Sheffield, 2:30; Leeds, 2:30; Manchester Oxford Road, 1:30.

ACCOMMODATION

There are nine colleges on campus and one (for three departments in the Faculty of Education) in Ambleside in the Lake District, which is a few miles to the north. Residences are mixed but with separate bathroom facilities and essential self-catering facilities.

ARTS AND ENTS

In terms of culture, the Uni dovetails into the city and vice versa. Students can enjoy The Duke's Playhouse; while the city population can enjoy the International Concert Series up at campus, which attracts major international performers (Julian Bream, Amanda Roocroft, the Halle and BBC Philharmonic up from Manchester, etc) - these are weekly events. Again, students can buzz down the hill into the city for the summer prom season in Williamson Park or the annual Litfest; while citizens can walk up the hill - and many thousands do, annually - to enjoy the Uni's contemporary art exhibitions at the Peter Scott Gallery or the student or professional productions at the Nuffield Theatre, which organises three seasons a year around Uni terms.

On the ents front, a miscellany of events is organised college-by-college by the JCRs around the bars and three times a week everyone - or not quite everyone, I suppose - dashes down the hill to the Sugar House, the Uni's own nightclub which can take well over a thousand, often for big name DJs or live bands. (There's minibus to take students back from Lancaster afterwards.) There are other clubs in Lancaster and masses of good pubs, some with live acts, but it is universally agreed, by citizens and students alike, that the Sugar House is where it's at.

SPORT

As you might imagine in this healthy atmosphere sport plays a big part and their facilities are good. There's a six-lane 25 metre swimming pool, a large and a smaller sports hall, eight squash courts, two aeroball courts, weights rooms, fitness room, sauna, solarium, dance facilities and a rock climbing wall. Some fourteen sports pitches, grass and synthetic, cater for the major competitive outdoor sports. There are eight tennis courts, a bowling green and a golf driving range. Everything culminates in the Roses Weekend, a happy rivalry between the Houses of Lancaster and York (York Uni, that is) - a sporting and social extravaganza, the like of which no other Uni sees.

ACADEMIA

Students are required to pass in all their three first year subjects, then the programme proceeds along modular lines. Faculties include Science & Engineering (including some interesting Ecology and Environmental courses); Management (with various international angles and a course in Advertising & Marketing); Social Sciences (this is where they scored 23 out of 24 in the Linguistics assessments); Humanities (including American, Chinese, Italian, French, German, Japanese and Spanish Studies - book your tickets now - and a good course in Creative Writing); Education; and Independent Studies, which brings a project element into combined courses or may be taken as a course on its own.

LEEDS UNIVERSITY

The University of Leeds
The University
Leeds
LS2 9JT

TEL 0113 2431751
FAX 0113 2336017

Leeds University Union
PO Box 157
Leeds
LS1 1UH

TEL 0113 2439071
FAX 0113 2448786

UNIVERSITY OF LEEDS

Founded **1887**

Situation/style **Campus**

UNDERGRADUATE PROFILE
Application acceptance rate **9%**
Medical AAR **7%**
Population **14,600**
Mature student population **12%**
Overseas student population **8%**
Male/female ratio **53:47**
1st year institut. accommodation **100%**
Approximate cost **£30-£80 pw**

ACADEMIC PROFILE
A-level requirements: **High-Very High**
Law, English, Psychology ABB, **Accounting & Finance** BBB, **E & E Engineering** BCC, **Broadcast Journalism/Studies** BBB/ABB, **Medicine** ABB:
- ★ Science 'A's required **Chemistry**
- ★ Additional Science 'A's preferred **Biology**
- ★ Addit. Non-Science 'A's acceptable **Yes**
- ★ Retakes considered **Ext. circs.**
- ★ Retake offer **AAB**

Clinical contact **3rd year**
Student/staff ratio **9:1**
1st class degree pass rate **9.4%**

HEFCE assessments (17 subjects assessed/approved):
1993 **Chemistry** Excellent
1994 **English, Geography, Music** Excellent
1995 **Geology** Excellent
1995 **Italian** 19
1995/6 **Sociology** 20
Iberian 22
1996 **French** 22 **Russian** 20

Joint Funding Council's research assessment 1996 (49 subjects assessed):
Food Science, Mechanical/ Aeronautical/ Manufacturing Engineering, Town/Country Planning, Italian. Grade 5*
Biochemistry, Chemistry, Physics, Earth Sciences, Pure Maths, Applied Maths, Geography, English, History, History of Art/Architecture/ Design, Music, Education. Grade 5

EMPLOYMENT PROFILE
Employability in Industry:
MPW national league table (1996) **5th**
Principal job market destinations:
Commerce (very strong), **Manufacturing** (strong **Electronic & Electrical, Pharmaceutical), Retail/Wholesale, Education, Public Admin./Law, Health** (incl. **Dentistry**), **Personnel, Computer, Arts/Media** (strong), **Engineering Design** (strong), good record **Market Research/ Advertising**

PIP 1996 employers' survey:
Top 3 subjects/national ranking
Construction & Civil Engineering 3rd
Science 7th
Engineering & Technology 8th=
Approximate % unemployed **13%**

VAG VIEW

'Leeds... A bit mixed. Very exciting city. My niece was there. Living accommodation after the first year was very difficult. She was in hall, but the hall was about 4 miles from the University, and they had to go back for an evening meal and then back into town if they were wanting to do anything. Bus fares were a bit of a problem. After that - private landlordism is rife in Leeds, and some of the [non-Uni] accommodation is really very grotty. Typically they don't repair anything and it can be downright

dangerous - the electrics, the fire hazards, really very dodgy. In fact one of their houses was burned down - a child put a petrol bomb through the front door - the Hyde Park area, up behind the University, where most of them live, is very mixed. She graduated three years ago. I wouldn't want to put off anybody who wants to go, but if you're from a sheltered environment, small town or rural background, you're going to have to sharpen up fairly quickly.'

Leeds University is part of the city, just as Liverpool is part of its city, and Bristol, and so on. You make a particular choice when you opt for the civic Uni. You belong to the university, you belong to the city. The comment from a schools careers teacher, above, was balanced by two others. The first lives in Leeds:

'The Hyde Park area? Poor people as well as students, unscrupulous landlords - very good quality terraced housing, but poorly maintained. But you can get places in better areas, paying say £10 a month more each than in Hyde Park. Leeds is excellent for its network of buses. If you get to the city centre you can go anywhere. It is a very vibrant city. It doesn't shut down at night, and it's not just a traditional night life; there's good variety. Very good student city. A lot stay. Have a look into The Town and Country Club for up and coming acts, well-known names and fringe.' (see The City below.)

'One reason we recommend Leeds is that you can do exotic languages, you can do Arabic. They are not run of the mill, and they've got good paramedical back-up for those who don't quite make it into medicine. And they are going in quite exciting new directions. They have got a good Sports Science course, which they are just developing now, sort of outward bound style, away from your soft option. I think they could develop quite interestingly.'

Leeds is indeed a great student city, possibly the best in the country at the moment. And the University has a lot to offer too.

SITUATION

Leeds is a campus university situated in the centre of the city.

GETTING THERE

★ By road: South - the M1 culminates in Leeds. The A1 for North and Eastern counties. The M62 for East and West. Extensive coach services.

★ By air: Leeds\Bradford airport for inland services and Western Europe.

★ By rail: London Kings Cross, 2:30; Liverpool Lime Street, 2:00; Manchester Piccadilly, 1:15; Newcastle, 1:45; Sheffield, 1:15; Birmingham New Street, 2:30.

ACCOMMODATION

The Uni guarantees all first years residence in Uni-owned halls, the majority of which have single study bedrooms. Some halls are on-site, some are a bus ride away. There are two single-gender halls (one for men, one for women). Typically these are catered residences, with a bar, a room for study and a TV room. There is a 'New to Leeds House Hunting Pack' for those wishing to find private accommodation, and both Leeds and Leeds Met. (Unis and Unions) own UNIPOL, Student Homes, an accommodation bureau at 8-12 Fenton Street, Leeds LS1 3EA. Telephone their New to Leeds Advice Line, 0113 243 8822.

ACADEMIA

'Very good on Modern Languages,' said one careers teacher, 'also on Eastern European, Middle Eastern Languages particularly - very good department, very friendly. Good too on History, and on the design based courses, but keeps its reputation pretty much across the board.'

Leeds has an excellent reputation, both in its undergraduate teaching and in its research departments, as the fact box shows. Its courses are now modularised in such a way as to open up a number of inter-disciplinary combinations, and those mentioned above - Humanities, Social Studies with Russian, with Arabic, with Modern European Languages (including Iberian languages), with Chinese and with Classical Literature certainly set it apart. There are also intriguing cross-Faculty schemes - for example, Computer Science - Music; Biology - History and Philosophy of Science, which demonstrate the significance of the modular opportunity.

It is also worth mentioning that on April 1st 1996, the Leeds College of Health became the University's new School of Healthcare Studies, which gives new strength to its already highly rated Medical and Dentistry School and courses related to Medicine, which now include Nursing, Midwifery, Radiography, as well as Medical Microbiology, Med. Biochemistry, Pharmacology, Medicinal Chemistry, etc.

Leeds also has an enlightened approach to BTEC or advanced GNVQ students, and to mature students, and has a dedicated approach to getting their undergraduates employed: 'Leeds has an excellent careers department,' we were told by an adviser who has worked for Leeds inspection services. 'They have a very good support network for students; they know what happens to their students; they know where they have gone; all the careers staff are professional - not people from industry who have just turned up. You can't say that about all universities. As well as doing the one-to-one support, they are going into the curriculum and linking back, working with departments, trying to raise awareness of skills, communication skills that will be needed, showing students how to market themselves. They are very pro-active.'

Leeds also has an impressive computer network for students. All students have passwords allowing access to network computers. PCs are available in more than 50 locations for teaching or private study, and there are plans to install stations in the largest hall of residence.

THE CITY

Leeds is a city on the make. Commerce and industry have combined to turn it into a shopping and nightlife fantasmagoria with a rather precious-cum-trendy cafe scene that'll make you Londoners feel homesick for Covent Garden. If you have money in Leeds you'll certainly have no difficulty in spending it, and if you don't they'll find ways of making your ends meet.

Smart modern offices sit alongside municipal dinosaurs like the Town Hall and Corn Exchange - magnificently renovated and decorated inside - a place that'll relieve you of your cash as deftly as Fagin might remove a silk handkerchief from your purse.

Explore the trendy arcades in the centre, but be wary and wise. Drop in perhaps at Roots and Fruits in Grand Arcade, one of the many cafe bars that have sprung up here. Sample the Victoria Quarter - a beautiful place to be if you're a beautiful person - but perhaps reserve your dwindling funds for not-to-be missed treats like the Way Ahead record store or Indie Joze café - cafe culture at its best, everything from Mexican to Swiss to Californian.

Alternatively, make your way over to Granary Wharf, under the arches by the canal. 'Granary Wharf is full of craft shops, aromatherapy and artists selling their goods. Thursday's open air market is groovy and cheap because it's all secondhand. You can pick up a pair of Levi's for a tenner. The indoor market is best for fruit, veg and meat, all of which are reduced on Saturdays around 4.00pm...' I can't think of a better tour round Student Leeds than that given by musician Sue-Lee Freeman - she of Leeds College of Music (see LCM's entry for the full works).

There are many times it'll occur to Londoners that Leeds is a smaller, not so provincial answer to home. There are still plenty of good pubs here, as Sue-Lee Freeman points out, but the really noticeable change is to this cafe culture. Leeds, prospering from business and commerce, has been gentrified, at least in parts. Just as London has its Camden Market, Leeds has Granary Wharf and Hyde Park corner, with its secondhand bookstores, specialist comic shops, Japanese raw fish parlours and workers co-operatives. But it is also an up-tempo, hip, happening place.

'Leeds cafe culture,' the SU tells us, 'has spiralled from a few cosmopolitan meeting places into a much more diverse collection of establishments, which range from the style of Indie Joze and Art's Cafe [in Call Lane: tapas, vegetarian dishes, grilled goats cheese], to the more chilled-out-crustiness of Dubterranean [Hyde Park: anything from chips to Continental fare], the not quite as cosmo World Café and Dare [Dare Cafe, Headingley: Earl Grey, Assam, Darjeeling, home made foccacia] as well as plenty in between.'

The word is, too, that the city has taken over from Manchester as night club capital: *Club Europa*, New Briggate; *The Cockpit*, Swinegate; *NATO*, Boar Lane; *Planet Earth*, City Square; *Pleasure Rooms*, Grand Arcade; *Ritzy's*, Swinegate; *Warehouse*, Somers Street - these and others offer a miscellany through the week of Indie, mainstream dance, disco/funk/hip hop, house, garage, Brit-pop, drum and bass. And Cookridge Street, the official site for both *Town and Country Club* and *The Underground*, is probably the most popular of all: Friday is Brutus Gold's Love Train at T&C; Sorted for Saturdays - 'Snap, Crackle and Loadsa Pop - all the best of 80s, 90s pop, indie and dance'. The Town and Country Club is for live bands too: Formerly the Coliseum, they tell us they first opened their doors in October 1992 and have since played host to 'INXS, Blur, Mark Knopfler, Jack Dee and The Stone Roses', amongst many others. April and May saw Cast, Tricky, Supergrass and Marillion. Meanwhile The Underground offers Latin/Salsa, live jazz, soul, RnB; and the new Monday regular spot is Corkers - top line TV comedians, music and dance.

THE UNION

They claim almost one million pints a year in The Old Bar at the Leeds Union - 'This makes it the second biggest beer outlet in Europe after the Munich Beer Festival.' There's also the Harvey Milk Bar - 'named after Harvey Milk, the gay activist shot by an assassin in San Francisco.' The Milk Bar is the official Union venue, booked not only by Ents but by outside promoters too, and with a licence extended beyond that of the Old Bar. Then there's The Doubles Bar - 'so called because of its former life selling cheap doubles' - and The RH Evans lounge upstairs, used for society club nights.

Elsewhere in the Union, in the basement next to the Old Bar, they boast 'the largest campus travel agency in England'. With an annual turnover of £3 million.

Leeds is also a campaigning Union. I caught an article in Essex Uni's *Parklife,* which was having a go at *Leeds Student*, their award-winning magazine. Essex put Leeds 'amongst the most politically correct higher educational institutes in the country' for banning an advert from the lingerie company, Knickerbox. The ad, which carried an NUS endorsement, showed a shapely lady removing her jumper to reveal a Knickerbox brassiere doing what it was meant to do. The ban came two weeks after Leeds had banned the *Sun* newspaper from the Union shop. 'I don't understand it,' one Leeds student was quoted as saying, 'This PC bollocks has gone too far.'

In fact Leeds's decision was absolutely in line with their policy. Whether it is women's rights or anti-racism, they have a clearly set out strategy. There is an anti-racist project called DART (Drive Against Racism Today), which goes into schools in the Leeds area. They employ drama workshop techniques to exercise the dangers of racism and discrimination in the minds of schoolkids. They also take coachloads of people all over the place to demonstrate against fascism, and have information packs setting out their thoughts on both these evils. I wondered that they had time for all this, and then learned that that too was the subject of a campaign. This campaign was against the University which was threatening to timetable away their free Wednesday afternoons, the one guaranteed time students had for such activities, as well as for sport and so on. They would seem to have a point, although their principal argument did appear to be a bit thin - 'It is now well recognised that the "transferable skills" grained from these activities complement academic achievement.' Mmmm, I suppose someone was bound to swallow that hoary old PTS chestnut in the end.

Nevertheless, Leeds keeps the pressure up. There is, for example, a Healthy Sex Campaign (HIV/AIDS), which deserves every encouragement. The idea here is to show that safe sex can be fun. So they threw a women-only sex toys party, screened the Woody Allen film, *Everything You Always Wanted to Know About Sex*, and promoted a live sex show. I imagine they were on to a winner with that.

SPORT

Leeds has two sports halls, one large enough to take 1,500 spectators. Sports facilitated include badminton, basketball, volleyball; there is also a gym, a weights room, a rifle range, fitness room, squash courts, table tennis, climbing wall, etc. Playing fields are sited about 5 miles from the Uni and include 28 pitches for football, rugby, lacrosse, American football and hockey; there are also cricket squares, a floodlit synthetic pitch and six floodlit tennis courts. Rowing is also catered for, both in Leeds and in York, as is sailing on nearby lakes and reservoirs. Hiking, climbing, canoeing and caving are undertaken not far north in the area of the Yorkshire Dales. Students may also use Leeds City's international swimming pool, and there are golf courses in the area. Spectators can of course enjoy cricket and rugby league at Headingley and suffer Leeds United at Elland Road.

City of Leeds College of Music

City of Leeds College of Music
3 Quarry Hill
Leeds
LS2 7PD

As of September 1997:
Cookridge Street
Leeds
LS2 8BH

TEL 0113 243 2491
FAX 0113 243 8798

CITY OF LEEDS COLLEGE OF MUSIC	
Founded	**1965**
Situation/style	**City site**
UNDERGRADUATE PROFILE	
Application acceptance rate	**19%**
Population	**250**
Mature student population	**42%**
Overseas student population	**3%**
Male/female ratio	**80:20**
1st year institut. accommodation	**None**
Approximate rent (accom. arranged by College through leasing agency)	**£35-£45 pw**
ACADEMIC PROFILE	
A-level requirements:	**Low**
Performing Arts: Music, Jazz Studies	EE
EMPLOYMENT PROFILE	
Principal job market destinations: **Arts/Media, Education**	

VAG VIEW

Moving into new purpose-built accommodation in September '97, facilities look set to improve beyond recognition at CLCM. Phase One will see a 5-storey teaching building with rehearsal rooms, workshops, recording studios, a recital room, a bar, library and learning resource centre. A 450-seat concert hall and residential accommodation are to come in Phases 2 and 3, which will turn it into the most up-to-date music college around.

Currently the Students Union leaves a little to be desired, but does provide annual bashes and several clubs, including the Ladies Club (see below). With the new facilities however, the ents look set to improve, as do sporting opportunities - negotiations are in progress with Leeds Uni to try and gain access to their facilities, clubs and socs on their campus 10 minutes away.

Foundation courses are offered to school leavers aged 16 and to mature students with or without qualifications. Degree courses are validated by the University of Leeds.

Jazz Studies (BA): *CLCM has been called 'The Jazz College' for years, students are taught by some of the big names in Jazz. You get to participate in bands and ensembles, workshops with visiting artists. Entrance requirements of two A-levels but an audition requiring improvisation and an entrance paper of a Grade VIII standard can substitute. Opportunities to study abroad on the Jazz Inter University Cooperation project with Finland, Norway, Netherlands, Austria.*

Bachelor of Performing Arts (Music): *Modular performance based degree with emphasis on composition and ensemble work. A Business and Professional Studies module is provided to equip you for self-employment. Entrance requirements are two A-levels or a BTEC diploma and Grade VIII practical (or equivalent at audition). Grade VIII theory and practical may be offered as an alternative to A-level Music.*

GETTING THERE

★ By road: From east - M62 (J39), M1. From west - M62 (J27), M621. From north A1, A58. From north-west, A65, A650.
★ By rail: Newcastle, (1:45); London Euston, 2:30; Birmingham New Street, 2:20.
★ By air: Inland and International flights from Leeds Bradford airport.

VIEW FROM THE GROUND
by Sue-Lee Freeman

The CLMC is brilliantly situated with the train station, coach station, markets, shopping centres and many banks all within five to ten minutes walking distance and many bus stops right outside. Bus and train fares are excellent especially between 9.0 a.m. and 3.0 p.m. and 6.0 p.m. - midnight when the dearest fare anywhere in West Yorkshire is around 80p. Day rovers (£2.30) are valid for one day and can be used for as many journeys as you like. However, roads are often busy (especially at peak times) which can slow things down. You might want to think about getting a bike! Pedal power is free and often faster (you don't get stuck at traffic lights). Recycle Engineers at 149 Victoria Road have quality secondhand bikes and offer 10% discount to students.

ACCOMMODATION

Accommodation is easy to find. Unipol at 8, Fenton Street (tel: 2430074) have many properties (usually shared) and take students in mini-buses to view; rents are reasonable and houses are generally well maintained. There are also numerous ads in papershop windows, on supermarket notice boards and in Thursday nights edition of the Yorkshire Post. If the worst happens you can always crash at the YMCA (22 Lovell Park Hill tel: 245 7840) which offers short stays at £33 per week. The Headingley/Woodhouse areas are a hive of student activity but also have the highest burglary rate in Leeds. Less risky areas include Harehills, Armley, Hanover Square and Kirkstall Road, all within two and a half miles of the city centre. Digs in Chapeltown are cheap but the area is dodgy; best avoided.

THE CLCM STUDENT

CLCM has lots to offer every kind of student although the ideal candidate would be an open-minded, independent thinker, with perseverance (the balls to badger tutors for extra information!), an inquisitive mind and not too much ego. There are many opportunities in Leeds for gigging and lots of music competitions; it's up to you to go out and get them. A philosophical outlook comes in handy when one gets knocked back.

Being a Fresher can be bloody scary but a smile works wonders to break the ice. The CLCM population is about 80% male, but there is surprisingly little sexism and most lads are not wanting to hit on the nearest available female. However, the SU Ladies Club organises girls nights out and offers moral support for fledglings!

STUDENT UNION

The SU is lively and strong, organising annual bashes and several clubs, including footy, basketball, cycling, fell walking, Christian Union meetings and a twice monthly jam session at the Felon and Firkin in Great George Street (done out with old fashioned cops and robbers regalia). This provides a wonderful and cool platform for all student musicians. The college also offers students free Alexander Technique sessions. Students from all over the country and abroad come to embark on the jazz and classical music courses here.

LEEDS CITY

City life is truly cosmopolitan and there are literally hundreds of nightspots to choose from. Some of the best clubs are the Underground at 55 Cookridge Street, playing jazz/latin grooves (also jazz gigs); Primos II at Westminster Buildings, New York Street, a gay club which opens til 6.0 a.m. on Fridays; the Pleasure Rooms at 9 Low Merrion Street, with three different floors of music; Stomp at Leeds Met SU, Calverley Street playing indie/alternative; and Scrumpies in Duncan Street playing rock music on Saturday nights. Of the vast multitude of pubs, well worth visiting are Whitelocks in Turks Head Yard, set in a Victorian alley with gas lamps to light the outdoor keg tables; The Bingley Arms at

37 Church Lane, Bardsey, said to be the oldest inn in the country; The Horse and Trumpet in The Headrow is a festival ale house, very intimate and decorated in the style of an old library/study; and the Headingley Taps, in North Lane Headingley, is converted from a disused water pumping station.

Eating out is not always expensive. Three of the best are The Suhana Restaurant at 194 Woodhouse Road, a curry and nan bread for £2.99; Zaks Bar at 43-45 Cookridge Street do lunchtime buffets of pasta and pizza for under £4 and Hansa's at 72-74 Worth Street (a vegi curry house) offer a three course meal during term time. Others worth mentioning are The Cornucopia Cafe, Corn Exchange, Call Lane, which is totally smoke free (good if you don't like fags) and The Dubterranean at 235 Woodhouse Lane which serves food and wine with live music and is open until 5.00am from Thursday to Saturday.

The Irish Centre in York Road, The Town and Country Club at 55 Cookridge Street and the Duchess of York in Vicar Lane are all live gig venues (featuring the likes of Jamiroqui, Chaka Khan and The Brecker Bothers), and when you've had enough of boozing and boogying there's a host of theatres, galleries, museums and parks to chill out in. Abbey House Museum has three streets of reconstructed Victorian shops and houses with costume and toy displays. The City Art Gallery and The Henry Moore Institute are an inspiration and Tropical World is home to exotic butterflies (living), nocturnal bats and iguanas, to name but a few. Theatres include the Grand Theatre which features touring musicals such as The Blues Brothers and The Rocky Horror Show, and The West Yorkshire Playhouse if you dig Shakespeare and contemporary productions. If you fancy a bit of fresh air and nature, Roundhay Park is ace. It has two lakes and lots of lovely walking.

Leeds folk are generally a welcoming lot when it comes to students (although you might meet the occasional Victor Meldrew who rattles on about students having a cushy time - not!) and are used to crowds and strangers. Some of the many events include a Summer Beer Festival (city centre), a West Indian Carnival, Jazz On The Waterfront (Brewery Wharfe), Opera in the Park (biggest outdoor opera in the country - Roundhay Park) and Leeds International Film Festival. The November firework display at Roundhay Park is free and attracts thousands even in the rain! (As was the case last year.)

There are five cinemas in Leeds with the MGM having the best deal for students. Sporting opportunities include the International Swimming Pool and The Metropolitan University Gym (only £2 for students - the cheapest in Leeds). Headingley of course is home of the famous cricket ground. And finally *shopping*! If you are window shopping (i.e. skint) or feeling flush, take a walk around the posh Victoria Quarter or Queens' Arcade. The Corn Exchange is hip if you're after something young and funky, and Granary Wharfe (by the canal) is full of craft shops, aromatherapy and artists selling their goods. Thursday's open air market is groovy and cheap because it's all secondhand. You can pick up a pair of Levi's for a tenner. The indoor market is best for fruit, veg and meat, all of which are reduced on Saturdays around 4.00pm. (Supermarkets apparently make the most profit from fruit and veg, which is why they are always near the entrance!) If you want your hair cut in the city centre, your wallet might need a general anaesthetic - it costs around £15 for a trim, never mind the rest. Go out of town.

I hope you have a wicked time studying in Leeds!

LEEDS METROPOLITAN UNIVERSITY

Leeds Metropolitan University
Calverley Street
Leeds
West Yorkshire
LS1 3HE

TEL 0113 2832600
FAX 0113 2833109

Leeds Metropolitan
Student Union,
City Campus
Calverley Street
Leeds LS1 3HE

TEL 0113 2430171
FAX 0113 2342973

Leeds Metropolitan
Student Union,
Beckett Park Campus
Headingley
Leeds LS6 3QS

TEL 0113 2430171
FAX 0113 2752796

LEEDS METROPOLITAN UNIVERSITY

Founded	**1970**
Situation/style	**City sites**
UNDERGRADUATE PROFILE	
Application acceptance rate	**9%**
Population	**8,200**
Mature student population	**54%**
Overseas student population	**6%**
Male/female ratio	**52:48**
1st year institut. accommodation	**70%**
Approximate cost (Uni)	**£33-£53 pw**
(City)	**£35-£45 pw**

ACADEMIC PROFILE

A-level requirements: **Medium**

Teacher Training 8-16, **Physiotherapy** BBC, **Nursing** BB-CCC, **Human Biology** 14, **Diatetics** CCD, **Computer Sciences** BBC, **Chem. Eng.** (incl. **Fire Science**) BCC-CCD, **Electronic, Manufacturing, Civil Eng.** DD,DD,EE, **Architecture** 16-20, **Law** BBC, **Leisure, Social Studies** 18,BCC, **Social Policy & Admin.** BC-CCD, **Accounting & Finance, Euro. Languages & Business** CDD, **Business, Int. Business** (also **Langs.**) CCD, **Retailing** 12, **PR** BBC

Student/staff ratio	**23:1**
1st class degree pass rate	**5.2%**

HEFCE assessments (10 subjects assessed/approved):
1996 **Modern Languages** 19

Joint Funding Council's research assessment 1996 (15 subjects assessed):
Grade 5/5* None

EMPLOYMENT PROFILE

Employability in Industry:
MPW national league table (1996) **44th=**

Principal job market destinations:
Manufacturing, Health, Commerce, Retail/Wholesale, Hotel/Restaurant, Public Admin./Law, Personnel, Computer, Arts/Media, Architecture, Sport

Approximate % unemployed **12%**

VAG VIEW

Leeds Met. has a clear sense of what it is about, is refreshingly uncomplicated and shows results. Its students also seem to have a good time. It really is as simple as that.

SITUATION

The Uni has basically two sites. The city site includes various buildings for teaching, accommodation and administration. The building in Calvery Street is one main focus. Beckett Park Campus is quite separate and situated three miles from the city site in Headingley

GETTING THERE

★ By road: South - the M1 culminates in Leeds. The A1 for North and Eastern counties. The M62 for East and West. Extensive coach services.
★ By air: Leeds\Bradford airport for inland services and Western Europe.
★ By rail: London Kings Cross, 2:30; Liverpool Lime Street, 2:00; Manchester Piccadilly, 1:15; Newcastle, 1:45; Sheffield, 1:15; Birmingham New Street, 2:30.

ACADEMIA

Roughly half Leeds Met. students are mature and study part time. They tend therefore to be particularly career orientated, which is not the same as saying they don't have a social life too. But there is a marked emphasis at Leeds Met. on work experience, sandwich courses and programming courses to the job market. A number of courses, for example, involve a participating European University like International Business Finance, European Marketing (run in cahoots with Hochschule Bremen, Germany, or the Groupe ESC Normandie at Caen, France). There are also a number of good BA courses focused on other specific work areas - Public Relations , Tourism Management , Landscape Architecture, Urban Development, etc. Then there is a range of Civil Engineering and Built Environment courses (BSc); of BSc Health Studies courses - including Nursing (Mental Health), Physiotherapy, Environmental Health, Dietetics; and interesting Electronics courses - including Electronics, Media and Technology (BEng).

Most students acquire skills in computing during the duration of their courses. And their USP is putting their students to work. 'They sell themselves on their links with small and medium-sized enterprises,' one school adviser told me. 'They have a very strong careers department, possibly a little under-staffed. But they are building bridges, making links.' In pursuit of this aim they are involved with Teaching Company schemes, putting recent graduates and Uni resources and expertise to work on major external company projects.

ACCOMMODATION

Uni-owned/managed halls or flats, self-catered student houses, private lodgings. They can't guarantee all first years accommodation, but with Leeds Uni they belong to UNIPOL, Student Homes, an accommodation bureau at 8-12 Fenton Street, Leeds LS1 3EA, which will help students find their own. Telephone their New to Leeds Advice Line, 0113 243 8822. And they are working hard on enhancing their own accommodation - 'Leeds Met. have upgraded their accommodation,' we were told. 'In Kirkstall, Leeds 5, they have converted a huge building into state of the art accommodation.' The project to which this school careers adviser was referring is the new £17 million development (including a gym, laundry and shop) of Kirkstall Brewery. So, who knows, you maybe even get to live in a brewery at Leeds Met. What's more they have made an arrangement to beat the risk of violence which exists in Leeds. 'If you simply show your Students Union card to a taxi driver, he will take you wherever you want to go, even if you haven't the money, and then charge it back to the Union, who will claim it back from you - just so you need never be caught in a tricky situation. You see, Leeds is a tricky place.'

VIEW FROM THE GROUND

by Rebecca O'Neill

Leeds Metropolitan really does have something to offer everyone. It has two campuses, one in the centre of Leeds and the other three miles out in an area of parkland, Beckett Park. Both campuses are served by cheap and frequent bus services.

Leeds Metropolitan appeals to all kinds of students. 62.5% of graduates go straight into employment. But that doesn't mean that there is a quiet and studious atmosphere; the emphasis is on having a good time at the same time as working. There is always something going on. It has also been said that you can spot a Leeds Metropolitan student because they look less 'studenty' than those at the other Leeds University.

The Student Union provides a bar on each campus and organises special events such as Healthy Sex Week and the weekly nights of: OTT (cheap drinks, mid-week), Stomp (Indie night), Saturday Night (formerly the Poly Bop, a mainstream night that is an institution) and, of course, regular Happy Hours and drinks promotions. The city site, Ents. Hall, also plays host to bands and comedy acts on tour such as Kula Shaker and Lee and Herring. Other facilities include: shops, banks, cafes, diners, sporting facilities (a health and fitness suite on both campuses) and photocopy shops. Leeds Metropolitan has a good reputation for sports. The main facilities are based at Beckett Park and competition takes place in all sports and at all levels. If this is not for you, stay well clear of Beckett Park SU bar on a Wednesday evening. Leeds is a fast growing city. It has lots to offer students; a wide range of bars, pubs and restaurants to suit all tastes and pockets. It is also home to some of the best clubs in the country, such as Back to Basics and Hard Times. There are also plenty of shops from boutiques and Harvey Nichols to chain stores and secondhand shops. Anything goes in Leeds from the young trendies to the traditional student look, and the city offers a wide range of activities, from football with Leeds United and cricket with Yorkshire Cricket, to Art at the Henry Moore Institute and history at the Royal Armouries. Headingley, the main student area, offers cheaper restaurants, take-aways, shops and the busiest pubs in the land - The Skyrack and The Original Oak - yet service is still remarkably quick.

Most students live in Headingley or the nearby areas of Burley, Hyde Park and Woodhouse. Headingley is by far the most popular place to live and rents reflect this. You can expect to pay £40 to £45 per week in the centre of Headingley compared to £30 a week in Burley.

About half the first year students can be housed in University accommodation, the majority of which is self-catering. Very few are accommodated on campus. This gives you more independence and makes you feel more like a part of the local community. By far the plushest of these is the modern Kirkstall Brewery Complex, which houses 1,000 students. Facilities include a gym and a Students' Union bar. Security is high.

Like any large city, Leeds has its fair share of crime. These are not specifically targeted at students, but it is wise to be cautious and security conscious.

LEICESTER UNIVERSITY

Leicester University
University Road
Leicester
LE1 7RH

TEL 0116 252 2522
FAX 0116 252 2200

Leicester University
Student Union
Percy Gee Building
Mayors Walk
University Road
Leicester LE1 7RH

TEL 0116 223 1111
FAX 0116 223 1112

UNIVERSITY OF LEICESTER

Founded **1921**

Situation/style **Campus**

UNDERGRADUATE PROFILE

Application acceptance rate **10%**
Medical AAR **7%**
Population **6,800**
Mature student population **16%**
Overseas student population **9%**
Male/female ratio **50:50**
1st year institut. accommodation **100%**
Approximate cost **£35-£70 pw**

ACADEMIC PROFILE

A-level requirements: **High**
Biological Sciences 18-20, **Physical Sciences** (incl. **Astronomy, Astrophysics**) 20, BCC-CCD, **Mech., General, E & E Engineering** 18, **Politics** 20, **Law** 24-26, **Psychology** BBB, **Sociology** BCC, **Archaeology** 20, **English** BBB, **History** BCC, **French & Italian, German & Italian** BCC, BCD, **Medicine** ABB:
★ Science 'A's required **Chemistry**
★ Additional Science 'A's preferred **1 other Sci.**
★ Addit. Non-Science 'A's acceptable **Yes**
★ Retakes considered **Yes**
★ Retake offer **AAA**
★ Clinical contact **1st year**

Student/staff ratio **9:1**
1st class degree pass rate **5.5%**
HEFCE assessments (13 subjects assessed/approved):
1993 **History, Law** Excellent
1994 **Chemistry, English** Excellent
1995 **Sociology** 19
1995/6 **French** 19 **German** 21 **Italian** 20
Joint Funding Council's research assessment 1996 (32 subjects assessed):
Pharmacology. Grade 5*
Biochemistry, Biol. Sciences, Physics, Archaeology, Economic & Social History Grade 5

EMPLOYMENT PROFILE

Employability in Industry:
MPW national league table (1996) **49th=**
Principal job market destinations:
Health, Commerce, Retail/Wholesale, Manufacturing, Public Admin./Law, Education
PIP 1996 employers' survey:
Top 2 subjects/national ranking
Science 32nd=
Accountancy, Finance & Banking 33rd=
Approximate % unemployed **7%**

VAG VIEW

'Leicester had been a rather good university of the Nottingham variety... They are very good on the Law course, but I have a sense that Leicester will take a lower grade. A good insurance choice.'

This was a reaction to Leicester from a school careers adviser, whose job it is to be aware of the strengths and weaknesses of all Unis so that her sixth-form pupils can come up with an optimum balance in their all-important UCAS application lists. She was casting Leicester in the role of fall-back option. If you look down their assessment record, Leicester has a fair wack of good scores. Its facilities are good. In their 1997 prospectus, they even quoted a student as saying that he had chosen

Leicester for the good accommodation. That seemed a rather odd thing to quote in a prospectus, but it is, nevertheless, a plus point. Perhaps it is just a question of fashion. Perhaps students aren't enamoured of the city, and the Uni, aware of that, has got itself into a bit of a defensive position with its offers.

What characterises the city is its culturally mixed population. The Leicester prospectus puts this rather quaintly, citing the great variety of cultural festivities which are celebrated there annually, beginning with the Chinese New Year and Christmas and moving through Navratri, Eid, Diwali, etc.

Another school teacher picked on this characteristic of the city as one source of De Montfort's rise - 'My impression is,' she said, 'that De Montfort have been successful in picking up on the ethnic minority population, which Leicester may have been less good at.'

You would expect the ex-poly De Montfort's student base to be essentially different to Leicester's (university founding date, 1921) - higher mature student intake, drawing more locally, etc. But it is interesting that Leicester's mature undergraduate population is now, in percentage terms, nearer to De Montfort's and a good deal larger than, say, Nottingham's, and it may well be that there is more direct competition for students between the ex-poly and the pucca university in Leicester than in many other university cities. If so, Leicester may be caught between two markets, offering a traditional university experience, academically and culturally, less suited to its real market than De Montfort's.

Again, unlike Nottingham's campus, Leicester's is situated right in the centre of the city, not far from the railway station. So any doubts among prospective students from afar about living in the city for three years are likely to weigh more heavily, which is a pity, for if you read Londoner Amanda Dodson's piece in the De Montfort entry you will see that the city is changing rapidly, in line with the increasing number of student residents since De Montfort's rise.

SITUATION

Leicester is some twenty miles south of Nottingham, by Junction 21 of the M1.

GETTING THERE

★ By road: M1 (J21 or J22).
★ By rail: London St Pancras, 1:20; Manchester Piccadilly, 1:30; Sheffield, 1:30; Birmingham New Street, 1:00; Nottingham, 0:30.
★ By coach: readily accessible.
★ By Air: Bus from Birmingham International Airport and East Midlands International Airport.

ACADEMIA

Single, joint or combined honours courses, all except the MBChB, modular in structure. Student Learning Centre with workshops and self-learning materials designed to develop study skills. Well equipped Language Centre and a policy of 'languages for all'. Their medical school leads the way with its new curriculum which integrates basic medical sciences with clinical education, devised in 1994 in response to the GMC's document *Tomorrow's Doctors* and approved. Six modules in Phase I are allocated to clinical work, and communication skills are to the fore. In science, the Uni's reputation stems from pioneering work in the field of Genetics - they discovered DNA 'fingerprinting'. Pioneering work, too, in water treatment technologies. Good academic reputation across the board.

ARTS & ENTS

Leicester has one bar and two venues, and a thriving ents scene. The Redfearn is the 'pub before the club' - pool, pinball, table football, arcade games, table games from behind the bar. There's a quiz on Tuesdays, TFI Saturday (variable but always culminating in two hours party music), Wozza's (disco) on

Sunday. The Venue has a 1,600 capacity, making it Leicester's No. 1 gig venue, the other being De Montfort Hall, next to campus. It's an eaterie during the day and usually a three-section venue at night - Mirage, Oasis and Concourse. Thursdays at Oasis is a re-vamped version of Freakscene ('Fugazi to Underworld, with a little bit of Goth and dodgy decor'), their ever-popular Indie night. The Mega is the high spot, three rooms, two DJs. The Asylum is smaller: Thursdays is Reagan's (80s); Fridays Rapture (Lesbian, Gay & Bisexual - retro, chart, dance) or Pants (Indie, rock, Britpop). On Saturdays it's either Rock night or their very own house night - High Spirits, fresh from a tour of Paris, Ibiza and Jersey.

In the city, two clubs do big student nights - Krystals and Le Palais; also Streetlife, The White Room, Luxor, Branigans, The Fan Club, Alcatraz. For more artistic fare, seek out The Phoenix - film, dance, theatre, comedy, folk music; also The Haymarket for London previews. Also masses of pubs and bars with live music - see De Montfort entry and Amanda Dodson's run-down on all these.

ACCOMMODATION

Halls include large Edwardian houses extended with modern refectories and study bedroom blocks; some en suite. Each has JCR committee common room, TV room and bar. First years guaranteed a place in these or Uni-owned self-catering property.

SPORT

Top class gymnasium, The Greenhouse, plus weights room, activity studio, squash courts. Outdoor facilities include 25 acres of parkland with pitches for soccer, rugby, cricket and lacrosse, fourteen tennis courts - three floodlit, an athletics track, full-size floodlit all weather pitch and cricket nets. Some forty Sports Association clubs (including horse riding and windsurfing). Many clubs belong to local Leicestershire leagues and play representative matches midweek.

LINCOLNSHIRE AND HUMBERSIDE UNIVERSITY

The University of Lincolnshire
and Humberside
Cottingham Road
Hull
HU6 7RT

TEL 01482 440550
FAX 01482 471836

Lincolnshire and Humberside
Student Union
Administrative HQ
Strand Close
Kingston-upon-Hull
HU2 9BT

TEL 01482 444584
FAX 01482 491911

UNIVERSITY OF LINCOLNSHIRE & HUMBERSIDE

Founded	**1983**
Situation/style	**4 site campus**
UNDERGRADUATE PROFILE	
Application acceptance rate	**21%**
Population	**8,240**
Mature student population	**25%**
Overseas student population	**6%**
Male/female ratio	**50:50**
1st year institut. accommodation	**85%**
Approximate cost (Uni)	**£60 pw**
(City)	**£35 pw**
ACADEMIC PROFILE	
A-level requirements:	**Low**

Law 12-18. **Modern Languages** D. **Applied Social Science, Accountancy, Architec. Technology, Engineering, Environmental Sci., Food Sci., Nutrition, Social Work** 12. **Architecture, Finance, Mgt., Marketing, Info. Systems, Interior Design, Museum/Exhibition Design, Agriculture, Countryside Mgt.** 14, **Business Studies, Computing, Graphic Design** 16

Student/staff ratio	**34:1**
1st class degree pass rate	**2.5%**
HEFCE assessments:	
6 subjects assessed/approved	
Joint Funding Council's research assessment 1996 (7 subjects assessed):	
Grade 5/5*	None
EMPLOYMENT PROFILE	
Principal job market destinations:	
Approximate % unemployed	**10%**

VAG VIEW

Lincolnshire & Humberside University is in a state of evolution. It has various sites in Hull, the main administrative site - the Cottingham Road site - also houses faculties of Engineering (Engineering, Computing, Information Systems and Technology) and Business (Accountancy, Administration, Business, Finance, Marketing and Languages). This is situated beside Hull University campus. Just north, in Inglemire Avenue, is the Inglemire site, which houses Social Science & Professional Studies (Applied Social Science and Social Work). In Hull city is a split City site, which has Architecture (plus Interior Design, Museum & Exhibition Design) and Art & Design (Fine Art and in Graphic Design). Then there's the Grimsby site, about 25 miles to the south, in Lincolnshire, which has the Faculty of Applied Science & Technology. This, however, is about to move to the Lincoln site, some thirty miles further to the south, which from May 97 has been offering Masters degree programmes in Manufacturing Systems, Environmental Protection and Management, Food Technology, Quality Management, and Tourism Management.

At Cottingham Road they have a

couple of bars and regular weekly discos, but a lot of students enjoy Hull Uni facilties, see Hull entry.

Looking at this scattered and movable feast you can begin to appreciate the problems they've been up against. The Lincolnshire site may well turn out to do well. It was launched as a project in 1993 to great fanfare and with support from local and regional professional and commercial groups, industrialists and employers, who now have an interest in it succeeding. Lincoln is already a centre for De Montfort University and indeed for Bishop Grosseteste (see entries elsewhere). It isn't exactly the most jumping city for students, though it is a lovely cathedral city with much potential for students, once the ball gets rolling.

There are typically characterful cathedral city pubs and some clubs, which already do student nights. There are two cinemas, the recently established Odeon and the unimaginatively named Cinema, both of which also offer student discounts. And there is the Theatre Royal for mainstream drama, concerts, exhibtions, etc. Enterprising entrepreneurs in the student ents/club scene line could do well, if there are any in the area. At the moment, at Lincs & Humberside Uni in Lincoln, the situation is more one of pleading for students to galvanise themselves into action. The Uni admits it has difficulty in getting the sports scene up and running, owing to poor resources - sports clubs are 'a bit thin on the ground,' as they put it, and they are exhorting students to set up extra-curricular activities on the basis that employers like to see them on their CVs, which is undoubtedly true. A large number of students at all sites in this Uni are, however, locals or fairly locally based, and it may take time.

GETTING THERE

★ By road to Lincoln: from the north (Hull) along the A15; from Sheffield way (NW) via the A57 onto A46 Lincoln by-pass.
★ By rail from London Kings Cross via Newark (on the main east coast line), 2:00; from Nottingham, 1:00.
★ By road to Hull: M62, A63, A1079, B1233.
★ By rail: Leeds, 1:00; Sheffield, 1:45; Manchester Piccadilly, 2:15; London Kings Cross, 4:30; Birmingham New Street, 3:00.
★ Fast connections to Cottingham; bus the two miles to Campus.

LIVERPOOL UNIVERSITY

The University of Liverpool
PO Box 147
Liverpool
L69 3BX

TEL 0151 794 2000
FAX 0151 708 6502

Liverpool University Guild
of Students
Liverpool University
PO Box 187
160 Mount Pleasant
Liverpool L69 7BR

TEL 0151 794 6868
FAX 0151 794 4174

UNIVERSITY OF LIVERPOOL

Founded	**1881**
Situation/style	**City campus**
UNDERGRADUATE PROFILE	
Application acceptance rate	**9%**
Medical AAR	**11%**
Population	**10,200**
Mature student population	**18%**
Overseas student population	**7%**
Male/female ratio	**50:50**
1st year institut. accommodation	**100%**
Approximate cost	**£40-£60 pw**
ACADEMIC PROFILE	
A-level requirements:	**High-Medium**

Law ABB, **Politics, Sociology** BCC, **Psychology** 22-24, **Architecture** BBC, **French, German** BBC-BCC, **English combinations** 12, **Biology and combinations** 18-22, **Physical Science** 12-20, **Economics & Math Statistics** BCC, **Computing combinations** 10-12, **Aerospace Engineering** 22, **General, E & E, Mech. Eng.** 18-20, **Nursing** BCC. **Medicine** ABB:

- ★ Science 'A's required **A Grade Chem. + 1 other Science**
- ★ Addit. Non-Science 'A's acceptable **Yes**
- ★ Retakes considered **Yes**
- ★ Retake offer **AAA**
- ★ Clinical contact **1st year**

Student/staff ratio	**8:1**
1st class degree pass rate	**6.4%**

HEFCE assessments (15 subjects assessed/approved):

1993 **History, Law**	Excellent
1994 **English, Geology Environmental Sciences**	Excellent
1995/6 **French** 22 **Iberian** 21 **German** 19	
1996 **Sociology** 21	

Joint Funding Council's research assessment 1996 (44 subjects assessed):

Physiology, Metallurgy, Music	Grade 5*
Anatomy, Pharmacology, Physics, Earth Sciences, Pure Maths, Mechanical Eng., Iberian	Grade 5

EMPLOYMENT PROFILE

Employability in Industry:

MPW national league table (1996) **22nd**

Principal job market destinations:

Health (incl. **Dentistry**), **Manufacturing** (strong on **Electrical & Electronic**), **Commerce, Retail/Wholesale, Public Admin./Law, Education, Architecture** (very strong), **Veterinary,** good record **Engineering Design**

PIP 1996 employers' survey:

Top 3 subjects/national ranking

Law	10th=
Electrical Engineering	15th
Science	17th=
Approximate % unemployed	**7%**

VAG VIEW

For some reason people don't think of Liverpool as an option in quite the same way that they used to. Maybe it has something to do with the reputation of the city for violence and drugs. Possibly it doesn't offer quite as clear-cut a market profile as, say, go-ahead Warwick or arrogant Nottingham or Rah-ridden Durham or Oxbridge-reject Bristol. In fact, a bit like Cardiff, it is, in our view, seriously under-rated academically. Liverpool is up to some interesting things in that area, and as a city, it is one of the most lively scenes available to sixth-form students in the premier league.

SITUATION

Liverpool is the original redbrick university. Established in 1881, The Precinct, which sounds like something out of an Ed McBain or police procedural but is in fact the name of the campus, sits but a few minutes walk from the city centre. Liverpool is famous for football, music, and the Mersey ferry, but with John Moores University and Liverpool Hope University College, it is now one of the major centres of Higher Education in Britain.

GETTING THERE

★ By road: M62 (East/West), which connects with M6 (North/South) at Junction 21a. Well served by National Express coaches.
★ By rail: Manchester, 0:40; Sheffield, 1:45; Leeds or Birmingham, 2:00; London Kings Cross, 3:00.
★ Liverpool airports for flights inland and to/from Ireland.

ACCOMMODATION

Eight halls of residence three miles from Uni are linked by a good bus service. Greenbank: Two halls, with own catering and bar. Carnatic: Six halls, all sharing dining room, bar, library, common room and games facilities. All-male hall (McNair); all-female (Salisbury).

Self-catering option - flats and houses for 3 to 6 - on Uni precinct and increasingly popular with first years.

Guaranteed first year Uni accommodation if form in by 2nd September.

Uni has set up Liverpool Student Homes with Liverpool John Moores to help sort out city accommodation. The office is at 140 Mount Pleasant, Liverpool L3 5SR (Tel: 0151 794 3296). It and the John Moores' web site have daily up-dated lists available.

ACADEMIA

Faculties include Arts, Engineering, Law, Medicine (including a School of Dentistry), Science, Social & Environmental Studies, and Veterinary Science.

Liverpool Medical School is ahead of most in developing the new curriculum required following the Medical Council's recommendations outlined in *Tomorrow's Doctors (1993)*. A completely new undergraduate medical curriculum has been in force since October 1996. Problem solving skills have come to the fore; the assimilation of theory is supported at every turn by small-group workshops, practicals, laboratory sessions; there is a stronger emphasis on clinical work, and assessments will focus most particularly on our future doctors' ability to apply the theoretical knowledge they glean from lectures. 'The course integrates at an early stage the basic sciences that are essential to modern clinical practice and research with exposure to clinical ideas and practice.' Undergraduate medical students also have the advantage at Liverpool of working alongside students involved in allied subjects - Diagnostic Radiography, Occupational Therapy, Orthoptics, Physiotherapy, Nursing, etc.

The university is one of only five offering a degree course in Veterinary Science, and a similar emphasis on clinical studies and practical work appertains.

Outside these clinical courses (Dentistry included), Liverpool has adopted a modular scheme - Single, Joint or Combined Honours being the framework. They offer a particularly interesting Combined Honours (BA), which involves an inter-disciplinary approach. A group of Languages, Humanities and Arts subjects have been opened up to another of Sciences, Maths and Social Studies. And there is an Arts and Social and Environmental Studies Joint programme (BA), offering further intriguing combinations such as French and Pure Mathematics, for example, or Maths and Philosophy. These are strategies which in an enlightened way offer a resolution to the old Arts/Science divide and demonstrate a whole different approach by what is regarded as a traditional redbrick university. 'Liverpool is coming up,' one careers master said to us, 'and I think that their asking grades are less than the excellence of some of their courses.'

The Academic Profile statistics of their course assessment results and A-level requirements (see fact box) would seem to back up this view. Some think of them as strong in Law, Archaeology, Geology, but Liverpool is coming to the fore in a number of areas. It has also adopted a concerted policy to encourage applications from mature and international students.

STUDENT GUILD

Some other schools careers advisers saw Liverpool's main problem as having to convince parents that the city is a safe place and that, as students, their children, if they went there, would not succumb to undue pressures to take drugs. Talking about York and Liverpool Universities, one said - 'York city has a very big drug problem, but how far that spills over into the Uni I can't be sure. Liverpool University is rather bad on that front, a difficult place for them to cope with.' Another said, 'Whispers of drugs at Liverpool, Glasgow, some people say Sussex.' The fact is that there are drugs at most, if not all, universities. Liverpool has a certain glamour due to its lively city - it may be better than Manchester on the local live band front. But it is no more dangerous than Leeds, or even Durham, where sporty public school Hoorays are regularly floored - even broken jawed - by recalcitrant Geordies. As LJM student Nicholas Wallis says, 'As a student in Liverpool, I have never been beaten, mugged or robbed, although God knows how many times I deserved it. Unfortunately many of my friends have suffered random violence, serial burglary and many other unpleasant incidents which have gone a considerable way to clouding their experiences of the place. Basically Liverpool is a modern city with more than its fair share of trouble for the uninitiated, unaware, or just plain unlucky. Having said that, only the truly paranoid would let this stop them from studying there.'

Liverpool Uni has one of the largest Guild buildings in Europe since its re-development in '95. All the usual amenities - launderette, barbers, photographers, stationers, printers, opticians, travel agents, plus an expansive, if not expensive, weekly market selling all kinds of goods from food to clothing, electrical goods to records, posters to jewellery.

Like John Moores Union, the Guild is strong in the student welfare department.

Clubs and societies are plentiful - over 100, including 45 sporting and 38 departmental (good social emphasis in these), the rest focused on pure/impure social, cultural, religious, political. The student newspaper is The Gazette.

The Guild has five bars, a cafe, TV lounge, rooms for table tennis, snooker, pool. The Mountford Hall at The Guild is one of Liverpool's major live venues and attracts big name bands. There are two additional, smaller venues for local and smaller acts, with strong local tradition maintained - e.g. Cast. Regular nightclubs - Saturday night Time Tunnel is its main attraction, as well as film screenings and comedy club. The Lark Lane area close to the Uni halls of residence is the best area for eating, Liverpool's Chinatown is a treat, and for the other city attractions - pubs, clubs (there are more than 130, Cream at The Nation is the big deal), see Nicholas Wallis's excellent resumé under Liverpool John Moores entry. Particularly interesting is what has happened to Liverpool's pubs - 'They're undergoing some sort of horrible transmogrification. The real pubs with shit beer, baseball bats behind the bar and frightening locals are being replaced by student-friendly venues run by the Firkin awful chains. As a result, the increasingly popular alternatives are the generic bar venues like Metz, The Milky Bar, Bar Zero, MelloMello, Beluga Bar, Arena etc. These questionable establishments offer you the opportunity to drink overpriced bottled lager and shout in the ear of the person next to you whilst eyeing down the achingly trendy students, posh scallies (gangsters to you and me), and fat office workers from Warrington.' Read on at LJM.

For the more cultured among you, the city's theatres offer everything from experimental/fringe to mainstream/touring. The internationally renowned Everyman Theatre is right by the Uni. The Playhouse Studio has a good reputation for contemporary drama, The Empire for ballet and opera, The Liverpool Philharmonic is home to The Royal Liverpool Philharmonic Orchestra. Then there's The Walker Art Gallery, with the largest art collection outside London, The Liverpool Tate for its impressive 20th century collection, and The Merseyside Maritime Museum and Museum of Liverpool Life for local cultural history. Though I shouldn't think many students spend much time in these, any more than they do in the commercial, touristy Albert Dock development, which the city makes such a shout about.

SPORT

The Sports Centre includes swimming pool, 4 squash courts, weight training, indoor cricket nets, climbing wall, sunbeds, facilities for aerobics, dance, trampolining. Hall at gymnasium for judo, fencing, archery, 4 additional squash courts, rifle and pistol range, weights room. The main sports ground near the halls of residence includes 2 floodlit artificial turf pitches for hockey, field sports, 5 rugby and 6 soccer pitches, 4 tennis courts, a lacrosse pitch, 2 cricket squares and 2 artificial wickets, bar and cafeteria. Two other grounds add a further 6 soccer pitches, and there's a base for climbing, walking, canoeing and field studies in Snowdonia, which accommodates 18 - good for a weekend away from it all.

This is the major Liverpool Uni for sport - in 1994/5 seven clubs had major local, regional or national success, 25 students represented their country, six becoming full internationals. Professional coaching is available. There are water sports amenities at Albert Dock, sailing centres at West Kirby and Hoylake, and spectator sport is a major plus - football (Liverpool at Anfield, Everton at Goodison Park), racing at Aintree, rugby league, rugby union, cricket, basketball, golf, and apparently an international tennis tournament on the Wirral.

LIVERPOOL HOPE UNIVERSITY

Liverpool Hope University
Hope Park
Liverpool
L16 9JD

TEL 0151 291 3000
FAX 0171 291 3100

Liverpool Hope
Student Union
Hope Park
Liverpool L16 9JD

TEL 0151 291 3663
FAX 0151 291 3535

LIVERPOOL HOPE UNIVERSITY

Founded	**1980**
Situation/style	**City sites**
UNDERGRADUATE PROFILE	
Application acceptance rate	**10%**
Population	**3,320**
Mature student population	**34%**
Overseas student population	**1%**
Male/female ratio	**40:60**
1st year institut. accommodation	**100%**
Approximate cost	**£55 pw**
ACADEMIC PROFILE	
A-level requirements:	**Low**

Teacher Training 10, **Combined Arts: English, Social Studies, Environmental Studies, Modern Langs., Art & Design, Performance Arts, Computing** 12

Student/staff ratio	**20:1**
1st class degree pass rate	**2.9%**
HEFCE assessments (7 subjects assessed/approved):	
1995 **Geography & Environmental Studies**	Excellent
1995 **Sociology** 22	
1996 **Modern Languages** 19	
Joint Funding Council's research assessment 1996 (9 subjects assessed):	
Grade 5/5*	None
EMPLOYMENT PROFILE	
Principal job market destinations:	

Education, Retail/Wholesale, Commerce, Arts/Media

Approximate % unemployed	**12%**

VAG VIEW

Liverpool Hope is a university college affiliated to Liverpool University, which validates its degrees. If the Pro-rector's introduction sounds a bit like a sermon - 'Hope is a great virtue with both sacred and secular connotations,' - you should not be surprised, for Liverpool Hope, once the Liverpool Institute, has its roots in an ecumenical amalgamation of two colleges for women, championed years ago by the then cricketing Bishop of Liverpool - David Shepherd. St Katherine's, an Anglican foundation, and Notre Dame, its Roman Catholic neighbour, were established in this city more than 150 years ago. The ecumenical spirit lives on - for example, rooms are provided for Muslim prayer and Buddhist meditation.

Liverpool Hope offers Liverpool University not only an opportunity to further its strategy to make Higher Education more widely available (hence, for example, that Uni's push into the mature student market) but course elements such as Theology and Religious Studies, which the Uni lacks. At the same time, Liverpool offers Liverpool Hope top-notch facilities for its Sport, Recreation & Physical Education courses. It is a good marriage - made in heaven you might say.

Key to understanding Liverpool Hope, besides its religious roots, is its determination to bring into the Higher Education system 'those who have hitherto not had the most distinguished or easy path to academic honours.' This is a college with a mission, eternally optimistic. Its foundation courses prepare students without the necessary grades to study a degree course. Lecturers even go out into the community and preach, sorry teach, those who for one reason or another can't take up a place at college. They call it their ReachOut degree route.

Pages of LHC's analysis of life in the city of Liverpool should be sent to all those parents of would-be students of Liverpool Uni worried lest their darlings fall foul of its evil drug pushers and baseball bat-wielding scallies. For here is a city not of degeneration but of regeneration, of colour and of peaceful co-existence among inhabitants from the four corners of the earth. Here, too, is a college bent on a wholistic approach to education - mind, body and spirit. How could you fault it? Liverpool Hope is running with a strong current in this vibrant, ever evolving city, and it has been rewarded with university college status because it is running with it rather well.

SITUATION

How disappointing (or how incredibly coincidental) that it has its name not from its approach to education but after its situation in Hope Park, some three miles from the centre of Liverpool.

GETTING THERE

★ By road: M62 (East/West), which connects with M6 (North/South) at Junction 21a.
★ Well served by National Express coaches.
★ By rail: Manchester, 0:40; Sheffield, 1:45; Leeds or Birmingham, 2:00; London Kings Cross, 3:00.
★ Liverpool airports for flights inland and to/from Ireland.

ACCOMMODATION

All first years accommodated in single study bedrooms either on-site or 4 miles away in Aigburth. There is a coach service which links the two. LHC is, like LU and LJM, a member of Liverpool Student Homes, a house/flat/bedsit agency for students (140 Mount Pleasant, Liverpool L3 5SR, telephone 0151 794 3296).

STUDENTS UNION

Traditional fare - bands, comedians, karaoke, jazz nights, and parties in the Pavilion Bar. Forceful campaigning on issues of more than campus relevance - racism, multicultural education, women's rights. This is a major point of recommendation (in our book) to Liverpool Hope. Other establishments which claim active student campaigners - Aberystwyth, Birmingham, etc, whine on about campus issues - rent increases, self-important Union execs. Absent is the political spirit of the 60s when issues of world significance were the thing - Vietnam, Capitalist exploitation of apartheid, etc. Here we have a university sector college that is anything but inward looking politically. Thatcher's spoiled children do not rule.

SPORT

They have recently installed a floodlit, all-weather astroturf pitch for hockey, tennis, football; there's a gym, and the Athletics Union is involved in all inter-Uni competitions.

ACADEMIA

Besides Theology, Single BA Hons programmes include European Studies, American Studies, and BSc Health & Physical Recreation. Combined Hons BA/BSC across American Studies, Art, Drama, English, Enviro. Studies, Euro. Studies, French, Geog., History, Biology, Info. Technology, Maths, Music, Psychology, Sociology, Sport, Theology. Plus BEd courses from Nursery through to Middle School.

They are becoming increasingly career-orientated in their approach. A module is in the works involving all students in work experience and they are part of the Merseyside, EU funded Business Bridge scheme, which alerts students to work placement opportunities in small businesses that operate in line with their course studies.

£5.5 million is set aside for a new library and multi-media Learning Resource Centre due to open September '97.

LIVERPOOL JOHN MOORES UNIVERSITY

Liverpool John Moores
University
Rodney House
70 Mount Pleasant
Liverpool
Merseyside
L3 5UX

TEL 0151 231 2121
FAX 0151 709 9585

Liverpool Student Union
Liverpool John Moores
University
The Haigh Building
Maryland Street
Liverpool L1 9DE

TEL 0151 794 1900
FAX 0151 708 5334

LIVERPOOL JOHN MOORES UNIVERSITY

Founded	**1970**
Situation/style	**City sites**
UNDERGRADUATE PROFILE	
Application acceptance rate	**7%**
Population	**11,000**
Mature student population	**36%**
Overseas student population	**8%**
Male/female ratio	**50:50**
1st year institut. accommodation	**45%**
Approximate cost	**£35-£40 pw**

ACADEMIC PROFILE

A-level requirements: **Medium**

Teacher Training CC-DD, **Accountancy & Finance, Business Stds.** 14-16, **Business & Law** BCC, **Law, Sociology combinations** 14-18, **Architecture** CCC, **Housing, Urban Planning** 14, **Media/Cultural Studies, Art & Design** 14-18, **Drama, Theatre Studies** 16, BB, **Computer Sci. & Eng.,** 12-16, **Environmental, Civil Engineering** 12,18, **E & E, Mech. Eng.** CC-DDD,DDD

Student/staff ratio	**19:1**
1st class degree pass rate	**4%**

HEFCE assessments
(14 subjects assessed/approved):
1995/6 **Modern Languages** 19
Sociology 18

Joint Funding Council's research assessment 1996
(28 subjects assessed):
Engineering, Sports. Grade 5

EMPLOYMENT PROFILE

Employability in Industry:
MPW national league table (1996) **36th=**

Principal job market destinations:
Education, Retail/Wholesale, Manufacturing (strong on **Pharmaceutical**), **Public Admin./ Law, Commerce, Health, Arts/Media, Hotel/Restaurant, Personnel, Construction, Computer, Property Development**

Approximate % unemployed **8%**

VAG VIEW

Of the three universities in Liverpool, John Moores can probably claim closest cultural contact with the city. To begin with it isn't campus-separate, it comprises some 24 buildings in and around the city. Then again, it draws more students from the area than Liverpool University, and has its roots deep in the city's industrial history. The founding date we give - 1970 - marks the year that it was established as Liverpool Poly, but it can in fact trace its origins back to 1823, as the Liverpool Mechanics' and Apprentices' Library. As a poly it brought together the City Colleges of Art and Design and Building, Commerce, and the Regional College of Technology, the City of Liverpool College of Higher Education, the IM Marsh College of Physical Education, the FL Calder College of Home Economics and the Liverpool College of Nursing and Midwifery - all of which give a good clue to its academic profile. Interesting, too, in getting to grips with the career-orientated personality of LJM is the fact that a group of businessmen were responsible for its original founding in 1823, and the Uni owes its name to one of Liverpool's most famous entrepreneurs, whose life spanned almost the entire 20th century. Sir John Moores CBE (1896 - 1993) built Littlewoods - the football pools organisation (responsible too for a host of charitable enterprises and hit recently by the National Lottery, with its similar gaming/charitable profile) from scratch. 'Sir John's business success was built upon his philosophy of the equality of opportunity for all,' the Uni says, 'echoed in his classic phrase "men and women can, if they want to enough, do anything". This fundamental belief...is a reflection of the University's commitment to higher education, to access, to flexibility and to participation.' One feature of their commitment to participation is the close relationship it enjoys with Liverpool University, which throws up all kinds of social and welfare opportunities and advantages. And it is LJM which has a proud association with what was arguably this country's most influential cultural event of all time - the Beatles - through its affiliation with Paul McCartney's Liverpool Institute for Performing Arts, opened in 1996. LJM awards its degrees in Acting, Community Arts, Dance, Enterprise Management, Music and Performance Design.

GETTING THERE

★ By road: M62 (East/West), which connects with M6 (North/South) at Junction 21a. Well served by National Express coaches.
★ By rail: Manchester, 0:40; Sheffield, 1:45; Leeds or Birmingham, 2:00; London Kings Cross, 3:00.
★ Liverpool airports for flights inland and to/from Ireland.

ACCOMMODATION

LJM offers around 1,650 places in halls, and flats and houses in the city, but guarantee a relatively small proportion of first years Uni-accommodation (students who come from 25+ miles away are given precedence. LJM and Liverpool Uni have set up Liverpool Student Homes to help you sort out city accommodation. The office is at 140 Mount Pleasant, Liverpool L3 5SR (Tel: 0151 794 3296). It and the LJM web site have daily up-dated lists available. Our correspondent, Nicholas Wallis, has something to say about accommodation, too, and we list popular student areas to live here, but your best bet, particularly if you are new to the city, is to give LSH a call, or call up the LJM web site via JANET.

CITY CENTRE

Popular for obvious reasons, but also competitive. Within walking distance of main Uni sites and city centre: L6 (Kensington), L7 (Kensington and Fairfield), and L8 (Toxteth and Dingle). Short bus trip away are these areas, also student-popular: L15 (Wavertree and Picton), L17 and L18 (Mossley Hill, Allerton Aigburth), L13 (Old Swan).

UNION AND ENTS

The Union Advice Shop is an active body, offering free, professional advice to students whatever their problems. Students also have access to Liverpool Uni's Job Shop for term-time casual employment in the city.

The LJM student magazine, *Shout*, was Student Magazine of the Year in 1993, and continues to be one of the best student mags around. The LJM radio station is Shout FM, and they have an enterprising link with Phil Redmond, creator of Liverpool-inspired TV drama, *Brookside*.

The Haigh is a magnet for students all over the city. Bars, quizzes, drinks promotions, live acts - bands, comedy - and cabaret-style film nights compose the ents menu, and students make use, too, of the Liverpool Uni's Guild building, particularly its Saturday night Time Tunnel club night. Comedy comes care of The Newcastle Brown Ale National Comedy Network, the national campus touring company which includes Alan Parker: Urban Warrior, Dan Freeman, Boothby Gafoe, The Landlord, Bill Bailey, newer stand-up talent and open-mic spots for wanabe's. Popular LMJ club nights include Tuesday's Crash (Indie), Wednesday's Isotonic (cheese), Friday's Liberty ('wild party tunes') and Saturday's Fever (classic dance). The live Haigh Venue is too small for the big acts, but the city's Royal Court Theatre and Mountford Hall at Liverpool Uni provide for these, and rest assured that there's no shortage of live music in Britain's NW live music capital. They also launch Campaign Weeks, an intriguing mix of cultural and political information (including, yes, Women's Awareness Nights) and getting totally out of your head. See Nicholas Wallis's piece for a run-down on what else LMJ and the city have to offer. 80+ Union societies/clubs on offer. Academia Vocational bias, strong on sandwich courses, good contacts with industry - professional associations offer direct employment routes, for example, in Pharmacy, Surveying and some Engineering programmes. Faculties include: Built Environment; Law, Social Work, Social Policy; Art; Business; Modern Languages; Media, Critical & Creative Arts; Education and Community Studies; Health; Human Sciences; Social Science; Biological and Earth Sciences; Biomolecular Sciences; Computing and Mathematical Sciences; Electrical Engineering, Electronics & Physics; Engineering & Technology; Pharmacy and Chemistry; and the European Institute for Urban Affairs. Note their Accountancy and Business college in Dublin (close proximity via airport), par of LJM's Business School since '89. Largest independent business college in Ireland: 800 full-time and 2,000 part-time students; good sporting and social activities too.

SPORT

Specatator sport good, of course - Liverpool FC, Everton FC, Tranmere Rovers, racing at Aintree, Pro Am golf at Royal Birkdale, rugby, League and Union, in easy reach. All usual facilities for Uni team sports, most 3 miles from city centre at the Education & Community base (IM Marsh) - gym, dance studios, sports halls, indoor swimming pool, pitches, all-weather athletics track - and at St Nicholas Centre by the cathedral - sports hall, gym, weight training room. LJM's proudest boast is its newish (October '95) Base Fitness Centre, amazingly well equipped and professionally staffed. There's a Student Sports Pass for free/reduced price access to sporting facilities - badminton courts, swimming pools, squash courts, athletics tracks. Note, in particular, LJM's research record in Sport (fact box).

VIEW FROM THE GROUND
by Nicholas Wallis

OK. Bad stuff first. As a student in Liverpool, I have never been beaten, mugged or robbed, although God knows how many times I deserved it. Unfortunately many of my friends have suffered random violence, serial burglary and many other unpleasant incidents which have gone a considerable way to clouding their experiences of the place. Basically Liverpool is a modern city with more than its fair share of trouble for the uninitiated, unaware, or just plain unlucky. Having said that, only the truly paranoid would let this stop them from studying there. Liverpool John Moores University is an ambitious institution which, despite its lowly league-table rankings, is easily the most visible and dynamic of the two (sorry, three) universities in the city. LJM has a number of beautiful buildings around the centre of town, which, surprisingly, is not a disadvantage, because Liverpool city centre is so remarkably small. The University of Liverpool, by contrast, is based on a campus overlooking the city, consisting of the original (and quite ugly) red brick clock tower made beautiful by the abundant Stalinist monstrosities surrounding it.

UNION

John Moores' students are represented by the Liverpool Students' Union, which is housed in your standard crap union building - badly designed and far too small. Nevertheless, it is very well run and serves as an excellent social fulcrum (or day centre) for both LJM and Liverpool University students. A stone's throw away lies the Liverpool Student Union's counterpart, the University Guild [see Liverpool University]. This place, by contrast, is huge, which allows it to host a mega club night on Saturdays called Time Tunnel, which, again, is well attended by students from both sides of the academic divide. You can, and in fact a lot of people do, drink all week in the Haigh, go to Time Tunnel every Saturday night and manage to avoid real life completely for three years.

Those who wish to broaden their horizons will find there are student and ever more esoteric club nights constantly cropping up all over the city in venues such as Heebiejeebies, Jaks, Fridays, The Blue Angel (known as the Raz), Mardi Gras, Cream, The Krazy House and, still the best night for my money in Liverpool (probably because I no longer have to pay to get in), Complicity at Garlands. Rest assured that by the time you read this the kids will be getting down somewhere entirely different.

Drinking-wise, Liverpool's pubs are undergoing some sort of horrible transmogrification. The real pubs with shit beer, baseball bats behind the bar and frightening locals are being replaced by student-friendly venues run by the Firkin awful chains. As a result, the increasingly popular alternatives are the generic bar venues like Metz, The Milky Bar, Bar Zero, MelloMello, Beluga Bar, Arena etc. These questionable establishments offer you the opportunity to drink overpriced bottled lager and shout in the ear of the person next to you whilst eyeing down the achingly trendy students, posh scallies (gangsters to you and me), and fat office workers from Warrington.

The best pub in Liverpool is The Brewery on Berry Street. Friendly, spacious, privately owned, it brews some very good beer, is cheap and open until 2am! It attracts locals, students, trendies, loonies and genuinely normal people.

The second-best pub in Liverpool is Bonapartes on Clarence Street. Drinkers need more landlords, and the world needs more people like Graham and Tina Fletcher who run the place. Make it your local, if you can afford it.

Having covered the important stuff I can give you a list of theatres you can pretend to visit regularly, like the Everyman, Unity, Playhouse and Empire. The Everyman is a good un but it seems to stage regular debacles, of which Gary of *Two Point Four Children*'s attempt at *Macbeth* was one.

There are a good number of mainstream cinemas and one arthouse one. I haven't been to the 10-screen Warner on Edge Lane since it became a Virgin, but I'm sure it's the best (creep, creep). Museums, yes, galleries, yes; and the Albert Dock. The Albert Dock is totally uninhabited by students apart from when relatives visit and everyone is afflicted by this strange desire to take them there. Why? I, like thousands of students before me, have dragged my poor parents round the overpriced gift shops, museums, galleries and Fred's weather map for no discernable reason. Must be the healthy sea air. Liverpool's two cathedrals are much more fascinating - visit them instead.

Liverpool's restaurants are totally hit and miss, but endlessly varied. For quality, quantity, good service and value for money there is no better than Caesar's Palace on Renshaw Street. You can also eat Chinese, Balinese, Greek, Turkish, Thai and vegi, but for Indian go to Rusholme in Manchester. The curry houses in Liverpool for some reason just don't quite cut it.

ACCOMMODATION

Finally, where to live. This is a pure lottery based on security, location and crucially, your landlord. Most University of Liverpool students spend their first year in massive halls next to Sefton Park, and in their second and third years move *en masse* into a giant student ghetto called Wavertree. I don't know why, but they do. LJM students seem to congregate around the city centre which is becoming a better idea as the place is sprucing itself up remarkably, and more buildings are being renovated for student use. Pretty much all university halls and LJM residences are fine except LJM's Crete and Candia Towers, which should be avoided at all costs. You have been warned.

To conclude, Liverpool is a super-fanny-tastic place. Whether it is a bit of top footie you are after (Anfield is as special as they say), a day at the races (Friday is much the better day of the Grand National festival), or, God help us, a degree, you will find the city has it all to offer. Not much of a gay scene, but if you are gay come anyway or there never will be one.

LONDON UNIVERSITY

University of London
Senate House
Malet Street
London WC1E 7HU

TEL 0171 636 6000
FAX 0171 636 5841

University of London Union
Senate House
Malet Street
London WC1E 7HY

TEL 0171 580 9551
FAX 0171 436 5688

VAG VIEW

Founded in 1836, London University is a federal body which allows its constituent, otherwise more or less autonymous, colleges access to certain facilities. The colleges and schools within LU, which are profiled in this book, are:

Birkbeck College, The British Institute in Paris, The Charing Cross & Westminster Medical School, The Courtauld Institute, Imperial College, King's College, The London School of Economics, Queen Mary & Westfield College, The Royal Free Hospital Medical School, Royal Holloway, The Royal Veterinary College, St George's Hospital Medical School, The School of Oriental & African Studies, The School of Pharmacy, The School of Slavonic & Eastern European Studies, University College, United Medical & Dental Schools (Guy's & St Thomas's), Wye College.

ACCOMMODATION

UL has eight fully catered halls of residence. Cost for a single room is just over £80 pw; for a shared room, between £69 and £75 pw. There are games rooms, common rooms, bars, launderettes, but no parking facilities.

'Halls, being "intercollegiate" (fetch your dictionary) are always interesting and provide an alternative social scene. The three biggies are: International (good social life, bad rooms), Commonwealth (average social life, average rooms) and Hughes Parry (bad social life, good rooms). There are also single-sex halls (best avoided)'

Gideon Dewhirst, student at The School of Slavonic & Eastern European Studies

Canterbury Hall
Cartwright Gardens,
WC1.
0171 387 5526.

College Hall
Malet Street, WC1.
0171 580 9131.

Commonwealth Hall
Cartwright Gardens, WC1.
0171 387 0311.

Connaught Hall
Tavistock Square,
WC1.
0171 387 6181.

Hughes Parry Hall
Cartwright Gardens,
WC1.
0171 387 1477.

International Hall
Brunswick Square,
WC1.
0171 837 0746.

Lillian Penson Hall
Talbot Square,
W2.
0171 262 2081.

Nutford House
Brown Street,
W1.
0171 723 5020.

★ *Canterbury and College Halls are men only; Connaught is women only.*

'If you're new in town, get a place in halls, meet tons of people, get pissed loads and eat unidentifiable slop (with rice). Grandmothers are sold to get into Hughes Parry and Commonwealth Halls.'

Peter Beveridge and Catherine Wynne, students at The School of Oriental & African Studies

University of London Library
This is housed in Senate House, comprises more than a million volumes and subscribes to more than 5,000 journals. Students may borrow books and use the library for reading.

University of London Union
'ULU possess all that you might want from a campus...discount shops, swimming pool, sports hall and a multitude of societies (as well as two cheap bars and an admittedly cheesy nightclub).' *SSEES student, Gideon Dewhirst*

There are squash and badminton courts and an international length pool in the basement of the Union building. There is also a sauna, steam room, sunbeds and a lounge area. The fitness centre includes a gym with weights machines, steppers, treadmill, ergometer rowers and bikes. Professional treatments are available as are a number of classes (aerobics, etc). There are charges for these facilities, but they are way below what you can expect elsewhere. Outdoor facilties include playing fields at Motspur Park, New Malden, Surrey, a boathouse on the Thames at Chiswick, and the Sailing Club does its stuff at the Welsh Harp Reservoir in Brent, where there is a clubhouse.

At Malet Street there's a bar, winebar and restaurant, and a nightclub which promotes club nights (Indie night, a Gorgeous Night) and top line live acts, which are very popular. In addition, you will find in the building a general store, travel agency, banks, a creche, a sports shop and an opticians.

The ULU newspaper, *London Student*, is also published from this building, and the NUS offices are housed there.

THE CITY

The club scene in London is second to none in Britain, whatever you hear elsewhere, but there are more over-rated clubs there than anywhere else too. The scene doesn't rely on the student market as it does in other big cities, so your choice may be wittled down by price, though many do offer student discounts. This is a starter selection of Clubs and interesting film and theatre venues. Ring to find out current programmes, student concessions and club nights. For the full works - all the London listings and advice about the best deals, get hold of ***Time Out's Student Guide***, probably the best £2.50 you'll spend after your *A to Z Streetfinder*.

CLUBS

Bar Rumba Shaftesbury Avenue, W1. 0171 287 2715. **The Wag Club** Wardour Street, W1. 0171 437 5534. **Limelight** Shaftesbury Avenue, W1. 0171 434 0572. **The Borderline** Manette Street, WC2. 0171 734 2095. **The Gardening Club** The Piazza, WC2. 0171 497 3154 **Heaven** Villiers Street, WC2. 0171 839 3863. **Velvet Underground** Charing Cross Road, WC2. 0171 439 4655. **Le Palais** Shepherd's Bush Road, W6. 0181 748 2812. **Subterania** Acklam Road, W10. 0181 960 4590. **Ministry of Sound** Gaunt Street, SE1. 0171 378 6528. **The Venue** Clifton Rise, SE14. 0171 326 0969. **Camden Palace** Camden High Street, NW1. 0171 387 0428. **The Garage** Highbury Corner, N5. 0171 607 1818. **HQs** Camden Lock, NW1. 0171 485 6044. **Jazz Café** Parkway, NW1. 0171 344 0044. **The Blue Note** Hoxton Square, N1. 0171 729 8440. **The Fridge** Town Hall Parade, Brixton Hill, SW2. 0171 326 5100.

INTERESTING & ARTHOUSE CINEMAS

Chelsea Cinema King's Road, SW3. 0171 351 3742. **Clapham Picture House.** Venn St, SW4. 0171 498 2242. **Curzon Mayfair** Curzon Street, W1. 0171 465 8865. **Gate Cinema** Notting Hill Gate, W11. 0171 727 4043. **Minema** Knightsbridge, SW1. 0171 235 4225. **Screen on the Green** Upper Street, N1 0171 226 3520. **Screen on the Hill** Haverstock Hill, NW3. 0171 435 3366. **Electric Cinema** Portobello Road, W11. 0171 792 2020. **Everyman** Hollybush Vale, NW3. 0171 435 1525. **ICA** The Mall, SW1. 0171 930 3647. **National Film Theatre** South Bank, SE1. 0171 928 3232. **Riverside Studios** Crisp Road, W6 0181 741 2255.

INTERESTING THEATRES OFF-WEST END

The Bush Shepherd's Bush Green, W12. 0181 743 3388. **The Gate** The Prince Albert, Pembridge Road, W11. 0171 229 0706. **Hampstead Theatre** Avenue Road, NW3.

0171 722 9301. **King's Head** Upper Street, N1. 0171 226 1916. **National Theatre** South Bank, SE1. 0171928 2252. **Orange Tree** Clarence Street, Richmond. 0181 940 3633. **Royal Court Theatre** Sloane Square, SW1. 0171 730 1745. **Theatre Royal Stratford East**, E15. 0181 534 0310. **Tricycle Theatre** Kilburn High Road, NW6. 0171 328 1000. **Young Vic** The Cut, SE1 (0171 928 6363).

London Guildhall University

London Guildhall University
31 Jewry Street
London
EC3N 2EY

TEL 0171 320 1000
FAX 0171 320 3488

London Guildhall University
Student' Union
2 Goulston Street
London E1 7TP

TEL 0171 247 1441
FAX 0171 247 0618

LONDON GUILDHALL UNIVERSITY

Founded	**1970**
Situation/style	**City sites**
UNDERGRADUATE PROFILE	
Application acceptance rate	**13%**
Population	**7,450**
Mature student population	**49%**
Overseas student population	**11%**
Male/female ratio	**48:52**
1st year institut. accommodation	**55%**
Approximate cost (Uni)	**£45-£68 pw**
(City)	**£55-£70 pw**
ACADEMIC PROFILE	
A-level requirements:	**Medium**

Psychology, Politics CD-DDD, **Law** BB-CCD, **Sociology** CC-CD, **Social Policy & Mgt.** 12-14, **Accountancy & Finance** CDD, **Business Admin.** CC-CDD

Student/staff ratio	**20:1**
1st class degree pass rate	**3.6%**
HEFCE assessments (5 subjects assessed/approved):	
1994 **Social Policy & Admin**	Excellent
Joint Funding Council's research assessment 1996 (14 subjects assessed):	
Grade 5/5*	None
EMPLOYMENT PROFILE	

Principal job market destinations:
Retail/Wholesale, Commerce, Manufacturing, Personnel, Arts/Media, Public Admin./Law

Approximate % unemployed	**13%**

VAG VIEW

London Guildhall is one of the largest providers of part-time professional business courses in the country, but there are more full-time students and some excellent courses other than business.

Note particularly that it was their Social Policy & Admin course which won the Excellent rating (see fact box). And you could study French, German, Sociology, Politics, Modern History, Law, all kinds of Design and Arts courses, Musical Instrument Technology, Psychology, etc. They offer two routes - Single Hons - 'early specialist' - degrees (traditional single honours), or modular programmes leading to deferred specialist, joint or combined degrees.

'One way to gauge a university is to test the litmus paper of life-after-graduation,' says current student, Stuart Harkness. 'LGU's offspring numbers a handful of celebrities, such as singers Alison Moyet and Sonya from Echobelly. Kate Hoey MP learned the ropes at LGU, which was also attended by pant-stroking comedy maestro, Vic Reeves. The big fish are undeniably drawn from the business courses, however, where you could have picked up a few inside tips from Barings broker, and breaker, Nick Leeson. The more successful figure of multi-millionaire Mark Thatcher, the former Tory PM's prodigal son, also did time at LGU. Indeed he of the mighty goatee, Richard Branson, is hopefully to be honoured by the institution.'

GETTING THERE

★ Nearest Underground stations are Aldgate (Metropolitan and Circle Lines), Aldgate East (Metropolitan and District Lines).

VIEW FROM THE GROUND
by Stuart Harkness

Welcome to the sprawling metropolis: London, where the streets are paved with a golden array of pubs, clubs, cinemas, cafes, concerts and empty Special Brew cans. In between such hedonism, however, you may wish to catch up on a little study, and at what better place that London Guildhall University?

One of the new breed, London Guildhall gained university status in 1992, being formerly known as The City of London Polytechnic. The institution has in fact been around in one shape or another for over 150 years, but hey - that's history. Nowadays the University's eight sites are scattered amidst London's famous square mile financial district. It's no surprise then that LGU's bent is business, with Calcutta and Central Houses, Jewry Street, Moorgate, Goulston Street, Whitechapel, Tower Hill and Commercial Road host to over 13,500 students.

STUDENT PROFILE
The resilience of the University largely stems from its streetwise student clientele, devoid of opulent silver spoons and armed with a left wing, if slightly lethargic, political bias. No one stands on ceremony at London Guildhall. They'll stand at the bar, or at the odd demo, but in general the attitude is more down to earth than a rattlesnake's belly in a wagon wheel rut.

Whether a typical student exists is arguable. It's the Jarvis Cocker school of learning, with a diverse array of mis-shapes and misfits. Nearly half of the 13,500 students are part-time, with many being professionals culled from the city. A large amount are therefore mature, with 49% of full-time and 96% of part-time students over the age of 21 on entry. Don't fear, however, as many have mental ages seemingly half this figure.

A high proportion of students originate from London (40%) with the surrounding South East accounting for a further 18%. Sure there are still the traditional farming defectors, who come for the beer, bright lights and big city. The indigenous prefer to keep a low profile though, content to keep studying to a vocation rather than lifestyle. Many juggle the two.

The melting pot is further fuelled by those from farther afield, to the tune of 110 countries. The cosmopolitan flavour makes LGU a truly multi-cultural university. 20% of students are black and 24% Asian. Multiple faiths are therefore evident and well catered for with prayer rooms at various University sites, a chaplaincy and numerous Students' Union funded cultural societies including Christian, Islamic, Muslim and Afro-Caribbean, to name but a few. All seem to respect each others' practices, with the threat of friction dispelled under the umbrella of LGU brotherhood.

ACADEMIA
Course-wise the University's strong suit is not limited to business. Excellent opportunities are also manifest in Law, Psychology, Musical Instrument Technology and Art and Design. Alternatively why not pick and mix courtesy of the incredibly flexible Credit Accumulation modular degree scheme, which is one of the country's best? The modular scheme works on the premise of 24 individual units, sixteen of which tally together to form an overall degree classification. Over 400 subject combinations exist, so you could, for example, graduate with a joint degree in Law and Computer Animation, with minors in Silversmithing and Spanish thrown in for good measure. Potential high flyers may be interested in the professional Civil Aviation course, which trains most commercial pilots and boasts its own flight simulator. Indeed London Guildhall University's academic offering is immense, not only at degree level but at HND, professional and Postgraduate as well. All courses are very much geared to the real world, so upon graduation you can apply your skills straight away.

LOCATION
Location is a definite asset with the University's eight sites juxtaposed between the City and East End, and all within walking distance of each other. There is a plethora of commercial banks on the doorstep, so students can gamble their grants on the stock market overlooked by the Nat West Tower and the futuristic blue glow of the Lloyds building.

The University's location also makes work

experience while studying an immensely viable option. Being so close to the country's financial nerve centre has definite practical applications, with the proximity acquainting students with the pace of life. Three years study in the capital can indeed arm you with several contacts before graduation. Not only bankers and lawyers thrive in such a climate, the east of the city also provides the gateway to the national press, in fact nearly all industries are prominent in London, which is undoubtedly a haven for head offices.

The craning mix of Legoland skyscrapers is offset by a maze of intimate side streets, stretching from the City to nearby Whitechapel, the home of Jack the Ripper and now besieged each evening by flocks of bloodthirsty tourists. The East End villainy does not stop there. A stone's throw away is Vallance Road, Bethnal Green - home to the infamous Kray twins, alias Ronny and Reggie, who, according to locals, rank somewhere up near Mother Theresa status. Tall buildings shadowed by tall stories, which should be taken with a pinch of salt.

FOOD

Seasoning in a more potent form can be found on nearby Brick Lane, a Balti paradise. The capital's curry epicentre is littered by inexpensive, yet excellent, Indian restaurants, revered throughout London and bombarded on a nightly basis by a heady mix of suits, students and locals. If the idea of a curry fails to move you for once, why not opt for a bagel instead. For those low on cash, dough in edible form can be found at the top of Brick Lane, starting at a mere 10p and climbing to a modest £1.50 for a top-of-the-range salt beef ensemble. More morsels of a salty origin can be caught at Tubby Isaac's famous seafood stand, located outside the Student Union, Goulston Street. Here you can savour the flavour of all things slimy - whelks, winkles, cockles, mussels and jellied eels. Tubby and his briny barrow can prove a little overpowering, however, first thing in the morning, so be prepared to open the gills when entering the SU feeling a little fragile from the night before. The SU also has a diner with surprisingly good food, whipped up by the resident chef. Curried goat and the like, plus a veritable feast of vegetarian cuisine can be yours for a paltry two quid. The University also provides catering facilities at various sites, alternatively, sandwich bars are spread thick and fast throughout the city.

UNION AND ENTS

The Student Union obviously competes with the wider attractions of London life. Where it succeeds is in both price (the cheapest SU bar in London according to an *Evening Standard* newspaper survey) and opportunity, with over forty subsidised clubs, sports and societies. This means you can snowboard, scuba dive, climb mountains and the like at drastically reduced prices. Furthermore, if none of the existing clubs, sports or societies tickle your fancy then you'll get full support in setting up your own.

The Student Union social forum spreads over three bars, one at Commercial Road and two in the SU's Goulston Street building. The first floor bar is the more pub-like of the two, open all day and well stocked with beers from around the world. Downstairs is the SUB bar, which hosts a diverse array of events, six days a week and is ideally the place to go for a nightcap, with its late license. Cheap entry (free - £3) is paired with excellent entertainments. Bands formerly treading the boards at LGUSU include The Stone Roses, Carter USM, Senser and, believe it or not, The Sex Pistols. A weekly showcase of live bands is accompanied by regular Jam nights, where you can merrily warble or beat the shit out of the drum kit and other instruments, provided gratis.

The comedy club has seen many an audience pissing themselves to the likes of Mark Thomas, Sir Bernard Chumley (aka *Shooting Stars*' George Doors, Jo Jo Smith, *Father Ted*'s Ardal O'Hanlon and Felix Dexter. London's heavy dance influence has seen DJs such as LUVDUP, Kiss FM's Paul Trouble Anderson and Youth from Killing Joke on the decks, plus a live PA from Baby 'Let Me Be Your Fantasy' D. The musical spectrum is diverse, ranging from Swing and Techno to Garage and Indie. Retro freaks are well catered for by the Sports' Societies, who throw a massive piss-up every Wednesday. The legendary Timewarp sees one and all get absolutely legless, burning up the dancefloor in their diamante disco slippers. The University's 50:50 gender ratio ensures that pulling is a fair, as well as a traditional, pursuit. Watch out for the beer goggles though, as at £1 a pint no one's ugly after 12 a.m. You might even make G:ECHO, the monthly SU magazine's ugly mug picture hall of fame.

LGUSU offers more than just cheap booze. Fair enough if you simply want to get shitfaced, play footy or hang off cliffs. The SU also offers a voice and representation. Its easygoing nature allows optimum involvement, with groups such as the Lesbian Gay and Bisexual Society thriving in such a positive climate. It's run by students, for students, which is why it works. The Union actively seeks to utilise the student body, providing what pocket money it can by employing nearly 100 student casual staff in its various outlets, which include cut-price stationery and art shops.

LGUSU's fun nature is offset by excellent welfare services. LGUSU is a pioneer in employing a Peer Support Officer, who co-ordinates a programme whereby second and third year students provide free advice sessions for first years. The University also offers support via its Student Counselling and Advice Centre, which includes a solicitor with free legal advice.

ACCOMMODATION

If you're not one of the many attending London Guildhall from the family home then it's likely that you're going to have to either rent digs or hit the Halls of Residence. The latter of these options comes in three forms at LGU. First up is Claredale House in Bethnal Green, which is about two miles from the University. 265 students are based here, split between 68 mixed-sex flats. Having been recently revamped at a cost of £1.5 million, each flat has its own kitchen and incoming phone. There's also a communal laundry and stacks of parties for budding insomniacs. Rents range between £45 and £59 per week, depending on room size, with bills inclusive. Next up is Sir John Cass, just down the road in Hackney. A bitter rival to Claredale, what with the annual soccer grudge match, Cass has 102 individual rooms, an upbeat atmosphere and regular social events. In return for £68 per week you'll get breakfast and an evening meal from Monday to Friday, with a full-monty fry-up on a Saturday and a big roast blow-out on Sundays. Again there's a communal laundry and kitchens, plus common rooms with satellite TV. Bills are inclusive and you even get your room cleaned for free!

Finally, Sir John Bell House is set in sunny Shadwell, which is about twenty minutes walk from the University. Communal kitchens, toilets and showers feature on single-sex floors. All three halls are well secured and have resident wardens, ideal when you've lost your keys at four in the morning.

The alternative to Halls is a house or bedsit-hell somewhere in London, probably the East End. But seriously, it's not as bad as it sounds. East London may not be scenic, but it's certainly colourful and has an eclectic community atmosphere to rival that of the TV soap. Looking early is essential, in order to secure the best deal. The University's excellent Accommodation Office may be able to help, but remember that you're going to be spending a minimum of £45 a week in the private sector, plus bills and travel.

GETTING ABOUT

Cars are not a great idea in the capital. For starters, you'll be going nowhere fast, due to the absurd amount of traffic. If you do finally get to London Guildhall, parking is a nightmare and will cost you a minimum of £4 per day. The Underground is a good option; we are relatively close to seven different tube lines. There's also the Docklands' Light Railway, whilst mainline trains terminate at nearby Fenchurch Street, Liverpool Street and Moorgate. Alternatively you could employ pedal power in order to get from A to B. Lights and a cycling helmet are essential in London, as is a decent lock, unless you fancy pedalling fresh air instead of your 1978 Raleigh Chopper. It's also advisable to invest in an anti-pollution mask.

Good luck! I'll see you in the bar...

THE LONDON INSTITUTE

The London Institute
65 Davies Street
London
W1Y 2DA

TEL 0171 514 6000
FAX 0171 514 6175

London Institute
Student Union
388-396 Oxford Street
London W1N 9HE

TEL 0171 514 6270
FAX 0171 514 6284

THE LONDON INSTITUTE	
Founded	1986
Situation/style	City sites
UNDERGRADUATE PROFILE	
Application acceptance rate	6%
Population	4,600
Mature student population	71%
Overseas student population	10%
Male/female ratio	40:60
1st year institut. accommodation	10%
Approximate cost (Institute)	£60-£90 pw
(City)	£55-£70 pw
ACADEMIC PROFILE	
A-level requirements:	Unspecified
Art & Design, Business, Marketing, Retail Management	
Student/staff ratio	16:1
1st class degree pass rate	8.9%
HEFCE assessments (1 subject assessed/approved):	
1994 **Business & Management**	
Joint Funding Council's research assessment 1996 (4 subjects assessed):	
Grade 5/5*	None
EMPLOYMENT PROFILE	
Principal job market destinations:	
Arts/Media, Retail/Wholesale, Manufacturing, Education	
Approximate % unemployed	**12%**

VAG VIEW

Comprising five of the key art and design colleges, The London Institute offers students a wide range of opportunities. Whether looking to study for a first diploma or a PhD, this is a world famous institution to join.

The five colleges are Camberwell College of Arts, Central Saint Martin's College of Art and Design, Chelsea College of Art and Design, London College of Fashion and London College of Printing and Distributive Trades. You can move between colleges if your interests change during your studies. Foundation courses, for example, are often taken at one college, and you progress to a degree course at another.

So, which college is good for what?

Camberwell *Foundation course in Theory of Art and Design or a BTEC National Diploma, with a more vocational focus are both available. Degree courses are as follows:*

- ★ *Art and Design courses specialising in Silversmithing and Metalwork, Ceramics and Graphic Design.*
- ★ *History of Art*
- ★ *Conservation course*

Joint Honours in Visual Arts allows a combination of two of the above.
MA courses are also available in Applied Arts, Conservation, History and Theory of Drawing, Printmaking and Book Arts.

The Camberwell Press (producing and publishing high quality books) and The Camberwell Collection of ceramic, metal and textile artifacts are assets unique to this college, which together with prime position and prestigious reputation make it a popular choice.

St Martin's
The largest of the colleges, it offers the most diverse programme of courses in the country. Foundation to MA studies are possible under these four subject areas:

★ *Art*
★ *Textiles and Fashion, including Journalism*
★ *Communication Design, including Film and Video*
★ *3-Dimensional Design*

Most courses include some placement or link with the industry, many abroad.

Chelsea

A small college providing specialist education in areas such as Painting, Sculpture, Printmaking, Combined Media and Interior Decor. Evening courses in Fine Art (BA) and a new fast stream 2-year BA in Design.

London College of Fashion

Only specialist college for Fashion, Design and Beauty. Consequently many courses are unique such as the degree in Make-up for Theatre, TV and video, Beauty Therapy, and there's a course for fashion models. Close links with industry lead to sandwich placements and employment contacts.
Undergraduate courses include:
★ *Costume and Make-up*
★ *Women's Wear and Accessories*
★ *Fashion Promotion (Journalism, Public Relations and Broadcast)*
★ *Product Development for the fashion industries*

London College of Printing and Distributive Trades

In its 104 year history, this college has produced world class professionals in printing, graphics, media, marketing and retailing. The college has good high-tec facilities. Employer links are a crucial aspect of college life, through placements, commissions and activities allowing contact with future employers. Courses offered range from Higher Education to Postgrad. Degree. New degrees on offer include:
★ *Marketing and Advertising*
★ *Business Communication*
★ *Interactive Multimedia*

London is a major centre for the worlds of fashion, media and design. Over 2,000 leading professionals working in areas such as fine art, fashion, product design, ceramics and printing are employed as visiting tutors to pass on their firsthand knowledge to students. The London Institute offers access to some of these. Indeed many lecturers started their careers studying here themselves.

New students are greeted with a student induction programme, where services such as welfare, nursery, money guidance and help finding accommodation are on offer. Only 10% of first years are actually housed in institute accommodation, so this could be useful.

London School of Economics

London School of Economics
and Political Science
Houghton Street
London
WC2A 2AE

TEL 0171 405 7686
FAX 0171 242 0392

London School of Economics
and Political Science
Student Union
East Building
Houghton Street
London WC2A 2AE

TEL 0171 955 7158
FAX 0171 955 6789

LONDON SCHOOL OF ECONOMICS & SCIENCE

Founded	**1895**
Situation/style	**City site**
UNDERGRADUATE PROFILE	
Application acceptance rate	**7%**
Population	**2,700**
Mature student population	**14%**
Overseas student population	**43%**
Male/female ratio	**58:42**
1st year institut. accommodation	**100%**
Approximate cost	**£70-£80 pw**
ACADEMIC PROFILE	
A-level requirements:	**Very High**

Economics and combinations ABB, **Social Policy and Population Studies** BBC, **Accounting and Finance** ABB, **Industrial Rel. & Human Resource Mgt.** ABB, **Management Sciences** BBB, **History, Law** ABB, **Psychology and Philosophy** BBB, **Anthropology, Social Policy** BBB, **Social Policy and Sociology, Social Policy & Admin and combinations** BBC, **Politics** ABB, **Social Policy and Government** BBC

Student/staff ratio	**14:1**
1st class degree pass rate	**8.1%**
HEFCE assessments (8 subjects assessed/approved):	
1993 **History**	Excellent
1994 **Anthropology, Applied Social Work, Business & Management Law, Social Policy & Admin.**	Excellent
1995/6 **Sociology** 20	
Joint Funding Council's research assessment 1996 (13 subjects assessed):	
Economics, Politics, Social Policy & Admin., History (Economic)	Grade 5*
Law, Anthropology, Business/ Management, Accountancy, History (International), Philosophy	Grade 5
EMPLOYMENT PROFILE	
Employability in Industry:	
MPW national league table (1996)	**22nd=**

Principal job market destinations:
Commerce (strong), **Arts/Media, Manufacturing, Public Admin./Law, Retail/Wholesale**

PIP 1996 employers' survey: Top 3 subjects/national ranking	
Accountancy, Finance & Banking	1st
Business	2nd
Social Science/Economics	3rd
Approximate % unemployed	**3.5%**

VAG VIEW

Heavyweight academic scene complete with crushingly boring heavyweight LSE Magazine. *Even when there's an article about condoms (Winter 1996) - filleted between load-bearing social and political issues of the day, the writer's campaign is led by a desire 'to maintain the salience of condom use'.*

However, it should be pointed out that this mag - The Beaver *- is a chance for academics to have a say. In any case 'salience', I note, means not only conspicuousness but an outward projection at an angle of less than 180 degrees, so perhaps the writer was engaged in a bit of nudge-nudge irony after all. So what's this place all about? Well, it's up there with Oxbridge at the* *pinnacle of scholarly achievement. Nine out of 13 research subjects assessed by the Joint Council achieved either a 5 or 5* rating, one of them (History) was split into 2 (International and Economic), making the full complement of 10 (see fact box). You can't do much better than that; only Oxford and Cambridge did. Six out of eight of the first degree subjects assessed by HEFCE received an 'Excellent' rating and Sociology had 20 out of 24, which means the same; only Geography scored a mere Satisfactory. Its Library of Political and Economic Science is famous the world over, and the school is hand in glove with Westminster, Whitehall, the city and the legal and media establishment. In fact its position in London ensures it closer contact with all departments of the Establishment than either Oxford or Cambridge, and its main, highly specialised subject areas - Economics, International Relations, Government, Law, Finance - are what you might call the active ingredients in the life of the Establishment today. In terms of fundraising the formula works a treat - the LSE Foundation has just hauled in £10 million. Research income has been increased by more than 50% since 1992. This, we must conclude, is a university whose public image is as important as its responsibilities to its undergraduates, perhaps more so. But then anyone bright enough to come here is not going to need spoon-feeding even if its academics had time between all their extra-mural commitments.*

In the departmental puff mag., academic gurus appear alongside their broadcasting C.V.s. Many are recognisable faces or by-lines in the media. If the media wants analysis or comment, it's the LSE they call up. How embarrassing all that anarchy in the 60s, Grosvenor Square and so on, must have been to this key Establishment establishment. And what a relief to them now that they have the student hordes under control.

You will read in the prospectus that the crucible for political debate is the weekly Union General Meeting, 'where left, right and centre compete for the hearts and minds of the uncommitted'. We are led to believe that students flock to these debates, but I doubt that more than a fraction visits, and then out of curiosity. 'LSE has rid itself of all it meant in the 1960s and is a very good university,' as one careers master put it.

A very large proportion of the undergraduate population has no more than an academic interest in the political scene in Britain for the very good reason that they are brought in from other countries. Twenty-five percent of students come from North America, 38% from Europe, 26% from Asia.

So what are we left with? Gone, certainly, are the days when the students would chant for Mick Jagger as Chancellor. What we have is a very rich school of international standing, where students of Economics, Political and Social Sciences are being groomed to join the Establishment.

SITUATION

LSE is situated off King's Way in the Strand. See the entry for The Courtauld Institute, which is nearby, for some of the cultural delights in this area.

GETTING THERE

★ The nearest tube station is Aldwych (Piccadilly line), but the most accessible may be Embankment (Northern, Bakerloo, Circle, District) and Holborn (Piccadilly, Central).

ENTS AND UNION

The bar at the Student Union (The Three Tuns) is open to the public and stages regular live events and discos, so if you're not a student there's no need to go to the ground floor SU shop to buy your regulation LSE socks and T-shirt (though it may be worth a visit if only for the sanitary products which are sold at cost price).

The Brunch Bowl is a popular hang-out for students as an alternative to the bar. That's located on the fourth floor of the building and it basically serves everything at a very reasonable price. At the Café, in the basement of the East Building, the food is good and cheap with a range for vegetarian students (even menus in Braille and table service for disabled students if they want it). Then there's the Prizza Burger and the Robinson Room, which is a bit more up-market and pricey.

Ents venues are held at the Tuns and the Café. The Chuckle Club has been resident at the Tuns for more than two years and is a regular winner of *Time Out*'s starred award for London's best comedy venue. (*Time Out* is London's famous listings magazine.) Ents include all the usual fare - the ubiquitous Regurgitator wooed Freshers last year with his swallowing and vomiting act, as did The Martin Taylor Hypnotist Show. Being in London you do get top-range DJs - DJ Cory (Limelight, Velvet Underground), Mark Chang (Turnville, The Complex). There are nights out at top London clubs, such as Scarlett in Holborn with its 20K sound system and Kiss FM DJ Graham Gold. There are good live acts too with all the works, late bars, inflatables, etc. Balls are held at key venues, such as Equinox last October with Dodgy or Shed Seven. And for all those overseas students who may be confused by the end of Freshers Week there's even a tour of London by the Christian Union.

The Beaver has all the listings of what's on ents-wise, sports, gossip, etc. See also the weekly News and Views listings which lists public lectures, films, and concerts. You can buy an ents card for £12 for the whole year. Finally, LSE is of course a member of ULU (see London), so you'll have access to all their facilities too.

ACCOMMODATION

Passfield Hall, Carr-Saunders Hall, Rosebery Avenue Hall are the three meal-catered halls of residence owned by LSE. All LSE halls and residences are within easy commuting and/or walking distance of the School except for Butler's Wharf, Docklands. Still, even from here, you can take a morning walk over Tower Bridge, a short trip on the tube from Tower Hill to Temple and then a breeze of a walk up from the Embankment to the school itself. Nowhere is really that far away from anywhere else in London.

There are also self-catering flats in houses which, unlike the halls, can be rented over the Christmas and Easter vacs. All these in addition to the ULU Intercollegiate Halls (see London).

SPORT

Again a mix of what LSE provides and caters for and what can be had at ULU. LSE has its sports grounds in South London and there are netball, tennis courts and 4 large swimming pools within 2 miles of Houghton Street. ULU has facilities for squash, basketball, rowing and a swimming pool. LSE cricketers can use the indoor facilities at Lords.

ACADEMIA

Among subjects pioneered at LSE are: Anthropology, International Relations, Social Policy and Administration. Almost all degree courses now require students to choose at least one outside option from a range of courses in another subject. In other words, LSE is into the inter-disciplinary approach. Looking down their published statistics on undergraduate courses in the 1995-96 session there was quite a spread of new subjects, including some interesting combinations with traditional subjects, such as Economic History with Population Studies, and new sub-subjects, such as Environmental Geography, Econometrics and Mathematical Economics.

LOUGHBOROUGH UNIVERSITY

Loughborough University
Ashby Road
Loughborough
Leics
LE11 3TU

TEL 01509 263171
FAX 01509 223905

Loughborough University
Student Union
Ashby Road
Loughborough
Leics LE11 3TT

TEL 01509 217766
FAX 01509 235593

LOUGHBOROUGH UNIVERSITY

Founded	**1909**
Situation/style	**Campus**
UNDERGRADUATE PROFILE	
Application acceptance rate	**13%**
Population	**7,600**
Mature student population	**14%**
Overseas student population	**12%**
Male/female ratio	**60:40**
1st year institut. accommodation	**100%**
Approximate cost	**£40-£65 pw**
ACADEMIC PROFILE	
A-level requirements:	**High**

Aeronautical, Automotive BBB, **E & E Engineering** BBC, **Chemical Engineering** 22, **Civil and Building Engineering** 20, **Sci. & Tech. Eng., Mech. Eng.** 20, **Ind. Design & Tech., Ergonomics** 18, **Maths, Math Eng.** BCC, **Computer Science** 20, **Psychology** 22, **Politics combinations** BCC, **Sociology, Social Policy** 18, **Information & Library Studies** 18, **Sports Science combinations** 18-24, **Accounting & Finance, Euro. Business** ABB,BBC, **Management combinations** 18-22

Student/staff ratio	**10:1**
1st class degree pass rate	**9.1%**
HEFCE assessments (7 subjects assessed/approved):	
1994 **Business & Management**	Excellent
1995 **Sociology** 23 **Chemical Engineering** 22	
Joint Funding Council's research assessment 1996 (24 subjects assessed):	
Subjects Allied to Medicine, Built Environment, Sociology, European Studies, Library & Information Studies, Sport.	Grade 5
EMPLOYMENT PROFILE	
Employability in Industry:	
MPW national league table (1996)	**8th**

Principal job market destinations:
Manufacturing (strong, including **Electronic & Electrical, Pharmaceutical**), **Commerce** (strong), **Retail/Wholesale, Education, Construction, Public Admin., Computer, Health, Industrial & Engineering Design** (strong), **Sport** (strong)

PIP 1996 employers' survey: Top 3 subjects/national ranking	
Construction & Civil Engineering	1st
Engineering & Technology	3rd
Electrical Engineering	8th=
Approximate % unemployed	**5%**

'Loughborough - very highflying on Sports Science, but very demanding on A-levels.'

'Loughborough was one of the first universities to offer these undergraduate taster courses. But it had more of a reputation in the 70s and 80s perhaps.'

VAG VIEW

Loughborough seems more popular among students than teachers for some reason, these quotes from careers teachers suggest. Yet the results in the academic assessments and employment statistics demonstrate that this is a university at the very top of its form. Perhaps there's a problem of communication. It was founded as a small technical institute in 1909. Nine years later it bought the land on which the campus stands today. In 1952, the institute was split into a teacher training college, an art college (which is Loughborough college of art & design today), and a technical college. In 1966 it was awarded full University status. The college of art and design is near by and shares the Uni's excellent facilities. There is talk of a coming together in the near future.

This is an exciting university, if rather plagued by selective aspects of its reputation.

SITUATION

Loughborough is a small market town, a mile or so to the east of the M1 (J23), between Nottingham to the north and Leicester to the South. Market days Thursday and Saturday; not a great deal else goes on, though it has some good pubs. The 216-acre Uni campus is a ten minute walk from the town.

GETTING THERE

★ By road: M1 (J23), A512.
★ By rail: London St Pancras, 1:45; Birmingham New Street, 1:30; Sheffield, 1:30; Nottingham, 0:20; Leicester, 0:15.
★ By air: East Midlands airport close by.
★ *Note:* rare for first years to get campus parking permits.

ACCOMMODATION

All first years are guaranteed places in halls. There are also cluster houses in the student village.

SPORT

Three sports halls, gym, fitness centre, dance studio, two swimming pools, seven squash courts, two flood-lit synthetic grass areas, an all-weather athletics stadium; numerous pitches for all outdoor games.

There are many international athletes studying here. Loughborough takes the honours at BUSA with almost monotonous regularity and have done for over a decade and a half. £1,000 sports scholarships available.

ACADEMIA

It is all too easy to fall for the line that all Loughborough does is sport and engineering, however, if you scan the assessments under Academic Profile in the fact box, you'll notice that the Uni achieved top results in Sociology and Business as well as Engineering, and if you look at the research facility you will see that they are present in-depth in a number of other areas too.

Loughborough offers degree courses in the following faculties: Engineering (their links with industry put these courses at the top of their employment successes nationally, see fact box); Science (their Ergonomics degree is the only full-time one of its kind; also see fact box for their research strength in Information & Library Studies); Social Sciences & Humanities (including the Business School, rated 'Excellent'; a discussion-based, performance-related English & Drama course growing in stature; the Sports Science courses are legendary; the Psychology course offers study from a social rather than biological perspective).

Two other points worth mentioning: first, they offer sandwich courses both thick (third year in industry) and thin (period split by academic study); second, there's a Foundation Studies course in Science and Engineering, which allows progression to a degree course if you don't have the high entry requirements required.

UNION & ENTS

There are five bars and a purpose-built nightclub, owned by the Union not by the Uni. The ents scene is the biggest thing in Loughborough; not too difficult, there are only two small clubs in the town. Regular programme includes Monday's Vibe, a mix of acid jazz, funk, trip hop; Tuesday's Flix (films); Wednesday's Hey Ewe, a miscellany of silly games 'and much other stuff that you'll regret the following day'; Thursday's Beano's (live bands); FND on Friday and Saturday is the big night with Fusion (guest DJs, club tours) and simultaneous ever-popular Carwash and Vogue Minogue at the

Rattlers.

Each bar has its own atmosphere - the Cayley is quiet but gets lively Thursday through Saturday; there are six pool tables and a games room. The Concert Bar is the main function bar when events are on in the Auditorium or Boardwalk. JC's is open every night - a real pub and favourite of the sporting fraternity - liveliest in the Union, with Sky TV and beer garden; Rattlers is of course the nightclub.

There's a three-studio campus radio station - LCR, which has been on the air since 1973 and is constantly upgraded by the Uni's dedicated engineers (openings too for students in the advertising dept.). The student Newspaper is published each Friday, and the Union has its own record label.

Loughborough College of Art and Design

Loughborough College
of Art and Design
Epinal Way
Loughborough
Leicestershire
LE11 3GE

TEL 01509 261515
FAX 01509 265515

LOUGHBOROUGH COLLEGE OF ART & DESIGN	
Founded	**1952**
Situation/style	**City site**
UNDERGRADUATE PROFILE	
Population	**700**
Mature student population	**13%**
Overseas student population	**1%**
Male/female ratio	**30:70**
1st year institut. accommodation	**100%**
Approximate cost	**£45 pw**
ACADEMIC PROFILE	
A-level requirements:	**Unspecified**
Student/staff ratio	**11:1**
1st class degree pass rate	**13%**
Joint Funding Council's research assessment 1996 (2 subjects assessed):	
Grade 5/5*	None
EMPLOYMENT PROFILE	
Principal job market destinations: **Creative Design, Manufacturing, Retail/Wholesale**	
Approximate % unemployed	**11%**

VAG VIEW

LCAD is right next door to the Loughborough University campus. Leicester, Nottingham and Derby are within easy reach. The college offers various degrees are validated by the University, of which it is increasingly becoming a part. They include Three Dimensional Design (Ceramics, Furniture or Silversmithing/Jewellery), Textiles Design (Multi-Media or Printed and Woven Textiles), Graphic Communication, Fine Art (Painting, Printmaking, Sculpture or Drawing), Illustration, History of Art and Design with Studio Practice, English and the History of Art and Design, which is a Loughborough Uni Joint Hons course based in the University Department of English and Drama. Courses are 3 years full-time or 6 years part-time. University students may be surprised to learn from our correspondent that full-time means literally what it says. None of this ten hours a week (or less) Uni arts stuff here!

GETTING THERE

★ By road: M1 (J23).
★ By rail: London St Pancras 1:45; Birmingham New Street, 1:30; Sheffield, 1:30.
★ Five minutes taxi from the station.

VIEW FROM THE GROUND
by Ayshea Corrigan

I'm studying Textile Design. My course is full-time which means 9-5, Monday to Friday. Even though I'm part of the Art College it is in the process of integrating with the university; already we are part of their Student Union. People at the Uni are really friendly, but there does seem to be a contrast between the University students and the Art students. For example, I am aware that as a subject, Art is not given as much weight as the more academic courses; this is understandable with the Sports students who have a complete lack of imagination and charisma.

Loughborough is around the middle of the country and is about an hour and a half away from London by train. However, because it is quite a small town, the train routes are via Nottingham, Leicester or Sheffield.

Loughborough has two markets (Thursday and Saturday), but Nottingham and Leicester - both around 10 minutes away - are the best places to go shopping for clothes, etc. As for leisure within the town there's a Sports Centre, which can be quite pricey, a six-screen cinema complex, which has student discounts on Mondays and Thursdays, making it quite busy, plenty of pubs to choose from, and two small nightclubs, which are full most nights.

On the University campus the Students' Union area is large with yet more pubs, clubs and takeaways. On the whole the Union has good facilities - bank cashpoints, hairdressers, opticians, mini-supermarket, sports equipment shop and a taxi rank.

There are lots of events organised at the Union - guest bands play every Thursday night - free entry, with cheap beer when you get inside. From 11 pm onwards there is a minibus which takes you straight back to your house or halls - door-to-door service, and it only costs 20p, so there's no excuse for not making use of it. There are plenty of clubs that you can join when you enroll at the beginning of your first term - besides sport, there's a cinema club, fishing club, real ale club, and clubs that you won't have heard of, and which wouldn't mean much to you if you had.

The University is best known for its Sports Studies, which means that there are loads of facilities, and every sport you can think of. For a non-sports person it can be quite amazing, and depressing, to walk up towards the Student Union bar on a Sunday morning and observe the energy that some students appear to have.

Quite a lot of money is being spent on different areas of the campus. The first to be redecorated was the Union Building; they put in better lighting, dotted sofas around, made it very different from the old cigarette-burned seats and chewing-gum encrusted floors.

Halls belonging to the University and the art college are extremely close. Rooms are either shared or single, and the safety aspect is seen to. All mod. cons. are available, and if not, they can be organised. The minus to Loughborough is that it is so small. It is very different from being in a large city. What you think about that depends on what kind of a person you are. Containment can prove to offer a feeling of security.

LUTON UNIVERSITY

University of Luton
Park Square
Luton
Bedfordshire
LU1 3JU

TEL 01582 34111
FAX 01582 743400

University of Luton
Student Union
Europa House
Vicarage Street
Luton
Beds LU1 3HZ

TEL 01582 489366
FAX 01582 457187

UNIVERSITY OF LUTON

Founded	**1957**
Situation/style	**City sites**
UNDERGRADUATE PROFILE	
Application acceptance rate	**11%**
Population	**7,700**
Mature student population	**29%**
Overseas student population	**6%**
Male/female ratio	**47:53**
1st year institut. accommodation	**100%**
Approximate cost	**£30-£46 pw**
ACADEMIC PROFILE	
A-level requirements:	**Low**

Vast number of combinations offered in **Business, Design & Technology, Health Care & Social Studies, Humanities, Management, Science & Computing, Modern Languages, Linguistics,** etc 6-16

Student/staff ratio	**29:1**
HEFCE assessments (15 subjects assessed/approved): 1995 **Linguistics** 21, 1996 **Sociology** 18, **Modern Languages** 20	
Joint Funding Council's research assessment 1996 (15 subjects assessed): **Grade 5/5***	None
EMPLOYMENT PROFILE	

Principal job market destinations: **Retail/Wholesale, Manufacturing, Commerce, Public Admin./Law, Health, Education, Arts/Media, Hotel/Restaurant, Computer**

Approximate % unemployed	**10%**

VAG VIEW

'Luton is up and coming among the new universities, and it has very good accommodation, all new.' So said one careers teacher in a school more than 200 miles away. The distance is not irrelevant, for this former College of Higher Education is no longer to be thought of as a contender only for local students.

You think of Luton, you think of Vauxhall Motors. Luton is a university heavily into links with commerce and industry, and it is ideally placed, between Junctions 10 and 11 of the M1, twenty miles or so north-west of London, and in the vicinity of Vauxhall Motors.

The Uni has a £2 million state-of-the-art design studio, a £250,000 media studio with hi-tech equipment; in the last three years they have committed more than £30 million to new projects (including the accommodation that the teacher mentioned), and there is a £5 million computer centre due to open in September.

Luton's good relations with the business and industrial sector is at the heart of its higher education strategy which, on a student-by-student basis is not complete until he or she has a job. Work experience is the key, vocational courses offered in the most bafflingly complex conglomeration of course combinations is one means to that end.

The Vice Chancellor's wry, even ironic, smile on the inside of the last prospectus says it all. For not only has he masterminded the strategy, but he has clearly assured himself that there isn't one error in the multiplicity of small-type tables which sixth-formers must read through in order to make their all-important choice. I believe him. For above all Luton is a live-wire place that oozes capability. Even when you ring the Student Union you feel it.

The Union probably has one of the best web sites on the Internet, good visuals that don't get in the way of the information, wicked but wise. It is a happening place; its facilities and ents nights are good and, against all reason, even Luton, the town, has been stirring of late, with Exodus Collective, the free party movement, on the prowl.

Exposed in a Channel 4 documentary and in The Guardian newspaper this wholly charitable institution takes over disused warehouses and holds raves to which up to 5,000 party people flock to fund the movement 'through donations' so that EC can refurb a hospice and give it back to the people. Well, whatever, at least there are parties to go to in Luton, or there were until recently ...when things fell quiet.

SETTING

Not to worry, there's always the football team. Park Square is the main campus in the centre of town. There's a rural mansion a few miles away, which is a bit like Chequers for the Cabinet, a conference centre and home to the Faculty of Management. Then there's a site in Castle Street in town.

GETTING THERE

★ By road: M1 (J10), head for the town centre: 1st r/about, take 1st exit; next r/about into Gypsy Lane; over two mini r/abouts and following r/about; at traffic lights turn left.
★ By rail: London Kings Cross Thameslink, 0:40; Nottingham, 1:45; Oxford, 2:15; Birmingham New Street, 2:30.
★ By air: London Luton Airport.
★ *Note:* Parking at the university is restricted.

ACADEMIA

Luton is, if not the inventor of the modular course structure, its principal exponent; there are some 450 combinations offered for Business alone in the Official UCAS Guide. They operate through six faculties: Business, Design & Technology, Health Care & Social Studies, Humanities, Management, Science & Computing. Their prospectus is clearly laid out and easy to handle. Just be prepared to spend a little time.

ACCOMMODATION

All first years are guaranteed Uni accommodation in halls or, possibly, in their managed accommodation in town.

ARTS & ENTS

Luton has two casinos, a triple-screen cinema and St George's Theatre, which sounds a delight. With a capacity of only 238, this intimate venue stages everything from Shakespeare (RSC tours) to popular musicals and occasionally top-line comedians and arthouse films. There's also the 33 Arts Centre with its 16-track recording studio, film and video equipment, art gallery, vegetarian eaterie and an intriguing line in happening shows, which might be a visit from a top-line jazz musician or local off-the-street talent, national calibre comedians or poetry readings - they are in Guildford Street: call to see what's on.

Then there are the pubs - if it's Luton it must be Irish. Pick of the bunch by the Union is J J Murphy's, near the main campus, with bands in the annex every night of the week. This town is full of pubs featuring live acts or DJs, or are just good for a drink: Brewery Tap, the Newt & Cucumber, Brookes, Yates, the Rat & Carrot and the new Fedora & Firkin are among those recommended by students for students. Clubs include Legends, Viva, the Zone (which now gets Club UK and United Nations), Peach, Mirage, Genies, and Rumours.

At the Union it's the SU Bar, the Stagger Inn and the Underground - 'Luton's only subterranean night club': Sunday is Quiz Night to sharpen your wits for the coming week; Monday is shots for 50p to get things back to normal, a request night where the DJ actually plays your request; comedy on Tuesday, cloths-and-candles cabaret style; Tribute Night on Wednesdays; TOTP on Thursday for chart, all drinks 75p; Bubbly on Fridays, 70s and 80s; and on Saturday it's either Addiction (indie) or Indulge (chart).

SPORT

The Uni makes use of extensive town facilities for all sports and has its own fitness centre, sauna steam room and solarium.

MANCHESTER UNIVERSITY

University of Manchester
Oxford Road
Manchester
M13 9PL

TEL 0161 275 2000
FAX 0161 275 2407

Manchester University
Student Union
Oxford Road
Manchester M13 9PR

TEL 0161 275 2930
FAX 0161 275 2936

UNIVERSITY OF MANCHESTER

Founded	**1851**
Situation/style	**Campus**
UNDERGRADUATE PROFILE	
Application acceptance rate	**9%**
Medical AAR	**10%**
Population	**14,000**
Mature student population	**9%**
Overseas student population	**8%**
Male/female ratio	**52:48**
1st year institut. accommodation	**100%**
Approximate cost	**£35-£70 pw**

ACADEMIC PROFILE

A-level requirements: **Very High**

Accounting ABB, **Law** 28, **Psychology** ABB, **Sociology** BBC, **Politics, Architecture** BBB, **Modern Languages** BBB-CCC, **Aerospace Engineering** 24, **E & E Engineering** BBC-BCC, **Civil, Mech. Engineering** CCC,18, **Maths** 22-24, **Physical Science, Computer Sci./Eng.** BBC-BCC, **Biology, Biochemistry, Biotechnology** BCC, **Nursing** BCC, **Medicine** ABB:

- ★ Science 'A's required **Chemistry + 1 of Maths, Biol.,Phys.**
- ★ Addit. Non-Science 'A's acceptable **Yes**
- ★ Retakes considered **Yes**
- ★ Retake offer **AAA**
- ★ Clinical contact **3rd year**

Student/staff ratio	**7:1**
1st class degree pass rate	**12.8%**

HEFCE assessments (19 subjects assessed/approved):

1993 **Chemistry, Law, Mechanical Engineering.**	Excellent
1994 **Anthropology, Business & Management, Computer Studies, English, Music**	Excellent
1995 **Geography, Social Policy & Administration**	Excellent
1996 **Geology**	Excellent

1995/6 **French** 19 **German** 21 **Linguistics** 21 **Sociology** 21
1996 **Iberian** 20 **Italian** 19

Joint Funding Council's research assessment 1996 (48 subjects assessed):

Metallurgy, Accountancy, Theology	Grade 5*
Clinical Dentistry, Pharmacy, Biochemistry, Physics, Pure Maths, Computer, Law, Anthropology, Sociology, Middle Eastern/African, French, German/Dutch/Scandinavian, Linguistics, History	Grade 5

EMPLOYMENT PROFILE

Employability in Industry:

MPW national league table (1996) **3rd**

Principal job market destinations:

Health (incl. **Dentistry**), **Retail/ Wholesale, Commerce, Manufacturing, Education, Personnel** (strong), **Arts/Media** (strong), **Public Admin/ Law, Computer, Dentistry, Market Research/Advertising** (strong), **Architecture** (strong)

PIP 1996 employers' survey:

Top 3 subjects/national ranking

Business	4th
Computing	5th
Engineering & Technology	6th
Approximate % unemployed	**5%**

VAG VIEW

Manchester is a serious place. It is the authentic, ready-to-wear entertainment capital of Britain, its haute couture pedigree through the Hacienda Club back to late 80s Acid House, with its tabloid press associations of powerful Manchester music moguls and gun-toting gangsters, an image - indeed the club itself - long reinvented as a tourist attraction. However suspect, its off-the-peg progeny now has a multi-faceted identity and credentials all of its own, and you can arrive in Manchester and be sure to find something to your taste. It is a large city, but it doesn't take long to get under its skin, though very few students - with only a grant cheque and three years to spare - will come, or probably want to come, within more than aortal distance of its vain and hungry heart.

Manchester is the place parents hate their children to go to (which may recommend it to you), partly because of the drugs scene, partly because of the violence. All big cities have violence, and we shouldn't be surprised to find violence here. Everyone has a story to tell - 'Two of my cousins went there,' said one school teacher responsible for advising the pupils of a leading girls public school on which Uni to go to. 'Both grew up in Inner London [the implication, they had seen life], and both found Manchester quite tough to the extent that when they went to get their money out of the hole in the wall, they used to go in groups - and these were big lads. Where students live tends to be verging on Moss Side and whereas the University itself is fine, non-University accommodation is very mixed.' Correspondent Nicola Chapman wrote, 'In such a large city security is a major issue and access to residences is usually limited by keys, card keys and intercoms, although this varies between halls.' But Nicola Sargent, who writes about Manchester Met, is wary of over-exaggerating the problem: 'It has an infamous club scene which has its advantages and disadvantages: you have to be street-safe, but the gang-related violence has been exaggerated by the national media.'

How fearful a place it seems to you will to a great extent depend on where you come from. The Student Union is active in this area, particularly as regards women. 'The Union runs a lot of services for women, including self-defence classes, a late night minibus, safety campaigns, cheap rape alarms, and confidential advice from the Women's Officer,' says the students' own Alternative Prospectus, which every intending student is advised to order from the Union. (See also the UMIST entry about a new swipe card initiative.)

The University is a compact safe haven in the middle of all this, with a far richer cultural recipe to offer than the Hacienda, as you may have heard. One of its strengths is the way it has brought on to the campus organisations such as the innovative Contact Theatre Company, which has its home at the University Theatre. Student actors and directors make daily contact with this renowned seed-bed of talent. Then there is The Whitworth Art Gallery, with its famous British watercolour and textile collection, and the Manchester Museum is also part of the Uni, offering its research and scholarship in a whole range of disciplines on site to students. The University is part of the culture of Manchester, with its art galleries, museums and six theatres, from the mainstream Royal Exchange to fringe venue The Green Room, with its Halle and BBC Philharmonic orchestras, and its more fashionable youth culture. The Uni's fairly recent addition to the Student's Union of The Academy, a 1,900-capacity disco and live band venue, completes the picture.

Manchester has the largest student population of any civic Uni and among the best teaching reputations in the land. The assessors have run their audits and found no hiatus between reputation and reality. On the contrary, it is excellent across the board - 'Our most recent experience - pupils that have gone there, to study History and Chemistry - is good,' said one teacher reflecting the view of many. 'It is good for both sciences and arts.'

Entry requirements are commensurately high and if you go there for interview, there is no reason to expect them to get down on bended knee and beg you to come - 'A member of staff's son applied to Manchester,' said another teacher, 'went there for an Open Day. No-one asked who he was, showed any interest in him as a person, so he turned them down.'

I dare say Manchester quickly recovered.

SITUATION

A short way from the city centre on the south-east side.

GETTING THERE

★ By road: M63 (J10), A34.
★ Coach services from Manchester good to all main destinations.
★ By rail: London Euston, 2:30; Leeds, 1:45; Liverpool Lime Street, 0:50.
★ By air: flights from Manchester Airport international and inland.

UNION AND ENTS

High profile Union, sabbatical editor of award-winning *Mancunian* magazine. Union active campaigners against two banks over Third World Debt issue, threats to student union, Green issues, Womens issues, though main body of students as apathetic as most anywhere. Weekly market - Academy Market for cheap clothes, records, posters, etc. Good on welfare, Community Action, rag, etc.

With the Academy and the Cellar, the Union now has, two nightclubs and two bars - The Serpent Bar, decorated with old newspaper clippings of famous graduates, and the Hop and Grape, smaller and generally quieter, though it too hosts the occasional lesser known band. Excellent ents programme and topline bands, lately at the Academy, M-People, The Orb, The Shamen. Their Friday nights are a major city attraction. Halls also organise their own ents.

City highlights include the Gay Village (by bus station, within Princess/Sackville/Portland/Whitworth Streets - Central Park, Follies, New York New York). Student recommended clubs: Boardwalk, Banshee, Brickhouse, Discotheque Royale, Hacienda, Home, Jabez Clegg, Man Alive, Paradise Factory, Rockworld (though not by our correspondent), Ritz (student night only), Squirrels (student village), Ministry, Severe, Venue, Wiggly Worm, plus Manchester Met's gay night.

See students' *Alternative Prospectus* (from Union) and *City Life Student Special* (on sale at vendors). See also below.

ACADEMIA

In the process of going modular, but it will never be a flexible free-for-all. They intend to take responsibility on themselves to present coherent strategies. Medicine and Dentistry, as elsewhere, will remain exempt.

ACCOMMODATION

Traditional halls of residence and student flats at the heart of the campus. Most single rooms, some twin (reserved for first years). Most res. a mile or so down Oxford Road towards the city centre (student village). See also below.

SPORT

Facilities include a boat house on the Bridgewater Canal, Yacht Club at Pennington Flash, Leigh, eighteen miles west of city. Pitches (31 acres) for rugby, soccer, hockey, lacrosse, cricket, netball, close to student village, also tennis courts, all-weather, artificial grass areas and pavilion. Further 90 acres ten miles south, below M63, at Wythenshawe Sports Ground. On campus itself is the McDougal Centre, which sports a swimming pool, indoor games hall, gym, squash and fives courts, outside 5-a-side court, rifle range, climbing wall, bowls carpets, sauna and solarium.

VIEW FROM THE GROUND
by Nicola Chapman

The sheer size of Manchester and its University can be enough to make even the most adventurous of newcomers feel like running straight back to Piccadilly Station and catching the first train home. That is, until you realise that everyone is in exactly the same position.

ACCOMMODATION
You will obviously have to choose where you want to live before you get here and the fact that the University and UMIST share accommodation (as they do facilities, clubs, etc) means that you are literally spoilt for choice. If it's self-catering you're after you can't go far wrong in UMIST's Grosvenor Street Building (edge of campus, only a few years old), Whitworth Park (on campus, but some rooms aren't that nice) or Oak House (in Fallowfield, next to OP). Owens Park is the favourite catered hall, but if you prefer something a bit more formal then I'm told Hulme Hall is good.

These halls are all mixed, but there are also some which are single sex, if you prefer. The rent is pretty reasonable, though it does vary from hall to hall. Basically you get what you pay for, so don't expect The Hilton and you won't be disappointed!

The social side of living in halls is excellent. Each has its own sports teams and bars, and organises its own events or formal balls, which are open to all students. The most notable ents are Owens Park's weekly Bop; then there's Oak House, home to Squirrels; Whitworth Park which has The Grovel; and Grosvenor, whose Grot Bar plays host to some rather mad parties every term and whose twice annual balls shouldn't be missed.

In the second year most students choose to live out in shared houses. The main areas are Victoria Park, Rusholme, Fallowfield and Withington with those few who are obviously fond of bus journeys choosing to live further out in Didsbury, or seeking Oasis in Burnage. Living out does prove a bit more expensive, but there are plenty of decent houses and at least you get to choose who you live with. You can return to halls in your final year, although a place isn't guaranteed.

FOOD
Wherever you live there will be a number of budget-priced take-aways just around the corner. Pizza, pasta and Indian remain the firm favourites with the odd fish and chip shop thrown in for good measure. For pizza, Babylon deserves special mention for feeding half of Grosvenor. Abduls do a good line in Indian food and if it's familiarity you're after there are a good few McDonald's dotted around. As a special treat, Queen of Hearts and Robinski's in Fallowfield offer some good bar meals at reasonable prices and, if you decide to venture into town, Yates' Wine Lodge and Moon Under Water are particularly good value.

The University Refectory has good variety and is handy for lunch, or tea if you've had a late lecture. If you feel like taking your taste buds on a bit more of an adventure then there's always the famous Rusholme 'Curry Mile', the only problem is deciding which restaurant to choose. Manchester also boasts its very own China Town, where there are quite a few nice, but more expensive restaurants as well as some authentic Chinese grocery stores.

CLUBS AND SOCIETIES
Joining a club can be the best way to meet like-minded people, and with such a diverse range between Uni and UMIST, there's bound to be something which appeals to you. Clubs vary from the sublime to the ridiculous - why not brush up on your 'Circus Skills', role-play with 'Almost Not Dungeons and Dragons' or go in search of other civilisations with the 'Alien Contact Group'? There are a good number which cater for those who have both feet firmly on the ground, or, if a soap box is where you prefer to have your feet, then there are plenty of campaign groups too. Many societies act as representatives for

different religions, nationalities and sexualities, meaning plenty of support whatever your background. If you fancy adding your name to Manchester's list of famous alumini then you could get a good start by taking part in the drama group productions, writing for the University newspaper, *The Mancunian*, or joining the Manchester Student Television Society.

The Union also boasts a vast range of high quality sports clubs, and we have excellent sporting facilities - two outdoor sports grounds and two sports centres incorporating a swimming pool, and a newly-installed fitness suite. Most sports clubs host their own social at some time during the year and the Athletic Union is famous for its annual socials, including the Christmas Charity Ball, where sports kit is swapped for formal dress but makes little change to the behaviour!

ACADEMIA

If it's a mickey-mouse-8-hours-a-week arts course you've chosen to follow, then I congratulate you, you are indeed a very sensible person. Unfortunately, the science bods have life a little bit harder and it's fair to say that we civil engineers have to put up with a lot. Surveying outside in all weathers, 20+ hours of lectures a week, 9 a.m. starts every day and have you looked under 'Boring' in the Yellow Pages recently? Being a female civil engineer is even tougher. The course is definitely male-dominated, and while a lot of the lads are great, there are still a fair number of stereotypical engineering geeks - females included - who sit at the front and ask questions every five minutes.

So why do it? you might ask. Well I've asked myself the exact same question many times during the past year-and-a-half. Students are encouraged to join the Engineering Society, whose main function is to organise paintballing trips and parties with the nurses. The atmosphere within the department is good between both students and lecturers, but just one word of warning girls - if the idea of a course with loads of blokes appeals to you then just remember...unfortunately they're all engineers!!!

OK, enough of the boring stuff, what about the ...

SOCIAL LIFE

Well, in the words of *The Shining*, all work and no play makes Jack a dull boy and, as Manchester night life is among the best in the country, you won't find many dull students here! Whatever your taste (or lack of it!) in music there's plenty for everyone. Every night is student night somewhere, guaranteeing your entry for next to nothing with cheap bar prices once you're inside. You're bound to hear all the old 'classics' but won't really care as you'll be too busy knocking back the cheap beer and trying to fight off the drunken idiot who keeps attempting to slobber all over you. If you prefer something a little more refined then the Paradise Factory is good if you like dance music. Normally a gay club, they have student nights twice a week when anyone is welcome. There are also plenty of clubs for all you indie kids. Fifth Avenue is probably the most popular, but by far the best would have to be The Hacienda's indie night, Stone Love. Watch out for celebrities too - namely Shed Seven and Mani from The Stone Roses, who have all been spotted strutting their stuff here of a Tuesday night. One of my favourites though has to be Love Train held at Discotheque Royale every Wednesday. Originating from Leeds and attracting far more people than is comfortable, Love Train is the ultimate in 70s nights. Brutus Gold spins the good old 70s tunes, while Bri Nylon, Peter Polyester and the Sequin Sisters, to name just a few, provide the dancing style, afro wigs, flares and platforms to match. More like a show than a disco, this really has to be seen to be believed! (Unlike the to-be-avoided-at-all-costs Rockworld. I think the name says it all!)

If you don't feel like clubbing then there's more than enough bars to keep you going for the duration. There are the typical student haunts, the pick of these being the Queen of Hearts in Fallowfield, Jabez Clegg on campus and, if dancing on tables is your thing, the Flea and Firkin, which all open late at weekends.

Towards UMIST a good alternative is Joshua Brooks, which is fairly dancey, as is The Overdraught which is quite new and whose decor is even louder than its music. If you're a fan of vodka then Revolution is an absolute must. With more different flavoured vodkas than you ever thought possible you could spend a week (and a fortune) here before sampling them all. Once you venture into town you can expect the bars to become a bit more expensive and clientele to become a bit more posey, especially at weekends when some places operate dress codes. Special mention has to go to Saturday night at the very stylish Athanaeum, where the clientele dress to impress and the music is strictly upfront house. Rothwells next door is also worth a look. The atmosphere here is more relaxed, unfortunately the bar prices are not! Dry 201 and Isobar are a poser's heaven but pricey, as is the whole Castlefield area, and the Gay Village also plays home to some pretty trendy bars such as Manto and Prague Five. And if you thought *Cocktail* was one of the best films ever made then don't miss Henry J. Beans and J. W. Johnsons where you can sample their cocktails with full Tom Cruise-style bottle juggling to boot.

The well-equipped Student Union also plays a large part in the social life of students. Besides all the usual stuff like a shop, travel agent, bank, advice centre, etc it is home to three bars and a nightclub.

The Serpent Bar opens at 12 p.m. and is perfect when your 2 p.m. lecture is just too much to cope with (the engineering building is just across the road by the way!). The Cellar is open five nights a week, the best of these being Saturday Night Fever, which should be experienced at least once, although you're bound to get beer spilt on you by a member of the rugby team! Next door, The Academy's most notable weekly event is the famous, or infamous 80s night Club Trop.

All the tired old stereotypes you've heard about students and drinking are absolutely true. Be warned - student life means alcohol-free nights out will be few and far between. But for those days when your liver really can't take any more then Manchester has all the alternative attractions you would expect from any large city, only bigger and better than most. There's a choice of multi-screen cinemas showing all the latest releases and well-renowned theatres which play host to the most popular shows, such as *Phantom of the Opera*, *Les Miserables* and *Grease*. For the music fans, not one, but four concert venues attract the biggest names in today's music (one of them being The Academy which is University owned) and if you enjoy watching sport then there's everything you could ask for. Manchester United are no doubt the world's most supported team (which means tickets for their matches are like gold dust) and there's still struggling City who would surely appreciate the support! If you fancy something a bit different then why not go see the Manchester Giants or Manchester Storm? What do you mean who? I am referring to the local basketball and ice hockey teams. Action-packed sport and a brilliant atmosphere will ensure you have a good time even if, like me, you haven't much clue as to what is going on.

SHOPPING

The famous Arndale Centre is still being rebuilt, but many shops are re-opening and M&S and Top Shop have claimed space in Lewis's and Debenhams respectively. Kendals, a slightly more upmarket department store, is worth a visit. If you're feeling a bit flush or fancy being a bit flash with your cash then the trendy King Street can't be beaten. Boasting names such as Hugo Boss, Morgan, Kookai, Ted Baker and Vidal Sassoon it is THE place to shop - window or otherwise! Affleck's Palace, however, is still the ultimate in student shopping. With four floors of everything from body piercing to hair extensions, designer originals to second-hand denims, whether you're an out-and-out gothic, a devotee of clubland or somewhere in-between there'll be the clothes, the music and the style to suit you and your budget. Let's face it, student life is all about enjoying yourself before settling down to the 9 to 5, while getting an education at the same time. Here at Manchester you get the best of both worlds - a top-class University which takes good care of the education part and a great city which takes care of the rest. And if all this hasn't made you at least think about coming to Manchester then you should check your pulse - you're probably dead! After all, it does have the highest student population in the country, and surely we can't all be wrong!

MANCHESTER INSTITUTE OF SCIENCE & TECHNOLOGY

The University of Manchester
Institute of Science &
Technology (UMIST)
PO Box 88
Sackville Street
Manchester
M60 1QD

TEL 0161 236 3311
FAX 0161 228 7040

University of Manchester
Institute of Science &
Technology Student Union
PO Box 88
Sackville Street
Manchester
M60 1QD

TEL 0161 200 3270
FAX 0161 200 3268

UNIVERSITY OF MANCHESTER INSTITUTE OF SCIENCE & TECHNOLOGY (UMIST)

Founded	**1824**
Situation/style	**Campus**
UNDERGRADUATE PROFILE	
Application acceptance rate	**14%**
Population	**4,400**
Mature student population	**17%**
Overseas student population	**17%**
Male/female ratio	**70:30**
1st year institut. accommodation	**100%**
Approximate cost	**£40-£65 pw**
ACADEMIC PROFILE	
A-level requirements:	**High**

Computer Science & Engineering 18-BCC, **Maths** BBC, **Materials Science** BCC-CCD, **Aerospace Engineering** BBB, **Chem., Civil, E & E, Gen., Mech. Eng.** BCC, **International Management with Langs.** ABB-BBC, **Building Services Eng., Management and Surveying** 18-20

Student/staff ratio	**8:1**
1st class degree pass rate	**14.4%**
HEFCE assessments (6 subjects assessed/approved):	
1994 **Business & Management**	Excellent
1995 **Chemical Engineering**	22
1996 **Modern Languages**	18
Joint Funding Council's research assessment 1996 (15 subjects assessed):	
Materials & Corrosion, Business/Management.	Grade 5*
Biol. Sciences, Pure Maths, Chemical Eng., Instrumentation & Analytical Science, Mechanical/Aeronautical/ Manufacturing Eng.	Grade 5
EMPLOYMENT PROFILE	
Employability in Industry:	
MPW national league table (1996)	**9th=**
Principal job market destinations:	

Manufacturing (good on **Electrical & Electronic**), **Retail/Wholesale, Commerce, Computer, Construction, Public Admin, Personnel,** good record **Engineering Design**

PIP 1996 employers' survey:	
Top 3 subjects/national ranking	
Engineering & Technology	1st
Electrical Engineering	1st
Science	3rd
Approximate % unemployed	**5%**

VAG VIEW

'There is no doubt at all that as far as head-hunting is concerned this is one of the best. Employers look to UMIST on a par with Oxbridge, particularly Engineering, IT, often with a French or a German connection. Science in general is well covered there. They have specialised. They are in the midst of one of the biggest, if not the biggest centre of Higher Education in Europe, and they are the best at what they do. I also think that they have had to develop their identity in a way that not many other universities have had to do. So they have looked at their strengths and developed them.'

This was the view of one boy's public school careers teacher, and no one would disagree with her. In the PIP Graduates Survey 1996, UMIST came out second only to Cambridge in terms of employability overall. They run what is probably the most extensive student sponsorship scheme with industry anywhere in the UK. We are not just talking about work placements, sandwich courses or guarantees of eventual employment, but sponsored places at the university.

UMIST is the No. 1 academic arm of industry. Full-time staff are in place to organise sponsorship for students on a one-to-one basis. It works because industry endorses the courses here and because UMIST is in constant touch with industry about new directions in engineering, science, management and related subjects, each year introducing new courses to reflect industry changes.

There is a happy feel to the place, an excitement about what they are doing and a sense of personal contact which reaches right up to the level of Principal Professor Bob Boucher, who signs off the UMIST web pages with a 'come back and see us again in the future - things will change... Happy surfing.'

SITUATION

UMIST is situated just north of the Mancunian Way A57(M), a walk away from Manchester University.

GETTING THERE

★ By road: M63 (J10), A34.

★ Coach services from Manchester good to all main destinations.

★ By rail: London Euston, 2:30; Leeds, 1:45; Liverpool Lime Street, 0:50.

★ By air: flights from Manchester Airport international and inland.

ACADEMIA

UMIST offers degrees through the following Departments: Biochemistry & Applied Molecular Biology; Building Engineering; Chemical Engineering; Chemistry; Civil and Structural Engineering; Computation; Electrical Eng. & Electronics; Language Eng.; Management; Materials Science; Mathematics; Mechanical Eng.; Optometry & Vision Sciences; Paper Science; Physics; Textiles. There is also an Integrated Engineering course for students who have not taken the necessary A-levels (Maths and Physics) for an engineering course but who wish to change directions. Individual consideration given to entrants, and prizes are awarded by UMIST and others funded by industry at various stages of the course.

ACCOMMODATION

Traditional and self-catering residential accommodation provided for all first years.

UNION

(See Manchester University for City and Ents run-down.) Although, as Nicola Chapman points out in her piece about Manchester University, UMIST does share their Union facilities, they have recently spent £600,000 on refurbishing their own, which includes a venue for live music and discos (licensed until 2 a.m.), as well as a second bar and all the usual facilities. The relationship with the Uni is very much two-way. Recently UMIST has organised the implementation on both campuses of student swipe cards aimed at improving personal safety and security. The cards will also be used to access shared facilities, such as libraries, photocopying and print services, even vending machines.

SPORT

UMIST have five acres of pitches and share Manchester Uni's, as well as their McDougal Centre (see entry). They have their own indoor sports facilities on campus and squash and tennis courts and a 5-a-side football court just opposite. There is a boathouse on the Bridgewater Canal and a new sports hall is due to open on campus in September.

THE MANCHESTER METROPOLITAN UNIVERSITY

The Manchester Metropolitan University
All Saints Building
Manchester
M15 6BH

TEL 0161 247 2000
FAX 0161 247 6390

Manchester Metropolitan Student Union
Martin Luther King Building
99 Oxford Road
Manchester M1 7EL

TEL 0161 273 1162
FAX 0161 273 7237

Manchester Metropolitan Student Union
Crewe & Alsager Site
Hassell Road
Alsager
Stoke-on-Trent ST7 2HL

TEL 01270 873 412
FAX 01270 882589

MANCHESTER METROPOLITAN UNIVERSITY

Founded	**1970**
Situation/style	**City sites**
UNDERGRADUATE PROFILE	
Application acceptance rate	**10%**
Population	**16,000**
Mature student population	**36%**
Overseas student population	**4%**
Male/female ratio	**45:55**
1st year institut. accommodation	**50%**
Approximate cost (Uni)	**£40-£75 pw**
(City)	**£35 pw**
ACADEMIC PROFILE	
A-level requirements:	**Low-Medium**

Law CCC-BCC, **Electronic & Computer Sci.** 12, **E&E/Gen Engineering** 10, **Mechanical Engineering** 12, **Applied Social Studies** CDD, **Euro Business/Modern Languages** BBC, **Art & Design** 4-12, **Interactive & Broadcast Media** CC

Student/staff ratio	**14:1**
1st class degree pass rate	**4.6%**
HEFCE assessments (12 subjects assessed/approved):	
1993 **Mechanical Engineering**	Excellent
1995 **Sociology** 21	
1996 **Modern Languages** 21	
Joint Funding Council's research assessment 1996 (34 subjects assessed):	
Grade 5/5*	None
EMPLOYMENT PROFILE	
Employability in Industry:	
MPW national league table (1996)	**41st**

Principal job market destinations:
Education, Manufacturing (strong), **Retail/Wholesale, Commerce, Public Admin./Law, Hotel/Restaurant, Personnel, Arts/Media** (strong on **Publishing & Printing**), **Health, Computer, Market Research/ Advertising, Sport, Architecture**

PIP 1996 employers' survey:	
Top subject/national ranking	
Electrical Engineering	27th
Approximate % unemployed	**11%**

VAG VIEW

Manchester Met., formerly Manchester Poly, is situated on various sites in the city of Manchester and in Crewe and Alsager, two towns some 35 miles away, either side of the M6 between Junctions 16 and 17. Together these two sites formed a single college until 1992.

The Manchester base is centred on the All Saints site very close to the University, making, with UMIST, a quite extraordinary concentration of students within the square mile.

Academically, in terms of the degree programme, the Met. retains the poly approach. Well over a third of its students are mature and many part-time, and the modular courses have a practical emphasis, tracing a clear vocational line to jobs in industry. More than 400 courses are offered from within the following faculties: Art and Design; Community Studies, Law and Education; Food, Clothing and Hospitality Management;

Humanities and Social Science; Management and Business; Science and Engineering. The Met. is the local people's Uni, which draws its undergraduates from the top academic echelons countrywide.

What is also notable in its approach to teaching, which has received some top class ratings in the HEFCE assessments (see fact box), is signalled by the relatively good student:staff ratio. As our student contributor, Anna Sargent, pointed out: 'There are small seminar groups with considerable personal contact with tutors.' This is particularly laudable when you consider that the Met. educates, in total, some 30,000 students.

Accommodation is offered in 21 halls of residence. Sport facilities at All Saints include sports hall/gym, two squash courts, a weight training area and a large multi-purpose sports centre. Elsewhere on its Manchester sites it has a swimming pool, tennis courts and more indoor training facilities and five football and rugby pitches. Much else is in development in the sports area, and at its farflung sites in Staffordshire there are 32 acres of playing fields, an athletics track, another swimming pool and more indoor facilities.

GETTING THERE

★ By road: M63 (J10), A34.
★ Coach services from Manchester good to all main destinations.
★ By rail: London Euston, 2:30; Leeds, 1:45; Liverpool Lime Street, 0:50.
★ By air: flights from Manchester Airport international and inland.

VIEW FROM THE GROUND
by Anna Sargent

The University has various sites, all, excluding the Crewe and Alsager sites, are near the city centre. All Saints is the central site, containing the main Student Union building and university facilities. It is on Oxford Road, possibly the most heavily student populated and polluted road in Britain.

The All Saints site has the best position, but all the sites in Manchester are pretty well located, while the Crewe and Alsager campuses are a bit out on a limb.

SOCIAL LIFE

There are six Union bars in total, the two at All Saints being the most popular. All have cheap beer and a very friendly atmosphere, not for quiet types.

There are weekly society socials and events of all kinds, as well as departmental parties. The main Student Union has comedy nights and discos on Wednesday and Friday nights, both of which are hugely popular and often sell out. The Athletic Union has termly balls which are great fun.

Good bands and DJs play at the Academy on Oxford Road, the Apollo and the G-Mex, Manchester being one of the top sites for tours. It is a vibrant city in which to live, geared towards the many students at the several univerities in the area. It has an infamous club scene which has its advantages and disadvantages: you have to be street-safe, but the gang-related violence has been exaggerated by the national media.

There are many new and stylish bars at which to drink, eat and be seen. Rusholme's curry mile offers a huge variety of good and cheap restaurants and China Town is well worth a visit. Vegetarians are catered for by the various cafes, such as On the Eighth Day. The city has a great choice of shops, both designer, such as the new Donna Karan shop, and those selling the more traditional student gear, of which there are several on the Oxford Road.

Manchester is also an important cultural centre with a great variety of theatres, cinemas and art galleries.

SOCIETIES & CLUBS

The University has lots of different societies, including film and theatre. Involvement is high among students and there are many opportunities to participate. There's a friendly feeling about Manchester Met, but it suits the sort of person who likes to get involved, rather than wander anonymously around a large institution. The Union is lively and active, welcoming people with lots of ideas and energy. The quality and range of sports clubs and societies is a particular strength of the university, it has excellent facilities spread over its sites. The huge range of sports clubs and societies means that many students are sporty but not fanatically so. The gyms, both at All Saints and Didsbury, have become very popular and membership is increasingly difficult to obtain.

Politics are not a major issue. As in most universities, apathy is common and students are disillusioned with the Government because of the present funding of Higher Education.

ACCOMMODATION

The University halls are good for first years wanting to meet people but are not cheap and it is fairly difficult to get your first choice. The halls at All Saints have the best location, those at Didsbury require a considerable bus journey.

There are many suitable houses for students in the city, of varying quality and price, as well as estate agencies through which to find them; the University Accommodation Office can also be of great help. Try to stay clear of Moss Side and the surrounding area, which do not particularly welcome students. Fallowfield has a great location, some of the best and most frequented student pubs and take-away joints, and the accommodation is reasonably priced, but can be of poor quality. Burglary is a problem, as it is in any student area, so precautions should be taken.

Withington village is on the Oxford/Wilmslow Road and has several cafes, shops and pubs. It is quieter and the accommodation is generally of good quality, though slightly more expensive. Didsbury is further out, it is a more affluent area with some great restaurants and shops, but the Didsbury Dozen pub crawl *must* be tried while a student in Manchester.

(See also Manchester Uni for Union and city social scene.)

MIDDLESEX UNIVERSITY

Middlesex University
Bramley Road
Trent Park
London
N14 4XS

TEL 0181 362 5000
FAX 0181 449 0798

Middlesex University
Student Union
(Trent Park Site)
Bramley Road
London N14 4XS

TEL 0181 362 6450
FAX 0181 440 5944

Middlesex University
Student Union
(Enfield Site)
Queensway
Enfield EN3 4SF

TEL 0181 362 6480

Middlesex University
Student Union
(Tottenham Campus)
Hendricks Building
White Hart Lane
London N17 8HR

TEL 0181 362 6470

Middlesex University
Student Union
(Hendon Site)
The Burroughs
Hendon NW4 4BT

TEL 0181 362 6475

Middlesex University
Student Union
(Bounds Green Site)
Bounds Green Road
London N11 2NQ

TEL 0181 362 6460

Middlesex University
Student Union
(Cockfosters Site)
Cat Hill
Cockfosters
Barnet
Herts EN4 8HT

TEL 0181 362 6465

MIDDLESEX UNIVERSITY

Founded	**1976**
Situation/style	**City sites**
UNDERGRADUATE PROFILE	
Application acceptance rate	**13%**
Population	**15,000**
Mature student population	**40%**
Overseas student population	**16%**
Male/female ratio	**45:55**
1st year institut. accommodation	**85%**
Approximate cost (Uni)	**£50 pw**
(City)	**£55-£70 pw**
ACADEMIC PROFILE	
A-level requirements:	**Low-Medium**

Law 16-18, **Business Studies/Accountancy/Finance** 16, **Computing** 12-15, **Media & Culture, Publishing, Performing Arts** 12-18, **Social Work/Health Studies** 12-16

Student/staff ratio	**20:1**
1st class degree pass rate	**5.4%**
HEFCE assessments (12 subjects assessed/approved):	
1995/6 **Sociology** 19	
Joint Funding Council's research assessment 1996 (23 subjects assessed):	
Grade 5/5*	None
EMPLOYMENT PROFILE	

Principal job market destinations:
Education, Arts & Media (especially strong on **Creative Arts & Publishing), Retail/Wholesale, Manufacturing, Commerce, Public Admin./Law, Health**

Approximate % unemployed	**10%**

VAG VIEW

Middlesex University, formerly the poly, offer a wide range of courses to full-time and part-time students. They are particularly strong on attracting mature students, substituting 'life skills and motivation' for traditional academic entry requirements in order to encourage them along. One year access courses lead automatically on completion to a place on one of their university degree courses. There is, too, a 'work based learning' scheme, whereby students, presumably part-time, can program their own courses out of modules directly related to things they know or are learning in the workplace. They do this, they say, in order to extend 'opportunities for people to take advantage of higher education'. It is a laudable ideal, and it also ensures that the university has a plentiful supply of undergraduate students.

Half their students come from Greater London, 16% from 'Europe and Overseas', 17% from South and East England and 17% from the rest of the UK. They, along with various other universities, claim to have invented the sandwich course, and there is certainly a strong career orientation to most of their courses. Accommodation is in halls of residence, or in study bedrooms grouped around a kitchen/dining area, some of which are en suite. There is a new Student Union Forum at the Enfield branch - the university is scattered around various sites in the area - which organises discos and live gigs; there are also many student productions.

Faculties include Art & Design; Business, Finance, Mgt., Economics and Law; Computing, IT, Maths and Statistics; Dance, Drama, Music and Performing Arts; Education; Engineering; The Environment; Health; Humanities, Languages and Media Studies; Social Sciences. Our correspondent is a mature student in the Department of Writing & Publishing Studies, who has been awarded a 2:1.

VIEW FROM THE GROUND
by Helen Gibbons

It took some guts to walk into Middlesex University at the age of forty-one, with a rusty English A-level under my arm and with no other serious writing experience, to join a Writing and Publishing Programme. Middlesex had more faith in my abilities than I had in myself, and this summer I will graduate with a 2.1 BA in Writing.

Middlesex welcomes all its students, but is exceptionally supportive of mature undergraduates who have family commitments. This, added to the varied and well designed programme on creative writing and the intricacies of getting published, has made it an exceptional experience.

The BA in Writing based at Tottenham, North London, offers the opportunity to develop in the wide spectrum of writing skills. This is based on the belief that writing is something which can be taught, and not an inherited talent. The programme offers script writing, poetry, narrative journalism and broadcast journalism, with the chance to use some of the up-to-date equipment in film and recording systems. There is also invaluable knowledge of the processes in editing and how to self-publish, with training on the latest publishing software.

All the lecturers on the programme are published writers or have invaluable knowledge of the world of broadcasting. Collectively, they provide a wide and extensive experience for the student. Throughout the course, other visiting published writers have given lectures on their work, and this has broadened the whole experience.

Middlesex offers all its students excellent sports facilities, new and improved residential accommodation, and the centre of London just down the road. The courses are in modular form, which enables switching and mixing subjects far more easily, and all the ten campuses are connected with the University's own bus service. The University is well respected locally and has established strong links with all surrounding communities.

NAPIER UNIVERSITY

Napier University
Craiglockhart Campus
219 Colinton Rd
Edinburgh
EH14 1DJ

TEL 0131 444 2266
FAX 0131 455 4666

Napier University Students' Association
12 Merchiston Place
Edinburgh EH10 4NR

TEL 0131 229 8791
FAX 0131 228 3462

NAPIER UNIVERSITY

Founded	**1964**
Situation/style	**City sites**
UNDERGRADUATE PROFILE	
Application acceptance rate	**14%**
Population	**6,100**
Mature student population	**44%**
Overseas student population	**6%**
Male/female ratio	**60:40**
1st year institut. accommodation	**85%**
Approximate cost (Uni)	**£50 pw**
(City)	**£45-£60 pw**
ACADEMIC PROFILE	
A-level requirements:	**Medium-Low**

Legal Studies CCC, **Accounting/Financial Services** CCD, **Journalism/Publishing** CCC-BC, **Math Sciences** CC, **Electronic & Comp, Civil Eng.** DD, **Applied Chemistry** DD, **Hospitality (Tourism Mgt.)** CC-DDD

Student/staff ratio	**15:1**
1st class degree pass rate	**3.8%**

SHEFC assessments (15 subjects assessed/approved):

1994 **Civil Engineering, Building & Surveying**	Highly Satis.
1995 **Chemistry, Hospitality Studies, Mass Communications,**	Highly Satis.
Maths & Statistics	Highly Satis.
Joint Funding Council's research assessment 1996 (10 subjects assessed):	
Grade 5/5*	None

EMPLOYMENT PROFILE

Principal job market destinations:

Manufacturing (strong on **Electronic & Electrical**), **Commerce, Retail/ Wholesale, Public Admin, Hotel/ Restaurant, Computer, Education, Construction,** good record **Engineering Design**

PIP 1996 employers' survey:

Top 3 subjects/national ranking

Social Science/Economics	13th=
Electrical Engineering	23rd=
Computing	23rd
Approximate % unemployed	**8%**

VAG VIEW

Napier became a university in 1992. Prior to that it was Napier Polytechnic. It carries with it all the hallmarks of the ex-poly in that the courses are vocational, they put their energies into training students for the workplace, and welcome mature students - in fact mature students account for 44% of their intake. This, of course, is precisely the new look to Higher Education which the government encouraged by giving the polys Uni status at that time, and it is important to realise that polys don't become universities overnight just because of the official status change. 'We just had a child come back from Napier - she jacked it in because she discovered that it really is a day college. There wasn't any social life; it closed down. There's not a unity to it. She was studying Business Studies. It was against my advice. I thought she would be happier at Oxford Brookes, where obviously there's a much more established university student life.' This was a careers teacher in a York public school. When she says, 'It closed down,' what she means is that students went home after lectures, and the university didn't at that time have much of a life of its own. In point of fact it has a Student Union presence at its Sighthill campus, and the Napier Students Association is ensconced at its Merchiston campus, and there is a Union bar, too, at its Craiglockhart campus. There is also a sports centre at the Sighthill campus where the girl would have been based for Business Studies. In addition, Napier is powering away at new developments. From September last year they took on a fifth faculty, Health Studies, following a merger with Lothian College of Health Studies and the Scottish Borders College of Nursing. Napier claims that the new faculty is the largest of its kind - Nursing and Midwifery - in Scotland. They are also in the throes of developing their newest campus, the former Craighouse campus. Things are happening. But old habits die hard. Napier's intake didn't change overnight in 1992. Students didn't suddenly come flocking in from the four corners of the earth. It remains an institution in development. They can pour as much money as they like into the place, but in the end it is the students who will change it into a University.

SITUATION

Napier is a conglomeration of eleven sites, nine of which are in Edinburgh. The two out of town sites - Melrose (10 miles), Livingston (25+ miles) - are hospitals, part of their Nursing and Midwifery faculty. This scattered setting, above all, makes it difficult to build an identity.

GETTING THERE

★ By road: M90 from the North across the Forth Bridge or the M9 down from Stirling. The A1 up from Newcastle. The M8 from Glasgow.

★ By rail, part of the fast north-east line which leads eventually to London Kings Cross (4:30). Glasgow Central is 50 mins. away; Newcastle 1:30.

★ By air: Edinburgh Airport offers inland and international flights.

ACADEMIA

Napier's five faculties are: Arts & Social Science (courses include Journalism; Photography, Film & TV; Publishing; Interior Design; Music; Industrial Design; Social & Mgt. Sciences), Engineering & Computing (Mechanical, Electronic & Electrical/ Computing, Software, Civil and Transportation), Business (including Hotel & Catering, Tourism Mgt., as well as the rest), Science (Maths Sciences, Applied Physics/Chemistry, Science with Mgt Studies, etc); Nursing & Midwifery. There is also a Combined BA/BA, BSC/BSC Studies programme. Napier has sold links with industry and continues to extend its sandwich course/work experience portfolio. Note especially its good record in the SHEFC assessments (see box).

SPORT

Sports centre with facilities for squash, volleyball, badminton, indoor hockey, judo, fencing, table tennis. There's also a gym and climbing wall, and, elsewhere, a swimming pool and fitness area.

ACCOMMODATION

85% of first years can be guaranteed accommodation in a mixture of one self-catering single and twin room hall of residence and a number of flats 'controlled' by the University.

UNION

There are three Union bars and standard ents - karaoke, pub quizzes, discos, etc. There is, too, a fortnightly newspaper called *Veritas,* which attempts to pull the thing together. See Edinburgh and Heriot-Watt for more about the city scene.

NENE COLLEGE

Nene College
Boughton Green Road
Moulton Park
Northampton
NN2 7AL

TEL 01604 735500
FAX 01604 720636

Nene College Student Union
Park Campus
Boughton Green Road
Moulton Park
Northampton NN2 7AL

TEL 01604 735500 x2818
FAX 01604 719454

NENE COLLEGE	
Founded	**1975**
Situation/style	**Campus**
UNDERGRADUATE PROFILE	
Application acceptance rate	**23%**
Population	**6,100**
Mature student population	**28%**
Overseas student population	**1%**
Male/female ratio	**37:63**
1st year institut. accommodation	**67%**
Approximate cost (College)	**£25-£50 pw**
(Town)	**£25-£45 pw**
ACADEMIC PROFILE	
A-level requirements:	**Low**
Law combinations 6-10. **Accountancy/Finance/Business Admin.** 10, **Sociology combinations** 6-10	
Student/staff ratio	**22:1**
1st class degree pass rate	**2%**
HEFCE assessments (12 subjects assessed/approved):	
1996 **Sociology**	
Joint Funding Council's research assessment 1996 (9 subjects assessed):	
Grade 5/5*	None
EMPLOYMENT PROFILE	
Principal job market destinations: **Education, Retail/Wholesale, Health, Manufacturing, Commerce, Public Admin./Law**	
Approximate % unemployed	**10%**

VAG VIEW

Nene is a College of Education which has exercised its powers to award degrees since 1995. Only a handful of degrees are awarded externally, by Leicester University. There are three faculties and a Combined Honours Programme.

The Faculty of Applied Sciences includes schools of Built Environment, Engineering & Technology, Environmental Science, Leather Technology, Health & Life Sciences, and Nursing & Midwifery, the latter awarding no degrees, but DipHE.

The Faculty of Arts & Social Sciences includes Art & Design, Behavioural Studies (including a BSc in Psychology), Cultural Studies (which includes a cross-cultural degree in Performance Studies - Drama, Dance, Music), education (BA Hons QTS Primary), and Social Studies (American Studies, History, Sociology).

The Faculty of Management & Business includes the schools of Business, Information Systems, Law & International Business, Professional Studies (Finance and Accounting) and Management (post-grad MMB, MSc Management Studies, which is where Leicester Uni comes in).

It is situated at 2 campuses with masses of green - Northants is one of the few counties (Shropshire might be said to be the only other), still largely undiscovered (or spoiled) by tourists and Nene is actually working on connecting their campuses with yet more acres of green space. Avenue Campus houses Art, Design, Technology and Performance Arts. Park Campus the rest.

There are sports halls, a dance studio and playing fields. Union ents are largely supplied by the students drawing on their performance skills in the School of Cultural Studies - there is a strong music and drama tradition. Single study-bedrooms in Hall comprise the Uni offered accommodation, which is guaranteed to only about two-thirds of the annual intake.

GETTING THERE

★ By road: Junctions 15, 15a, 16 of M1, and easy access to M5/6/25/40, A1 and A45.
★ By train: Roughly equidistant from London and Birmingham, an hour from each.
★ By air: Luton, Birmingham, East Midlands airports (all with international flights) are each about an hour away. Northampton is well set.

NEWCASTLE UNIVERSITY

The University of Newcastle-upon-Tyne
6 Kensington Terrace
Newcastle-upon-Tyne
NE1 7RU

TEL 0191 222 6000
FAX 0191 222 6229

The Union Society
The University of Newcastle-upon-Tyne
Kings Walk
Newcastle-upon-Tyne NE1 8QB

TEL 0191 232 8402
FAX 0191 222 1876

UNIVERSITY OF NEWCASTLE -UPON-TYNE

Founded	**1834**
Situation/style	**City campus**
UNDERGRADUATE PROFILE	
Application acceptance rate	**10%**
Medical AAR	**7%**
Population	**9,500**
Mature student population	**21%**
Overseas student population	**16%**
Male/female ratio	**55:45**
1st year institut. accommodation	**100%**
Approximate cost	**£38-£57 pw**
ACADEMIC PROFILE	
A-level requirements:	**High**

Medicine ABB:
★ Science 'A's required **Chemistry**
★ Additional Science 'A's preferred **Biology**
★ Addit. Non-Science 'A's acceptable **Yes**
★ Retakes considered **Yes**
★ Retake offer **AAB**
★ Clinical contact **1st year**

Student/staff ratio	**7:1**
1st class degree pass rate	**9.1%**
HEFCE assessments (15 subjects assessed/approved):	
1994 **Architecture**	Excellent
1995 **English, Geology, Social Policy & Admin**	Excellent
1995 **Modern Languages** 22	
1995/6 **Chemical Engineering** 21	
Joint Funding Council's research assessment 1996 (42 subjects assessed):	
Civil Engineering	Grade 5*
Physiology, Agriculture, Earth Sciences, Computer, Geography, Law, Education	Grade 5
EMPLOYMENT PROFILE	
Employability in Industry:	
MPW national league table (1996)	**14th=**

Principal job market destinations:
Health (incl. **Dentistry**), **Manufacturing** (good on **Electrical & Electronic**), **Commerce, Retail/Wholesale, Public Admin./Law, Education, Arts/Media, Hotel/Restaurant, Personnel, Computer, Agriculture** (strong)

PIP 1996 employers' survey:	
Top 3 subjects/national ranking	
Construction & Civil Engineering	12th=
Engineering & Technology	16th
Electrical Engineering	16th
Approximate % unemployed	**6.5%**

VAG VIEW

Newcastle is the capital of the north-east. With a population of less than 300,000 it is tiny in comparison to London. Yet where it scores over London is in packing in an incredible number of cultural, artistic, hedonistic, sporting, educational power centres into a relatively small space (and at relatively low cost). So much is going on, and all of it is so concentrated, that the buzz on the street at night is ten times what you will feel in the greater but more dispersed metropolis. The Uni's Academic and Employment Profiles speak for themselves. The student population is taken countrywide. If you are up to this cocktail, a city more exciting than any down south, less self-conscious than Manchester, less violent than Liverpool, in the premier league nationally, put it near the top of your list.

SITUATION

Northern edge of city centre.

GETTING THERE

★ By road: A1 to Junction with A167/A696, signed City Centre. Take A167 exit marked 'Universities & Royal Infirmary'.
★ Good National Express coach service.
★ By rail: Edinburgh, 1:30; Leeds, 1:45; London Kings Cross, 3:00; Manchester Piccadilly, 3:00; Birmingham New Street, 4:00.
★ By air: Newcastle International airport, also for London, Manchester, Birmingham, Cardiff, Aberdeen, Glasgow.

ARTS AND ENTS

It would be impossible to list all the clubs and pubs in the city. Susannah Bell gives a good idea of student haunts in her Northumbria Uni piece. For student nights or special deals check out Bliss in Market Street, Cooperage or Julie's or Tuxedo Royale on the Quayside, Planet Earth in Low Friar Street, The Powerhouse in Waterloo Street (gay), but these are only a few. For the full works, pick up a copy of *The Crack Guide to the North East*; it's second to none.

For live venues the Newcastle Arena's the big one, then, a fifth of the size, Newcastle City Hall for bands and classical (it's the home of the Newcastle Sinfonia Orchestra and the Royal Philharmonic and Berlin Symphony have played there recently), and there are two dozen or more smaller venues for local and bigger bands. At the Uni Union, they have all the big acts and comedians, discos, etc. Then there are the halls of residence, where the JCRs handle ents on their own account.

For theatre Newcastle is a feast. At the top end is The Theatre Royal (Royal Shakespeare Company, Scottish Opera, The Birmingham Royal Ballet, the D'Oyly Carte). On campus is The Playhouse (student productions from RSC to Hull Truck) and the Gulbenkian just behind it (a smaller studio type place, vigorous - dance, drama, experimental, student and national/prestigious). And there is a host of small theatres in the city, like the hugely popular Little Theatre (in Gateshead, strong on local writers), the Live Theatre on Quayside, and so on.

Newcastle has two television stations, four radio stations, a broadcasting station for the BBC and three newspapers. The Uni has only *The Courier* - a great newspaper, but what about radio and TV? There's a gap or two there for anyone wanting to fill them.

For cinema the city is spoiled with two massive 9 and 10 screen cinemas (Warner and Metrocentre), an Odeon, the Ashington (student discount) and one of the few arthouse/foreign independents left, the little Tyneside Cinema, where you can feel the metro rattling along beneath your feet.

ACADEMIA

Academically it is good right across the board. 'Those who live in the North perhaps understand how good it is better than those from the South,' said one Yorkshire-based school careers teacher. 'It is very popular among students who go there.'

Its medical school is especially forward thinking - 'At Newcastle they get you on the ward rounds fairly soon on,' said another teacher, 'whereas on some of the more traditional courses you don't.'

★ *Moral: don't get ill in Newcastle.*

ACCOMMODATION

Guaranteed place for first years. Halls are mostly single study bedrooms and all provide breakfast and evening meals. They have strict rules about cars/motorcycles; permission from Hall must be sought.

Castle Leazes

Three halls (Havelock, Freemen's, Eustace Percy), ten minutes walk from the University precinct, 2 squash courts, mini-gym.

Henderson Hall

Three miles east of Uni precinct by the University playing fields and tennis courts at Cochrane Park. Computer room, snooker room, weight training room, darkroom and stage.

Ethel Williams Hall

Three miles north-east of Uni with own tennis courts. Also near University sports grounds. Music practice room with grand piano, table-tennis room, computer room, nearby Metro station.

SELF-CATERING ACCOMMODATION

The Uni has realised that their lazy clientele find the catered hall scene a bit of a bind - getting back for the evening meal is a drag, and breakfast is too early generally to be of much use. As a result, all new accommodation is self-catering. There are five complexes of flats. Student houses at Leazes Terrace on the edge of the University precinct are an alternative. Three houses (Embleton, Garnett and Lake) provide single and twin study bedrooms, TV lounges, computer facilities, etc.

SPORT

Professional sport in the city can't be passed over without a mention: Kenny Dalglish and Newcastle United; Rob Andrew and the Newcastle Falcons; international athletics at the Gateshead Stadium; and there's the annual Great North Run, the half-marathon that anyone can enter.

On campus, the Claremont and King's Walk Sports Centres provide variously for aerobics, badminton, basketball, indoor hockey soccer, netball, squash, tennis, trampolining, volleyball, fitness training, martial arts, dance, gymnastics. Swimming pools hired by the University for water sports. Track and field use the Gateshead International Stadium. See also facilities at halls (Accommodation). Pitches and courts (cricket, tennis, rugby, hockey, etc) at Cochrane Park, Heaton (Medicals), Longbenton (with its new all-weather pitch), and at Close House, the Uni estate ten miles to the west. Rowing also a popular and successful Uni sport.

VIEW FROM THE GROUND

by Miles Starforth

Ask anyone what they think of when you mention Newcastle-upon-Tyne and it is more than likely they will mention beer. And the Bigg Market. And, of course, football. Moving to Newcastle - with its alcohol and football obsession - is, hardly surprisingly, an increasingly popular option for prospective students from all across the country.

Virtually every night of the week the bars and clubs are thronged with locals and students out for a good time. The heart of Newcastle's nightlife can be found in the infamous Bigg Market and its assortment of fun pubs and disco bars. While it may not be to everyone's taste, the vibrance of the area by night has to be seen to be believed.

Newcastle's attractive Quayside, and its more sophisticated charms, is another favourite with the city's huge student population. It is also the place to spot Newcastle United's, and even Sunderland's, footballers letting their hair down after a big match (or even before one if you believe Newcastle's well oiled rumour mill).

But of course Newcastle has a lot more to offer than its pubs and clubs. The city has restaurants, shops, cinemas and theatres in abundance, with many offering special deals on production of that all important NUS card. Also, the North East's beautiful coast is only a short Metro-ride away, with Tynemouth and its pubs and chip shops a popular day trip destination for many undergraduates.

Students are also well catered for by the two main Union buildings near the city's Haymarket. Both offer excellent welfare and advice services, as well as cheap beer and good entertainments all through the week. Equally importantly they are both bang in the middle of town, with the city's main commercial centre only a short walk away. Also a short distance away are many of the university halls, though private sector accommodation is further out.

The city has student housing in abundance, and most students live out of the University in their second and third years. As a result, Jesmond, Heaton and Fenham all have thriving and lively student communities. A walk along Fenham's Brighton Grove any Friday or Saturday night will soon lead you to a student party.

And here lies a key difference between studying at one of Newcastle's two universities and local rivals Durham. While Durham students find themselves largely confined to the University's colleges, Newcastle's undergraduates have a real and vibrant city to discover, a city recently voted one of the best in the world for a good time. This is something Newcastle students have known for a long time. Howay th' Toon!

NEWMAN COLLEGE

Newman College
Genners Lane
Bartley Green
Birmingham
B32 3NT

TEL 0121 476 1181
FAX 0121 476 1196

Newman College
Student Union
Genners Lane
Bartley Green
Birmingham B32 3NT

TEL 0121 476 1181

NEWMAN COLLEGE	
Founded	**1968**
Situation/style	**Suburban site**
UNDERGRADUATE PROFILE	
Application acceptance rate	**9%**
Population	**1,000**
Mature student population	**30%**
Overseas student population	**5%**
Male/female ratio	**22:78**
1st year institut. accommodation	**30%**
Approximate cost (College)	**£52.50 pw**
(City)	**£35pw**
ACADEMIC PROFILE	
A-level requirements:	**Medium-Low**
Theology combs. incl. **Biol. Sciences** CC, **Education incl. Sports/Social Psychol.** CC, **Teacher Training** CC	
Student/staff ratio	**23:1**
1st class degree pass rate	**7.9%**
Joint Funding Council's research assessment 1996 (5 subjects assessed):	
Grade 5/5*	None
EMPLOYMENT PROFILE	
Principal job market destinations: **Education**	
Approximate % unemployed	**18%**

VAG VIEW

Newman is a Roman Catholic foundation, originally dedicated to teacher training. It takes only around 1,000 students, so you can expect a pretty close-knit community. You do not, however, have to be a Roman Catholic to be accepted.

It is situated in suburban Birmingham and has one over the University, which is always at pains to point out the leafy environs of its campus, because Newman overlooks its campus site on one side and the Worcestershire countryside on the other.

The teacher/education aspect still remains (BEd and BA/BSc QTS, but Newman also offers some interesting BA/BSC cross faculty courses, including Art & Design and Biological Science, Biological Science and Social Psychology, Expressive English (Drama and Literature) and Maths Studies. There are interesting combinations, as is their PE & Sports Studies with Theology. I have seen this in action on the playing fields of Ampleforth School in North Yorkshire (another Roman Catholic foundation). A team of 17-year-old rugby players completely shattered their youthful opponents from another public school by getting into a huddle minutes before kick-off and reciting the Lord's Prayer by way of motivation. It worked then, and it (or something similar) seems to work at Newman, which regularly competes in rugby, football, basketball and hockey with some of the best university teams in the country.

GETTING THERE

★ By road: north/south M5 (J3), A456 Kidderminster exit, first road on left (Lapal Lane), right at end, over island into Woodgate Lane, left into Adams Hill, which becomes Genners Lane.

★ By rail: London Euston, 1:40; Bristol Parkway or Sheffield, 1:30; Liverpool Lime Street or Manchester Piccadilly,1:40; Leeds, 2.15.

★ Bus No. 22 from station to top of Jiggins Lane, Bartley Green (30 mins); or 21A direct to the college from the city centre.

NEWPORT UNIVERSITY

University of Wales
College
Caerleon Campus
PO Box 179
Newport
NP6 1YG

TEL 01633 430088
FAX 01633 432006

University of Wales
College,Newport
Student Union
College Crescent
Caerleon
Newport
S. Wales NP6 1XJ

TEL 01633 432076
FAX 01633 432688

UNIVERSITY OF WALES COLLEGE, NEWPORT

Founded	**1975**
Situation/style	**2-site campus**
UNDERGRADUATE PROFILE	
Application acceptance rate	**14%**
Population	**2,100**
Mature student population	**69%**
Overseas student population	**3%**
Male/female ratio	**43:57**
1st year institut. accommodation	**100%**
Approximate cost	**£38-£50 pw**
ACADEMIC PROFILE	
A-level requirements:	**Low**
Law, Health & Social Care, Business Admin., Archaeology, Art/Design 10, **Education Primary** 10, **Electrical & Instrumentation Systems** 4	
Student/staff ratio	**31:1**
1st class degree pass rate	**6.8%**
HEFCW assessments: 8 subjects assessed/approved	
Joint Funding Council's research assessment 1996 (4 subjects assessed):	
Grade 5/5*	None
EMPLOYMENT PROFILE	
Principal job market destinations: **Education, Manufacturing, Arts/Media** (strong on **Printing**), **Public Admin/Law**	
Approximate % unemployed	**15%**

VAG VIEW

Newport College of Wales, until a couple of years ago, Gwent College of HE, offers courses in three faculties - Business & Engineering; Art & Design; Education, Humanities & Science. There is also an introductory foundation course programme.

Activities are split between two towns, Newport, which is the first town of any size you come to down on the south-east corner of Wales, just South of the M4 between Junctions 25 and 26, and Caerleon - 'City of Legions and Court of King Arthur' (according to Geoffrey of Monmouth) - which sits just north of the M4 between the same junctions.

Most of the students are over 21 and from the locality. Though the college claims to attract students from overseas (as far away as Australia and Japan) this is not terribly relevant as the total of overseas students is only 3%.

Accommodation is laid on, however, for anyone who wants to come, with a choice of 'traditional' or en-suite rooms. There is a good ents scene in the Union, with the usual comedy nights, live bands and May Ball, and various clubs in Newport offer students nights - The Big Bang at the Cotton Club (chart & mainstream, cider £1) and Squelch at TIs (they have a way with words down here). There's also Rumours (DJs, video music, live bands), Heights 2000 (swingbeat & Jungle), and the Newport Centre itself, which pulls all the big bands before they find their way up the road to Cardiff.

Sport is also big in this area (see Cardiff entry) and there's fishing on the Usk, boating the Brecon canal, and good facilities on campus at Caerleon - gym, pitches, floodlit artificial pitch, tennis courts, health & fitness suite. They get involved with the Welsh Rugby Union and Cricket Association, as well as with local groups.

GETTING THERE

★ By road: M4 (Junctions 25/26).

★ By rail: London Paddington, 1:50; Birmingham New Street, 2:00; Manchester Piccadilly, 3:30; Cardiff, 0:40; Bristol Parkway: 0:25.

NORTH EAST WALES INSTITUTE

The North East Wales Institute
of Higher Education
Plas Coch
Mold Road
Wrexham
Clwyd LL11 2AW

TEL 01978 290666
FAX 01978 290008

North East Wales Institute
Student Union
Plas Coch
Mold Road
Wrexham
Clwyd LL11 2AW

TEL 01978 293225/6
FAX 01978 290008

NORTH EAST WALES INSTITUTE OF HIGHER EDUCATION

Founded	**1975**
Situation/style	**Campus**
UNDERGRADUATE PROFILE	
Application acceptance rate	**17%**
Population	**1,550**
Mature student population	**20%**
Overseas student population	**4%**
Male/female ratio	**40:60**
1st year institut. accommodation	**90%**
Approximate cost	**£35-£45 pw**
ACADEMIC PROFILE	
A-level requirements:	**Low**

Teacher Training 8, **Art & Design, Computing, Built Environment, Management & Business** EE, **Humanities Joint Honours (English, History, Welsh, Media etc)** 10, **Sociology, Social Work** 12, **Geography, Biology** EE, **Environmental Studies** 8

Student/staff ratio	**18:1**
1st class degree pass rate	**3.8%**
HEFCW assessments: 11 subjects assessed/approved	
Joint Funding Council's research assessment 1996 (6 subjects assessed):	
Grade 5/5*	None
EMPLOYMENT PROFILE	
Principal job market destinations: **Education, Health**	
Approximate % unemployed	**5%**

VAG VIEW

NEWI, as the institute is known, is a small college of the University of Wales, but well equipped for accommodation, and fortuitously well situated. Wrexham is on the borders of Wales and England within easy motoring of Chester and Liverpool in particular. But NEWI is very much part of the local community, which has a sound artistic tradition. Theatre Clwyd at nearby Mold, for example, is a draw to top flight theatre and opera companies, the International Music Eisteddfod Fest. is held at nearby Llangollen, and they don't find it too difficult to haul in fairly decent live bands to the Union.

Other than the teacher/education base, NEWI offers degree courses through the following faculties: ***Humanities*** *(some interesting Media mixes with History, Geography, English),* ***Business Management & Computing*** *(including elements of Leisure & Tourism, Estate Mgt., Multimedia Computing),* ***Engineering*** *(including Aeronautical),* ***Built Environment*** *(from Architecture to Quantity Surveying),* ***Science*** *(some interesting Environmental courses/Biology, Chemistry).*

They have got their accommodation together, always a good sign that an institution is on the way up. All first years are guaranteed a place, and a phase development of their Student Village has already produced apartment groupings of en-suite study-bedrooms.

Union good on ents - discos, quizzes, live bands, etc, and there's an 890-seater theatre on campus which gives classical concerts - well, we are in the land of song: choirs and soloists come from all over the place.

Sport is strong - they compete at football, rugby (Union and League) and netball in the Welsh Division of BUSA - though mainly use facilities in Wrexham, and why not? There's an international athletics stadium, playing fields abound, as do leisure centres, and swimming pools, and there's a golf club. Centres for squash, cricket, etc. Some of the best fishing can be had on the River Dee, too.

NORTH LONDON UNIVERSITY

The University of North London
166-220 Holloway Road
London N7 8DB

TEL 0171 607 2789
FAX 0171 753 5166

North London University Student Union
166-220 Holloway Road
London N7 8DB

TEL 0171 609 1212
FAX 0171 753 7065

North London University Student Union
Ladbroke House
UNLSU
62-66 Highbury Grove
London N5 2AD

TEL 0171 359 6174
FAX 0171 354 8933

UNIVERSITY OF NORTH LONDON	
Founded	**1896**
Situation/style	**City sites**
UNDERGRADUATE PROFILE	
Application acceptance rate	**8%**
Population	**7,800**
Mature student population	**75%**
Overseas student population	**13%**
Male/female ratio	**45:55**
1st year institut. accommodation	**55%**
Approximate cost (Uni)	**£46-£61 pw**
(City)	**£55-£70 pw**
ACADEMIC PROFILE	
A-level requirements:	**Low**
Business, Environmental, & Social Studies, Humanities & Education, Science, Computing & Engineering EE-CCC	
Student/staff ratio	**20:1**
1st class degree pass rate	**6.8%**
HEFCE assessments (11 subjects assessed/approved):	
1995 **English**	Excellent
Joint Funding Council's research assessment 1996 (20 subjects assessed):	
Grade 5/5*	None
EMPLOYMENT PROFILE	
Principal job market destinations: **Education, Retail/Wholesale, Commerce, Manufacturing, Health, Public Admin./Law**	
Approximate % unemployed	**12%**

VAG VIEW

This was once the North London Poly and became a university in 1992. Mature population some 75% of its intake and mainly local. In the prospectus they promise accommodation to all first years coming to the Uni from 25 or more miles away, but it's just as well that that means only a fraction of any year's intake, as they've only got 850 places available.

That's not to say that UNL isn't building for the future. For starters, the Union Building has had a face lift, no, 'it has been transformed'. There are three bars (one non-smoking) and still plenty of space for club nights, live bands, meetings, a shop, welfare facilities... Its old stage, now with sophisticated sound and lighting system, has been re-installed a floor above, complete with changing rooms and all mod cons for concerts and plays.

The 'Rocket', as it's known, has been around as long as the Poly, 100 years. The building holds the entire history of this institution within its walls, and John Izbicki, UNL's Director of Public Affairs, used its transformation in an issue of Fusion, UNL's news sheet, as a taster for a full blown centenary history of the Poly in 1996. The Rocket began as the Great Hall. When the North London Poly's first students arrived in 1896 it was a venue for concerts, some of them conducted by Sir Henry Wood. By 1929 it had been re-named The Polytechnic Theatre, some while after its proscenium arch had been picked up for a song from the old Marlborough Theatre down the road, opposite the Nag's Head, when it was turned into a cinema.

The Poly Theatre moved from concerts to become a hive of theatrical activity - locals poured through its doors, all of it arranged by the Poly. Its centrepiece was an organ that was played by William Lloyd Webber, the father of Julian and Andrew, a resident of the area. This organ remained the centrepiece of the theatre for over half a century, until it was sold to St Joseph's RC Church on Highgate Hill.

Reading the full story of this Hall-come-Theatre-come-Rocket is like trespassing on a family's personal history. What was the Poly is now the Uni and nothing has changed. And yet everything has. The trades for which its students were trained are no more. UNL's students now study business, environmental & social studies, and humanities, as well as education, science, computing and engineering.

What hasn't changed is that the courses are still driven by the need for jobs, and what the university is up against is shown in notes it published for a Student Profiling Project Plan undertaken from the end of 1995 through 1996. They begin, 'The University has long recognised the general difficulties faced by all graduates in gaining employment and UNL graduates in particular. Reasons for this include the preponderance of mature students and a general misunderstanding of the quality and type of education provided here.'

It sounds like an uphill battle. But this is no ordinary university. It is as far away from the punts and gowns of Oxbridge as you can get. It is a people's university, as much a part of the local scene as the Arsenal up the road. Eighteen-year-olds who come here to study do so because they live in North London and it's the obvious thing to do. Mature students may arrive with a particular course in mind, because they can see an opening for a better job if they study at UNL part-time. But as often they'll come because the opportunity arose, like Angela Cameron, who gave up work to have a baby and after two years at home with her child decided, as she was eligible for a grant, she would take the degree she'd passed over in order to get a job straight after school, a job that had led nowhere in particular.

UNL is a great place, good relations between lecturers and students - everyone is part of the same scene, and they've got a flashy new Learning Centre (opened in 1995) within the mirrored walls. They are, as they put it, 'Equipped for Study'. But they have this problem that people aren't taking their graduates seriously. So they started this Student Profiling Project 'to increase as far as possible the potential of our students to compete equally in the market for jobs and opportunities in the late twentieth century and beyond.' What was needed, they saw, was more than an academic education. Students had to learn to look at themselves closely, to build up a picture of their strengths and weaknesses, and to develop personal skills, communication skills, personal transferable skills, which would put them on the same par as students elsewhere.

And so, among the six preliminary modules of the Business Studies course, we find one dedicated to learning techniques, evaluation and analysis, identifying, tackling and solving problems, writing (communication) skills, oral communication skills, self-knowledge and interpersonal skills, group work. PTS is all the rage. But it may be that once they get that first floor of The Rocket up and running, they'll discover that a lot of those sort of things will fall into place anyway, and their students can get down to the real business of business.

SITUATION

Collection of sites around the Holloway Road in north London.

GETTING THERE

★ Holloway Road Underground (Piccadilly Line).

Northern College

Northern College
Hilton Place
Aberdeen
AB24 1FA

TEL 01224 283500
FAX 01224 283900

Northern College
Students Association
Aberdeen Campus
Block G
Hilton Place
Aberdeen AB9 1FA

TEL 01224 283565
FAX 01224 283900

Northern College
Students Association
Dundee Campus
Gardyne Road
Dundee DD5 1NY

TEL 01382 455091
FAX 01382 450446

NORTHERN COLLEGE	
Founded	**1987**
Situation/style	**Campus**
UNDERGRADUATE PROFILE	
Application acceptance rate	**16%**
Population	**1,000**
Mature student population	**30%**
Male/female ratio	**15:85**
1st year institut. accommodation	**100%**
Approximate cost	**£40-£60 pw**
ACADEMIC PROFILE	
A-level requirements:	**Low**
Teacher Training BC-DD, **Social Work** EE	
Student/staff ratio	**17:1**
HEFCE assessments (2 subjects assessed/approved):	
1996 **Social Work**	Highly satis.
Joint Funding Council's research assessment 1996: (1 subject assessed)	
Grade 5/5*	None
EMPLOYMENT PROFILE	
Principal job market destinations:	
Education, Health	

VAG VIEW

Northern College adds to the undergraduate population of both Aberdeen and Dundee (see Robert Gordon, Aberdeen University, Dundee University and Abertay Dundee) following the marriage in 1987 of Aberdeen and Dundee Colleges of Education. Here, besides its BEd degrees, Northern offers a BA/BA (Hons) in Community Education and a BSc in Maths & Computing with Education. Both sites have very good sporting facilities: Dundee has outdoor pitches, three gyms, a games hall for indoor sports (including cricket nets), a swimming pool, dance studio, tennis and squash courts; Aberdeen has two gyms, a multi-gym, pitches, tennis courts and a swimming pool. The Aberdeen accommodation is in halls or purpose-built flats, but I suspect many students are very local, Dundee caters for 32 students only.

NORTHUMBRIA UNIVERSITY

The University of Northumbria at Newcastle
Ellison Building
Ellison Place
Newcastle-upon-Tyne
NE1 8ST

TEL 0191 232 6002
FAX 0191 227 4017

University of Northumbria
Student Union
Coach Lane
Benton
Newcastle-upon-Tyne

TEL 0191 266 1913
FAX 0191 233 0827

University of Northumbria
Student Union,
University of Carlisle Campus Site
Paternoster Row
Carlisle

TEL 01228 512277
FAX 0191 227 4820

UNIVERSITY OF NORTHUMBRIA AT NEWCASTLE

Founded	**1969**
Situation/style	**Campus/ City sites**
UNDERGRADUATE PROFILE	
Application acceptance rate	**11%**
Population	**11,000**
Mature student population	**34%**
Overseas student population	**10%**
Male/female ratio	**38:62**
1st year institut. accommodation	**95%**
Approximate cost (Uni)	**£40-£65 pw**
(City)	**£30-£48 pw**

ACADEMIC PROFILE

A-level requirements: **Medium**

Accountancy, Financial Studies CCC,CCD, **Business Studies, Marketing** CCC, **Psychology & Sport Studies** CCC, **Art & Design** (incl. **Fashion**) 18, **Law** BBB, **Sociology, English & Women's Cultures** BC,BCC, **Community Health Care Studies** CC, **Midwifery, Nursing** CCC, **Biomedical Sciences** 14, **Architectural Design & Mgt.** 16, **Planning** 14, **Computer Science** 8-12, **E & E Engineering** 18 **Mech., Building Services Eng.** 12, **Modern Languages** CC

Student/staff ratio	**14:1**
1st class degree pass rate	**5.7%**
HEFCE assessments (12 subjects assessed/approved):	
1994 **Business & Management, English, Law**	Excellent
1995/6 **Modern Languages** 23 **Sociology** 20	
Joint Funding Council's research assessment 1996 (24 subjects assessed):	
Grade 5/5*	None

EMPLOYMENT PROFILE

Principal job market destinations:
Manufacturing (strong on **Electrical & Electronic**), **Education, Health, Retail/Wholesale, Commerce, Public Admin/Law, Personnel, Computer, Arts/Media, Eng. Design** (strong)

PIP 1996 employers' survey: Top 3 subjects/national ranking	
Business	36th=
Approximate % unemployed	**6.5%**

VAG VIEW

'I think what is important about being a student in Newcastle is that the poly and the University mix very well. There is little snobbery, rather a healthy competitive rivalry, especially when it comes to sport. Very often students find themselves living in a house with both Uni and poly students, which is unheard of in places such as Oxford. The poly has a far greater mix of people (the Uni being overrun by people from public school). But don't be put off by this - Newcastle, as a city, caters for every taste and every person, and I have not heard of anyone who has not enjoyed it.'

Current student Susannah Bell makes a good point about the lack of snobbery between the two universities, and it's underlined by her calling Northumberland Uni 'the poly'. Everyone does, with no stigma attached. This is a fun city, even the Geordies tolerate this huge student influx into their capital city, problems only arising when the natives are provoked.

The fact is that they, the Geordies, have made it the fun city that it is and seem to be happy enough for anyone to enjoy it in the same spirit. (It's a different picture at Durham.)

Northumbria has a reputation among school careers teachers as one of the best of the poly-turned-universities, and the HEFCE assessments back this to the hilt, as does Northumbria's employment record. The ents scene may not be as highly geared as Newcastle Uni's, but what does it matter if everyone mixes anyway.

SITUATION

The main site, the **City Campus**, is in the centre of the city opposite the Civic Centre. Student Union, library, sports centre, language laboratories, art gallery, computer services are all here, as are the Faculties of Arts & Design (all humanities, languages, fine art, design, fashion), Social Sciences (geography, psychology, sports studies, law, politics, sociology, economics), Business, and Science & Technology.

The Faculty of Health, Social Work & Education ,and departments of Chemical and Life Sciences of the Faculty of Eng., Sci. & Tech., are at **Coach Lane Campus**, three miles from the centre, out towards the coast at Benton. This also has Union, sports, library and computing facilities.

Management students from the Business Faculty are out on the **Longhirst Campus** near Morpeth, fifteen miles north up the A1. Longhirst is a joint project with the NTEC to provide a smart residential conference centre, which sounds rather stiff from a student's point of view. But clearly they like to concentrate the minds of their business students, because they cast a whole lot more adrift on the **Carlisle Campus**, essentially a different experience from Newcastle.

GETTING THERE

★ By road to Newcastle: A1(M) from the south and north; A19 from York; A69 from the west; M6 from the south-west.

★ Good National Express coach service.

★ By rail: Edinburgh, 1:30; Leeds, 1:45; London Kings Cross, 3:00; Manchester Piccadilly, 3:00; Birmingham New Street, 4:00.

★ By air: Newcastle International airport.

A VIEW FROM THE GROUND
by Susannah Bell

Newcastle probably has the best student night life in the country, but there is plenty of potential for students to do well on the academic side. The poly, as it is still regarded by a majority of students, has one of the best Business Schools, Law Schools and Fashion Departments in Britain. My course, the History of Modern Art, Design and Film, is also very highly esteemed in the Art world. However, courses do tend to be less structured than at some other universities, so self-motivation is the key.

The Poly campus is right in the centre of town and no more than a five minute walk to Haymarket and Jesmond Metro stations and to the extensive array of shops and pubs. The University campus is also very close, and poly students make use of many of their facilities.

ACCOMMODATION

First year accommodation consists of a variety of halls of residence and self-catering flats. Probably the most popular hall is Claude Gibb, which has the advantage of being on campus and in crawling distance of town and lectures. There is a great mixture of people here and more of the public school crowd than in most of the other halls. I was there in my first year and loved it.

Other halls include Moorlands Hall (more commonly known as Gosforth Halls), from which it is a bit of a trek into town. It is also very small - only about a hundred students and, as my flat mate says, it is very close knit. When she was there about thirty of them all went around in one huge group.

Then there is Lovaine Halls, also on the poly campus, handy but a bit pokey inside. All the other first-year accommodation are blocks of flats. It tends to be a bit harder to meet people here than in halls. However a friend of mine was in Glenamara and had great fun with a really nice bunch of people. Glenamara and Stevenson Building both have the advantage of being very central in location. Marlene Court is the Brookside Close of

Newcastle and situated a bit far out in Heaton.

The Larches are evidently the Halls to avoid, not only do they resemble a prison block but are situated in a very rough area with the security not too hot.

There are also halls on the other campuses of Coach Lane, Longhirst and Carlisle. Friends who've been at Coach Lane have loved it but it is very small and quite far out of the centre of town. The one problem about all the poly accommodation is the lack of social activities. None of them have bars or balls. Entertainment is very much up to the individual to provide.

SOCIAL SCENE

The social life surrounding the Student Union is fairly limited (the Newcastle University one is ten times better), although it is quite good for an after-lecture cheap pint and does have the odd good night such as Innocence on a Friday. Student night life, however, has no need to rely on the Union, with Newcastle's huge array of cheap drinking and eating establishments. I don't believe there is any other city in Britain that is so geared towards students.

Probably the most famous venue is the Tuxedo Royale, more commonly known as the Boat, where students as far as Durham and Edinburgh will come for a Monday night. Not only is it famous for its cheap triples (£1 plus mixers), but also for its revolving dance floor, which is not always great for the balance, even when you're sober! The Boat is definitely best enjoyed when drunk, as it does tend to get very overcrowded. A word of advice, *do not* get on the wrong side of the bouncers, they have no qualms about throwing you off (quite literally) if you misbehave. Monday nights are Student Night and you can start getting worried if you spend much over a pound for a drink.

Other Monday night venues include Legends, Ritzy (a bit of a cattle market) and Planet Earth, all of which are great fun. Wednesday nights are also big student nights especially for the rugby boys. The University tend to go to NE1, whereas the poly tend to frequent Bliss. Friday nights are well spent down the Quayside, at pubs such as Offshores, Bob Trollops and the Akenside, then moving on to Diva or Planet Earth and for those more rave-inclined, Viva is a good option. There are also plenty of visiting DJ's, with Arcane coming once a term. Bands such as Babybird and the Lightening Seeds played at the City Hall and the Riverside last term.

On Friday and Saturday nights students have to be more careful with the locals, as this is *their* night out and things can get a bit nasty especially when both have had a bit too much to drink. Students should be aware that the Bigg Market is primarily for the Geordies, although unprovoked they will not bother you. As with any university town, drugs are readily available but Newcastle does not have the reputation of, say, Manchester, for being particularly druggie.

What the poly really lacks is a good ball. There are the sports balls, of which the Rugby one is probably the best, and there are course balls, but there are no summer balls. I and some friends have started a Caledonian Society this year and we are organising a Burns Night Ball for students of the poly and the Uni.

CLUBS & SOCIETIES

For sporty people, the poly has a lot to offer - a very good sports hall, with fully equipped gym and indoor tennis court. One can do anything from scuba diving to sky diving to OTC (army). They have a very good rugby team who continually beat Newcastle University, much to their delight as well as good hockey teams (for both men and women), football teams and good tennis teams. The list goes on. But other than for sporty, there are very few clubs and societies, unless you are into chess or politics.

Talking of politics, there are very active societies for just about every kind of party from Fascist to Communist. Emphasis tends to be on the left, but it was interesting at this year's Societies Fair that there was far more interest in the Young Conservative Party than in any of the other parties.

ARTS

The poly also has a very good art gallery. They get big names to exhibit. For example, recently there was a very impressive exhibition of Lucian Freud Etchings. In the city the main art gallery is the Laing, which primarily exhibits paintings by northern artists, and which has been greatly improved by recent refurbishment. There are less traditional galleries, such as the Zone, which exhibits contemporary photography.

As far as music is concerned there is little potential unless you are doing a music course. They have recently started a choir (before, people generally joined the Newcastle University ones), but music is very badly publicised. Drama, on the other hand, is more impressive and good use is made of slightly limited resources. Newcastle also has two theatres, the Theatre Royal for your Shakespeare and Opera, and the Playhouse for more contemporary plays. The Playhouse caters well for students with its concessions.

There are also plenty of cinemas, such as the Odeon and the cinema in the Metro Centre, and the multi-screen Warner Brothers, which offers cheap student prices (although the pick and mix counter is highly over-priced). If you are bored on a Sunday afternoon, I highly recommend the fun park in the Metro Centre with its nauseating Pirate Ship and Roller Coaster. For more artistic films there is also the Tyneside Cinema, which shakes every time the metro goes underneath.

NOTTINGHAM UNIVERSITY

The University of Nottingham
University Park
Nottingham
NG7 2RD

TEL 0115 9515151
FAX 0115 9515733

University of Nottingham
Union
Portland Building
University Park
Nottingham NG7 2RD

TEL 0115 935 1100
FAX 0115 935 1101

UNIVERSITY OF NOTTINGHAM

Founded	**1881**
Situation/style	**Campus**
UNDERGRADUATE PROFILE	
Application acceptance rate	**6%**
Medical AAR	**6%**
Population	**11,400**
Mature student population	**11%**
Overseas student population	**8%**
Male/female ratio	**50:50**
1st year institut. accommodation	**100%**
Approximate cost	**£31-£64 pw**

ACADEMIC PROFILE

A-level requirements: **Very High**

English, French Studies, Music ABC, **Architecture, Management Studies** BBB, **Psychology** ABC, **Law** AAB, **Politics** BBB, **Sociology** BBC, **Geography** ABB-BBC, **E & E Engineering, Mechanical Eng., Chemical Engineering** BBB-BCC, **Agriculture & combinations** CC-CDD, **Physical Science** AAB-BBC, **Biology, Biochemistry & Genetics, Pharmacy** ABB-BBB, **Nursing** CCC, **Medicine** ABB**:**

- ★ Science 'A's required **Chemistry + any Sci**
- ★ Addit. Non-Science 'A's acceptable **Yes**
- ★ Retakes considered **Rarely**
- ★ Clinical contact **3rd year**

Student/staff ratio	**8:1**
1st class degree pass rate	**9.9%**
HEFCE assessments (16 subjects assessed/approved):	
1993 **Chemistry, Law, Mechanical Engineering**	Excellent
1994 **Architecture, Business & Management, English, Geography**	Excellent
1995 **Music**	Excellent
German 22	
1995/6 **Sociology** 21	
1996 **Chemical Engineering** 21	
Russian 19	
Joint Funding Council's research assessment 1996 (46 subjects assessed):	
Pharmacy, Genetics, Food Science, French, German/ Dutch/Scandinavian, Russian.	Grade 5*
Agriculture, Chemistry, Applied Maths, Civil Eng., Law, Economics, American Studies, Iberian, Theology, Music.	Grade 5

EMPLOYMENT PROFILE

Employability in Industry:

MPW national league table (1996) **4th**

Principal job market destinations:

Health, Manufacturing (strong **Pharmaceutical, Electronic & Electrical), Commerce** (strong)**, Retail/Wholesale, Education, Public Admin./Law, Computer, Construction, Arts/Media, Agriculture** (strong), good record **Architecture & Engineering Design**

PIP 1996 employers' survey:

Top 3 subjects/national ranking	
Engineering & Technology	7th
Construction & Civil Engineering	5th=
Languages	6th=
Approximate % unemployed	**3.9%**

VAG VIEW

Nottingham has come a long way since the radical 60s. Just about the only thing that hasn't changed is the three CCCs required by would-be Theology undergrads. It is now the in place to be for the rich and cocksure. But watch out, the school Careers Officers we spoke to have got it in for you! - 'Sporty, arrogant and unpleasant,' said one; 'Going the same way as Bristol,' opined another. But they all agreed it is popular with students. Perhaps they just need to brush up their PR to schools, make them feel a bit wanted. Though the truth may be that Nottingham doesn't need to feel wanted...yet.

So much for the bitter sweet truth, the Uni is top-rated by all the League Tables; employers love it, even if the Uni's Research Assessment results were a little disappointing.

What's more the city is a gas, and with a bit of luck you'll forget all mythic associations of the place with Robin Hood within minutes of getting there. The only myth you'll never forget is the 3:1 ratio of women to men. It's not true of the Uni (despite what our mole suggests), but for some unknown reason it is true of the city, and neither gender can be heard complaining. Perhaps it's just a question of appetite.

You'll read about the splendid views from the campus over the Trent valley in the Uni prospectus, but it's not really that staggering. OK, the lake is fine in front of the Portland (SU) Building, and the Downs over the back sweep away into the distance just as they should, but the architects have lost it any sense of tranquility.

Be that as it may, Nottingham itself is great, not just because it is a thriving, lively and artistic city (the Theatre Royal has particularly lusty roots), but because it is on the edge of some stunning countryside . There's the tidal River Trent, immortalised by George Eliot in 'The Mill on the Floss', and half an hour away there is still something left of D H Lawrence country (they've even named a bar after him in the Uniuon) - 'the red sandstone and the oak-trees of Nottingham, and the cold limestone, the ash-trees, the stone fences of Derbyshire.' (That's the Peak District of TV's Peak Practice for any cultural morones.)

CAMPUS SATELLITE

The Faculty of Agricultural and Food Sciences is located ten miles away from the main cammpus at Sutton Bonington (near Loughborough, another Uni whose star has risen). It has its own teaching buildings, hall of residence and sports facilities, and a shuttle coach service operates during the day to University Park. Tel: 0115 951 5151. Medics operate across Clifton Boulevard, linked to main campus by a footbridge.

GETTING THERE

★ The M1 dominates. J 25 and then east on the A52. You can't get lost. Agri students bound for Sutton Bonnington Campus take J24, A6 south for a moment and then left turn to SB.

★ Or taxi from the station - London St Pancras, 1:50; Edinburgh Waverley, 4:30; Exeter, 4:00; Birmingham New Street, 1:30

★ *Beware!* Limited parking on campus and you can't even bring a car or motorcycle on site without a permit. What's more if you live off-campus within a three-mile radius you can forget the permit. It just won't happen. This policy is very tight. Getting to and from the city (about three miles) is irksome without wheels (though buses to town are good).

But then students at Nottingham these days are just grateful to be there, aren't they? Perhaps we'd better let Joanna Witt, editor of SU Magazine *Impact* , put us right...

VIEW FROM THE GROUND
by Joanna Witt

'It's the most popular university in the world ever...!' or something like that.

First of all Nottingham University is a campus about ten minutes by bus from town. Great if you need a push to get stuff done (once you're on campus you tend to stay there for a while), crap if you have no motivation to get there in the first place (and hate walking - campus is quite hilly).

Medical students study in the Queen's Medical Centre and are therefore quite separate from campus life. Agricultural students study at Sutton Bonington, miles away from anywhere and nobody ever sees them.

Nottingham is not a radical university. It's conservative. It's rich. It's apathetic. And the students are the same. Half public school/middle class rich kids. Half grammar school/comprehensive school. Lots of trendy, clubby types. Sporty types. Few radical socialists/punks/etc. Yeah, yeah...loads more women than men allegedly.

Politics just don't exist. Who needs to worry when you've got money right? Conservative/Labour/Liberal/Socialist student parties exist, but don't tend to get radical. Union fails to promote demonstrations/protests (or casually forgets to publicise them). Trent University more militant. More people get political. about sport.

Media openings are good. Whilst there are no vocational journalism courses, Nottingham boasts an award-winning radio station (URN), which runs all year round on campus and two months on FM. The student magazine (Impact) has spawned numerous aspiring journalists and has attracted praise from the *Guardian* awards.

ACADEMIA

Nottingham is renowned for Medicine and Engineering. Other departments with excellent ratings include Geography, Management and Finance and Law, but basically all faculties are well respected. Medics and Engineers tend to have ten times more work than anyone else (and let everyone know about it). Geography and Theology tend to have less work (or so it seems). Erasmus schemes figure in most degrees (if you want to spend a year abroad). American Studies spend a year in the States. Field trips aren't all that abundant, but do feature in Geography and History, etc.

Degreees are taught in modules (courses). Each academic year is split into two semesters (over three terms). Each semester you take a number of modules and then have exams at the end (January and June). This means you can cram for exams and then forget everything you learnt, without worrying about final exams, cos every one counts. Great if you work well consistently. Crap if you like to build up information and take final exams where final means *final*.

CAREER PROSPECTS

Generally good, with the University being part of the milk round, whereby large firms come to Nottingham to interview and recruit. Excellent openings for management and financial appointments in particular.

THE ACTION

Nottingham Union pales into insignificance with Unions such as Sheffield, Leeds and Cardiff. It comprises two bars...and er... that's it. They're located in the main Union building in the centre of campus, where's there's also Union offices, restaurants and stuff. The main bar area being the Buttery. There is no gig venue whatsoever, except a small hall which never gets used anyway. Themed nights are beginning to take off (especially Comedy Night) and Soda Pop discos until 2 a.m. on Friday and Saturday. Location means only first years really go, everyone else goes into town, or to student pubs in Lenton [half way between campus and town].

Nottingham is the place to be if you're a clubber. Trendy clubs are everywhere with obnoxious bouncers, labels galore and top tunes. Popular dance clubs include the Marcus Garvey, Deluxe, Essance, the Lenton, the House and Beatroot. Designer shops thrive in the centre of town, it's trance, house or garage...indie wise - Rock City has a capacity of 1,700 (equivalent to the Sheffield Leadmill or the Manchester Apollo). Not that much scope for anything else (acid jazz or funk, etc), except for a few nights at smaller clubs. Plenty of cheesy clubs, Ritzy, MGMs all offer cheap student nights/£1 a pint nights, etc. Athletic Union offers Wednesday night piss-ups here, after you've been all fit playing fixtures in the afternoon. The Theatre Royal and the Royal Concert Hall get family bands such as Lighthouse Family, as well as plays and stand-up comics (Eddie Izzard, etc). Trent University Student Union gets bands. Local live band circuit good and improving in pubs and smaller clubs. Lots of cool cafes and pubs serving veggie stuff.

City also great for shopping and fantastic for just mooching about. It's got everything a city needs but is manageable in size. Compact and practical with the social life of Leeds or Newcastle, and the calmness of Bath or Guildford.

Too many Union clubs/societies to mention. Cock-Soc - pay £4 membership fee, get in cheap parties (held in cheesy clubs in town). 50p per drink. Drink. Get drunk. And dance. Bit of a cult thing. Rock Society/Band Society/Soul Society all have nights at different clubs. Loads of environmental societies/amnesty/conservation/etc. Bell ringing/ballroom dancing. Most departments have societies too.

New Theatre - Cambridge footlights of Nottingham. Regular performances scripted, produced and acted by students - opportunities to get into the technical side (TEC) or stage management.

Record Library growing in strength and size every year. £3 membership and 50p per CD for two days.

ACCOMMODATION

First years (and some second/third etc) live in Hall. Eleven in all. All guys - Hugh Stu, Cripps (public school but cool building) and Lincoln. All gals - Cavendish, Nightingale and Florence Boot. Other halls mixed. Rutland always wins *Karni* week (charity fund raising activities). Derby known as the most social hall. Sherwood pretty good at sport. Archaic rivalry Hugh Stu/Cripps (no-one really gives a toss). Good structure - hall presidents and social secretaries make sure you know what's going on. Inter-hall sport gets people involved. All halls are on campus with great surroundings, greenery, quads, trees and five minutes from lectures! Catering is fairly ordinary. In some all meals are included, in others you pay as you eat (better if you want to eat out/go home/aren't hungry). Every hall has its own bar. Great way to get to know everyone/skive off from studying/get pissed cheaply. Each has parties throughout the year from Sex Change to Barn Dance to full scale balls. Brilliant first year, but tendency for halls to get a bit cliquey and claustrophobic.

Alternative is self-catering. Broadgate flats situated just outside the university campus, share with five usually. Good if you don't fancy hall, but a bit of a nightmare if you need to feel secure amd like being in the thick of it.

Life after hall? Three main areas of student housing. Most live in Lenton (between campus & town). Streets off Derby Road into town are mainly student. Great location, plenty of pubs/off licences/chippies etc. Can walk to and from town or campus. Burglary is rife. Take all valuables home in the holidays. Try to avoid living in Radford (borders with Lenton) - crime rates higher. Beeston is the other side of the University [south west] - better quality housing and lower rents, but further from town. Tends to be more subdued than Lenton and full of Postgraduates and keenies. Dunkirk is sort of middle land. Very close to the University. Pain to get to town/Lenton, but good for lectures and cheap, warm houses. Rents tend to average £35-£40 per week, but you can find cheaper hovels. Insurance rates high (if not impossible to obtain!).

SPORT, RELIGION...

The Athletic Union is the prominent player in the Union. Hundreds of sporting activities (wind surfing/bowling/snowboarding/ canoeing/ rambling/rowing/ju jitzu, etc) as well as University teams (football, rugby, etc). Women also well represented in football and rugby, as well as netball, etc. Sports centre - £15 membership to join. Handy location if you're in hall. Pain in the arse if you live off campus. But numerous gyms/swimming pools and sports centres in Nottingham, which are closer to most student housing and offer discounts. Tennis courts also on campus and astro-turf. *[New prospectus says £20, £12.50 for all facilities at main campus and Sutton Bonnington. Plus user fee per visit at the new 25 x 18metre swimming pool. Alternatively free usage with £30 season ticket.*

The Christian Union is strong, with regular meetings and chapel in Union building, many trips and free meals. Community Action is also well represented.

Nightline operates all night if you're suicidal or just can't remember a pizza number.

NOTTINGHAM TRENT UNIVERSITY

The Nottingham Trent University
Burton Street
Nottingham
NG1 4BU

TEL 0115 941 8418
FAX 0115 947 3523

Union of Students
Nottingham Trent University
Byron House
Shakespeare Street
Nottingham NG1 4GH

TEL 0115 952 8800
FAX 0115 952 8801

NOTTINGHAM TRENT UNIVERSITY	
Founded	**1970**
Situation/style	**City sites**
UNDERGRADUATE PROFILE	
Application acceptance rate	**12%**
Population	**13,800**
Mature student population	**18%**
Overseas student population	**3%**
Male/female ratio	**55:45**
1st year institut. accommodation	**90%**
Approximate cost (Uni)	**£40-£50 pw**
(City)	**£40 pw**
ACADEMIC PROFILE	
A-level requirements:	**Medium**
Law BBC, **Physiology & Pharmacy, Biomedical Sciences** DDE, **Social Sciences** BB-CCC, **Psychology** 18-20, **Civil Engineering** CDD, **E & E Engineering** 10, **Design Studies** 14	
Student/staff ratio	**22:1**
1st class degree pass rate	**5.3%**
HEFCE assessments (11 subjects assessed/approved):	
1993 **Chemistry**	Excellent
1994 **Business & Management**	Excellent
1996 **Sociology**	19
Joint Funding Council's research assessment 1996 (24 subjects assessed):	
Grade 5/5*	None
EMPLOYMENT PROFILE	
Employability in Industry:	
MPW national league table (1996)	**44th=**
Principal job market destinations:	
Manufacturing (strong **Pharmaceutical**), **Education, Retail/Wholesale, Commerce, Construction, Public Admin./Law, Arts/Media** (strong, especially **Creative Arts**), **Personnel, Computer, Health, Engineering Design** (strong), **Market Research/Advertising**	
PIP 1996 employers' survey:	
Top 3 subjects/national ranking	
Construction & Civil Engineering	7th
Business	21st=
Law	30th=
Approximate % unemployed	**7%**

VAG VIEW

'The city is enormously popular with students and it's partly geographical. It's about equidistant from a lot of places. If you're in the South you can go to Nottingham without considering that you're in the North. If you're coming from the North you can go without having crossed that gin-and-tonic line as we call it.'

This interesting socio-geographical observation came with one from a different sixth-form careers adviser, about Trent's competitor up the road: 'Nottingham University considers itself to be the best. I think it's bordering on the arrogant. I think it's going to go the same way as Bristol. Bristol actually got to the stage where they were writing to people in my position asking why we were not recommending students to apply to study Law at Bristol, and the answer was that they never even bothered to call people for interview, and I think Nottingham's going to go the same way.' It might be tempting to suggest that Trent is benefiting from this situation, were it not for the fact that its appeal lies in more positive directions.

They are indeed both very good

universities, and where you get two in a town - as in Newcastle - the success of each seems to rub off on the other.

SITUATION

Three sites in the city:
City Site Burton Street,
Nottingham,
NG1 4BU,
where most of the nine faculties may be found - Art & Design; Business; Environmental Studies; Law; Economics and Social Sciences; Engineering and Computing.
Clifton Campus
Clifton Lane,
Nottingham,
NG11 8NS,
some four miles away, where students study in the faculties of Humanities and Science & Mathematics.
Clifton Hall
Clifton Village,
Nottingham,
NG11 8NJ,
where Education is in a Georgian manor house, a walk away from Clifton Campus.

GETTING THERE

★ By road: M1 (J 25/6).
★ Very well served by National Express coach service.
★ By rail: London St Pancras, 1:50; Edinburgh Waverley, 4:30; Exeter, 4:00; Birmingham New Street, 1:30.
★ By air: East Midlands airport twelve miles away.

ACADEMIA

'Nottingham Trent offers some exceedingly good courses - Law, good on European Studies (a very good course on Modern Languages with European Studies). Again, like Northumbria University, you've got a big conglomeration of students in a pleasant, not too big, city, with its own theatre, its own good pub life and so on. I have also spoken to staff there and noticed that on the whole there is quite a high level of job satisfaction - you get people who go there and stay there, feel that it's good and stable - York is similar.'

This, again, was a school teacher, but a student of the Law faculty here picked out one reason why Trent has become so successful, pointing to the fact that the lecturers were more or less all *practising* lawyers - solicitors or barristers. They offer full-time or sandwich honours and a European course, grounded in English Law but requiring an expertise, too, in either French or German Law, as well of course as fluency in the chosen language. The A-level requirement, compared to some, is not that high (see fact box).

The European Studies course to which the teacher was referring is Modern European Studies (BA Hons), which moves from a broad-based, cultural foundation through increasing language fluency to job placements abroad.

All are modular courses at Nottingham Trent, semester structured, and half the full-time courses are sandwich courses. The career orientation is strong and the Uni has excellent contacts with industry. Boots is big in the city and Nottingham Trent's record of getting graduates jobs in the pharmaceutical industry is good. Partnership with industry, commerce and the professions is made through services they provide, courses and training, commercial research, consultancy, inspection, testing, etc.

Their Art & Design is particularly dynamic and the courses they offer widely varying - from fashion to print media, from furniture to photography, from contemporary arts (dance, drama, performance, visual art) to knitware and fine art. And in the Dept. of English & Media Studies a new degree course in Media and Cultural Studies, which aims at the advertising, journalism and PR sectors looks tempting.

It is an impressive array across the board, and when another teacher said to me that Trent is 'at the top end of the former polys,' I couldn't help wondering what you have to do to be accepted as a university.

ACCOMMODATION

With their success has come a need to house increasing numbers of students coming from afar. £30 million committed since 1992. By the end of this year there'll be well over 4,000 beds - modern facilities - often en-suite, in halls of residence and University-managed properties.

SPORT

High tec, sumptuous health & fitness studio - Summit - managed by the Union. Summit II at great expense on Clifton Campus. Sport halls at City and Clifton, pitches and athletics track at Clifton, squash courts everywhere. Rowing of course is a feature on the tidal Trent.

SOCIAL SCENE

See Nottingham Uni for a piece about the city, though the possibilities are endless. Recommended here as student venues are the Hippo, Ritzy's, the Irish, out of town Black Orchid, the Cookie Club for hip-hop to jazz, Rock City for live gigs and disco - everyone seems to offer student nights and the choice is endless. The Union is much more together than the one on that *other* campus out of town - SUB is the nightclub (Submerge on Fridays, Pure on Saturdays), live bands play in the refectory. Then there's Le Metro specialising in more laid-back continental bar culture with jazz, which if anything's going anywhere is probably where it will go, though no doubt everything will have changed by the time you get there.

The Open University

The Open University
Milton Keynes
MK7 6AA

TEL 01908 274066
FAX 01908 653231

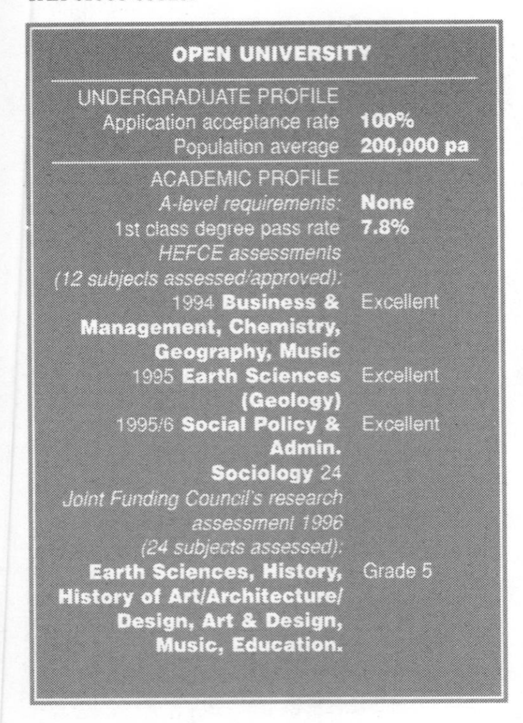

OPEN UNIVERSITY

UNDERGRADUATE PROFILE

Application acceptance rate	100%
Population average	200,000 pa

ACADEMIC PROFILE

A-level requirements:	None
1st class degree pass rate	7.8%
HEFCE assessments (12 subjects assessed/approved):	
1994 **Business & Management, Chemistry, Geography, Music**	Excellent
1995 **Earth Sciences (Geology)**	Excellent
1995/6 **Social Policy & Admin.**	Excellent
Sociology 24	
Joint Funding Council's research assessment 1996 (24 subjects assessed):	
Earth Sciences, History, History of Art/Architecture/ Design, Art & Design, Music, Education.	Grade 5

VAG VIEW

One of the best things about the Open University is that it is what it says it is - Open. Open to all, regardless of age, gender, geographical situation and most importantly previous academic qualifications - you don't need ANY.

Distance learning isn't for everyone though, self-motivation and the ability to work alone whilst juggling work/family commitments are an essential. Regular tutorials (non-compulsory) are a way of meeting other students, and the setting up of self-help groups is encouraged. Each student is given the telephone number of a tutor to whom they can call for help/support when necessary, and of course there is the summer school giving OU students a taste of student life at a University location of their choice. Whatever the social implications it seems this is the highlight of the academic year. (The academic year for most courses runs from February to October).

There is no 'typical' OU student, although the one thing all students have in common is the desire to learn. The request for a short article about life as an OU students for inclusion in this guide produced a flood of articulate, well-written information, every piece positive with the general theme being that it was a 'life changing' experience. Many become perpetual students since the thought of abandoning their studies would leave such a gap (it takes - on average - six years to gain a degree). And you will require iron self-discipline. Dee McArthur's experience, we discovered, was far from unique. In fact one lady fell in love with a man in her tutorial group and lost her husband and her home, though she doesn't for one moment regret the liberating experience which her Open University experience gave her.

For those students concerned about their ability, the OU recommends Level 1 Foundation Courses 'designed to be accessible to adults who have few formal educational qualifications or no recent experience of academic learning'. And stress that 'by the end of a foundation course you will be working at the same academic standard and using the same study skills as a first-year undergraduate in any other UK university'.

VIEW FROM THE GROUND
by Dee McArthur

I was 45, falling apart physically and mentally. So what could I do? Start an OU course! I first thought of it at 25 (too busy with the career and wild social life), then at 35 (too bogged down in childcare to send off the completed application form). But now, at last, desperate at my accelerating decay, determined to achieve some of my aims in this ever-shortening lifespan, I did it.

It all started well - each week I marked up a tick on the OU study calendar as I completed the set reading. But, oh so soon, those virtuous red ticks petered out, and there was I, with only two weeks left to do the last and most important Tutor Marked Assignment. Doing TMAs (there are only two words you absolutely need to study with OU, one is TMA, the other is paradigm) is physically sweaty stuff. Books and notes everywhere, the ever-present danger of coffee and crumbs in the word processor - thank God for cut and paste - dreaming deadlines (why does your computer always break down a week before the deadline?), yelling at the kids, family feeding and watering themselves... and 'Get the hell out of here!' I will never do it this way again. Until next time.

Then the exam. Why, oh why did I decide to do all the extra reading (eighteen books) three weeks before the exam? Why did I try to assimilate every line of those copious notes until not one sentence came out straight? Why did I stay up until 2 a.m. the night before? Why did I spend half an hour just looking at the paper in sheer brain-fused panic? Nevertheless I passed. I'm now an OU graduate. So did the OU course help me to remember my neighbours' names again? Or phone numbers with more than six digits? Did it change my life? Well, yes it did. It opened my mind again, engendering an explosion in my intellectual capacity. It gave me an enormous increase in confidence, boosted my career aims, led me to reconsider my whole direction in life, made me think about becoming a grown-up standing on my own two feet for the first time in my life.

And as for the summer schools, they tell you that they are politically correct these days. Don't you believe it! The 'let's get laid' brigade are still out there in full force.

The funny thing was, I hadn't given a thought to that side of things. I was only worried about leaving my three-year-old overnight for the first time so I was like a lamb to the slaughter. For the first time in fifteen years, there were men hanging on my every word! And they fancied me too! I could not believe it. Nobody had listened to me for years, let alone made a pass. There's a lot more desperate 40 year olds out there than I ever imagined, especially when let loose from the restraints of colleagues, neighbours and that little accessory called a family.

But it wasn't the sex. In fact, there wasn't any. It was much much worse. I fell in love. With the course. With the tutor. Silly, silly, stupid, stupid me. And, even now, at the end of the course, degree in hand, the effects are still with me.

I'm falling apart physically and mentally. I burst into tears at unexpected inopportune moments.

Well, whoever said being fifty was easy? It's wonderful, liberating, exciting, full of a sense of your own identity, your own path, indented with great pitfalls of physical decay and plummeting confidence. But, as they say, you can't have the ups without the downs, and, as someone who has cycled the canals of Holland, I can verify that the flat path gets awful boring.

Before the OU, my life seemed to centre on such critical early morning issues as whether or not the socks in the airing cupboard were in matched pairs, and if not, why not. Suddenly, back from summer school, I found myself deep in conversation about existentialism and social justice with the vicar, about globalisation with the local distribution manager, about liberation from the demands of home and family with the mums at the school gates. It was like being high on something, and OK, it didn't last, but it sure was fun while it lasted.

The OU has liberated me from unmatched socks. You have to appreciate that for a recommendation surely.

OXFORD UNIVERSITY

The University of Oxford
University Offices
Wellington Square
Oxford
OX1 2JD

TEL 01865 270000
FAX 01865 270708

Oxford University Student Union
New Barnett House
28 Little Clarendon Street
Oxford OX1 2HU

TEL 01865 270777
FAX 01865 270778

UNIVERSITY OF OXFORD

Founded	**12th Century**
Situation/style	**City collegiate**
UNDERGRADUATE PROFILE	
Application acceptance rate	**31%**
Medical AAR	**14%**
Population	**10,700**
Mature student population	**2%**
Overseas student population	**10%**
Male/female ratio	**60:40**
1st year institut. accommodation	**100%**
Approximate cost	**£70+ pw**
ACADEMIC PROFILE	
A-level requirements:	**Very High**

Medicine AAA:
★ Science 'A's required **Chemistry A or AS + 1 other sci. or 2 AS**
★ Addit. Non-Science 'A's acceptable **Yes**
★ Retakes considered **No**
★ Clinical contact **4th year**

Student/staff ratio	**6:1**
1st class degree pass rate	**15%**

HEFCE assessments
(11 subjects assessed/approved):

1993 **Chemistry, History, Law**	Excellent
1994 **Anthropology, Applied Social Work, Computer Science, English, Geography**	Excellent
1994/5 **Geology**	Excellent
1996 **Modern Languages**	21

Joint Funding Council's research assessment 1996
(45 subjects assessed):

Clinical Lab. Sciences (Dunn School of Pathology), Community/ Clinical, Hospital/Clinical, Biochemistry, Psychology, Chemistry, Physics, Earth Sciences, Pure Maths, Applied Maths, Computer, Engineering, Metallurgy, Law, Economics, Politics, Asian, English, French, German/Dutch/Scandinavian, Classics/Ancient History, Archaeology, History, Philosophy.	Grade 5*
Clinical Lab. Sciences, Anatomy, Physiology, Pharmacology, Zoology, Sociology, Middle East/ African, Celtic, Italian, Russian, Spanish, Linguistics, Theology, Art & Design, Education.	Grade 5

EMPLOYMENT PROFILE
Employability in Industry:
MPW national league table (1996) **1st**
Principal job market destinations:
Commerce (very strong), **Manufacturing, Education, Arts/Media** (very strong, especially **Publishing**), **Health, Retail/Wholesale, Public Admin./Law, Computer, Market Research/ Advertising** (very strong)
PIP 1996 employers' survey:
Top 3 subjects/national ranking

Law	1st
Languages	1st
Social Science/Economics	1st
Approximate % unemployed	**3%**

VAG VIEW

'I think people look at particular colleges, rather than making a choice between Oxford and Cambridge, and that is a very difficult choice to make. We had somebody here who had a very bad interview at one college. - "Oh, you are from an Independent School, what do you think you know?"- "Oh, you are having a gap year, mummy and daddy paying for that?" That was our head girl last year. She was really treated quite badly by the college. It seems to me some colleges do treat people in a certain way. It is a minefield without a map.'

This quote from a schools careers adviser suggests you'd do well to mug up on your college beforehand. We give you a start, but both Oxford and Cambridge provide student derived Alternative Prospectuses (as do some colleges too). So take our advice and call the Unions of both and order these now. Much is being said about Oxbridge drawing more from the public schools than the comprehensives and sixth-form colleges, and we discuss this under the Cambridge entry. In fact, even with the Target Schools Scheme, Oxford still takes about 50% from public schools, which is clearly unrepresentative. But there is an additional problem which lies with schools, and that is the obstinate way in which some schools refuse students the chance to apply to Oxbridge. Take a look at the Application Acceptance rates of Oxford and Cambridge (fact boxes) - they are about three times as lenient as most other universities, which suggests not that they are easier to get in to, but that in both cases the University is not getting sufficient numbers of sixth-formers from which to make their selection.

The Oxford Alternative Prospectus raises this issue - 'The Student Union still receives letters from candidates,' they write, 'describing their problems in convincing their school to allow them' to apply. I have seen this policy in action in a leading girls school in London, and it is hard to understand why. Sometimes it may be an active dislike of the Oxbridge way of teaching or ethos - we found quite a number of schools careers teachers against Oxbridge per se, and with the new HE strategies in place at a number of other universities, strategies which favour Higher Education for all, it is not impossible that there is a political edge in this policy. The Oxford Union's advice is to apply anyway, whatever your school says. Many do 'and get in, leaving lots of red faces behind them.'

GETTING THERE

★ By road: From the north, A423 or A34 or A43. From London, M40. From the south, M4 (J13), A34.
★ National Express coach service good.
★ By rail: London Paddington, 1:00; Birmingham, 1:30; Bristol, 1:45; Sheffield, 3:30.

THE COLLEGES

Balliol
Broad Street
Oxford OX1 3BJ
TEL 01865 277777
Founded 1264. Thick with tradition, once Left Wing but now heavily into 'effortless superiority' in political, journalistic, drama activities in particular. Strong in Classics, History, PPE and Philosophy. Down on formal entertainment and women apparently, although it boasts a formidable women's rugby team. Newish Target Schools' program makes it attractive to State sector sixth-forms. Active ents, 'sweaty bops and karaoke', outings and annual summer 'Event' (ball). The main tradition is Gordouli, which amounts to abuse shouted over the wall to Trinity.

Brasenose
Radcliff Square
Oxford OX1 4AG
TEL 01865 277830
Founded 1509. Central and picturesque situation in Radcliff Square, low profile, easy-going, friendly, supportive. 'Not the place from which to carve fame at Oxford,' said one student. Strong on sport - rugby, rowing, hockey. Key subjects, PPE and Law.

Christ Church
St. Allgates
Oxford OX1 1DP
TEL 01865 276150
Founded 1546. The model for Brideshead Revisited by Evelyn Waugh (1945) but increasingly broad intake, and, astonishingly, 'rugby lads think they run the College now'. Punt through Christ Church Meadows to sports grounds - cricket, hockey, tennis and there's even croquet in the Master's Garden. Strong Classics and PPE. Fortnightly bops, live bands, karaoke, bar quizzes - eat your heart out, Sebastian.

Corpus Christi
Merton Street
Oxford OX1 4JF
TEL 01865 276700
Founded 1517. Backs onto Christ Church Meadows. Small, around 220 undergraduates - warm, intimate (or claustrophobic, depending on your view). A JCR Cultural Relations officer overseas cosmopolitan intake policy. Strong on History, English, Medicine and Classics. Bop orientated ents. Annual tortoise race.

Exeter
Turl Street
Oxford OX1 3DP
TEL 01865 276900
Founded 1314. Traditional college, beautifully traditional buildings, cosmopolitan intake (including Martin Amis). Bops, big name summer event, boisterous bar, gym.

Harris-Manchester
Mansfield Road
Oxford OX1 3TD
TEL 01865 271006
Founded at some point in the 18th century and moved from its original site in Manchester to Oxford in 1889. In 1990 its name changed from Manchester College when it received its Royal Charter. Admits only mature students and its population represents the entire 1.5% mature student intake to Oxford, way below the national average of 10% incidentally. Strong on Arts subjects and Biology.

Hertford
Catte Street
Oxford OX1 3BW
TEL 01865 279400
Founded 1740. Long term reputation for enlightened intake policy. Warms to State School and 'Northern' applicants in particular apparently. Multi-gym and rowing machine, high profile sport, especially football. Popular student-run bar and bop cellar. First men's college to admit women.

Jesus
Turl Street
Oxford OX1 3DW
TEL 01865 279700
Founded 1571. Accommodation to all its students. 'Small, beautiful and very rich'. Good State School intake, traditionally large Welsh contingent. Bops, theme nights and the Elizabethans, the College drinking society. Strong on men's soccer, rugby, women's hockey, but not a particularly sporty college.

Keble
Parks Road
Oxford OX1 3PG
TEL 01865 272727
Founded 1870. Red brick architecture, unpretentious, large but friendly and mixed intake. Far less insular than most colleges. Strong on sport and good facilities. Good for drama, music, especially choirs.

Lady Margaret Hall
Norham Gardens
Oxford OX2 6QA
TEL 01865 274300
Founded 1878. First women's college, mixed gender since 1979. Beautiful situation

leading down to the river, yet ten minutes away from the city centre. Unintimidating to those not obsessed with sport or academia. High profile entry. Good on sport.

Lincoln
Turl Street
Oxford OX1 3DR
TEL 01865 279800
Founded 1427. Good atmosphere and strong loyalties. Good for Arts, Law and Medicine. Low on ents, but great annual ball. Strong on darts. Not obsessed with sport, though successful in rowing, football, hockey, boxing. Good collection of whiskeys in the bar. Lincoln undergraduates beat the boundary stones on Ascension Day, drink ivy beer and throw hot pennies at choirboys.

Magdalen
High Street
Oxford OX1 4AU
TEL 01865 276000
Founded 1458. Pronounced Maudlin. Rich musical life, one of the oldest colleges, steeped in tradition but relaxed and social. Undergraduates highly motivated academically. Low on ents but spectacular ball once every three years. Lowish sports profile but good facilities, strongest at rowing, squash, tennis, badminton and cross-country. On May Morning, at 5 a.m., the goddess Flora is saluted from the top of the tower.

Mansfield
Mansfield Road
Oxford OX1 3TF
TEL 01865 270999
Founded 1886. Welcoming to State School sixth-formers, cosy, close but liable to be gossipy. Ents popular and broadly based, from bops to slave auctions. Joins Merton for sport, good for non-professionals. Only fifty undergraduates.

Merton
Merton Street
Oxford OX1 4JD
TEL 01865 276310
Founded 1264. Ancient, traditional, but waking up to State School sixth-formers. Good line in journalism, drama and music. Academically exacting. Frequently tops the Norrington Table, the Finals league table of Oxford Colleges. Very Rich. Wide ranging ents. Twenty-year-old tradition of walking backwards round the Fellows' Quad quaffing Port as the clocks go back in autumn.

New
Holywell Street
Oxford OX1 3BN
TEL 01865 279555
Founded 1379. Large, progressive, busy, almost too good to be true. Central position amidst old Oxford. Mixed population not hidebound by tradition, though it is possibly the oldest college in Oxford. Strong on drama, music. Predominantly Left Wing politically. Strong at football, cricket, rugby (women's too). Best bar in the university.

Oriel
Oriel Square
Oxford OX1 4EW
TEL 01865 276555
Founded 1326. Oriel means bay window, which probably has little to do with its appeal to a predominantly lively, unacademic, sporty clientele - rowing is key - though the College has other sides including drama. Poor ents, concentration on boozing.

Pembroke
St. Aldates
Oxford OX1 1DW
TEL 01865 276444
Founded 1624. 'If your aim in life is to have a good time and scrape by, then Pembroke is the college for you.' Strong at hockey and rowing and in more or less every other sport Pembroke figures. Barnstormers is the Drama Society, the Johnson Club is a discussion group; there are also dining clubs as well as the usual bops, karaoke, etc. Long standing rivalry with Christ Church and Pembroke.

Queen's
High Street
Oxford OX1 4AW
TEL 01865 279120
Founded 1341. Self-sufficient, unpretentious

but a bit insular. Great ents scene (especially Blind Date, a termly event), a lively Beer Cellar. Good presence in sport and academia (Maths, Sciences, PPE and History). Very cheap bar. Traditionally a Northern stronghold.

St. Anne's
Woodstock Road
Oxford OX2 6HS
TEL 01865 274800
Founded 1879. A State School Mecca, it is on the fringe of the Oxbridge myth. Strong tradition of student journalism apparently, ents good and varied. Wide range of sport played to fairly low success level. Rent equalisation scheme for those living out.

St. Catherine's
Manor Road
Oxford OX1 3UJ
TEL 01865 271700
Founded 1963, but many of its buildings Grade I listed. Away from the centre. Enthusiasms include sport and drama, but not one for sports trophies. Cheap food and masses of it. Rooms small.

St. Edmund Hall
Queen's Lane
Oxford OX1 4AR
TEL 01865 279000
Founded 1278. Thirty years ago you could get into Teddy Hall, as it's known, with a cauliflower ear and a couple of Es but the macho image is a distant memory. Sport is still fairly strong, but so is journalism, music and drama. Ents active and it is the Fresher Bop Venue.

St. Hilda's
Cowley Place
Oxford OX4 1DY
TEL 01865 276884
Founded 1893. The only single-gender college left and a safe second choice for women. Draws widely from among overseas applicants. City centre situation hidden away from tourists. Hildabeasts roam and return replete to their tranquil sanctuary. College ents limited.

St. Hugh's
St. Margaret's Road
Oxford OX2 6LE
TEL 01865 274900
Founded 1886. Set apart a long way out, but fourteen acres of grounds, a magnet for undergraduates especially in Summer. Academic but boisterous social life too and ents increasingly imaginative. Sport OK, rowing good. In-house gym.

St. John's
St. Giles
Oxford OX1 3JP
TEL 01865 277300
Founded 1555. Central location. Strong academically and in drama (the St. John's Mummers), ents week, bar cheap. Squash courts, weights room, good reputation in rowing and football. Richest college and apparently the most 'spoddy'.

St. Peter's
New Inn Hall Street
Oxford OX1 2DL
TEL 01865 278900
Founded 1929. Young, city centre college. Strong on drama. Overall light academically. Sport popular. Sweaty ents bops, beer fests, a laddish time.

Somerville
Woodstock Road
Oxford OX2 6HD
TEL 01865 270600
Founded 1879. Margaret Thatcher, Indira Gandhi, Iris Murdoch, also Shirley Williams and Esther Ranzen. And, since 1994, men. A college in transition, set apart geographically but wholly involved. Active Women's Group. Academically keen. Cheap bar, ents focus.

Trinity
Broad Street
Oxford OX1 3BH
TEL 01865 279900
Founded 1554. Open to charge of insularity, but most like it that way and there is a good social scene here. Academic and sport profile mediocre, but Trinitarians enjoy themselves.

University
High Street
Oxford OX1 4BH
TEL 01865 276602
Founded 1249. Another college whose close-knit students are only too happy to enjoy their own scene. Beautiful architecture, oldest college in Oxford. High academic profile, good at drama. Accommodation available to all students. Underground bar the social fulcrum. Strong on sport, rowing bias.

Wadham
Parks Road
Oxford OX1 3PN
TEL 01865 277900
Founded 1610. Described as 'the most radical Oxford college', Wadhamites get involved at Uni level in most every way - politics, sport, drama. They have their own theatre. Ents popular, focus the bar. Academically relaxed but serious.

Worcester
Worcester Street
Oxford OX1 2HB
TEL 01865 278300
Founded 1714. Public school orientated until recently but now 60:40 with State. Friendly but a bit cliquey, fairly conservative. Strong on drama and music. Laid back academically. Ents include barn dances, slave auctions, as well as bops, but the Cave Bar is focus. Fair on the sporting front with excellent facilities all within college grounds.

VIEW FROM THE GROUND
by Fern Miller

City of dreaming spires, bicycles, geniuses (should that be genii?), white bow ties, champagne, punting, dusty old books, dusty old professors...I could tell you that all of this is a cliche and a fallacy, but then you wouldn't believe me. Actually, all these joys are there should you want to live that cliche at Oxford, but whilst some people choose to knock back the port and troll round town in full dinner suits, the majority get on with their lives like any other impoverished, beer drinking, essay shirking student. Thing is, in a University of this many undergraduates (about 10,000) you are bound to find people you get on with. This is made easier by the collegiate system, which splits the population up into handy bit sized chunks of around 200 to 800 people, making it all the easier to settle in with new mates in the first term, whereas a large campus style Uni can often be more intimidating...which leads me neatly on to...

COLLEGES
Make sure you investigate the differences between them. They all offer roughly the same subject options, but each has its own character (sporty, politically active, academic, more posh, less posh, etc) as well as gender breakdown so its worth finding out where you'd prefer to be, since you have the choice, and three years in a college which is famous for rowing, rugby and rabble rousing will be less than perfect if your three rs are rambling, Rembrandt and relaxation, for instance.

CITY
The city itself has two faces: term time and vacation time. Term time finds the already narrow streets packed with scarved 19(ish) year-olds on old bikes complaining of their essay crisis on the way to a college bar to buy very cheap drink (about £1.10 a pint), where they will complain about their financial crisis, before hitting one of the clubs in town, which range from the tack centres banging out Abba and Take That to the more trendy, playing house, techno and jungle to the small, expensive, jazz bistro/cocktail bars. Whilst lots of townspeople aren't over keen on the student community, you make you own luck like anywhere else. Act like a prat and you'll be treated like one. Vacation time empties the streets of these types entirely, leaving Oxford to its state as a large-ish city, well served for shops, pubs and cafes, with various diverse housing areas, from the vibrant and ethnically diverse Cowley Road, area favoured by the young and trendy, to the artsy *Guardian* reading, chic cafe society of Jericho (home of Morse).

ACCOMMODATION

Many students won't have to make any such decisions, as lots of colleges are now in a position to offer accommodation in college for all their time at University should they want it, although some still chuck you out for your second or third year. However this year 'living out' can be a blessing, allowing you to sample real life to a certain extent: something you can feel lacking in at times at Oxford. College accommodation ranges from the devastatingly beautiful 'set' (flat, essentially) located in a turret overlooking the river, to a small cupboard on a long corridor populated by smelly and loud kitchen abusers. You pays your money and you takes your chance, but it is still much cheaper than the extravagant rents Oxford landlords are fond of demanding (£55 per week on average for a shared house) and tends to include all sorts of benefits: food, hot water, not having to argue about who paid for the last bottle of washing up liquid...oh yes, and someone who comes in once a week to hoover your room, and empties your bin every day, affectionately known as a 'scout', whose other responsibilities include gossiping with you about your neighbours and having a bad back. (Don't ever, ever entertain the idea that once you enter an Oxford college, you will be able to maintain any sort of privacy, by the way.)

ACADEMIA

Terms lasts for only eight weeks. This has the effect of allowing you to spend huge amounts of your University career at home. However, don't think this makes academic life easier for Oxford students. Oh no. Term time itself tends to be high pressured, most tutors setting at least one essay a week, if not two or three. The system is tutorial based, meaning that you have one meeting with each of your tutors per week, for which you do work which you get on with throughout the week, generally by yourself. This differs between courses, arts students tending to find themselves carrying out more research on their own in libraries, bided by lengthy reading lists, whereas science subjects demand more time in labs and lecture halls. During the vacation you will not be let off to put your feet up in front of Australian soaps for six weeks. Instead you will be sent off with another extensive reading list, a few essays, dissertation, or project to finish, plus the work you didn't finish during the term when you were busy catching up on valuable social activities...

Still, there's plenty to take your mind off it. No one at Oxford lives by essays alone. You will find that from your closest friends, two will be talented musicians, another two will have played hockey/football/chess for their county, perhaps one of them will be a future prime minister, another edits the Oxford student newspaper, or is playing the lead in a production of Hamlet, and another will large it for England. The Freshers Fair, organised by the Student Union, which is the chance to sign up for a range of clubs and societies within the Uni, is the largest in Europe. Whatever you like, be it stamp collecting, indie music or ballroom dancing it will be represented there, along with some intriguing activities you've never heard of.

Whether you think it should or not, Oxford continues to send its graduates to great jobs and postgraduate courses. Some say that the atmosphere here, stressful, busy, demanding and competitive is ideal for training tomorrow's leaders. Others put it down to the old boys' network, and the fact that those that go for the places at Oxford tend to be pushy anyway. Still, I have to say, that these are huge generalisations. Just like anywhere else, Oxford houses a range of types, and, whilst the image of Oxford is one of toffs and boffins, the reality is that most of the student population here is bending over backwards to try to get people put off by that image to apply, through visiting schools, printing alternative prospectuses and so on. Look at it this way: either you'll find loads of people here just like you, or you'll be surrounded by people like no one you've ever met before. What can you lose?

OXFORD BROOKES UNIVERSITY

Oxford Brookes University
Gipsy Lane Campus
Gipsy Lane, Headington
Oxford
OX3 0BP

TEL 01865 741111
FAX 01865 483073

Oxford Brookes University
Student Union
Helena Kennedy Student Centre
Headington Hill Campus
London Road
Headington
Oxford OX3 0BP

TEL 01865 484750
FAX 01865 484799

OXFORD BROOKES UNIVERSITY

Founded	**1864**
Situation/style	**Campus**
UNDERGRADUATE PROFILE	
Application acceptance rate	**9%**
Population	**6,200**
Mature student population	**36%**
Overseas student population	**14%**
Male/female ratio	**45:55**
1st year institut. accommodation	**80%**
Approximate rent (Uni)	**£55-£70 pw**
(City)	**£50-£55 pw**

ACADEMIC PROFILE

A-level requirements: **Medium**

Law, Psychology BBB, **Publishing** CCC, **Building** CC-DDD, **Civil Engineering** CD-DDE, **Teacher Education** CC-DDD, **Human Biology** DD, **Nursing** CD

★ Large no. of combinations offered across all disciplines on the module system, High to Low requirements

Business/Admin/Mgt combs. AB-DD, **Modern Languages combs.** BB-DD, **Accountancy/Finance combinations** BBB-DD, **English, Sociology, Anthropology** AB-DD

Student/staff ratio **16:1**

1st class degree pass rate	**7.8%**	
HEFCE assessments (17 subjects assessed/approved):		
1993 **Law**		Excellent
1995 **Anthropology, English, Geography**		Excellent
German 19		
1995/6 **Modern Languages** 22		
French 22		
1996 **Sociology** 21		
Joint Funding Council's research assessment 1996 (26 subjects assessed):		
Grade 5/5*	None	

EMPLOYMENT PROFILE

Principal job market destinations:

Health, Education, Manufacturing, Retail/Wholesale, Commerce, Hotel/ Restaurant, Public Admin./Law, Personnel, Computer

PIP 1996 employers' survey: Top 3 subjects/national ranking

Languages	19th
Law	26th=
Construction & Civil Engineering	29th
Approximate % unemployed	**7%**

VAG VIEW

Darling of the ex-poly/New University League Tables, Oxford Brookes has, we are assured, made the grade. It has certainly become the model of other new and would-be new universities. OB's success, if measured only in financial terms, is truly impressive, it turns over some £60 million a year. Its modular programme, by which it has built its reputation, didn't happen overnight, it has been constructing it for more than 24 years. Among many courses which lead the way are European Business Studies, a Single Honours BA modular course which leads to a dual award - a British degree and German or French equivalent from the European end. Its Law Single Honours modular course raised plaudits from school careers teachers we spoke to. OB was the first to offer a Publishing degree and it is one of the few which commands respect in the industry. Its Languages for Business Single Honours modular course marries a linguistic, cultural approach with work placement, an introduction to the principles of business and microcomputing for European business and a final specialism in Marketing or Human Resource Mgt., which must surely rate as one of the most useful vocational/business courses around. Their Nursing and Midwifery degrees, which together with its Health Care Studies courses makes up its second most popular area of study after Business, has an attractive practical bias following a common foundation programme. And so on. OB has worked hard not only in drawing up a flexible programme but in exploring the benefits of the modular system in terms of employment, student interest and subject exploration, using the inter-displinary nature of the system to that end. What's more, the student environment in which all this takes place is itself something of a modular experience - a model of intra-cultural influences. There is a vast range of students, in terms of age, ethnic and social backgrounds. The great irony, of course, is that the OB revolution is happening in the very heartland of traditional university education.

SITUATION

Set in the beautiful University city of Oxford, the University is based on three sites. The Gypsy Lane site, the original 10-hectare campus, is on Headington Hill looking out over the city centre. Across the road is the newest campus, Headington Hill Hall, once home to the bouncing Czech, Robert Maxwell, though he was always proud to admit that he never owned it, describing it as the most impressive council house in England, which indeed it was - all six hectares of its parkland estate. Opened in 1994, Headington Hill Hall houses the newest and potentially most impressive Student Union Building in Britain (if Ed Balleny is to be believed, see below!), parts of the Business School, Arts, Publishing and Music. Finally, the Schools of Business and Education are based at The Wheatley Campus, 21 hectares, five miles or so away from Gypsy Lane.

ACCOMMODATION

There are twelve halls of residence. Most of the 2,200 rooms are found in the larger halls of residence, some of which are self-catering flats and others catered accommodation. 300 rooms are provided in smaller halls, and single sex accommodation is available if required. In addition to the halls there is a Housing Association which provides around 350 places in shared houses either leased from private landlords, or owned by the Association itself. These are usually allocated in the summer term, but mature freshers are encouraged to make late applications if they so desire. Priority for hall accommodation is given to first years, and you are advised to get your applications in as soon as you receive your Accommodation Handbook.

SPORT

Brand new sports centre - sports hall, five badminton courts, a health suite, weights training room, plus sports pitches, tennis courts, pitch and putt and playing fields at the Wheatley Campus. Characteristically, OB has an approach to sport, designed to galvanise enthusiasm among the strictly amateur sportsperson and to maximise potential among those with professional capabilities. It's known as a twin track programme.

GETTING THERE

★ By road: From the north, A423 or A34 or A43. From London, M40. From the south, M4 (J13), A34. The Wheatley campus is just off the M40 (J8), A418 signed Thame and Aylesbury.

★ National Express coach service good. Coaches and buses from Heathrow and Gatwick will stop outside Gypsy Lane campus by request.

★ By rail: London Paddington, 1:00; Birmingham, 1:30; Bristol, 1:45; Sheffield, 3:30.

VIEW FROM THE GROUND
by Ed Balleny

Oxford Brookes University is the top new university in the country.

The very fact that it is in Oxford has enough associations to attract a great number of people, but it stands on its own as a 'happening' new university, leading the others in almost everything, but most importantly as a pioneer of the modular system. As Oxford University reputedly offers the best in academic traditional university courses and education in the country, Oxford Brookes is undoubtedly the leader in vocational courses and modern university education. It offers hundreds of courses in literally everything under the sun, including Honours Degrees in Brewing and Beer appreciation (only kidding).

The main campus - Gypsy Lane - is about a mile and a half from the city centre in a part of Oxford called Headington. The Wheatley campus is about four miles from the city centre and is only of importance if you are doing Business, Education or you live there. If so, have no fear, there is a free, yes, free bus service that runs from the main campus every half an hour.

Cars are not permitted in most halls of residences or at the main campus, but Wheatley campus loves cars. If you live there a car is useful but, with the bus service, not necessary. If you are living elsewhere don't bother chums, it is not allowed, the campus will be within walking or cycling distance and who needs the hassle of potential car break-ins and friends constantly bumming lifts!

What is in my opinion one of the greatest assets of Oxford and Brookes is the access to London, by coach. This is great if you live in London, want to visit friends, go clubbing or shopping! The coach service goes from right outside Brookes to the centre of London every ten minutes at peak times, 24 hours a day. It takes about an hour and only costs £6.50 return. Beat that.

The Gypsy Lane campus is situated in a leafy suburb that seems a million miles away from the chaos of the city centre but literally only a ten minute bus ride or a 25 minute walk. The campus is modern but not an eyesore. It has separate buildings for most subjects, four 24 hour computer rooms and a food court with six different styles of food to choose from.

The Wheatley campus is also modern but the teaching facilities and sports facilities are excellent. It is a classic green field site with a lot of space for sports and it gives it a relaxing countryside environment to contrast the stress of Oxford city centre. The Wheatley bar is the epicentre of a lot of collective student piss-ups. There are two 24 hour computer rooms here too, a gym, floodlit tennis courts and football pitches, basketball courts and a 9-hole pitch and putt golf course! It is a great place for first years.

STUDENT PROFILE

There are a fair few mature students and part-time students due to the modular system. They don't make up that large a proportion of the students so don't start thinking you might find yourself the only person under twenty in your class, and they have their advantages as they always work hard and are very useful to have in your seminar group!

Foreign students and ethnic minorities are also well represented at Brookes. There are students it seems from almost every country in the world and from every ethnic background which means you will be exposed to new cultures and people that you might not have had much contact with. These students add a very cosmopolitan and international flavour which ties in with the international and in particular European outlook of the university and courses. And though this does have its advantages, it must be said some of the foreign students are very reserved and only socialise with their compatriots. Their interest in being at university in England rubs off on you, making you appreciate everything more. Also if you like travelling you can make contacts all over the world.

In general, British students are very mixed state/independent and there seems to be no divide. At Brookes there are few cliques. But if you are very inward looking and see university as purely a chance for a piss up with a bunch of people like you, then Brookes is probably not the place for you.

SOCIAL SCENE

There are 20,000 or so students in Oxford, hundreds of pubs (pretty much London pub prices), four cinemas, three theatres, art galleries, bars, four reasonable clubs and some good restaurants. Whatever you are into there is something for you and if you are really into serious clubbing, you can always jump on a bus to London and go to arguably the best clubs in the world.

Students in Headington tend to stay there. Prices are cheaper and a lot of socialising revolves around hall bars. The hall bars are the centre of socialising in the first year and they are all really good with Sky TV, pool tables, juke box, food and a wide range of beers, spirits, bottled beers and basically anything you could find at a normal pub but at half the price. There are also discos organised weekly at each bar which are mad fun.

The Union is the newest in the country and still trying to sort out its entertainment. There are two club nights, gigs and a weekly comedy night, a huge bar, food and lots of shops and things to do. It is purpose built and will be one of the most kicking university Unions in the country. Oxford has been granted the first full-time Student Radio licence in the country, so this will be an exciting and novel part of the social life at Brookes. On Monday evening everybody goes to the Park End club in Oxford for a monster night out that is run for Brookes students by Brookes students.

ACCOMMODATION

Accommodation in Oxford is notoriously expensive and this to a certain extent applies to university accommodation. It is roughly £66 a week in catered accommodation and about £50 in self-catered - 70:30 self-catered to catered for first year students. The majority of accommodation is near the Gypsy Lane campus and is mostly self-catered flats for about six. It is all very new and the facilities at each hall are first rate. As I mentioned before there is also accommodation at the Wheatley campus. This comprises six or so catered blocks. They are all brand new except for the tower which is due to be refurbished in '97/'98.

ACADEMIA

The quality of teaching at Brookes is second to none. The lecturers have often come from the real world of employment. The teaching support is extremely good and they do a lot to make life easier for you, with very good communication of work deadlines and handy hints, advice sessions, problem clinics and seminars on time management and so on. If you are planning to do a vocational course then there is no better place than Brookes and if you are looking to do Business or a course that is part of the Built Environment then these two schools are quite possibly the best in the country!

SPORT

If you are a post rugby game, ten point drinking man (or woman! - there is a ladies' rugby team) then Brookes can satisfy those needs! Brookes rugby club is well established, with a current England International as an ex- student, namely Tim Rodber. There is also a large hockey club and football club. Minor sports are also catered for with things like basketball and badminton. Brookes also has the newest university sports centre in the country with a large sports hall, its own sports shop, weights gym, fitness gym, indoor climbing wall, bar and astro turf.

One final thing, if *The Times* is to be believed Oxford Brookes students are the third most employable students after Oxford and Cambridge, something to think about, heh!

PAISLEY UNIVERSITY

The University of Paisley
High Street
Paisley
Renfrewshire
PA1 2BE

TEL 0141 848 3000
FAX 0141 887 0812

University of Paisley
Students' Association
17 Hunter Street
Paisley PA1 1DN

TEL 0141 889 9940
FAX 0141 848 9693

University of Paisley
Students' Association
Craigie Campus SRC
Beechgrove
Ayr KA8 0SR

TEL 01292 268392/610811

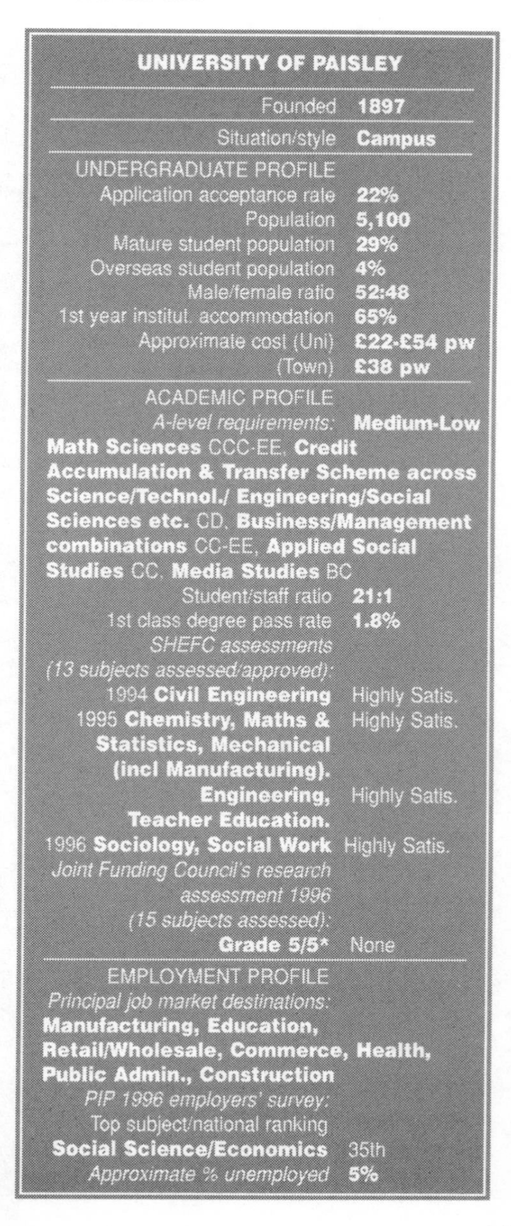

UNIVERSITY OF PAISLEY	
Founded	**1897**
Situation/style	**Campus**
UNDERGRADUATE PROFILE	
Application acceptance rate	**22%**
Population	**5,100**
Mature student population	**29%**
Overseas student population	**4%**
Male/female ratio	**52:48**
1st year institut. accommodation	**65%**
Approximate cost (Uni)	**£22-£54 pw**
(Town)	**£38 pw**
ACADEMIC PROFILE	
A-level requirements:	**Medium-Low**
Math Sciences CCC-EE, **Credit Accumulation & Transfer Scheme across Science/Technol./ Engineering/Social Sciences etc.** CD, **Business/Management combinations** CC-EE, **Applied Social Studies** CC, **Media Studies** BC	
Student/staff ratio	**21:1**
1st class degree pass rate	**1.8%**
SHEFC assessments (13 subjects assessed/approved):	
1994 **Civil Engineering**	Highly Satis.
1995 **Chemistry, Maths & Statistics, Mechanical (incl Manufacturing).**	Highly Satis.
Engineering, Teacher Education.	Highly Satis.
1996 **Sociology, Social Work**	Highly Satis.
Joint Funding Council's research assessment 1996 (15 subjects assessed):	
Grade 5/5*	None
EMPLOYMENT PROFILE	
Principal job market destinations: **Manufacturing, Education, Retail/Wholesale, Commerce, Health, Public Admin., Construction**	
PIP 1996 employers' survey: Top subject/national ranking	
Social Science/Economics	35th
Approximate % unemployed	**5%**

VAG VIEW

The University came out of Paisley Technical College and School of Art (founded 1897). In 1992 it was authorised to award its own degrees, and it became a fully fledged university in 1995, and in the same year began its development into Nursing and Midwifery. It is a new university, high on PTS and the career-orientated benefits which the modular programme brings - languages and work placements are key.

Paisley - both uni and town - seem part of the spirit of change, most of it optimistic, which is taking Glasgow from a depressed industrial city into new prosperity. Paisley is five miles to the west of Glasgow, a short way inland from the south bank of the Clyde. It is famous of course for the Paisley pattern. But this is its past out of which it is weaving a very different future.

The Uni is developing in line with the town, which has moved into Engineering, Computing and Business, and is entering into a sound relationship with these neighbouring industries, which is benefiting students in terms of work placement and careers. But it has also spread its wings further afield, some 30 miles to the south to Ayr.

This was Robbie Burns country, where, on market day, Tam o' Shanter set off for home in drunken mood to fall foul of his amorous urges. But today it is a popular dormitory town for Glasgow, where sadly you are least likely to find some 'winsome wench' pursuing you across the famous Brig' o' Doon, except in your dreams. However, Ayr does offer students a nightlife of sorts. Cub de Mar has a student night on a Thursday, and there's heavier stuff at The Powerhouse; pubs also abound.

The Uni's Ayr site accounts for Education, Media Studies, Business, Nursing & Midwifery. At Paisley it's Engineering, Information Sciences, Science & Technology, Social and Management Sciences (and more Midwifery and Nursing).

Each campus is set in twenty acres of grounds. Preference is given to first years from 25 miles out of the area for the five Paisley halls of residence, but their furnished flats go to later years. Some work is being undertaken to increase the number of flats available to increase the number of first years it can accommodate. In Ayr the accommodation is more limited, a hundred or so students in campus flats and individual study bedrooms.

Most Paisley students use Glasgow for their nightlife (see Glasgow Uni and Glasgow Caledonian), though there is an active arts centre in the town (folk, jazz, comedy), a cinema and a theatre. The Union is five minutes away from campus. It has a subterranean Subway bar, which doubles as venue for clubs nights, usual events and film screenings, and the Precinct bar, which includes a pool table. Late licences Thursday through Saturday.

GETTING THERE

★ By road: M8 links to the M74, A77 and M80, for easy access to Paisley from the rest of Scotland and the South. The A77 northbound links Ayr to Glasgow and Paisley under the hour.

★ By rail: Fast and regular service from Glasgow Central along Clyde Coast routes via Paisley Gilmore Street (0:15) and Ayr Central stations. Glasgow Central for London (6:00), Liverpool, Manchester and Birmingham (5:30). Glasgow Queen Street station (just minutes from Glasgow Central) for Edinburgh (0:50), Aberdeen (2:45), Dundee (2:00).

★ By air: Glasgow International airport is on the outskirts of Paisley.

Plymouth University

The University of Plymouth
Drake Circus
Plymouth
Devon
PL4 8AA

TEL 01752 600600
FAX 01752 232011

Plymouth University
Student Union
City Site
Drake Circus
Plymouth
Devon PL4 8AA

TEL 01752 663337
FAX 01752 251669

Plymouth University
Student Union
Faculty of Art & Design
Earl Richards Road North
Exeter
Devon EX2 6AS

TEL 01392 475039
FAX 01392 475012

Plymouth University
Student Union
Exmouth Faculty of Art
& Education
Douglas Avenue
Exmouth
Devon EX8 2AT

TEL 01395 264783
FAX 01395 222463

Plymouth University
Student Union
Seale Hayne Faculty of
Agriculture
Ashburton Road
Newton Abbot
Devon TQ12 6ng

TEL 01626 60557
FAX 01626 335181

UNIVERSITY OF PLYMOUTH

Founded	**1970**
Situation/style	**City/town**
UNDERGRADUATE PROFILE	
Application acceptance rate	**12%**
Population	**11,800**
Mature student population	**44%**
Overseas student population	**7%**
Male/female ratio	**50:50**
1st year institut. accommodation	**33%**
Approximate cost (Uni)	**£38-£50 pw**
(Out)	**£40 pw**

ACADEMIC PROFILE

A-level requirements: **High**

Law BCC-BBC, **Building/Quantity Surveying** 10, **Biological Sciences** 14-16, **Marine Biology** BCC-CCC, **Geography** 16, **Geology** CC **Civil Eng.** 10-30, **Social Policy/Sociology combs.** 14-18, **Business combinations** 12-18

Student/staff ratio	**21:1**
1st class degree pass rate	**4.4%**

HEFCE assessments (14 subjects assessed/approved):

1994 **Environmental Science, Geography, Geology, Oceanography**	Excellent
1996 **Sociology** 20	

Joint Funding Council's research assessment 1996: 20 subjects assessed

Grade 5/5*	None

EMPLOYMENT PROFILE

Employability in Industry:

MPW national league table (1996)	**49th=**

Principal job market destinations:

Manufacturing (strong on **Electrical & Electronic), Education, Retail/ Wholesale, Commerce, Public Admin./ Defence/Law, Health, Arts/Media** (strong on **Printing), Agriculture, Computer, Architecture, Eng. Design**

PIP 1996 employers' survey:

Top subject/national ranking

Electrical Engineering	39th=
Approximate % unemployed	**13%**

SITUATION

Plymouth University is spread across four sites. At the main Plymouth campus are the Faculties of Science, Technology, Human Sciences, and Business. At the Exeter and Exmouth sites are Arts and Education. While the students of *Agriculture, Food and Land Use* are stationed at the Seale-Hayne Campus in Newton Abbot.

VAG VIEW

These easterly campuses are a long way off; it's 35+ miles from Plymouth to Exeter (Exmouth is about ten miles further) and it's a good 25 from Plymouth to Newton Abbot. They are very much outposts. Seale-Hayne gets its own sports complex and Student Union and seems to be a lively place; they also have halls of residence, and all told can accommodate around 200. Overseas students get priority, the rest must find lodgings round and about, which is not difficult. In Exeter they have some Uni-managed properties, and it's a great city with plenty of activity (see Exeter Uni entry). Exmouth has a Union and about the the same amount of accommodation as Seale-Hayne, but you're much more cut off here, beautiful as it is.

The beauty of the whole area is not in doubt, and the various sites cover practically every aspect going. Plymouth has most of the resources. There is a bar on every campus, but in Plymouth they've also got a nightclub with a 2 a.m. licence every Friday and Saturday. Union club nights and live acts, and plenty of action in Plymouth itself (like the student favourite Club Oz) keep most people occupied.

Plymouth is a large post-war city that looks out across Drake's Island and the Sound to the English Channel. There are four theatres (The Drum offering 'alternative' fare), two commercial cinemas, with The Plymouth Arts Centre producing an imaginative programme of cult releases. But the real bonus to students at this Uni is the sea.

It seems to be why many come, though I dare say as many are drawn by the Uni's vigorous rise since gaining university status: four 'Excellent' assessment ratings and a 20 out of 24 can't be bad. Oceanography is one of these and therein lies the key.

Marine and Maritime courses also take in Business, Law, History, Navigation, Technology. Ocean Science - Chemical Oceanography - offers other intriguing combinations - Astronomy, Underwater Studies, Hydrography, Geology, Fisheries Studies... Students come down to the coast and pick up their BScs while winning the Offshore sailing group in the British Yachting Nationals, or finishing second while representing Britain in the World Student Yachting Cup, or winning the national Student Surfing championship, or the White Water Canoeing finals.

Plymouth's water sporting record is astonishing. At one point they had three amateur surfing champions studying there, and last year they had a mature student participating in a 3,000-mile round the world race. If Plymouth needed a niche, they have found it.

But there is more to their development than that. One of the impressive aspects of their rise is the way they are doing it in consultation with their students. They have what they call a Student Perception Questionnaire, designed to get students to identify which way to push the boat out next. And the response is there. In 1996, 45% of the total student population completed the survey, and it wasn't new rigging they were after, but a boost to the library and computing provision. Action was taken, and now a new scheme is in motion. Students are in active discussion in faculty groups about the questions to be asked in the 1998 Questionnaire.

It's the kind of strategy that may even bring the Exmouth crew into the swim of things.

ADDRESSES

Plymouth Campus, as above.
Seale-Hayne Campus,
Newton Abbot,
TQ12 6NQ
Tel: 01626 325606.
Exeter Campus,
Earl Richards Road North,
Exeter EX2 6AS
Tel: 01392 475009.
Exmouth Campus,
Douglas Avenue,
Exmouth,
EX8 2AT
Tel: 01395 255324.

GETTING THERE

★ By road: A38 from Plymouth links to the motorway network at Exeter (M5). Find Seale-Hayne (Newton Abbot) on the way (A383 off the A38) and Exmouth at Junction 30 of the M5, then the A376. Journey time London to Plymouth by road about four hours.
★ Good coach services to Exeter and Plymouth.
★ By rail to Exeter from London Paddington, 2:30; Bristol Parkway, 1:30; Birmingham New Street, 3:00; some trains go through to Newton Abbot, otherwise change.
★ By rail to Plymouth: London Paddington, 3:30; Bristol Parkway, 3:00; Southampton, 4:00; Birmingham New Street, 4:00.
★ By air: Exeter airport or Plymouth City Airport, which is four miles from campus.

PORTSMOUTH UNIVERSITY

The University of Portsmouth
University House
Winston Churchill Avenue
Portsmouth
Hampshire
PO1 2UP

TEL 01705 876543
FAX 01705 843082

Portsmouth University
Student Union
Main Site
Alexandra House
Museum Road
Portsmouth
Hants PO1 2QH

TEL 01705 843640
FAX 01705 843675

Portsmouth University
Student Union
Milton Site
Foster Hall
Locksway Road
Milton
Portsmouth
Hants PO4 8JS

TEL 01705 844185
FAX 01705 739312

Portsmouth University
Student Union
School of Art, Design
& Media Studies
Winston Churchill Avenue
Portsmouth
Hants PO1 2DJ

TEL 01705 826435

UNIVERSITY OF PORTSMOUTH

Founded	**1900**
Situation/style	**Campus**
UNDERGRADUATE PROFILE	
Application acceptance rate	**14%**
Population	**12,250**
Mature student population	**25%**
Overseas student population	**6%**
Male/female ratio	**52:48**
1st year institut. accommodation	**100%**
Approximate cost	**£38-£60 pw**
ACADEMIC PROFILE	
A-level requirements:	**Medium**

Architecture CCC, **Sociology/Social Policy & Admin.** 12, **Psychology** 20, **Geography** 18, **Business Studies** 16, **E & E/Mech./Gen. Engineering** 16, **Modern Languages** 12-14

Student/staff ratio	**14:1**
1st class degree pass rate	**5.2%**
HEFCE assessments (14 subjects assessed/approved):	
1994 **Geography**	Excellent
1996 **French** 23 **Socilogy** 20 **Italian** 20 **Russian** 18	
Joint Funding Council's research assessment 1996 (24 subjects assessed):	
Russian/Slavonic/East European Languages	Grade 5
EMPLOYMENT PROFILE	
Employability in Industry:	
MPW national league table (1996)	**44th=**

Principal job market destinations:
Manufacturing (strong on **Electronic & Electrical**), **Retail/Wholesale, Commerce, Public Admin./Defence/ Law, Computer** (strong)**, Health, Education, Construction** (strong)**, Hotel/Restaurant, Personnel, Arts/Media** (strong on **Publishing**), good record **Architecture**

PIP 1996 employers' survey: Top 2 subjects/national ranking	
Construction & Civil Engineering	27th=
Engineering & Technology	37th
Approximate % unemployed	**9%**

VAG VIEW

Portsmouth is one of the polys that have recently been transformed into universities, and it has got itself together very efficiently, with military precision you might say.

Its five faculties are Business; Environment (Art, Design & Media, Architecture, Civil Engineering, Geography, Land Mgt. & Construction), Humanities & Social Science (English, Nursing, Languages, Politics, Social Policy, Sociology, History), Science (Physical and

Biological Sciences, Pharmacy, Psychology, Sports Science), Technology (Electrical & Electronic Engineering, Mech. and Manufac. Eng., Computer Science, Maths).

Its assessments have been good, particularly in the languages area; it has no difficulty in attracting a large undergraduate contingent, even though it is beset with competition on all sides (Bournemouth, Southampton, Brighton Unis); and its employment record is good. One particular thing that Portsmouth has over other new universities, however, is its connections.

As a Fresher you are likely to hear a little more about joining the military services than you do from your average Uni OTC. You will be offered a training opportunity with either the army, the airforce or the Royal Navy Unit, and you will be told that you should apply 'before or during the first week'. Subject to passing a selection board, you will pick up experience and training, which will 'lead you to a service career, should you wish it.' There will be no hard sell, but the offer will be there, on the table. What's more, whether you do wish it or not, you will be required to read and accede to a set of university regulations. Short of the Official Secrets Act you may never see such a set of rules again. The rules will be framed in a document called, 'The Code of Student Discipline', and will relate to 'improper interference in the broadest sense'. Essentially you will have to agree not to bring the university down or into disrepute or to harm it in any way at all. You will then be given a set of Disciplinary Procedures relating to misconduct, and be advised of the tariffs of penalty, your right of appeal, and so on.

And there you were, thinking wouldn't it be nice to have a dossy three years on the Solent.

You may then be introduced to a document called 'The Use of Radioactive Materials in the University - an overview', which makes the perfectly reasonable request that you do not bring any radioactive materials on to campus, unless you've cleared it with the area RPS. Then, presumably, you can.

Do all that they say and you will have a fine time. They'll look after you very well. You'll have ents at the Union bars and thrill to live bands in the Ents Hall, and before, and/or afterwards, you will trip into town and visit any number of its clubs and pubs, which by all accounts aren't bad. You may even glow in the dark.

SETTING

Portsmouth lies on a peninsula between Southampton and Bognor Regis. The land has a harbour either side, its tip is named Southsea, and it looks on the map like the male end-piece of a jigsaw awaiting fit. The harbours which flank it are well hidden from view and the whole landpiece protrudes into the Solent well out of harms way, behind the Isle of Wight. For this reason, originally, it was earmarked as an ideal naval stronghold and for centuries it has been an important Government base.

GETTING THERE

★ If you live in Cherbourg or in the Channel Islands you could hop on a ferry, but assuming an approach by land, it's the A3(M), about two hours from London.
★ By rail: London Waterloo, 1:30; Bristol Parkway, 2:15; Birmingham New Street, 3:30; Sheffield, 4:45.
★ By air: Southampton airport.

QUEEN MARGARET COLLEGE

Queen Margaret College
Clerwood Terrace
Edinburgh
EH12 8TS

TEL 0131 317 3000
FAX 0131 317 3256

Queen Margaret College
Student Association
36 Clerwood Terrace
Edinburgh EH12 8TS

TEL 0131 339 1990
FAX 0131 317 3402

QUEEN MARGARET COLLEGE, EDINBURGH

Founded	**1875**
Situation/style	**Campus**
UNDERGRADUATE PROFILE	
Application acceptance rate	**8%**
Population	**2,500**
Mature student population	**33%**
Overseas student population	**7%**
Male/female ratio	**20:80**
1st year institut. accommodation	**60%**
Approximate cost (College)	**£46-£56 pw**
(City)	**£45 pw**
ACADEMIC PROFILE	
A-level requirements:	**Medium**

Nursing CD, **Food Sci. subjects** CC-DE, **Tourism Management** BB-CC, **Physiotherapy** ABB **Health Sci. subjects** CC-DD, **Media/Communications** CCD-BC

Student/staff ratio	**14:1**
1st class degree pass rate	**3%**
SHEFC assessments (3 subjects assessed/approved):	
1995 **Consumer Studies, Hospitality Studies**	Highly Satis.
Joint Funding Council's research assessment 1996 (5 subjects assessed):	
Grade 5/5*	None
EMPLOYMENT PROFILE	
Principal job market destinations:	

Health, Retail/Wholesale, Hotel/Restaurant, Public Admin.

Approximate % unemployed	**6%**

VAG VIEW

Queen Margaret College is mainly for women. Its history suggests this. It began in 1875 as the Edinburgh School of Cookery and was re-named in 1930 as The Edinburgh College of Domestic Science. In 1971 came the big break. Following the introduction of a range of new courses it changed its name again.

Today it is located at four sites. Its main Corstorphine campus is out towards the airport, west of Edinburgh. Then they have a campus to the northeast of the city centre just off Leith Walk. This is one of most characterful parts of Edinburgh. It was here, down 'the wide thoroughfare that joins the city of my childhood with the sea' that Robert Louis Stevenson used to walk as a child, standing and staring at the great ships in the Western Harbour, listening to the sailors as they pulled on their ropes, firing his imagination with thoughts which would later produce the novels 'Kidnapped' and 'Treasure Island'. QMC even have a hall of residence named after him.

The other two Uni sites are a Business Development Centre near Edinburgh's Haymarket Station and the Gateway Theatre, also on Leith Walk, which QMC has recently acquired as a base for its Department of Drama, and which will be a major venue for theatre during the international Edinburgh Festival. A better shop window for QM would be hard to find.

So we should not be surprised perhaps suddenly to find Drama on the menu of this college linked so definitively to the food, consumer and hospitality industries, and I

suspect that it will be an increasingly important aspect of QMC, as it is highly geared to vocational courses, and Drama can teach PTS skills better than any other discipline.

In any case, the widening of its academic scope in the 70s has long taken it beyond its original specialism. The Leith Campus is exclusively into Health: Occupational Therapy, Physiotherapy, Podiatry and Radiography. And its other focus, on business management, provides a wholly modern vocational slant to its original preoccupation with domestic science.

'Queen Margaret's is making a big push towards Media and Business Studies,' said one school careers teacher. 'Also the professions supplementary to Medicine - physiotherapy and so on.'

QMC sees higher education as a route to employment - 'People who choose Queen Margaret's mostly do so with a specific career in mind.' What's more, its Business Development Centre, which provides a training and consultancy service to the business community, offers an ideal link with industry to ensure that the passage from higher education into employment is as smooth as possible. Altogether, it has to be a winning strategy.

Accommodation at Corstorphine is in three halls of residence, some catered, some self-catered. They have a swimming pool, a gym, squash courts and an all-weather surface for tennis, football, hockey and netball. The Student Association has a bar and provides ents throughout the week, including a popular Wednesday club night, EH2, as well as the usual karaoke, quizzes, comedy acts, celtic ceilidhs, etc. See also Edinburgh Uni and Heriot-Watt for city delights - there is a night bus service, incidentally, which gets students back from Edinburgh centre to Corstorphine in the early hours.

GETTING THERE

★ By road: M8 (J2), A8 takes you first past the airport, then past Corstorphine Campus. By rail, Edinburgh to London Kings Cross, 4:30; Birmingham New Street, 5:30. Glasgow Central is 50 minutes away; Newcastle 1:30.
★ By air: Edinburgh Airport, which offers inland and international flights is nearby.

QUEEN MARY AND WESTFIELD COLLEGE

Queen Mary and Westfield College
Mile End Road
London
E1 4NS

TEL 0171 975 5555
FAX 0171 975 5500

Queen Mary and Westfield College
(University of London)
Student Union
432 Bancroft Road
London E1 4DH

TEL 0171 975 5390
FAX 0181 981 0802

QUEEN MARY AND WESTFIELD COLLEGE

Founded **1934**

Situation/style **City sites**

UNDERGRADUATE PROFILE

Application acceptance rate **13%**
Medical AAR **8%**
Population **6,500**
Mature student population **18%**
Overseas student population **12%**
Male/female ratio **58:42**
1st year institut. accommodation **100%**
Approximate cost **£55-£67 pw**

ACADEMIC PROFILE

A-level requirements: **Medium-High**
Law ABB, **Politics** BCC, **Geography, English, Modern Languages** 18-20, **Drama combinations** 20, **Computer Science, Statistics** BCC, **Aerospace, Civil, Mech. Engineering** BBB-CCD, **E & E Engineering** 18, **Biology** 16.
Medicine BBB:
★ Science 'A's required **Chemistry**
★ Additional Science 'A's preferred **Biology**
★ Addit. Non-Science 'A's acceptable **Yes except Art/Music** ★ Retakes considered **Ext. circs.**
★ Clinical contact **3rd year**

Student/staff ratio **14:1**
1st class degree pass rate **8.3%**
HEFCE assessments
(9 subjects assessed/approved):
1994 **English, Geography** Excellent
1996 **Modern Languages** 23
Joint Funding Council's research assessment 1996
(28 subjects assessed):
Pure Maths, Applied Maths, Statistics & Operational Research, Electrical & Electronic Eng., Metallurgy & Materials, English, Iberian & Latin American. Grade 5
Russian, Slavonic & E. European Languages. Grade 5*

EMPLOYMENT PROFILE

Employability in Industry:
MPW national league table (1996) **15th=**
Principal job market destinations:
Health (incl. **Dentistry**), **Retail/ Wholesale, Commerce, Manufacturing** (strong **Electronic & Electrical, Pharmaceutical), Arts/Media, Public Admin./Law, Computer, Education**
PIP 1996 employers' survey:
Top subject/national ranking
Law 30th=
Approximate % unemployed **7%**

VAG VIEW

Queen Mary and Westfield came originally out of two colleges. One - Queen Mary's - establishes its geographical and cultural roots in London's colourful East End. Founded in 1885 (though not named Queen Mary's until 1934), the college was located at the People's Palace, as it was known - QMW's base in Mile End Road today - ideally situated for its essential purpose, which was to educate the East End poor.

Westfield College, also a 19th century institution, was a pioneer in higher education for women. Men were not in fact admitted until 1964.

QMW has a later, medical foundation

too, which arises out of a merger in 1995 between the Royal London School of Medicine & Dentistry and St Bartholomew's Hospital Medical School and the formation of a new medical school within Queen Mary & Westfield. Medical students spend their first two years at Mile End and then undergo their clinical training at the Royal London in Whitechapel and Barts in West Smithfield.

There is, then, this caring, pioneering, local and culturally robust mainspring, which the Uni sees as its defining characteristic. In terms of its research record alone it is continuing to prove its pioneering spirit. The position of its campus and clinical bases certainly keeps its true to its original cultural and geographical base, and its relatively high overseas student contingent - they draw from some 100 countries worldwide - reflects the multi-cultural character of the area as it is today, though on a rather more academically selective basis than, say, East London Uni, for the entry requirements at QMW are high.

Central to this strategy is a Study Abroad programme (in arts, sciences, engineering and maths), which attracts a wide range of overseas students for a year (or even at a pinch a semester) of their Uni study period at home. QMW also have a special Unit teaching English to overseas students to prepare them for study at QMW, a programme which works in tandem with foundation courses in the students' chosen subjects. The other side of the coin is the benefit of this strategy in terms of UK students' study abroad, not only in Europe but in particular at various universities in Japan and America, where again students may opt to study either for a semester or for a full year.

Languages are to the fore throughout QMW's course programme. Being a pioneer of the modular system, which has been running here for more than twenty years, they have some experience in guiding students in their choice of module mix (every student is assigned a personal tutor). But the language element is not only part of the modular programmes, it is open to everyone whether or not they wish to combine it with a course.

They also have a higher than average local mature student population and have every intention of increasing it, seeing the benefit not only to the students themselves, but to the student community as a whole, in terms of their strong academic commitment and the experience of the real world they bring to seminars and tutorials. Optional two-week bridging courses are offered to mature students, designed to familiarise them with courses and the general ethos of the place.

All in all, what goes on at QMW is not some cleverly worked out strategy, but one which seems to flow naturally from its history and origins. What they are good at is recognising and capitalising on the advantages with which their origins and history present them. As Prof Zellick, the Principal, declares, 'It has taken over a century to shape Queen Mary and Westfield into the institution it is today.'

SITUATION

The People's Palace - the main campus - is farthest east on Mile End Road, near Stepney Green Underground station. The Royal London is a walk up the road, opposite Whitechapel Underground. Bart's is hard by Smithfield market, nearest Underground St Paul's.

QMW is part of the federal University of London, in fact it is the fourth largest constituent college.

GETTING THERE

★ QMW - Mile End Underground station is also near (5 min. walk);
★ the No. 25 bus travels Mile End Road from Oxford Circus, and the 277 from Islington way will drop you at Mile End tube. Two night buses, N76 (from Trafalgar Square) and N98 (from Victoria via Trafalgar Square).
★ Difficult parking a car round here and on campus.

ACCOMMODATION

All single first years guaranteed accommodation in traditional, catered halls, self-catered houses and flats, or UL's intercollegiate halls (see London).

UNION AND ENTS

The QMW undergraduates are a fairly cosmopolitan lot and certainly don't depend on the Union to spoonfeed them entertainment. London is their gritty oyster (again, see London University entry). However, there are good facilities at QMW Union. There's e1, the nightclub for regular hip-hop, jazz, indie, mixed dance nights and live bands, bar and cafe, and the Drapers' Arms, a pub with CD jukebox and games room. The St Valentine's Day Ball takes the whole place over - bands, bars, dinner, fairground rides. Fearful medical and dentistry students may escape to their bars.

Community Action is strong here, students get involved in the HIV/AIDS day care centre and other community works.

SPORT

There's a multigym, squash courts and gymnasium on site, and a sports ground at Theydon Bois, 45 minutes away by tube: 2 rugby pitches, 3 football, a non-turf cricket pitch. ULU provides additional facilities (see London), and there are hockey astro-turf pitches and the ULU boathouse in Chiswick.

ACADEMIA

QMW is organised academically around nine faculties: Arts (English & Drama - they have the Harold Pinter Studio Theatre, History, Politics, Modern Languages - incl. combinations within faculty and beyond, with Linguistics, Maths, Business, and Social Sciences; they have a particular strength in Russian), Basic Medical Sciences (Anatomy, Physiology, Biochemistry, Pharmacology, vigorously inspired by QMW's research programmes), Clinical Dentistry, Clinical Medicine, Engineering, Informatics & Maths Sciences, Laws (Law and Commercial Law Studies), Natural Sciences (Biol. Sciences, Chemistry, Physics) , and Social Sciences (Economics, Geography).

Medicine & Dentistry is the largest faculty, then Arts. All degree courses, with the exception of Law, Medicine and Dentistry, are modular in structure.

Queen's University Belfast

The Queen's University
of Belfast
University Road
Belfast
Northern Ireland
BT7 1NN

TEL 01232 245133
FAX 01232 247895

The Queen's University
of Belfast Student Union
University Road
Belfast BT7 1PE

TEL 01232 324803
FAX 01232 236900

QUEEN'S UNIVERSITY OF BELFAST

Founded	**1845**
Situation/style	**Suburban sites**
UNDERGRADUATE PROFILE	
Application acceptance rate	**11%**
Medical AAR	**18%**
Population	**9,200**
Mature student population	**12%**
Overseas student population	**11%**
Male/female ratio	**50:50**
1st year institut. accommodation	**88%**
Approximate cost (Uni)	**£26-£54 pw**
(City)	**£35 pw**

ACADEMIC PROFILE

A-level requirements: **High-Medium**
English, Psychology/Social Policy, Sociology, Modern Languages BCC, **Ethnomusicology, Music** BCC,CCC-CCD, **Law** ABB-AAB, **Aero./E & E/ Mech. Engineering** BCC, **Geology, Physics & Combinations** CCC, **Biological Sciences** 18. **Medicine** AAB

★ Science 'A's required **Chemistry**
★ Additional Science 'A's preferred **Biology**
★ Addit. Non-Science 'A's acceptable **Yes**
★ Retakes considered **Yes**
★ Retake offer **AAA**
★ Clinical contact **1st year**

Student/staff ratio	**14:1**
1st class degree pass rate	**8.9%**

HEFCE assessments
(18 subjects assessed/approved):

1994 **Applied Social Work, History, Law**	Excellent
1995 **English, Geology, Music**	Excellent
1995/6 **Chemical Engineering** 21 **Sociology** 19 **Modern Languages** 19 **French** 20 **Iberian** 21	

Joint Funding Council's research assessment 1996
(45 subjects assessed):

Mechanical/Aeronautical/ Manufacturing Engineering.	Grade 5*
Agriculture, Physics, Electrical & Electronic Eng., European Studies, Archaeology, Music.	Grade 5

EMPLOYMENT PROFILE

Employability in Industry:
MPW national league table (1996) **49th=**
Principal job market destinations:
Education (very strong), **Health** (incl. **Dentistry**), **Retail/Wholesale, Manufacturing** (strong on **Electronic & Electrical**), **Commerce, Public Admin./Law, Computer, Construction, Architecture** (strong)
PIP 1996 employers' survey:
Top 3 subjects/national ranking

Law	21st
Construction & Civil Engineering	27th
Engineering & Technology	27th
Approximate % unemployed	**6.5%**

VAG VIEW

Sound academically, a great number of its research subjects which didn't hit the 5 or 5 rating last year made it to 4. It was a very good result. They offer a consistently high standard of teaching. Most of their students are drawn from Northern Ireland, a few from the South. From a social point of view it might represent quite a challenge.*

SITUATION

South side of the city, a suburban area, not the most volatile.

GETTING THERE

★ An hour by air from London, with at least 24 flights a day each way.

ACADEMIA

Courses are modular in structure, the academic year is split up into two semesters of 15 weeks. Faculties include Agriculture; Arts; Economics & Social Sciences; Law; Science; Theology; Medicine; Engineering; Education.

Arts consists of English, American Studies, many Classics courses (from Byzantine Studies to Hebrew to Ancient History), Modern History, Music, courses in Philosophy and in Anthropology.

Psychology may be taken in three faculties - in Arts as a BA, in Economics & Social Sciences as a BSSc, in the Science Faculty as a BSc. There's no need for a Science A Level to read it as a BSc, which is unusual and welcome news to many arts students normally confined to reading Psychology as a Social Studies/BA course.

Medicine and Dentistry schools are part of the Medical Faculty, and there are courses in Medical Genetics, Podiatry, Nursing too. Belfast is re-vamping its medical degree like everyone else; clinical contact comes half way through second year; in the the new course programme it will occur in the second semester of the first year.

SOCIAL LIFE

City clubnights at Storm (Lisburn Rd) - retro Thursdays otherwise chart, dance & soul, The Parliament Bar (Dunbar Link), The Crow's Nest (Skipper Street). Gay venues - Network (Lower North Str) - 'UK's top house DJs every Saturday, and Club Rmani (Botanic Avenue) - 'Climatic weekend party experience every weekend.'

The Student Union ents venues comprise The Bunatee, a 'very popular, comfortable drinking establishment', situated in the basement and used as a venue for comedy, quiz nights and Sky TV, but 'mostly hangover recovery sessions'. The recently refurbished Speakeasy on the 1st Floor is for live bands, club nights, sports coverage, theme nights and comedy shows. The Mandela Hall hosts mid-week discos, concerts and Shine, 'a Friday night club that offers the best in dance music with resident and international DJs'. Then there's the Snack Bar, largest of the four venues in the Union, used on Thursdays for concerts, discos... and exams.

Union clubs and societies are not legion, right now they amount to sixteen and range through Gaelic Football, Science Fiction & Fantasy, the Christian Union (the only religious club) to Seidokan Karate.

There's a two-and-a-half week International Arts Festival, hosted by the University each November. The Festival offers more than 200 performances in every area of the arts - theatre, classical music, jazz, rock, folk music, and a whole host of lighter events, plus film at the Queen's Film Theatre.

ACCOMMODATION

Queen's Elms halls of residence are within the university area, which adds to a city campus feel. There are single, double and a few treble rooms (which may add to the cosy feel yet further.) Accommodation also offered in self-catering houses and centres.

SPORT

2 swimming pools (diving, subaqua, water polo and canoeing facilities), 3 conditioning rooms, 10 squash courts, 12 badminton courts, 4 basketball courts, 2 tennis courts, 3 volleyball courts, 2 handball courts, an Olympic handball court, a hockey court, a netball court, 2 judo squares, 4 cricket nets, 4 trampolines, a purpose-built mountain wall and facilities for Olympic gymnastics, athletics, fencing, golf, karate, bowls, yoga and archery. 17 pitches for rugby, soccer, gaelic, hockey, hurling, camogie and cricket. In addition there are 3 netball courts, a floodlit training area, 9 tennis courts and an athletics arena where the Mary Peters Track is situated.

Opportunities for golf at Malone Golf Club (3 miles away), sailing at Belfast Lough and Lough Neagh, waterskiing at Craigavon, gliding and parachuting at Magilligan, mountaineering in the Mourne mountains, caving in Fermanagh and rowing on the nearby River Lagan.

Sports bursaries available, sponsored - you guessed it - by Guinness. 15 awarded annually.

READING UNIVERSITY

The University of Reading
Whiteknights
PO Box 217
Reading
RG6 6AH

TEL 0118 987 5123
FAX 0118 931 4404

Reading University
Student Union
Main Site
PO Box 230
Whiteknights
Reading
Berks RG6 2AZ

TEL 01734 860222
FAX 01734 750337/755283

Reading University
Student Union
Bulmershe Court
Woodlands Avenue
Earley
Reading RG6 1HY

TEL 01734 318693
FAX 01734 318693

UNIVERSITY OF READING

Founded	**1892**
Situation/style	**Campus**

UNDERGRADUATE PROFILE

Application acceptance rate	**8%**
Population	**7,500**
Mature student population	**20%**
Overseas student population	**12%**
Male/female ratio	**50:50**
1st year institut. accommodation	**95%**
Approximate cost (Uni, £20 termly discount prompt pay)	**£40-£75 pw**
(City)	**£40 pw**

ACADEMIC PROFILE

A-level requirements: **High**

Law ABB, **Agriculture** CDD, **Geography** BBC, **Cybernetics & Control Eng.** BBB, **Mechanical Engineering** BBC-CCC, **Maths & Meteorology, Soils & Environ., Psychology and Zoology, Archaeology, Sociology, Modern Languages** BCC, **Building Construction, Surveying** 20

Student/staff ratio	**10:1**
1st class degree pass rate	**9.5%**

HEFCE assessments (16 subjects assessed/approved):

1994 **Geography, Mechanical Engineering**	Excellent
1995 **Environmental Sciences, Geology**	Excellent
1995 **Linguistics** 19 **French** 21	
1996 **Sociology** 22 **Italian** 20	

Joint Funding Council's research assessment 1996

Agriculture, Environmental Science, Built Environment.	Grade 5*
Psychology, Business and Management, French, Classics/Ancient History, Archaeology.	Grade 5

EMPLOYMENT PROFILE

Employability in Industry:

MPW national league table (1996) **36th=**

Principal job market destinations:

Manufacturing, Education, Commerce, Retail/Wholesale, Public Admin./Law, Health, Arts/Media, Computer, Agriculture (strong)

PIP 1996 employers' survey:

Top 3 subjects/national ranking

Computing	10th=
Languages	20th=
Construction & Civil Engineering	23rd=
Approximate % unemployed	**5%**

SITUATION

The main 300-acre Whiteknights Campus is situated between one and two miles from the centre of Reading, not the most inspiring city, last stop before London if you're a West Country boy. But you are on the verge of Kenneth Grahame country, that section of the stripling Thames between Streatley and Goring in the west to Cranbourne and Windsor Castle in the east, which so enslaved the creator of Ratty and Toad.

Education and Community Studies (Nursing - psychiatric, community nursing, youth studies, etc) are a mile away from Whiteknights, at Bulmershe Court (Woodlands Avenue).

GETTING THERE

★ By road: M4 (J11), A33.
★ An express bus service to London leaves from outside the university.
★ By rail: London Paddington, 0:30; Birmingham, 2:15; Oxford, 0:40; Bristol Parkway, 1:00; Sheffield, 3:45.
★ By air: Heathrow and Gatwick are served by bus and train.

ACADEMIA

Reading finds a place on many a sixth-former's UCAS list, though not always at the top. Yet their assessment ratings are good. It isn't an easy university to pin down. Notice the mature student population, higher than average for a pukka Uni, and there's a lean towards part-time courses, daytime and evening. Courses include Geology, Geography, Environmental Science, Agriculture, Archaeology, Zoology, Sociology, Languages, Education... There is certainly a sciences slant and yet no hard-edged definition.

One of the reasons perhaps is its Faculty of Letters and Social Sciences - central to the university's academic profile and, indeed, geographically on campus. There is no other Faculty quite like it, and some 50% of Reading's undergraduate population belongs to it. Subjects include American Studies, Sociology, Psychology, Archaeology, Politics, Languages, Economics, English, Linguistic Science, Music, Film & Drama. On the surface it's a mish-mash of arts and social sciences. But these are courses which Reading has taught throughout its history (though the faculty wasn't formed until 1957), and in the light of current thinking about the virtue of interdisciplinary course programmes, the faculty could be said to have been way ahead of its time.

Besides the 300-acre campus there are 2,000 acres of farming land for the students of agriculture, and on site is the Museum of English Rural Life, a popular tourist attraction on the one hand, but serious research business on the other. In addition to the hardware (everything from haycarts to combines) there is a unique photographic collection of rural life, which goes almost as far back as the camera (c. 1840).

Reading has a way of collecting museums on campus. The Cole Museum of Zoology resides in the foyer of the Animal and Microbial Sciences building, the Ure Museum of Classical Archaeology on the ground floor of the Faculty of Letters and Social Sciences. There are other presences too: in 1972 Reading became the first Uni to integrate an industrial R & D Group on its campus (the Philip Lyle Building). A decade later it welcomed the National College of Food Technology to Whiteknights. And Gyosei International, the Japanese founded business school (see entry) occupies its old premises on London Road. These were not chance moves. If you look at their research strengths in the 1996 assessments (see fact box) you will begin to appreciate where one of Readings' real interests lies.

ACCOMMODATION

There are halls of residence, most single study bedrooms, fully catered. Car parking is limited at some. There's also student housing. In a nice sideswipe at those who stuck Reading on their UCAS list as a back-up/insurance measure, they get Uni-managed landlady accommodation or they're out on their own in the private sector. If you want to flirt with a job in Japan, opt for St David's Hall (self-catered, en-suite) or Mansfield Hall (fully-catered). They're owned by Gyosei International.

SPORT

Sports centre (badminton courts, squash courts, fitness room, dance studio, solarium). Pitches for all outdoor team games are in abundance, and on campus, 5 floodlit tennis/netball courts, 12 grass tennis courts, and boathouses on the Thames (rowing, sailing, canoeing). Then there's a sports hall and other facilities at Bulmershe.

SOCIAL LIFE

A bit bland. I'm sure everyone has a good time on campus - Tony's Bar is the happening place on a Wednesday night, the main hall is a live hive for some of the best bands on tour, but Reading itself is a bit docile. They'll tell you about the Reading Festival, but that's in August when most Reading students have returned home. There is much artistic activity, however, from the Uni Drama Soc. and the Reading Film Theatre does its stuff on campus, as indeed does the Film & Drama Department - at the Bridges Theatre at Bulmershe. Should all else fail you could always take yourself off to 'the cool and secluded reaches of the stripling Thames, remote and dragonfly haunted,' and look for Toad.

RIPON & YORK ST JOHN UNIVERSITY COLLEGE

University College of Ripon & York St John
Lord Mayor's Walk
York
YO3 7EX

TEL 01904 656771
FAX 01904 612512

University College of Ripon & York St John Students Union
Cordukes Building
Lord Mayor's Walk
York YO3 7EX

TEL 01904 629816
FAX 01904 620559

University College of Ripon & York St John Students Union
Wilkinson Building
College Road
Ripon HG4 2OX

TEL 01765 603221

UNIVERSITY COLLEGE OF RIPON & YORK ST JOHN

Founded	**1841**
Situation/style	**Campus/ City sites**
UNDERGRADUATE PROFILE	
Application acceptance rate	**15%**
Population	**3,000**
Mature student population	**23%**
Overseas student population	**5%**
Male/female ratio	**35:65**
1st year institut. accommodation	**90%**
Approximate cost (College)	**£40-£70 pw**
(City)	**£40 pw**
ACADEMIC PROFILE	
A-level requirements:	**Medium-High**

Teacher Training CCC-DD, **American Studies** CCD, **Linguistics combinations** BC-CCD, **Film, TV, Lit. & Theatre** AB-BBC

Student/staff ratio	**21:1**
1st class degree pass rate	**4.5%**
HEFCE assessments (7 subjects assessed/approved):	
1995 **Linguistics** 19	
Joint Funding Council's research assessment 1996 (8 subjects assessed):	
Grade 5/5*	None
EMPLOYMENT PROFILE	
Principal job market destinations:	

Education, Health, Retail/Wholesale, Arts/Media, Manufacturing

Approximate % unemployed	**8%**

VAG VIEW

Founded by the Anglican Church in 1841 as a teacher training college, this is, since 1990, a College of the University of Leeds. Now, besides its BA/BSC degrees with Initial Teacher Training, Ripon and York offers a number of degrees in the areas of Performing Arts (music, Dance, Drama), Social and Cultural Studies and Social Sciences, Languages, Humanities (including Theology and History), and Environmental Sciences, Health Sciences (including Occupational Therapy to professional qualification), Leisure & Tourism Mgt., and Physical Education.

'Some of the performing arts, some of the therapies, counselling, linguistics [they offer English Studies - Literature & Language, as well as other combinations], I have heard some very good reports about,' said one school careers teacher. 'We had someone with straight As, could have gone anywhere, but chose Ripon.'

The college is situated on a very attractive, quadrangle campus in the city of York, close to the Minster, on one or two other sites in the city, and on a 50-acre site close to the centre of Ripon, another cathedral city, 25 miles to the north. It is a

beautiful and historic area, and close to both the Dales and the moors. The college operates a daily bus between the two, though students are mostly involved academically with one or the other.

With their presence in counselling, student welfare is no doubt pretty effective. There is in fact a Union presence on both campuses, bars, eateries, etc, and ents committees devise programmes which follow a similar pattern - club nights, discos, live music - with college balls in Summer and at Christmas. There are squash courts and a swimming pool on the York campus and playing fields out by York University (see York) and on the Ripon campus. Accommodation is in mixed, catered halls of residence on campus or nearby.

GETTING THERE

★ By road: north/south, the A1 feeds both York and Ripon; east/west it's the A64 for York.

★ By train: north/south, York is on the main east coast line, the fastest in Britain. Leeds, 30 mins; Sheffield: 1:15; Manchester 1:30; London Kings Cross, 2:00; Birmingham New Street, 3:00. Ripon is via York to Thirsk, the nearest station, 0:25.

ROBERT GORDON UNIVERSITY

The Robert Gordon University
Schoolhill
Aberdeen
AB10 1FR

TEL 01224 262000
FAX 01224 263000

The Robert Gordon University
Students Association
60 Schoolhill
Aberdeen AB1 1JQ

TEL 01224 262262
FAX 01224 641980

THE ROBERT GORDON UNIVERSITY

Founded	**1881**
Situation/style	**City sites**
UNDERGRADUATE PROFILE	
Application acceptance rate	**13%**
Population	**5,250**
Mature student population	**18%**
Overseas student population	**5%**
Male/female ratio	**50:50**
1st year institut. accommodation	**99%**
Approximate cost (Uni)	**£36-£50 pw**
(City)	**£45 pw**
ACADEMIC PROFILE	
A-level requirements:	**Low-Medium**

Law & Management CE, **Food Science Nutrition** EE, **Physiotherapy/Radiography** BBC/CD, **Pharmacy** CCC, **Business** CCC, **Architecture** CC, **Chemistry, Mechanical Engineering** EE, **Applied Social Studies** DE

Student/staff ratio	**14:1**
1st class degree pass rate	**6.5%**
SHEFC assessments (14 subjects assessed/approved):	
1995 **Chemistry**	Excellent
1994 **Physics**	Highly Satis.
1995 **Business & Management, Graphic/Textile Design, Maths & Statistics, Mechanical (incl Manufacturing) Engineering, Architecture**	Highly Satis.
1996 **Social Work**	Highly Satis.
Joint Funding Council's research assessment 1996 (31 subjects assessed):	
Grade 5/5*	None
EMPLOYMENT PROFILE	
Principal job market destinations:	

Health, Retail/Wholesale, Hotel/Restaurant, Manufacturing, Public Admin., Commerce, Computer

PIP 1996 employers' survey:	
Top 3 subjects/national ranking	
Social Science/Economics	27th=
Languages	29th=
Law	30th=
Approximate % unemployed	**5%**

VAG VIEW

RGU owes its foundation to philanthropist Robert Gordon, from whose estate the Robert Gordon's Hospital was created in 1750, and which developed into a college half a century later. RGU is also the beneficiary of another Aberdeen entrepreneur, an architect by name of Tom Scott Sutherland, who presented them with the grounds and mansion at which RGU's Scott Sutherland school of architecture is based, a beautiful site overlooking the River Dee. Another of RGU's constituent parts is the Gray's School of Art. It too bears the name of an Aberdeen entrepreneur, engineer John Gray; it was founded in 1885.

RGU, it would seem, is pretty well set up. And today, it makes the most of its situation in Britain's Oil Capital. It claims strong links with the oil and gas industry. Its Offshore Management Centre is part funded by the oil industry and many of its courses reflect a close knowledge of, and partnership with, this rich industry on its doorstep.

There is a School of Mechanical and Offshore Engineering and a School of

Applied Sciences, which offers a range of courses designed in collaboration with industry. But these are not the only masts to RGU's rig.

Besides Design (Architecture, Art), Science & Technology (Applied Physical Sciences, Maths Science, Engineering), the Faculty of Health & Food offers degrees in Social Studies, Food & Consumer Studies (Hospitality/Consumer Product Management) Health Sciences (Occup. Therapy, Physiotherapy, Radiography), Nursing, and Pharmacy.

There is a Faculty of Business Management, with a European flavour and a well tried passage for its Accounting & Finance graduates into the local industry (which must be unique). Post-grads are working hand-in-glove with the oil industry through applied research at the Offshore Mgt. Centre. The Faculty also incorporates degree courses in Law and Publishing.

As if to emphasise their no-nonsense, businesslike approach the student welfare services at RGU are known as Customer Services.

There is a Union, with two bars, one rig-style for roughnecks, which is apparently a regular venue for local bands (including Runrig and the Shamen). There are the usual theme nights, events and discos, and a monthly student newspaper, Cogno.

The Uni is in fact a scattered conglomeration of sites, some of which are residential. They can't quite guarantee first years a place, and their advice is to get in quick. Sporting facilities are not generous, but access allows athletics, rugby, rowing, football, archery, badminton, basketball, and of course all those outward bound activities - skiing, hillwalking, etc. which are naturally available in this beautiful area (see Aberdeen).

GETTING THERE

★ By road: approach from the south on the A92, thence onto the ring road where you'll pick up signs. From the north, approach on the A96 or the A92.

★ By air: Aberdeen International Airport links with Heathrow, Gatwick, Stansted and Luton - just over one hour's flight time.

★ Taxis from the airport cost about £8.

★ By rail: links via Edinburgh, Newcastle, find their way in around seven hours to London King's Cross; Glasgow, 2:45; Edinburgh, 2:30; Newcastle, 4:30; The line from Edinburgh to Aberdeen can be gruellingly slow.

Roehampton Institute

Roehampton Institute
Roehampton Lane
London
SW15 5PU

TEL 0181 392 3000
FAX 0181 392 3131

Roehampton Institute
Student Union
Roehampton Lane
London SW15 5PH

TEL 0181 392 3221
FAX 0181 392 3287

ROEHAMPTON INSTITUTE

Founded	**1975**
Situation/style	**City sites**
UNDERGRADUATE PROFILE	
Application acceptance rate	**10%**
Population/Full-time	**5,250**
Part-time	**600**
Mature student population	**39%**
Overseas student population	**2%**
Male/female ratio	**25:75**
1st year institut. accommodation	**55%**
Approximate cost (Institute)	**£45 pw**
(City)	**£55-£70 pw**
ACADEMIC PROFILE	
A-level requirements:	**Low**

Teacher Training CC-EE, **Performance Arts combinations** 16-CC, **Combined Humanities** CC, **Sociology or Women's Studies combs.** CC-EE, **Studies** DE, **Sport Studies combinations** 10-16

Student/staff ratio	**23:1**
1st class degree pass rate	**5.4%**
HEFCE assessments (9 subjects assessed/approved):	

1995/6 **English Lang. & Linguistics** 22 **Sociology** 20

Joint Funding Council's research assessment 1996 (13 subjects assessed):	
Grade 5/5*	None
EMPLOYMENT PROFILE	

Principal job market destinations:
Education, Retail/Wholesale, Manufacturing, Personnel, Commerce, Arts/Media, Hotel/Restaurant, Health, good record **Sport**

Approximate % unemployed	**11%**

VAG VIEW

Roehampton Institute is heavily into vocational courses in the Arts, Education, Social Sciences, Sciences and Sports areas. Degrees are validated by Surrey University, though they are empowered to award their own. Their Mission Statement emphasises the 'humanistic and Christian principles of its four historic foundations', which would sound like a bit of a contradiction if it were not for the fact that they are not in the business of pushing religion down your throat. What they do push is the humanist/cultural influence - it's a caring environment which does specially well in caring profession courses such as healthcare and therapeutic work (and teaching too, under their regime). Digby Stuart College (Arts & Humanities) has a Roman Catholic foundation; Froebel College (Education) follows the teachings of Friedrich Froebel, the caring chappie who invented Kindergartens; Southlands College (Social Sciences) has a Methodist inheritance; and lastly Whitelands College (Science) has a Church of England base, with a Rev. at the top.

It sounds like it might be a geographically scattered base, but it isn't.

In fact all but Whitelands, which is not far away, by Putney Heath and Wimbledon Common, will be together at Roehampton Lane by the 1997 intake. It is a pleasant place to be, if a bit off the public transport map. They'll tell you that you are most unlikely to get an Institute parking permit, and without one you can't bring a car on to the premises. Somehow Gina Wright, our ballet dancing correspondent, made a case for one, but I was too polite to ask how.

They are not dispersing the College framework after Southlands joins Digby and Froebel at Roehampton Lane. Why should they? This is a collegiate institute, which enjoys the distinct academic and social character of its colleges, though there is a move to make one Union only.

ADDRESSES

Digby Stuart College,
Roehampton Lane,
London SW15 5PH
Tel: 0181 392 3200, Fax: 0181 392 3231.
Froebel College,
Roehampton Lane,
London SW15 5PJ,
Tel: 0181 392 3300, Fax: 0181 392 3331.
Southlands College,
Wimbledon Parkside,
London SW19 5NN,
Tel: 0181 392 3411, Fax: 0181 392 3431.
Whitelands College,
West Hill,
London SW15 3SN,
Tel: 0181 392 3500, Fax: 0181 392 3531.

GETTING THERE

Roehampton campus is a fifteen to twenty minute walk from Barnes British Rail station and is served by the No. 72 bus from Hammersmith Underground (Piccadilly, Metropolitan, District Lines), and the No. 265, which runs from Putney Bridge Underground station (District from Earls Court). Whitelands College is twelve minutes walk from East Putney or Southfields Underground stations. The No. 170 bus connects the college with Clapham Junction British Rail station.

ACCOMMODATION

Good if you can get it. Variously in single/shared study bedrooms, halls or houses. Halls are mixed with 'a few restrictions on visitors'. Amenities include launderettes, kitchens, TV and games room, coffee bars, refectories, snack bars, common rooms. Colleges cater for vegetarians. If you miss out, call the Accommodation Office.

UNION

At present each of the four colleges has its own Union facilities and bureaucracy, which provides individually tailored ents programmes - weekly discos, live bands, debates, quiz nights, etc.

High point is the Summer Ball. (See also London for clubs, etc.)

SPORT

Very strong department and while its egalitarian principles ensure sport for all, the big boys make it at regional and national student level. They have a strong rugby side and it is worth noting (for the game's real aficianados) that arguably the best rugby club in the world - Rosslyn Park - is more or less just over the road. At Froebel there are indoor and outdoor facilities for football, hockey, basketball, volleyball, and badminton. Plenty of local pitches for other team sports.

ACADEMIA

With the exception of Psychology & Counselling, and Teaching Studies, all courses may be studied part-time at the Institute, typical three-year course durations (four years in the case of some language specialisms) stretch to four to seven years part-time. They follow a modular scheme, and exploit well the opportunities for inter-disciplinary combinations which the system encourages, as our correspondent notes. Within timetable limitations, Combined Honours degrees allow students to design their own programmes to suit interests and career aspirations.

Academic Faculties include Arts and Humanities (from Bookbinding and Calligraphy to Dance and Music Therapy, from Eng. Lit. to Film & TV Studies, from Art in the Community to Theology); Education offers imaginative combined studies programmes; Sciences include various courses in Applied Technology and Computing, Life Sciences (from Health Studies to Biology, from Nutrition to Neurobiology & Stress Management), Psychology & Counselling, Sport Studies; Social Sciences includes the Departments of Business Studies, Environmental & Geographical Studies, Sociology & Social Policy., and the Dept. of Women's Studies.

VIEW FROM THE GROUND
by Gina Wright

Roehampton combines the best aspects of living in London. I cannot imagine a more perfect site - a peaceful green campus set in landscaped grounds with lakes and trees, yet near enough to buses and tubes to make the journey into central London in about half an hour. Froebel, Digby and the newly built Southlands College are situated on the edge of Richmond deer park, Barnes Common and the River Thames close by. Whitelands College is by Putney Heath and Wimbledon Common. Regular sightings of foxes, badgers, herons and of course many squirrels make you feel in the middle of the countryside, yet at the same time it is on the edge of the city. These four idyllic natural parklands are perfect for walking, running, cycling, riding, picnicking, blackberrying, mushrooming (mushroom forays regularly take place in the autumn), and anything else you can think of.

The regular inter-college link bus is an excellent free way of getting around. For myself, as a part time student dashing in and out at odd times, my Froebel student car parking permit is an essential plus. Especially now Roehampton Institute is located on a red route.

Being small in comparison to many other Unis, Roehampton is a friendly place, and although as a part-timer my contact with other students is limited, when preparing for group seminar activities in twos and threes you get to know one another pretty well. The students I have met come from a wide area and bring with them an assortment of earlier experiences. This is partly because Roehampton operates a successful student exchange programme.

ACADEMIA

For my part, as a mature student studying Education part-time, I find my course fascinating. From the philosophical angle to the sociological and psychological aspects, it's challenging, stimulating stuff, professionally delivered with never a dull moment - loads better than I ever imagined it could be.

There is a strong research culture at Roehampton. The Institute's Research and Commercial Development Unit is substantial and dynamic, and the library and Learning Resource Centre, Computer Unit, Reprographics Unit and Television Production Unit all provide state of the art support facilities on site. Even the first recorded episodes of 'Neighbours' are available to view in the library!

There is also a free internal, inter-departmental telephone service plus 'e-mail' accounts for all students, which makes vital communication simple, fast and effective. And for students with children there is a creche and nursery, although inevitably over-subscribed.

SPORT

For serious sportsmen and women and budding sporty types Roehampton has a formidable record of achievement countrywide. All the usual games are offered, and there are many more ladies teams than are generally found. (Is it not every man's dream to have a ratio of about three ladies to one man - at Froebel it's more like 24:1!)

The ladies teams challenge top clubs and universities around the country, occasionally teaching 'the boys how to play the game!' The men's football team won the BUSA Cup in 1996, beating Edinburgh in the final. Rugby, hockey, basketball and badminton teams are all of a high standard and got through to final matches last year. The hockey team train near Chiswick bridge on the acclaimed, 'Hounslow Pitch'. The Dangerous Sports Society include paintballing and parachuting among their less conventional activities.

Should injury on the sports field occur, the Roehampton campus medical centre comes into play, and I can say with confidence (as it's staffed by two of my best friends - a GP and a nurse) that whatever your illness or injury, sick undergraduates a long way from home couldn't have a more friendly, caring team.

Wednesday afternoons are for sports training, but Wednesday nights are when the real fun starts. The social side of all the sports clubs is a must, and in the case of men's hockey it can be seriously dangerous! The initiation ceremony to join the team involves swallowing vast quantities of beer laced with liqueurs and even Mars bars, and all without falling off the rim of a bucket!

UNION, ARTS & ENTS

For part-time job opportunities to supplement the grant or for work experience Roehampton is very active. The student employment officer works hard on this, as does the Union, and the notice boards everywhere are packed with information. This year the Roehampton Institute Student Union (RISU) is responsible for the recruitment of temporary staff for the pre-championship and the Wimbledon Tennis Championship itself, which is only a short walk from Whitelands College. Among intriguing jobs on the notice board recently were positions in playschemes, holiday camps, the Chelsea Flower Show, the Volvo PGA gold championship, the Henley Royal regatta, the Paris Air Show, the Open Golf Championships and Buckingham Palace garden parties, and there are regular ads for nannying, tutoring and helping out at special needs schools.

For entertainment, as a lover of dance I enjoy the many reasonably priced concerts promoted by the active Dance Department. A series of open events in the outstanding Michaelis Theatre attracts audiences from both inside and outside the Institute. Students are given every opportunity to perform their own works, view professional companies and share the results of collaborating with well known dance companies. Only today on the notice board I caught sight of a lunchtime ballet class with live pianist - perfect for me, but there is something for everyone whatever their interest.

On the relaxation side, life begins at Roehampton with a bang - a brilliant Freshers Week, which for me included a boat party on the Thames and a trip to the 'Ministry of Sound' (Elephant and Castle). Then the year culminates in the infamous, extravagant Summer Balls. Froebel boasts one of the best in Britain - my friends in the Union told me that last year RIL had to obtain special clearance from the flight authorities at Heathrow airport for the dazzling light show. Club UK dee-jayed.

Besides the on-site bar and cafes, and local pubs, regular fun is had at the local nightclub, the Theatre, which hosts a student night every Tuesday (and, incidentally raised money to donate a minibus to RIL. Another favourite for lovers of trippy, way out, ambient dance music is the Whirly-gig club - a roving nightclub at present in nearby Hammersmith... Oh to be twenty years younger!

Rose Bruford College

Rose Bruford College
of Speech & Drama
Lamorbey Park
Burnt Oak Lane
Sidcup
Kent DA15 9DF

TEL 0181 300 3024

Rose Bruford College of Speech
& Drama Student Union
Lamorbey Park
Burnt Oak Lane
Sidcup
Kent DA15 9DF

TEL 0181 300 4949
0181 694 9021

ROSE BRUFORD COLLEGE	
Founded	**1950**
Situation/style	**Campus**
UNDERGRADUATE PROFILE	
Application acceptance rate	**6%**
Population	**430**
Mature student population	**40%**
Overseas student population	**6%**
Male/female ratio	**40:60**
1st year institut. accommodation	**30%**
Approximate cost (College)	**£60 pw**
(Town)	**£45 pw**
ACADEMIC PROFILE	
A-level requirements:	**Unspecified**
★ Often performance related	
Student/staff ratio	**18:1**
1st class degree pass rate	**5.2%**
EMPLOYMENT PROFILE	
Principal job market destinations: **Arts/Media, Education**	
Approximate % unemployed	**24%**

VAG VIEW

Rose Bruford was the first drama school to get into the business of awarding degrees to its undergraduates (see also Central School, where Rose herself was a student in 1921). They are validated by Manchester Uni. On the face of it, the idea seems rather odd in a profession which spins on personal contacts, luck and ingrained talent which is either evident or it is not. It seems less odd at Central, which includes Speech Therapy and a teaching bias.

There are three faculties: Theatre (Acting, Actor Musician - an actor with an extra bow to his string, Directing, and Acting USA/UK - the plum course which guarantees you a sojourn in Texas); Production (Costume, Lighting, Music Technology - composition, performance and recording), Scene Construction & Props, Stage Management, Theatre Design; and finally Distance Learning. This last faculty includes a correspondence course in Opera Studies which on the face of it seems like a very good idea. Materials are also available for Theatre Studies, and Theatre & Performance Studies.

All said, this is a leading drama institution with a fine reputation and two excellent campuses, one in Creek Road, Greenwich (specialist recording studios, MIDI lab, lighting workshops, performance studios) and one in Sidcup - an 18th century Kentish park called Lamorbey Park. It could be that pretty soon all operations will be at Lamorbey. At time of writing they have in a Lottery bid, which, if successful, will transform Rose Bruford. At present, however, first years spend most of their time at the Sidcup campus, travelling to Greenwich when required (there's a regular train service to New Cross station). Accommodation in London is extended to halls of residence owned by Greenwich Uni and Goldsmiths College, so our figure of 30% first years may well be out of date. Certainly they claim to ensure, one way or another, that every student is housed before they arrive. There is a Studio theatre at Greenwich, and at Lamorbey Park the 100 seater Barn Theatre, and, just completed, a theatre-in-the-round with a 450 seat capacity, which as yet is still wanting a name.

THE ROYAL AGRICULTURAL COLLEGE

The Royal Agricultural College
Stroud Road
Cirencester
Gloucestershire
GL7 6JS

TEL 01285 641404
FAX 01285 650219

ROYAL AGRICULTURAL COLLEGE	
Founded	1845
Situation/style	Campus
UNDERGRADUATE PROFILE	
Application acceptance rate	25%
Population	450
Mature student population	15%
Overseas student population	11%
Male/female ratio	60:40
1st year institut. accommodation	100%
Approximate cost	£67-£100 pw
FEES	
Approx. annual tuition fee	£4,250-£6,500
ACADEMIC PROFILE	
A-level requirements:	Medium

VAG VIEW

The Royal Agricultural College is involved at the forefront of research with bodies like the Long Ashton Research Station and other research centres in the EU. On its 770-hectare farms it conducts experiments in farming practice (they include a 50-acre site which has been farmed organically for nearly a decade) and through its Industry Associate Scheme it calls on industry (farming, food processing, agrochemical companies) to keep it abreast of changing markets and management techniques. So what you get at its impressive campus in Cirencester is a completely up-to-date education, and not only in farming but in Agribusiness and Land Management, all from an international perspective - they run the largest agri. student European exchange programme in the country. They were the first agri. college and the strong impression they give is of strength in depth. It's the Principal's boast that there's 'hardly a major farming/business or land management employer in the UK and beyond that doesn't have a former RAC student in a decision-making position.'

Degree courses offered include: Agriculture & Land Management, Crop Production, Ecology & Mgt., Farm Mechanization & Mgt., International Agribusiness Mgt., Int. Agric. and Equine Business Mgt., Int. Agric., Land and Business Mgt., Rural Estate Mgt. and Rural Land Mgt.

They don't seem to be the kind of courses you'll need for 400 acres up on the moors, and anyone who comes here will have serious intentions not to have his hands in the soil all his life, I dare say. Tuition fees alone will weed out the uncommitted - £6,500 per year for 1997 (you get a little more than 10% back from the LEA). Some bursaries and scholarships are available, however, and if you look at it in terms of your average fees at a decent public school, it's a pretty good deal, for the best.

Set, as it is, in the midst of some glorious Cotswold countryside, you're really better off studying farming her than most anything else. Accommodation guaranteed for first years is in twin or single study rooms. All-in price around £3,000 per year. There is a bar and Union organised ents, which include four balls a year. Sports are big news, especially rugby - Richmond/England flanker, Ben Clarke is former student - and hockey. Then there is clay pigeon shooting, karate, squash, riding, etc. It makes you feel tired just thinking about it.

GETTING THERE

★ Within easy reach of national rail and motorway links (M5, M42 - Birmingham Airport two hours), (M5 and M6 - Manchester three hours), (M4 - Severn Bridge/Wales one hour) and (M4 to Heathrow Airport and London - two and a half hours).

★ By rail: two hours to Oxford, London Paddington; Birmingham New Street around 3:30.

ROYAL FREE HOSPITAL SCHOOL OF MEDICINE

Royal Free Hospital
School of Medicine
Rowland Hill Street
London
NW3 2PF

TEL 0171 830 2686

ROYAL FREE SCHOOL OF MEDICINE	
Founded	**1874**
Situation/style	**City site**
UNDERGRADUATE PROFILE	
Application acceptance rate	**7%**
Population	**540**
Mature student population	**10%**
Overseas student population	**6%**
Male/female ratio	**48:52**
1st year institut. accommodation	**100%**
Approximate cost	**£50-£80 pw**
ACADEMIC PROFILE	
A-level requirements	**ABB**
★ Science 'A's required	**Chemistry**
★ Additional Science 'A's preferred	**Biology**
★ Addit. Non-Science 'A's acceptable	**Yes**
★ Retakes considered	**Ext. circs.**
★ Retake offer	**AAB**
★ Clinic contact	**3rd year**
Student/staff ratio	**2:1**
1st class degree pass rate	**1.9%**
Joint Funding Council's research assessment 1996 (7 subjects assessed):	
Anatomy, Pharmacology.	Grade 5*
Community/Clinical, Biochemistry.	Grade 5
EMPLOYMENT PROFILE	
Approximate % unemployed	**0%**

VAG VIEW

There seems to be a polarisation going on in the Medical Establishment. Along with the current merger plans of Charing Cross/Westminster with Imperial, and the pulling together into Queen Mary & Westfield of Barts and the Royal London in 1995, the Royal Free is expected to join with University College London to form a new Medical School in 1998/9. A new curriculum will be active from some time in 1998, but is unlikely to affect students until the 1999 intake. The Royal Free has established a 'goals and objectives' group to research thoroughly their response to the GMC's recommendations for new clinical and practical emphases in medical schools' curricula. The Free has a reputation for leading the way and is unlikely to be pushed in any direction which it has not considered in depth. Current practice is for no regular clinical contact before Year 3, a fact which may suit many of the hospital's patients. Principal among its firsts is that the Royal Free was the first medical school to accept female undergraduates - in fact it was founded in 1874 with the idea of qualifying female practitioners - and after 1948, when a mixed gender intake became obligatory, it was the first to achieve equality of intake.

As members of the University of London, students automatically have access to ULU's facilities, sporting and social (see London), but most of the socialising centres on the bar at the Free and there is no shortage of sporting facilities of their own. As James Varley points out below, there is a keen sporting interest at the Free. It shares a 24-acre athletic ground in Enfield with The School of Pharmacy and has on-site facilities for netball, football and badminton, and a gym, weights room, two squash courts and swimming pool. But whatever are the many arguments in favour of the Free over other medical, sporting or social training grounds, its position in one of the most sought-after areas in London, overlooking Hampstead Heath, must, as James suggests, surely be counted among them.

GETTING THERE

★ Belsize Park Underground (Northern Line) or overland railway, Hampstead Heath.
★ Bus routes: C11, C12, 24, 26, 46, 168, 268.

VIEW FROM THE GROUND

by James Varley

I came to this hospital through the lottery of Clearing, and from the north, so had never heard of it before. Not having a real look round at the interview (as I was going to take the place if I got it, there seemed little point), it was only when I started my studies here that I saw what it was like. Personally, I think the place is great, but then I would, wouldn't I? I hope I get across a flavour of it so that you'll want to come to, but I have made more sure of listing the downsides than the upsides, so nobody gets any nasty surprises and comes looking for me with an axe.

Hampstead is one of the safest, most aesthetically pleasing and cultured boroughs of London. Not having the terrible snobbery and superficiality associated with Kensington and Chelsea, its artistic charm and history attract a wide range of trendy intellectuals, celebrities and literati. The main area of Hampstead, around the High Street and Heath Street, is smothered with attractive small cafes and restaurants (Pellicano, the Dome, House in the Hill); clothes shops such as Gap, Kookai, Monsoon; and other types such as Waterstones, Our Price et al. Basically everything your average middleclass type requires.

Hampstead is also blessed with the Heath, the largest area of parkland in London, and the extensive studies of it painted by Turner can be seen in the stately home it possesses - Kenwood House.

The area is well connected in the travel sense. Hampstead, and closer to the hospital itself, Belsize Park have tube stations on the Northern Line. Close to the hospital is the overland North London line, and the area is well serviced with buses. You can be in the centre of London within twenty minutes easily.

However, all these attributes do have their downside, in that it's a very desirable location to live, and as a result is expensive to rent property. All the students manage despite this, either through the possession of wealthy parents, part-time jobs or shrewd money management. Alternatively you can live a bit further afield in Golders Green, Kentish Town or other areas, which can work out twenty quid cheaper than the seventy-five pounds average in Hampstead.

SOCIAL SCENE

The Free Bar is what everything revolves around. Meeting up for sports, relaxing between ward rounds/lectures, cheap parties held there every month or so. Food is OK, but this is a hospital so it won't be winning any Michelin awards. Hampstead, and Camden are stuffed with good pubs and clubs: Hampstead being pub (of the nicer variety), cafe and restaurant orientated. Camden is more clubby. Camden is a great place. More downmarket than Hampstead its markets attract crowds, its nightlife brings in even more people. In the surrounding area there are plenty of sports facilities, cinemas, bars, restaurants to cater for any taste and wallet. Not including all the amazing galleries, concerts, theatres and museums that come with being in London.

I have never heard of any racism at the Free, there being such a diverse mix it would be difficult. Nor are there any student-local tensions. Medicine being a well respected, intellectual profession, it's probably the ideal higher education establishment to put in the middle of Hampstead.

STUDENT PROFILE

The Free's biggest selling point has to be how friendly it is. Everyone always says this about wherever they study, but here it is actually true. The majority of first years say it's the big reason that swayed them, having got a feel for the place on their interview day. As pre-clinical and clinical students are all taught on the same site, there isn't the snobby split between the two phases of Medicine that commonly exists elsewhere. Because of this, everyone has friends in every year.

This is very useful, as someone will have been there whatever problems you may have. As the Free is quite a small place the type of person that gets the most out of being here is someone who's not afraid of trying to get to know everyone. The quieter types with the smaller social circles might find it a bit difficult sometimes.

There is a broad range of people, although if anything there is a small majority of the public schooled, monied types. Overall it is one of the more laid-back teaching hospitals, though we do get some of the best Final results in the University of London - receiving several times in the last few years the Gold Medal, a prize for the best Medical finalist in London. As the Free started out as a teaching hospital purely for women, the mix between male female is always at least 50:50, if anything there being slightly more females. We do take a few foreign students, maybe 5% of each year's intake, some of whom integrate into the social life, some of whom don't.

Politics aren't a major theme of the Free, but neither is it all based around getting pissed up. If anything the Free is sporty, there aren't great numbers into debating or any of the more obscure university pursuits. Being in London, there is nothing you can't do if you want to. This is different from, say, a provincial or campus university where if they haven't got it, that's it. At the Free, if we haven't got it, go look for it - it's out there somewhere.

ACCOMMODATION

The majority of first years stay in Frances Gardner Halls. These are situated in West Hampstead, which is not a bad area, and are about half an hour's walk away from the hospital. The halls themselves are not amazing, but are warm in the winter, equipped with washing machines and dryers, and pretty much everything works. You won't impress anyone by living there, but you will have a good time as a 'we're all first years together' sort of atmosphere soon develops. It's pretty likely you'll have to share a room though, and it's self-catering.

The other main choice for Freshers are the University of London Inter-collegiate halls in Euston. Their upsides are that you get to meet people not doing Medicine, they are catered, and you get to spend time right in the centre of London. Downsides include having to be there on time for meals, taking a bit long to get to know the rest of your year group, and travelling back late can be a hassle, as tubes stop around half past twelve. First years do sometimes stay in private accommodation, but this is rare. The big second year challenge is to form a flat with a suitable group of friends, and then to find a suitable flat, which is no mean feat. It can be quite difficult to find a suitable place, within your price range and within whatever distance of the Free you're looking for. However, people always manage sooner or later, and the standard of accommodation is generally quite high. There aren't any student ghettos as such, although there are better and worse areas.

This being London, accessibility isn't ever really ever a hassle. People who live further afield, past Golders Green, don't have it quite as convenient as the rest of us though.

CLUBS, SPORTS

The biggest four clubs are the main sports: rowing, rugby, football and hockey. These have the most members and the biggest social circles. The Free also has a large and successful Sub-Aqua society, which is threatening these four in number of members and socially. Rugby and football have mixed fortunes, one year being promoted and Hospital Cup finalists, the next relegated/mid-table and knocked out at the first round. Other clubs include hiking and trekking, badminton, water polo, golf, cricket, photographic, art, Tolkein society (drinking), and many others that I can't think of at the moment. Religiously speaking there is the Christian Union and the Islamic society. Musically and dramatically the Free is quite active, the Music Soc. putting on a few concerts every year, the Drama Soc. having a musical and play every year.

ROYAL HOLLOWAY COLLEGE, UNIVERSITY OF LONDON

Royal Holloway and
Bedford New College
Egham
Surrey
TW20 0EX

TEL 01784 434455
FAX 01784 437520

Royal Holloway
Student Union
Egham Hill
Egham
Surrey TW20 0EX

TEL 01784436045/439839
FAX 01784 433864

ROYAL HOLLOWAY COLLEGE

Founded	**1886**
Situation/style	**Campus**
UNDERGRADUATE PROFILE	
Application acceptance rate	**13%**
Population	**4,600**
Mature student population	**21%**
Overseas student population	**16%**
Male/female ratio	**45:55**
1st year institut. accommodation	**100%**
Approximate cost	**£45-£65 pw**
ACADEMIC PROFILE	
A-level requirements:	**High-Medium**

Biol./Phys./Math Sciences BBC-CCC, **German** ABC-BBC, **Italian** BBC, **Geology** CCC, **Sociology combinations** ABC-BCC

Student/staff ratio	**14:1**
1st class degree pass rate	**14.2%**

HEFCE assessments (11 subjects assessed/approved):

1993 **History**	Excellent
1995/6 **Geology**	Excellent

1995/6 **French** 21 **German** 19
1996 **Italian** 21 **Sociology** 21

Joint Funding Council's research assessment 1996 (19 subjects assessed):

Drama/Dance/ Performing Arts, Music.	Grade 5*
Psychology, Geography, French, Russian, Classics/ Ancient History, History.	Grade 5

EMPLOYMENT PROFILE

Employability in Industry:

MPW national league table (1996)	**41st=**

Principal job market destinations:
Retail/Wholesale, Commerce, Arts/Media (strong), **Manufacturing, Computer, Public Admin.**

Approximate % unemployed	**5%**

VAG VIEW

Royal Holloway is no ordinary college. To begin with it is one of only two rurally based colleges of the University of London, Wye being the other. It is situated on a 120-acre campus at Egham in Surrey, to the south-west of London.

Royal Holloway has been called 'London's Country Campus', and it is certainly a beautiful spot, made distinctive by the so-called Founder's Building, an extraordinary 'surprise' of a building, which covers a very large area. It is not a house, more like a castle with a huge internal space or quadrangle, the actual building only marking out the limits of this space, not covering it at any point other than when an errant 'wing' cuts the huge quadrangle into two, joining one side of the building to the one opposite. It is red brick, with stone columns and porticos, but delicately multi-turreted, looking fairytale-like from afar. Students, when they see it for the first time, are amazed. It begs the term picturesque or perhaps exuberant and it is something of a foible, a copy of the Chateau de Chambourd in the Loire. It was built by Thomas Holloway, who in 1886 founded a college for women there.

Nearly a century later, in 1985, this college merged with another college founded for women (by Elizabeth Jesse Reis in 1849) called Bedford College, to form Royal Holloway's full name, Royal

Holloway and Bedford New College.

Here University of London degrees are offered in Biological and Physical Sciences, Maths, Computer Science, Humanities, Languages, Arts, Social Sciences, and Management. Altogether 31 subjects are offered, but they are deliberately not grouped in faculties or schools as I have done because over the years RH has developed a course unit method of study, which is not modular, but which allows imaginative but coherent groupings, for example Maths and Psychology.

It is a setting which favours concentrated and imaginative work, and students interviewed almost uniformly mention the workload. But when you look at the Department of Drama, Theatre & Media Arts, for example, which just earned a 5 rating in the Joint Council assessments (that's international excellence), you can begin to appreciate Royal Holloway's purpose.*

Being relatively close to London, you would think that it'd be easy enough to get away when things got a bit too claustrophobic. But, as one of the students says, it can take 45 minutes to an hour to get where you're going to in central London, door-to-door. From that point of view RH's position will not be to everyone's taste. But others will warm to the inherent advantages of being away from the bustle and noise of London (and yet near enough to its resources and entertainment to make use of the city).

The RH experience does incorporate quite a lot of its own entertainment. There are 5 or 6 events each week - discos, live bands (D:Ream, Baby D, Dreadzone), comedy, etc, and there are four or five bars around campus. The main watering holes are The Stumble Inn, Holloways and Crosslands, and Times Square, a coffee bar, is a popular meeting place. The ents programme reaches its zenith with the Summer Ball and Champagne Breakfast in the Founder's Quad, dusk to dawn.

There are also concerts and plays throughout the year, performed by the undergraduates in these particularly good departments as part of their course programmes.

Sport also figures strongly. There are pitches on campus for hockey, football, rugby and cricket, tennis courts, a sports hall and multi gym, and a new all-weather pitch is probably by now completed. A swimming pool may be used at nearby Windsor. They are ranked third in the BUSA small Uni division.

GETTING THERE

★ By road: M25 (J13), A30.

★ By rail: London Waterloo, 0:35; Woking, 0:45 (change at Weybridge); Reading, 0:40.

The Royal Veterinary College

The Royal Veterinary College
Royal College Street
London
NW1 0TU

TEL 0171 468 5000
FAX 0171 388 2342

ROYAL VETERINARY COLLEGE	
Founded	**1791**
Situation/style	**Rural & city campus**
UNDERGRADUATE PROFILE	
Application acceptance rate	**8%**
Population	**460**
Mature student population	**17%**
Overseas student population	**6%**
Male/female ratio	**37:63**
1st year institut. accommodation through UL	
Intercollegiate system, *see* London University	
Approximate rent (city)	**£55-£70 pw**
ACADEMIC PROFILE	
A-level requirements:	**AAB**
Student/staff ratio	**4:1**
Joint Funding Council's research assessment 1996 (31 subjects assessed):	
Grade 5/5*	None
EMPLOYMENT PROFILE	
Approximate % unemployed	**1.4%**

VAG VIEW

One of only six places to offer a degree in Veterinary Science. The others are universities - Bristol, Cambridge, Edinburgh, Glasgow and Liverpool.

Founded in 1791, this college was the first establishment of the veterinary profession in this country. The Camden Town campus is its original position, but RVC has since acquired a country estate in Hertfordshire, where the departments of medicine and surgery are located.

For the first two years you will be based at Camden, where the Department of Veterinary Basic Sciences is housed, along with part of the Department of Pathology and Infectious Diseases.

There is a refectory, bar and common rooms. During your course you will also gain experience at the Beaumont Animal's Hospital, also in Camden, examining case histories, and assisting with animal diagnosis and treatment.

The 230 hectare campus at Hawkshead is in Hertfordshire (Potters Bar) and includes the Departments of Farm Animal and Equine Medicine and Surgery, Small Animal Medicine and Surgery and the rest of the Department of Pathology and Infectious Diseases. In addition there is an Equine Hospital, the Queen Mother Hospital for Animals and a Large Animal Practice on site. The College's working farm is just next door. There is also a library and computing service here, and two halls of residence.

GETTING THERE

★ By road to the Hawkshead campus: A1/M25 (J23).
★ By rail: half hourly to Potters Bar from Kings Cross London, and from Stevenage. Takes twenty minutes. There's a College minibus, or taxis from station. Camden Campus: ten minutes walk from Kings Cross Station, right down St. Pancras Road, second right after it becomes Crowndal Road.
★ By Underground, it's the Northern Line, Mornington Crescent, Camden Town or Kings Cross (Victoria, Piccadilly, Northern).

UNION, ENTS AND SPORT

Hawkshead is also where the Student Union and Sports and Leisure facilities are located. The RVC is affiliated with the London Union (see London) and the Association of Veterinary Students or AVS. It provides a social calendar of discos, barbeques, barn dances, fireworks displays and Christmas inter-year dinners. It also has a variety of sports clubs, including rowing, rugby, football, hockey and riding (having won the AVS Riding Competition for the last five years). With only 460 students there is a very strong community emphasis, and with practically everyone attending all the events. As a member of ULU you have use of their sports facilities, Union building, pub, clubs and societies.

ACCOMMODATION

The two halls based on the Hawkshead campus offer only 86 rooms, but as part of the University of London, students at the RVC can benefit from the UL Intercollegiate halls of residence. Some half dozen of these, which give priority to first years, are within walking distance of the Camden campus. This is a great opportunity to mix with students of other colleges and faculties and gets over the problem of your academic specialism intruding socially. Demand is very high though. If application is unsuccessful you will have to rent privately. The University of London Accommodation Office can help.

THE COURSE

A full-time five-year course covers preclinical, paraclinical and clinical groups of subjects. Entrance requirements are high (AAB), and your two A grades must be in Biology and Chemistry, though the final A-level can be substituted with two independent AS levels, also of a grade B standard. If Physics is not your other subject, you must have passed it with at least a grade C at GCSE (or as part of a combined sciences GCSE syllabus).

ST. ANDREWS UNIVERSITY

The University of St. Andrews
College Gate
North Street
St. Andrews
Fife KY16 9AJ

TEL 01334 476161
FAX 01334 462543

St. Andrews University
Students Association
St. Mary's Place
St. Andrews
Fife KY16 9UZ

TEL 01334 462700
FAX 01334 462740

UNIVERSITY OF ST ANDREWS

Founded	**1410**
Situation/style	**Town sites**
UNDERGRADUATE PROFILE	
Application acceptance rate	**12%**
Medical AAR	**14%**
Population	**5,000**
Mature student population	**9%**
Overseas student population	**12%**
Male/female ratio	**48:52**
1st year institut. accommodation	**100%**
Approximate cost	**£33-£82 pw**
ACADEMIC PROFILE	
A-level requirements:	**High**

Medicine ABB:
★ Science 'A's required **Chemistry**
★ Additional Science 'A's preferred **Biology + Maths/Physics**
★ Addit. Non-Science 'A's acceptable **Yes**
★ Retakes considered **Yes**
★ Clinic contact **Postgrad/changing**

Student/staff ratio	**10:1**
1st class degree pass rate	**10.8%**
SHEFC assessments (12 subjects assessed/approved):	
1994 **Physics**	Excellent
Computer Studies	Highly Satis.
1995 **Chemistry, Economics, Geography, Maths & Statistics.**	Excellent
Business & Management, Geology.	Highly Satis.
1996 **History**	Excellent
History of Art, Philosophy, Theology	Highly Satis.
Joint Funding Council's research assessment 1996 (24 subjects assessed):	
Psychology.	Grade 5*
Applied Maths, Classics/ Ancient History, History, Philosophy, Theology.	Grade 5
EMPLOYMENT PROFILE	
Employability in Industry:	
MPW national league table (1996)	**26th=**
Principal job market destinations:	
Commerce, Education, Manufacturing, Public Admin., Retail/Wholesale	
PIP 1996 employers' survey:	
Top 3 subjects/national ranking	
Social Science/Economics	5th=
Languages	3rd
Law	15th=
Approximate % unemployed	**5%**

VAG VIEW

This University has a very old foundation (1410) and some of its traditions immediately reach into the lives of Freshers. Jargon is as prevalent here as in the old days in the English Public School system, and you are advised to contact the Union before you arrive, order a copy of their very good Student Handbook and mug up on all their idiosyncratic ways.

In many ways the Uni is the town. With staff and postgrads, it accounts for well over a third of the town's population, and this dominating student influence has been the case for so long, the town itself is so tranquil, and the Uni buildings are so well integrated with the town, that there's no great town/gown issue. Judging by the warnings about where and where not to go in said handbook, there is more dissension between public school Rahs and mere mortal students.

This Uni has a fine record in the assessments and a reputation, which has stood the test of time, for being among the very best in the premier league - see also its performance in the PIP Survey (1996), Employment Profile, fact box. Asking grades are correspondingly high. There is a good mix of English and Scottish students - better than at most of the Scottish Unis.

The only caveat about St Andrews is that it is a long way away from a lot of places and the poseur or streetwise may find it a bit soft. For those who like a close-knit family feel it is ideal, and for those who can appreciate beauty it is a must. If they'll have you.

SITUATION

St Andrews is out on its own, a small, ancient seaside town in the north-east of Scotland, surrounded by open countryside and sea. However, Dundee is only thirteen miles to the north, over the Firth of Tay, and Edinburgh is but 45 miles to the south.

GETTING THERE

★ By road: Forth Road Bridge, M90 (J3), A92 to Kirkcaldy, A915 to St Andrews; or M90 (J8), A91.
★ By rail: Nearest station on main line London (King's Cross) - Edinburgh - Aberdeen line is Leuchars (5 miles). A few trains have bus connection for St Andrews station; service bus runs from Leuchars every twenty minutes between 9.00 a.m. and 6.00 p.m.; otherwise taxi.
★ By air: Edinburgh Airport, airport bus to Edinburgh (Waverley station), thence by rail to Leuchars.

UNION, ENTS & ARTS

There is a coffee house scene in St Andrews - some seventeen non-alcoholic venues where students gather. There are also, you'll no doubt be relieved to hear, 25 pubs, an extraordinary number for the size of the town, each with its own personality. For music, try The Thirsty Whale (DJs Thursdays, Fridays; live music Saturdays, licence till 2, pinball, pool table), The Tudor (juke box, live music, licence till 1), The Featherie & Firkin (usual Firkin fare and live music occasionally).

There are three Union bars: Main Bar (promo nights, Thursdays), Beer Bar (small gigs, discos - mainly chart, dance, indie - and comedy) and Fraser Suite (Societies ents, 'Alternative' disco night Friday, student DJs, compensates for sweatier, 1,000-strong Friday disco - the BIG night of the week, Megabop - at the Union Theatre).

Not the most sophisticated ents scene, but the best in town and everyone enjoys themselves. The Union is attracting increasingly good guest DJs for the Thursday spot. Recent live acts include Credit to the Nation, Thrum, Frank Black.

Mermaids, the Drama Soc, is especially active - large productions in 450-seater Union Theatre, smaller at Crawfords Arts Centre and Buchanan Lecture Theatre, plus open air productions at the Castle. Debating tradition also strong, with numerous awards.

ACADEMIA

There are only three faculties at St Andrews - Arts, Science, and Divinity. Entry is by faculty rather than department, but this does not exclude cross-faculty course programming. Modular structure, 12-week semester system. They have a system of Adviser assignments, where students can get advice on course programming and anything else. In the Science and Divinity faculties it's on a one-to-one basis. Good self-study (audio, video and computer) facilities in the Language Teaching Services building.

ACCOMMODATION

Eleven halls of residence, 22% are twin rooms. First year students are normally allocated these. In New Hall all rooms are en suite. Self-catered student houses also available, each with six single-study bedrooms, kitchen with dining room, shower room and toilet.

SPORT

Golfers paradise. Student discounts on five courses. Otherwise, there's a sports centre with sports hall, gym, activities room, weight training room, squash courts, solarium. Extensive playing fields, jogging and trim tracks.

Golf bursaries funded by the Royal and Ancient Golf Club - £650 first year then £1,300 each subsequent year.

St George's Hospital Medical School

St George's Hospital
Medical School
Cranmer Terrace
Tooting
London
SW17 0RE

TEL 0181 672 9944
FAX 0181 672 6940

St. George's Hospital
Medical School
(University of London)
The School Club
Cranmer Terrace
London SW17 0RE

TEL 0181 725 2709
FAX 0181 725 2709

ST GEORGES HOSPITAL MEDICAL SCHOOL

Founded	**1751**
Situation/style	**Campus**
UNDERGRADUATE PROFILE	
Application acceptance rate	**6%**
Population	**900**
Mature student population	**10%**
Overseas student population	**4%**
Male/female ratio	**52:48**
1st year institut. accommodation	**100%**
Approximate cost	**£40 pw**
ACADEMIC PROFILE	
A-level requirement	**ABB**

★ Science 'A's required **Chemistry or Biology + AS Chemistry**
★ Addit. Non-Science 'A's acceptable **Modern Euro. Langs, Social Science**
★ Retakes considered **Ext. circs.**
★ Retake offer **AAA**
★ Clinical contact **Day one**

Student/staff ratio	**3:1**
1st class degree pass rate	**4.4%**
Joint Funding Council's research assessment 1996 (4 subjects assessed):	
Grade 5/5*	None
EMPLOYMENT PROFILE	
Approximate % unemployed	**0%**

VAG GUIDE

After Imperial College teams up with Charing Cross & Westminster in 1997 and the Royal Free merges with University College London the following year, St George's Hospital Medical School will be the only free standing medical school left in the UK. No other school will contain within its own campus the entire pre-clinical and clinical infrastructure required to teach medical students. And as they rightly crow this will put them in an ideal position to implement the GMC's recommendations for a more clinically orientated medical undergraduate course. Everything is on hand to make it happen. Indeed, even at this point, you could say that St George's is more enlightened as a teaching hospital than most. They only insist on one science A-level for entry; it can be Chemistry or Biology; if Biology then AS Chemistry is required; but if Chemistry you can submit the other two A-levels in the form of a modern Euro language and a Social Science. In other words they, unlike many others, recognise the benefit to medicine of practitioners with high level attainment in a broad based educational culture. On the question of how soon their students are set loose on patients, while most schools will be talking about

Year 3 of the course, St George's replies, 'From Day 1.' Leaving aside what patients may feel about this, it is precisely in accord with what the GMC is after. 'Medicine is on the verge of a complete change of curriculum, so they say,' said one school careers adviser not as disbelieving as one could make that sound. 'They are looking for skills, for the problem solvers, maybe allowing an Arts subject at A-level. They are wanting to bring the clinical training in earlier, so they say (as Newcastle has done from the word go).' On that basis, at least, it would seem that St George's is well set to be in the vanguard of Tomorrow's Medicine. Indeed they have long taken the view at St George's that the traditional departmental specialism approach to medical education is not the way forward, and have experimented with inter-disciplinary teaching based on the systems of the body. Since 1976 they have had a course which mingles basic medical sciences with clinically relevant topics.

The school teacher added a caveat, however. During our discussion about the pros and cons of the various schools, she said that 'in London, on the other hand, your social life can be quite hard work, you have to transport yourself distances and so on.' I wouldn't agree with her about a lot of the medical schools in London, but as far as St George's is concerned she could have a point. Rootin' Tootin' can be something of an acquired taste, colourful culture certainly, plenty of curry houses, but a dusty, traffic-busy sort of place, rather depressed, not the kind of area in which I would imagine your typical medical student choosing to spend a night out. But apparently there's a busy nurses home there and the school does have cavernous common rooms and bar with adjoining snooker hall, a TV room, a games room, a dance floor, and apparently a balcony overlooking the poor peasants outside. They also have the Monkton Theatre, which the students use for theatrical and musical productions.

It is quite an interesting story as to how St George's got there in the first place. The old hospital site was of course on Hyde Park Corner, elegance personified, but shortly after the Second World War they found themselves short of patients to practise on round Hyde Park way, which was why they relocated to Tooting, where presumably they hoped to find people dying all over the place. Certainly Lambeth cemetery was and is across the road. Such dedication on the part of a teaching hospital is to be applauded. Clearly the roots of their practical, clinical obsessions run deep.

Like Charing Cross their sports grounds are down in Cobham, Surrey - nine winter pitches and two cricket squares in summer, plus grass and hard court tennis. They also keep an eight and a four in the UL boathouse on the Thames and have facilities for sailing. And back at the hospital there's the Lowe Sports Centre, six squash courts, gym and areas to play badminton, basketball, etc.

GETTING THERE

★ Tooting Broadway Underground station (Northern Line), Tooting overland.

ST MARK & ST JOHN, PLYMOUTH

College of St Mark & St John
Derriford Road
Plymouth
PL6 8BH

TEL 01752 636700
FAX 01752 636820

College of St Mark & St John
Student Union
Derriford Road
Plymouth
Devon PL6 8BH

TEL 01752 636825
FAX 01752 636825

COLLEGE OF ST MARK & ST JOHN	
Founded	**1840**
Situation/style	**Campus**
UNDERGRADUATE PROFILE	
Application acceptance rate	**11%**
Population	**2,200**
Mature student population	**34%**
Overseas student population	**7%**
Male/female ratio	**32:68**
1st year institut. accommodation	**100%**
Approximate cost	**£40-£56 pw**
ACADEMIC PROFILE	
A-level requirements:	**Low**
Teacher Training 4-8, **Sociology/Community Studies combs.** 4-12, **English Literary/ Language Studies** 12	
Student/staff ratio	**19:1**
1st class degree pass rate	**2.5%**
HEFCE assessments (7 subjects assessed/approved):	
1995 **Linguistics** 21	
1996 **Sociology** 22	
Joint Funding Council's research assessment 1996 (5 subjects assessed):	
Grade 5/5*	None

VAG VIEW

This College, which is situated on the outskirts of Plymouth and likes people to call it Marjon, is a teacher training college offering a modular (arts/humanities based) honours degree, awarded by the University of Exeter.

Marjon began as two colleges, St Mark and St John, both founded 150 years ago in London by the Church of England.

They offer a sound teacher training programme, well proven, and where they have been assessed they have done very well indeed. The striking element of the degree course, which mainly covers subjects they have been teaching for years, is the PR and media content.

The first year of the PR course, which may be taken as a Major or Minor, combines modules concerning communication theory, sociology and psychology (areas in which Marjon has its proven track record), matched by practical courses in design, media, photography, DTP and employee relations. The second year focuses on the PR industry, where and how it operates and intersects with marketing, advertising, sponsorship, market research, etc, and carries a welcome element about moral issues appertaining to PR. This may well ensure that none of its pupils make it to the top of the tree in this dog-eat-dog profession. On the other hand, in a small but effective way, it spells out the potential of higher education in the evolution of our media obsessed society, and should certainly be encouraged. In year three students become involved in major PR projects. Some combine this with Media Studies, which adds depth of understanding about the world in which they will engage as spin doctors.

There's a growing international presence owing to a well worked out International Education Centre, which looks after the teacher trainer requirements of particular countries, and the contacts Marjon are making with governments and institutions abroad (they have students from 50+ countries, which is impressive for an establishment this size), are clearly part of its strategy of growth.

Accommodation is on campus for first years unless they want to ensure a campus place in their last intensive year of study. The campus 'village houses' have five or six study bedrooms, bathroom and kitchen; halls of residence have single study bedrooms, shared bathroom and kitchen. Ents are pretty limited beyond Freshers Week and big dates through the year. And there is a large locally drawn student population (34% are mature), so it would be unwise to expect a vibrant social scene.

Sporting facilities have recently been greatly enhanced on campus - there's a 25 metre indoor swimming pool, a fitness suite, three squash courts, a gym, three sports halls, badminton courts and rock climbing wall. Besides playing fields there is an all-weather floodlit astro-pitch for hockey and a floodlit astro training area. Sailing dinghies are moored in Plymouth Sound; there's an outdoor pursuits centre, a fleet of plastic canoes, and a trim trail, which seems to encompass the entire campus - fair to assume that they have plans to extend their degree course Physical Recreation programmes.

GETTING THERE

★ By road: A38 (picks up M5 at Exeter).
★ By rail: London Paddington, 3:30; Bristol Parkway, 3:00; Southampton, 4:00; Birmingham New Street, 4:00.
★ By air: The College is close to Plymouth Airport - daily flights to Newquay and London.

ST MARTIN'S COLLEGE

University College of
St Martin
Bowerham Road
Lancaster
Lancashire LA1 3JD

TEL 01524 63446
FAX 01524 38485

University College of
St Martin Student Union,
Bowerham Road
Lancaster
Lancashire LA1 3JD

TEL 01524 65827
FAX 01524 841924

ST MARTIN'S COLLEGE, LANCASTER	
Founded	1963
Situation/style	Campus
UNDERGRADUATE PROFILE	
Application acceptance rate	14%
Population	3,500
Mature student population	30%
Overseas student population	4%
Male/female ratio	30:70
1st year institut. accommodation	100%
Approximate cost	£55-£65 pw
ACADEMIC PROFILE	
A-level requirements:	**Medium-Low**
Education Studies combinations BC-DEE, **Science/Technology/Society combs.** CC-CDE, **English combinations** BC-CD	
Student/staff ratio	28:1
1st class degree pass rate	2.5%

VAG VIEW

St Martin's is a teacher training college with a Church of England foundation, which is the base for a number of courses leading to employment in what they describe as the caring professions (health, education, the Church). Degrees are awarded by nearby Lancaster Uni.

Outside the BA/BSc Teacher Status degrees, undergraduate courses are geared to BA/BSC modular degrees; to Single Honours degrees (BA) in Christian Ministry, Community & Youth Studies, and Performing Arts; to BSc Single Hons in Imaging Sciences, and Sports Science; and to BSc Single Hons in Nursing, Occupational Therapy and Diagnostic Radiography. There is also a range of part-time BA/DipHE courses in Health.

On the modular degree course, you opt for one of two routes, leading either to a Joint Honours degree, or to a named Major subject. The subjects covered include Sport, Drama, Music, Art & Design, English, Community Studies, Humanities, Languages, Information Technology, Maths, Business, Social Ethics and Health.

It seems likely that the best career prospects lie in the teacher training option rather than the modular degree course, though not all of the above can be taken with QTS. The Health degrees, however, are more clearly vocational, and the Sports Science grows out of St Martin's experience with this faculty. The BA (Hons) in Christian Ministry is an interesting option because it's aimed uniquely at employment in overseas aid work and work within national Christian organisations. Some students do go into education from it, and some will be ordained, but that is not the main thrust of this course.

The main campus is located a mile or so from the central shopping area of Lancaster and has one or two outlying sites in Carlisle to the north, Barrow, Whitehaven and Kendal. The proximity of the Lake District is clearly a plus to its sporting bias, and within the college there are grassed games areas, 2 indoor halls, tennis courts, squash courts, a floodlit, all-weather pitch and a weights and conditioning room. Students also avail themselves of the facilities at Lancaster Uni.

There are 6 halls of residence, single sex and mixed, all but 1 on campus. Mill Hall is a 10 minute walk away in the city centre and is mainly reserved for first year Nursing, Radiography and Occupational Therapy students.

A large proportion of the students are mature. Drama and Music courses spill talent over into the entertainment/arts side of social life, with the Nuffield Theatre on campus staging student productions and hosting outside productions. The Students Union organise Ents, but it seems fairly low key.

GETTING THERE

★ By road: M6 (Junctions 33, 34).
★ By rail: Manchester Oxford Road, 1:30; Leeds, 2:30; Newcastle, 3:00; London Euston, 3:30.

ST MARY'S UNIVERSITY COLLEGE

St Mary's University College
Waldegrave Road
Strawberry Hill
Twickenham
TW1 4SX

TEL 0181 240 4000
FAX 0181 240 4255

St. Mary's University College
Student Union
Strawberry Hill
Twickenham
Middx TW1 4SX

TEL 0181 891 6123
FAX 0181 744 1700

ST MARY'S UNIVERSITY COLLEGE	
Founded	**1850**
Situation/style	**Campus**
UNDERGRADUATE PROFILE	
Application acceptance rate	**10%**
Population	**2,250**
Mature student population	**16%**
Overseas student population	**8%**
Male/female ratio	**36:64**
1st year institut. accommodation	**95%**
Approximate cost (College)	**£65-£85pw**
(City)	**£55-£70pw**
ACADEMIC PROFILE	
A-level requirements:	**Low**
Teacher Training 8-14, **History combs./Sociology combs.** 4-14	
Student/staff ratio	**14:1**
1st class degree pass rate	**4.5%**
HEFCE assessments (5 subjects assessed/approved):	
1996 **Sociology** 20	
Joint Funding Council's research assessment 1996 (7subjects assessed):	
Grade 5/5*	None
EMPLOYMENT PROFILE	
Principal job market destinations:	
Education, Retail/Wholesale, Public Admin.	
Approximate % unemployed	**6%**

VAG VIEW

St Mary's is situated south of the Twickenham rugby ground between Richmond and Kingston. It is a good setting, close to the River Thames, near enough to London to benefit from all the city has to offer and yet enjoying a measure of campus seclusion. It is a campus that has both geographical and cultural completeness. For this is a Roman Catholic foundation which doesn't care to bury its traditions. In fact you could say it succeeds on the back of them. Religious disciplines are at the core of its ethos and its community life.

Degrees are awarded by Surrey Uni, and in recent years between 30 and 38% of students have managed either Firsts or Upper Seconds. 40% are studying for teaching degrees; the rest, BA Hons in Drama, English, History, Theology; BSc Environmental Science, Geography; or a BA/BSc Combined Hons degree, which introduces Biology, Classical Studies, Irish Studies, Maths, Sociology, Sport Science to the other degree subjects. There are sports halls and pitches on site and an athletics track.

Accommodation is mainly single study bedrooms. Two halls (Cashin and Cronin) offer en-suite facilities. There are good local pubs. Richmond has two cinemas and is home to the Richmond and Orange Tree Theatres. See Kingston Uni entry for nightclub life there. There's a new Students Union at St Mary's, with three bars and a concert hall. There are weekly discos.

GETTING THERE

★ By rail: Waterloo Station to Strawberry Hill station, which is close to the college, takes thirty minutes.
★ By Underground, it's the District Line to Richmond, then overland to Strawberry Hill , or by Nos. 33 or R68 buses. No. 33 travels directly from Richmond Bus Station to the college.

SALFORD UNIVERSITY

The University of Salford
The Crescent
Salford
M5 4WT

TEL 0161 745 5000
FAX 0161 295 5999

Salford University
Student Union
University House
The Crescent
Salford M5 4WT

TEL 0161 736 7811
FAX 0161 737 1633

UNIVERSITY OF SALFORD	
Founded	**1967**
Situation/style	**Campus**
UNDERGRADUATE PROFILE	
Application acceptance rate	**13%**
Population	**8,700**
Mature student population	**40%**
Overseas student population	**9%**
Male/female ratio	**60:40**
1st year institut. accommodation	**100%**
Approximate cost	**£35-£65 pw**
ACADEMIC PROFILE	
A-level requirements:	**Medium**
Physical Sciences BCD-CDD. **Engineering:** ★ High: **Aeronautical** 22 ★ Low: **Civil** 16. **Sociology** BCC-CCD. **French combinations** BBC-BCC	
Student/staff ratio	**14:1**
1st class degree pass rate	**8%**
HEFCE assessments (9 subjects assessed/approved):	
1996 **Sociology** 20	
Joint Funding Council's research assessment 1996 (11 subjects assessed):	
Built Environment	Grade 5*
European Studies	Grade 5
EMPLOYMENT PROFILE	
Employability in Industry:	
MPW national league table (1996)	**36th=**
Principal job market destinations: **Manufacturing** (strong **Electronic & Electrical**), **Commerce, Construction** (strong), **Public Admin, Retail/Wholesale, Computer** (strong), **Education**	
PIP 1996 employers' survey: Top 3 subjects/national ranking	
Construction & Civil Engineering	11th
Business	12th=
Electrical Engineering	20th=
Approximate % unemployed	**9%**

VAG VIEW

Salford sounds a good Uni at which to be. It may not yet have the caché of its neighbour in the city, but for certain subjects, and for its campus social life, it is up there with the best.

SITUATION

Two miles from Manchester city centre.

GETTING THERE

★ By road: Approach via the M62 (which connects with the M6, M63)/M602.
★ Coach services from Manchester good to all main destinations.
★ By rail: Salford Crescent station is on-campus; Manchester Oxford Road is a few minutes away; Liverpool Lime Street, 1:20; Sheffield, 1:30; Birmingham New Street, 2:30; London Euston, 3:30.
★ By air: flights from Manchester Airport international and inland.

ACADEMIA

Faculties include Art & Design Technology; Business, Management & Consumer Studies; Engineering; The Environment; Health Care & Social Work; Media, Music & Performance; Science; Social Sciences, Languages & Humanities.

Salford is known for its Engineering, Science & Technology and Social Studies programmes. It is the pioneer of sandwich course work placement schemes and its links with local firms are legendary, and this is a Uni which is very much part of the locale - for example, they have a hand in the National Industrial Centre for Virtual Reality, which is to be housed alongside the largest collection of L .S. Lowry paintings in the world at Salford Quays (Lowry is a son of Salford).

But it isn't only local firms that benefit from Salford graduates. The big push recently has been abroad - most courses have an international dimension. All courses are modular, and the system has been used to add social, cultural and economic elements to main subject interests as often as possible. They have excellent relationships with countries throughout Europe and farther afield, which have produced interesting Science/Arts groupings, such as Information Technology with Studies in Japan. Languages are an important department, Hispanic and Arabic are strong.

SOCIAL SCENE

Students have the benefit of Manchester just minutes away by train from the campus, and their own vibrant scene, organised by the Union. Pavilion is the Union nightclub, more about that from our correspondent. There's also the Sub nightclub. Crescent & Campus is a Uni arts promotion to bring leading outside as well as student companies and productions to various venues on campus - music as well as theatre, and appealing to a range of tastes.

SPORT

Student operated leisure centre facilities include 2 sports halls, 3 fitness rooms, a snooker room, a climbing wall and 5 squash courts. The wide range of indoors sports catered for - from cricket to martial arts, from volleyball to fencing, from aerobics to badminton - is matched by the caving, canoeing, parachuting, windsurfing, mountaineering, sailing options on the outdoor side of things. It's a premier league Uni for sporting facilities and they engage in all the BUSA team sports, with one special event - the Northern Boat Race with Manchester Uni on May Day.

ACCOMMODATION

Halls of residence, self-catering student houses and student flats. See also Accommodation below.

VIEW FROM THE GROUND

by S. M. Ashton

Salford is a great place to study because it either has, or is near, everything a student could possibly want. It has all the advantages of a town cheap rent, everything close by, a friendly atmosphere and yet still has the facilities of a city nearby. Manchester is home to one of the largest student populations in the country so is the most student-friendly place imaginable. The food and drink is cheap, particularly on weekdays and down Oxford Road; there are countless venues for concerts and shows, whatever your tastes may be; and the majority of nightclubs (which there are hundreds), cinemas and shops give student discounts on production of an NUS card. If you want to have a brilliant time while you study for your degree, Salford is definitely the place to do it.

UNION, ENTS, SPORT & CLUBS

The city of Salford is not like a city at all. Really it seems more like a smallish town, which means that there is not a massive amount of entertainment for us students unless you have a penchant for bingo and supermarkets. Luckily though, not only is the Salford University Students Union pretty good at organising events but the campus is only a short distance from Manchester city centre which is much more student-friendly and offers a wide range of entertainment (most of which involves drinking a lot, but what student activities don't?).

On the subject of drink, following a merger with University College Salford last year, the University has increased in size and the number of Union-run bars has more than doubled, so you are never far from one. The only downside to the Union bars is that the beer is not subsidised like it is at most universities so it is not as cheap as it could be. Prices are similar to those in local pubs, which means beer is considered reasonably priced by students from the north of the country, and a bargain by those from the South. The good side to this, though, is that the union makes a decent amount of money so can afford to subsidise other things, such as sports clubs, and special events, such as balls.

The Union also runs its own night club, the Pav, which is situated at Castle Irwell Student Village. The Pav also houses a cafe which is very cheap and perfect if you can't be bothered to cook your own tea! Since most first years live there it's easy to meet new people when you first arrive, so you're not short of friends for long when you come to Salford.

Castle Irwell is also the site for the University's sports fields, it only takes around thirty seconds to walk from your room to the pitches. Joining a team is highly recommended - there are plenty to choose from so it's very likely you'll find something you enjoy. It's often worth joining a team for the social life, because the nights out are nothing short of brilliant. In fact, one of the best nights of the entire year is Rec Night, a Union-arranged night of drinking and games at The Pav, and entry is restricted to members of sports clubs so it's worth joining a team just for that! The teams themselves enjoy varying success, but a good time is most definitely had by all. If sports clubs are not really your cup of tea, there are loads of different societies you can join, from the political to the environmental to the just plain bizarre. And if you still can't find one that interest you and your like-minded friends you can always start your own.

There is also a Community Services organiser who can put you on the right lines if volunteer work is more your thing. This varies from helping out in a local school or college, to taking disadvantages children on outings or helping the families of international students with their English. As well as being rewarding, these activities look great on a CV.

ACCOMMODATION

Most accommodation, including Castle Irwell, is situated around fifteen to twenty minutes walk away from the campus although some is actually on the campus itself. The University also has a direct leasing scheme, where it acts as 'middle-man' between students and private landlords, so the old problem of being stuck in a hell-hole for a whole year doesn't happen often, although, by and large, University accommodation is usually better. In recent years the University has rented ex-council tower-blocks from private landlords and sublet the flats to groups of students. These flats are convenient not only for lectures but also for shopping, but as with all accommodation in Salford the areas where they are situated are not particularly safe. They are not trouble-spots by any means but going out alone at night is definitely not advisable, especially for women. Attacks on students are rare, since locals like to keep themselves to themselves, but it is still important to be careful because they do happen from time to time. There is really no excuse for walking around at night, since buses are frequent and taxis are quite cheap.

ACADEMIA

The variety of courses at Salford University is enormous, so it's hard to say anything specific about them. Salford has a good reputation for Engineering and Science based courses, so has invaluable links with industry in these fields and in many others. If you are considering a course that involves a sandwich year or work experience, these links make it much more likely that you'll get a worthwhile placement instead of spending all your time making coffee. A good number of students get jobs with their work experience host on finishing their degree.

The workload varies a great deal from course to course, from five hours of lectures a week to thirty. The lecture timetable for my course, which is sociology, is quite sparse, but lecturers expect the rest of the timetable to be filled with reading and personal study. The first year is mainly A-level standard work, to enable students who did not do Sociology A-level to get up to speed with everyone else. No-one feels out of their depth this way, which means the drop-out rate for the course is low. That is not to say that there is nothing to learn for students who passed their Sociology A-level, since new skills are learned from day one. These include computer literacy, which is a relatively new addition to the early stages of the course and includes lessons in how to use computer packages, which can cut down time spent on research and data processing for essays and projects in years two and three. In the second and third years there is a great deal of choice when deciding what modules to take (you have to pick three modules for each semester in year two, but in year three there are other options as well, such as a project on a subject which you pick yourself). The range of module topics is diverse - football, class, drug use, gender, and crime are just a few - so everyone can find something which interests them.

Scarborough University College

University College
Scarborough
Filey Road
Scarborough
North Yorkshire
YO11 3AZ

TEL 01723 362392
FAX 01723 370815

Students Union
University College
Scarborough
Filey Road
Scarborough
North Yorkshire
YO11 3AZ

TEL 01723 373864
FAX 01723 360665

UNIVERSITY COLLEGE SCARBOROUGH

Founded	**1948**
Situation/style	**Campus**
UNDERGRADUATE PROFILE	
Application acceptance rate	**34%**
Population	**1,400**
Mature student population	**20%**
Overseas student population	**1.5%**
Male/female ratio	**20:80**
1st year institut. accommodation	**95%**
Approximate cost (College)	**£70 pw**
(Town)	**£35 pw**
ACADEMIC PROFILE	
A-level requirements:	**Low**

Teacher Training DD. **Combined Performance Arts** (incl. **Theatre, Dance**) DD-EE, **Arts/Sciences/Social Sciences/ Humanities combs.** CC-DE. **Environmental Studies** (incl. **Coastal Management**) DD-EE **Management Studies, Leisure & Tourism** DD

Student/staff ratio	**21:1**

VAG VIEW

This is a small, emerging university college with close local ties and a strong sense of belonging to the community.

Scarborough means different things to different people: Britain's first Spa town, seaside resort, a conference centre once favoured by Westminster, the internationally famous home of Alan Ayckbourn's Theatre in the Round, the confluence of a unique set of topographical features - the moors, the Wolds and a wind-lashed coastline so sublime that it brought Charlotte Brontë to real tears of wonder and persuaded Bram Stoker to coax Dracula ashore a few miles to the north.

Today Scarborough's stormy seas are among the most polluted around England. Its once proud fishing industry is a sorry plaything of the EEC. Its Edwardian elegance, favoured by the Sitwells, is overrun by DHSS fugitives. Its holiday-by-the-sea tourist strategies outmoded by time and circumstance. And yet, out of this is growing a university college that is worth more space than your average establishment with a three-year track record. Why? Because University College Scarborough has in an enlightened way sought to focus upon precisely this set of natural resources and depressing environmental, social and economic developments, and set out to resolve them in its courses. *(See Academia)*

GETTING THERE

★ By road: A1, A64
★ By rail: Trains run regularly the 45 miles from York (ultimately from Manchester airport).

ACCOMMODATION

On Campus is the Cayley Hall of Residence,

built in 1994, so it's all mod cons. 214 students get this sort of treatment, the rest herd into the main college building, various annexes, or chance their arm in the town. There's the usual backup from college admin and Scarborough landlords have hospitality bred in the bone.

CITY/TOWN LIFESTYLE

Behind the glitter of what might now more accurately be called the Strip, with enough one-armed bandits to give you gambler's elbow, there are a few remnants of the old town and pubs, like the Leeds, where you'd do well not to tread unless you're one of the fishermen or lifeboatmen who frequent it. The student pub is the Cask; other favourites include the Alma, Tap & Spiel, Real Ale haven the Hole in the Wall, Raffles, the Salisbury, Scruffy Murphey's. Clubs include Toffs (student discounts), Laughtons, Boleyns, Bacchus, the Underground.

The Futurist has live acts (Billy Connelly) and films; Stephen Joseph Theatre (in the old Odeon, has Alan Ayckbourn, arthouse films and a restaurant; the Spa has classical concerts; the Corner has touristy fare.

ACADEMIA

Scarborough began as a training college for teachers in 1948 and the OFTSED assessments show their continuing ability in this area. The first non-Tteaching university degree courses - Combined Honours - were offered in 1993, validated by Leeds. The first Single Honours courses appeared in 1994. Degree courses undertaken from 1995, will be validated by York.

In September 1996 UCS streamlined the Combined Honours curriculum, each minor subject extending the depth of a course in which a student is majoring or giving it a practical dimension (English with Problem Solving Science, Dance with Management Studies, etc).

The character and environmental problems associated with the Scarborough coastline and seashore, is material for the School of Environmental Studies (Environmental Science, Coastal Marine Biology, Geography), as do the diverse landscapes and land uses of the nearby moors, the Wolds and Vale of Pickering. Its problematic tourism and leisure industry informs its Leisure & Tourism Management course, and the whole Management School is inspired by the socio-economic profile of the locality. Representatives from local, national and international businesses (this is the home of the mighty independent printer, Pindar, and gravure printer D H Greaves), agriculture (an industry bolstered by the monster Canadian potato-fries company, McCains), communications, aviation and specialist engineering, are all lively participants in the process of UCS's academic evolution.

Again, Alan Ayckbourn's influence on theatre studies is crucial. Drama has always been a strong theme in UCS and it is the home of the NUS Drama Festival. Ayckbourn gets involved personally with UCS, and students work at his Theatre in the Round.

VIEW FROM THE GROUND
by Ian Montgomery

When people think of Scarborough (if they've heard of it at all) they think of sun, sea and excitement. Trying not to sound like an advert for Haven, I do have to say that Scarborough is a very nice town. However, it is fairly small and off the beaten track and has been described as a bit of a cul-de-sac. If you want to go to a very friendly, small town on the seaside, surrounded by lovely countryside, then Scarborugh is the place for you. UCS was a Teacher Training College up until 1993, but you wouldn't know that now as several new buildings have been added to the campus and others refurbished and the teacher training students are a diminishing minority.

The College has a family atmosphere. I worked there for a year on placement from Sheffield Hallam, and got to know everybody (staff and students) very quickly. The College is situated on one site, even the new halls of residence, which are very nice. This means that everyone, no matter what course they're on, mixes in together. This is helped by having a single dining hall, bar and library within ten metres of each other; and because there is a small student population, you'll always see the same faces around. The staff also build a good rapport with the students more easily as the class sizes are small.

The new halls have en-suite bathrooms. The older halls, of which there are few, have shared bathrooms but, they are still of a reasonable standard. All halls are catered, so if you're not Delia Smith you won't have to worry about living on pot noodles, and the choice and standard of food available is better than school dinners, i.e. you *can* identify what it is you are eating. If you'd rather not live in halls, the accommodation office has a large list of accommodation in the town. As there is so much holiday accommodation, there is plenty for students out of season which, generally, is of a reasonable rent and standard.

The Students Union, like the College, is small, but it still runs several sports cubs and other societies and organises regular events in the College bar. The SU also organises a Freshers Week, which involves pub-crawls, karaokes, discos, a Freshers Fair and other activities which involve having a good time and getting to know everyone. The College bar is not an SU bar but it is well-furnished, sells cheap drinks and does have live music as well as the other events run by the Union. Unfortunately the College does not have a large range of sport facilities. It has a couple of football pitches and a hockey pitch and a small indoor hall, but that's about it. However, there is a sports centre just down the road which has a gym, tennis courts, etc., and offers a discount for students.

The College itself is about one and a half miles from the town centre up a hill. If you don't fancy the walk, there is a regular bus service. There is a College car park but it is not very big.

Surprisingly there are four or five nightclubs in town. One has a student night mid-week, with cheap entry and drinks promotions. Please do remember that this is Scarborough, so do not go in a club expecting it to be the Ministry of Sound.

As it is a seaside town, there are a lot of pubs. Do take care though because Scarborough is the karaoke capital of England. After a certain amount of exposure, what you once thought was an embarrassing thing to do in public could turn into a hobby!

There is a nice new theatre in the town centre, but no cinema, although the Futurist Theatre on the seafront does show new releases on certain nights of the week. Scarborough is also a bit limiting in terms of shopping, but York is only a 45 minute train journey away, and being a large city it has a large shopping area, a multiplex cinema and a train museum.

Scarborough's shortcomings are only due to its size. If you are the type of person who would like to study in a small, friendly town in a picturesque location, at a college where you can really get to know everybody without trying too hard, then UCS is the ideal place for you.

THE SCHOOL OF ORIENTAL AND AFRICAN STUDIES

The School of Oriental and African Studies
Thornhaugh Street
Russell Square
London
WC1H 0XG

TEL 0171 637 2388
FAX 0171 436 3844

School of Oriental and African Studies
Student Union
Thornhaugh Street
Russell Square
London WC1H 0XG

TEL 0171 580 0916
FAX 0171 637 5008

SCHOOL OF ORIENTAL & AFRICAN STUDIES

Founded	**1916**
Situation/style	**City sites**
UNDERGRADUATE PROFILE	
Application acceptance rate	**13%**
Population	**1,500**
Mature student population	**53%**
Overseas student population	**19%**
Male/female ratio	**37:63**
1st year institut. accommodation	**50%**
Approximate cost (School)	**£70-£80 pw**
(City)	**£55-£70 pw**
ACADEMIC PROFILE	
A-level requirements:	**Medium**
200+ **African/Asian/Oriental combs.** 16-24	
Law 24 **Anthropology combinations** 22	
Comparative Religion, Music Studies 20	
Student/staff ratio	**10:1**
1st class degree pass rate	**8.2%**
HEFCE assessments (5 subjects assessed/approved):	
1994 **Law, Music**	Excellent
1995 **Anthropology**	Excellent
1996 **Linguistics** 20	
Joint Funding Council's research assessment 1996 (12 subjects assessed):	
History, Music.	Grade 5*
Anthropology, Linguistics, History of Art/Architecture/ Design, Theology.	Grade 5
EMPLOYMENT PROFILE	
Principal job market destinations: **Retail/Wholesale, Education, Commerce, Arts/Media, Public Admin./Law, Manufacturing**	
Approximate % unemployed	**8%**

VAG VIEW

This is a specialist School of the federal University of London, situated in a huddle with Birkbeck College, SSEES, London University Union and University College (see entries) in the Bloomsbury area of London.

The courses concern the full diverse range of language, culture and history of Africa and Asia. All are awarded either BA or BSc Honours degrees, excepting Law, which attracts a LLB (Hons).

Accommodation is provided in a Student Residence (500 single en-suite study bedrooms in cluster flats) fifteen minutes walk away on the Pentonville Road. Alternatively students may use the London University Intercollegiate Halls (see London).

There are two squash courts on site, otherwise their sports ground is at Greenford, and, again, they may use the ULU facilities in nearby Malet Street.

SOAS has a close working relationship with branches of the Civil Service, especially the Foreign Office - it actually teaches their staff - and with overseas governments, industry and commerce, which facilitates, among other things, the compulsory study-abroad aspects of some of the courses. Students, as our correspondent tells, live rather a different life.

GETTING THERE

★ Russell Square Underground station (Piccadilly Line) is closest; Goodge Street ((Northern Line) is also nearby, as are Tottenham Court Road (Central, Northern), Euston Square ((Metropolitan & Circle) and Warren Street (Victoria, Northern).

NOTES FROM A TOPICAL ISLAND

by Peter Beveridge & Catherine Wynne

SOAS is one of the smaller, specialist Colleges of the University of London. Its size and the type of student it attracts make it radically different. Its students come from different age and ethnic groups, and it offers the opportunity to meet people from all over the world.

SOAS students are always asked the same two questions: 'What languages do you study, and what drugs do you take? Do not think of coming if you haven't dragged a backpack through either; (a) Thailand or (b) India, and claim to have gained a unique insight into unspoilt and indigenous cultures. If, however, you haven't - lie!

A typical conversation in the bar concerning Summer activities, 'I'm just back from three months in South East Asia, saving villagers from Acid Rain'. Oh, how did you get that? 'Dad got me the job.'

On your travels (or in Camden Market), don't forget to stock up on big jumpers from Nepal, and collarless Indian shirts.

SOAS has only 2,500 full-time students which gives it a relaxed and friendly atmosphere. This compares favourably with other London Colleges with a mob of 15,000 students where you'll be lucky to bump into someone you know once a month. Unfortunately, it's also harder to hide from your tutor at SOAS. Top tip: don't get a locker near your department.

There are 421 more females than males. At the time of going to press, the Student Union was said to have no plans of instituting a 'Blokes Officer'.

Buzz-words: Be sure to be able to use these words with confidence and flair (without necessarily knowing what they mean); 'diaspora', 'post-modern', and state that everything is 'neo-colonialist'.

Academically Speaking SOAS does all the usual disciplines, but with specific reference to Africa and Asia. This means that in Geography you're more likely to be looking at the 'Biogeography of Savannahs in Sub-Saharan Africa' than the spatial planning of Birmingham town centre. Strong on languages from Chinese and Japanese to a whole shitload that you probably won't have heard of. Colloquial Cambodian, for example, looks great on your CV, and unless you're in Pnom Penh the interviewer is unlikely to challenge you on it. Forget Oxbridge, this is the place to come for experts on Africa and Asia. Law students whinge that they're the only people who ever do any work. But generally students are highly motivated and courses are demanding. Beware, language courses are very intense. Teachers say that languages should become your life. Be prepared to decorate your bathroom with Vietnamese verbs!

The University of London purports to be a federal system, which means that a decreasing number of people every year get the chance to do courses at other London colleges. For those interested in a different part of the Developing World, UCL does good courses in Latin American culture and history.

SOCIAL LIFE: SOAS Action

Once a 'hot-bed of left-wing activity', the Student Union now fills its days drinking instant coffee out of polystyrene cups. Occasional single-issue activism and petition signing to stop evil, multi-national corporations destroying native cultures, flora and fauna, abound. Most activities are organised by SOAS's many societies. Every shade of political opinion and liberation struggle is represented. Many are worth getting involved in as they have interesting debates and guest speakers. You could find yourself chatting over wine and nibbles with some chap who could get you a flash job in the UN or the World Bank. SOAS has its own rugby, football and netball teams, but the University of London Union (ULU) offers a much wider range, as well as swimming pool and gym facilities.

Every once in a while, a mate of someone in the Union turns up and plays some old reggae records. The world renowned Bar (not SU run) is open from 11-2 p.m. and 5-8 p.m. When people moan, Chris, the much-loved Bar Manager, replies, 'Get a life, there's the whole of London out there' (sic).

Drugs: In 1996, drug dealing in SOAS Bar was generally seen to have become 'excessive'. The School launched a clean-up drive which involved a series of undercover police operations. This destroyed the widely-held myth amongst students that SOAS had some kind of immunity from being raided. One alleged dealer was surprised when the woman he was chatting up produced hand-cuffs and a warrant card! ULU, supposedly packed galore with fun and excitement, is just round the corner. UCL is also a stone's throw away, and Kings College is a short walk, both offering the opportunities and delights of a larger Union; more members of the opposite sex, beer, bands, etc. London is full of good, cheap places to eat, drink and be merry. You'll soon learn where they are; or starve! There are some great cheapie Indians behind Euston, for example, and many cinemas and theatres do discounts, or pay-what-you-can nights.

SOCIAL LIFE: General London Stuff and Accommodation

SOAS is secreted in the leafy heart of central London; close to Camden, host to all manner of houses of disrepute, and the West End - the celebrated domain of Sir Andrew Lloyd Webber and accomplices.

SOAS owns one mixed self-catering residence in the smashing Kings Cross area. It opened in September 1996, and facilities are good, but the residence has been dogged by allegations of mismanagement and that students' complaints about security and safety have been ignored. If you're new in town, get a place in halls, meet tons of people, get pissed loads, and eat unidentifiable slop (with rice). Grandmothers are sold to get into Hughes Parry and Commonwealth intercollegiate halls of residence. Most are within staggering distance of SOAS for a nine o'clock lecture.

The worst thing you could possibly do is find yourself in the unbelievably popular Green Lanes area of North London. There is absolutely nothing to do, but everyone seems to end up there. Alternatively, live in Camden, where a bed-sit can be had cheaply. Console yourself with the thought that someone who once had a Top 20 hit in the late 80s may pass your door. Ideally, move to the East End, darling of the style pages. Puffa jacket obligatory. Get used to sleeping on friends' floors as you can guarantee that they will live at least an hour away and there will be no night bus. Accommodation and travel make London more expensive than everywhere else, but don't let that put you off. The Holy Grail of living in London is finding a place that is central and cheap, but the two rarely come together. Take into account travel time and what zone the house is in when considering anywhere. Spending too much time on the tube is hazardous to your health!

School of Pharmacy

The School of Pharmacy
29-39 Brunswick Square
London WC1N 1AX

TEL 0171 753 5800
FAX 0171 278 0622

SCHOOL OF PHARMACY	
Founded	**1842**
Situation/style	**City site**
UNDERGRADUATE PROFILE	
Application acceptance rate	**7%**
Population	**375**
Mature student population	**24%**
Overseas student population	**22%**
Male/female ratio	**43:57**
1st year institut. accommodation	**100%**
Approximate cost	**£60-£85 pw**
ACADEMIC PROFILE	
A-level requirements:	**BBB**
Student/staff ratio	**9:1**
1st class degree pass rate	**7.4%**
Joint Funding Council's research assessment 1996 (1 subjects assessed)	
Pharmacy	Grade 5
EMPLOYMENT PROFILE	
Principal job market destinations: **Health, Retail/Wholesale, Manufacturing (Pharmaceutical)**	
Approximate % unemployed	**3.7%**

VAG VIEW

The School of Pharmacy is a specialist School of the University of London, the most specialist. It offers two degrees: BPharm Hons. in Pharmacy and BSc Hons. in Toxicology and Pharmacology. It has the best record in the country for what it does.

The School is situated within walking distance of the British Museum, and the nearest Underground Station is Russell Square (Piccadilly Line). For sport it shares the Royal Free grounds out at Enfield, but closer to home you'll find facilities for squash, badminton, swimming, etc., and the London University centre in Malet Street is close at hand (see London). Students at the school have their own Union, bar, ents programme (there's a regular disco Friday nights and film shows) and Common Room facilities for table tennis, billiards, etc.

SCHOOL OF SLAVONIC AND EAST EUROPEAN STUDIES

School of Slavonic and
East European Studies
Senate House
Malet Street
London WC1E 7HU

TEL 0171 637 4934
FAX 0171 436 8916

Student Union
School of Slavonic and
East European Studies
21-22 Russell Square
London WC1E 7HJ

TEL 0171 637 4934 x4069

SCHOOL OF SLAVONIC & EAST EUROPEAN STUDIES

Founded	**1915**
Situation/style	**City site**
UNDERGRADUATE PROFILE	
Application acceptance rate	**33%**
Population	**350**
Mature student population	**40%**
Overseas student population	**8%**
Male/female ratio	**48:52**
1st year institut. accommodation	**90%**
Approximate cost (School)	**£40-£75 pw**
(City)	**£55-£70 pw**
ACADEMIC PROFILE	
A-level requirements:	**Medium**

East European Languages/Lit./Studies CCC, **History & combinations/Russian/ Jewish** BCC
★ Special provision for mature/overseas students. Adequate written & spoken English a prerequisite.

Student/staff ratio	**10:1**
HEFCE assessments (3 subjects assessed/approved):	
1995 **Russian** 23	
1996 **E. European Studies** 18	
Joint Funding Council's research assessment 1996 (3 subjects assessed):	
None	Grade 5/5*
EMPLOYMENT PROFILE	
Principal job market destinations:	

Public Admin./Defence, International Charities, Industry, Banking, Media

VAG VIEW

SSEES is one of those University of London colleges situated in a huddle - (along with Birkbeck College and SOAS) - close to London University Union and University College in the Bloomsbury area of London (Russell Square - Piccadilly Line - Underground).

As its name suggests, 'SSEES is the best college in the country for the language, culture and history of Eastern Europe: Poland, German Democratic Republic, Czech Republic, Slovakia, Hungary, Slovenia, Croatia, Bosnia-Herzegovena, Serbia, Yugoslavia, the Hapsburg Empire, the Soviet Union, Ukraine, Bulgaria, Roumania, Albania, Macedonia, former Soviet Republics, Finland and more,' as our correspondent so kindly listed for us. In fact Gideon has tackled so well every aspect of life at SSEES, other than sport - (they guarantee you access to facilities for football, rugby, netball, aerobics, hockey and mountaineering and to ULU sporting facilities round the corner) - that it may be as well to give him his rein.

VIEW FROM THE GROUND
by Gideon Dewhirst

The School of Slavonic and East European Studies (SSEES - pronounced 'cease') awaits to impose its twisted vision of 'permanent [university] revolution' upon you! SSEES is the largest institution for the study of Eastern Europe in Britain. It holds the academically-acknowledged best lecturers in their fields, and the largest East European library in Britain. Amongst our luminaries were Tomas Masaryk, professor here then first President of Czechoslovakia, and Jonathon Ross, though apparently he now denies it and says he went to LSE (snob). SSEES is very fortunate regarding its position, being placed in the pulsating heart of London, and it possesses such a friendly, cosy atmosphere (prompted, no doubt, by its small size) that you have no excuse to have anything but a brilliant time.

SITUATION
Two buildings, both centrally placed, adjacent to Russell Square: the imposing granite Stalinist/Gotham City edifice of Senate House (academia) and 21-22 Russell Square (the social hub of SSEES). In Russell Square is the JCR (also smoking room) with armchairs, informatiques and daily newspapers. Across the way is Irene's Canteen, with reasonable quality food at rather dubious prices. Next to the hallowed institution of the bar - the one and only and focal point of SSEES life - is the Pool Room, housing (absolutely free!) pool, subject to an almost continual battle of wills and very bad jokes (e.g. What's the queue? A piece of wood you hit the balls with...) The Rainbow Room houses free-use TV and Video (self-explanatory).

MORE BROKEN PIECES OF SSEES LIFE
SSEES also offers a bi-termly news magazine, SSEESFIRE - 'a reflection of the truth' - full of news, rumours (rife at a small college), etc., and SSEES Man's column: more drunken pontificating as patented at the SSEES bar. There are societies aplenty; the Masaryk society, a Czech-o-slovak society named after the former professor. Studies into Czech beer, culture and dumplings are undertaken. The Polish/Russian/Hungarian society, likewise, studies Polish/Russian/Hungarian vodka etc....And yet there is more! The Debating Society deliberates topically in a civilised and wine-fuelled atmosphere, the Mountaineering Society undertakes trips to the (bleak) Isle of Skye...Sports are undertaken at the premises of the University of London Union, less that four minutes walk from the college, and which are furnished with much more cash and space than the limited funds of the college, for no cost to you or your college.

SOCIAL THINGYS
And now to the SSEES bar, the Hammer and Sickle, the only part of SSEES that really matters. Forget those boring lectures, the Hammer and Sickle is really where it's at. The Bar is renowned for its cosy, comfortable, bijou atmosphere. A place where people come to enjoy themselves, relax, and try to forget about that coursework essay. The size is modest, with a complex of different rooms to choose from; there's even a TV and video on offer. And hey, in most bars you wouldn't get the friendly atmosphere that these conditions offer - the Bar isn't just for getting drunk, it's a social experience all by itself. You can rely on making friends even as a timid fresher dude(ss). Oh, and by the way, the bar sells draught and bottled beer, including Czech and East European beers/spirits, crisps and snacks... As well as this continual bar party, SSEES has regular PARTIES(!), thrice-termly, with alky promos, discos, stupid themes, and live bands. Academic departments and societies often have their own parties too.

The atmosphere of SSEES is what really sticks it out from the crowd. Unlike the snobbish, stilted cliques of much of mass-student universities' life, SSEES's small population means you will soon know everyone by their first name and they will know you. Mature and post-sixth-form college students mix amicably. The smaller size does limit pulling potential, but lots of other colleges are nearby waiting for the kill. And

SSEES being so small, any intended victims can't get away. Another joy is that citizens can use the University of London Union (ULU), only four minutes walk from college. ULU possess all that you might want from a campus that SSEES might possibly lack. Discount shops, swimming pools, sport halls and a multitude of societies (as well as two cheap bars and an admittedly cheesy nightclub) are all within easy grasp.

ACADEMIA

An interest in Eastern Europe is recommended. Your lecturers will probably have written the books you will be working from. History and languages are special strengths, and the college is (surprisingly) sympathetic towards overloaded students, though the workload is usually medium in range. SSEES's library is the largest East European library in Western Europe, and the University of London Library, a huge complex, is located within the same building as SSEES's.

Living in Eastern Europe for an extended period of time is a normal part of most courses, and has been the highlight of most students' time at SSEES. Trips go to the Czech Republic, Poland and many cities within the Russian Federation for a period varying according to the student from three months to one year. This is worked through the Erasmus scheme and financial aid grants are available.

MY HOUSE

Turning to the less exciting subject of accommodation, the situation is, although not overwhelmingly so, hazard-free. The extremely local intercollegiate halls (see London Uni) tend to be people's first year (and virtually guaranteed) choice, and they move out to the private sector after getting to know the place better. Halls, being 'intercollegiate' (fetch your dictionary), are always interesting, and provide an alternate social scene. The three biggies are: International (good social life; bad rooms), Commonwealth (average social life; average rooms) and Hughes Parry (bad social life; good rooms). There are also single-sex halls (best avoided).

Private accommodation (this IS London) is easy to find, especially with the aid of the University of London Accommodation Office (ULAO). The city does have dodgy areas, which common sense or ULAO should warn you away from. Average rent away from the absolute centre is £55 per week - you pay £15 for your weeks' travelcard tho'. To live centrally is too expensive to consider (£80 per week on average, if you do). A popular (and happening) place to be is Camden, but Sseesonians tend to live all over, usually with friends they made in their first year.

In conclusion, to flourish at SSEES you should not be a teetotaller or have a hatred of Eastern Europe. There is no typical SSEES citizen - male/female, mature/immature, Britisher/East European mix well in the cosy atmosphere. The quality of teaching is high and so, those with the necessary cast iron gut and high-minded ideal should enjoy themselves and come out with a fairly decent degree.

SCOTTISH AGRICULTURAL COLLEGE

SAC Auchincruive
Ayr
KA6 5HW

TEL 01292 520331

SAC Aberdeen
The McRobert Building
581 King Street
Aberdeen
AB24 5UD

TEL 01224 711000

SAC Edinburgh
West Mains Road
EH9 3JG

TEL 0131 667 1041

SCOTTISH AGRICULTURAL COLLEGE	
Founded	**1899**
Situation/style	**City campus/ sites & farms**
UNDERGRADUATE PROFILE	
Application acceptance rate	**32%**
Population	**320**
Mature student population	**43%**
Overseas student population	**5%**
Male/female ratio	**70:30**
1st year institut. accommodation	**40%**
Approximate cost (College)	**£60 pw**
(City)	**£45 pw**
ACADEMIC PROFILE	
A-level requirements:	**Low**
Agriculture D, **Biol. Sciences: Aquaculture** CD	
Student/staff ratio	**5:1**
1st class degree pass rate	**7.7%**
Approximate % unemployed	**7%**

VAG VIEW

Doug Page covers it all - SAC is to Scotland what the Royal Agricultural College is to England.

VIEW FROM THE GROUND

by Doug Page

SAC is no different from any other Higher Education Institution - it does not have a typical student. The College has three different Centres of Study at Aberdeen, Ayr and Edinburgh, and although the name suggests agriculturally based courses, the College has diversified into other areas such as Leisure and Tourism, Conservation Management, Aquaculture, Environmental Protection, to name but a few. Approximately 1000 students are scattered over the three Centres with Ayr being the largest. The proportion of male to female is approximately 70:30 and 35%+ are mature (i.e. 21 and over on entry). The College is filled with all colours, creeds and nationalities and because of its smallish size, can truly guarantee a community type atmosphere at each of its Centres. By common consensus, staff at all three Centres, are, in the main friendly and approachable, with high regard placed on the 'informal' which has led to good staff/student working relationships. Money is always a problem for students but one good thing is that everyone is in the same boat. Skint! The usual war cry can be heard for miles around the College campuses 'I've no money for food'. However, everyone meets up at night to discuss who is the most impoverished over a few beers in each of the student bars.

SAC ABERDEEN

Situated about fifteen minutes drive from the city centre on the Craibstone Estate, there are three halls of residence, Sutton Hall being the most recent and luxurious with all rooms en suite - but you pay a little bit more for that. Craibstone has good sporting facilities on site with the new astro-turf being regularly used for football, hockey and basketball. There is also a fitness centre and indoor facilities. An enthusiastic Agricultural Society runs the sports teams, mainly for those who believe that it's the taking part that is important and whose emphasis is on post match analysis in the various hostelries in and around Aberdeen! Talking of which, Craibstone boasts its own special bar which offers immense ceilidhs and awesome discos and is certainly the hub of social life on Campus. In Aberdeen there are hosts of pubs and clubs which SAC students frequent, namely, the Bobbin, Ma Cameron's, Smart Alec's, ZUU, to name but a few. Aberdeen is also fortunate to attract a good selection of live music throughout the year with the Lemon Tree being a popular haunt for students. Like any other large city, Aberdeen has a wealth of diverse eating houses, cinemas and leisure facilities and the scenery round and about the city is not bad either, e.g. forty minutes and you are on Royal Deeside for your afternoon tea at Balmoral.

SAC AUCHINCRUIVE

This campus is also approximately three miles from the town centre [of Ayr] and is surrounded by rolling countryside - God's Country to the locals. There is one hall of residence but further student self-catering residences are planned. Buses run frequently past the front door but students also cycle and bring their four wheel drive jeeps (agrics only). Living on campus allows you to be the rural visionary by day and urban warrior by night, plus the fact we are only 45 minutes by car/train to the centre of Glasgow.

Social life at Auchincruive can certainly test not only your stamina but courage. With its own bar, entertainments revolve around ceilidhs, discos, quizzes, revues, etc, etc. Charities Week has had great successes, the Summer Ball is one of the biggest events on the student social calendar...

One good thing about Ayr is that it is not that big and finding your way about doesn't take long. Times change from year to year but the most popular watering holes at the moment are O'Brien's, a busy bar with basic cheap food and good live Irish music. Flannigan's in Prestwich is the same and runs a bus from the College. Elliot's have regular promotions and many of the other bars offer Happy Hours on various nights and at various times, the list of bars is endless and offers something different to everyone. Cub de Mar (or Club Too Far as it is affectionately known) is the most popular with students, especially on a Thursday with a ticket obtained from the Club allowing students entry for £1.00 rather than £4.00. All forms of dance, house and rave music are found here, but in contrast is The Powerhouse which is a bit more 'Heavy' than Club Too Far. Here you can really let your hair down. Prices vary between £4.00 and £6.00 depending on whether or not a band is playing. Bobby Jones has an older crowd and would suit the more 'mature student' as Club de Mar would do on Wednesday night. There is also a newish club which has recently opened but not really rated as a student hangout - yet! Ayr has a plethora of eating places in the form of fast foods, Chinese, Indian, Italian, Turkish, as well as those establishments offering good Scottish cuisine. The Odeon cinema gives discount to students during the day and some evening performances and although this is the only cinema, Craigie College has a Film Club on Wednesday nights which show more arty films.

Sport is high on the list of priorities for many students at Auchincruive and there are the usual teams and clubs which take playing and socialising very seriously, especially against cross Centre fixtures and visiting Colleges. There is also an active Outdoor Pursuits Club for the Chris Bonnington types, a well equipped fitness centre for the Mr Motivator types and line dancing classes for the very sad types. South Ayrshire's wet and dry leisure facilities are excellent and well within reach of the College.

SAC EDINBURGH

The Scottish Agricultural College (Edinburgh) is situated at the furthest and most inaccessible corner of King's Buildings - a range of buildings which houses the scientific branch of Edinburgh University and which bears an uncanny resemblance to an industrial estate from the 1970s. The campus is approximately four miles from the city centre but has no accommodation on site. However, the nice ladies in the Education Office at KB can usually provide you with help and information. As its name suggests, until a few years ago the campus catered mainly for Agricultural students, however, over the past few years it has begun to diversify by including courses in Rural Resource Management, Environmental Protection and Management and Horticulture with Plantsmanship.

Edinburgh pubs and clubs are legendary in their own right and any student new to the city will find their own favourite watering hole - which you have to as there is no SAC Bar on campus (but you can infiltrate into Edinburgh Uni's with your SAC matriculation Card). Finally, a word of advice. If you can fit all that in with the various balls, orgies and toga parties that are an everyday part of a SAC student's life, then you are not doing enough work mate!

GETTING THERE

Ayr:

★ By road: The A77 northbound links Ayr to Glasgow and Paisley under the hour. Link with M74 (J2), A71, A77 from the east.

★ By rail: Fast and regular service from Glasgow Central to Ayr Central station. Glasgow Central for London (6:00), Liverpool, Manchester and Birmingham (5:30). Glasgow Queen Street station (just minutes from Glasgow Central) for Edinburgh (0:50), Aberdeen (2:45).

Aberdeen:

★ By road: From the south on the A92, thence on to the ring road where you'll pick up signs. From the north, it's the A96 or the A92 .

★ By rail: links via Edinburgh, Newcastle, find their way in seven hours or so to London King's Cross.

★ By air: Aberdeen International Airport links with Heathrow, Gatwick, Stansted and Luton - just over one hour's flight time.

Edinburgh:

★ By road: M90 from the north across the Forth Bridge or the M9 down from Stirling. The A1 up from Newcastle. The M8 from Glasgow.

★ By rail: Kings Cross (4:30). Glasgow Central; Newcastle, 0:50, 1:30.

★ By air: Edinburgh Airport offers inland and international flights.

SHEFFIELD UNIVERSITY

The University of Sheffield
Firth Court
Western Bank
Sheffield
S Yorks
S10 2TN

TEL 0114 222 2000

University of Sheffield
Union of Students
Western Bank
Sheffield S10 2TG

TEL 0114 222 8500
FAX 0114 275 2506

UNIVERSITY OF SHEFFIELD

Founded	**1905**
Situation/style	**Campus**

UNDERGRADUATE PROFILE

Application acceptance rate	**8%**
Medical AAR	**7%**
Population	**12,200**
Mature student population	**17%**
Overseas student population	**10%**
Male/female ratio	**56:44**
1st year institut. accommodation	**99%**
Approximate cost (Uni)	**£40-£65 pw**
(City)	**£40 pw**

ACADEMIC PROFILE

A-level requirements: **High-Medium**
Law AAB, **Architecture, Planning** BBC-BCC, **History, English Literature** BBB, **Music** BBC-BCC, **Chemical Engineering** BBC-CCD, **E & E, Civil Engineering** BBC-BCC **Mechanical Engineering** 24, **Russian** BCC-BCD, **Social Policy and Sociology** BBC.
Medicine ABB:
★ Science 'A's required **Chemistry + 1 from Biology, Physics, Maths**
★ Addit. Non-Science 'A's acceptable **Yes**
★ Retakes considered **Yes**
★ Retake offer in retake **A**
★ Clinical contact **Stage 1**

Student/staff ratio	**11:1**
1st class degree pass rate	**8.3%**

HEFCE assessments
(19 subjects assessed/approved):

1993 **History, Mechanical Engineering, Law**	Excellent
1994 **Applied Social Work, Architecture**	Excellent
1995 **English, Geography, Music, Social Policy & Admin.**	Excellent
German 20	
1995/6 **Russian** 24	
Linguistics 22	
1996 **Iberian** 21 **Chemical Engineering** 21 **French** 21	

Joint Funding Council's research assessment 1996
(40 subjects assessed):

E & E Engineering (Automatic Control & Systems), Metallurgy & Materials, Archaeology, Library & Information, Theology.	Grade 5*
Psychology, Mechanical/ Aeronautical/Manufacturing Eng., Built Environment, Town & Country Planning, Geography, Law, Politics, Russian, History, Philosophy, Music, Education.	Grade5

EMPLOYMENT PROFILE

Employability in Industry:

MPW national league table (1996)	**13th**

Principal job market destinations:
Health (incl. **Dentistry**), **Manufacturing, Commerce** (strong), **Retail/Wholesale, Public Admin./Law, Education, Hotel/Restaurant, Personnel, Arts/Media, Computer, Engineering Design** (strong)

PIP 1996 employers' survey:
Top 3 subjects/national ranking

Engineering & Technology	8th=
Science	9th=
Accountancy, Finance, Banking	14th=
Approximate % unemployed	**7%**

VAG VIEW

Sheffield is a long-established university, and like others of its founding time, is adapting to change. All its courses are now modularised except for Architecture, Medicine and Dentistry. Students, like our correspondent Emily McGarr, are feeling the change. But in the prospectus the impression you get is of a Uni that was already doing what was needed to attain its impressive record of employment and academic success. For example, they pick up on the buzz phrase 'personal transferable skills', which is sweeping the new higher education establishments as what is wanted by today's employer, and they liken them to the basic academic skills, as if there is really no change at all. They define them as analytical and evaluative skills, mentioning presentation too, and show that their academic course will supply them. In terms of new teaching techniques and employment-related coursework Sheffield has led the way and they don't need pressure from outside to show them how. Their School of Biological Studies has for many years used computer-assisted methods. Students in their Mechanical Engineering department are already integrated project-wise with local companies. There is a course on World Civilisations (History) taught almost entirely through video and information technology.

In the midst of great change, when the new Uni strategies have all the running, it is reassuring to sample the depth of work that has gone into a more traditional Uni's world-class record of achievement in research and graduate employment.

GETTING THERE

★ By road: M1 (J33), A630, A57. From the west, A57.
★ By rail: London, 2:30; Liverpool Lime Street, 1:45; Manchester Piccadilly, 1:00; Nottingham 1:00; Leeds, 0:30.
★ By air: Manchester airport for international and inland flights.

VIEW FROM THE GROUND
by Emily McGarr

Fed up reading prospectuses trying to decide which university is best? Just want to throw the UCAS forms in the bin? Well, worry no longer. Make sure you're the one who comes to Sheffield. Why? Well, where do I start...?

SITUATION

Sheffield is an established, yet modern, city in the geographical centre of England, renowned years ago for its steel and fast becoming famous for sport and leisure. It boasts two major footballs teams (Wednesday and United), an international sports centre, Don Valley Stadium and The Arena, home of Sheffield Steelers ice hockey team. Manchester is an hour west, Leeds an hour north and London about three hours south.

Sheffield is huge but the University and student ghettos are all on one side of the city centre, so there ís a friendly community feeling to the place, although Sheffield is most definitely not a campus university.

The central concourse is about 15 minutes walk from the main city shops, with departments scattered through the surrounding area. It is not uncommon to find a house, a solicitor's and an annex of the English department all in one street. The Crookesmoor Building (Law) and Mappin Street (Engineering & Management School) are furthest from the concourse, and though still only ten minutes walk from the Union they are 20 minutes from each other, so don't pick Law and Economics unless you can run real quick in between lectures.

In truth, one word describes Sheffield and that's hilly. Make that two actually, hilly and *wet*. It rains loads. Most students walk everywhere, but public transport is reliable and cheap and Sheffield also has Supertram, which runs from the city centre to numerous places, including Meadowhall, the famous out-of-town shopping complex. It's very pretty with glass lifts and posh malls, although not brimming with bargains (so take your parents when they come to visit).

A car is a real bonus as it gets you up the hills and keeps you dry, although there isn't an abundance of parking spaces and getting a permit is hard. Having your own transport helps you enjoy weekends though - Sheffield is on the edge of the Peak District where you can walk, cycle or abseil to your heart's content. Bakewell, home of the famous tart, is just one little country village great to escape to on Sunday afternoons when you should be working. But remember the umbrella or hooded top, or just get a wet look haircut and be done with it.

STUDENT PROFILE

There is a highly diverse student population and in 1996/7, the 18-21 year-old undergraduates made up just under half of Sheffield students. Considering the high proportion of international students, there isn't a great deal of multi-cultural mixing. Students come from a variety of backgrounds and areas and you can expect to meet people whose parents support them well and those trying to make a grant and loan stretch to the summer. You can be as studious as you want, the libraries are open until 9 o'clock most nights and weekends which might not sound like much but you'll be grateful in essay week. Similarly there are many computer rooms, most open for general use, and one open 24 hours every day - free tuition is available at any time, from the real basics (turning it on) to making your own homepage on the Internet.

There isn't an average student at Sheffield anymore, but this is certainly not the place to come if your idea of a good time is Saturday night in watching TV alone. The Union is a sociable, active and lively place, giving you the perfect chance to do all the things you didn't have time to when doing A-levels - joining a football team, auditioning for a play, raising money for charity. You can comfort yourself in the knowledge that being captain of the History Football team is improving your job prospects because employers are looking now for graduates with interesting life experiences rather than a first class degree. What a relief.

SOCIAL LIFE

The Union building has just undergone a major refurb, and there are now two bars. The original, named Bar One, is the classic cheap student hole with loud music, a constant haze of smoke (the only place to smoke in the day), bar quizzes, drink promotions and snack bars selling junk food and the best pizza you've ever tasted. There's an arcade, a pool room and a beer garden which is a magnet for living beings when the sun finally comes out. The new Interval Cafe Bar is aimed primarily, but not exclusively, at postgraduate, mature and international students or the 'quieter types', and provides another place to eat lunch. The U-Zone is the shopping bit of the Union, including a shop with extra low prices, a free advice centre, a laundrette, numerous banks, a travel agent and loads of grub places.

More opportunities to buy beer appear in the evening when The Park changes from a cafe to a pub/club and speakers in The Foundry pump out the music for the night's gig or event. This year we've seen Skunk Anansie, Squeeze, Perfecto, The Chemical Brothers, Incognito and numerous others in the Union.

In the city, the Arena and City Hall play host to major names for music and comedy, Jamiroquai, Manic Street Preachers, Lighthouse Family, Eddie Izzard, Lee Hurst, Ben Elton to name but a few. Most of the major tours stop at Sheffield and you can usually get discount tickets for £12-ish.

The Union puts on events almost every night, ranging from Pop Tarts (70s and 80s) to El Tel's Midweek Fixture (current pop and chart to coincide with sports events) to Stomp for Indie kids. Most gigs and events are organised and run by Ents and TSC (Technical Services Committee), students looking after bands and setting up events.

There is a good variety of clubs in the city and Sheffield is fast becoming a rival to Leeds for northern nightlife, bringing in top DJs and famous bands. For true hardened clubbers, Rise on Fridays at the Leadmill is just the best and the Music Factory is home to the infamous Love to Be... on Saturdays. These aren't your usual 10-2, 'curtain and carpet' cheesy clubs, although we've got a fair share of them too, but are true warehouse venues open until early morning. Most clubs and pubs have at least one student night with free or cheap entry and drink at unmissable prices (50p a shot/£1 a bottle), catering for a range of musical tastes. Drugs are available if you want them, but nobody forces it if you're not interested. The locals are pretty reasonable, although they are going to complain if you keep coming back at 2 a.m. after a curry singing 'Alice the Camel...' really loud. Obviously.

ACCOMMODATION

Broomhill, home to the University residences, is the place to live in your first year because it has top pubs and is only fifteen minutes walk from the central concourse. Everyone who firmly accepts a place and gets their forms back on time (strongly advised) gets in university managed accommodation. This makes life easier as you automatically meet at least 300 housemates, pay lower rent and get a cleaner. University accommodation has improved recently offering a greater range, from a cheap two person room with shared facilities to an individual en-suite room for those who like their privacy (and are rich).

Halls are very popular with first years and the atmosphere in the first few weeks is comparable only to that of a holiday, meeting new people and non-stop partying. Ranmoor is the biggest and has a bar to rival no other, although smaller halls like Stevenson or Halifax are friendlier. Self-catering accommodation is popular with those who appreciate their independence and enjoy cooking. Some like Crewe Flats offer entertainment like a hall, others like Riverdale Flats are cheaper and quieter. Housing Services help find accommodation for all students and sort out domestic problems, such as collapsed ceilings and other minor disasters.

After a year though, it can get claustrophobic and a student house without oddbods knocking on your door at 3 a.m. for a coffee, may seem an attractive option. The student houses in Broomhill are very popular and therefore very expensive (£40+ rent a week with no summer reduction) so you may end up in Crookes or Hunters Bar, both major student living areas (rents more like £35 - £40 with reductions). All three areas have loads of pubs, the noisy, student orientated ones and quieter ones for first dates and daytime pints, and offer a superb range of restaurants and takeaways with students discounts and special deals as good as 'Buy one pizza, get another free'. You'll probably be visiting a lot of takeaways after a few weeks of hall food or washing up. Sheffield is surprisingly safe although like any big city, there are dodgy areas and rents are inevitably cheaper there. Broomhall, just south of University, is a less popular housing area, famous for prostitutes and high crime rates. Check the insurance premium before you sign a contract.

ACADEMIA

For most students on average type courses, the year is divided into two semesters, which run from September to January and then February to June with exams in the last three weeks of each semester. Holidays are long with three weeks at Christmas, four weeks at Easter and three months in the summer which gives you time to get a horrible factory job to pay back your overdraft or go travelling if you get organised.

Sheffield University have jumped on the modularisation bandwagon which has swept through higher education as a ploy to confuse older lecturers and get them to retire. The result? Each semester, you are expected to complete 60 credits, which means studying three to six modules, depending on whether the module is worth 10 or 20 credits (confused yet?). The nice coloured flow charts in the handbooks explain this better, but basically you end up with two to three hours of lectures and anything from one to six hours of tutorials/seminars/lab classes per module. Lectures aren't compulsory and it only takes a few weeks to decide which lecturers are reading from the key text and which are worth getting up for. Sadly registers are taken at tutorials and labs, and official warnings are given by some departments if you miss more than two. In truth, this all happens in the last few weeks of a semester when essay deadlines and exams get close, the libraries get busy and the bars mysteriously empty.

Sheffield University has a reputation of excellence which helps get a job - the Psychology, Medicine and Law courses are highly acclaimed and the Sociology department has won many awards for research. Sheffield is currently the only 'old' university to offer a BA in Journalism. All language courses enable you to spend a year abroad and study away is available to students on most courses through Erasmus. Many courses involve fieldwork, from measuring river speeds in the Peaks to market research in the city.

Medicine and Dentistry are without doubt the most demanding courses, with shorter holidays than most and a large amount of work experience. But medics have the last laugh when they get a job easily.

POLITICS, ARTS, SPORT, RELIGION, CLUBS

As people come from varying backgrounds, there isn't a general lean towards left or right in voting. Sheffield students are often seen as being apathetic although there are political groups and campaigns to get involved in and the Union is always represented at NUS and local demos.

The free fortnightly student newspaper, DARTS, covers local community and student issues and is written by students with editorial control independent of the Union. The Theatre Company use the Drama Studio 3 times a term for productions ranging from Shakespearean tragedy to student written plays on pornography to musicals. Both the Crucible and Lyceum theatres in the city and the 10 screen Odeon cinema offer big student discounts, especially mid-week. The extension to the Union involved the building of a new 400-seat auditorium which is used by the Film Unit as a cinema 3 times a week, showing films well before they are released on video.

The Goodwin Sports Centre which includes a first class (but cold) swimming pool, gym and numerous astro-turf pitches, is planning major improvements to its facilities at a cost of £14 million. There are currently some 60 sports clubs with the policy 'sport for all', covering traditional sports like rugby, hockey and cricket and newer sports like frisbee, step and skiing. You can be as involved as you like, many aerobics classes work a 'pay as you go' system for example.

There are 127 societies covering almost everything including political and campaigning societies like Amnesty International, societies for particular departments, religions and cultures and general interest societies including Debating, Guinness Appreciation and Shiatsu Massage. The word is 'if it isn't there and you want it, start it yourself' - the Radio Society started as an individual's idea last year and they'll soon be broadcasting around the Union from their own studio.

The Workspace, the first of its kind in the country, is the heart of sports clubs and societies and consists of meeting rooms and work areas with telephones and computing facilities which members can use to contact each other, meet and organise events. The manned information desk here is the place to find out about any club, society or working committee.

Still undecided? Every November (when it's getting freezing), the Uni and Hallam student charities appeals come together and organise Pyjama Jump, the only ticketed street pyjama party in the UK. Girls dress up in pyjamas and men in women's underwear and everyone goes out to the pubs, ending up at a club with the intention of drinking as much alcohol as possible and copping off with anyone (policemen, horses, lamp-posts included). This event raises about £50,000 for charity and almost 20,000 students take part making it quite simply superb - so good the locals don't complain too much and it's worth queuing all day for a ticket (an event in itself). Double your snog count in one night - easy.

THE FINAL BIT

I have never regretted my decision to come to Sheffield. The Union is one of, if not THE best in the country, offering so many exciting opportunities, it's a wonder anybody ever does any work. But don't believe a word I say. Student Reception (contact (0114) 2228546) are a group of students who spend their time taking sixth-formers around the Union and to the other exciting places no one else will show you. For a measly £5.50 a night, they'll even find you a student house to stay in so you can get a real taste of Sheffield social life. This experience is invaluable; arrange your visit now and you'll never have to look at another prospectus.

SHEFFIELD HALLAM UNIVERSITY

Sheffield Hallam University
Pond Street
Sheffield
S1 1WB

TEL 0114 2720911

Sheffield Hallam University
Union of Students
Nelson Mandela Building
Pond Street
Sheffield S1 2BW

TEL 0114 253 4111
FAX 0114 253 4140

SHEFFIELD HALLAM UNIVERSITY

Founded	**1905**
Situation/style	**Campus**
UNDERGRADUATE PROFILE	
Application acceptance rate	**8%**
Population	**11,200**
Mature student population	**36%**
Overseas student population	**3%**
Male/female ratio	**55:45**
1st year institut. accommodation	**35%**
Approximate cost (Uni)	**£35-£55 pw**
(City)	**£40 pw**
ACADEMIC PROFILE	
A-level requirements:	**Medium-Low**

Business Studies (Sandwich) AB-CCC, **Finance/Accounting** 14-18, **Law** 18-20, **Physioth./Occup. Therapy/** CCC, **Biomedical Sciences combined** 8, **Nursing** CC, **Civil Engineering** CD-DDE, **Electronic Engineering** DD

Student/staff ratio	**16:1**
1st class degree pass rate	**3.8%**

HEFCE assessments (9 subjects assessed/approved):

1994 **English**	Excellent
1995/6 **Modern Languages** 19	
Sociology 22	
Joint Funding Council's research assessment 1996 (17 subjects assessed):	
Grade 5/5*	None

EMPLOYMENT PROFILE

Employability in Industry:	
MPW national league table (1996)	**36th**

Principal job market destinations:

Manufacturing (**Pharmaceutical, Electronic & Electrical** strong), **Education, Commerce, Health, Retail/Wholesale, Public Admin./ Law, Computer,** good record **Arts/ Media, Construction, Sport**

PIP 1996 employers' survey:
Top 2 subjects/national ranking

Business	18th
Construction & Civil Engineering	29th=
Approximate % unemployed	**7%**

VAG VIEW

First, what's the view of what goes on from the schools? - 'They've got mainly Business and Hotel/Catering, Tourism - very good at what they do on those. And it has a lot of sandwich courses.'

'Sheffield is one of our more attractive cities despite all the re-routing going on at the moment. It's got contours hasn't it? The surrounding area is very pleasant. Sheffield Hallam is on the way up and popular among students.'

Their faculties include Business, Computing & Mgt. Sciences, Construction, Cultural Studies, Education, Engineering, Financial Studies & Law, Health & Community Studies, Leisure & Food Mgt., Science & Maths, Urban & Regional Studies. It has done very well on its course assessments (see fact box), and its graduate employment record puts it into the league tables. At the start of the section of its prospectus about its Combined Studies Programme, SH declares its aim clearly enough - 'Each of the University's named courses...is a set of units which has been put together to suit a particular range of careers.' The question is whether you consider that is what the university experience is about? Many do.

Try as he might, Ian Montgomery, our correspondent, doesn't really convince us that SH gives him such a good time. You get the feeling he is there for the course. SH is the former Sheffield City Poly. It has some very good courses, and excellent teaching, and its rise to university status has lifted it onto a more visible and significant stratum, no longer only defined by what it has shown itself to be good at. SH has an edge with some of its courses, but you don't build a university only on courses or on your record of employment or on a spanking new built environment (recently £40 million was spent on its award-winning Atrium, the university's hub).

Although these are part of it, in the end it is students who make a university, and the problem all the newer ones have is a cultural one, setting that ball rolling. It isn't chance that SH's prospectus opens with pages of photographs of what Sheffield, the city and surrounding countryside, are like, while its neighbour, Sheffield Uni, launches straight into the vibrant student life at their Uni, a piece entitled 'The Sheffield Experience'.

SH has a large proportion of mature students, 36%, which is absolutely in line with its commitment to satisfying the need for re-training and re-education in a job market which no longer offers jobs for life. But the employment angle, which is sharp, and the age of its students, are bound to affect the culture of the place.

In re-defining Higher Education we are re-defining what our Unis are about in more ways than academically, and yet the revolution that has brought polys to university status was clearly much more than a marketing exercise. Perhaps the fault lies with us if we assume that the new Unis see the university experience in the same way as the old. It is as yet too early to tell.

SITUATION

Sheffield Hallam has five campuses, one in the city centre - City Campus (address above), and four in the Southwest of the city. Most courses are campus based.

ADDRESSES

Telephone, the same as for City.
Collegiate Crescent Campus,
Sheffield S10 2BP.
Hallamshire Business Park,
Napier Street, Sheffield S11 8HD.
Psalter Lane Campus,
Sheffield S11 8UZ.
Totley Campus,
Totley Hall Lane, Sheffield S17 4AB.

GETTING THERE

★ By road: M1 (J33), A630, A57.
From the west, A57.
★ By rail: London, 2:30; Liverpool Lime Street, 1:45; Manchester Piccadilly, 1:00; Nottingham 1:00; Leeds, 0:30.
★ By air: Manchester airport for international and inland flights.

VIEW FROM THE GROUND
by Ian Montgomery

★ Sheffield is built on seven hills and I've lived on three of them. Apart from the occasional slope Sheffield is a great city (and the University is not bad either).

★ Sheffield is for the city dweller. If you're a country bumpkin who likes nice quiet walks in the fields don't even think about going to Sheffield.

Personally, I like the University, so I haven't got many bad words to say about it. Although, because of its size it can sometimes be a bit impersonal, there is such a diverse range of cultures and interests at the University, nearly everyone will fit in.

The facilities at the University are excellent, the new buildings and teaching areas create a good, quality atmosphere. The new learning centre is very nice, although there is always a queue to use the PCs, so you use the computers (of which there are many) in other parts of the campus.

Although 50% of first year students are over 21, the number of mature students varies widely across the many different courses, so don't worry about being the only 18-year-old on your course. The older students may even be just as nervous about working with younger people, especially if it has been several years since they last studied.

There's a great atmosphere in Sheffield. What with about 30,000 students the town is very student-friendly. You can get student discounts for almost anything, from cheap drinks to hair cuts.

You'll find there's at least one nightclub offering a special student night every day of the week. These are cheap to get into and there are also drinks promotions, so you can have a good night without hurting your wallet.

There are more pubs than you can shake a stick at. The most popular areas are West Street and Ecclesall Road. Just as with the nightclubs, many of the pubs run drinks promotions and student nights, so you can always find somewhere that stretches your measly grant or student loan that little bit further.

The Students Union bar is where I spend a lot of my time. It's a great place to meet your friends, with cheap drinks and a groovy disco open until 3 a.m. and as with other clubs, there are different styles of music on different nights.

There are also many venues for live music, the Leadmill, the Students Union, the City Hall and the Octagon are the most well-known. If you're into dance music, check out Rise at the Leadmill or the Music Factory.

I don't aspire to being a football-loving lager lout and museums and art galleries are not really my field, but for the more cultured student, there are two theatres, the Crucible and the Lyceum, close to the city campus.

The transport network in the city is excellent. There are enough fume pumping buses to ruin anyone's lungs, but there is a good regular service all over the city. There is also the Supertram, but I would only use it for longer journeys, such as to the Meadowhall shopping centre, as you have to pay a uniform fare, regardless of your destination. If you own a car, beware! Parking in Sheffield is a nightmare. Even if you can park in the town centre it will cost you a fortune. Unless you live miles away from the campus I'd say take the bus, or walk for free.

There is a large number of chip shops, kebab shops, Indian and Chinese takeaways all over the city. As well as expensive restaurants there are more grant-friendly eateries, such as Groucho's on Ecclesall Road or the Forum on Division Street, where you can get snacks and hot food from around £3 up to £8.

There are several places to eat in and around the city campus, all are very reasonably priced. Whether you want a sandwich or a hot meal, you can always find somewhere.

The Students Union has societies and clubs that cater for everyone, from sports to rock music, and campaigning groups, such as the hunt saboteurs. If you want to do a sport run by the Students Union you have to pay to join that (currently £6-£9). Ponds Forge is a huge leisure centre in the middle of town. Again you can get a student discount on the facilities there, but you have to buy a leisure card (£6 this year). The Union organises a Freshers Week of course, at the beginning of the semester. This is a bit like the 1960s: if you can remember it, you weren't there!

Probably my only criticism of the University is that some of its halls of residence are not very nice. I stayed in halls at Totley for two nights whilst looking for a house. They were six miles outside the town and weren't particularly pleasant, but halls are a great way of getting to know a large number of people quickly, so if you're not a mingler, these may be the place for you. Contrary to my experience, several of my friends lived there and they like it.

I have always lived in shared houses and the house-hunting days run by the University help you find people to share with and give you plenty of addresses to look at. However, this can be a bit hit and miss. You may find a nice house with the house-mates from hell, or you may end up in a real hovel. Try and look at a few houses which charge the same rent, you'll get a better idea of the standard of housing you can expect for your money. If you don't like the first few houses you look at, don't despair, there is so much student accommodation in Sheffield you're bound to find somewhere eventually.

If I was to sum up Sheffield Hallam in one phrase it would have to be, 'Life is what you make it'. It's so large and diverse, anyone could enjoy themselves. I know I have.

SOUTHAMPTON UNIVERSITY

The University of Southampton
Highfield
Southampton
SO17 1BJ

TEL 01703 595000
FAX 01703 593939

Southampton University Student Union
University Road
Highfield
Southampton
Hants SO17 1BJ

TEL 01703 595200
FAX 01703 595252

UNIVERSITY OF SOUTHAMPTON

Founded	**1862**
Situation/style	**Campus**
UNDERGRADUATE PROFILE	
Application acceptance rate	**9%**
Medical AAR	**6%**
Population	**9,250**
Mature student population	**13%**
Overseas student population	**6%**
Male/female ratio	**48:52**
1st year institut. accommodation	**100%**
Approximate cost	**£40-£60 pw**
ACADEMIC PROFILE	
A-level requirements:	**High**

Medicine ABB:
★ Science 'A's required **Chemistry**
★ Addit. Non-Science 'A's acceptable **Yes**
★ Retakes considered **No**
★ Clinical contact **Term 1**

Student/staff ratio	**7:1**
1st class degree pass rate	**9%**
HEFCE assessments (14 subjects assessed/approved):	
1993 **Chemistry**	Excellent
1994 **Applied Social Work, Computer Studies, Geography**	Excellent
1995 **English, Oceanography, Geology, Music**	Excellent
Modern Languages 18	
1995/6 **Sociology** 21	
Joint Funding Council's research assessment 1996 (17 subjects assessed):	
Nutrition, Electrical & Electronic Engineering.	Grade 5*
Chemistry, Environmental Sciences, Operational Research, Law, Computer, Mechanical/ Aeronautical/ Manufacturing Eng., Geography, Economics, Business and Management, Archaeology, Music.	Grade 5
EMPLOYMENT PROFILE	
Employability in Industry:	
MPW national league table (1996)	**26th=**

Principal job market destinations:
Health, Commerce, Retail/Wholesale, Manufacturing (strong on **Electronic & Electrical**), **Education, Public Admin./Law, Personnel, Computer,** good record **Engineering Design**

PIP 1996 employers' survey:	
Top 3 subjects/national ranking	
Electrical Engineering	11th
Engineering & Technology	15th
Computing	19th=
Approximate % unemployed	**5%**

VAG VIEW

The Medical faculty at Southampton is one of the forward thinking ones, already ahead of the recommendations of the GMC for a more clinically, practically orientated curriculum. They are looking for the committed, well-rounded applicant, he or she may only have one science A-level among the stipulated AAB: it will have to be Chemistry, but the remaining two could be arts. This is revolutionary thinking. They want to take, well, wiser students, students drawing on a richer educational font, students capable of approaching problems with a certain flair, not confined by specialism, tunnel visioned.

The course is geared towards problem solving, which is why patient contact is made in the first term, again unusual, in order to develop communication skills. It is the newest school, established only in the 70s and it still has among the smaller intakes, yet the number of applicants is among the highest and their acceptance rate commensurately low, indeed among the lowest (6% in 1995).

If you look at another area in which Southampton is renowned - Geography, you see a similar sort of picture. Two degrees are offered - BA and BSc. Analytical skills, computing, field and laboratory techniques, problem solving, written and oral expression are to the fore. This is the method which they use to tackle a broad-based course at the start, leading to increasing specialism. It is also the kind of approach to which future employers will relate.

Again, the Oceanography Centre gives Marine Sciences and other undergraduates on the waterfront access to exceptional analytical and research facilities and produces the partnership degrees with Biology, Geology, Geography, Maths, Physics, which have led to 'Excellent' ratings in the assessments. And now another range of Marine science degrees has emerged - it is a niche area for Southampton, there are few others offering such degrees, and they have one with French, involving a year abroad.

But if you look at Southampton's assessments, what is noticeable is that they are 'Excellent' across the board, sciences and arts. So it is that, as in Oceanography, in the Department of English, integration of research with the teaching of undergraduates is of primary importance, and students are again taken from a broad base of different critical perspectives and topics to a specialism in some aspect of the culture - literature, language, cultural theory.

Southampton, it seems, has an academic strategy which is constant throughout the curriculum, designed to set students up for whatever discipline - employment or research - they eventually choose. One school careers teacher to whom I spoke worked at the University from 1969 to 1972, which was when these ground rules were being laid and their medical school was being set up - 'They'd got the staff appointed when I left; the faculty is that new. It was very impressive.'

CULTURE & SOCIAL SCENE

The University is heavily into organic culture, they don't see each School as a distinct specialist entity, but as an integral part of the whole. The Uni has its roots in the 19th century as the Hartley Institute. For a time it was even a College of London University, but the growth of Southampton as a university since it was granted its Royal Charter in 1952, has been deliberately organic. Equally, the University is an integrated part of the locale, its preoccupation with Oceanography and Marine Sciences, for example, flowing naturally from its position on the coast, its Ocean Village, its maritime history (The Mayflower, The Titanic), and you will find the arts lecturers actively involved with the culture of the town.

Of the two large theatres which are a cultural focus in the area - staging opera, ballet, music, film - the key one, the Nuffield Theatre, is on the Uni campus. In town, at the Phoenix Theatre, the programme of films is run by the Uni.

The careers teacher I spoke to added that besides the vibrant academic scene, she had enjoyed her time there because, 'It is also a lovely town to be in.' There is an emphasis on the arts in both campus and town. Southampton has its own annual film festival, a multiplex in Ocean Village and a newish film theatre called Harbour Lights. On campus there's the Turner Sims Concert Hall (classical concerts, lunchtime and evening, more than sixty a year), and the John Hansard Gallery (art, photography and craft).

The whole southern coastline from Bournemouth in the west, through

Southampton, Portsmouth, Chichester, Bognor, Brighton has become something of a university strip. The presence of students of Bournemouth University, Southampton University, Southampton Institute, LSU, King Alfred's Winchester, Portsmouth University, The Chichester Institute, Brighton Uni, Sussex Uni has helped to transform it, but perhaps never more completely than in Southampton, where the Uni itself has taken a hand.

Presented with a 20,000-strong student market, Southampton has provided a wide choice of clubs, pubs, live music venues. Some are student only places; elsewhere - for example the Penguin Club and New York New York - student nights are routine. Even the shopping mall has been transformed. *Punter: Student Guide*, the mag to grab for what's on along the South coast, describes it as 'the UK's first youth mall...the interior sculpted in chrome and white... curving stairways snake through three levels to cafes and eateries in the basement...four video walls...a spectacular 72-screen drum broadcasting music, visuals.' And it isn't only fashion, there's even a New Age vendor called Body and Soul.

SPORT

Needless to say, water sports are the big splash here. The sailors have won the BUSA championship more times than Portsmouth would care to remember. There's water everywhere, even a stream flowing through the campus, and the nearby River Itchin takes the boats from the Uni boathouse down to the Solent. The sports grounds are just the other side of the M27; on campus facilities include sports hall, fitness studio, squash courts, martial arts area (Zen Shorin Do karate is the thing), and there's a rifle range.

ACCOMMODATION

Guaranteed place in mixed halls, close to the hub, for all first years. Ents organised on a hall basis as well as by the Union. All halls well kitted out with common rooms, games, rooms, TV rooms etc; some have sports facilities too.

GETTING THERE

★ By road: M3 (J 14), A33, then left into Burgess Road (first set of lights); or M27 (J5), A335, take a right at Burgess Road (fourth set of lights).

★ National Express Coaches run to and from Southampton Coach Station.

★ By rail: London Waterloo, 1:40; Bristol Parkway, 2:15; Birmingham New Street, 3:30; Sheffield, 4:45.

★ By air: Southampton international airport.

VIEW FROM THE GROUND
by Tristan Negus

Coming to university, I had three worries:

1 Spending three precious years of my life in an urban wasteland.

2 All the leisure activities available would be dominated by hyper-talented ex-Head Boys of schools across the country.

3 I'd wake up one morning face down in a puddle in an unfamiliar street, with a hangover as huge as my overdraft.

Still, I came to Southampton. This is where the UCAS tour actually came in handy. I knew I was coming to a campus with a cute stream running through it. I knew I was coming to a campus with a large common nearby. The details of my degree evaded me, but....well....it didn't seem important at the time! So, worry number 1 was mercilessly vanquished. I should mention also that the city centre is only two miles away, and travel to London, Bournemouth or even France is easy. Plus you have the New Forest. Upshot? Escapism (if you need it: depends on the course usually!).

Luckily the Students Union here is large, so the services it provides are comprehensive. More to the point, there are two bars and over 200 societies, ranging from sailing to politics to wine appreciation. You name it....Worry number 2 sprang to mind. Is it possible to leap into any society with negligible talent? Well, yes it is, more or less....and if you don't like it? Try something else.

So, my attentions turned to

entertainment. What did this city have in store? Admittedly, coming from Cornwall anything would've dazzled my eyeballs off, but I digress. Basically, there are two opposite poles; near the University you have the studenty pubs and clubs (i.e. wear what you like, and be prepared to DRINK), whilst at the Waterfront you have the 'trendy' clubs (i.e. drink as much as you like, as long as you worship the bouncers). More civilised pursuits? A five screen MGM cinema, the Mayflower Theatre, the Guildhall (recently featuring Gene, Skunk Anansie, Radiohead), even dry skiing and of course Southampton Football Club, a half-hour walk from the university. Water sports your thing? Get the Students Union to sort it out for you. Sorry, this is starting to sound like a prospectus.

My opinion of life at Southampton University? I love it here. Okay, it's quiet compared to London but what isn't? I've been involved in running a student radio station and I'm playing guitar in a band....things I wouldn't have dreamed of at home. Recommended philosophy: try it!

You may be wondering what came of my third worry. Well, it was pound-a-pint night so my overdraft was spared. Pity about the rest..
(Tristan Negus is Editor of the Uni's radio station, University Radio Glen.)

SOUTHAMPTON INSTITUTE

Southampton Institute
East Park Terrace
Southampton
Hampshire
SO14 0YN

TEL 01703 319000
FAX 01703 222259

Southampton Institute
Student Union
East Park Terrace
Southampton
SO14 OYN

TEL 01703 232154
FAX 01703 235248

SOUTHAMPTON INSTITUTE	
Founded	**1984**
Situation/style	**Campus**
UNDERGRADUATE PROFILE	
Application acceptance rate	**22%**
Population	**8,250**
Mature student population	**48%**
Overseas student population	**5%**
Male/female ratio	**58:42**
1st year institut. accommodation	**100%**
Approximate cost	**£50-£70 pw**
ACADEMIC PROFILE	
A-level requirements:	**Low**
Law + combinations 10-18, **Accountancy/Finance/Business Studies** 10	
Student/staff ratio	**25:1**
1st class degree pass rate	**1.3%**
HEFCE assessments (7 subjects assessed/approved):	
1996 **Sociology** 19	
Joint Funding Council's research assessment 1996 (12 subjects assessed):	
Grade 5/5*	None
EMPLOYMENT PROFILE	
Principal job market destinations: **Retail/Wholesale, Manufacturing** (strong on **Electrical/Electronic**), **Commerce, Personnel, Arts/Media, Public Admin./Law, Computer, Construction, Education,** good record **Advertising**	
Approximate % unemployed	**9%**

VAG VIEW

Southampton Institute will soon be a university like its neighbour, but it has a different undergraduate profile. Almost half its students are mature, many are local and part-time. The courses lean towards particular jobs and careers, sometimes with a technical bias, and in some areas (e.g. Maritime) provide an interesting extension/balance to courses offered at Southampton University.

SITUATION

The main campus is in the heart of Southampton. Marine Ecology, Ocean Science Labs and floating facilities of the Maritime faculty are located on a second campus in remote Warsash near the mouth of the River Hamble, close to the Solent.

GETTING THERE

★ By road: M3 (J 14), A33. Warsash: M27 (J8), A27 east, right turn at Sarisbury.
★ National Express Coaches run to and from Southampton Coach Station.
★ By rail: London Waterloo, 1:40; Bristol Parkway, 2:15; Birmingham New Street, 3:30; Sheffield, 4:45.
★ By air: Southampton international airport.

ACADEMIA

9 faculties are: Built Environment; Business Finance; Design; Business Management; Law; Maritime; Social Science; Media Arts; Systems Engineering. Nottingham Trent Uni awards its degrees.

Intriguing courses include Fine Arts Valuation (for some reason part of Built Environment), it must be one of the few available for budding antiques/auction house merchants. Among the Business Finance courses are ones in Accountancy, and Accountancy & Law. A lot of their courses are closely linked to work experience, study abroad, some, like Marketing Design, involving a consultancy project for an outside organisation (with clear potential prospects). A BSc Hons in International Transport Management falls within the Maritime faculty; otherwise this faculty gears students to maritime technology, environmental management or science, maritime leisure management, yacht manufacture or design, and a special course - Shipping Operations - for students looking to work in Shipping or Port Management, Film Study and Journalism courses are included in Media Arts.

Computer-aided guidance packages provided for career opportunities. Extensive information about careers, employers, vacancies, further study and destinations of past graduates.

ACCOMMODATION

There is a major accommodation building programme to provide 2,350 places a few minutes walk from the main campus by October 1997. Some en suite, most halls have common rooms with Satellite TV.

UNION

3 bars, ents include balls, bands, discos, cabaret. Big name bands in recent years include D:REAM, Alison Limerick, the Pasadenas, K-Klass, Sub Sub, Jools Holland and Mica Paris. (See also Southampton Uni.)

Part-time jobs available through a Jobshop to eke out grants.

SPORT

Sports hall and fitness suite with sauna and solarium. Fitness classes include circuit training, step aerobics and aerobics. Coaching for netball, rugby, soccer, waterpolo, basketball, fencing and Tae-kwon-Do. Playing fields, 4 miles from the city with licensed pavilion; additional playing fields at Warsash Campus.

South Bank University

South Bank University
103 Borough Road
London
SE1 0AA

TEL 0171 928 8989
FAX 0171 815 8155

South Bank University
Student Union
Keyworth Street
London SE1 6NG

TEL 0171 815 6060
FAX 0171 815 6061

South Bank University
Student Union
Wandsworth Road
London SW8 2JY

TEL 0171 815 8350
FAX 0171 815 8351

SOUTH BANK UNIVERSITY

Founded	**1892**
Situation/style	**Campus**
UNDERGRADUATE PROFILE	
Application acceptance rate	**13%**
Population	**8,600**
Mature student population	**43%**
Overseas student population	**9%**
Male/female ratio	**52:48**
1st year institut. accommodation	**75%**
Approximate cost (Uni)	**£60 pw**
(City)	**£55-£75 pw**
ACADEMIC PROFILE	
A-level requirements:	**Low-Medium**

Law 14-20, **Maths combinations** 12-18, **Chemical Engineering** DE, **Architecture** CC, **Media Studies combinations** 14-BCC, **Sociology combinations** 12-18, **Business Studies** BC, **Management combinations** 12-18

Student/staff ratio	**25:1**
1st class degree pass rate	**5.7%**

HEFCE assessments (9 subjects assessed/approved):
1995/6 **Modern Languages** 22 **Sociology** 19 **Chemical Engineering** 18

Joint Funding Council's research assessment 1996 (13 subjects assessed):
Grade 5/5* None

EMPLOYMENT PROFILE

Principal job market destinations:
Retail/Wholesale, Health, Education, Manufacturing, Commerce, Construction, Hotel/Restaurant, Computer, Property Development, Arts/Media, Architecture and Engineering Design (strong)

Approximate % unemployed **15%**

VAG VIEW

Faculties at South Bank include Built Environment, Business & Management, Computing, Engineering, Health, Science, Education. There is also a Combined Honours programme. The University grew out of the South Bank Poly, which in turn grew out of the Borough Poly, founded in 1892.

It became a University in 1992. Characteristically it has a large percentage of mature and part-time students, and students who live locally, which, as our correspondent points out, makes for a rather fragmented social scene in comparison with a traditional campus university. The course programme is modular in structure, the academic year is divides into two semesters, and on appropriate courses they offer sandwich courses.

Accommodation is provided near campus and guaranteed to students from overseas; otherwise priority is given to first and third year students. All residences are managed by 24-hour security.

VIEW FROM THE GROUND
by Richard Neville

The location of the main university campus is excellent given its close proximity to Waterloo main line station (two minutes by bus) and also to Elephant and Castle Underground (100m). Problems can arise, however, as some students that live in the halls of residence at the main campus can find themselves travelling to Stockwell on the Underground for their lectures (faculty of the Built Environment), the Underground is not at its best during the rush hours and the lecture theatres at Stockwell are about eight minutes walk from the Tube station. The Elephant & Castle is slightly infamous as not one of the best parts of London, but if you can overlook this then the location is fine.

The main student profile is that of someone who already lives in London and has done for quite some time. Students that live outside of London and stay in the halls of residence are likely to make the best use of the facilities laid on for students because they may not have an active social life outside of the University already. As previously stated the majority of the students live *in* London and so already have friends from school and college rather than throwing themselves in at the deep end as far as student life goes.

The University itself has 4 union bars. 3 are located on the main campus, in Keyworth Street, the 2 on the ground floor are the Revolution Cafe, which at most times is devoid of people, next to that is The Void, which provides most of the student end of term clubs and can be an excellent night out. The best of the bars on the main campus, however, is the Tavern, which has a more traditional and relaxed feel to it. The bar on the Wandsworth Bridge campus benefits slightly from a pool table but the 'atmosphere is one of . . . just walked from Stockwell tube and it's raining again!'

It can be a bit of a challenge for the student union at South Bank to provide excellent nights on the campus because of its close proximity to central London, which has some of the best clubs in the country - The Ministry of Sound on Gaunt Street, The End on West Central Street and the Hanover Grand are a few examples, but the main point is that there is something for everybody. The West End of London is about 5 minutes away by bus and needs no introduction as 'theatreland'. The problem with being this close to the capital is that the prices do take an exceedingly large bite out of any student's pocket, so going out every night is definitely not recommended! Prices for most of the London nightclubs are between £5 and £15, with Saturdays usually being more expensive.

There are 4 main halls of residence in the University that range in prices from £40 per week self-catering to £66 per week all in. The halls are all fairly easy going, and unlike most universities, none has a particular reputation because of Class, Academia or Sports.

Most of the courses are well structured with an average workload. From personal experience the courses do take some getting used to because of the high volume of students and the need to review all work after lectures (regardless of whether work has been set or not).

'It's not the winning it's the taking part,' I think best describes sports at South Bank, with the Rugby team possibly more interested in pints than points! For most popular sports there is the opportunity to go to trials and join a team. There is a large outdoor facility in Dulwich with football, rugby, hockey and cricket pitches. There are also indoor facilities in the main campus building that provide for indoor football, basketball, etc. It can be unnerving at times as all students going in and out of the main building, and waiting for lectures in the main hall, can view the various games going on from the gallery.

SITUATION
Much of South Bank Uni is either in or clustered around a triangle of ground demarcated by Borough Road, London Road and Southwark Bridge Road, just south of the Thames in Elephant and Castle.

GETTING THERE
★ Elephant and Castle Underground (Bakerloo and Northern Lines) and the mainline overland station of Waterloo are nearby.

STAFFORDSHIRE UNIVERSITY

Staffordshire University
College Road
Stoke-on-Trent
ST4 2DE

TEL 01782 292752
FAX 01782 745422

Staffordshire University
Student Union
Stoke Site
College Road
Stoke-on-Trent
Staffs ST4 2DE

TEL 01782 294628
FAX 01782 744588

Staffordshire University
Student Union
Stafford Site
Beaconside
Stafford ST18 0AD

TEL 01785 353311

STAFFORDSHIRE UNIVERSITY

Founded	**1903**
Situation/style	**Campus/ town sites**
UNDERGRADUATE PROFILE	
Application acceptance rate	**12%**
Population	**10,300**
Mature student population	**34%**
Overseas student population	**6%**
Male/female ratio	**57:43**
1st year institut. accommodation	**67%**
Approximate cost (Uni)	**£33-£55 pw**
(Town)	**£35 pw**
ACADEMIC PROFILE	
A-level requirements:	**Medium-Low**

Law BCC, **Biological/Physical Sciences** 4-12, **Applied Statistics combinations** 8-14, 100+ combs. **Sociology/Developmental 8-18 Business Studies** 16

Student/staff ratio	**20:1**
1st class degree pass rate	**3.6%**
HEFCE assessments (13 subjects assessed/approved):	
1996 **Modern Languages** 21	
Joint Funding Council's research assessment 1996 (24 subjects assessed):	
Grade 5/5*	None
EMPLOYMENT PROFILE	

Principal job market destinations:
Manufacturing (strong **Electronic & Electrical), Retail/Wholesale, Commerce, Computer** (strong)**, Education, Public Admin./Law, Arts/Media, Hotel/Restaurant**

Approximate % unemployed	**10%**

VAG VIEW

Here we are in Arnold Bennett's Potteries, with a university geared up to get you a job with the best ceramic designers to be found anywhere - at the Hothouse design centre in nearby Longton. Staffs is altogether a career orientated Uni, and although it may seem geographically a bit fragmented, the whole area is made over to students it seems. (See also Keele.)

SITUATION

There are 2 sites in Stafford, close to one another, and two in Stoke, 12 miles to the north, again close by one another and opposite the railway station, one and a half miles from the town centre. Call 01782 292752 for prospectus.

ADDRESSES

Stoke Campuses:
College Road,
Stoke-on-Trent
ST4 2DE;
Leek Road,
Stoke-on-Trent
ST4 2DF.
Stafford Campuses:
Beaconside,
Stafford ST18 OAD;
Blackheath Lane,
Stafford
ST18 OAD

GETTING THERE

★ By road: Stafford - M6 (J14), A513. Stoke - M6 (J15 from south; J16 from north), A500.
★ By rail: both on same line, approx. times: Birmingham New Street, 0:40; Manchester Piccadilly, 1:20; London Euston, 1:45; Nottingham, 2:00; Sheffield, 2:15.

ACADEMIA

Faculties include Arts, Business, Computing, Design & Ceramics, Engineering, Health, Law, Sciences, Social Sciences.

Stoke campuses: College Road for Arts, Design & Ceramics, Sciences (Biology, Chemistry, Geology, Physics). Leek Road for Business, Law, Sciences (Geography, Sport, Health, Exercise).

Stafford campuses: Beaconside for Business (Enterprise, Innovation, Communications), Computing, Engineering. Blackheath Lane for Health.

Staffs Uni comes out of Staffordshire Poly. Modular degrees on offer; many mature students; many part-time. Strong on Computing. Purpose-built computing centre at the Octagan, Beaconside Campus (Stafford). Also strong on Sport (five degrees offered). Interesting Product Design Technology cross-faculty course with Design & Ceramics and Engineering. Uni has strong contacts with local industries, not least the Ceramics industry on which this area built its reputation. The Arts faculty offers Film/TV/Radio studies.

ACCOMMODATION

Stoke-On-Trent: 6 on-campus halls of residence, 8 off campus. Student houses: 30 six-bedroom houses on Leek Road. Student Flats: blocks of flats, two thirds sharing, within 2 miles of Leek Road. Up to 300 additional bedrooms in planning stage. All self-catering.
Stafford: 1 hall on site (some en suite in annexe). Student flats: off-campus block, 4 sharing. All self-catering.
Further accommodation at both Stafford and Stoke for 1997/98.

UNION & ENTS

Union hosts regular indie, alternative, 70s, chart dance, acid jazz and comedy club nights - at Legends on the Beaconside site (Stafford), also pool competitions and bar promotions at its Sleepers Bar. There's also club venue and bar at Leek Road, and another, more alternative, venue and bar - Odyssey - in College Road (swing, soul, hip hop, alternative rock, metal, punk, indie). Jazz nights at the Pavilion in Stoke and classical concerts at the Octagon in Stafford. Both Stafford and Stoke and nearby Newcastle-Under-Lyme variously strong on student pubs and clubs, since besides Staffs Uni there's Keele, Stoke College, Newcastle-Under-Lyme College and Stafford College of Higher Education. Staffs Uni provide excellent Survival Guide, Get Knotted (student mag) and a Student Diary. There's a good bus service right to Keele campus from Stoke and they lay on good ents too (see entry). Pubs wise, the Firkin chain has quite a grip - Stoke, Newcastle, Hanley, Stafford. The Terrace in Leek Road (Stoke) does student nights; live bands at the Wheatsheaf. There's the Market Tavern & Dew Drop (alternative and Indie) at Hanley, also the Stage for live acts; the Locker Room, also in Hanley, has a student night Thursday, music till 2 a.m. There are student nights at club Zanzibar in Newcastle and various other clubs in Newcastle and Hanley.

There are theatres in both Newcastle and in Stoke. The King's Hall (Stoke) is a concert venue and there's the Trent Film Theatre on campus, and at Festival Park (also Stoke) there's a 10-screen cinema

SPORT

Academic influence brings good facilities for all and fame for some. Facilities to be found at Stoke and Stafford include: sports halls, squash courts, floodlit synthetic surfaces, grass pitches for football or rugby, fitness suites, gym with multi-gym, weights and fitness machines. There's also a floodlit training pitch at Stoke, and a dance and aerobics studio at the Sir Stanley Matthews Sports Centre, Leek Road. 1995 was a good, but not especially good year: the athletics teams finished second in the BUSA championships, an improvement of one place on the previous year. 2 selected for third successive appearance in World Student Games.

STIRLING UNIVERSITY

The University of Stirling
The University
Stirling
FK9 4LA

TEL 01786 473171

Stirling University of
Students' Association
Robbins Centre
Stirling FK9 4LA

TEL 01786 467166
FAX 01786 467190

STIRLING UNIVERSITY

Founded	**1967**
Situation/style	**Campus**
UNDERGRADUATE PROFILE	
Application acceptance rate	**9%**
Population	**4,400**
Mature student population	**30%**
Overseas student population	**15%**
Male/female ratio	**50:50**
1st year institut. accommodation	**100%**
Approximate cost	**£30-£40 pw**
ACADEMIC PROFILE	
A-level requirements:	**Medium**
Economics combinations BBB-CCC, **Environemntal Science** CCC, **Film & Media Studies** BBC, **Law/Business/Management/ Accountancy/Finance/ Psychology/Sociology combs.** BBC-CCC, **Teacher Training combs**. BBC-CCD	
Student/staff ratio	**13:1**
1st class degree pass rate	**7.1%**
SHEFC assessments (13 subjects assessed/approved):	
1995 **Economics, Environmental Science**	Excellent
Business & Management, Maths & Statistics, Teacher Education.	Highly Satis.
1996 **Sociology**	Excellent
Finance & Accounting, History, Philosophy, Mass Communications, Politics, Social Work	Highly Satis.
Joint Funding Council's research assessment 1996 (21 subjects assessed):	
Communication/Cultural/ Media, Education	Grade 5
EMPLOYMENT PROFILE	
Employability in Industry:	
MPW national league table (1996)	**31st=**
Principal job market destinations:	
Commerce, Education, Retail/ Wholesale, Public Admin./Law, Health, Manufacturing, Hotel/Restaurant	
PIP 1996 employers' survey:	
Top 3 subjects/national ranking	
Social Science/Economics	18th=
Computing	24th=
Accountancy, Finance & Banking	28th=
Approximate % unemployed	**6%**

VAG VIEW

Suzane says it all, Stirling is at the apex of a triangle of which the other two points are Edinburgh and Glasgow. A premier-league university with a reputation for leading the way, it was the first traditional Uni to grasp the nettle of semesterization and has shown the others how to make it work.

GETTING THERE

★ By road: M9 (J11), A9; or, from the east, A91, A907, A9.
★ National Express coach destination.
★ By rail: Glasgow or Edinburgh, about 55 minutes; Aberdeen, 2:30; Newcastle, 3:00; London Kings Cross, 6:00.

VIEW FROM THE GROUND
by Suzane Bush

★ Beautiful surroundings.
★ Small, friendly campus atmosphere.
★ 7 weeks Christmas holiday and no study.

SITUATION

Stirling is a classic example of a campus university. Typical 60s breezeblock buildings, but set in beautiful surroundings with a small loch in the centre, hills in the background, and more than enough ducks, rabbits, and squirrels. It's situated a mile or so outside Stirling itself and, if you so desired, you could spend the whole semester there without leaving once, as all your basic everyday needs are catered for on campus.

In their first year most students find the campus pleasantly secure, while by second year it can become slightly claustrophobic, as the chances that you'll bump into last night's conquest on the loch bridge the next day are very high.

There are plenty of buses into and out of campus. Lower fares and more night and weekend buses wouldn't go amiss, but still, it's not essential to have your own wheels.

Stirling itself is by no means a big city, but with a mixture of old and new buildings it's nice enough. For its size the shops are quite good, a combination of high street and speciality shops as well as an abundance of charity shops, and a second shopping centre is currently under construction. There is a good Tesco, the next best place after the Library for bumping into people you know, and Stirling has plenty of places to take your parents if they decide to come up for the day. Mel Gibson liked it so much he decided to hold the premiere of his film *Braveheart* there! But if there's not enough going on to suit you, then it's only a quick train ride to Glasgow or Edinburgh for a day or night out.

STUDENT PROFILE

Being a small campus university makes Stirling a very friendly place, like a community, and one that's home to a great mixture of people. However, it should be warned that by the time you reach fourth year you will probably know virtually everyone else in your year, and if you don't, then you obviously didn't get out enough.

Stirling students generally fit into four broad categories; foreign students, mature students, rich sporty types and your stereotypical broke studenty types. Each category has its own haunt: studenty students can usually be found in the bar; your sporty types, unsurprisingly, in the Sports Centre; most mature students in the library, snaffling all the best books first; and foreign students either hiding in their room or round in someone's flat at a wild party.

It's a good place to develop yourself, you will have loads of opportunities to get involved in a whole range of things. If you're an outdoor type you'll have a field day at Stirling, though it has to be said, most Stirling students are far more interested in the bars than the hills around them.

While a small percentage of students could be described as rich kids, a large number are fairly poverty-stricken. Around half are Scottish, and Stirling attracts a lot of students from Ireland. Most come from State Schools and the male/female ratio is roughly 50:50, though this looks set to change as a new nursing and midwifery course is due to start next year. So guys, if the thought of girls in nurses uniforms appeals to you....

SOCIAL LIFE

SUSA, Stirling's Students Association is situated in the Robbins Centre and consists of a discobar and three other bars. There is the Ye Olde Worlde Alehouse for the philosophical types, Maisies for your arty types and the Long Bar, the heart of the University. It has a bar, it's long and it has a great atmosphere.

Stirling isn't a big enough venue to have a really good Ents scene, the biggest names to come here recently are Steven Frost, the Gyres and Mrs Woods, but it does have some excellent discos, providing music to suit most tastes: Britpop, dance, jungle and ambient sounds, rave and the highly popular Up the Glitter, playing all those tacky records you'd never usually dare listen to such as Big Fun and Boney M. On Saturday nights there are also discos in the Gannochy, the sporty part of the Students Association, but as a rule you either go to one place or the other; rarely are sporty types to be seen down the Robbins or vice versa.

The food is very good in the Gannochy and each bar in SUSA has it's own speciality foodwise. Maisies puts on specials every lunchtime and caters well for veggies as well as serving excellent breakfasts. The University has its own catering department, with coffee bars and dining rooms around campus serving top notch food at very reasonable prices. Watch out in particular for the h-u-u-u-ge wedges of carrot cake!

Moving away from the Students Association, the halls of residence hold parties each semester, an excellent opportunity to get pissed and finally profess your undying love to the guy/girl across the corridor who you've fancied all semester. Some academic departments also have parties at the end of the year. But the best ones are those put on by assorted sports clubs every Thursday night in the meatmarkets, sorry, clubs in town. Everyone starts off by taking advantage of the 2-for-1 drink offers in various bars around town before dancing/snogging the night away in the FUBAR or the Rocks. These are Stirling's only two clubs. The FUBAR is supposed to be the best club in Scotland, though most students remain dubious of the claim.

Stirling does have a bit of a town/gown divide. There have been one or two attacks on students, but compared to most other universities it is still a safe place to study and it does have some excellent pubs; the Cafe Saloon and the Courtyard on a Thursday night, and the Barnton Bistro, Whistle Binkies and O'Neills any time.

Despite its size, Stirling has restaurants of all kinds; Mexican, Indian, Italian, French, most of which offer good food at good prices. Students also have a good supply of theatre, cinema and music on their doorstep in the form of the MacRobert Arts Centre, situated in the middle of the campus. In the past semester the MacRobert has brought us the Royal Shakespeare Company's *Comedy of Errors*, *Animal Farm*, the Australian Pink Floyd show and screenings of *The Godfather* Parts I and II and *Stealing Beauty*, to name but a few.

For all the current film releases there is another cinema in Stirling offering a student discount that means you only have to part with £2 to see a film.

ACCOMMODATION

At Stirling the majority of students live on campus. The accommodation varies greatly; from halls where you may be as many as 18 to a kitchen, to the Uni-owned Bridgehaugh flats in town where you can enjoy en-suite facilities. Or, if you're in the fourth year, you could go for a swiss-style chalet at Spittal Hill.

When applying for a university flat, you must decide whether to go for prison-style breezeblocks, which keep the noise out, or paper-thin walls, which will really allow you to feel a part of your next-door neighbour's nocturnal activities! Some of the flats could be a lot better, but you do get what you pay for, and breezeblocks can always be covered over with posters.

Commercial facilities for halls and flats aren't bad, but be prepared to queue to make telephone calls in halls. All accommodation is self-catering and mixed and if you live on campus nothing is very far away; the Sports Centre, shops, and Students Association are all just on the other side of the loch.

Living out in Stirling can work out quite cheaply rent-wise as the average is £30-40 a week. Most students live in Stirling centre or one of the small towns around it. There are one or two rough areas such as the Raploch Estate and Cornton where walking at night isn't the most pleasant of experiences. But at the other end of the scale there are many flats available in the affluent Bridge of Allan, nearby the University. Stirling centre is the best place to live for proximity to pubs, clubs restaurants etc, as the smaller towns don't have much to offer.

ACADEMIA

Strong subject areas in Stirling are Marketing, Environmental Science, Aquaculture and Film & Media. The great thing about Stirling is its flexibility, it allows you a freedom to change your degree in your first year or two at least. They also allow you to a wide choice of combinations.

In terms of workload, it is probably wise to choose an arts subject over a science one. But this can vary. English and Film & Media are commonly thought of as the lightest subjects, but it depends on the particular course - some can involve a lot of reading or studio work. One course notorious throughout the University is the dreaded fourth year Marketing course M7, which involves marketing for an actual company and is known to cause very high stress levels.

Stirling provides many opportunities to travel and in third year a large number of students study abroad for a semester, whether it's language students in France, Germany, Spain or Japan, or students from other departments in Sweden, Holland, Lapland... Many courses involve doing placements (Education and Social Work), or fieldwork (Aquaculture and Environmental Science).

What really sets Stirling apart from other universities is its semester system. Other universities have half-heartedly moved over to semesters while sticking to their three terms, but for several years now Stirling has been doing it properly, in two blocks of 15 weeks. The first is fitted in before Christmas. Then follows a 7 WEEK CHRISTMAS HOLIDAY (yes, I kid ye not) before another 15 week semester, which finishes at the very end of May. Students study three courses per semester and for most of these the coursework content is high, keeping the pressure on throughout the whole semester. The first couple of weeks are reasonably relaxed while courses get going, but the last two most definitely aren't. However, with coursework counting towards the semester mark it's rare for any exam to be worth 100%. Grades are awarded for each course and these determine whether you get on to honours, and later on they determine what degree you get. All in all it's a very tidy, well-organised structure, offering incredibly long holidays with no study to do and the chance to snap up all the best holiday jobs first.

POLITICS

Politically, Stirling students are very apathetic. The last General Meeting attracted eleven students out of around five thousand. The most active political groups are the Scottish Nationalists and the Labour Club.

ARTS

SUDS, the Drama Society aims to put on at least a couple of productions each semester. The Musical Society works towards one big production every year, staging *Grease* four years ago and the challenging *West Side Story* a year later. The University Choir brings students and people from the community together and puts on a big concert every semester in Dunblane Cathedral. Also, the University has recently started an orchestra and there's a thriving live music society which gives students the chance to perform on a Sunday night in Maisies.

SPORT

Sport is very important - particular strengths are tennis, swimming and golf. Many bursaries are available for these and rugby as well, although anyone can join, you just need to be able to drink a lot of beer. High performance sportsmen/women are catered for very well, but there is plenty of provision for all levels of skill at anything from trampolining to mountaineering. Stirling University can boast the biggest indoor tennis centre in Scotland, as well as a swimming pool, gym and everything else you need.

CLUBS

The Students Association has around fifty clubs and societies from the Birding Society to the Role-playing Society, and others catering for photographers, jugglers, linguists, sci-fi lovers, videomakers and so on.

SUSA also offers a very good support service for Stirling students. There are Welfare advisers available during the day to provide information and help, and Nightline runs every night, which you can phone for information or to talk about anything you want to, completely confidentially. The University also has a Student Information and Support Service, with a full-time counsellor and a Careers Advisory Service.

Finally, Stirling has a thriving media, with a monthly student newspaper, BRIG, which was shortlisted for Best Student Newspaper of the Year in 1996. There is also a campus radio station, Airthrey 963, offering music, and news programmes covering all the current news and student issues.

STRATHCLYDE UNIVERSITY

The University of Strathclyde
McCance Building
16 Richmond Street
Glasgow
G1 1XQ

TEL 0141 552 4400
FAX 0141 552 0775

Strathclyde University
Students Association
90 John Street
Glasgow G1 1JH

TEL 0141 552 1895
FAX 0141 552 8083

University of Strathclyde
Students Association
Jordanhill Campus
76 Southbrae Drive
Glasgow G13 1PP

TEL 0141 950 3256/7
FAX 0141 950 3680

STRATHCLYDE UNIVERSITY

Founded	**1964**
Situation/style	**Campus**
UNDERGRADUATE PROFILE	
Application acceptance rate	**14%**
Population	**10,230**
Mature student population	**30%**
Overseas student population	**5%**
Male/female ratio	**53:47**
1st year institut. accommodation	**100%**
Approximate cost	**£35-£60 pw**
ACADEMIC PROFILE	
A-level requirements:	**High-Low**

Law ABB, **Biochemistry with Food Science** CCC, **Forensic & Analytical Chemistry** ABB, **Pharmacy** BBC, **Physiology** DD, **Physical/Maths Sciences** BBB-DD, **Engineering** ★ High: **Chemical** ABB, ★ Low: **Chemical, E & E** CCD, **Engineering/Accounting** BBB, **Maths/Statistics/Accounting or Finance** BBC or CD, **Business/Management combs** (incl **Hort.**) BBB-CD, **Teacher Training** BC-CD

Student/staff ratio	**14:1**
1st class degree pass rate	**6.6%**
SHEFC assessments (19 subjects assessed/approved):	
1994 **Physics**	Excellent
Civil Engineering, Computer Studies	Highly Satis.
1995 **Business & Management, Architecture, Electrical & Electronic Engineering, Geography, Mechanical (incl Manufacturing) Engineering, Chemistry.**	Excellent
Hospitality Studies, Maths & Statistics, Teacher Education.	Highly Satis.
1996 **Politics**	Excellent
History, Law, Sociology, Social Work.	Highly Satis.
Joint Funding Council's research assessment 1996 (35 subjects assessed):	
Subjects Allied to Medicine.	Grade 5*
Biochemistry, Engineering, Electrical & Electronic Eng., Politics, Business/ Management, Accountancy, History.	Grade 5
EMPLOYMENT PROFILE	
Employability in Industry:	
MPW national league table (1996)	**15th=**

Principal job market destinations:
Education (very strong), **Manufacturing** (strong **Electronic & Electrical, Pharmaceutical**), **Retail/Wholesale** (very strong), **Public Admin./Law** (very strong), **Commerce, Health, Hotel/ Restaurant, Architecture & Engineering Design** (strong)

PIP 1996 employers' survey:	
Top 3 subjects/national ranking	
Electrical Engineering	4th
Business	5th=
Construction & Civil Engineering	8th
Approximate % unemployed	**6%**

VAG VIEW

Strathclyde is first a technological university and first again a Glaswegian university. The first 'first' is evident not principally in the huge number of Engineering and Technology students on its books, and certainly not because it specialises only in these fields, for there are many other strings to its bow, but in its research and approach to teaching. The second 'first' - its Glaswegian nature - is characterised in the number of Glaswegians who attend and the way they know how to have a good time, as well, of course, as in the Uni's location in the very centre of the city.

It became a university in 1964, following a merger of the Royal College of Science and the Scottish College of Commerce, which fact alerts us to Strathclyde's second largest faculty, known today as The Strathclyde Business School. In 1993, its third largest faculty, Education, was formed when it took over Jordanhill College of Education, also Glasgow based.

Strathclyde leads the way in Scotland for Excellence in the SHEFC subject assessments, and would be well into the top six in the UK, were there a fair comparison (different subjects have been assessed in the four countries). Employment-wise it is right up there at the top of the tables.

SITUATION

The John Anderson Campus is a walk from Queen Street station. It bears the name of the man who founded Anderson's Institution, to which the Uni is proud ultimately to trace its roots. AI was founded in 1796 as 'a place of useful learning'. The Jordanhill Campus is in the west end of the city between Jordanhill Drive and Southbrae Drive.

GETTING THERE

★ By road: The John Anderson Campus from the south, M74, M8 (J15); from the north, A82, M8 (J15); from the west and east, M8 (J15). The Jordanhill Campus from the south, M74, M8 (J19); from the north, A82, M8 (J19); from the west and east, M8 (J19).
★ Parking will be a problem at John Anderson without a permit. Good coach services to Buchanan Street bus station, a short way away from John Anderson Campus.
★ By rail: Edinburgh, 0:50; Newcastle, 2:30; Aberdeen, 2:45; Birmingham New Street, 5:30; London Kings Cross, 6:00.
★ By air: Glasgow Airport, 15-20 minutes drive.

ACCOMMODATION

In the city, most of the Uni accommodation is single/shared rooms in self-catering flats, some of it at a student village on JA Campus, some of it a walk away. At Jordanhill it's all on-campus, catered halls of residence.

ACADEMIA

The key thing is the way they teach: audio-visual, video, visual materials, computer-assisted learning programmes are all to the fore. Very close links with industry and commerce ensure a real-world, highly practical emphasis.

The Uni operates out of the following faculties: Education (Jordanhill exclusively); Arts & Social Sciences (including Scottish Studies, Russian & Eastern European Languages, other Modern Languages, as well as Psychology, Politics, English, Euro Studies, Geography, History, Sociology); Business (BA except for Law (LLB) and BSc in cross-faculty Technology & Business - technology could be Computer Science, Electronic Technology, Engineering); Engineering (everything you might expect Architecture, Environmental Health, Prosthetics & Orthotics - engineering for the disabled, and Naval Architecture & Offshore Engineering - fast lane into the oil/gas industry); Science (included here their well-thought-of Statistics courses, Laser Physics & Optolectronics, Pharmacy, various interesting Biochemistry combinations, and the rest).

We are of course into the credit-based

modular system and, except at Jordanhill, a semester structure. They have a Learning Resources Base which, among other things, is there to help you in adjusting to study methods, curriculum design etc; also, every student is assigned a personal tutor, and there's a built-in early warning system to prevent any first year getting lost along the way.

SOCIAL LIFE

Level 8 is the live venue, and disco on Thursday, Friday, Saturday. Bob Geldof, Dodgy, Sonic Youth, Stereo MCs, Fluke, Del Amitri, Inspiral Carpets, The Fall, Happy Mondays, The Sawdoctors were first seen here by Strath students (some of them a while ago), as was Deacon Blue, whom they claim as their own, as does Abertay Dundee.

Reds is the theme night disco, also three nights a week - Indie, 60s/70s, etc, plus comedy, cabaret, ceilidh nights.

Then there's the Barony Bar and Bar 5, a veggie cafe. What looks like the very best deal of all is the Games Room jukebox and five full-size, top of the range snooker tables.

See also Glasgow Uni and Glasgow Caledonian for the city and these Unions' events - all within easy reach.

SPORT

At John Anderson Campus, there are indoor facilities for basketball, netball, archery, volleyball, tennis, badminton, handball, martial arts, fencing, table tennis, gymnastics, circuit training, yoga, indoor training facilities for track & field, cricket, golf and hockey, a weight training & conditioning room, 6 squash courts, 1 glass-backed, and swimming pool. Outside campus there are 7 grass pitches, artificial floodlit pitches, and a pavilion - team games include hockey, rugby, American football and soccer.

Jordanhill have a similar range of indoor and outdoor facilities on campus.

Proximity to river, sea and mountains enables a whole range of other sports - from mountaineering to sailing, from rowing to skiing.

There are 8 bursaries available for low handicap golfers from The Royal and Ancient, each worth £1,250 p.a. (max. four years).

SUFFOLK UNIVERSITY COLLEGE

University College Suffolk
Rope Walk
Ipswich
Suffolk
IP4 1LT

TEL 01473 255885
FAX 01473 230054

UNIVERSITY COLLEGE SUFFOLK	
Founded	**1957**
Situation/style	**Campus/ town sites**
UNDERGRADUATE PROFILE	
Application acceptance rate	**14%**
Population	**1,850**
Mature student population	**42%**
Overseas student population	**2%**
Male/female ratio	**50:50**
1st year institut. accommodation	**None**
Approximate town rent	**£30-£35 pw**
ACADEMIC PROFILE	
A-level requirements:	**Low**
Law combinations EE-E, **Education Studies or Business/Management combs.** (from **Media** to **Info Technology**) CE-EE	
HEFCE assessments	
4 subjects assessed/approved	

VAG VIEW

University College Suffolk is situated on a 12-acre campus on the outskirts of Ipswich and became a university college of the University of East Anglia (see entry) on August 1st, 1996, so there is not a great deal to go on as yet. Even they are clutching at straws, leading off with their close links with BT at nearby Martlesham, which have enabled them to get on the Internet.

They offer a large modular programme, which doesn't quite mix every subject with every other. Faculties offering degrees include Art & Design, Business, Cultural Studies, Education & Childhood Studies, Hospitality (Hotel & Catering), Leisure & Tourism, Info. Technology, Community Health Care Nursing, Performing Arts, Product Design, Radiography, Science (Biology, Environmental), Social Studies (Behavioural, Social Policy).

There is a Union, which has a cafe, common room, TV lounge and games room. Sports-wise there's a gym, squash courts and a polygym. No accommodation as yet. This is a college in transition, mainly for locals, a large percentage of whom are mature students. London is an hour away by train.

We are in at the beginning, as it were.

SUNDERLAND UNIVERSITY

The University of Sunderland
Chester Road
Sunderland
Tyne & Wear
SR1 3SD

TEL 0191 515 2000

Sunderland University
Students Union
Wearmouth Hall
Chester Road
Sunderland SR1 3SD

TEL 0191 514 5512
FAX 0191 515 2441

UNIVERSITY OF SUNDERLAND

Founded	**1860**
Situation/style	**Campus**
UNDERGRADUATE PROFILE	
Application acceptance rate	**18%**
Population	**9,300**
Mature student population	**34%**
Overseas student population	**9%**
Male/female ratio	**52:48**
1st year institut. accommodation	**100%**
Approximate cost	**£35-£55 pw**
ACADEMIC PROFILE	
A-level requirements:	**Low-Medium**

Pharmacy BBC-BCC, **Business & Legal Studies** 18, **Physiology & combinations** 10 & 8-12, **Biomedical Sciences/Health Studies** 10/12, **Maths Sciences** 8-12, **Engineering:** High: **Civil** 14, Low: **E & E DD, Sociology & combinations** CC & 10-12

Student/staff ratio	**26:1**
1st class degree pass rate	**2.9%**
HEFCE assessments (12 subjects assessed/approved):	
except **Geography**	
1996 **Sociology** 21	
Joint Funding Council's research assessment 1996 (14 subjects assessed):	
Grade 5/5*	None
EMPLOYMENT PROFILE	
Principal job market destinations:	

Education, Retail/Wholesale, Manufacturing (Pharmaceutical strong), **Public Admin./Law, Health, Commerce, Hotel/Restaurant, Arts/Media**

Approximate % unemployed	**13%**

VAG VIEW

Bisected by the River Wear, the city of Sunderland lies 5 miles or so south of the mouth of the Tyne, South Shields (and up river of course Newcastle). It was an area devastated by the demise of its core industries a few decades ago and it is an unlikely place to go unless you have a very good reason, so perhaps you are unaware that the city has been reborn and its Uni with it.

Sunderland became a university in 1992 and is engaged in a huge expansion programme, both in terms of buildings and, more especially, in endeavouring to build its academic infrastructure in partnership with the locality. 'Partnership' is the buzz word of all applications to the National Lottery, and it was only recently that Sunderland's School of Computing, in partnership with the National Glass Company, copped £6 million from the Lottery charity/national gaming addiction.

Glass and Sunderland go together. Glass is one of the 19th century industries on which the wealth of this city - or town as it was then (it became a city, rather appropriately, in the same year that Sunderland Poly became a Uni) - was created. Glass, along with shipbuilding, coal mining and pottery, are what Sunderland was once all about. And their award-winning new St Peter's Campus at the mouth of the River Wear attests to this - it is all glass. St Peter's houses the Business School, and the recently completed second phase of building has taken in the School of Computing. The Student Union's purpose-built Manor Quay nightclub is also here, and this year will open...the National Glass Centre. The association is evident too in what must be a unique Art Faculty degree course - in 3D Design in Glass and Ceramics, and the tie-up is but one of many which demonstrate the route that Sunderland Uni is taking.

Sunderland, the city, has seen an extraordinary development over recent years, the old industries giving way to some sixty new ones, from hi-tec to manufacturing. Over £1,000 million has been injected into the area, and the Uni sees itself at the heart of this regeneration.

In 1969 a merger between the local Tech. and Art Colleges designated Sunderland a Poly. 6 years later, a further merger added the School of Education. Today, as a Uni, it comprises eight Schools: Arts, Design and Communications; Business; Computing & Information Systems; Education; Engineering & Advanced Technology; Environment; Health Sciences; Social and International Studies.

Since 1992 they have been feverishly building up a learning/cultural resource support system for these - a new university library, language laboratories, a media centre, an art gallery, specialist research centres such as the industry centre, an ecology centre, a centre for Japanese studies. Hang on a minute, Japanese? Well, the mighty Nissan's in town, why not? It will be interesting to see how long it takes for the language to work its way on to the curriculum.

Nor is this some kind of smash-and-grab sponsorship strategy. The city backed the National Glass Centre because it is a glinting piece of its heritage. And Sunderland Uni is working along the same lines in areas other than industry. For example, the Uni's Vardy Gallery, 'supported by the local company Reg Vardy PLC', promotes artists like John Hoyland and Gillian Ayres and has developed links in the art world as far afield as Russia. Oh, and one of their exhibitions was... Finnish Post War Glass.

Barclays Bank sponsors prizes for Fine Art at the Uni, as does the local Sunderland Echo in all kinds of art forms attended to in their Faculty of Arts, Design & Communication. What's more the Royal Shakespeare Company, Northern Playwrights and Ballet Rambert do workshops with the drama and dance elements of the faculty, and one of their design projects has been sponsored by...Pilkington Glass.

This strategy is what impresses about their teaching method - students not only exhibit and perform in the Arts and Communications faculty, they must go out and seek sponsorship for what they produce. If that is not the real world, what is? Sunderland, you may be unaware, was the first institution in England and Wales ever to offer a work placement 'sandwich' programme...in 1903. Today their synergy with the locality goes a lot further than the usual work placements in engineering, business and computing (though it does that better than most as well). They live in the real world up here, hardened perhaps more than a little by the devastation of their root industries. And having had its fingers burned by economic changes beyond its call, they are getting on with life on their own terms and in their own way. The fact that the underlying principle of everything they do - 'collaboration and partnership between students, staff and outside bodies,' - is the underlying principle of the new career-orientated concept of Higher Education country-wide is a happy coincidence, for they wouldn't have done it any other way. Sponsorship carries its own set of risks of course; it can, in the course of serving the sponsor's interests, pervert the sponsored institution's. But there is no evidence of that at Sunderland yet.

Of course many of Sunderland's students are at this point in time from the locality, and local businesses like that, but the big companies, such as Nissan, couldn't care less where their employees high from. Sunderland's local students are also often part-timers and mature. They are people who will be happy to stay and work in the local companies with which they are sandwiched. And they are getting the offers. Local companies are only too pleased to snap up what the Uni is turning out. But what about the future. Will Sunderland become premier-league, on a national scale, through this strategy? I asked the question of a sixth-form college careers teacher not quite so far north. He replied, 'Sunderland are getting their act together. It used to be, if you can't get in anywhere else go to Sunderland. But it is now going very well.'

Faint praise? Perhaps not, it is only five years since Sunderland became a university. Already it is among the largest providers of pharmaceutical education in the country, and as their Profile shows (see fact box), it is one of their great employment strengths. You could do worse than to look at their Pharmacology and Pharmacy courses. One of the interesting things about the Pharmacy degree is the emphasis not only on practical and professional skills, but on the legal and ethical aspects too. Again, the Business School's emphasis on vocational skills, as well as core academic skills, is likely to appeal to any future employer.

And maybe Sunderland isn't such a bad place to be. There's this artistic streak for a start - the Royal Shakespeare Company was so knocked out by the response they received at the Seaburn Centre that they are making it an annual event. Then there's the Empire Theatre for top acts - comedy, opera, ballet. Having got itself up and running again, Sunderland is the perfect host to anyone who has something else to contribute to it. And the North East has some of the best nightlife going - clubs and bars abound. Annabel's, Ku Club and Chambers/Gossip in High Street West, Fino's in Park Lane, Pzazz in Holmside are all popular with students. Pubs like the Borough in Vine Place, Rosie Malone's in Burdon Road and the Washington Arts Centre to the west of the city are all popular live venues - rock, folk, Irish. Manor Quay, the Uni's own club, has a capacity of 1,200, and they do things in style - from formal balls to wild party nights, from live acts (comedy events, bands) to USSU Club Nights five days a week. Then there are sudden surprising delights, like the Screen on the River, a sister cinema to Newcastle's Tyneside Cinema, based in the 400-seat Tom Cowie Theatre on campus - arthouse and mainstream. On top of all this, Gazza threatens to return!

ACCOMMODATION

The great thing about the Uni accommodation is that most of it is new. Two-thirds of it has been built in the last four years; all first years are accommodated either on the main campus or at new St Peter's.

SPORT

The sports centre consists of a two-storey fitness and cardiovascular suite, a 25 metre swimming pool with canoeing facilities, and a sports hall for badminton, football and basketball. Otherwise it's the Silksworth Sports Complex for outdoor team sports, tennis, athletics, orienteering.

GETTING THERE

★ By road: A1(M), A690 or A19, A690.
★ By rail: Newcastle, 0:25; Leeds, 2:15; Edinburgh, 2:30, Manchester Piccadilly, 3:30, London Kings Cross, 3:45.
★ By air: Newcastle International airport.

SURREY UNIVERSITY

The University of Surrey
Guildford
Surrey
GU2 5XH

TEL 01483 300800
FAX 01483 300803

Surrey University Student Union
Union House
Guildford
Surrey GU2 5XH

TEL 01483 259223
FAX 01483 34749

SURREY UNIVERSITY

Founded	**1966**
Situation/style	**Campus**
UNDERGRADUATE PROFILE	
Application acceptance rate	**14%**
Population	**4,500**
Mature student population	**19%**
Overseas student population	**19%**
Male/female ratio	**52:48**
1st year institut. accommodation	**100%**
Approximate cost	**£40-£50 pw**
ACADEMIC PROFILE	
A-level requirements:	**Medium**

Law combinations 18-22, **Chem, E & E, General, Mech. Eng.** 18-24, **Civil Engineering** CCC, **Music** BC-BCC, **Music & Sound Recording** ABB-BBC, **Nursing** CCC, **Business combinations** 18-20, **German combinations** 22, **Computing & Information Technology** AB-BBC

Student/staff ratio	**12:1**
1st class degree pass rate	**9.6%**
HEFCE assessments (8 subjects assessed/approved):	
1994 **Business & Management, Music**	Excellent
1995 **Chemical Engineering** 18	
1995/6 **Sociology** 21	
Modern Languages 18	
Joint Funding Council's research assessment 1996 (21 subjects assessed):	
Electrical & Electronic Eng.	Grade 5*
Toxicology, Sociology	Grade 5
EMPLOYMENT PROFILE	
Employability in Industry:	
MPW national league table (1996)	**31st=**
Principal job market destinations:	

Manufacturing (strong on **Electrical & Electronic**), **Health, Public Admin/Law, Commerce, Hotel/Restaurant, Education, Computer, Retail/ Wholesale, Arts/Media, Engineering Design** (strong)

PIP 1996 employers' survey:	
Top 3 subjects/national ranking	
Languages	12th
Construction & Civil Engineering	18th=
Electrical Engineering	20th=
Approximate % unemployed	**3%**

SITUATION

Surrey University's self-contained and landscaped campus lies just off the A3 in the ancient city of Guildford, next to the Cathedral. But before you run away with the idea that it has managed the impossible - a real campus within the environs of a small Cathedral City, you should know that its rising concrete buildings were built in the 60s, the architecture of the Cathedral is itself relatively modern and its lines pretty severe and both are distinct in style and position from the city's old cobbled streets, which might find a place on the film set of a Trollope novel. Still, it is better than compromise, and the campus landscape, with its lakes and gardens, is attractive enough, and it *is* only half an hour on the train to London and a few minutes walk from Guildford's centre.

GETTING THERE

★ By road: A3, signs to University.
★ By rail: thirty minutes from London on the Waterloo/Portsmouth line.
★ By air: Gatwick and Heathrow are accessible.

ACADEMIA

Surrey has its roots in Battersea Poly and its rise as University, characterised in its course assessments and in particular by its Employment Profile (see fact box), is a triumph of the career orientation of its courses and course methodology. There seem to be no secrets as to how it has succeeded. It has only understood and managed the vocational nature of its courses, and its work placement and overseas exchange strategies, better than most.

Faculties include Engineering (many courses have a European language or some other useful add-on, such as Offshore and Maritime Eng.); Science (these courses include physical, biological, maths, health and food sciences, again sometimes associated with a subject which will define the student's main interest in the career market); Human Studies (which embraces social sciences and studies - from sociology or psychology to economics or law, from dance or music to retail management or hotel & catering). Many of the courses are modular and are made to work in a similar way, profiling their students for work. Many courses are accredited by professional bodies and release the student from elements of further training. Work placements are real, salaried, often courses stretch to four years to accommodate them. There is a USA exchange scheme which substitutes for a student's second year; semesters have been geared to facilitate this. A student may spend a year in the States and come back to spend the third year on professional placement. At Surrey they plan to see you grow and not confine you in the artificial environment of a university campus.

ACCOMMODATION

All first years are guaranteed accommodation in self-catered courts of residence at reasonable cost, with cafes and restaurants on campus providing meals.

ARTS, UNION & ENTS

There are three nightclubs in Guildford and threebars in the Union, and the club nights (often with name guest DJs) on Friday and Saturday (licensed till 2 a.m.) are the biggest attraction in the area. Students societies are also active on the social scene, providing specialist club nights of acid jazz, folk, rock, Indie. Then there are the comedy acts, films and usual quizzes and drinks promo nights, and the big black tie events, Graduation, Colour and Charter Balls.

Departments - Music, Dance - evolve their own series of concerts and the Uni choir, orchestra, chamber orchestra and student Drama Society regularly perform. In Guildford there's the well respected Yvonne Arnaud Theatre.

There is both a student radio station - Guildford Campus FM - and Bare Facts, the student magazine which apparently has lived up to its name by being banned from the Internet by the University authorities. If you look for it, you will find a message from its disenfranchised editor who needs your sympathy.

SPORT

The Campusport Centre is the sports hall for indoor sports. The Varsity Centre is for field , squash and tennis, and pitches. Guildford's Spectrum Leisure Centre provides facilities for swimming, ice skating and athletics, and the Uni provides a bus linking Spectrum with other pick-ups in the city and the Uni campus.

SURREY INSTITUTE

Surrey Institute
of Art and Design
Falkner Road
Farnham
Surrey
GU9 7DS

TEL 01252 722441
FAX 01252 733869

Surrey Institute of Art &
Design Student Association
Main Site
Farnham Site
Falkner Road
Farnham
Surrey GU9 7DS

TEL 01252 710263/732222
FAX 01252 713591

Surrey Institute of Art &
Design Student Union
Epsom Site
Ashley Road
Epsom
Surrey KT18 5BE

TEL 01372 723609

SURREY INSTITUTE OF ART & DESIGN

Founded	**1969**
Situation/style	**Campus**
UNDERGRADUATE PROFILE	
Application acceptance rate	**5%**
Population	**2,200**
Mature student population	**30%**
Overseas student population	**4%**
Male/female ratio	**45:55**
1st year institut. accommodation	**60%**
Approximate cost (Institute)	**£35-£50pw**
(City)	**£40-£45 pw**
ACADEMIC PROFILE	
A-level requirements:	**Low**
Design Management 12-16, **Journalism** 12-16, **Media Studies** 14-18	
Student/staff ratio	**27:1**
1st class degree pass rate	**3.9%**
Joint Funding Council's research assessment 1996 (3 subjects assessed):	
Grade 5/5*	None
EMPLOYMENT PROFILE	
Principal job market destinations: **Arts/Media** (very strong especially **Printing, Radio & TV**), **Manufacturing, Retail/Wholesale, Hotel/Restaurant**	
Approximate % unemployed	**6.3%**

VAG VIEW

The Institute drives home a few key points to its prospective students. Their leafy locations, they make it perfectly clear, are not going to satisfy students hungry for a nightlife. Epsom, you might think, is near enough to London for it not to be a problem. But that is not really the point. At the Institute you're going to work hard, probably stay late into the evening. The kind of people they want are totally committed to making whatever talent they have their life, and the Institute sees its job as making that happen. Teaching is one element, and they run a rigorous self-assessment and development programme for their lecturers, spending around £100,000 each year to ensure that they can deliver what they promise. Another element is a partnership approach to professional practice. One of their principal aims is to get their students into work. They do this by facing them with the market realities, integrating into their courses the processes and disciplines which they will have to understand. They put the onus on students of certain courses to 'produce' their own projects, finding sponsors for a film project becomes as important as finding locations. They work into courses skills students will need to negotiate themselves into a position to put their talent to work. That may mean students on some courses organising their own work placements; by the time they come to it they will have learned how. Meanwhile the Institute is constantly involved with the industries and professions and agencies on which their students livelihoods will depend, in one year bringing into contact with the Institute more than 400 organisations to that end. It's an impressive proposal, and it seems to work. Their students win awards and they're not content if they get fewer than three-quarters of their graduates viably employed by the end of their graduation year.

Degree courses include Animation, Film & Video, Fine Art, Media Studies, Photography, Design Management, Visual Communications (Graphics processes), Interior Design, Packaging Design, Textiles, 3D Design (Ceramics, Glass, Jewellery, Metalwork), Design History (brings in museum curatorial considerations, critical studies, languages, professional practice), Fashion (Design and Processes), Fashion (Promotion and Illustration), Graphic Design.

SITUATION

Besides the 16-acre campus in Farnham the Institute operates from a site in Surrey: Ashley Road, Epsom, Surrey, KT18 5BE. Tel: 01372 728811.

GETTING THERE

★ By road to Farnham: Approach from the west via the A325 towards the centre of town; turn left up The Hart. To Epsom: Approach from the east via the A24 to town centre, pass under the railway bridge; turn left at lights into Ashley Road.

★ By train to Farnham: London Waterloo, 0:45. To Epsom: London Waterloo or Victoria, 0:30.

ACCOMMODATION

None on Epsom campus. At Farnham there's a new student village - self-catered flats.

Sussex University

The University of Sussex
Sussex House
Falmer
Brighton
BN1 9RH

TEL 01273 606755
FAX 01273 678335

Sussex Student Union
Falmer House
Falmer
Brighton
Sussex BN1 9QF

TEL 01273 678555
FAX 01273 670230/678875

UNIVERSITY OF SUSSEX

Founded	**1961**
Situation/style	**Campus**
UNDERGRADUATE PROFILE	
Application acceptance rate	**10%**
Population	**6,500**
Mature student population	**31%**
Overseas student population	**13%**
Male/female ratio	**45:55**
1st year institut. accommodation	**100%**
Approximate cost	**£40-£45 pw**
ACADEMIC PROFILE	
A-level requirements:	**High**

Law ABB, **English, Psychology, Social Policy** BBB, **Social Anthropology, Music** BBC, **Modern Languages** BCC, **Maths** BCC, **Computer Science** BBC, **E & E, Mechanical Engineering** BBC,BCC, **Biochemistry, Biology** BCD,BCC, **Physics** CCC

Student/staff ratio	**17:1**
1st class degree pass rate	**11%**
HEFCE assessments (16 subjects assessed/approved):	
1994 **Civil Eng.**	Highly satis.
1994 **English, Music**	Excellent
1995 **Anthropology**	Excellent
1995 **Linguistics** 22	
1995/6 **Sociology** 24	
French 22	
Joint Funding Council's research assessment 1996 (29 subjects assessed):	
History of Art/Architecture/ Design.	Grade 5*
Biol. Sciences, Chemistry, Pure Maths, Computer, Politics (Science Policy Research Unit), American Studies, English, French, German/Dutch/ Scandinavian, History, Communication/Cultural/ Media.	Grade 5

EMPLOYMENT PROFILE
Principal job market destinations:
Commerce, Education, Retail/ Wholesale, Manufacturing, Health, Arts/Media, Personnel, Public Admin./ Law, Computer
Approximate % unemployed **8%**

VAG VIEW

Sussex was the first of the so-called 'plate glass' universities (Warwick, York, etc) founded in the 1960s, its award-winning design by Sir Basil Spence. It admitted its first students in October 1961. Since then it has been up, way up in the late 1960s and 70s. But then for some reason it seemed to slip away from the student imagination - fickle things. But just now it is re-emerging, some things stronger than ever. Take a look at what's going on in Brighton-by-the-sea, and then a long cool look at what the Uni has to offer in terms of its teaching and courses.

SETTING

The Sussex campus, an 18th century park designated as an area of outstanding beauty, is set a few miles north-east of Brighton, on the edge of the South Downs near the village of Falmer, more or less mid-way between Brighton and Lewes, a few minutes from either.

GETTING THERE

★ By road: M23 (past Gatwick), A23 to Brighton, onto A27 eastbound for Falmer. From east or west, A27.
★ By rail: Frequent trains from London Bridge/Victoria 1:10; Portsmouth, 1:30; Birmingham New Street, 3:45; Leeds, 4:15; Manchester Piccadilly, 5:00. Change at

Brighton for Falmer.
★ Taxis available at Brighton Station.
★ Coaches to Brighton leave from London Victoria Coach Station and arrive at Brighton Pool Valley Coach Station.
★ By air: Gatwick better than Heathrow, but both accessible. From Gatwick take train to Lewes and change for Falmer. From Heathrow, it's Underground to Victoria and then train to Brighton/Falmer.

ACADEMIA

Sussex's course programming strategy was way ahead of its time in 1961, and might be said to take best advantage of the cross-faculty potential inherent in the modular ideal. Sussex's timetables and Schools of Study are designed for interdisciplinary course programming of a discriminating kind. The Uni brings some forty years experience to patterning undergraduate courses, the object to enhance perspectives rather than to massage employment prospects by shovelling in a language here or a computer course there.

The Schools are African and Asian Studies; Biological Sciences; Chemistry, Physics and Environmental Science; Cognitive and Computing Sciences; Cultural and Community Studies; Engineering; English and American Studies; European Studies; Mathematical Sciences; Social Sciences.

Research links with industry are a key element in their real world strategy: 'Many of the University's research grants and contracts have direct application to industry both locally and nationally.' They have a regional Innovation Centre concerned with developing ideas both in technology and in business. These links are further enhanced by consultancy contracts, by lab analysis and testing arrangements, by design and development contracts.

Sometimes the strategy brings industry literally to the Uni's door: 'For many years companies have rented space in existing buildings.' One company set up beside the University to exploit campus developments in AI and computer software, for example. Also on campus are a number of Research Institutes which work a similar symbiotic strategy: The Science Policy Research Unit (like Sussex's courses) works in an interdisciplinary way, looking at how scientific and technological developments impact on economic, social and political processes. The Trafford Centre for Medical Research and Education brings Sussex's research scientists and staff and consultants of local hospitals together. The Sussex Centre for Neuroscience is based in the School of Biological Sciences. The Thermo-Fluid Mechanics Research Centre has recently been designated as a Rolls Royce University Technology Centre in Aero-Thermal Systems. And so on.

Partnership is the key and it all flows through to undergraduate level - 'American Studies is a great strength,' said one sixth-form teacher. 'They have very well established links with the States, with universities out there.' Sussex in fact pioneered the American Studies degree in the 60s. Some of the undergraduate course assessments have been quite extraordinary - for example, 24 out of 24 for Sociology; this is very rare. It is an exciting subject as taught here. If you're in doubt, get hold of a copy of the *Alternative Prospectus* from the Union and read what the head of it has to say. The Schools are not just academic but socially active and welfare conscious; it's all that interdisciplinary strategy, you see, it's bred in the bone.

SOCIAL

Sussex has a more mixed undergraduate population than most premier-league universities (see fact box); a high mature student element and a higher than average overseas contingent. 'This mature student aspect is something that sixth-formers need to be aware of when considering a new university. An 18-year-old may discover that more than half the students in a particular course are mature students. There are plusses in that, but from an 18-year-old perspective there are also some minuses. It is a different experience,' said a careers adviser in a leading girls' public school. The plusses she was referring to were the different perspectives in seminar work, and what she meant about all those wrinklies not matching with the girls' expectations of what a Uni was like is plain enough. But the Uni experience is changing, faster in some places than in others, to be sure. Imagine how it must be for the mature student overwhelmed by her hyperactive teenage student scene.

Brighton is famed for its nightlife. Among clubs are The Basement, The Escape, Cuba, The Shrine, The Caver, Enigma, The Jazz Rooms, Beachcomber, The Zap, Revenge, Volks Tavern, Skid Row Bar, The Paradox, Orianas, The Warehouse, Event II, Concorde. Then there are the beach parties in the summer, and the warehouse parties you'll get to hear about at The Green Dragon or The Concorde on the seafront. Not to mention the pubs - Irish, Gay.

Not so long ago the first edition of the USSU's LGB (Lesbian, Gay, Bisexual) newsletter saw the light of day. Unusual at Sussex, where they say it's hard to get people involved politically, on Wednesday 12th February, 1997, LGB joined with students from all over the south-east on a march through Brighton 'to celebrate queer diversity, to raise public awareness of queer issues, and, in the run up to the General Election, to remind MPs of our demand for civil equality.'

There's a fair old (and not so old) gay scene in Brighton and a dozen or more gay bars in town - WonderBar, Simone on Top, Skirt and Just Sisters. 'Outside of maybe Manchester and London, it really is one of the best places to be if you are gay,' Ella Jackson of WonderBar was quoted as saying in essential ents mag, *Punter Student Guide*. If you're not convinced, stick around until the summer for Brighton Gay and Lesbian Pride.

Brighton comes alive in summer, and summer starts here in February with the Music Breaks Free Festival in the Gardner Arts Theatre on campus. The Gardner is the innovative 500-seater centre of performance in Brighton - jazz, contemporary plays, films, dance, cabaret, concerts, and a purpose-built art gallery. Then in May comes Britain's biggest arts celebration - The Brighton Festival brings performers from all over the place to Brighton for three weeks.

Back on campus there's the club scene and live gigs, Park Village Bar and main venue the Hothouse, which has different DJs every night of the week, ranging from house to indie to acid jazz. The bigger gig venues are in town at the 2,000-seater Dome or the Brighton Centre. Then there are the cinemas - ABC, Odeon, Virgin, and the choice moviehouse, the Duke of York at Preston Circus for arthouse and cult.

Oh, and there's a campus student radio station - University Radio Falmer (URF) and a Radio Current Affairs and Drama Society (RCADS), which broadcasts five, 'Slope to Slope', speech-based programmes a week. And the student weekly newspaper, *The Badger*.

ACCOMMODATION

All the accommodation is self-catering, single or shared, groupings of six to twelve. Plenty of campus eateries if you prefer not to cook. The Uni also has managed accommodation in Brighton and Hove, more popular with some.

SPORTS

Two large multi-purpose sports halls, a fitness room with multi-gym and training facilities, four glass-backed squash courts, sauna, solarium, cafe and bar. Elsewhere on campus are the pitches, tennis courts, and five more squash courts.

SWANSEA UNIVERSITY

University of Wales
Singleton Park
Swansea
SA2 8PP

TEL 01792 205678
FAX 01792 295157

University of Wales,
Swansea Student Union
Mandela House
Singleton Park
Swansea SA2 8PP

TEL 01792 295466
FAX 01792 206029

UNIVERSITY OF WALES, SWANSEA

Founded	**1920**
Situation/style	**Campus**
UNDERGRADUATE PROFILE	
Application acceptance rate	**13%**
Population	**7,000**
Mature student population	**12%**
Overseas student population	**6%**
Male/female ratio	**45:55**
1st year institut. accommodation	**100%**
Approximate cost	**£35-£65 pw**
ACADEMIC PROFILE	
A-level requirements:	**High**

Law ABC-BBB, **Sociology** BBC, **German** BBC, **Computer Science** BBC-BBD, **Biological Sciences** BCC, **Engineering: Mech., Civil** 18-20 **: E & E** CCC-BCC **: Chemical** 12-24

Student/staff ratio	**12:1**	
1st class degree pass rate	**6.7%**	
HEFCE assessments (20 subjects assessed/approved):		
1993/4 **History, Computer Science**	Excellent	
1994/5 **Geography**	Excellent	
1995/6 **Psychology, Physics, Electrical & Electronic Engineering, Modern Languages (German/ Italian/ Spanish)**	Excellent	
Joint Funding Council's research assessment 1996 (32 subjects assessed):		
Civil Engineering, Metallurgy & Materials.	Grade 5*	
German/Dutch/ Scandinavian.	Grade 5	
EMPLOYMENT PROFILE		
Employability in Industry:		
MPW national league table (1996)	**44th=**	

Principal job market destinations:
Manufacturing (strong on **Electronic & Electrical**), **Retail/Wholesale, Commerce, Education, Public Admin./Law, Hotel/Restaurant, Arts/Media**

PIP 1996 employers' survey:	
Top 3 subjects/national ranking	
Electrical Engineering	27th=
Engineering & Technology	28th
Science	30th=
Approximate % unemployed	**6%**

SITUATION

The Gower peninsula in West Glamorgan (South Wales) is one of the loveliest stretches of sea coast in the whole of Britain. Some of its tiny villages are as lovely as they were a hundred years ago. The University campus is set on the seafront, a couple of miles from the centre of Swansea, not far from where the peninsula begins.

GETTING THERE

★ By road: M4 (J42B).
★ By rail: London Paddington, 2:50; Bristol, 2:00; Cardiff, 0:50; Birmingham, 3:15; Manchester, 4:30.
★ By air: Cardiff airport.

ACADEMIA

Its performance in the course assessments has been very good, and in percentage terms places it third within Wales after Bangor and Cardiff. It uses the modular scheme and offers an enormous number of choices, particularly in the arts and social science disciplines.

ARTS & ENTS

Swansea itself, the town, has a surprisingly lively club scene. There's Escape Swansea, with pre-club and 1,000-capacity superclub; Neptunes Niteclub in Bracelet Bay, Mumbles, mopping up the Baywatch manque watersport talent from this old fishing village turned wind-surfing, water-skiing Mecca; Sloanes is at the Swansea Marina - house, garage and often name DJs; but Tramps in Kingsway is the people's choice - trance, Detroit techno, progressive house. At the Uni they manage to hold on to some of their club-crazed custom with two ents bars, one at the Union and the other in the Student Village, two miles away at Hendrefoelan. Both work a weekly programme of discos, quizzes, cabarets, comedy nights, live bands and Party Nights.

For art there's the annual Swansea Fest every autumn, hosted by the Grand Theatre and Brangwyn Hall, galleries like The Glynn Vivian, which last year ran an Egyptology exhibition inspired by the Uni's major collection of Egyptian artifacts, held at its Wellcome Museum. There's also the Arts Workshop Gallery in the Maritime Quarter, and on campus the arts focus is the building named after Taliesin, the poetic spirit of Wales, whose story is among the oldest of Welsh myths. Here is a constantly unfolding programme of drama, dance, film and concerts from classical through jazz and rock. The building also has a bar and a bookshop.

ACCOMMODATION

Six halls of residence, all mixed gender-wise. The Hendrefoelan site, the student village, has self-catering houses and flats, and a facility for herding together Welsh speakers if they want it. Swansea isn't alone among Welsh Unis in this strange mono-cultural tendency, while the civic Unis in England make a sales point out of their cultural diversity. But the Welsh have had a hard time keeping their culture together over the centuries, so perhaps its understandable and they justify the strategy by pushing a few novice Welsh speakers into their midst for a taste of the concentrated cultural recipe.

SPORT

Sports centre with sports hall, five squash courts, weight training room, climbing wall and indoor swimming pool. Two sets of playing fields include a new floodlit synthetic grass pitch, athletics track, field sport areas, six tennis courts, two netball courts, a rifle range and fishing lake. There's also of course sailing, rowing (on the River Tawe), surfing and canoeing, and a £700 p.a. sports scholarship; apply before you join up.

SWANSEA INSTITUTE

Swansea Institute
Student Union
Townhill Campus
Townhill
Swansea SA2 0UT

TEL 01792 298845/481000
FAX 01792 208376/655400

SWANSEA INSTITUTE	
Founded	**1976**
Situation/style	**Campus**
UNDERGRADUATE PROFILE	
Application acceptance rate	**17%**
Population	**1,800**
Mature student population	**60%**
Overseas student population	**3%**
Male/female ratio	**47:53**
1st year institut. accommodation	**25%**
Approximate cost (Institute)	**£36-£40 pw**
(Town)	**£35 pw**
ACADEMIC PROFILE	
A-level requirements:	**Low**
Student/staff ratio	**18:1**
1st class degree pass rate	**2.9%**
HEFCW assessments (8 subjects assessed/approved):	
1993/4 **Business Studies**	Excellent
1995/6 **Art & Design**	Excellent
Joint Funding Council's research assessment 1996 (5 subjects assessed):	
Grade 5/5*	None
EMPLOYMENT PROFILE	
Principal job market destinations: **Education, Retail/Wholesale, Manufacturing**	
Approximate % unemployed	**14%**

VAG VIEW

The Institute, which is accredited by West of England University (see entry) has three sites in Swansea, from which it operates eight faculties: Business; Education; Art & Design; Applied Design & Engineering; Tourism, Leisure & Transport; Computing; Law; Built Environment, with faculty populations descending in that order. Most of their students are Welsh (about three-quarters), most are local and most are mature. (See also Swansea University)

TEESIDE UNIVERSITY

The University of Teeside
Borough Road
Middlesbrough
TS1 3BA

TEL 01642 218121
FAX 01642 342067

Students Union
Teeside University
Borough Road
Middlesborough TS1 3BA

TEL 01642 342234
FAX 01642 342241

TEESIDE UNIVERSITY	
Founded	**1970**
Situation/style	**Campus**
UNDERGRADUATE PROFILE	
Application acceptance rate	**15%**
Population	**5,800**
Mature student population	**41%**
Overseas student population	**5%**
Male/female ratio	**55:45**
1st year institut. accommodation	**80%**
Approximate cost (Uni)	**£35-£45 pw**
(Town)	**£30-£35 pw**
ACADEMIC PROFILE	
A-level requirements:	**Low**
Law 12-18, **Business Studies** 12, **Computing** 8-12, **Engineering:** High: **Chemical** 8-20, : Low: **Electronic 8, Psychology & Sociology** 14-16	
Student/staff ratio	**21:1**
1st class degree pass rate	**6.7%**
HEFCE assessments (11 subjects assessed/approved):	
English on 2nd visit, 1995	
1994 **Computer Science**	Excellent
1995 **Sociology** 19	
EMPLOYMENT PROFILE	
Principal job market destinations: **Manufacturing, Public Admin./Law, Retail/Wholesale, Health, Commerce, Computer, Education,** good record **Industrial & Engineering Design**	
Approximate % unemployed	**9%**

VAG VIEW

Between 1850 and 1914 the glory of the North Eastern Coalfield was that it provided the energy for the urbanisation and industrialisation of Western Europe. Teeside was at the hub of this revolution as a major exporter of coal and later as a centre for the production of iron and steel. Those days are over and like Sunderland (see entry), Teeside has, in modern times, had to claw its way back from the edge of disaster and rebuild itself in a partially different mould. Now it is business and commerce, high-tec and offshore engineering, which make the running. Although British Steel is in the area to remind us of its past traumas, they are joined now by ICI, BASF, Phillips Petroleum; and the giant electronics firm, Samsung, is in the process of developing a multi-million pound manufacturing base on Teeside. This is good news for a university whose expertise lies in many similar areas and which is dedicated to giving its undergraduates employment experience, and eventual employment, in such industries.

Teeside was the local poly, and its student profile reflects this; it has a large mature student population, operates dozens of part-time courses. It appeals, in particular, to sixth-form colleges all over the North, which see it as in tune with what they are doing.

'Vocational, business, engineering. Teeside is important to us,' said one careers master. 'We have a number of students doing GNVQs (General National Vocational Qualification), a parallel qualification to A-level, but only in certain subject areas; it also covers areas which A-levels don't - Business, Leisure & Tourism, Health & Social Care and Science, Sports, Computing... So, Teeside is important to us

because it offers the sorts of courses that a lot of our students do, or which are end-on to what a lot of our students do. And they are offering entry grades which our students achieve.'

SITUATION

The campus is located within a few minutes walk of the centre of Middlesborough, on the south bank of the River Tees. No smoking on campus.

GETTING THERE

★ By road: A19, or A1(M), A66.
★ National Express coach service good.
★ By rail: Newcastle, 1:15; Leeds, 1:45, Manchester Piccadilly, 2:45, Liverpool Lime Street, 3:45, London Kings Cross, 3:30.
★ By air: Teeside International airport for Europe and inland flights is ten miles away.

ACADEMIA

Modular degree programme. Both full- and part-time degrees available.

Faculties include Design (usual coverage of fine art, computer graphics/visualisation, marketing/packaging, but also a practical, specialist course for the Entertainment Industry - theatre/film/TV/museum/leisure industry; also Industrial Design, Interior Architecture, Photography); Business & Management; Computing & Maths (including language-involved International Business Information Technology); Health (Radiography, Occupational Therapy, Physiotherapy); Law, Humanities & International Studies (including Journalism and Law amongst others); Science & Technology (from Engineering to Food Technology, a cross-faculty course involving Chemistry, process Engineering, Business); Social Sciences (Criminology, Politics, Psychology, Social Policy, Sport, etc, plus a cross-faculty course in Information Technology & Social Science).

ENTS

The Union has two floors and two bars - Above and Beyond for club nights (70s/80s/Hardcore/Techno) and live bands (2 a.m. licence); Union Central is the cavernous alternative downstairs, where also The Pizzeria is found. Friday night is the big student night. The Union building is on Southfield Road, which is also a friendly area for pubs.

Probably the best club is Arena, Newport Road (student night Monday); Blaises, Albert Road, is also popular; Bong, Bridge Street, for local colour, tread warily; the Empire, Corporation Road (disco, house, dance); Visage, High Street, Stockton (house, chart); Waterfront, Castle Quay, Stockton (student night Thursday).

Live acts at Redcar Bowl, Redcar; Middlesborough Town Hall; also Arena and their other place, the Corner House, Albert Road - there's theatre here too, now - pub theatre! Also the Dovecot Arts Centre, Stockton, for cinema, dance and theatre, and even courses. In Middlesborough itself, the Little Theatre runs a varied programme of dance, drama and music. Cinemas in Middlesborough include the Odeon and, on Teeside Leisure Park in Stockton, there's the 14-screen Showcase.

ACCOMMODATION

Five mixed halls of residence - 'segregated into male and female rooms', you'll not be surprised to hear - all within walking distance of main site. They also have Uni-managed properties in the town, equipped with the essentials. Apply early for any accommodation as there isn't enough to go round.

SPORT

On-site sports hall, indoor climbing wall, fitness centre with weights, exercise machines, sauna and solarium. Off-site, sixty acres of playing fields at Saltersgill for all team games, including American Football, women's rugby, women's soccer.

Newish Sports Pavilion includes a bar. Uni hires local squash and indoor tennis courts, swimming pool, etc. Coaching provided at all levels (and including athletics). For county standard sports people the Uni operates four High Performance Centres for squash, tennis, badminton and golf.

THAMES VALLEY UNIVERSITY

Thames Valley University
St Mary's Road
Ealing
London
W5 5RF

TEL 0181 579 5000
FAX 0181 566 1353

Thames Valley University
Students' Union
Ealing Campus
St Mary's Road
Ealing
London W5 5RF

TEL 0181 231 2276
FAX 0181 231 2589

Thames Valley University
Students' Union
Wellington Street
Slough
Berkshire SL1 1YG

TEL 01753 697745
FAX 01753 552930

THAMES VALLEY UNIVERSITY

Founded	**1991**
Situation/style	**Campus**
UNDERGRADUATE PROFILE	
Application acceptance rate	**16%**
Population	**4,800**
Mature student population	**55%**
Overseas student population	**29%**
Male/female ratio	**40:60**
1st year institut. accommodation	**None**
Approximate cost (Slough)	**£35-£50 pw**
(Ealing)	**£60-£70 pw**
ACADEMIC PROFILE	
A-level requirements:	**Low**

Law, Psychology, Social Policy 10-12, **Humanities** or **Business combinations** 8-12, **Sciences** 8-10

Student/staff ratio	**25:1**
1st class degree pass rate	**2.6%**

HEFCE assessments (13 subjects assessed/approved):
Computing on 2nd visit, 1994
1995/6 **Modern Languages** 18
Sociology 22 **Linguistics** 22

EMPLOYMENT PROFILE
Principal job market destinations:
Retail/Wholesale, Commerce, Education, Hotel/Restaurant, Manufacturing, Health, Public Admin./Law, Arts/Media

Approximate % unemployed **9%**

VAG VIEW

Formerly West London Poly, TVU is based on four sites in Ealing and in Slough (as in plough). With most students from the local area, 29% from overseas and 55% belonging to the mature student population, its boast of a diverse mix of students is certainly valid.

Their mission is 'Mass participation in Higher Education as a contribution to equality and social justice'. It works with local HE colleges on access programmes, allowing successful completion of an access course as an alternative to usual entry requirements. Experience equivalent to entry qualifications is also considered (contact the Guidance team), and part-time day and evening access programmes are offered to mature students to enable them to qualify for a degree course.

All courses can be studied full- or part-time, and combinations are limited only by timetable clashes. You can pick and mix your combinations and your degree will be titled so as to reflect the depth of study in each area. So if you pick a Criminal Justice module, a bit of Sociology and some Psychology, your degree will be named BA in Criminal Justice, Sociology and Psychology.

Relatively large range of subjects are on offer, Accounting, Business, Law, Languages, History, Tourism, Media Studies, Video Production, Womens Studies to name a few.

Really the essence of this place is that it lives up to its New University title. Its aims are to take a step away from the traditional university stereotype, and it does so very successfully, a revolutionary attitude led, it would seem, from the top. A careers adviser at an Independent Boys, school described for us a recent conference - 'a typical Independent School conference, though they are trying to sort of spread it [to include State School representation]. As one of the speakers made his way to the microphone I could feel the guy next to me - he had on a very dark suit and a very stiff collar - bristle slightly when this chap advanced upon the microphone. This chap, the speaker, he had something hanging from his ear [an earring] and his hair was not quite... Anyway he was the Vice Chancellor of Thames Valley University, a Liverpudlian, and he was absolutely magnificent! He got right to the heart of the matter and he was very entertaining. He had a standing ovation. The chap next to me, with the stiff collar, he did soften. This Vice Chancellor is the youngest of our VCs, and he had shown his metal. Before that, one would never have thought of Thames Valley, not unless a boy was desperate and had low grade expectations.'

Honorary professors at TVU include Neil Kinnock, David Frost, Alexei Sayle, Chief Executive of Channel 4 TV, Controller of Radio 5 live... TVU is, as Merseyside Poet Roger McGough, writes:

'Not an ivory tower cut off from its roots
But a place not afraid to get mud on its boots. To be flexible and willing to change
To tighten its belt or widen its range...
A new University for a new millennium.'

GETTING THERE

Ealing:

★ Ealing Broadway Underground (Central and District Lines) plus overland linking with Slough and London Paddington.

Slough:

★ Site is across the road from the railway station (London Paddington to Reading route, 25 minutes to Slough)

★ By road: M4 (J6), A4.

VIEW FROM THE GROUND
by Ian Draysey

Where? is usually the first question ever asked of a TVU student, and with good reason, no one's heard of the place. Thames Valley University is another new university still building its reputation. Based in Ealing, West London, the main campus is reasonably small but well equipped. There's a library, a student welfare office, health centre, Students Union and teaching centre. There are other university buildings around Ealing, and another campus at Slough. A new library has recently been built on the Slough campus and there is a free mini-bus between the two sites, although most of the subjects are taught at Ealing. The majority of courses are modular, a bonus if you're not keen on exams, and the workload seems to be pretty acceptable for most students. The modular scheme is fairly flexible, meaning that you can pretty much choose to do exactly what you want and when you want to do it.

ACCOMMODATION

There are no halls of residence! Well, there were rumours concerning the availability of a converted children's home for thirty foreign students, but apparently it's been sold now. Accommodation is probably the biggest problem for TVU students. The accommodation office is really only useful if you are a first year looking for lodgings. As a Fresher I was allocated a room which was already inhabited, and spent my first week of university homeless. The Ealing YMCA is practically on the campus, and ought to have been a hall of residence. It isn't, and they charge students about £90 a week to stay there. Rents are high in Ealing, and if you're looking to live with five minutes of the University then expect to pay between £60 - £70 for a room. West Ealing is a popular choice for many people, it's only about twenty minutes walk and there are loads of buses about. Acton is nearby, and probably best avoided. The University noticeboards are useful when looking for potential housemates, and it's worth checking these out as soon as possible. Expect hassle when looking for somewhere to live and you won't be disappointed; many of the estate agents don't deal with students, and those that do suffer from a shortage of properties.

SOCIAL SCENE

High rents aside, Ealing is a reasonable place to live as a student. There are plenty of pubs in the town and most of them are worth visiting. Ealing provides a good base as it's on the tube and night bus routes which makes visiting London a possibility. The Broadway Boulevard is Ealing's answer to a nightclub, their student night is a particularly predictable affair but is a popular alternative to the bus home. The Students Union offers something for someone, but I've never been able to work out who. Entertainment at the Union is typically centred around cover bands (Queen, Abba, Nirvana, etc.) and sports society nights. There aren't any big name bands or DJs fighting to play at TVU, but that isn't to say that the potential isn't there, the Union building is modern and fairly well equipped and things have improved since I started my course. There is a sense of community that you might not find at a larger university, and although the atmosphere could be described as apathetic it certainly isn't intimidating.

STUDENT PROFILE

The most positive point to be made about TVU concerns the diversity of students. Students of all ages come to TVU from all over the world and studying there has given me the opportunity to meet people I never would have otherwise. The majority of universities make similar claims, but in this case it's true, honest! It's this mix which makes it difficult to describe a typical TVU student. You might not have heard of the place before, but it's definitely worth having a look if you want to study in London.

TRINITY & ALL SAINTS COLLEGE

Trinity & All Saints College
Brownberrie Lane
Horsforth
Leeds
LS18 5HD

TEL 0113 2837100
FAX 0113 2837200

Trinity & All Saints College
Student Union
Brownberrie Lane
Horsforth
Leeds LS18 5HD

TEL 0113 258 5793/283 7241
FAX 0113 283 7200

TRINITY & ALL SAINTS COLLEGE

Founded	**1966**
Situation/style	**Campus**
UNDERGRADUATE PROFILE	
Application acceptance rate	**8%**
Population	**2,000**
Mature student population	**19%**
Overseas student population	**23%**
Male/female ratio	**35:65**
1st year institut. accommodation	**100%**
Approximate cost	**£57-£78 pw**
ACADEMIC PROFILE	
A-level requirements:	**Low**

Teacher Training CC-EE, **Management** 14, **Media** 10-24, **Sociology combs.** 16

Student/staff ratio	**20:1**
1st class degree pass rate	**1.6%**
HEFCE assessments (6 subjects assessed/approved):	
1995 **Sociology** 20	
Joint Funding Council's research assessment 1996 (7 subjects assessed):	
Grade 5/5*	None
EMPLOYMENT PROFILE	
Principal job market destinations:	

Education, Commerce, Retail/ Wholesale, Manufacturing, Arts/Media

Approximate % unemployed	**6%**

VAG VIEW

Trinity and All Saints is a College of the University of Leeds, situated on a 40-acre campus about six miles out of the city.

'It's a bit introspective,' said one careers teacher/sometime inspector, 'but it's a good community, and they do have increasing numbers of mature students, local people.' Courses are modular and focus on three areas - Management, Media and Teacher Training. One of the HEFCE assessments - Sociology - produced a good score, the rest (English, History, Modern Languages, Business & Management, Geography) were approved.

Four of the research subjects assessed (Sociology, Business & Management, English, Education) were accorded only 1 point; French and Iberian Languages scored 2, and History 3b.

GETTING THERE

★ By road: From east - M62 (J39), M1. From west - M62 (J27), M621. From north A1, A58. From north-west, A65, A650.

★ By rail: Newcastle, 1:45; London Euston, 2:30; Birmingham New Street, 2:20.

★ By air: Inland and International flights from Leeds Bradford airport.

TRINITY COLLEGE CARMARTHEN

Trinity College Carmarthen
College Road
Carmarthen
Dyfed
SA31 3EP

TEL 01267 237971
FAX 01267 230933

Trinity College
Student Union
College Road
Carmarthen
Dyfed
SA31 3EP

TEL 01267 237794

TRINITY COLLEGE CARMARTHEN	
Founded	**1848**
Situation/style	**Campus**
UNDERGRADUATE PROFILE	
Application acceptance rate	**22%**
Population	**1,400**
Mature student population	**18%**
Overseas student population	**1%**
Male/female ratio	**40:60**
1st year institut. accommodation	**80%**
Approximate cost	**£48-£62 pw**
(Town)	**£35 pw**
ACADEMIC PROFILE	
A-level requirements:	**Low**
Teacher Training CC-DD	
Student/staff ratio	**15:1**
1st class degree pass rate	**3.8%**
HEFCW assessments:	
2 subjects assessed/approved	
Joint Funding Council's research assessment 1996	
(3 subjects assessed):	
Grade 5/5*	None
EMPLOYMENT PROFILE	
Principal job market destinations:	
Education	
Approximate % unemployed	**16%**

VAG VIEW

Set on a hill overlooking Carmarthen, and part of the University of Wales, Trinity College was established 150 years ago by the Anglican Church as a teacher training college. Today, besides the BA (Ed) courses, it offers BA degrees in Archaeology, English, History, Language and the Media, Religious Studies, Theatre Studies and Welsh Studies. BSc courses are also offered, in Health and the Environment, Heritage Conservation, Information Systems and Technologies and The Rural Environment.

On the face of it, Trinity Carmarthen sounds unexceptional, a teacher training college that has spread its wings. It is, however, quite other than this. Its peculiar mix of religion, rugby and raucousness seems to cut a sliver off the backside of Welsh culture, and must seem to the inhabitants of Carmarthen, as they look nervously up the hill and listen to their revelries, like a permanent exhibition of mooning. The SU President explains:

VIEW FROM THE GROUND
by Robin Zulkiffly Rowlands

Carmarthen is a small and busy agricultural/administrative town, set against a beautiful rural backdrop of valleys and enchanting medieval castles. Summer time is made by the proximity of some of the cleanest, picturesque beaches, and October is full of surprises for the amateur walker - lovely rolling hills full of wild herbs and muscaria that can add spice to a student's budget-catering.

Trinity, or Drindad, as we all like to address our humble institution, is one of the oldest colleges in Wales, founded as a Church of Wales College in 1848 by Chadwick's Education Committee to train teachers in Wales. Trinity maintains its religious links and is still a strong teacher training college, but has, over the years, produced a number of BA, BSc and MA graduates, and many serious drinkers.

Campus itself is very friendly and compact, everything is a two minute walk away - the Merlin Restaurant, Chapel, lectures, but most important the Student Union bar, my favourite place, where a cool, refreshing pint can happily be had for a mere £1.20.

The town itself is not much further, a ten to fifteen minute walk down the hill.

Night life can be a bit rough, but the pubs are good and busy. There are also three nightclubs, but they are small and always packed full of Celtic tribes out on a hunt. The local supermarkets, chainstores, hotels and pubs are always looking for students, and there are also job opportunities in College. Speaking Welsh is helpful, for Carmarthen is a predominantly Welsh speaking town. Personally, I have been lucky because I spent a year working in a supermarket deli in town and my knowledge of Welsh... well, it's getting better.

STUDENT PROFILE

There are places for academics and career-minded teachers, but neither outnumber the legendary drinkers and sports people here. The Student Union hall can take 800 students. Wednesday and Friday are the big disco nights, where everybody gets howlin', steamin', stinkin' intoxicated and dance to songs they can't remember. Strictly hedonistic, this is no place for radical political debating societies. It's sport/booze only...and a bit of scholarly work in between.

There is only one mixed hostel - the one for first year female students.

The majority of students are Welsh - about 72% - the rest are English and Irish. There is some animosity, but generally everyone gets on well with each other, apart from the Five Nations Championship when England plays Wales. Then the Union bar is like a scene out of Braveheart.

Trinity, you see, has strong sporting traditions, especially rugby. 1996 has proved successful, the 1st XV is unbeaten at time of writing and has recently been promoted to Division One of the Welsh College/University League. The women's netball and hockey teams are also of a very high standard and deserve every credit.

We are a small college with just under 1,700 students; everybody knows each other, and the single best characteristic of Trinity is the fine sense of camaraderie which makes it, to my mind, the finest college in Wales.

GETTING THERE

★ By road: M4, A48, A40. From Lampeter to the North, A495, A40.

★ By rail: Cardiff Central, 1:30; Birmingham New Street, 4:10.

ULSTER UNIVERSITY

University of Ulster
University House
Cromore Road
Coleraine
Co. Londonderry
BT52 1SA

TEL 01265 44141
FAX 01265 324901

University of Ulster
Student Union
Cromore Road
Coleraine BT52 1SA

TEL 01265 56321
FAX 01265 324915

University of Ulster
Student Union
Jordanstown Site
Shore Road
Co. Antrim BT37 0QB

TEL 01232 365121
FAX 01232 366817

University of Ulster
Student Union
Derry Site
Magee College
Northlands Road
Derry BT48 7JL

TEL 01504 262978
FAX 01504 260292

University of Ulster
Student Union
Belfast Site
York Street
Belfast BT15 1ED

TEL 01232 230939
FAX 01232 267351

UNIVERSITY OF ULSTER

Founded	**1984**
Situation/style	**Urban sites**
UNDERGRADUATE PROFILE	
Application acceptance rate	**8%**
Population	**11,000**
Mature student population	**25%**
Overseas student population	**19%**
Male/female ratio	**40:60**
1st year institut. accommodation	**44%**
Approximate rent (Uni)	**£35 pw**
(City)	**£30 pw**
ACADEMIC PROFILE	
A-level requirements:	**Medium**

Law BBC, **Nursing** BBC, **Health Care** - High: **Optometry** ABB, - Low: **Biomedical Engineering** CCC, **Biological Sciences** CDD, **Maths/Stats/Computer** BCC, **Engineering - Civil, Mechanical** CCD-,DDD - **Electronic** CCC-CDD, **Business & combinations** BBC-CCC, **Housing** CCC

Student/staff ratio	**16:1**
1st class degree pass rate	**6.4%**
HEFCE assessments (16 subjects assessed/approved):	
1995 **Music, Social Policy & Admin**	Excellent
1995/6 **Environmental Studies,**	Excellent
Iberian 18	
1995/6 **German** 19	
Joint Funding Council's research assessment 1996 (25 subjects assessed):	
Biomedical Science	Grade 5*
History	Grade 5

EMPLOYMENT PROFILE

Principal job market destinations:
Manufacturing (strong on **Electronic & Electrical, Pharmaceutical**), **Health, Education, Retail/Wholesale, Commerce, Public Admin./Law, Computer** (strong), **Hotel/ Restaurant, Arts/Media, Market Research/Advertising**

Approximate % unemployed	**7%**

VAG VIEW

The Uni came out of a merger in 1984 between Ulster Poly and the New University of Ulster (which was the old university, if you follow).

It is a collection of four disparate sites: Belfast (city centre, see also Queen's University); Jordanstown at Newtownabbey just north of Belfast, on the coast; Coleraine (far north-west of Belfast, on the coast, near the Giant's Causeway); and Magee College in Londonderry, yet further away to the West.

The Faculty of Art & Design is at the Belfast site, but it is not at all clear where you will have to be to study a particular

course. The Faculty of Informatics (Computing & Maths, Information & Software Engineering) is spread over the Jordanstown, Coleraine and Magee College campuses. Engineering is largely at Jordanstown, but increasingly, too, at Magee College, and so on. Fact is that most of the students are local and what appear to us confusions are no doubt part of the rich pattern of Northern Irish culture. There is at least one course, however, which brings students from far and wide, BA Hons Peace and Conflict Studies, which is part of the History, Philosophy & Politics School in the Humanities Faculty. There is a similar course in Bradford, but they are rare, and clearly especially relevant here. All courses are modular. Contact the Coleraine office with queries.

Ulster has done well at the HEFCE assessments of late. After reams of 'satisfactories' they've been scoring high over the last couple of years.

The merger was probably a more constructive idea than turning the poly into a University.

GETTING THERE

★ An hour by air from London, with at least 24 flights a day each way.

★ Ulsterbus operates a fast and frequent service across Northern Ireland.

ACCOMMODATION

Low percentage of first years get Uni residences, but there doesn't seem to be a problem in finding local accommodation. In Coleraine 400+ students live in self-catered blocks and a new complex of Uni houses; the rest in Coleraine or the coastal resort towns of Portrush and Portstewart.

700-odd Jordanstown and Belfast students live in similar housing or in residential Halls, and at Jordanstown there is some Uni-managed private housing. There are three halls of residence at Magee College, catering for just under 300 students.

ARTS & UNION

There's quite a bit of friendly rivalry between the Belfast based Ulster students and the Queen's Uni. Ulster responds to the Queen's arts fest (see entry) with a regional festival, the arts programme revolving around all four of its campuses. Coleraine has a 500-seat recital room, the Octagon and the 1,200-seat concert hall the Diamond, and, best of all, the Riverside, which is the third largest professional theatre in Northern Ireland and an established touring company. The Coleraine programme comprises, drama, music, rock, contemporary dance, ballet and opera. The Music Department is based at Jordanstown and has several recital rooms and the Assembly Hall, a 1,000-seater. Magee College's Great Hall is the other large auditorium.

A Student Union administration operates at each of the four sites. Belfast has a big hall for functions, but it's upstairs in a balcony area which is the ents area at night and an eats-and-bar during the day - 'the beer is cheap and the craic is great'. It's a fixture on the Belfast music circuit. These are in a building known as the Conor Hall, which links the two main Uni buildings. There's also an Art Shop, as the Uni's Art & Design students are based here, a creche, and welfare/accommodation/health offices.

At Jordanstown they've recently redesigned the Union, there's a new club bar and major ents hall (discos, live bands), photocopying service, catering facilities, etc. There's also a lounge bar with satellite TV, video games, pool, snooker tables.

At Coleraine, a complete refurbishment of club and (two) disco bars is underway and there's a lively ents programme through the week. The Triangle bar is the main ents venue.

At Magee, the Bunker room has bar and catering, and becomes ents venue at night; there's also a lounge bar.

SPORTS

Jordanstown: two large sports halls, gym, fitness suite, five squash courts, eight-lane swimming pool and hydrotherapy pool. Playing fields are on-campus, sports include athletics, camogie, gaelic football, hockey, hurling, rugby, soccer, tennis. There's also a floodlit synthetic pitch for training. Belfast students use Jordanstown and city facilities.

Coleraine: sports hall and adjoining minor hall for all indoor sports, and it includes five squash courts, fitness suite, solarium and steam room.

The playing fields and pavilion are close to the residences. Floodlights have been installed on a soccer pitch, a training area and a synthetic pitch. Their cross-country course has been used for the World Student Cross-Country Championships. Rowing, sailing, canoeing, sub-aqua and water skiing operate out of the Water Sports Centre on the banks of the River Bann.

Magee College is well situated for outdoor activities - sailing, and rowing and canoeing on the River Foyle, and climbing in nearby Donegal. There's a new sports complex, sand-carpet pitch for soccer and a synthetic training pitch for hockey, 5-a-side football and training. There's also a sports hall with fitness suite and solarium. Sports bursaries available.

UNITED MEDICAL & DENTAL SCHOOLS OF GUY'S & ST THOMAS'S

United Medical & Dental Schools
of Guy's and St Thomas's
Hospitals
Lambeth Palace Road
London
SE1 7EH

TEL 0171 922 8013
FAX 0171 928 0069

UNITED MEDICAL & DENTAL SCHOOLS OF GUY'S & ST THOMAS'S

Founded	**1769**
Situation/style	**City sites**
UNDERGRADUATE PROFILE	
Application acceptance rate	**7%**
Population	**1,560**
Mature student population	**10%**
Overseas student population	**5%**
Male/female ratio	**50:50**
1st year institut. accommodation	**100%**
Approximate cost	**£40 pw**
ACADEMIC PROFILE	
A-level requirement	**ABB**
★ Science 'A's required: **Chemistry + 1 other in Science/Maths**	
★ Addit. Non-Science 'A's acceptable: **Yes**	
★ Retakes considered: **Ext. circs.**	
Clinical contact	**2nd year**
Student/staff ratio	**2.4:1**
1st class degree pass rate	**5.5%**
Joint Funding Council's research assessment 1996 (5 subjects assessed):	
Clinical Dentistry	Grade 5*
EMPLOYMENT PROFILE	
Principal job market destinations: **Medicine, Dentistry**	
Approximate % unemployed	**1.2%**

VAG VIEW

St Thomas's Hospital is situated on the south bank of the Thames by Westminster Bridge; Guy's is four bridges further east by London Bridge. They have had a special association since the 1720s when a rich philanthropist, Thomas Guy, a Governor of St Thomas's, built Guy's nearby to take in patients other than the acutely ill in which, up until then, most hospitals specialised. They were geographical neighbours, which presumably explains the presence of St Thomas's Street in Southwark, and from the start there was a tie-up in the teaching of students, which was formalised in 1769.

Things went along like this until 1836, when there was a fight between students from the respective hospitals during an operation, which had to be abandoned. Shortly afterwards St Thomas's de-camped to Vauxhall, and then settled finally on its present site. It was only a decade and a half ago that the Schools were merged, and now there are plans for a merger between UMDS and King's College School of Medicine and Dentistry, already associated as colleges of the federal University of London.

First year accommodation is guaranteed in self-catering hostels close to the hospitals and UMDS have access to all UL's facilities, including the Intercollegiate Halls (see London University). Their sports facilities (for rugby, hockey, cricket, tennis, croquet) are in Honor Oak Park in south London and near Cobham in Surrey. There is sailing at Burnham-on-Crouch, rowing on the Thames at Chiswick, and both hospitals have on-site swimming pools, squash courts, and gyms. Recreation is also through The United Clubs, some of which (drama, music, etc) also provide regular entertainment to balance the rather less artistic weekly bops. There are, in addition, a number of annual Balls.

University College London

University College London
Gower Street
London
WC1E 6BT

TEL 0171 387 7050
FAX 0171 387 8057

University College London
Student Union
25 Gordon Street
London WC1H 0AH

TEL 0171 387 3611
FAX 0171 383 3937

UNIVERSITY COLLEGE LONDON	
Founded	**1826**
Situation/style	**City sites**
UNDERGRADUATE PROFILE	
Application acceptance rate	**10%**
Medical AAR	**7%**
Population	**8,700**
Mature student population	**19%**
Overseas student population	**14%**
Male/female ratio	**50:50**
1st year institut. accommodation	**100%**
Approximate cost	**£40-£80 pw**
ACADEMIC PROFILE	
A-level requirements:	**High**

Medicine ABB:
★ Science 'A's required: **Chemistry**
★ Additional Science 'A's preferred: **Biology**
★ Addit. Non-Science 'A's acceptable: **Yes**
★ Retakes considered: **Ext. circs.**
★ Retake offer: **AAB**
★ Clinical contact: **3rd year**

Student/staff ratio	**6:1**
1st class degree pass rate	**13.6%**
HEFCE assessments (16 subjects assessed/approved):	
1993 **History, Law**	Excellent
1994 **Anthropology, Architecture, English, Geography**	Excellent
1995 **Geological Sciences**	Excellent
Iberian 19 **Italian** 20	
1995/6 **German** 23 **French** 21	
Linguistics 22	
Joint Funding Council's research assessment 1996 (40 subjects assessed):	
Anatomy, Pharmacology, Electrical & Electronic Eng., Geography, Economics, English, French, Italian, Classics/Ancient History, Art & Design, Hospital/Clinical (Inst. of Ophthalmology) History.	Grade 5*
Community/Clinical, Psychology, Biochemistry, Biol. Sciences, Physics, Pure Maths, Applied Maths, Computer, Chemical Eng., Civil Eng., Built Environment, Mechanical/Aeronautical/Manufacturing Eng., Law, Anthropology, Dutch, Linguistics, Archaeology, History of Art/Architecture Design, Hospital/Clinical (Inst. Child Care). Clinical Dentistry (Eastman Dental Inst.), Hospital/Clinical (Inst. Neurology).	Grade 5
EMPLOYMENT PROFILE	
Employability in Industry:	
MPW national league table (1996)	**26th=**

Principal job market destinations:
Health (very strong), **Commerce, Retail/Wholesale, Arts/Media** (strong), **Education, Public Admin./Law, Manufacturing, Market Research/Advertising**

PIP 1996 employers' survey: Top 3 subjects/national ranking	
Law	9th
Languages	12th=
Social Science/Economics	18th=
Approximate % unemployed	**6%**

VAG VIEW

UCL was inspired by the first principle of the Philosophy of Utilitarianism, 'the greatest happiness of the greatest number'. It was a pioneering move by a group of heavy thinkers, John Stuart Mill among them, for an alternative approach to Higher Education, which, in 1826, meant an alternative to the privileged education dished out by Oxford and Cambridge. The idea was to open the doors of education to the rising middle classes and to free the educational establishment from the doctrinal prejudices of the Anglican Church. Roman Catholics, Jews and Nonconformists were barred from an Oxbridge education in those days. To ensure freedom from dogma, it was decided not to have subjects appertaining to religion taught at UCL.

There is a mural by Henry Tonks, who died in 1937, in the dome above the Flaxman Gallery of the UCL library depicting an architect submitting plans of the building to a man, who is often assumed to have been UCL's founding father. The figure is Jeremy Bentham, and the architect, William Wilkins. But the scene was intended as a symbolic representation of the ideal which inspired the founding of the university, for Bentham was the father of Utilitarianism. He was not UCL's founder.

UCL's foundation was revolutionary. Today, it appears rather traditional. The administrative revolution in Higher Education is going on elsewhere - 'none of that fancy 'modular' approach here mate,' as the author of UCL's Alternative Prospectus puts it - UCL concerns itself with revolutionary matters in the area of research.

Although, its campaigning spirit was exercised not so very long ago when UCL championed black South Africa in its struggle against apartheid, invited Nelson Mandela to become its Honorary President (at a time when Mandela was under arrest), and funded a scholarship to allow a black South African to study at UCL free. The Scholarship continues to this day and there is an on-going Scholarship appeal.

However, UCL hardly fills the bill as 'the Cockney College' (the name given it in the 19th century by those who feared widespread education would demolish their ivory tower); nor, indeed, does the tag, 'the Godless Institution of Gower Street' quite ring true, if only because a majority of institutions are, today, also fairly Godless. It is interesting, however, to attach this historical class perspective to the current demand for Higher-Education-for-all if it helps to explain why such a movement should be as necessary in the dog-eat-dog meritocracy in which we live today as it was then.

UCL has this sort of effect on one. It is a seriously academic place, great circles of thought spinning out over its Bloomsbury campus to aerate the collective subconscious and have us examine the very roots of thought.

It is situated hard by the University of London Student Union Building and as a College of UL it shares in its privileges, I mean facilities. See London University entry for what that entails. UCL has its own halls of residence and undertakes to house all single first-year undergrads. It has, believe it or not, an Ents Committee, which promotes live acts, D:REAM, James Taylor Quartet, Credit to the Nation, Mike Flowers Pops, Fabio, Farley Jackmaster Funk et al...though it isn't clear how long ago or how often such acts appear. There are between 100 and 150 clubs and societies, depending which version of things you read. Especially active is the Drama Society - productions ten weeks of the year. UCL has its own West End Bloomsbury Theatre for drama, music and comedy, and there is a Theatre Workshop on the College site. There is an active musical life, an orchestra, choir, chamber orchestra, chamber choir and jazz band. Operatic Society is renowned and puts on a full-length opera each year.

Sports-wise they have a fitness centre and squash courts, and make use of ULU's pitches for outdoor team games.

GETTING THERE

★ Euston Square (Metropolitan, Circle, Hammersmith & City Lines), Warren Street (Victoria, Northern), Euston (Victoria, Northern).

WALES COLLEGE OF MEDICINE

University of Wales College
of Medicine
Heath Park
Cardiff
CF4 4XN

TEL 01222 747747
FAX 01222 742914

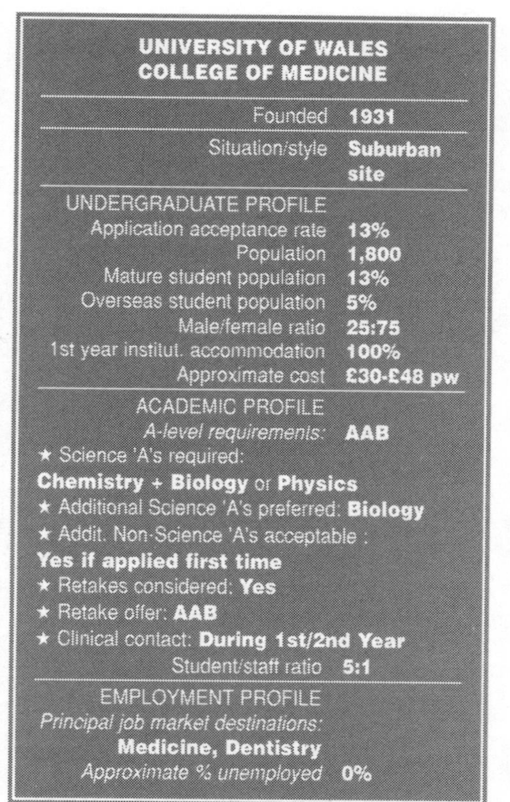

UNIVERSITY OF WALES COLLEGE OF MEDICINE

Founded	**1931**
Situation/style	**Suburban site**
UNDERGRADUATE PROFILE	
Application acceptance rate	**13%**
Population	**1,800**
Mature student population	**13%**
Overseas student population	**5%**
Male/female ratio	**25:75**
1st year institut. accommodation	**100%**
Approximate cost	**£30-£48 pw**
ACADEMIC PROFILE	
A-level requirements:	**AAB**

★ Science 'A's required:
Chemistry + Biology or **Physics**
★ Additional Science 'A's preferred: **Biology**
★ Addit. Non-Science 'A's acceptable :
Yes if applied first time
★ Retakes considered: **Yes**
★ Retake offer: **AAB**
★ Clinical contact: **During 1st/2nd Year**

Student/staff ratio	**5:1**
EMPLOYMENT PROFILE	

Principal job market destinations:
Medicine, Dentistry

Approximate % unemployed	**0%**

VAG VIEW

The college is situated on a 53-acre, 70s-built campus, a few miles north of Cardiff city. Roughly 40% of the intake is Welsh. They make a particular point in their A-level requirements that applications are welcome from students offering a European language as third subject - there is an optional two month research project abroad in the fourth year.

There is also a pre-med foundation course for applicants with three Arts A-levels or two Arts + one Science A (though two of Chemistry, Biology or Physics must be offered at GCSE). Straight Bs are required for Dentistry, and degree courses are also offered in Occupational Therapy, Physiotherapy, Diagnostic and Therapeutic Radiography - requirements range from BB-CCD - and in Nursing (CCC).

There is a close working relationship with Cardiff Uni, which includes use of the Uni's teaching as well as social and recreational facilities. The college has the Med Club bar, with pool table, weekly discos, live bands, etc., and there are annual balls. There's an active sports scene - again Cardiff Uni's facilities are on offer, and the College has its own swimming pool, squash courts, gym and fitness room.

Accommodation is both self-catering and full board, some shared with the Uni, some in the college's own high rise block on site, and there are also college-owned properties (houses & flats) beyond. For Cardiff city ents, see Cardiff Uni entry.

GETTING THERE

★ By car: M4 (J29), A48 and you'll see a sliproad to College campus signposted.
★ By rail: London Paddington, 2:30; Birmingham New Street, 2:45; Manchester Piccadilly, 4:00; Nottingham, 4:30.
★ Airport for USA and inland. City centre coach station. Good local bus services to campus.

UNIVERSITY COLLEGE WARRINGTON

University College Warrington
Padgate Campus
Fearnhead
Warrington
Cheshire
WA2 ODB

TEL 01925 814343
FAX 01925 816077

UNIVERSITY COLLEGE WARRINGTON	
Founded	1946
Situation/style	Campus
UNDERGRADUATE PROFILE	
Application acceptance rate	23%
Population	760
Mature student population	30%
Overseas student population	1%
Male/female ratio	46:54
1st year institut. accommodation	100%
Approximate cost	£30-£35 pw
ACADEMIC PROFILE	
A-level requirements:	Low
Media Studies 16, **Sports Studies** 12	

VAG VIEW

The College became affiliated to Manchester University in 1993, which means that it has faculty status within the University, and Manchester validates its degrees. UCW offers vocational courses in Business Management, taken neat or laced with either Sports Studies, Leisure Industry, Performing Arts or Media Studies. Work placements play a major role in the course programmes. 'All degrees are focused on future employment,' they declare, and many students stay with their placement employers, earning money during the vacations.

Warrington is a small but busy place, on the edge of the Cheshire plain. Since the 60s it has developed massively, into a major distribution centre and high-tech industry base.

The Padgate Campus is the College's base, a 55-acre site close to the town centre. All accommodation is here, and provides residence for first and third year students domiciled more than twenty miles away. Rooms are single or shared study bedrooms.

With the sports bias come good sports facilities, including a modern sports hall, an all-weather 400m athletics track, tennis courts, playing fields and a new fitness centre.

For relaxation there is a bar, which also serves food, and a hall for discos, etc. Warrington has a few nightclubs, a cinema and bowling alley. Manchester and Liverpool, you'll be pleased to hear, are only 40 minutes away on the train.

GETTING THERE

★ By road: M6 (J21) and M62 (J10).
★ By rail: either Padgate or Birchwood stations on the Liverpool to Manchester line.

WARWICK UNIVERSITY

The University of Warwick
Senate House
Coventry
CV4 7AL

TEL 01203 523523
FAX 01203 461606

Warwick University
Students Union
Gibbet Hill Road
Coventry
Warwickshire CV4 7AL

TEL 01203 427220
FAX 01203 692083

UNIVERSITY OF WARWICK	
Founded	**1965**
Situation/style	**Campus**
UNDERGRADUATE PROFILE	
Application acceptance rate	**9%**
Population	**7,000**
Mature student population	**10%**
Overseas student population	**9%**
Male/female ratio	**50:50**
1st year institut. accommodation	**100%**
Approximate cost	**£35-£65 pw**
ACADEMIC PROFILE	
A-level requirements:	**High**
Law AAB, **Sociology** BCC, **English Literature** ABB-BBB, **French** BBC-BCC, **Maths with Computing** AAB-ABB, **All Engineering** 20	
Student/staff ratio	**12:1**
1st class degree pass rate	**10.4%**
HEFCE assessments *(9 subjects assessed/approved):*	
1993 **History**	Excellent
1994 **Business & Management, Computer Science, English, Law**	Excellent
1995 **Italian** 21	
1996 **Sociology** 24	

Joint Funding Council's research assessment 1996 (25 subjects assessed):	
Pure Maths, Computer, History.	Grade 5*
Biol. Sciences, Statistics, Economics, Sociology, Social Work, Business/ Management, French, Communication/Cultural/ Media, Drama/Dance/ Performing Arts.	Grade 5
EMPLOYMENT PROFILE	
Employability in Industry:	
MPW national league table (1996)	**9th=**
Principal job market destinations:	
Commerce (strong especially on **Accounting**), **Education, Manufacturing** (**Electronic & Electrical** strong), **Retail/ Wholesale, Public Admin/Law** (strong), **Computer, Arts/Media** (strong)	
PIP 1996 employers' survey:	
Top 3 subjects/national ranking	
Business	1st
Accountancy, Banking & Finance	3rd=
Computing	4th
Approximate % unemployed	**6%**

VAG VIEW

Warwick has exploded upon the university scene in the last ten years and there can be few who wouldn't want to have it on their UCAS list. We heard only one critical voice - a careers teacher at a girls' independent school. I wouldn't begin with even this mildest of criticisms if I didn't know that Warwick could take it:

'Warwick is very high in all the employment ratings, the league tables. Part of their strength is their location. They have a lot of inward investment from local industry. But as far as some arts subjects are concerned there's a tendency to churn out students, a certain lack of personal touch. We had someone there for English recently and it took her a long time to settle because, she said, it is so impersonal. You go along to your big lectures, you write your essays, you have large seminar groups...not a lot of contact.' *More typical were the following, the first from a boys' independent school careers adviser, the next two by current Warwick students:*

'Definitely in the top League. Part of it is to do with the Vice Chancellor, who is much more of a high flyer than your average British academic...I get people going to Warwick whatever course they want to do.'

'I knew from the first time that I visited the University of Warwick that it was the place for me. As far as I could see, it had the ideal balance of having a good reputation, offering a sound education and an excellent social life... The students vary immensely in terms of background. You get the usual private school boys and girls, for whom going to a university is the first time they haven't had to wear a uniform. However, you get all kinds of other students, including those who are not really that well off, and lots of international students. From my own experience, the ones who fit in best are those who are out for a laugh, enjoy drinking and are open-minded, basically your average student really!'

Emma Burhouse

'Warwick University is a self-contained pit of riotous hedonism that provides fun for every Thomas, Richard and Harold that ever sets foot in it. It's ace, eventful and memorable. These are the best days of your life times ten. Don't let things that surprise you in the first week be a yardstick. If shit happens, it happens. If not, why not?'

Ben Jones & Chris Wilding

SITUATION

Warwick is a campus university, set, not in Warwick, but three miles south-west from Coventry city centre. The reason it was called Warwick is that it was part-funded by Warwickshire County Council. A second campus, ten minutes walk away - it was once a College of Education - houses the University's Education Institute and Westwood Halls of Residence.

GETTING THERE

★ By road: From the north and east: M1 (J21), M69, A46, signs to University. From the south: M1 (J17), M45, A45, or M40 (J15), A46, signs to University. From the west: M5 (J4a), M42 (J6), A45 (East), signs to University. Regular coach services to Coventry, then bus to campus.
★ By rail: Birmingham New Street 30 minutes; Manchester Piccadilly 2:30; Nottingham, 1:45; Bristol 2:30; London Euston, 1:20.
★ By air: Birmingham International Airport - eleven minutes to Coventry by train.

ACCOMMODATION

Guaranteed on-campus accommodation for all first years who apply, but not for Clearing students. Six halls of residence, four groups of flats.

SPORT

Excellent facilities for all team sports - soccer, rugby, hockey, tennis, cricket, croquet...also a five km trim track with exercise stations, an eight-lane Olymprene all weather running track, a sports centre with six-lane swimming pool, squash courts, climbing room, and on the Westwood Campus there's a sports hall with games area, swimming pool, specialist facility for Olympic gymnastics and a dance studio. 70+ sports clubs - from Gliding to 'Zhuan Shu Kuan'. National champions in Men's Coxless Pairs, Ultimate Frisbee, Lifesaving. Plans for new outdoor pitch complex and sports pavilion.

ACADEMIA

No Medicine, Health Sciences, Veterinary, Agriculture, Architecture, Media/Publishing/ Journalism/etc. Heavy on Social Studies (Politics, Economics, Law), Maths Sciences, Engineering & Technology, Languages, Education, Biological Sciences, Business, Humanities, Physical Sciences, etc.

VIEW FROM THE GROUND

by Ben Jones & Chris Wilding

Warwick is, apparently, the largest campus in England. This is good in that it gives the 13,000 inhabitants a bit of space and bad in that it can a mean a 45 minute yomp across field to get to your nine o'clock lecture. Try that in January.

While cynics and the under-endowed may sneer that size isn't everything, if you don't like the idea of a crowded, claustrophobic city college, then Warwick, with its acres of fields, lakes and woods (to say nothing of its car parks and building sites) will seem like heaven.

Being a young University (just over thirty years old) it is continually expanding. A much larger venue for bands and functions is currently being built next to the Union, and many of its verdant acres have already been condemned to concrete death. It seems that no one knows when to stop. Indeed the grassy knoll where you drink and play footy in the first year could well become your lecture theatre two years on, giving rise to many 'I remember when all this was nowt but fields' speeches. Tragic.

But despite the relentless march of the builders, it remains a campus rather than a suburb of Coventry (praise be) and the excellent social atmosphere ensures that the 'we're in this together so let's have a laugh' attitude prevails.

ACCOMMODATION

'All first years get a room on Campus,' the official prospectus will gloat. What this means in practice is that every year, some healthy percentage of innocents is dumped into temporary accommodation, usually sharing a single room. It is for this reason that the personality section of the accommodation form should be filled in thus: 'Messy. Likes thrash metal. Burns dogs. Masterbates loudly and frequently.' The only downside of this ploy is that you may actually end up sharing with one of the above. It's a lottery to be honest.

There are several halls from which to choose. Jack Martin, the University's flagship hall, has en-suite bathrooms, reasonable rooms, and convenient location; but is ruthlessly overpriced, and the rest of the campus looks down at the occupants as 'Rich Southern Jessies'. Westwood has colossal rooms, but it's miles from anywhere, the bar is criminal, and the dining scheme is ludicrous and costly. Rootes is the most popular choice. The rooms are adequate, it's right next to the Union, and it's fairly priced. It was, however, built according to the plans of a Swedish women's prison the corridors are so designed that it's impossible to throw a punch, play football or pass your fat friend going the other way.

STUFF THAT GOES ON

It's the Union that's the centre of first year life. It likes to pass itself off as a debonair hive of activity, but instead is a big building with bars in. Fair enough. These bars are named after various luminaries including Des Lynam, 'Grumpy' John, and Harvey Milk, the first openly gay lawyer in San Francisco, who was shot dead for the revelation. Those that run the Union, despite their capitalistic opulence, feel the need to support the impoverished. Thus, while settling down for a quiet ale, the table will be scattered with leaflets saying things like: 'If you're reading this leaflet, you've got eyes. Xiao Xing hadn't had eyes since the Chinese Secret Police poured battery acid over his face'.

The appearance of this sort of propaganda does nothing but desensitise the majority, and bar conversations often include the, 'Well he must have done something wrong in the first place', line which is probably undeserved.

When the revolution comes, sure as top hats are top hats, it won't start at Warwick. There's an active political/debating scene here, but if the vast majority of students were summoned to march on Downing Street and overthrow the Government, it would depend on the weather, if it was after 12 o'clock and if they could make it back for Blind Date.

One way to corrupt the mindless minds of the masses is to join the Warwick media. This consists of a radio station pioneered by Simon Mayo and Timmy Mallett that broadcasts to three top floor bedrooms of Rootes residences on a clear day, or the unfortunately and inappropriately monikered Warwick Boar newspaper. The Boar is read by 12,000 people each week and comes with a bi-weekly lifestyle section focusing on the arts and music scenes of the day. Former editors have gone on to write for the *Guardian, The New York Times* and...erm...*Razzle.*

Clubs and societies range from political forums and wind orchestra to football watching and drum 'n' bass. If you want it, you can find it. And if you can't, with thirty signatures and you can start your own club. Personally I think there's a niche in the market for twenty thrusting nubile first years to form an orgy society. I, for one, would support it to the hilt.

On a lighter note, the Union organises an event every night, ranging from Monday night's Top Banana (dubiously advertised as the best free disco in the West Midlands, in fact a drunken pull-fest), to The Whipround on Saturday nights, where such bands as Oasis and Kula Shaker have played, albeit a year before their stardom, giving the Indie Snobs a chance to say they were there, whereas in reality, they were probably eating pizza in their room with Ned's Atomic Dustbin on the stereo.

The beer at the Union is grossly overpriced. If you come from London, the 'three pints for less than a fiver', will impress, but the cheapest beer is £1.30, and that's watered down piss.

Food is pricey and often cold, but for those inept in the kitchen it provides a reasonable meal. It ranges from rubbery kebab to meaty slop, but it doesn't stop me, and thousands of others eating shedloads.

The policy on drugs at the University is confusing. You can be kicked out of hall for smoking a joint, but last year there was a furore when the University re-admitted a convicted dealer. Suffice to say, if you go looking, recreationals are refreshingly easy to unearth, but it's safer to wait until you have your own house, as most landlords wouldn't care if the toilet was blocked with brown needles as long as you paid your rent.

But that's not all. Warwick also boasts the largest Arts Centre in the country apart from the Barbican in London, where the rich and pretentious can watch anything from Kafka to Tarantino, which almost makes up for the fact that every two days the Arts Centre is populated by visiting school hordes with eight-year olds forming a loud, disorganised crocodile, wearing claret uniforms and gazing at you as if you were an adult. Hah! Then they troop off under the watchful eye of 'teach' to see the King's Players do Postman Pat. Class.

Nestling next to the Arts Centre is the book shop. In the day it looks like a lego turd, by night it's transformed into an ultra-violet white-walled fantasy, which honestly looks more impressive than it sounds. All this glamour fails to hide the fact that it does nothing other than sell books to those stupid enough to believe the lecturers' myth that they actually need them.

The sports centre is apparently quite decent, despite Warwick's lowly position in every league in the land. If you want to do sport, go to Loughborough.

The library is a current talking point. Those in the know say there aren't enough books, and that the photocopying is extortionate. Most don't care.

Oh! And there's one more minor thing that goes on, and that's the courses. The details aren't important and are available from other publications. It may sound arrogant, but you're getting a degree from Warwick University and that's all that matters.

Drink, eat and be merry, for time here won't last long.

COVENTRY - The City

Forget Manchester, Barcelona and Marseilles - Coventry, for the record, has the highest inner-city violent crime rate per head of population in Europe. And then some. But so long as you don't run multi-million pound narcotic rings, spill pints of lager over shaven-headed locals called Bubba or start talking about astrophysics in Canley Working Men's Club, then trouble will have a hard time locating you. Sure, you will see various characters who more than resemble the photofits on Crimewatch, but they've got hitmen to look out for, and don't give a monkey's toss-tissue about a few students living nearby.

As a first year student, the mere mention of a night out in Coventry may fill you with dread and terror. However, should you choose to dodge the bullets of the bright lights, it is possible to find satisfactory entertainment and lubrication in the festive West Midlands haven of Coventry.

Back to Basics have a resident night at the pleasingly efficient Foundry, and Coventry poly (sorry, University) have recently opened a new £3 million venue called The Planet, boasting big name DJs such as Jeremy Healy, Carl Cox and Paul Oakenfold. Nice one. Elsewhere, Mr G's, Scholar's and Brown's offer lamentable excuses for nightclubs. The Dog and Trumpet has an alternative rock night on a Friday. Should you decide to take on the Dog and Trumpet, be prepared for sweat, long hair and fat men who haven't seen the Imperial Leather for several weeks. Actually, it's a good night. So is Thursday at the Colosseum. It's basically an Indie/Britpop/60s kind of affair, but it has cheap beer, and plenty of top tunesmithery.

As for pubs, the Cottage in Earlsdon (two miles north of the university) offers a quiet drinking haunt with a plethora of old men, cheap beer, and a rather fetching beer garden complete with fashionable gazebo. The City Arms and the Dolphin are sure fire pubs to take a beating, and the Royal Oak enforces a 'No Hat' policy.

Nourishment can be found for Coventry residents amidst a ravishing waterfall of assorted chip shops, kebaberies, balti houses and greasy spoons. Curry prices in Coventry are competitive with the rest of the country, but steeper than an mountain goat's erection for the West Midlands.

Earlsdon is good for a haircut (there are nine hairdressers within half a mile), and has churches, golf courses and art shops for the cultural elites. For the rest of the world, there is Suzy Q's splendid American pool and snooker bar, which offers the obscenely low price of £2 per day for unlimited play.

So there you have it - Coventry. It has three cinemas, isn't far from Birmingham and has a statue of a naked bird on some old nag in the city centre. It's not exactly like home, but with a few Jedi mind tricks, you can survive.

Then there's Royal Leamington Spa. Despite being a daunting eight miles from the University, Royal Leamington Spa is the most popular choice for students when cruelly hurled off campus in the second year. The main reason for this impressive claim is, quite simply, that it isn't Coventry. A smallish town in Warwickshire, it boasts a vast selection of pubs, fast food outlets and dirt cheap curry houses that more than make up for its distance from the Students' Union.

Leamington's nightlife is decent enough. The pubs fall into several categories: there are those designed with the student in mind; there are those where students are accepted (if not welcomed); and there are those with signs outside bearing adverts of 'Wacky Prices' and 'Ker-azy Student Offers'. This last bunch are to be avoided, as they are the shocking pubs trying to drum up trade. However, should a group of pissed up 'Wacky' students enter, the reception is frostier than a Midlands morning. Brr.

There are a couple of clubs. The clientele is either 15-19 year-old townies trying to pull, or 25-40 somethings persuading themselves that yes, they can still fit into that little dress. They can't.

Eating in Leamington is easy and enjoyable. McDonald's and Burger King trade BSE free blows, several pizza places vie for the student vote, kebabs and chip shops are prolific, but it's the curry that really stands out. Here, the competition is the connoisseur's friend, and if you pay over a fiver for a huge Balti, manhole coveresque naan and frisbee sized popadoms, then you've been swindled. For shame. Next time, got to the one next door. For those not put off by a year of cooking for themselves, there is an in town Tesco, Asda and Sainsbury's if you don't mind walking, and a Mini-mart on every street. Couldn't be easier.

To work off your excess, there are gyms, snooker halls and even golf courses. Nothing quite like a swift nine holes to see off that fried breakfast.

Leamington is quite the quintessential student town, locals are accommodating, and it's not too expensive. What more could you ask for? Free shuttle between town and Uni? Proper club scene? Lottery win? Now you're just being greedy.

WELSH COLLEGE OF MUSIC & DRAMA

Welsh College of Music
& Drama
Castle Grounds
Cathays Park
Cardiff
CF1 3ER

TEL 01222 342854
FAX 01222 237639

Student Union
Welsh College of Music
& Drama
Castle Grounds
Cathays Park
Cardiff
CF1 3ER

TEL 01222 372700

WELSH COLLEGE OF MUSIC & DRAMA	
Founded	**1949**
Situation/style	**City site**
UNDERGRADUATE PROFILE	
Population	**450**
Mature student population	**36%**
Overseas student population	**6%**
Male/female ratio	**40:60**
1st year institut. accommodation	**None**
Approximate rent	**£35-£40 pw**
ACADEMIC PROFILE	
A-level requirements: **performance related**	
Student/staff ratio	**6:1**
1st class degree pass rate	**12.5%**
HEFCW assessments (2 subjects assessed/approved): **Music, Drama**	
EMPLOYMENT PROFILE	
Principal job market destinations: **Arts/Media** (especially **Creative Arts**), **Education**	
Approximate % unemployed	**4%**

VAG VIEW

The College was founded in 1949 and in those days it actually occupied Cardiff Castle. Today, and since 1974, its purpose-built premises nearby are 'more suitable for people blowing trombones,' as someone there told me. They are presently engaged in enhancing their teaching facilities by refurbishing a listed property alongside, which will be open by the 98 intake. There is also an opera studio planned and a new concert hall and premises for the design department. There is, however, no student accommodation, though it is not difficult to find in the city. See Cardiff entries for more about the city.

The College offers BA degrees in Music, and Theatre Studies - Acting or Stage Management. All applicants are invited for audition, for a fee of £33 (music), £20 (drama).

UNIVERSITY OF THE WEST OF ENGLAND

University of the West
of England
Coldharbour Lane
Frenchay
Bristol
BS16 1QY

TEL 0117 9656261
FAX 0117 9763972

University of the West
of England Students Union
Coldharbour Lane (Main Site)
Frenchay
Bristol BS16 1QY

TEL 0117 965 6261 x2577
FAX 0117 976 3909 x2577

UNIVERSITY OF THE WEST OF ENGLAND

Founded	**1969**
Situation/style	**Campus & sites**
UNDERGRADUATE PROFILE	
Application acceptance rate	**8%**
College of Health AAR	**9%**
Population	**11,400**
Mature student population	**24%**
Overseas student population	**2%**
Male/female ratio	**52:48**
1st year institut. accommodation	**72%**
Approximate rent (Uni)	**£40 pw**
(Uni managed private sector)	**£40-£50 pw**
ACADEMIC PROFILE	
A-level requirements:	**Medium**

Law BBB-BBC, **Biological Sciences** 10, **Psychology & Health Science** 20, **Accounting & Finance, Business** 16, **Architecture & Town Planning** 18, **Computer Science, Statistics** 12, 8, **Engineering** 14, **Physiotherapy** BBC, **Cultural & Media, Literary** BBC

Student/staff ratio	**19:1**
1st class degree pass rate	**4.5%**
HEFCE assessments *(12 subjects assessed/approved):*	
1993 **Law**	Excellent
1994 **Business & Management, English**	Excellent
1995/6 **Modern Languages** 21 **Sociology** 23	
Joint Funding Council's research assessment 1996 (20 subjects assessed):	
Grade 5/5*	None
EMPLOYMENT PROFILE	
Employability in Industry:	
MPW national league table (1996)	**49th=**

Principal job market destinations:
Manufacturing (strong **Pharmaceutical, Electrical & Electronic**), **Education, Commerce, Health, Retail/Wholesale, Public Admin/Law, Arts Media** (strong on **Publishing, Radio/TV, Creative Arts**), **Health, Computer, Personnel, Construction, Property Development**

PIP 1996 employers' survey: Top subject/national ranking	
Construction & Civil Engineering	23rd=
Approximate % unemployed	**9%**

VAG VIEW

West has joined the select group of 'new' universities which have made it, or at least the heels of the first division runners are in sight. The Uni has five sites in and around Bristol, and regional centres in Bath, Gloucester and Swindon. But UWE's reputation is enough to bind them. Some of its strengths are clear from the assessments (see fact box), but there are some intriguing ones, such as Time-Based Media, which put them way ahead of the crowd.

VIEW FROM THE GROUND
by Richard Silver

On first learning that I'd be moving to Bristol (to study Business at UWE), the reaction of my Brummie friends gave me some cause for concern. Some assumed that I'd be lodging with a West Country farmer in the middle of a turnip field. Others congratulated me for making a choice so close to the sea. Still others questioned the fact that UWE was in Bristol at all.

FIRST IMPRESSIONS

The University extends over four campuses throughout Bristol, the largest of which, Frenchay, is where the Business School is situated, and where I found myself on the September morning I arrived. Corridors led off in all directions, stairs ascended and descended all around me. The timetable was baffling, instructing me to reach room 4E11A for an induction. Which way now? If only I'd taken A-level Geography...

After just a few days, however, the layout of the building and the room numbering system begins to make sense, and reaching fifth floor rooms at 9:29 a.m. for an Economics tutorial becomes less of a problem. Be prepared for extremes though - lectures at UWE can be with as many as 600 others from assorted courses, whereas tutorials can be with as few as five, including tutor. This is an ideal way of meeting peple of course, but whether you find it easier to talk to people en masse or on more intimate terms will affect the outcome here.

So, what 'type' of student might benefit from what UWE has to offer? The studious might feel at home exploring the newly extended Bolland Library, though it is now unfeasibly huge (and has to be seen to be believed). However, it is conveniently located opposite the refectory, so energy lost exploring it can be replenished with a fry-up. The computer literate and illiterate will find a large part of life at UWE spent on exercising or evolving these skills. All students get their own e-mail file (perfect for communicating with your buddies to see who's going clubbing that night, for free!), and have access to the Internet (anyone know the address for the *Baywatch* site?) and most major software packages. There are loads of computers too, and lots are open 24 hours. So, if you feel the need to surf the Net at 2:00 a.m. on Saturday, then hey, go for it. Linguaphiles will have their needs more than catered for with the latest audio-visual aids and Language Laboratory, which has rows of monitors showing Satellite TV from around Europe (sadly not Eurosport, though).

The on-campus facilities are, generally speaking, more than adequate for a university of this size. Frenchay boasts a shop (selling everything from Crunchies to condoms), bookshop, NatWest bank and cashpoints, a vast refectory, numerous smaller eateries, travel agency, launderette and, of course, the bars. Opinion is divided as to which is best. Both serve food (pizzas, cookies, baguettes, etc.); both serve all types of booze.

However, the Escape bar has a juke box, MTV and fruit machines, giving a pub atmosphere, whereas Traders bar has piped music, uniformed staff and is decorated in pastel shades of green, giving a more refined image. Coffee from Traders comes in a delicate cup and saucer with an Almond biscuit. From Escape it comes in a brown mug.

Should UWE be your choice, be prepared to PARTY like you never have before. There are limitless events on all year on UWE's campuses, which cater for all tastes. (Hey, if you want to work you should be at Bristol Uni, spit! spit!) Every Friday night UWE holds Sin at Frenchay. It's a strange phenomenon, but nobody ever admits to going to this boozy, dancy night, though it frequently turns out to be the best (and cheapest) night out in Bristol. All the campuses have similar events and organise bands and quiz nights, but Frenchay seems to get the lion's share.

The renowned House of Sutra visits regularly for all types of dance freaks, whilst anything goes at the Ruffneck Ting night. Apparently.

Also worth a mention are the balls, particularly the Freshers Ball and Snow Ball. These are hugely popular and have to be seen to be believed. They attract a wide range of acts too. Recent ones have included Michelle Gayle, the Outhere Brothers, Sunscream, Reel 2 Reel, and the Mike Flowers Pops.

One major selling point of UWE has to be its proximity to Bristol city centre. The nightlife here should suit everyone, as the pubs and clubs are so diverse. Also, Bristol is home to some of the most acclaimed clubs outside London. These include hip-hop favourite Blue Mountain. The Thekla (a club inside a huge, moored boat) and, of course, Lakota, the creme de la creme of clubbing. Gain instant street cred by going here. Odyssey and Club I.Q. are more mainstream and offer excellent student nights. UWE student union actually owns a club in the centre called The Tube. Never been there, but I've heard it's good.

But if clubbing 'aint your thing, then the centre offers cinemas, an ice rink, markets, museums, and the historical docks. The Hippodrome and Colston Hall also have the latest and greatest in shows and concerts. I've always found that all these places are very student friendly and are accepted as valuable customers, rather than traffic-cone-wearing yobs. The centre is well lit too, with one of the biggest police stations known to man.

SPORT AND CLUBS

Should you still feel the need for something to do during the day, you can join a club. There's football (mens and womens), rugby (ditto), skiing, squash, kick boxing, cycling, waterpolo, snooker (is snooker a sport?) and loads more. Political covers all the major parties. Laid-back means sailing, canoeing, golf, American football (that woke you up), photography, fellwalking. Nutter suggests Gaelic football, splatball, Tequilla Society, Bungee.

If you do excel in a particular area of sport, please consider UWE as we badly need to maintain our competitive edge against the evil Bristolians and their various teams. Particularly rugby players. Kieran Bracken studied here, you know. That said, sporting facilties at UWE are sparse to say the least. We've just one astro-turf, a scattering of playing fields and a gymnasium/squash courts thing. How you feel about that depends on how highly you rate the need for such facilities; things are supposedly improving.

ACCOMMODATION

An area where UWE is much more efficient is in student accommodation. There is a dedicated team of housing officers who make it their mission to assist in the provision of good quality housing, particularly for freshers and foreign exchange students. There are extensive on-campus villages for many students, although Ashley Village at Frenchay appears to be the worst, resembling a series of grey bomb shelters rather than houses. For my first year I lived with two girls and two guys, none of whom turned out to be psychopathic axe murderers, as I'd initially imagined they would.

That said, accommodation can be a bit of a lottery in Bristol - I viewed a three-floor squat with 10 bedrooms and 2 bathrooms. Sure the rent was just £25 a week, but I value my health and so left quickly.

The main student areas are Bishopston, Redland, Fishponds and Horfield, all are within easy reach of either Gloucester Road or Whiteladies Road, 2 sprawling high streets crammed with pubs, restaurants, shops, banks and fast-food places. Whiteladies Road features the cocktail heaven of Henry J. Beans and the notorious club Kickers, whilst Gloucester Road has the world famous Pizza King and the renowned pub, The Bristol Flyer. It now even boasts Bristol Rovers F.C. at the Memorial Ground. Enjoy.

So, if any of the above appeals to you, then maybe you should consider UWE. It's in the top 5 biggest Uni's in the country, so I'm told. Sure, it's not Oxford or Cambridge, but then who'd want it to be? Become an honorary Bristolian and develop that unique West Country burr. Ooh Arr...

WESTHILL COLLEGE

Westhill College
Weoley Park Road
Selly Oak
Birmingham
B29 6LL

TEL 0121 472 7245
FAX 0121 415 5399

Westhill College of Higher Education Students Union
Guild of Students
Melville Hall
The Close, Bristol Road
Selly Oak
Birmingham B29 6LT

TEL 0121 471 1720
FAX 0121 471 1720

WESTHILL COLLEGE	
Founded	**1907**
Situation/style	**Campus**
UNDERGRADUATE PROFILE	
Application acceptance rate	**11%**
Population	**1,000**
Mature student population	**42%**
Male/female ratio	**20:80**
1st year institut. accommodation	**100%**
Approximate cost	**£65 pw**
ACADEMIC PROFILE	
A-level requirements:	**Low**
Combined programmes **(Humanities, Social, Educational Studies)**	CC
Student/staff ratio	**22:1**
1st class degree pass rate	**1.7%**
Joint Funding Council's research assessment 1996 (5 subjects assessed):	
Grade 5/5*	None
EMPLOYMENT PROFILE	
Principal job market destinations: **Education**	
Approximate % unemployed	**15%**

VAG VIEW

Westhill College is situated three miles south-west of the centre of Birmingham and its degrees are validated by Birmingham University. It has a particular contribution to make to teaching by providing students with a BA degree, first step to a PGCE (Post Graduate Certificate in Education), though graduates do go on into other professions.

Westhill offers four alternative routes or faculties. Each route has a number of strands or subjects, from which you choose four. Each strand comprises several modules. The idea is to compose an interdisciplinary course programme which will 'develop new and consistent ways of looking at the world'.

Essentially Westhill is describing the modular system. But what makes Westhill's approach interesting is the one compulsory element in the programme. Your strands or subjects must be Interdisciplinary Studies.

Interdisciplinary Studies is like a touchstone throughout your degree, for these studies show you how to maximise the interdisciplinary approach by discovering and exploring the areas of connection between your various subject strands which are the very areas in which these 'new and consistent ways of looking at the world' will be developed.

Westhill has a clear statement of the

purpose of modular education (the clearest I have read from any university or college). They also frame their statement well by explaining that the modular revolution is occurring not for the sake of allowing students into the Higher Education system who might not be up to specialism, but because the value of an interdisciplinary approach - with this potentiality for new and alternative perceptions - is now being recognised at the sharp end of research. It is what is taking the world forward.

GETTING THERE

★ By road: M42 (J1), A38.
★ By train to Birmingham New Street: London Euston, 1:40; Bristol Parkway or Sheffield, 1:30; Liverpool Lime Street or Manchester Piccadilly,1:40; Leeds, 2:15.

WESTMINSTER COLLEGE

Westminster College
Oxford
OX2 9AT

TEL 01865 247644
FAX 01865 251847

Westminster College Oxford
Student Union
Westminster College
Oxford OX2 9AT

TEL 01865 200067
FAX 01865 201393

WESTMINSTER COLLEGE OXFORD	
Founded	**1851**
Situation/style	**Campus**
UNDERGRADUATE PROFILE	
Application acceptance rate	**23%**
Population	**1,000**
Mature student population	**34%**
Overseas student population	**1%**
Male/female ratio	**20:80**
1st year institut. accommodation	**95%**
Approximate cost	**£70 pw**
ACADEMIC PROFILE	
A-level requirements:	**Low**
Teacher Training CE-EE, **French combinations** CE, **Theology** CE	
Student/staff ratio	**23:1**
1st class degree pass rate	**4%**
Joint Funding Council's research assessment 1996 (3 subjects assessed):	
Grade 5/5*	None
EMPLOYMENT PROFILE	
Principal job market destinations: **Education**	
Approximate % unemployed	**15%**

VAG VIEW

Westminster College moved to its present site on Harcourt Hill, just outside Oxford, off the A34 Newbury Road, in 1959, and now, although they have their own accommodation, sporting and teaching facilities, enjoys a unique relationship with the University of Oxford. Its students, for a fee, can partake of the University's Fresher Fair, they can even play sport for the University and gain half-blues, and all but one of their degrees are validated by the University. The college has a Methodist foundation and there is a degree in Theology, though its main thrust remains Education, their BEd (Hons) degree being a four year course. The exception to Oxford Uni's validation is a BA degree in Contemporary Studies, which is an exploration of 'the cultural, economic, political and value dimensions of modern societies' and is validated by the Open University. It is possibly the clearest statement of what Westminster is about, for the main theme of all their degrees is that the multi-cultural nature of society is its strength, and an awareness of the implications of this is the purpose of their educational programme.

WESTMINSTER UNIVERSITY

The University of Westminster
309 Regent Street
London
W1R 8AL

TEL 0171 911 5000
FAX 0171 911 5103

University of Westminster
Student Union
Kathrada House
104-108 Bolsover Street
London W1P 7HS

TEL 0171 636 6271
FAX 0171 911 5192

University of Westminster
Student Union
Watford Road
Harrow
Middlesex HA1 3TP

TEL 0171 911 5000 x4022
FAX 0171 423 2794

UNIVERSITY OF WESTMIMSTER

Founded **1838**

Situation/style **City site**

UNDERGRADUATE PROFILE

Application acceptance rate **9%**
Population **7,500**
Mature student population **63%**
Overseas student population **6%**
Male/female ratio **50:50**
1st year institut. accommodation:
★ guaranteed to ex-London UK-based students
Approximate cost **£60 pw**

ACADEMIC PROFILE

A-level requirements: **Medium**
Law BCC, **Sociology, Media Studies** BC
French combinations BCC-CC,
Computational Maths, Maths Sciences CD,
Architecture CC, **Engineering:** High: **Civil, Industrial Systems & Business Management** 12, Low: **Mechanical** 8
Student/staff ratio **19:1**
1st class degree pass rate **9.1%**
HEFCE assessments (13 subjects assessed/approved):
1996 **French** 23 **Russian** 18
Sociology 18 **Linguistics** 20
Italian 19
Joint Funding Council's research assessment 1996 (19 subjects assessed):
Communication/Cultural/ Media Grade 5

EMPLOYMENT PROFILE

Principal job market destinations:
Retail/Wholesale, Manufacturing, Arts/Media (strong on **Publishing, Radio/TV**), **Health, Commerce, Education, Public Admin./Law, Construction, Computer, Property Development,** good record **Architecture**
Approximate % unemployed **15%**

VAG VIEW

The University comes out of The Royal Polytechnic Institution, established in 1838 by Sir George Caley, of whom you may not have heard, but who hailed from a tiny village in North Yorkshire in the lea of the moors, where, amongst other things, he invented the aeroplane (it is true!), wisely getting one of his lackey's sons (a boy of ten) to ride in it down Brompton Dale. When he had his butler do the same, the man's nerves were so shot that he promptly gave in his notice.

Some of Sir George's relatives still live in the village. I know his eldest great, great...etc. granddaughter, and I can vouch that he would be quite tickled to hear what is going on today at Westminster.

Following its founding, at a time when it was still de trop, *even considered dangerous, to educate the working classes, the curriculum included manufacturing (preparation for the new Industrial world) and they managed to sneak in a few language courses apparently and even some arts. It became a university in 1992, and today Westminster University is involved in another educational revolution. Its course structure is modular and it organises its assessments in terms of the CATS points system. But where it succeeds is in becoming totally involved in a student's choice of which modules to study. In their prospectus - which is probably the first occasion that a prospective student will have any meaningful contact with the university - they point out in the clearest and most interesting way the purpose of the modular system to prepare students for a particular avenue of employment, and then go on to show why it is imperative that the module mix is right. Not only have they given due consideration to what, day to day, a particular profession will require a student to have mastered, in terms of educational and other skills, but they have consulted with employers to that end. In the matter of skills, as distinct from knowledge, they and their students have been involved with more than 3,500 employers in real, practical projects in which students can identify and rehearse the skills they will require. Two particular skills underly the whole programme - linguistic skills and numeracy. Westminster offers 26 languages, taught at various levels from beginner to postgraduate, to all its students, the idea being to open up an international dimension to their plans for employment. At Westminster, language is a core skill and their Self-access (audio/ visual) Language Centre allows students to practise their languages in their own time. On the numeracy side, their parallel 'mathematics for all' initiative offers a collection of modules which explain mathematical thinking in non-technical lingo to non-technical students.*

Among Westminster's degree departments are Architecture & Civil Engineering; Biological & Health Sciences; Business, Economics & Mgt. Studies; Communication (Design & Media); Computer Science, Information Systems & Maths; Construction, Housing & Surveying; Electronic & Manufacturing Systems Engineering; Law, English Studies; Social & Policy Sciences; and Urban Development & Planning.

What I liked about their presentation was not only its clarity but the spirit in which it was delivered. So many prospectuses issued by institutions desperate to capitalise on their new university status are over-eager to attract custom from the student marketplace. Westminster issues theirs as a challenge which, far from putting you on the back foot, enthuses you to become a part of what they are up to.

SITUATION

Westminster operates from a new, multi-million pound site in Harrow in Middlesex and seven sites in London, five of them clustered around the Post Office Tower and a stone's throw from Regent Street, where The Royal Polytechnic Institution itself once stood (from 1881 it was actually re-named The Regent Street Poly). The Harrow site is home to the Harrow Business School and courses in Communication, Design and Media. It includes TV, radio, photography and music studios, and the student population here is growing rapidly - they expect its population to reach 7,000 within the next three years. This scattered base includes a Student Union in London and one in Harrow, and all the various teaching departments, research facilities and learning resource mechanisms are linked by a sophisticated computer system.

GETTING THERE

★ Oxford Street Underground (Victoria, Central and Bakerloo lines) to 309 Regent Street, Westminster's Headquarters.

VIEW FROM THE GROUND
by Calvin Holbrook

The University of Westminster is, in fact, quite a misleading title for a centre of academic excellence. For increasingly students are studying at the Harrow campus, based in Middlesex, rather than at wonderful Westminster. The central London sites still exist, and students are taught there, but because of the distance involved students from each campus rarely interact - it's more like two universities than one.

Fret not, as central London is still easily accessible from Harrow - just a twenty minute tube journey away. The location has its advantages. If you're not too keen on living in the hustle and bustle of the world's liveliest capital, then the pace of life at Harrow will appeal. Better still, weekly rent in this area should be £50 to £60 a week, significantly less than other parts of London. And that extra wonga will come in very handy for beer...errr, I mean books!

The University itself offers halls of residence accommodation for over 400 students. Each flat houses six, and each room has its own shower and WC, so no communal nastiness in the hygiene department. The kitchen is well equipped for those pasta 'n' sauce opportunities, and the washroom saves you nipping to the launderette every other month.

Initial, planning permission traumas meant that students enroling in 1995 and 1996 were forced to move into the local hospital's nursing accommodation, instead of the halls of residence. And believe me, it's not a pretty sight.

ACADEMIA

If you want to study at a traditional university then don't come to Westminster. The courses here have a mainly 'hands- on' approach, that set students up for the real world. Bookworms need not apply. Certain courses such as Fashion BA (Hons) and Media Studies BA (Hons), are highly regarded by their respected industries for churning out skilled, intelligent workers, who can easily settle into a job.

Westminster is the only university offering to teach 'Commercial Music' - a fantastic chance for musicians and bands to learn about the business and to record their own tracks.

We don't have a library here, we have an Information Resource Service (IRS). This three-floor building holds masses of comprehensive information for all you busy bees, not just books. It holds stores of current national and specialist publications, a CD and video library, video and stereo units, everything you could possibly need for looming deadlines. You can also access your E-mail and the Internet in the computer rooms, and if you're a technophobe - don't worry, it really is simple.

SOCIAL SCENE

Enough of this though, what you really want to know about is the nightlife, right? Harrow campus has a friendly, well- stocked bar, soon to be enlarged, and is open seven days a week. It is host to various specialist nights where all musical genres are covered. There are also comedy nights for those up for a bit of a giggle. What the campus currently lacks is a music venue for major, established bands to perform at - the current bar simply couldn't accommodate the band and the crowd. However, if you're a music lover, you can easily get to the main venues in London. Drinks are priced favourably for students, with regular promotions. Harrow town itself is a tad dreary, with only one nightclub, which is abysmal anyway, but does have a vast amount of stylish, student-friendly pubs. It is, however, a sprawling town, with two shopping centres which hold the majority of chainstores, well Virgin's here anyway. (Ha!) There are plenty of charity shops for those on a cheap style mission. Harrow may not be the most happening place to live if you're a bit of a funkster, but remember central London is never far away. You can even get back to Harrow using the nightbus at 6 a.m., which is an experience in itself. The entertainments department have teamed up with major clubs such as SW1, Blue Note and Turnmills, to ensure exclusive, bargain deals for party animals.

COMMUNICATIONS

The Smoke is Westminster's own publication and is created almost entirely by students. So if you're a budding journalist you have the opportunity to gain valuable experience here. If you'd prefer to be a DJ then you may like to get involved in M-Factory radio, broadcast on campus. Our own live television programmes are also put out live on air. The technical equipment at Harrow is up to industry standard and makes for creating professional students. Past students have gone on to great success, for example, Michael Jackson, head of BBC1 and Danny Kelly, editor of Q magazine. This place is a boiling pot for personalities. With all races and nationalities, as well as sexualities. This makes for a lot of interesting individuals. There are lots of different tribes here: fashion victims, nerds, G-force, wannabies - people who want to succeed and get ahead of the crowds. As a university it's way ahead of its time - if you want to be on the cutting edge of technology and resources, and gain professional qualities - then come to Westminster.

WOLVERHAMPTON UNIVERSITY

The University of
Wolverhampton
Wulfruna Street
Wolverhampton
West Midlands
WV1 1SB

TEL 01902 321000
FAX 01902 322680

Wolverhampton University
Student Union
Telford Campus
Shifnal Road
Priorslee
Telford
Shropshire TF2 9NT

TEL 01902 323980
FAX 01902 323886

Wolverhampton University
Student Union
Wulfruna Street
Wolverhampton WV1 1LY

TEL 01902 322021
FAX 01902 322020

Wolverhampton University
Student Union
Dudley Campus
Castle View
Dudley DY1 3HR

TEL 01902 323333

Wolverhampton University
Student Union
Walsall Campus
Gorway Road
Walsall WS1 3BD

TEL 01902 323035
FAX 01902 323036

UNIVERSITY OF WOLVERHAMPTON

Founded	**1969**
Situation/style	**Campus/ city sites**
UNDERGRADUATE PROFILE	
Application acceptance rate	**13%**
Population	**11,600**
Mature student population	**30%**
Overseas student population	**2%**
Male/female ratio	**47:53**
1st year institut. accommodation	**80%**
Approximate cost	**£40-£47 pw**
(City/town)	**£30pw**
ACADEMIC PROFILE	
A-level requirements:	**Low**

Teacher Training B-E, **Law** 12-20, **Biomedical Sciences, Food Biology, Biology, Ecology, Computing, Math Sciences, Business,** etc DD, **Sociology** 14

Student/staff ratio	**31:1**
1st class degree pass rate	**3.3%**

HEFCE assessments (15 subjects assessed/approved):
1995/6 **Russian** 22 **Iberian** 20 **French** 19
1996 **Linguistics** 21 **Sociology** 20

Joint Funding Council's research assessment 1996 (19 subjects assessed):
Grade 5/5* None

EMPLOYMENT PROFILE

Principal job market destinations:
Education, Retail/Wholesale, Health, Manufacturing, Commerce, Public Admin./Law, Hotel/Restaurant, Arts/Media (strong on **Creative Arts**), **Computer, Construction, Personnel, Market Research/Advertising** (strong), **Engineering Design** (strong)

Approximate % unemployed **13%**

VAG VIEW

Wolverhampton is a dynamic operation. Besides their five campus sites, this former Wolverhampton Poly has associations with no less than eleven colleges. Close association with industry in this high density industrial area, as well as commerce and the professions, gives confidence in terms of future employment. If you want to know how their module system works, call up their web site on JANET and make up your own personalised programme. Then pick up the phone!

SITUATION

Based at five sites, two basically in Wolverhampton (the Compton Park site is in a leafyish suburb three miles to the West of the city centre, off the A454 to Bridgnorth), one in Walsall six or so miles East of Wolverhampton city centre, one in Dudley five miles to the south of the city, and one twelve or so miles to the Northwest, near Telford (Shropshire), just off the M54 between Junctions 4 and 5.

ADDRESSES

Telephone all via central switchboard, see above

Wolverhampton Main Campus:
Address as above. Applied Sciences, Art & Design, Computing, Construction, Engineering, Health Sciences, Languages, Law. Students Union.

Compton Park Campus,
Compton Road West,
Compton,
Wolverhampton
WV3 9DX.
Some Business (Business Admin, Info. Mgt., some Human Resourcing, Marketing), some Computing. SU bar, sports facilities nearby.

Walsall Campus,
Gorway Road,
Walsall WS1 3BD.
Education (incl. Sports Studies, Music).
Sports Hall, playing fields, swimming pool, dance studio, tennis courts.

Dudley Campus,
Castle View,
Dudley DY1 3HR.
Humanities and Social Sciences, also Education (Design & Technology). Sports Hall, tennis courts, playing fields, refurbished Students Union.

Shropshire Campus,
Priorslee Hall,
Shifnal Road
Telford TF2 9NT.
Business, Computer-aided Product Design. 18th century mansion, green field site, best accommodation.

GETTING THERE

★ By air: 30 miles Birmingham International Airport.
★ By road: Wolverhampton - From north M54 (J2), A449. From south and east, M6 (J10), A454. From north-east A4124. Walsall - From south M5, M6 (J9), A4148 (ring road, Eastbound). From Birmingham M6 (J7), A4148. Dudley - From north/south M6 (J2), A4123, A461, A459. From north-west A459. Telford (Shropshire) - From east M54 (J4). From west M54 (J5) signs first for Priorslee before those for University).
★ By train: Wolverhampton two hours from London, good for all destinations, station five minutes. walk from campus. Walsall, trains from Birmingham New Street, or 529/966 bus from Wolverhampton, then 51 from Walsall bus station to Jesson Road.. Dudley, train to Wolverhampton, 558 bus to Dudley. Telford, train from Birmingham New Street.

ACCOMMODATION

Halls of residence on or near all sites. Accommodation guaranteed to first year overseas students. Laundry, pay phones, TVs, games rooms. 460 en suite study bedrooms on Wolverhampton campus.

ARTS, ENTS AND UNION

Wolverhampton good for music venues, house, garage, rock, indie, bhangra, jungle techno, acid jazz, folk, classical. Cinemas include The Light House (mainstream and foreign); 10-screen mutiplexes at Walsall, Dudley and Telford. Uni's Arena Theatre for alternative, touring, student drama and music. Wolverhampton Art Gallery for one of finest collections of British and American Pop Art in the country.

Student Union provides ents with enthusiasm seven nights a week. Six bars across the sites, each with its own individual programme. Recent investment of more than £500,000 on venues, sound & light systems. Top name live bands, comedians, cabaret performers. Acts have included Charlie Chuck, Mark Lamarr, hypnotists, The Regurgitator, Secret Cabaret; bands - Jools Holland, Australian Pink Floyd Show, Desmond Decker, Bob Marley Tribute, Credit to the Nation; special Events last term included BeerKeller, Casinos, Foam/Laser discos, Steel Band Nights, Clairvoyants, Gyrowheels, Cajun Bands, Live Jazz, Karaoke, Dr. Fox. Regular events include Poco Loco, top DJ club night, Bavarian evenings, Gladiators Nights and Foam Parties. (See also Birmingham.)

SPORT

Multi-purpose sports halls at Wolverhampton, Dudley, Walsall. Playing fields and tennis courts at Dudley, Walsall. Running track, swimming pool and dance studio at Walsall. New fitness suite and weights room at Wolverhampton. Compton Park use nearby Wolverhampton facilities or neighbouring Compton Park Activities Centre. Wolverhampton students have discounts on many of town's facilities, including a swimming pool. Shropshire-based students use facilities in Telford.

ACADEMIA

Part- as well as full-time degrees, sandwich courses where appropriate. Integrated computer network incorporating over 1,500 microcomputers on all sites, 750 student workstations.

Ten academic schools. Modular Degree Scheme and the BSc Applied Science scheme allows inter-school programming. Special one-to-one counselling arrangements for course programming. Schools are:

Applied Sciences, Art and Design, Computing and Information, Technology, Construction, Engineering and Technology, Education, Health Studies, Humanities and Social Sciences, Languages and European Studies, Legal Studies, Wolverhampton Business School.

Worcester College

Worcester College
Henwick Grove
Worcester
WR2 6AJ

TEL 01905 855000
FAX 01905 855132

Worcester College
Students Union
Henwick Grove
St. Johns
Worcester WR2 6AJ

TEL 01905 740800
FAX 01905 740801

WORCESTER COLLEGE

Founded	**1946**
Situation/style	**Campus**
UNDERGRADUATE PROFILE	
Application acceptance rate	**11%**
Population	**2,800**
Mature student population	**53%**
Overseas student population	**1%**
Male/female ratio	**30:70**
1st year institut. accommodation	**100%**
Approximate cost	**£40-£60 pw**
ACADEMIC PROFILE	
A-level requirements:	**Low**

Teacher Training 12, **Sociology & combinations** CD, **Women's Studies & combinations** CC-DE

Student/staff ratio	**26:1**
HEFCE assessments (6 subjects assessed/approved):	
except **Music**, 1994	
1996 **Sociology** 21	
Joint Funding Council's research assessment 1996 (8 subjects assessed):	
Grade 5/5*	None
EMPLOYMENT PROFILE	
Principal job market destinations:	

Education, Retail/Wholesale, Public Admin.

Approximate % unemployed	**14%**

VAG VIEW

Worcester offers full-time and part-time degrees in the areas of Arts, Social Studies, Humanities and Science. The intake is mainly local to Worcester and includes a number of mature students. It is the kind of friendly local college every town and city should have. Its campus is two miles from the centre of the city and its degrees are validated by Coventry University. Accommodation and sporting facilities are in place for its bid to become a university - there are even sports scholarships on offer (cricket - Worcester is mad on cricket - rugby and netball) to the tune of £1,000. Precisely what distinguishes your typical college of higher education from a university is ever difficult to define when the very concept is in a state of constant re-definition. Only time can tell.

WRITTLE COLLEGE

Writtle College
Lordship Road
Writtle
Chelmsford
Essex CM1 3RR

TEL 01245 420705
FAX 01245 420456

Writtle College Student Union
Lordship Road
Writtle
Chelmsford
Essex CM1 3RR

TEL 01245 422752
FAX 01245 422611

WRITTLE COLLEGE	
Founded	1893
Situation/style	Campus
UNDERGRADUATE PROFILE	
Application acceptance rate	18%
Population	600
Mature student population	43%
Overseas student population	6%
Male/female ratio	50:50
1st year institut. accommodation	70%
Approximate cost (College)	£57-£80 pw
(Town)	£40-£50 pw
ACADEMIC PROFILE	
A-level requirements:	Low
Agriculture, Horticulture, Equine, Landscape etc 10-16	
Student/staff ratio	7:1
Joint Funding Council's research assessment 1996: 1 subject assessed	
Grade 5/5*	None
EMPLOYMENT PROFILE	
Principal job market destinations: **Agriculture, Education**	
Approximate % unemployed	19%

VAG VIEW

Writtle is just outside Chelmsford in Essex. Over the period since the college's founding in 1893 it has built up some impressive resources for degree programmes ranging from Rural Environmental Management through European Horticulture to Equine Studies. Its arboretum has more than 1,000 trees; its grounds more than 70,000 bulbs, besides numerous other plants; its farmland runs to 135 hectares; its relatively new laboratories (opened in 1994) are state of the art.

There is also a thriving sports scene - there's a sports hall and squash courts and all the usual pitches and playing fields, with rugby teams, soccer, cricket and so on. And a lively Students Union too - discos, dances, folk nights, jazz nights, quizzes and, yes, cocktail evenings! Well, bully for them, perhaps they'll set a trend, certainly beats swallowing goldfish. There is a bar for these events, but anything big is held in the sports hall.

Writtle has a way of making best use of resources and a clear sense of priorities. When a number of industrially sponsored research projects (fertiliser trials and cultivar trials) required their attention recently and they couldn't find anywhere free to carry them out, they weren't fazed for one moment. They turned over the sportsfields.

Writtle's degrees are validated by Anglia Polytechnic University (see entry). First year accommodation is generally in one of their nine halls of residence.

GETTING THERE

★ By road from the Northwest: M11 (J8), A1060; from the West, M11 (J7), A414; from the Southwest, M25 (J28), A12; and A12 from the Northeast.

★ By rail: Chelmsford is 35 minutes away from London Liverpool Street.

WYE COLLEGE

Wye College
Wye
Ashford
Kent TN25 5AH

TEL 01233 812401
FAX 01233 813320

Wye College Student Union
Olantigh Road
Wye
Ashford
Kent TN25 5AH

TEL 01233 812091

WYE COLLEGE	
Founded	**1894**
Situation/style	**Campus**
UNDERGRADUATE PROFILE	
Application acceptance rate	**15%**
Population	**520**
Mature student population	**33%**
Overseas student population	**11%**
Male/female ratio	**50:50**
1st year institut. accommodation	**100%**
Approximate cost	**£67-£80 pw**
ACADEMIC PROFILE	
A-level requirements:	**Low**
Agriculture, Equine, Horticulture, etc 14, **Countryside Management** 16	
Student/staff ratio	**8:1**
1st class degree pass rate	**5%**
HEFCE assessments:	
1 subject assessed	
Grade 5/5*	None
EMPLOYMENT PROFILE	
Principal job market destinations: **Agriculture, Retail Wholesale, Public Admin., Education**	
Approximate % unemployed	**5%**

VAG VIEW

The University of London in the heart of Kent'. With only 520 undergraduates, and set in the middle of a quaint village in Kent, it's probably as far removed from your image of London University as it could get. Small, friendly and full of farmers, the setting is picturesque. The college has been an educational establishment since the 15th century, and the buildings around the College quadrangle are beautiful.

GETTING THERE

★ By road from London: M20 (J9), A28 towards Canterbury and follow the signs to Wye.

★ By rail: From London Charing Cross or Victoria, to Ashford, where you may need to change to get to Wye on the Canterbury line.

VIEW FROM THE GROUND

by Chloe Shears

The first hurdle to be overcome for the potential Wye student is the incessant barrage of poor jokes you will receive when you say that you are going to college: 'Where are you going to?' 'Wye.' 'Because I want to know where you are going.' 'I'm going to W...' and so on. As if that wasn't enough we are constantly referred to as the country bumpkins of London University, those slow farmers who couldn't hack the pace of city life! Well you couldn't be further from the truth. Yes we do have fields as opposed to concrete, and manure instead of smog, but I think you'll find if you come to Wye that we the students have more to talk about than our new combine harvester!

SO WHERE AND WHAT IS WYE?

Well, we are about four miles outside Ashford, a fine town with its new and very shiny Eurostar station, and 12 miles from Canterbury, the lovely crumbly old cathedral city. Wye itself is a rural Kentish village, comprising lots of very loud students and many long suffering residents! It has a station (the only one still around with manually operated crossing gates!), as well as a regular bus service to Ashford and Canterbury. A car is useful if you want to get out and see the surrounding area, but not essential.

Generally the Wye student is a fairly relaxed character, who does not let the world rest on their shoulders. If you are a keen political activist then this probably isn't the place for you. Warning to all feminists, the average Wye guy is still in the Dark Ages about equal rights and may try to strap you to his tractor and carry you back to his hay loft. However, due to the concerted efforts of us girlies he is being tamed and his bank balance is generally better than your typical student!

We're good at making our own entertainment and also doing the occasional bit of study, though as a student here you can set your own pace. There is a healthy mix of backgrounds, quite a few colonials and public school kids, but these are actually outnumbered now by the State sector. Wye also attracts many foreign students and of course mature students.

UNION AND SOCIAL SCENE

We can boast three pubs and the Union bar, a full range of shops, banks and a rather fine Indian takeaway. The three nightclubs, leisure complex and golf course are currently under development (in our dreams!). Until then we make do with the Union and the lovely surrounding countryside to entertain us.

Monday nights are fairly dead, a good opportunity for a quiet drink and a game of pool. Tuesday and Friday nights are function nights, these range from theme discos, live bands, cocktail nights, Sumo wrestling, quizzes, the list goes on. On Wednesday nights the sport clubs invade the union, either to celebrate their victories or drown their sorrows. Usually a very vocal night, singing and drinking games are compulsory until 10.0 p.m., not for the faint hearted or those with sensitive hearing! Thursday is club night. One of Wye's many eccentricities is its 'Elite Clubs', basically drinking clubs which can be entered by invitation only - general requirements for prospective recruits are a cast iron liver and a healthy bank balance. These include the Jock Strap Farmers (JSF), complete drunkards and loud with it, a barrel of ale won't be enough to keep these guys quiet! The Beaus, the gentlemen drinkers, partial to gin and tonics and wooing young ladies, the Garters, girlies out to have a good time, generally blonde and not the most intellectual of students. Finally the Druids, a secret society who have the rather annoying habit of kidnapping young innocent Freshers and whoever else they fancy!

Wye also has regular balls, normally two a term, live music, discos and late bar - black tie and ball dresses are wardrobe essentials! The biggest is the Commemoration Ball, featuring fairground rides, bouncy castles and champagne breakfast for those who survive the whole night.

Freshers week is a big event and Charity Week occurs in the middle of the first term. Activities range from tractor pulling through the village, Druids' Disco (held out in the woods), bonfire and torchlit procession and so on. In the summer term there is Cricket Week - a bit of sport, a bit of beer and a whole load of fun. Due to its small size there is great integration between years, which leads to a really friendly and fun atmosphere. You can't help but enjoy yourself.

When the pace of country life has bored you to tears, Canterbury and Ashford offer student-friendly restaurants, pubs, bars as well as a few nightclubs. Canterbury also has a cinema. If you are a serious clubber then I would not recommend Wye, but in general most things are available.

Do the students get their say at Wye? Yes, they do. Wye has a Student Exec. Council, who are responsible for organising the social scene, supplying services to students and generally making sure that their views are expressed and their rights protected. Elections are held every February and anyone can stand who does not mind standing up and making a fool of themselves in front of the rowdy student population. As part of London University we also get a say concerning wider issues.

SPORT

Sports facilities are limited, but all major sports are undertaken and we still manage to maintain a high position in our respective leagues. Our men's hockey and rugby both play in the University of London's first divisions. The great thing about sport at Wye is that everyone gets a chance to play. Wye also has its own beagle pack and there are regular hunts on a Wednesday and a Saturday.

ACCOMMODATION

All first year undergraduates receive places in halls of residence. These range from the luxurious heights of Dunstan Skilbeck Hall, flats of six students with en-suite showers and brand new kitchens, to the more basic accommodation at Withersdane Hall, communal bathrooms and kitchens, accommodation is arranged on corridors, rooms are large but basic. All halls are mixed. Accommodation is reasonably priced ranging from £670-£800 a term depending on the halls. Food is included in your rent although there is no catering service at weekends. After the first year most students choose to live out, although places in halls are available. Houses in Wye are generally more expensive and limited in number so a large number of students live in the surrounding villages. Rents range from £30-£55 a week, excluding bills. A car is very useful or a housemate who can taxi you around, as some good places are quite remote.

ACADEMIA

Yes, there is an academic side to life at Wye. Although perceived as an agricultural college there is in fact a wide range of courses. Currently the largest degree course is Business Studies, the college has a particularly good reputation for the subject and strong links with a lot of the big names in the market. Animal Sciences is another popular course, attracting lots of failed vets, some of whom go on to qualify. Agricultural Business Management is one of Wye's renowned courses and their Environmental degrees also have a good reputation. There are several new degrees being launched for the new academic year, including Business and the Environment and International Business.

The facilities at Wye have recently been updated with the development of a new library and computer centre, which is an excellent resource for all students. All the computers are connected to the Internet, which is really useful for research and for keeping in touch with friends at other universities.

Every student has a Director of Studies who keeps an eye on your progress, gives sound advice and is basically a shoulder to cry on. They are there to help with academic problems, as well as any other hassles you may have. A benefit of Wye's size is the small teaching groups, you are less likely to feel swamped by hundreds of other students in the lecture theatres. Good relations with staff mean that any problems you may have can be solved quickly, you will not need to struggle by yourself.

To conclude, Wye is what you make of it. Its a great place to study if you want to have a good time, but also if you want to have your own space. Wye's motto should be 'no pressure'. Everyone here can do their own thing, have an excellent university life and get a highly respected University of London degree at the end, providing they do not go out on the beer *every* night!

YORK UNIVERSITY

The University of York
Heslington
York
YO1 5DD

TEL 01904 430000
FAX 01904 433433

York University
Students Union
Student Centre
Heslington
York YO1 5DD

TEL 01904 433723
FAX 01904 433724

YORK UNIVERSITY

Founded	**1963**
Situation/style	**Campus**
UNDERGRADUATE PROFILE	
Application acceptance rate	**8%**
Population	**4,600**
Mature student population	**14%**
Overseas student population	**10%**
Male/female ratio	**50:50**
1st year institut. accommodation	**100%**
Approximate rent	**£33 pw**

ACADEMIC PROFILE

A-level requirements: **High**

English ABC, **Psychology** BBB, **Sociology, Social Policy** BCC, **History/French** ABC, **French, German** 20-22, **Archaeology, Music, Music Technology** BBC, **Avionics, Electronic Engineering** BBB, **Biological Sciences** BBC-BCC, **Physics** BCD, **Maths, Computer Sci., & combinations** 20-24

Student/staff ratio	**7:1**
1st class degree pass rate	**11.8%**

HEFCE assessments
(10 subjects assessed/approved):

1993 **History**	Excellent
1994 **Applied Social Work, Architecture (MA), Computing, English**	Excellent
1995 **Music, Social Policy & Admin.**	Excellent
1995/6 **Sociology** 23 **Modern Languages** 22	

Joint Funding Council's research assessment 1996 (23 subjects assessed):

Psychology, Computer.	Grade 5*
Biol. Sciences, Economics, Social Policy & Admin, Social Work, English, Music.	Grade 5

EMPLOYMENT PROFILE

Employability in Industry:

MPW national league table (1996) **31st=**

Principal job market destinations:

Manufacturing (strong on **Electronic & Electrical**), **Commerce, Retail/Wholesale, Education, Public Admin., Health, Computer, Arts/Media**

PIP 1996 employers' survey:

Top 3 subjects/national ranking

Languages	8th
Computing	10th=
Social Science/Economics	11th
Approximate % unemployed	**8%**

VAG VIEW

'York requires a lot from their students, but provides more for them in terms of contact than Warwick.' School careers adviser.

'A good university is a university which is prepared to say where their students end up - not just the majority, into commerce, but where their Archaeology students went and so on. York is probably the best at that, very informative, very well researched. York hasn't hidden anything.'

(You can obtain a copy of After a Degree...? *, to which this schools career adviser refers, from the Director of the Careers Service at the Uni, and, as she implies, there are some surprises in it.)*

Founded in 1963, York has, along with some other universities which sprang up in the 60s - Sussex, Warwick, East Anglia, for example - an unfair reputation of being a place for Oxbridge rejects. Unfair, because if you have a reputation, as York has, for being uniformly good across your particular academic spectrum - Arts, Sciences/Engineering, Social Sciences (modular structure) - you are bound to find a place on a majority of sixth-form UCAS forms. York's high application/low acceptance rate reflects this state of affairs.

However, the university is anything but complacent, as its deep research into first destinations for its graduates shows. Also, far from sitting back and waiting for applications to flood in, York is actually looking closely at alternative/additional recruitment routes - 'They have been monitoring GNVQ students,' one careers master informed me. 'They have started to accept a few in some areas, but have looked very closely at what those students have done along the way. It's a route to the more vocational courses.' (Information Technology, Business Mgt. and Language, Engineering might fall into this category.)

What this shows is that even though York has enviable recruitment sources it recognises that it would be limiting its evolution by drawing only from the traditional Independent School and top level of State School areas, and that the GNVQ route trains students in a way that may be particularly well suited to its vocational degree offerings. Indeed, York's whole attitude to education is an enlightened one, as was demonstrated recently when the Vice Chancellor publicly encouraged local people to make use of its marvellous library resources.

SITUATION

Purpose-built, rather unattractive campus at Heslington, on the south-east edge of the city. Colleges, including accommodation and social facilities, are set around a large lake in 200 acres.

York is one of our most beautiful cathedral cities, a magnet for tourists from all over the world owing to the wealth of Viking and Roman remains, as well as its Medieval resonances in the Minster, in streets like the Shambles, where buildings lean inwards and over you as if out of a fairytale, in street names like Whip-Ma-Whop-Ma-Gate, and in the Snickleways which offer an alternative way about for those in the know. Then there are the waters of the Ouse, lapping over green-field banks or warehouse walls, redolent of the city's merchant past. It is also within a short distance of the North York moors, one of our most sublimely beautiful wilderness retreats.

GETTING THERE

★ By road: Make for the A1237 ring road (part of which is the A64) from any of a dozen routes which lead to the city. Heslington is on the south-east side and the university is well signposted.
★ By train: York is on the main East Coast line, the fastest in Britain. Leeds, 30 mins; Sheffield: 1:15; Manchester 1:30; London Kings Cross, 2:00; Birmingham New Street, 3:00.
★ Buses from the station are Nos. 4 and 5; a taxi will take about fifteen minutes.
★ By air: Nearest airport is Leeds.

ACCOMMODATION

Guaranteed mixed, mainly single study rooms on campus for first years.

Colleges have common rooms, bar, TV room, laundry, telephone, 24 hour portering. Ex-campus accommodation includes Eden's Court about five minutes walk away, Fairfax House, again within five minutes walk. Garrow house close to campus but also convenient for York. Fulford Road Residence is a couple of miles to the south of the city. Scarcroft Road Residence, well placed for the city centre is given for final-year students. Holgate's Hall is about 20 minutes walk from campus.

ARTS

The Arts Centre in York is very active. The Theatre Royal sometimes has good touring companies. Forty minutes away in Scarborough is Alan Ayckbourn's Theatre, staggering along financially since it moved to the old Odeon by the station, but a world beater for his brand of comedy. Hull is also near, and Leeds and Bradford (see separate entries). Multi-screen cinema out at Clifton Moor Estate (on the north side of the city), Odeon in York. Active student journalism - University Radio York and York Student Television, plus two fortnightly newspapers and other occasional magazines.

SPORT

Forty acres of playing fields - rugby, football, hockey, cricket - floodlit artificial hockey pitch, all-weather (three floodlit) tennis courts, squash courts. Sports centre for archery, badminton (seven courts), basketball, climbing, cricket (five nets), fencing, five-a-side soccer, judo, karate, netball, sauna, table-tennis, tennis, trampoline, volleyball. 400 metre, seven-lane athletics track, Uni lake for fishing, canoeing, sailing, rowing and windsurfing.

Rowing and sailing boathouse on the Ouse about a mile from the University. Rowing is particularly strong at York. Golf at Fulford Golf Club. Swimming at the Barbican Centre half a mile from campus. Gliding, hang-gliding, riding and other facilities also found locally.

VIEW FROM THE GROUND

by Kevin Murphy

Come to York University - land of sixties prefab concrete buildings, lakes of silt, more Oxbridge rejects than you can shake a UCAS form at, an impoverished SU, student apathy, and a campus you can walk across at weekends meeting nobody but the ducks.

The bastard offspring of an LSD-inspired architect and a bent set-square, York University campus sits like an open concrete wound, a hideous pseudo-futuristic nightmare, on the periphery of one of the North's most beautiful cities. In a vain attempt to adhere to the Oxbridge tradition of a collegiate system, the University is split into six main colleges, each equally dreadful to behold in all their monotone glory, set around an extensive man-made lake. To be fair, in the Summer term, when the ducklings outnumber the students, the grass is a lush green, and the trees are in full bloom, the campus is a pleasure to inhabit. But during the winter months it is difficult to imagine anything more dreary.

However, the singularly uninteresting topography and architecture is strangely conducive to obtaining a good degree with minimal distraction. Indeed, the University thrives on its respectable record for academic achievement in all departments. This may be why the University throngs with people who fell at the last hurdle at Oxford or Cambridge.

STUDENT PROFILE

All sections of society are represented here, more or less proportionally. It would be fair to say that the majority of politically-inclined students are the kind who claim to be New Labour but will vote Tory as soon as they get a job. The acerbic mutual abuse of the Conservatives and the Socialist Workers is regarded by most students more as comic relief during Union General Meetings than a source of political intrigue. Those who are political, however, tend to lean toward the militant demonstrating student stereotype, with the exception of the SU Officers, who tend to toe the New Labour/NUS line on almost everything.

York's limited size makes forming a very large circle of friends near impossible. There are a fair number of gothics, hippies, ravers, indie-kids, and rockers, and they all know each other. There lies the source of the phenomenon of the York Clique System. It is impossible not to acknowledge its existence, and some students have been known to leave due to not being able to integrate themselves into their chosen clique. However, a normal well-balanced person should have no trouble making friends. Although, as with any university, there are short-sighted minorities who refuse to look beyond the confines of the clique they establish in Week 0, the average student will be able to claim by the end of their first year that they know almost every body who's anybody. And if they don't, they'll know someone who does.

All in all the students here fall into two broad categories. There's the aforementioned Oxbridge rejects, who adopt the stereotype of taking everything far too seriously and honestly believing the man in the street gives a damn what students think and do. Then there's the majority (or 'the masses') who conform to the other stereotype, their biggest concern being where their next pint/spliff is coming from. York may have more than its fair share of middle-class, public school Southerners, but they are by no means indicative of the student population as a whole. No matter what background, most students have one thing in common: they want to have as good a time as possible. And here is where the problems starts.

SOCIAL

For the average student, the grant-sponging hedonist we all secretly know ourselves to be, York may initially be seen as a bit of a disappointment. City-folk will stand open-mouthed in astonishment when they discover there are only three nightclubs, whereas country yokels such as myself will be impressed by such a vast quantity before realising they're all a bit crap really.

Silk's, Toff's and Ziggy's, the unholy trinity, are virtually identical in their clientele and musical output. We're talking chart dance every night, with a break to indiepop reserved for student nights. Those people requiring specialist music to survive are advised to check out the Arts Centre, which puts on fairly regular decent club-nights from the more obscure ends of the dance spectrum, or alternatively get on the train to Leeds.

What York lacks in clubs it more than makes up for in pubs. Local tradition holds that York has a pub for every day of the year. Although this is almost certainly not the case, there is still a considerable choice, taking in everything from neon-infested theme bars to pokey living-rooms which serve the cream of local brewing talent. Wine bars, live music pubs, tourist pubs, gay bars, cellars, CAMRA award winning pubs, York has something for everybody.

On the campus itself, each college has its own bar. These are universally accepted, however, to be a bit rubbish, although they do try. Alcuin bar, for instance, has an American theme, which means you can't move for Marilyn Monroe posters and replica Cadillacs bursting from the wall. Langwith bar has a more traditional pub-like feel to it, whereas Derwent and Vanbrugh look like hotel foyers and Wentworth looks like the bridge of the USS Enterprise.

Once the Fresher's Week hangover wears off, the new York student might want to investigate some university-based activities. The SU Entertainments Reps try hard to provide students with the big names, but with the lack of a large enough central venue (ever since Bob Geldof caused a ban on Central Hall by trashing it back in the early eighties) most performers are restricted to 400-capacity Alcuin Dining Hall. This inevitably means that whereas your mates in other universities will be boasting of having the very latest chart music live on their own campus, the best you will be able to claim seeing are the likes of Menswear or Audioweb, and bands that have yet to establish themselves.

CLUBS AND SOCIETIES

York has its fair share of societies, however, which provide students with a break from the tedium of academia. Every interest from the more obscure sports to rock/dance/metal/indie music, film drama and UFOs is catered for, and it is impossible not to find the society you're looking for. Among the many societies which provide a service for students, York Student Cinema screen classic movies and the best of recent releases three times a week, and there's a radio station, a TV station, and two student newspapers. But it's all a bit pathetic really. Nobody can receive the radio, the TV station plays irregularly to an audience of about half a dozen, and a 6,500 population campus hardly needs two newspapers. York has nothing, though, if not an awareness of its own patheticness and a keen sense of irony. Perhaps this is the secret of its main charm - this sense of fellowship. If we're not playing for the same team, we're sinking in the same boat.

You may think from reading this that I don't like York. Untrue, I'm having a great time here. The York student, like students at any other university, has to put up with all the faults and idiosyncrasies of the place they find themselves in, and this is just to give you a taste of the negative aspects of what you'll be living with for the duration of your degree. Everybody finds their own positive aspects. If anything, this should give you an impression of what the typical York student is like: a moaning bastard, never content with his lot.

WHICH UNIS FOR WHICH SUBJECTS?

It used to take a long while for news to filter through to public consciousness as to which universities were coming up and going down on which subjects. Now, one great advantage of the HEFCE, SHEFC, HEFCW assessments is that we have a continuing independent analysis of it - a massive and unprecedented undertaking. Here, subject by subject, are lists of those Unis which have been passed **Excellent** or given a score of **20 points or more** out of the maximum 24 (see Introduction for what this means) after close assessment. Not all subjects have been covered by these assessments yet, but year to year a complete picture begins to emerge until, like the painters on the Forth Bridge, it is time to start all over again.

SOCIAL STUDIES

Anthropology (England, N. Ireland)
Brunel, Cambridge, Durham, Kent at Canterbury, LSE, Manchester, Oxford, Oxford Brookes, SOAS, University College London.

Law (England, N. Ireland, Scotland)
Aberdeen, Bristol, Cambridge, Dundee, Durham, East Anglia, Edinburgh, Essex, Glasgow, King's College London, Leicester, Liverpool, LSE, Manchester, Northumbria, Nottingham, Oxford, Oxford Brookes, Queen's (Belfast), Sheffield, SOAS, Strathclyde, Warwick, West of England.

Sociology with Anthropology (England, N. Ireland)
Hull.

Sociology with Social Policy and Administration (England, N. Ireland)
Coventry, Durham, Leeds, Loughborough, Nottingham, Royal Holloway, Sheffield, Southampton, Sheffield Hallam, Warwick, West of England.

Social Policy and Administration (England, N. Ireland)
Bath, Brunel, Edge Hill, Hull, Kent at Canterbury, Lancaster, LSE, Guildhall, Manchester, Newcastle-upon-Tyne, The Open, Sheffield, Ulster, York.

Applied Social Work (England, N. Ireland)
Anglia, Bradford & Ilkley, Bristol, Durham, East Anglia, Huddersfield, Hull, Keele, Lancaster, LSE, Oxford, Queen's (Belfast), Sheffield, Southampton, West London Inst. HE, York.

Politics (Scotland, Wales)
Aberdeen, Aberystwyth, Dundee, Edinburgh, Glasgow, Stirling, Strathclyde.

Sociology (England, N. Ireland, Scotland)
Aberdeen, Anglia, Bath College, Birmingham, Bristol, Brunel, Cheltenham & Gloucester, St. Edinburgh, Essex, Exeter, Glasgow, Glasgow Caledonian, Greenwich, Goldsmiths, Keele, Kent at Canterbury, Kingston, Lancaster, Liverpool, Liverpool Hope, LSE, Manchester, Manchester Met, Nene, Northumbria, Oxford Brookes, Paisley, Plymouth, Portsmouth, Reading, Roehampton, St. Mark & St. John, St. Mary's, Salford, Stirling, Strathclyde, Sunderland, Surrey, Sussex, Thames Valley, The Open, Trinity & All Saints, Wolverhampton, York, Worcester.

Social Work (England, N. Ireland, Scotland)
Anglia, Bradford & Ilkley, Bristol, Dundee, Durham, Edinburgh, East Anglia, Glasgow, Glasgow Caledonian, Huddersfield, Hull, Keele, Lancaster, LSE, Northern, Oxford, Paisley, Queen's (Belfast), Robert Gordon, Sheffield, Stirling, Southampton, Strathclyde, West London, York.

PHYSICAL SCIENCES

Chemistry (England, N. Ireland, Scotland, Wales)
Aberdeen, Abertay Dundee, Bangor, Bristol, Cambridge, Cardiff, Durham, Edinburgh, Glasgow, Glasgow Caledonian, Heriot-Watt, Hull, Imperial College of Science, Leeds, Leicester, Manchester, Napier, Nottingham, Nottingham Trent, Oxford, Paisley, Robert Gordon, St. Andrews, Southampton, Strathclyde.

Geology (England, N. Ireland, Scotland)
Aberdeen, Birmingham, Cambridge, Derby, Durham, Edinburgh, Glasgow, Kingston, Leeds, Liverpool, Imperial College, Manchester,

Newcastle-upon-Tyne, Oxford, Plymouth, Queen's (Belfast), Reading, Royal Holloway, St. Andrews, Southampton, The Open, University College London.

Geography (England, N. Ireland, Scotland, Wales)
Aberdeen, Birmingham, Bristol, Cambridge, Canterbury Christ Church, Cheltenham & Gloucester, Durham, East Anglia, Edinburgh, Exeter, Glasgow, Lancaster, Leeds, Liverpool Inst. of HE, King's College London, Queen Mary & Westfield College, University College London, Manchester, Manchester Met, Nottingham, The Open, Oxford, Oxford Brookes, Plymouth, Portsmouth, Reading, St. Andrews, Sheffield, Southampton, Strathclyde, Swansea.

Environmental Studies (England, N. Ireland, Scotland)
Bath College HE, Dundee, East Anglia, Greenwich, Hertfordshire, Lancaster, Liverpool, Liverpool Inst. of HE, Plymouth, Queen Mary & Westfield College, Reading, Stirling, Southampton, Ulster.

Physics (Scotland, Wales)
Dundee, Edinburgh, Glasgow, Glasgow Caledonian, Heriot-Watt, Robert Gordon, St. Andrews, Strathclyde, Swansea.

HUMANITIES

History (England, N. Ireland, Wales)
Birmingham, Cambridge, Canterbury Christ Church, Durham, Hull, King's College London, Lancaster, Leicester, Liverpool, LSE, Oxford, Queen's (Belfast), Royal Holloway, Sheffield, Swansea, University College London, Warburg Institute, Warwick, York.

Philosophy (Scotland, Wales)
Aberdeen, Cardiff, Edinburgh, Glasgow, St. Andrews, Stirling,

Theology and Religious Studies (Scotland, Wales)
Aberdeen, Bangor, Edinburgh, Glasgow, St. Andrews, Stirling.

ARCHITECTURE, BUILDING, PLANNING

Architecture (England, N. Ireland, Scotland, Wales)
Bath, Cambridge, Cardiff, Central England, East London, Edinburgh Coll. of Art, Edinburgh, Glasgow School of Art, Robert Gordon, Greenwhich, Kingston, University College London, Newcastle, Nottingham, Sheffield, Strathclyde, York.

Building and Surveying (Scotland)
Napier.

BUSINESS AND ADMINISTRATIVE STUDIES

Finance and Accounting (Scotland)
Aberdeen, Dundee, Edinburgh, Glasgow, Glasgow Caledonian, Heriot-Watt, Stirling.

Business and Management Studies (England, N. Ireland, Scotland, Wales)
Bath, City, Cranfield, De Montfort, Edinburgh, Glamorgan, Kingston, Lancaster, London Business School, Imperial College, LSE, Loughborough, Manchester, UMIST, Northumbria, Nottingham, Nottingham Trent, The Open, Robert Gordon, St. Andrews, Scottish College of Textiles, Stirling, Strathclyde, Surrey, Swansea Institute of HE, Warwick, West of England.

Hospitality Studies (Scotland)
Dundee, Glasgow Caledonian, Napier, Queen Margaret, Strathclyde.

LANGUAGES AND RELATED DISCIPLINES

Modern Languages Including Russian and Eastern European Languages and Studies (England, N. Ireland)
Coventry, Queen Mary & Westfield, Brighton, Cambridge, Northumbria, Oxford.

Russian (England, N. Ireland, Wales)
Bangor, Birmingham, Bristol, Durham, Exeter, Keele, Leeds, Sheffield, SEES, Wolverhampton.

German (England, N. Ireland, Wales)
Aston, Birkbeck, Bristol, Durham, Exeter, Hull,

King's College London, Leeds, Leicester, Liverpool, Manchester, Nottingham, Portsmouth, Reading, Sheffield, Swansea, Warwick, Westminster.

Iberian Languages and Studies (England, N. Ireland, Wales)
Birmingham, Bristol, Exeter, Hull, King's College London, Lancaster, Leeds, Liverpool, Manchester, Queen's (Belfast), Sheffield, Swansea, University College London, Wolverhampton.

English (England, N. Ireland, Wales)
Aberystwyth, Anglia, Bath, Birkbeck, Birmingham, Bristol, Cambridge, Cardiff, Chester College of HE, Durham, East London, Kingston, Lancaster, Leeds, Leicester, Liverpool, Newcastle-upon-Tyne, North London, Northumbria, Nottingham, Oxford, Oxford Brookes, Queen's (Belfast), Queen Mary & Westfield College, Sheffield, Sheffield Hallam, Southampton, Sussex, University College London, Warwick, West of England, York.

French (England, N. Ireland)
Aston, Birmingham, Bristol, Durham, Exeter, Hull, Keele, King's College London, Lancaster, Leeds, Liverpool, Oxford Brookes, Portsmouth, Queen's (Belfast), Reading, Sheffield, Sussex, Ulster, University College London, Warwick, Westminster.

Italian (England, N. Ireland)
Birmingham, Bristol, Durham, Exeter, Hull, Lancaster, Leicester, Portsmouth, Reading, Royal Holloway, University College London, Warwick.

Modern Languages Including Italian (England, N. Ireland, Wales)
Anglia, Brighton, Cambridge, Central Lancashire, Coventry, Luton, Manchester Met, Oxford, Oxford Brookes, Queen Mary & Westfield, Swansea.

Linguistics (England, N. Ireland)
Central Lancashire, Durham, Essex, Hertfordshire, Lancaster, Luton, Manchester, Newcastle-upon-Tyne, Roehampton, SOAS, St.Mark & St. John, Sheffield, Sussex, Thames Valley, University College London, Westminster, Wolverhampton.

Modern Languages Including Linguistics (England, N. Ireland)
Brighton, Cambridge, Central Lancashire, Oxford, Queen Mary & Westfield, West of England, York.

ENGINEERING

Civil Engineering (Scotland)
Aberdeen, Dundee Institute of Technology, Dundee, Edinburgh, Glasgow, Heriot-Watt, Napier, Paisley, Strathclyde.

Electrical and Electronic Engineering (Scotland, Wales)
Cardiff, Edinburgh, Heriot-Watt, Strathclyde, Swansea.

Chemical Engineering (England, N. Ireland)
Bath, Birmingham, Bradford, Cambridge, Imperial College, Loughborough, Newcastle-upon-Tyne, Nottingham, Queen's (Belfast), Sheffield, UMIST, University College London.

Mechanical Engineering (England, N. Ireland, Scotland)
Aberdeen, Abertay Dundee, Bath, Bristol, Coventry, Cranfield, Glasgow, Glasgow Caledonian, Heriot-Watt, Manchester, Manchester Met, Nottingham, Paisley, Reading, Robert Gordon, Sheffield, Strathclyde, UMIST.

MATHS SCIENCES AND INFORMATICS

Computer Science (England, N. Ireland, Wales)
Cambridge, Exeter, Imperial College, Kent at Canterbury, Manchester, Oxford, Southampton, Swansea, Teeside, Warwick, York.

Mathematics and Statistics (Scotland)
Aberdeen, Abertay Dundee, Dundee, Edinburgh, Glasgow Caledonian, Glasgow, Heriot-Watt, Napier, Paisley, Robert Gordon, St. Andrews, Stirling, Strathclyde.